HUMAN SEXUALITY
brief edition

HERANT A. KATCHADOURIAN, M.D.
Stanford University
DONALD T. LUNDE, M.D.
Stanford University
ROBERT J. TROTTER

HOLT, RINEHART AND WINSTON

New York   Chicago   San Francisco   Dallas
Montreal   Toronto   London   Sydney

Credits

Cover illustration *Eternal Springtime* by Rodin (marble, 1884). Photograph courtesy Lee Boltin. Excerpts pp. 49, 185, 202, copyright © 1976 by Shere Hite. Reprinted by permission of The Macmillan Company from *The Hite Report* by Shere Hite. Excerpts pp. 50, 185, copyright © 1977 by Anthony Pietropinto. Reprinted by permission of Times Books, a division of Quadrangle/The New York Times Book Co., Inc. from *Beyond the Male Myth* by Anthony Pietropinto and Jacqueline Simenauer. Figure 4.5 copyright © 1974. Reprinted by permission of Addison-Wesley Publishing Co. from *Sex and Human Life* by Eric T. Pengelley. Quotation p. 311 from "Murder in the Cathedral," Part I, by T. S. Eliot, 1935. Reprinted by permission of Harcourt Brace Jovanovich, Inc.

Library of Congress Cataloging in Publication Data

Katchadourian, Herant A
  Human sexuality.

  A briefer version of the 2d ed. of Fundamentals of
human sexuality, published in 1975.
  Bibliography: p. 323
  Includes index.
  1. Sex. I. Lunde, Donald T., joint author.
II. Trotter, Robert J., joint author. III. Title.
HQ31.K36 1979   612.6   79-705
ISBN: 0-03-045051-9

Preface to the Brief Edition

Fundamentals of Human Sexuality is a text with which we and numerous students and teachers have been well pleased over the years. But since the book was first published in 1972, and especially since it was revised in 1975, we have come to recognize the growing need for a text on human sexuality that could reach a larger audience. In an attempt to fill that need, we have revised, updated, and rewritten in slightly less technical terms our own 1975 edition. We have done this in collaboration with a new co-author, Robert Trotter, a skilled free-lance social science writer. The result, *Human Sexuality,* Brief Edition, is a briefer, but current and more accessible, version of *Fundamentals of Human Sexuality.*

In rewriting our text we were forced to abbreviate and omit certain components that helped give the original book its well-rounded and solidly-based approach to human sexuality. In doing so, however, we were careful not to sacrifice our coverage of the subject matter. Biological, psychological, and social aspects of human sexuality are dealt with thoroughly and presented in the light of the most recent research findings. While we continue to emphasize the cultural aspects of sexual behavior, the separate chapters on the erotic in art, literature, and film do not appear in this brief edition.

Chapter 1 offers a brief overview of sexuality and poses the fundamental questions that will be addressed throughout the book. Chapters 2 and 3 cover the anatomy and physiology of the sex organs and reproductive systems, including the mechanisms of sexual arousal and the role of the brain in sexual functioning. Chapter 4 examines the increasingly complex but fascinating data on hormonal systems. Chapter 5 covers conception, pregnancy, and childbirth and includes discussions of such things as predetermination of the sex of the baby, drugs for the treatment of infertility, and various methods of natural childbirth. Chapter 6 has been updated to include the most recent information on contraceptive devices and abortion procedures.

With Chapter 7 we turn to the behavioral aspects of human sexuality and discuss, among other things, gender identity. The behavioral section of the book contains not only data from the Kinsey surveys but more current findings (along with evaluations of those findings). Chapters 8 and 9 are updated to reflect current data and attitudes on autoerotic behavior and sexual intercourse. The same is true of chapters 10 and 11, which examine variations and deviations in sexual behavior and sexual disorders and therapies. And finally, in Chapter 12, we turn to questions of sexual morality and legality, discussing them first from an historical point of view and then focusing on contemporary trends and attitudes.

We would like to express our gratitude to Nancy Cozzens and to John and Janice Baldwin, who offered invaluable suggestions in the planning stages of the Brief Edition and then provided detailed critiques of the manuscript as it took shape. Though we were not able to follow all of the recommendations, this edition has benefited greatly from their care and hard work.

Our appreciation goes also to Jeanette Ninas Johnson of Holt, Rinehart and Winston, who coordinated all of the activities necessary to turn a manuscript into a bound book.

We would also like to acknowledge Susan West and Judy Klein for their help in preparing the manuscript.

Preface to Fundamentals of Human Sexuality
Second Edition

Authors who have the pleasant task of introducing second editions of their textbooks usually offer a variety of justifications which can be classified into several categories: correcting errors of commission and omission, updating the material, reorganizing the method of presentation.

During the three years that our text has been available we have received numerous comments and reactions from students, instructors, and other readers. While these comments have been favorable, we nevertheless came to the conclusion that a revision was called for based on the following considerations:

It was necessary to include information that had been omitted in the first edition. Abortion, for example, has been legalized in many states since the first edition was published, and many of the techniques explained here were not discovered or in general use in 1972. Most important, the field of human sexuality has been expanding rapidly and even during the short interval between the first edition and this one, substantial contributions have been made in this field that must be presented.

We must confess that when we undertook the revision we did not fully anticipate the magnitude of the task. The book looked like a reasonably clean and tidy room. But as we started moving the furniture around, pockets of dust and lurking cobwebs kept coming into view—so in retrospect, the need for a revision is even clearer now than it was at the outset.

In the acknowledgments to the first edition we indicated that the text was an outgrowth of our course on human sexuality at Stanford University and went on to say that it is appropriate that we first give due recognition to those who helped initiate and sustain the course. Robert M. Moulton, Jr., chaired the committee on university health where the need for such a course was first discussed. His interest and support, along with that of Robert R. Sears (who was at the time Dean of Humanities and Sciences at Stanford and a member of the committee) were crucial. Since then help and encouragement have come from many quarters. David A. Hamburg's broad conception of psychiatry legitimized our involvement in this field. The university unfailingly provided the necessary financial and administrative support. We have been the grateful recipients of much encouragement from the faculty as well as from other members of the Stanford community. Ultimately our most important supporters have been our students, for without their enthusiastic response neither the course nor this book would exist today.

• • •

During the early phases of the preparation of this book we profited greatly from visits to the Institute for Sex Research at the University of Indiana. Director Paul Gebhard and others of his staff have been helpful in numerous ways. The Institute is well known for its publications, but deserves wider recognition for the informal, yet important, educational job it fulfills.

A number of colleagues and friends read parts of the manuscript and made specific, as well as general, comments. We are particularly grateful in this regard to Frank A.

Beach, Fred Elmadjian, Julian M. Davidson, Paul H. Gebhard, H. Duane Heath, Raeburne Heimbeck, Erich Lindemann, George L. Mizner, Stephen A. Robins, John Romano, Judge George W. Phillips, Jr., Sherwood L. Washburn, Archdeacon John Weaver, and Lee H. Yearley.

In the preparation of this book we were assisted by David P. Boynton, Jane Mayo Roos, Jan Hughes, Estelle Whelan, Susan F. Riggs, and Carol Lee Smith. The manuscript was typed by Ann Dunn Morey and Ann Edmonds.

The division of labor between co-authors was as follows: Katchadourian wrote the introductory chapter, the chapters on anatomy, physiology, sexual behavior, autoeroticism, sexual intercourse, the introductory section on contraception, and the section on sexual malfunctions; Lunde wrote the chapters on hormones, conception and pregnancy, morality, law, the concluding chapter, and the sections on contraceptive methods and diseases of the sex organs. The chapter on sexual variations and deviations was written by Lunde and revised by Katchadourian.

Several of our colleagues and friends mentioned above once again came to our aid in the preparation of the second edition. We must also gratefully add to our list Anthony Amsterdam, Paul and Anne Ehrlich, Donald Laub, John Messenger, Karl Pribram, and Leslie Squier.

In our collaboration with Louise Waller, we found out what a tremendous difference an editor of her caliber makes. Finally, in ending our remarks to the first edition we indicated that since this book was written over a period of two years, mostly in the evenings and on weekends, our families had labored with us throughout this process. Furthermore, from the book's conception to its birth, we had benefited from the good judgment and critical sense of our wives. They have continued to sustain us during the process of revision.

January 1975
Stanford, California

—H.A.K.
—D.T.L.

Contents

CHAPTER 1 Fundamental Questions about Human Sexuality

Everything you always wanted to know about sex—whether you were afraid to ask or not—possibly cannot be told. Sex has always been an important and universal aspect of the human condition, so we would expect a great deal to be known about it. But such is not the case. There is so much variety in human sexual behavior that even the most sophisticated and experienced individuals cannot generalize adequately from their personal experience. Because all societies regulate sexual activity to some extent there have usually been restrictions on both the observation of sexual behavior and access to information about it. The result is that many questions about this basic human activity remain unanswered or only partially answered.

Of the many questions that can be asked about the sexual life of human beings, three are of primary importance: Why do we behave sexually? How do we behave sexually? How should we behave sexually?

Our task in this book is to provide information to help answer these questions.

WHY WE BEHAVE SEXUALLY

There are certain physiological functions, like eating, whose primary purpose is imme-

diately obvious. Food preferences may vary widely among individuals and groups, but everyone must eat. Similarly, unused food matter must be eliminated from the bowels regardless of the social customs attached to the process.

What about sex? Can it be compared to either of these two functions? Both comparisons have been made, but neither is adequate. We can, of course, refer metaphorically to "sexual hunger." In fact, at certain times people and animals may prefer copulating to eating. Nevertheless, sex is not necessary to sustain life (except in the broad sense of species preservation), and there is no generally agreed-upon evidence that lack of sex is harmful to one's health. The comparison with elimination also has some validity since most men do ejaculate periodically. But women experience orgasm and do not ejaculate, so the comparison fails.

Comparisons with other bodily functions may be inadequate, but we cannot deny that the origins of sexual behavior are biological. Biology, however, is not all there is to sex. All human behavior is the result of three types of forces—biological, psychological, and social. These forces work together in a complementary and integrated fashion, and all three must be considered in any attempt to understand sexual behavior.

1

Biological Origins of Sexuality

Sex and reproduction are intimately linked in most living creatures (although there are asexual modes of reproduction among some species), so it is understandable that one explanation of sexual behavior is simply the biological need to reproduce. Sex, in this sense, is considered part of a reproductive "instinct"—a deep-rooted biological incentive for animals to mate and perpetuate their species. Biological explanations of sexual behavior based on the concept of instinct—an innate, or built-in, force—have proved useful, but so far scientists have failed to explain exactly what an instinct is. Furthermore, lower animals cannot possibly know that mating results in reproduction. For that matter, we do not know who made the momentous discovery, at some point in prehistory, that coitus leads to pregnancy. If lower animals are ignorant of this association, what mysterious force propels them to mate?

Although the reproductive consequences of copulation are obvious to us, sexual behavior cannot be scientifically explained as behavior in which animals engage in order to reproduce. Besides, a great deal of animal and especially of human sexual activity serves no reproductive function.

A simpler and more likely explanation is that human beings and other animals engage in sex because it is pleasurable. The incentive is in the act itself rather than in its possible consequences. Sexual behavior in this sense arises from a psychological need associated with sensory pleasure, and its reproductive consequences are a by-product (though a vital one).

What about sex hormones? They are a fascinating but currently problematic subject of study. We know, for instance, that they begin to exert their influence before birth and are vital in sexual development. Yet, in the mature animal they seem relatively dispensable to the maintenance of sexual functioning. Although these hormones are intimately linked to sexual functioning, the link is clearly not a simple one, and we have yet to discover a substance that might represent a true "sex fuel."

Thus, the biological basis of our sexual behavior involves certain physical "givens," including sex organs, hormones, intricate networks of nerves, and brain centers. How these components are constructed and how they work will occupy us in Part One of this book.

Psychological Determinants of Sexual Behavior

If biological explanations of sexuality were totally satisfactory, it would not be necessary for us to go farther. But they do not tell the full story, so we must look for additional factors to explain sexual behavior.

In discussing psychological determinants of behavior, we often must deal with different levels of analysis of the human organism. In one sense, psychological or social forces are merely reflections and manifestations of underlying biological processes. For example, Freud argued that the libido, or sex drive, is the psychological representation of a biological sex instinct.

In another sense psychological factors are independent of the biological, even though they must operate through the mechanisms of the brain, for neither thought nor emotion can occur in an empty skull. But these mechanisms are considered only as the intermediaries through which thought and emotion operate, rather than as their primary determinants. Let us again use hunger as an example. When the brain motivates a person to eat, in response to a feeling of hunger (due to certain sensations in the gastrointestinal system or to a decrease in blood sugar), the response of the individual is relatively independent of psychological and social considerations. Although such factors have some influence on the individual's behavior, they are not the main determinants. Yet someone who dislikes pork or is expected to abstain from eating it acts from personal preference or religious conviction. The motivation is still mediated through the brain, but it originates in learned patterns of behavior rather than in biological factors. We have used the example of hunger, rather than of sex itself, because in the latter the biological imperative is less clear.

Theories of the psychological motivation for sexual behavior are fundamentally of two types. In the first, which includes psychoanalytic theory, psychological factors are considered to be representations or extensions of biological forces. In contrast, many learning theories assume that patterns of sexual behavior are largely acquired through a variety of psychological and social mechanisms.

While the causes or determinants of a given type of behavior must not be confused with the purposes that it serves, and though such distinctions are not always easy to recognize, it is also useful to examine the various aims of sexual behavior. For instance, when a person engages in sex expressly to satisfy physical desire or to relieve "sexual tension," we may say that sex occurs "for its own sake." But for most people sex has an emotional component as well; it takes on added significance as an expression of affection or love for the partner. We can argue whether this affective component ought to be a basic part of sex or a desirable addition to it, and this question will be considered later in this chapter.

If we assume that the primary goals of sexuality are reproduction and the attainment of pleasure, a number of secondary, though by no means unimportant, goals can be seen that are "nonsexual." First among these is the use of sex as a vehicle for expressing and obtaining love. This may involve deep and genuine affection or its shallow and stereotyped parodies. Women have been traditionally more likely to yield their bodies for such emotional security and reassurance. Some women go through the motions of sexual intercourse for the satisfaction of being held and cuddled. Adolescent girls may indulge in promiscuous but joyless sexual encounters to maintain popularity and acceptance by their peers. Underneath such behavior is a defense against loneliness, which is effective at best for a brief period. This same consideration applies to males who are likely also to be driven to sexual exploits to defend against self-doubts about masculinity and power or to gain status

among their peers. The contribution of sex to self-esteem is most important. Each of us needs a deep and firmly rooted conviction of personal worth. Although no one can hope to be universally loved and admired, we must receive some appreciation from "significant others" and from ourselves. Our sexual standing in our own eyes as well as in the eyes of others is an important aspect of self-esteem.

Sexuality is clearly an important component of an individual's self-concept or sense of identity. Awareness of differences between the sexes precedes that of all other social attributes in the child: The child knows the self as a boy or girl long before it learns to associate the self with national, ethnic, religious, and other cultural groupings.

Although developing an awareness of one's biological sex is a relatively simple matter, the acquisition of a sense of sexual identity is a more complex, culturally relative process. Traditionally we have assumed that biological sex (maleness and femaleness) and its psychological attributes (masculinity and femininity) are two sides of the same coin. In traditional and stable societies this assumption may have been (and may still be) valid. But in the technologically advanced and structurally more fluid societies such direct correspondence between biological sex and psychological attributes is being challenged more and more vigorously as occupational and social roles for men and women become progressively blurred.

Finally, sex figures prominently in an individual's moral or spiritual identity. At least in Western cultures sex is used as a moral yardstick more consistently than any other form of behavior, at both the personal and public levels. Many of us feel greater guilt and are often punished more severely for sexual transgressions than for other offenses. Common as sexual themes are in our mass media, the level of tolerance is nowhere near that for aggression and violence.

Although both personal and public attitudes are changing in this regard, a common first reaction as to whether or not a person (particularly a woman) is moral or "honorable" is to think in sexual terms. We are not implying that this should or should not be so, but are merely pointing out the enormous influence that sex has on our standing as individuals and members of society.

Social Factors in Sexual Behavior

Just as psychological functions are intimately linked with biological forces, so they are equally tied to social factors. In fact, distinctions between what is primarily psychological and what is social often tend to be arbitrary. As a rule, in referring to social or cultural factors the emphasis is on the interpersonal over the intrapsychic and on group processes over internal ones.

Sexuality is often considered a cohesive force that binds the family unit together. In this sense it has a social goal, and social organizations help make this goal easier to achieve by providing sexual partners and contacts. Sexuality can also have a divisive influence, and this potential may be one reason for the ambivalence with which sex is viewed in many societies.

Sex also functions as a form of communication. Through it we express affection and love—as well as anger and hatred. When, after coming home from a party, a wife who is herself sexually aroused refuses to sleep with her husband because he has been flirting with other women, she is using sex to communicate a message ("I am angry") and a lesson ("Next time behave yourself"). On the other hand, a woman who is sexually unstimulated may engage in coitus to reward her husband for good behavior. Similarly, promiscuous sexual activity may communicate messages like "I am lonely," "I am not impotent," "I dare to misbehave," and so on.

Sex also symbolizes status. The dominant male animals in a troop and the men with power in society often have first choice of the more desirable females. Beauty is naturally pleasing to the eye, but beyond this attraction the company of a beautiful woman is a testimony and a tribute to a man's social standing. A woman's status is more often enhanced by the importance than by the looks of her man, although attitudes in this regard are currently in a state of change.

For some people sexual activity is a form of self-expression in a creative, or esthetic, sense. What matters most is not simple physical pleasure, but the broadening of sensual horizons with each experience, and the opportunity to express and share these experiences in a very special and intimate way with another person. Such feelings, though very real, are difficult to describe.

In various places and at various times sex has been used for the loftiest, as well as for the basest, ends. Although sexuality is foreign to the major modern Western traditions of religious worship, other religions have had distinctly sexual components, as the erotic statuary adorning Indian temples (*see* Figure 1.1) and phallic monuments from Classical times (*see* Figure 1.2) attest. Some Muslim men still offer brief prayers before coitus.

FIGURE 1.1 Temple reliefs, sixteenth century A.D., Srirangam Temple, Trichinopoly, India.

FIGURE 1.2 Phallic monument, the Dedication of Karystos (from the Sacred Road on the Island of Delos), fourth-third century B.C.

end insomnia. Sex can thus be used for "nonsexual" as well as "sexual" ends. Conversely, sexual gratification can be achieved through orgasm as well as by the displacement of the sexual drive with countless ordinary and extraordinary "nonsexual" activities.

HOW WE BEHAVE SEXUALLY

Why we behave sexually is a complex question, so it is understandable that we do not have satisfactory answers to our first question. We might hope, however, that answers to our second question would be relatively easy, for all that is theoretically required is the observation of behavior rather

On balance, sex has been more crassly and mercilessly exploited than any other human need. The female body in particular has been a commodity since remotest antiquity. Although women have benefited financially from prostitution, men have had more than their share of profits from this commerce. Prostitution is the most flagrant example of the use of sex for practical gain, but it is by no means the only one. Sexual favors are exchanged for other services between spouses and friends. Sex is used to maintain social standing, to gain popularity, to ensnare and hold spouses and mates, and so on. The overt and covert use of sex in advertising hardly needs to be pointed out.

Other uses of sex are legion. The ancient Romans wore amulets in the form of male sex organs (*see* Figure 1.3). Some people use sex to cure headaches, to calm their nerves, or to

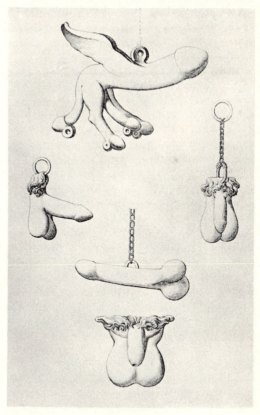

FIGURE 1.3 Roman amulets.

than attempts to fathom human motivation. But, in fact, we are frequently in the dark on questions of how we behave sexually as well, and this ignorance may be an important cause of our being unable to fully answer the first question. After all, if we do not know enough about *how* people behave, how can we investigate *why* they behave as they do?

A comprehensive view of human sexual behavior would require knowledge of current sexual behavior in our own society, the history of sexual behavior and how it has changed over the centuries, sexual behavior in other cultures and its historical roots, and, finally, the sexual behavior of animals.

Although it is customary (for good reason) to decry our ignorance in these matters, we actually do have a great deal of information (and a great deal more misinformation) on human sexual behavior, even though it is uneven and scattered. Most of this information can be found in three sources: art and literature, clinical reports, and ethnographic and statistical surveys.

Since the Paleolithic cave painters of *c.* 15,000 years B.C., artists have portrayed sexual activities. As a result we have a wealth of information, despite repeated and often successful attempts to conceal, distort, and destroy it. Writers of all periods have also recorded descriptions, observations, and speculations on the sex life of humans. More recently, films have become an important vehicle for the portrayal of sexual behavior.

Clinical interest in sexual functioning also goes back to antiquity, but more intensive concern with sexual behavior is a twentieth-century phenomenon. The primary interests of the clinician have been aberrations and malfunctions. We can also learn a great deal about the normal through studies of the abnormal, as long as inferences are made with full awareness of the potential pitfalls.

Surveys of sexual behavior are generally of two types. In the first, observations are primarily descriptive. Anthropologists and travelers have, for instance, provided fascinating accounts of sexual activities in distant lands. The second type of survey is more systematic

in attempting to describe sexual behavior in quantifiable terms, relating the activities of specially selected samples to other significant characteristics. The Kinsey studies are the best-known examples of this type of survey. In Chapters 7–11 we shall make extensive use of data from both types of surveys, as well as from clinical sources. The more important sources of information that we have used are discussed later in this chapter.

Interest in animal behavior has until recently been restricted to zoologists. Now, however, we are becoming more aware of the relevance of data on animal behavior (particularly that of primates) to the understanding of human behavior. Just as cross-cultural data provide us with comparisons of how various societies organize certain behaviors, cross-species comparisons may eventually permit us to trace the biological roots of our behavior. We can also learn about biology from cross-cultural studies and about social systems from cross-species comparisons, for there are biological constants in all cultures, and social organization is not an exclusively human characteristic.

HOW WE SHOULD BEHAVE SEXUALLY

Our third question is primarily, though not exclusively, a moral one. In addition to more strictly moral judgments, we must take into account, for instance, health considerations, factors that will enhance sexual satisfaction, and social customs and conventions that carry no moral weight but define courtesy, decency, and so on. At worst these codes are hollow rituals that needlessly complicate life, offer arrogant badges of status, and serve as tools of intimidation. At best they make social intercourse more comfortable and gracious. Although we must bear in mind these wider implications of the question, we shall be concerned here mainly with the more specifically moral aspects of sexual behavior.

To live in society in reasonable peace we

have to know its rules and to be able to differentiate between those that can be broken with relative impunity and those that cannot. But what if the rules are irrational or unfair? Is adjustment to society the ultimate goal? The answers again involve personal choices. Most people follow the main trends of sexual behavior, and this majority provides stability. Many people, however, refuse to conform, and some attempt to change others' behavior as well. Despite these complexities, can we isolate some components of a fundamental standard of sexual behavior? There are at least five that seem worthy of major consideration.

Accepting Sexual Realities

Knowledge and acceptance of sexual realities are indispensable to sexual fulfillment and honesty. First comes the willingness to recognize biological facts, including practical knowledge (not necessarily from formal study) of the sexual organs and their functions. More important is acceptance of sexual feelings as legitimate biological and psychological manifestations, rather than as afflictions that must be exorcised or only grudgingly tolerated.

Next is a willingness to accept behavioral facts, to recognize how people behave, regardless of how we think that they ought to behave. People have remarkable capacities for self-deception. When an investigator reports statistics on the prevalence of some socially unacceptable behavior, there is always a public outcry. People object not because they have more reliable data but because the findings "don't make sense." "There cannot be so many homosexuals," they may say; but what they mean is that they think there should not be so many homosexuals.

The behavioral realities are there, whether we recognize them or not. By ignoring, distorting, or denying them we merely fool ourselves. On the other hand, recognizing reality does not necessarily require condoning it.

Of all the various phases of our sex lives perhaps the most crucial is how well we face up to our own sexual thoughts and feelings. It is not possible to come to terms with ourselves as long as we refuse to confront our own sexuality. Some extraordinary individuals willingly recognize their sexual needs, yet delay or inhibit satisfying those needs for what they consider to be higher causes. That is one thing; simply to look away is another. We must be honest with ourselves and others in all things, but especially in sex, for in this area pretense wears thin, bravado sounds hollow, and in bluffing others we bluff ourselves.

Enhancing Sexuality

Sexuality is not a wild horse that must be tamed and then exercised periodically. It is a potential with which we are born and which must be developed and nourished. It is every bit as important to be concerned about fulfilling our sexual capabilities as about fulfilling our intellectual or artistic capabilities.

The biological origins of sexual functioning do not insure its automatic operation. Monkeys raised in isolation, for instance, do not know how to interact sexually. They are physically healthy and the sex drive is present, but the behavior that would lead to gratification is disorganized. Sexuality thus requires a certain milieu in which to develop. It needs warm contacts with other people, and it needs nurturing.

To start with, there must be acceptance of the fundamental value of sex, in addition to acceptance of its reality. Such acceptance must come early and be incorporated into the personality structure of the child. Intimate relationships must enhance this feeling and permit the growth of sexuality while instilling the restraints required for successful social living.

A fundamental standard must therefore include incentives as well as prohibitions. There is at times the assumption that one can do no wrong sexually as long as one does nothing at all. This approach is too negative and makes sexuality appear a necessary evil at best.

When a person enters a relationship that has a legitimate sexual component, is not that person obligated to act effectively in a sexual way? We rightfully condemn a parent who does not provide for the family to the best of his or her ability or fails to care for the children. But what about the spouse who makes no effort to maintain and improve his or her sexual attractiveness, who is lazy and inept in bed, and who tries to pass off sexual incompetence as innocence or decency?

Integrating Sex into Life as a Whole

Ultimately, sex must make sense in the context of one's overall life. At certain periods sexual pressure is overwhelming, and sometimes we go to great lengths for its sake. But these instances are unusual and transitory and generally give way to more prosaic but steady sexual needs.

The place that sex occupies in our overall lives varies from one person to another. It is possible that we are born with different genetic predispositions in this regard. Physical characteristics certainly have great influence on personality development and sexual behavior. For example, a pretty child discovers very early the impact of that fact on others. The families that rear us and the community values that we learn to share or reject combine to shape our sexual behavior.

For some people sex becomes the pivot of their lives. Others hardly seem to care. The important point is not how many orgasms we achieve during a week or in a lifetime but whether or not our sexual needs are satisfied in a manner consistent with the strength of our desires, the requirements of our consciences, and the basic goals and purposes of our lives.

As we shall discuss in Chapter 11, some sexual dissatisfactions are caused by false or excessive expectations. Gratifying as sex may be, we can derive only so much from it. It cannot be substituted for all other needs, just as substitution of other satisfactions for those of sex can also be stretched only so far.

A fundamental standard that does not facilitate the integration of sexuality into life as a whole has limited usefulness. There are those who feel or act morally in all respects but sexually; sex is thus their secret vice. To a degree such schisms are unavoidable, but beyond certain limits they constitute points of weakness that are vulnerable to stress.

The Relation of Sex to Marriage

The aspect of heterosexual intercourse that raises the most frequent moral concern is whether it occurs within or outside of marriage. Marriage in its various forms is a universal institution. Sex almost always plays a part in it, but, of course, marriage involves much more than sex. At least in principle, however, there are important cultural differences in whether or not sex is restricted to marital partners.

In the West the traditional expectation has been that sex will be restricted in this way. In practice there have been many departures from this expectation, particularly among men. Currently the trend is toward less rigidity on this point for both sexes, particularly in relation to premarital sex. Statistical estimates of the incidence of virginity have been one of the more popular forms of sex research on university campuses. Current assessments vary, but half the student population in some colleges may well be engaging in coitus with some frequency. Extramarital coitus poses different kinds of problems, for it involves consideration of the spouse's feelings as well as of one's own conscience. The incidence of extramarital sex is apparently also on the rise, but again there are wide variations among social groups.

Because of the long-term mutual commitments of married couples, marital sex has particular significance. The marital relationship entails much more than sex. Nevertheless, sexual imcompatibility is a frequent cause of marital discord. Marital discord arising from other sources also leads to sexual problems. The issue is not how much sex is necessary or "good" for the couple but whether or not sex plays a mutually satisfactory role in the relationship.

These areas are the ones to which a fundamental standard must apply. The matter has been discussed time and again and continues to be a major topic.

Sex and Love

Each era and culture has had its views on love, and many of our most eloquent expressions have been those of love. It is a tribute to the enduring strength of the sentiment to which it refers that the word "love" — hackneyed, abused, and exploited as it has been — still retains so much meaning.

A common, and justified, criticism of "sex manuals" is that they neglect appropriate consideration of love: Either they omit mention of it altogether, or they include only insipid platitudes. By the same token, essays on love tend to neglect or etherealize sex to a point at which it seems more suited to angels than to human beings.

The relation of sex to love, like that of sex to marriage, is a frequent source of controversy. The well-known Western ideal attempts to combine all three: sex, love, and marriage. But relatively few people seem able to attain this ideal or to sustain it over periods of years. Currently, some people are willing to settle for love and sex alone, and love too may be on its way out as a necessary condition for sex. This change is viewed as moral degeneration by some people and as sexual regeneration by others.

There is a vast literature on love, as well as many historical and analytical studies of the concept of love. Love is generally viewed as a complex emotion. There are different kinds of love, and each act of love has a number of components. Thus, we differentiate *sex* (or lust), *eros* (or the urge toward higher states of being and relationships), *philia* (friendship, or brotherly love), and *agape* (or *caritas*), selfless love as exemplified in the love of God for human beings, and so on.

Should sex, which is equally complex, not be viewed as an entity in its own right? If we can have love with or without sex, why can we not legitimately have sex with or without love? Everyone must ultimately face this

question, and a well-thought-out, individual, fundamental standard may be preferable to the usual compromises reached under the pressures of the moment.

SEXUALITY IN HISTORICAL PERSPECTIVE

Part of the confusion regarding sexual behavior arises from our inability and unwillingness to view sexual matters in an historical and cross-cultural context. We become so bound up in our immediate needs and fears that we lose perspective both at the personal and the societal level. Adolescents have little inclination to remember how they felt about sex as a child or how they are likely to view it as an adult. Adults likewise readily forget what it was like to be an adolescent. When a longitudinal view is finally forced on us in old age, there is relatively little time or energy left to do very much about it.

We are just as shortsighted and ahistorical as a society. Our views of history are often at the level of homilies about the "good old days" or how "the more things change, the more they remain the same." We learn about ancient times and remote places in school, but such knowledge is rarely seen as having any immediacy for our lives.

We are pressed by the present and preoccupied with the future. As a consequence we have difficulty in determining whether changes we see in sexual behavior constitute regular installments in the normal course of events or whether a process of more drastic change is afoot. It is altogether easy under such circumstances for some people to cry "sexual revolution" in the face of any startlingly real, just imagined, or wished-for change; and for others to sit placidly through profound upheavals in sexual attitudes and behavior as if nothing new were happening.

Arthur Schlesinger, Jr., in an informal essay on the history of love in this country, has outlined some of the major shifts that have occurred in sexual attitudes over the past three centuries. We often think of the Puritan founders of this nation as prudes. Yet the Puritans in the seventeenth century were quite open about sex and viewed it as a natural and joyous part of marriage. One James Mattock was expelled from the First Church of Boston for refusing to sleep with his wife. Puritan maidens with child were married by understanding ministers, as is indicated in the town records of the time. The Puritans were stern and God-fearing people who could be very harsh with adulterers. Yet their wrath was aroused not because of the sexual element but because such behavior threatened the sanctity and stability of marriage. The lack of a general sexual repressiveness was even apparent to outsiders. A visitor from Maryland who was in Boston in 1744 reported: "This place abounds with pretty women who appear rather more abroad than they do at [New] York and dress elegantly. They are for the most part, free and affable as well as pretty. I saw not one prude while I was there."

With the coming of national independence in the eighteenth century, there was a reaction to romantic notions that were associated with Old World feudalism and aristocracy. The republic was pledged to liberty, equality, and rationality. Marriage became more and more a service institution geared to populate the nation and strengthen the labor force. Native as well as visiting observers were quick to comment on this victory of rationality over romantic love. "No author, without a trial," complained Hawthorne, "can conceive of the difficulty of writing a romance about a country where there is no shadow, no antiquity, no mystery, no picturesque and gloomy wrong, nor anything but a commonplace prosperity, in broad and simple daylight, as is happily the case with my dear native land." The French writer Stendhal observed that Americans had such a "habit of reason" that abandonment to love became all but impossible. In Europe, he wrote, "desire is sharpened by restraint; in America it is blunted by liberty."

In the nineteenth century American men became progressively more obsessed with achievement and making money. American

women, on the other hand, had become quite self-assertive, having successfully used the leverage provided by their scarcity when the country was being settled and later during its expansion to the West. Between male preoccupation and female coolheadedness, love and romance seem to have been more and more dissociated from the relationship between the sexes.

To further complicate matters the nineteenth-century marriage attempted to make up for the lack of passion with a certain gentility and oppressive inhibitedness. Men and women could not visit art galleries together in Philadelphia because of the potential embarrassment that classical statues would cause. Prudery was carried to extraordinary lengths and Victorian standards of decorum seem to have been more oppressively enforced in this country than even in England.

The separation of sexuality from respectable relationships resulted in increasing reliance by men on the services of prostitutes to satisfy urges that were considered too beastly to impose on their wives and the mothers of their children. This is not to say that many individuals did not achieve a workable harmony between sex and affection within their marriages. But the tendency, at least among the financially better off classes, was toward idealizing women on the one hand and robbing them of their sexuality on the other.

There were occasional female voices of protest, but these usually involved radical feminists. Victoria Woodhull, for instance, proclaimed in one public lecture: "Yes, I am a free lover! I have an inalienable, constitutional, and natural right to love whom I may, to love as long or as short a period as I can, to change that love every day if I please!"

The upheaval of World War I accelerated dramatically the changes that were already in ferment at the turn of the century. Wars have a jarring impact, since people under stress are driven to and allow themselves behaviors that they ordinarily would not engage in. In the postwar period additional influences, including the spread of the tenets of psychoanalysis and the social sciences, further secularized and liberalized the common culture. Other important influences that helped liberalize sexual attitudes were related to increasing leisure and prosperity and the availability of contraceptives. The development of the automobile and the movie industry also had widespread impact, since the former provided a certain mobile privacy and the latter reached large numbers of individuals and often dwelt on romantic and, for the time, sexually explicit themes.

The changes following World War II further eroded traditional sexual attitudes. With the spread and entrenchment of psychoanalytic views in psychiatry and the social sciences the notion that sex is a central moving force in life came to be more widely accepted. The studies of Alfred C. Kinsey and his associates in the late 1940s and early 1950s, as well as the writings of the anthropologist Margaret Mead, combined to force people to reconsider their traditional views about how people behave or ought to behave sexually. Further advances in the development of contraceptives made the separation of sex and reproduction more feasible for a wider sector of the population. The discovery of penicillin virtually eliminated for a while the threat of syphilis and gonorrhea. Children reared according to permissive standards grew up to be parents themselves and allowed more latitude in behavior to their own children, so that by the early 1960s a new generation of youth developed a distinctive life style, a more radical political philosophy, and more liberal sexual attitudes. This trend carried over into the 1970s, though there are indications of a slight return to less radical attitudes.

Common observation indicates that during the past two decades there have been sweeping changes in public attitudes toward the expression and discussion of sexual themes. The publications of Masters and Johnson brought sex into sharp focus both within the professions and among the general public. The astonishing success of Reuben's *Everything You Always Wanted to Know about Sex (But Were Afraid to Ask)*, the "Sensuous" series (Woman, Man, Couple, and so forth), and, more currently, Comfort's *The Joy of Sex* and *More Joy* (the most sophisticated and intelli-

gently written books in this "genre") indicate an apparently insatiable interest in such literature by the reading public.

In the literary world sexually explicit themes are becoming commonplace. There have always been such books on the market, but now the authors are established writers like Philip Roth and John Updike. Nor is such literary license any longer the prerogative of male writers, as witness Erica Jong's *Fear of Flying*. The theater, too, has stretched the boundaries of the acceptable to include explicit scenes of coitus (*Oh! Calcutta!*), oral-genital sex (*The Beard*), and homosexual acts (*Fortune and Men's Eyes*). The *Last Tango in Paris* represents this same trend in film, which in the more "hard core" variety is already suffering from the boredom of redundancy. That sexual attitudes have been changing markedly in large segments of the population is quite clear. But what about actual behavior? Until lately the prevailing opinion among professionals was that there was no significant change in sexual behavior commensurate with changes in attitude. Recent studies show that this may no longer be the case. Real and impressive changes have taken place in premarital sexual behavior and possibly in other areas as well, as we shall discuss in Chapter 7.

It may not be an exaggeration to say that currently the area of human sexuality is in a state of flux. Our knowledge of sexual biology is expanding as research in this field gains in respectability. The same applies to some extent to studies of sexual behavior, which unfortunately continue to remain more subject to methodological pitfalls. Notions of sexual normality, norms, and morality are timely topics of conversation among youth, as well as the older generations. These issues are in turn intertwined with the expanding concerns of the women's liberation movement.

Now that we are free to talk about sex and freer to act than before, an additional measure of responsibility is called for. If we do not want others to provide us with set formulas, we must have the necessary information to formulate our own opinions. The profusion and diversity of conviction and advice require that we sharpen our critical judgment to sort out the sense and nonsense in our sexual lives. Rapid change involves higher risks. In ridding ourselves and our institutions of anachronistic attitudes and practices we may inadvertently discard the useful with the useless in the manner of the proverbial baby and the bath water. An informed and reasoned approach is therefore called for, not only to gain anew what we need but also to not lose what we already have that is of demonstrable value. To this end the following chapters are dedicated.

Biology

PART ONE

THE ANATOMY
of the SEX ORGANS

THE PHYSIOLOGY
of SEXUAL FUNCTIONS

SEX HORMONES
and the REPRODUCTIVE
PERIOD

CONCEPTION, PREGNANCY,
and BIRTH

CONTRACEPTION

THE ANATOMY of THE SEX

cHAPTER 2 ORGANS

Did You Know That . . .

penis is the Latin word for "tail"?

the scrotum contracts when the inner side of the thigh is stimulated?

the clitoris is an erectile organ that grows larger when stimulated?

fertilization usually takes place in the fallopian tubes, not the uterus?

the organ of the body that normally goes through the most dramatic changes in size is the uterus?

during the first six or seven weeks of intrauterine life male and female embryos cannot be told apart?

if the gonads of an embryo are removed during the early weeks of intrauterine life an embryo— whether male or female—will develop anatomically as a female?

INTRODUCTION

Poets have sung its praises. Artists have sculpted and painted its fascinating form more than a million times. It has been described as everything from "the temple of the soul" to "an ingenious assembly of portable plumbing." It is, of course, the human body—a marvelous, exquisitely tooled, and perfectly designed biological machine whose workings and form have been objects of fascination and wonder throughout history.

Much of our fascination with the human body has focused on the genitals, the sex organs that provide both erotic pleasure and a means of reproducing our species. Cave drawings and Stone Age carvings dating back thousands of years depict the human genitals in a variety of ways. The ancient Greeks and Romans had religious cults dedicated to the worship of the human genitals. Phallic worship (**phallus** is the Greek word for "penis") is one of the oldest religious practices known and has been seen in a variety of cultures around the world. In societies that relied on the forces of nature much more than today's technological societies do, fertility—of crops, animals, and humans—was an important issue. Symbols of fertility, such as the penis and the female form, became objects of worship in the fertility cults and religious practices of such societies. Representation of the genitals of both sexes in prehistoric cave drawings, Renaissance paintings, modern art, and popular magazines (to mention only a few, *see* Figures 2.2 and 2.3) suggests that our interest in the human body and its sex organs always has been and always will be high.

Our interest in the sex organs often centers on their external appearance because of what they symbolize (erotic pleasure, sexual love, fertility, and human reproduction). But the structure and function of these organs—their design and the way they operate—is equally fascinating. As we will see in this chapter, the male and female sex organs, though dramatically different in appearance, are basically similar and complementary in their functions. In fact, the male and female sex organs grow from similar tissues and develop along almost identical lines during the early stages of fetal growth.

At maturity the male and female sex organs are equal parts of the human reproductive system. They are designed so that the male's penis fits perfectly inside the female's vagina. This sexual joining, called **coitus** ("coming together"), copulation, or sexual intercourse, makes possible the union of male and female germ cells (the sperm produced by

Figure 2.1 Mochica pottery.
Courtesy of William Dellenback, Institute for Sex Research, Inc.

Figure 2.2 *Pair of Lovers,* late copy after an engraving by Marcantonio Raimondi, based on design by Giulio Romano.

the male and the egg, or ovum, produced by the female). When these germ cells unite they form one fertile cell capable of developing into a human being.

For a long time the sex organs were objects of mystery as well as of fascination. Most people knew little or nothing of how the sex organs worked or of the processes involved in reproduction. Even without such knowledge, however, people have been engaging in sexual activity, giving and receiving a great deal of erotic pleasure, and successfully reproducing the species for hundreds of thousands of years. Much of the mystery that once surrounded sex has been cleared up by modern science, and even though up-to-date scientific information is not essential for most people to lead successful sex lives, a basic knowledge of the sex organs can add to whatever appreciation we may already have of such matters.

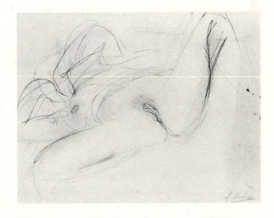

Figure 2.3 *Nude, c.* 1910, drawing by A. Rodin.

17

Anatomy is the study of the structure of organs and organisms. Physiology is the study of the functions and activities of organs and organisms. In this chapter we will examine the anatomy of both the male and the female sex organs. In the next chapter we will discuss the physiology of the sex organs.

THE MALE SEX ORGANS

There is more to the sex organs than meets the eye. In both males and females the sex organs are located partly outside and partly inside the body cavity. The internal sex organs are suspended in a sort of hammock connected to the bones of the **pelvis,** which houses and protects them (*see* Figure 2.4). The pelvis is made up of the **sacrum** (the triangular end of the spinal column) and the two hip bones. The hip bones are attached to the sacrum at the rear and to each other (at the **pubic symphis**) in front, forming a bottomless bowl—the pelvic cavity. Organs of the reproductive, urinary, and digestive systems are located within this cavity (*see* Figure 2.5) and are separated from one another and supported by various fibrous structures and cords. These, along with muscles in the

area, form the hammock in which the internal sex organs are suspended.

Although the internal and external sex organs belong to a single system, the external organs, the genitals, are usually thought of in terms of sexual activity itself, and the internal organs in terms of reproduction. The entire system, both external and internal components, is generally referred to as the reproductive system (though reproduction is only one of the possible goals of sexual activity).

The reproductive system of the male consists of three units: the sperm-producing **testes;** a system of *ducts,* or tubes, for the storage and transport of sperm; and an apparatus for the delivery of sperm. The first two units of this system are the internal sex organs. The components of the third unit, the **penis** and the **scrotum,** or sac, that holds the testes, are the external organs.

External Sex Organs

The Penis

The male organ through which sperm are transported is the penis (from the Latin word for "tail"). It has two notable features: It is an extremely sensitive and excitable organ, and it has the ability to become hard and

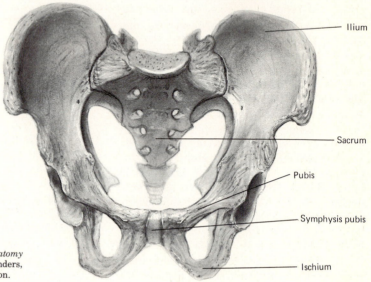

Figure 2.4   Male bony pelvis.

From Dienhart, *Basic Human Anatomy and Physiology* (Philadelphia: Saunders, 1967), p. 35. Reprinted by permission.

Ilium

Sacrum

Pubis

Symphysis pubis

Ischium

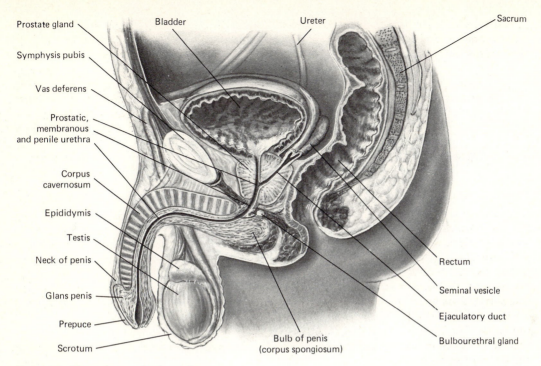

Prostate gland
Symphysis pubis
Vas deferens
Prostatic, membranous and penile urethra
Corpus cavernosum
Epididymis
Testis
Neck of penis
Glans penis
Prepuce
Scrotum

Bladder
Ureter
Sacrum

Bulb of penis (corpus spongiosum)

Rectum
Seminal vesicle
Ejaculatory duct
Bulbourethral gland

Figure 2.5 The male reproductive system.

From Dienhart, *Basic Human Anatomy and Physiology* (Philadelphia: Saunders, 1967), p. 207. Reprinted by permission.

stand erect. In its unexcited state, the penis is a soft tube of flesh that hangs between the legs of the male. When excited, it becomes larger, harder, stands erect, and can be inserted into the female vagina. The penis in its erect state has been described (in the vernacular) as a pricking, piercing, or probing instrument.

The penis has three main sections: the root, the body, and the head, or **glans penis.** The root is attached to the pelvis. The body is the free-hanging portion. And the glans (from the Latin word for "acorn") is the smooth, rounded tip of the penis.

The glans penis has particular sexual importance because it contains a great many nerve endings and is extremely sensitive— much more so than the rest of the penis. An especially sensitive area is the rim, or crown (**corona**), of the glans. This is the raised edge of the glans that slightly overhangs the neck, the boundary between the glans and the body of the penis. An even more sensitive and ex-

citable area is the underside of the glans where a thin strip of skin (the **frenulum**) connects it to the body of the penis.

Although the penis looks like a tube, it actually consists of three parallel cylinders of spongy tissue (*see* Figure 2.6). Two of these cylinders are called the cavernous bodies (**corpora cavernosa**), and the third is called the spongy body (**corpus spongiosum**). Running through this third cylinder is a tube called the **urethra** that carries both urine and **semen** (liquid that contains the sperm) out of the body. The opening of the urethra, located at the tip of the glans, is called the **meatus.**

The inner tips (**crura**) of the cavernous bodies are attached to the pubic bones, but the spongy body is not attached to any bone. Instead, its inner end expands to form the **bulb** of the penis, which is fixed to the fibrous hammock that stretches in the area beneath the pubic symphysis. The front end of the spongy body expands to shelter the tips of the

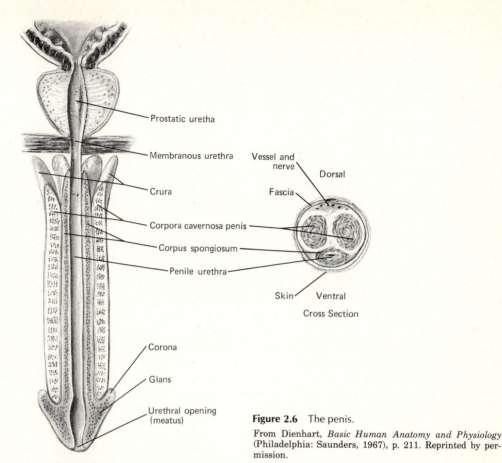

Prostatic uretha

Membranous urethra

Vessel and nerve

Dorsal

Fascia

Crura

Corpora cavernosa penis

Corpus spongiosum

Penile urethra

Skin   Ventral

Cross Section

Corona

Glans

Urethral opening
(meatus)

Longitudinal Section

Figure 2.6   The penis.

From Dienhart, *Basic Human Anatomy and Physiology*
(Philadelphia: Saunders, 1967), p. 211. Reprinted by permission.

cavernous bodies and to form the glans penis.
The crura and the bulb make up the root of
the penis. Muscles (the **bulbocavernosus**
and the **ischiocavernosus**) that surround
the bulb and crura help eject urine and semen
through the urethra.

Each cylinder of the penis is wrapped in a
tough fibrous coat, with the two cavernous
bodies having an additional common wrap-
ping that makes them appear as a single structure for most of their length. When the penis
is flaccid, or soft, these bodies cannot be seen
or felt as separate structures, but when the
penis is erect, the spongy body stands out as a
distinct ridge on the underside of the penis.

The penis is richly supplied with blood vessels, and it is the flow of blood into the penis

that gives it its ability to become stiff and
hard during an erection. As the terms "cavernous" and "spongy" suggest, the penis contains a great many irregular cavities and
spaces — very much like a sponge. When the
penis is flaccid, its cavities contain little
blood, but during sexual arousal the caverns
become engorged, or filled, with blood. And
because the three cylinders of the penis are
constricted by their fibrous coats, pressure
builds up within them, giving the erect penis
its characteristic stiffness. (The mechanism of
erection will be discussed more fully in the
next chapter.)

The skin of the penis is hairless and unusually loose, which permits expansion during erection. Although the skin is fixed to the

20

penis at the neck, some skin folds over and covers part of the glans (except during erection), forming the **prepuce,** or **foreskin.** Beneath the prepuce and in the corona and neck of the penis are small glands that produce a cheesy substance (**smegma**) that has a distinctive odor. This substance, which has no known function, is not the same as semen, which is discharged through the urethra.

Circumcision Circumcision ("cutting around") is an ancient practice in which the foreskin is removed. The operation is simple: The prepuce, or foreskin, is pulled forward and part of it is cut off, leaving the glans and the neck totally exposed at all times.

There are several reasons why circumcision is performed. In some cultures it is done as a ceremony marking a boy's passage from childhood to manhood. In some instances circumcision is a mark of membership in a religion (such as Judaism). There is also a rare condition known as phimosis in which the prepuce is so tight that it cannot be pulled back over the glans. In this case, circumcision is considered medically necessary. Otherwise it is optional—although it is still performed (with parental consent) in most hospitals in the United States on the second day after birth.

Size of the Penis Variation in size and shape from individual to individual is the rule for all parts of the human body. Even though most of us are aware of this rule, the size and shape of the penis are often the cause of curiosity and amusement as well as of apprehension and concern. One reason a man may feel inadequate with regard to the size of his penis is that many men and women tend to believe that a large penis is more virile, stronger, and more potent than a small penis. Such beliefs are reinforced by jokes and pornographic movies and literature that often emphasize penis size. Despite such attitudes, virtually all penises are neither too small nor too large to function as a reproductive tool or to give and receive sexual pleasure.

The average penis is from 3 to 4 inches (7.6 to 10.2 centimeters) long when flaccid and about 6 inches (15.2 centimeters) long when erect. The diameter of the penis is about 1.2 inches (3.2 centimeters) in the relaxed state and about 1.5 inches (3.8 centimeters) during erection. Penises can, however, be considerably larger or smaller. Differences in penis size are less marked in the erect than in the flaccid state.

The Scrotum

Suspended beneath the penis is the scrotum, the multilayered pouch that holds the testicles. The outermost skin of the scrotum is darker in color than the rest of the body and contains many sweat glands. At puberty, when the reproductive organs begin to mature, the scrotum becomes sparsely covered with hair.

The second layer of the pouch consists of loosely organized tissues and muscle fibers. These muscles are not under voluntary control but do contract, or tighten, in response to cold, sexual excitement, and other stimuli. The scrotum contracts, for instance, when the inner side of the thigh is stimulated. When the muscles do contract, the scrotum appears compact and heavily wrinkled. Otherwise it hangs loose and has a smooth surface.

Internal Sex Organs

In reproductive terms, the task of the male sex organs is to produce and deliver sperm to the female sex organs. The penis, as we have seen, is the delivery apparatus. Production and storage of sperm are the tasks of the internal sex organs. Sperm are produced in the testes, and long tubes running from each testicle carry them to the penis and out of the body. At various points along this journey the system of tubes is called by different names—epididymis, vas deferens, ejaculatory duct, and urethra.

The Testes

The reproductive glands, or **gonads,** of the male are the testes (from the Latin word for "witness," as in *testify,* from the ancient custom of placing one hand over the genitals when taking an oath). The testes produce sperm as well as testosterone, the male hormone. (Hormones, which will be discussed in Chapter 4, are body chemicals that control various functions, including growth and sexual development.)

The two testicles are about the same size (2 × 1 × 1.2 inches [5.1 × 2.5 × 3.2 centimeters]), although the left one usually hangs a little lower than the right one. The weight of the testicles varies from one person to another, but averages about 1 ounce (28.3 grams) and tends to lessen in old age. The testes are housed in the scrotal sac, which contains two separate compartments, one for each testicle and its spermatic cord. This cord is the structure from which the testicle is suspended in the scrotal sac. It contains the tube (**vas deferens**) that carries sperm from the testicle, as well as blood vessels, nerves, and muscle fibers. When these muscles contract, the spermatic cord shortens and pulls the testicle upward within the scrotal sac.

Inside the scrotum each testicle is enclosed within a white, fibrous sheath that is thickest at the rear of the testicle. There it penetrates and spreads out within the testicle, subdividing it into conical lobes. The structures in which sperm are produced are located within these lobes (*see* Figure 2.7, which shows only a few of the many lobes). The tight, white covering of the testicles is indirectly responsible for one type of sterility (inability to reproduce) that sometimes follows an adult case of the mumps. When this virus infection involves mature testicles, they swell and push against their unyielding covers. The resulting pressure destroys the tubes in which sperm are produced.

The process of **spermatogenesis** (production of sperm) takes place completely within the **seminiferous** (sperm-bearing) **tubules.** At birth these threadlike structures are solid cords, but at puberty they develop hollow centers (*see* Figure 2.8). Each seminiferous tubule is from 1 to 3 feet (30.5 to 91.4 centimeters) long but is highly convoluted (compactly folded and curved) and takes up very little space. The combined length of the seminiferous tubules of both testicles is several hundred yards—allowing for the production and storage of hundreds of millions of sperm.

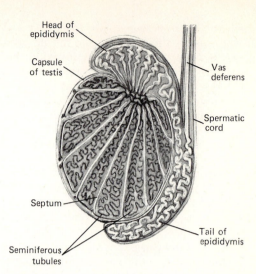

Figure 2.7 Testis and epididymis.

From Dienhart, *Basic Human Anatomy and Physiology* (Philadelphia: Saunders, 1967), p. 207. Reprinted by permission.

The Duct System

Once the sperm are produced, they begin a long and tortuous journey full of repeated twists, bends, and turns. The journey begins as the sperm leave the seminiferous tubules. These tubules come together and fuse into a single tube in each testicle, forming the beginning of a system of paired genital ducts.

The Epididymis The **epididymis** ("over the testis") is the first part of this duct system. Each epididymis is a remarkably long, convoluted tube (about 20 feet [6.1 meters] when stretched out) that appears as a C-shaped structure not much larger than the testis over the surface of which it runs.

The Vas Deferens The vas deferens, or **ductus deferens** ("the vessel that brings down"), is the less tortuous and shorter continuation of the epididymis through which the sperm continue their journey up out of the scrotal sac (*see* Figure 2.7). The vas deferens is the easily located cord that can be felt in the scrotal sac. It is also the most convenient target for sterilizing men. The operation, called a **vasectomy** ("cutting the vas") is

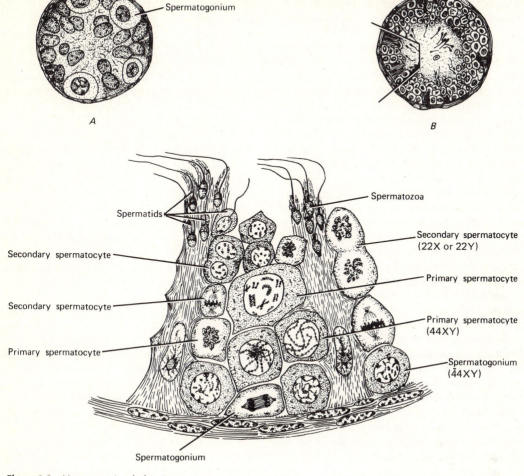

Figure 2.8 Human testis tubules, in transverse section. *(A)* Newborn (×400); *(B)* adult (×115); *(C)* detail of the area outlined in *(B)* (×900).

From Arey, *Developmental Anatomy,* 7th ed. (Philadelphia: Saunders, 1965), p. 41. Reprinted by permission.

simple: Under local anesthesia, a small incision, or cut, is made in the scrotum, and the vas of each testicle is either tied shut or cut. A man who has had a vasectomy will still be able to ejaculate, but his semen will contain no sperm (which remain in the testicle and are reabsorbed). The result is sterility, but sex drive and the ability to have orgasms are not affected. The effects of a vasectomy can be reversed sometimes and fertility reestab-

lished by untying or by sewing together the cut vas. This procedure, however, is very delicate and not always successful.

The vas deferens runs up out of the scrotal sac and through the abdominal cavity. Near its end it widens into an area called the **ampulla** ("flask"). From there it passes behind the urinary bladder, narrows to a tip, and joins the ejaculatory duct. This last portion of the paired genital duct system runs its entire course within the prostate gland and is less than 1 inch (2.5 centimeters) long. It opens into the urethra.

The Urethra The **urethra,** which is about 8 inches (20.3 centimeters) long, is the tube that carries both urine and semen out of the body. It is divided into prostatic, membranous, and penile parts (*see* Figures 2.5 and 2.6). The prostatic portion of the urethra is more easily dilated (widened) than are the others. The two ejaculatory ducts and the multiple ducts of the prostate gland open into it (*see* Figure 2.6).

The short membranous portion of the urethra is surrounded by muscle fibers (the **urethral sphincter**) that make possible voluntary control of urination. When sufficient urine has accumulated in the bladder, a slight discomfort results and the person is prompted to relax the urethral sphincter and allow the passage of urine. Because the sphincter is located at the root of the penis rather than at the head, some urine remains in the penile portion of the urethra after the sphincter is closed. This remaining urine is squirted out by contractions of the muscles that surround the bulb of the penis.

The penile portion of the urethra has already been mentioned. It pierces the bulb of the corpus spongiosum, travels the length of the penis, and opens in the glans at the meatus (*see* Figure 2.6).

Accessory Organs

Several additional organs play roles in the reproductive system of the male: the prostate gland, two seminal vesicles, and two bulbourethral glands.

The Prostate The **prostate** is a structure about the size of a chestnut located at the bottom of the bladder. It consists of three lobes and contains glandular tissue with some smooth muscle fibers. The secretions of the tissues account for much of the seminal fluid and for its characteristic odor. These secretions empty into the urethra through a "sieve" of multiple ducts. As mentioned earlier, sperm are also poured into the prostatic

part of the urethra through the ejaculatory ducts.

The prostate, which is small at birth, enlarges rapidly at puberty and usually shrinks in old age. Sometimes, however, it becomes enlarged and interferes with urination. In such cases, the prostate can be removed in open surgery or piece by piece through the urethra.

The Seminal Vesicles The two seminal vesicles also contribute fluid to the semen. Each is a small sac, about 2 inches (5.1 centimeters) long, that ends in a straight, narrow duct at the tip of the vas deferens to form the ejaculatory duct. The seminal vesicles were once thought to be storage areas for sperm (each holds from 2 to 3 cubic centimeters of fluid), but it is currently believed that they are primarily involved in contributing fluids that activate the sperms' tails and aid in the movement of sperm.

The Bulbourethral Glands Another fluid that enters the urethra is produced by the bulbourethral glands (**Cowper's glands**), two pea-sized structures that flank the penile urethra and empty into it through tiny ducts. During sexual arousal these glands secrete a clear, sticky fluid that appears as a droplet at the tip of the glans. (The fluid has been called the "distillate of love.") It is an alkaline substance that probably serves to neutralize the acidic surface of the urethra and prepare it for the passage of sperm, which are harmed by acid. Although the fluid produced by the bulbourethral glands is not the same as semen, it often contains some stray sperm—which explains pregnancies that may result from intercourse without ejaculation (the release of sperm). This is one of the reasons that the withdrawal method of birth control (*see* Chapter 6) is not very effective.

THE FEMALE SEX ORGANS

"I'll show you mine if you'll show me yours," little boys and girls have been known to say to each other; and their curiosity is just another indication of our fascination with the sex organs. Part of the attraction probably has to do with the apparent difference between the sexes. The female and male sex organs look nothing alike, yet they are closely related in both design and function. They develop from similar tissues, and at maturity they fit together like parts of a well-designed machine. They both contain erectile tissue, change sizes, and consist of systems of tubes and ducts. They both have internal and external components, and they have the same three basic functions. In the female these are the production of germ cells, or eggs (in the **ovaries**), the transport of those cells (through the **fallopian tubes** to the **uterus**), and the reception of semen from the penis (in the **vagina**). In addition, the female sex organs have a uniquely maternal function. Because fertilization of the egg occurs inside the female body, the female duct system carries sperm as well as eggs and the fertilized product of those two germ cells. The uterus is also the organ in which the embryo develops.

External Sex Organs

The external sex organs of the female are collectively called the **vulva** ("covering"). They include the **mons pubis** (or **mons veneris,** "mount of Venus," the goddess of love), the **major** and **minor lips,** the **clitoris,** and the **vaginal opening.**

The mons pubis is the soft, rounded mound of fatty tissue that covers the pubic symphysis. It becomes covered with hair at puberty and is the most visible part of the female genitals.

The Major Lips

The major lips (**labia majora**) are two elongated folds of skin that run down and back from the mons pubis. Their appearance varies from woman to woman. Some are flat and hardly visible behind thick pubic hair. Others bulge prominently. Ordinarily these lips are close together, and the female genitals appear "closed."

The major lips are more distinct where they meet in front. Toward the anus they flatten out and merge with the surrounding tissues. The outer surfaces of these lips are covered with skin of a darker color, which grows hair at puberty. The inner surfaces are smooth and hairless. Within these folds of skin are bundles of smooth muscle fibers, nerves, and vessels for blood and lymph. The space between the major lips is visible only when the lips are parted (*see* Figure 2.9).

The Minor Lips

The minor lips (**labia minora**) are two fleshy, hairless folds of skin located between the major lips. The space the minor lips enclose contains (from front to back) the clitoris, the opening of the urethra, the opening of the vagina, and the openings of the two Bartholin's or greater vestibular glands. The **anus,** which is completely separate from the external genitals, lies farthest back.

The minor lips merge with the major lips in the rear (toward the anus). In front each divides in two. The upper portions form a single fold of skin over the clitoris and are called the **prepuce of the clitoris.** The lower portions meet beneath the clitoris as a separate fold of skin called the **frenulum of the clitoris.**

The Clitoris

The **clitoris** is the female embryonal counterpart of the penis. It is smaller than the penis but similar to it in several ways. The clitoris consists of erectile tissue (two corpora cavernosa but no corpus spongiosum) attached to the pubic bone. Most of the body of the clitoris is covered by the upper folds of the minor lips, but its free rounded tip, the glans, projects beyond the lips. Like the glans of the penis, the clitoris is richly endowed with nerves, highly sensitive, and a major focus of sexual stimulation. In fact, sexual stimulation is the only function of the clitoris. During sexual arousal it becomes engorged with blood and grows slightly larger. But because of the way it is attached it does not actually stand erect.

Clitoridectomy, or removal of the clitoris, is a rare procedure, but it has been practiced

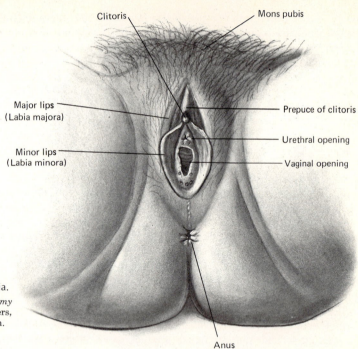

Clitoris

Mons pubis

Major lips
(Labia majora)

Prepuce of clitoris

Urethral opening

Minor lips
(Labia minora)

Vaginal opening

Anus

Figure 2.9 External female genitalia.

From Dienhart, *Basic Human Anatomy and Physiology* (Philadelphia: Saunders, 1967), p. 217. Reprinted by permission.

ritually in the Middle East and in certain tribes of Africa and Latin America. This mutilating procedure, for which there is no medical justification, has even been performed in Europe and the United States (as recently as the early part of this century) as a means of preventing masturbation. A related procedure, removal of the prepuce, or foreskin, of the clitoris has been performed in attempts to enhance sexual responsiveness. The procedure is reported to be effective in some instances, but it is not considered routine and is rarely recommended.

Slightly to the rear of the clitoris is the opening of the female urethra, a small slit with raised edges. The female urethra carries only urine and is totally independent of the reproductive system.

The Introitus

The opening, or orifice, of the vagina is called the **introitus.** It is not a gaping hole but is visible only when the inner lips are parted. The appearance of the vaginal orifice depends to a large extent on the shape and condition of the hymen. This delicate and exclusively human membrane, which has no known physiological function, varies in shape and size. It may surround the vaginal opening (annular), bridge it (septate), or serve as a sievelike cover (cribriform) (*see* Figure 2.10). There is usually always some opening to the outside, but in rare instances the hymen consists of a tough fibrous tissue that has no opening (imperforate hymen). This condition is usually detected after a girl begins to menstruate and the products of several menstrual periods begin to accumulate in the vagina and uterus. The condition is corrected by a simple surgical incision.

Most hymens will permit passage of a finger (or a sanitary tampon) but usually not an erect penis without tearing. Occasionally, however, a very flexible hymen will withstand intercourse. This fact, along with the fact that the hymen may be torn accidentally, makes the condition of the hymen unreliable as evidence for or against virginity.

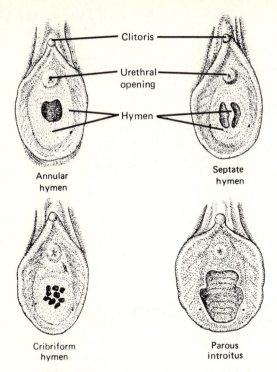

Clitoris

Urethral opening

Hymen

Annular hymen

Septate hymen

Cribriform hymen

Parous introitus

Figure 2.10 Types of hymens.

From Netter, *Reproductive System* (Summitt, N.J.: Ciba, 1965), p. 90. Reprinted by permission.

Virginity on the wedding night is not emphasized in our culture as forcefully as it once was, but in many societies the intact hymen has been used as an indication of virginity, and there is hardly a culture that has not been preoccupied with the proper disposal of the hymen—often called **defloration,** or **deflowering.** In medieval times some lords are said to have claimed the prerogative of "plucking the maidenheads" of their female subjects on the women's wedding nights. Where defloration has been thought to pose a magical threat, special men have been assigned to carry it out. Among the seminomadic Yungar of Australia girls were deflowered by two old women a week before marriage. If a girl's hymen was discovered at this time to be not intact, she could be starved, tortured, mutilated, or even killed.

The old custom of parading the bloodstained bed sheets on the wedding night is well known. In various cultures horns, stone phalluses, or other assorted implements have been used in ritual deflorations.

Internal Sex Organs

The internal sex organs of the female include the paired ovaries and fallopian tubes, the uterus, and the vagina, along with a few accessory structures. These organs are housed in the pelvic cavity and are supported by a multilayered hammock suspended across the opening of the pelvis. The female pelvis is broader than that of the male in order to permit passage of the infant's head during birth (*see* Figure 2.11).

The Ovaries

The ovaries correspond to the testes. They are the gonads, or reproductive glands, of the female and have two functions: They produce germ cells called **ova** ("eggs") and the female hormones **estrogen** and **progesterone.** The ovary is almond-shaped, smaller ($1.5 \times 0.7 \times 1$ inches or $3.2 \times 1.9 \times 2.5$ centimeters) and lighter (0.2 ounce or 7.1 grams) than the testis. In their usual positions the ovaries lie vertically, flanking the uterus (*see* Figures 2.12, 2.13 and 2.14). They are held in place by a number of folds and ligaments, including the **ovarian ligaments,** which attach them to the sides of the uterus.

The ovary contains numerous capsules, or **follicles,** in various stages of development. They are embedded in the tissues and are located near the surface of the organ (the **cortex,** or "bark"). The central portion of the ovary (the **medulla,** or "marrow") is rich in convoluted blood vessels. Each follicle contains an ovum, and every female is born with several hundred thousand immature ova. At puberty some of the follicles start maturing, and each month usually one follicle reaches maturity and releases its ovum. The egg leaves the ovary by bursting through its wall. The empty follicle becomes a yellowish struc-

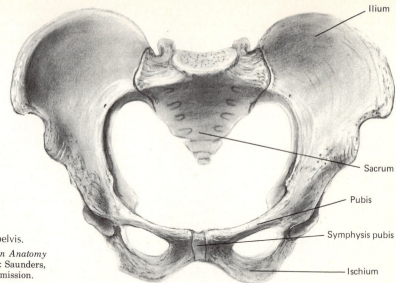

Ilium

Sacrum

Pubis

Symphysis pubis

Ischium

Figure 2.11 Female bony pelvis.

From Dienhart, *Basic Human Anatomy and Physiology* (Philadelphia: Saunders, 1967), p. 35. Reprinted by permission.

ture called the **corpus luteum.** This ovarian cycle has great reproductive and hormonal significance and will be discussed in more detail in Chapters 4 and 5.

The Fallopian Tubes

Both male and female reproductive systems consist of sets of tubes for the transport of germ cells. But the ovary, unlike the testis, has no tubes leading directly out of it. When eggs leave the ovary, they become caught in the fringed end of the fallopian tube. These tubes were named after a sixteenth-century Italian anatomist, Gabriello Fallopio, who mistakenly thought they were "ventilators" for the uterus. Instead, they are the tubes through which eggs are transported from the ovary toward the uterus.

The fallopian tubes, which are about 4 inches (10.2 centimeters) long, extend from the ovaries to the uterus. The ovarian end of the tube, the **infundibulum** ("funnel"), is cone-shaped and fringed by irregular projections, or **fimbriae,** that cling to or embrace the ovary but are not attached to it. This arrangement aids the ovum, which must find its way to the fallopian tube after leaving the ovary. Although not every egg finds its way to the fallopian tube, there have even been in-

stances in which women missing an ovary on one side and missing a fallopian tube on the other side became pregnant—all the more remarkable considering that the ovum is about the size of a needle tip and the opening of the fallopian tube is a slit only about the size of a printed hyphen.

The second portion of the fallopian tube (the **ampulla**) accounts for more than half its length. It has thin walls and is joined to the less tortuous **isthmus,** which resembles a cord and ends at the uterine border. The final segment of the tube (the uterine part) runs within the wall of the uterus and opens into its cavity.

The ovum, unlike sperm, cannot move on its own. Its movement through the fallopian tube depends on the sweeping motions of tiny hairlike structures (**cilia**) that line the tube and on contractions of the uterine wall during the passage of the ovum.

The fallopian tubes do more than provide a passageway for the ovum. The fertilization of the ovum usually occurs in the outer third of the tube, where sperm that have traveled through the vagina and the uterus meet the ovum. Passage of the ovum through the tube takes several days, and if fertilization has occurred, the structure that reaches the uterine

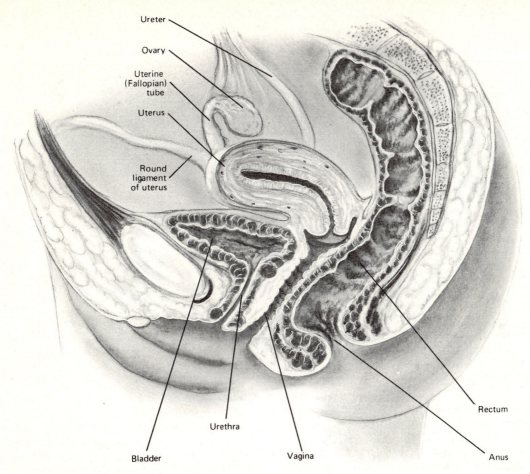

Figure 2.12   The female reproductive system.

From Dienhart, *Basic Human Anatomy and Physiology* (Philadelphia: Saunders, 1967), p. 213. Reprinted by permission.

cavity is already a complex, multicellular organism. On rare occasions the fertilized ovum becomes implanted in the wall of the fallopian tube itself, causing one form of **ectopic** ("out of place") **pregnancy** that ultimately results in the death of the fetus and may cause the tube to rupture—with potentially serious consequences for the woman.

Although the fallopian tubes are not as easy to get to as the vas deferens of the male, they are the most convenient targets for the sterilization of females. The usual procedure is to tie or cut the tubes (**tubal ligation**) on both sides. The result is sterility without in-

terference in sexual characteristics, desire, or ability to reach orgasm (*see* Chapter 6).

The Uterus

The uterus, or **womb,** is a hollow, muscular organ in which the fertilized ovum, or **embryo** (called a fetus after the eighth week), is housed and nourished until birth. The Greek word for uterus is *hystera,* a term that supplies the root for words like **hysterectomy** (surgical removal of the womb) and *hysteria* (a condition believed by the ancient Greeks to be the result of a uterus wandering through the body in search of a child).

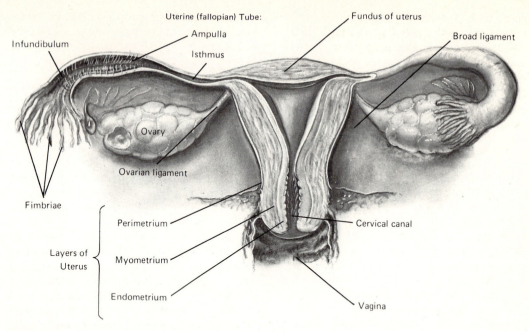

Infundibulum

Uterine (fallopian) Tube:

Ampulla

Isthmus

Fundus of uterus

Broad ligament

Ovary

Ovarian ligament

Fimbriae

Layers of Uterus

Perimetrium

Myometrium

Endometrium

Cervical canal

Vagina

Figure 2.13   Internal female reproductive organs.

From Dienhart, *Basic Human Anatomy and Physiology* (Philadelphia: Saunders, 1967), p. 215. Reprinted by permission.

The uterus is shaped like an upside-down pear and is usually tilted forward (*see* Figure 2.12). It is held, but not fixed, in place by various ligaments. Normally 3 inches (7.6 centimeters) long, 3 inches (7.6 centimeters) wide at the top, and 1 inch (2.5 centimeters) thick, the womb expands greatly during preg-

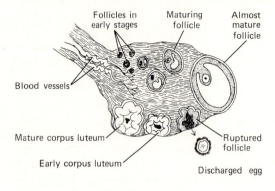

Follicles in early stages

Maturing follicle

Almost mature follicle

Blood vessels

Mature corpus luteum

Early corpus luteum

Ruptured follicle

Discharged egg

Figure 2.14   Composite view of ovum.

From Crawley, Malfetti, Stewart, and Vas Dias *Reproduction, Sex, and Preparation for Marriage* (Englewood Cliffs, N.J.: Prentice-Hall, 1964), p. 16. Reprinted by permission.

nancy. No other body organ goes through such changes in size.

The uterus consists of four parts (*see* Figure 2.13): the **fundus** ("bottom"), the rounded portion that lies above the openings of the fallopian tubes; the **body,** which is the main part; the narrow **isthmus** (not the same as the isthmus of the fallopian tube); and the **cervix** ("neck"), the lower part of which projects into the vagina. The cavity of the uterus is wider at the top, where the uterine tubes enter, and narrows toward the isthmus. Because the front and rear walls are ordinarily close together, the interior of the uterus appears as a narrow slit (*see* Figure 2.12). The opening of the cervix, which is no larger than the head of a pin, expands to a width of 4 inches (10.2 centimeters) in order to permit passage of an infant's head at birth.

The uterus has three layers (*see* Figure 2.13). The inner **mucosa,** or **endometrium,** consists of numerous glands and a rich network of blood vessels. The second, or muscular, layer (**myometrium**) is very well developed with intertwined layers of smooth muscle fibers that give the uterine wall tremendous elasticity and strength. It is these muscles that propel the fetus at the time of birth by means of a series of contractions. The third layer, the **perimetrium** or **serosa,** is the external cover.

The Vagina

The female reproductive tube system continues as the cervical canal of the uterus opens into the upper end of the vagina. The vagina ("sheath") is the female organ of copulation and the recipient of semen. Discharge during menstruation and the baby during birth also pass through the vagina.

The vagina is ordinarily a collapsed muscular tube, a potential, rather than a permanent, space. It is slanted downward and forward. Its front and rear walls are about 3 and 4 inches (7.6 and 10.2 centimeters) long, respectively. Its side walls are quite thin, and like the uterus, its interior appears as a narrow slit (*see* Figure 2.12).

The inner lining, or vaginal mucosa, is like the skin covering the inside of the mouth. In adult, premenopausal women the vaginal walls are corrugated, or wrinkled, but fleshy and soft. Menopause is the natural cessation of menstruation that usually occurs between the ages of 45 and 50 years. Following menopause the vaginal walls become thinner and smoother. The middle vaginal layer is muscular but far less developed than that of the uterine wall. The outer layer is also rather thin. The vaginal walls are poorly supplied with nerves, and like the body of the penis, most of the vagina is not very sensitive. The area surrounding the vaginal opening, however, is very excitable.

The vagina opens at its lower end into the vestibule between the minor lips. When the major and minor lips are removed, the ring of muscular fibers that surrounds the external vaginal opening, or introitus, can be seen (*see* Figure 2.15; the muscles are shown to the left of the vagina only). Muscular rings that act to constrict, or close, bodily orifices are known as **sphincters.** The bulbocavernosus muscle, in this case, acts as a vaginal sphincter even though it is not as highly developed as, for instance, the anal sphincter. Both voluntarily and sometimes without being aware of it, women can flex this muscle and narrow the opening of the vagina.

Underneath the bulbocavernosus muscles are the **vestibular bulbs,** two elongated masses of erectile tissue. These structures are connected at their upper ends with the clitoris and like that organ become congested with blood during sexual arousal. They too play an important role in the female sexual response cycle and together with the muscular ring determine the size, tightness, and "feel" of the vaginal opening.

Behind the vestibular bulbs are two small glands (**Bartholin's,** or **greater vestibular glands**), the ducts of which open on each side of the lower half of the vestibule in the ridges between the edge of the hymen and the minor lips. These glands are the female counterpart of the male bulbourethral (Cowper's) glands. Their function is also somewhat obscure. Although these glands were thought to play a major role in lubricating or moistening the vagina, the main source of vaginal lubrication is now known to be the walls of the vagina itself (*see* Chapter 3).

Size of the Vagina Because of its function in sexual intercourse, the size of the vagina, like that of the penis, has been the subject of great interest and speculation. There is rarely reason for concern, however. In most normal, adult women the vagina is neither "too tight" nor "too loose." Because the vagina stretches so easily, any sufficiently stimulated adult vagina should be able to accommodate even the largest penis. No penis is as large as a normal infant's head, which must pass through the vagina during birth.

Some vaginas may not return to normal size after childbirth, and tears produced during the birth process may weaken the vaginal walls. Exercising the muscles that surround the vagina can help counteract this effect. Even after childbirth, however, the vagina expands only to the extent that the penis requires. Most of the time there is no problem of "fit" between the penis and vagina.

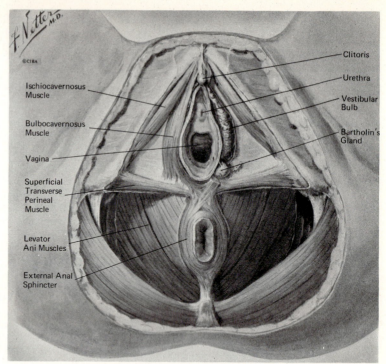

Clitoris

Urethra

Vestibular
Bulb

Bartholin's
Gland

Ischiocavernosus
Muscle

Bulbocavernosus
Muscle

Vagina

Superficial
Transverse
Perineal
Muscle

Levator
Ani Muscles

External Anal
Sphincter

Figure 2.15 External female genitalia.

From Netter, Frank H., *The Ciba Collection of Medical Illustrations:* Volume 2, Reproductive System, p. 92.

If there does seem to be a problem of fit, it probably has to do with the introitus, the opening to the vagina. The arrangement of the erectile tissue of the bulb of the vestibule and, more important, the muscular ring around it make a great deal of difference in how relaxed or tight it will be.

Although the muscles surrounding the vagina can "grip" the penis during intercourse, there is no reason to fear stories that the penis can be "trapped" inside the vagina, although some such cases have been reported. This concern usually arises from observations of dogs since the penis of a dog expands into a "knot" inside the vagina and cannot be withdrawn until ejaculation or loss of erection occurs. Other horror stories haunt some men: Fantasies that the vagina has teeth (*vagina dentata*) or is full of razor blades or ground glass are known and understandably influence sexual functioning.

The Breasts

Breasts are characteristic of the highest class of vertebrates (mammals), which suckle, or breast feed, their young. The breasts are not part of the reproductive system proper, but they do have a related function in females. Female breasts also have a high degree of erotic significance in many cultures. Although males also have breasts, their breasts are not as fully developed as those of females. (Male breasts can be stimulated to enlarge by injections of female hormones, as in the case of male transsexuals.)

The adult female breasts are located in front of the chest muscles, extending between the second and sixth ribs and from the midline of the chest to below the armpit. Each breast consists of lobes or clusters (about fifteen to twenty) of glandular tissue, each with a separate duct opening at the nipple. The lobes are separated by loosely packed fibrous and fatty tissue, which gives the breast its soft consistency (*see* Figure 2.16).

The **nipple** is the prominent tip of the breast. The area surrounding it, the **areola,** becomes darker during pregnancy and remains so thereafter. The nipple consists of smooth muscle fibers that can contract and make it stand erect. The nipple also contains a great many nerve endings, is highly sensitive, and plays an important role in sexual arousal. (However, not all females find it sexually stimulating to have their nipples kissed, and some males do find nipple stimulation arousing.) The sensitivity of the nipples and breasts is not related to their shape or size. The shape and size of the breasts do, however, play a role in their erotic appeal, especially in our culture. As a result, women with small breasts may feel self-conscious quite unnecessarily.

DEVELOPMENT OF THE SEX ORGANS

As we have seen throughout this chapter, the male and female sex organs, even though

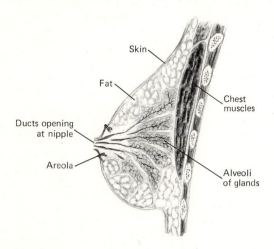

Figure 2.16 Vertical section of the breast.

From Dienhart *Basic Human Anatomy and Physiology* (Philadelphia: Saunders, 1967), p. 217. Reprinted by permission.

dramatically different in appearance, have quite similar and complementary functions (the production, storage, and transportation of germ cells). This similarity between the sexes is even more obvious during the early stages of development—as a quick look at the developmental process shows.

The sex of each individual is determined by the chromosomal makeup of the sperm (*see* Chapter 5) at the moment of fertilization. From this union of two cells, either a male or female will develop. For the first six or seven weeks, however, the male and female develop along almost identical lines and look quite similar.

The reproductive system makes its appearance during the fifth to sixth week of intrauterine life, when the embryo has attained a length of 5 to 12 millimeters. At this stage the embryo has a pair of gonads (reproductive glands) and two sets of ducts (*see* Figure 2.17), as well as the beginnings of the external genitals (*see* Figure 2.18). As development proceeds the gonads contribute chemicals necessary to sexual differentiation. If the gonads are removed at this stage, the embryo—even if it is a male—will develop anatomically into a female.

Differentiation of the Gonads

The gonad that is destined to develop into a testis becomes more and more compact as it develops. Some of its cells are organized into strands that will become the seminiferous (sperm-bearing) tubules. Others form the basis of the internal duct system, and by the seventh week enough development may have taken place for the organism to be recognizable (under a microscope) as a future testis. If by this time the basic architecture of the testis is not evident, it may be assumed that the gonad will develop into an ovary. Better evidence that the baby will be a girl comes near the tenth week when the forerunners of the follicles begin to become visible. After these basic patterns are set, the testis or ovary will continue to grow and eventually reach maturity at puberty.

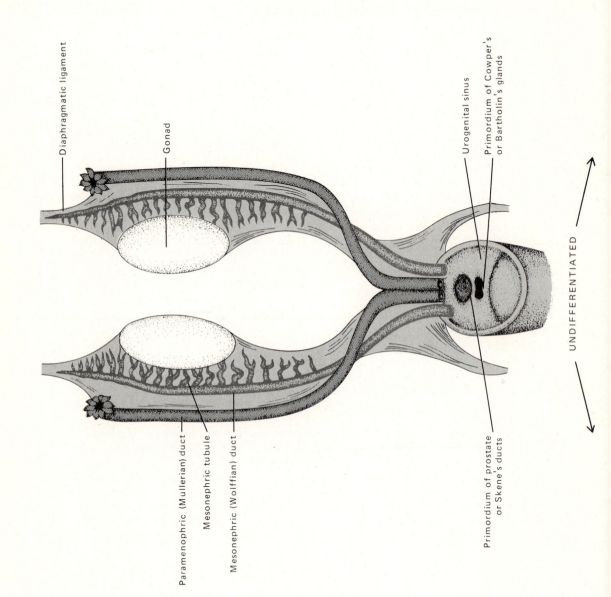

Diaphragmatic ligament

Gonad

Urogenital sinus

Primordium of Cowper's or Bartholin's glands

Paramenophric (Müllerian) duct

Mesonephric tubule

Mesonephric (Wolffian) duct

Primordium of prostate or Skene's ducts

UNDIFFERENTIATED

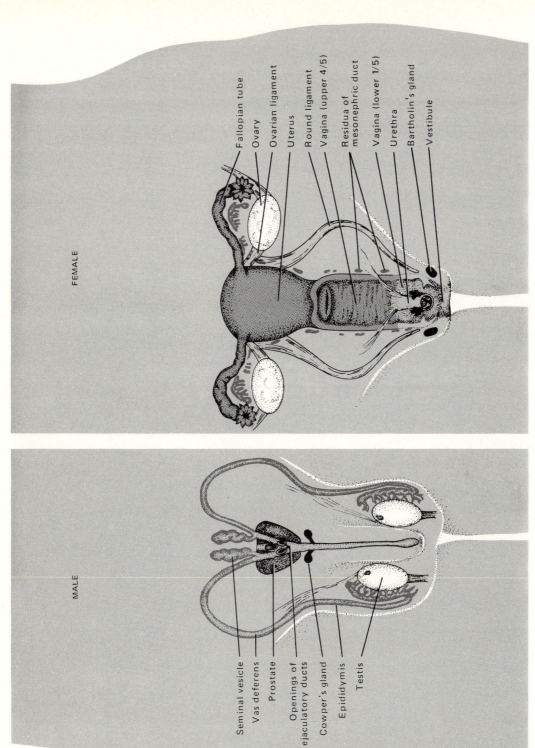

MALE

FEMALE

Seminal vesicle

Vas deferens

Prostate

Openings of
ejaculatory ducts

Cowper's gland

Epididymis

Testis

Fallopian tube

Ovary

Ovarian ligament

Uterus

Round ligament

Vagina (upper 4/5)

Residua of
mesonephric duct

Vagina (lower 1/5)

Urethra

Bartholin's gland

Vestibule

Figure 2.17 Similar components of internal male and female genitalia; development from undifferentiated into differentiated stage.
From Netter *Reproductive System,* The Ciba Collection of Medical Illustrations, vol. 2. (Summit, N.J.: Ciba, 1965), p. 2. Reprinted by permission.

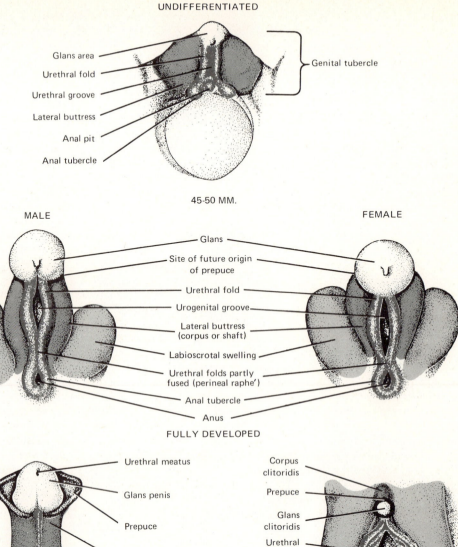

UNDIFFERENTIATED

Glans area
Urethral fold
Urethral groove
Lateral buttress
Anal pit
Anal tubercle

Genital tubercle

45-50 MM.

MALE

FEMALE

Glans
Site of future origin of prepuce
Urethral fold
Urogenital groove
Lateral buttress (corpus or shaft)
Labioscrotal swelling
Urethral folds partly fused (perineal raphe')
Anal tubercle
Anus

FULLY DEVELOPED

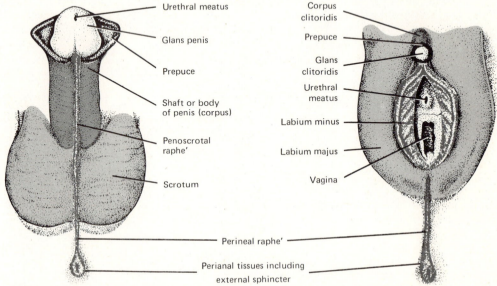

Urethral meatus
Glans penis
Prepuce
Shaft or body of penis (corpus)
Penoscrotal raphe'
Scrotum

Corpus clitoridis
Prepuce
Glans clitoridis
Urethral meatus
Labium minus
Labium majus
Vagina

Perineal raphe'
Perianal tissues including external sphincter

Figure 2.18 Similar components of external male and female genitalia; development from undifferentiated into differentiated stage.

From Netter, *Reproductive System*, The Ciba Collection of Medical Illustrations, vol. 2. (Summit, N.J.: Ciba, 1965), p. 3. Reprinted by permission.

Descent of the Testis and Ovary

As the gonads develop, they change in shape, size, and position. At first they are high up in the abdominal cavity, but by the tenth week they have grown and moved down to the level of the upper edge of the pelvis. The ovaries remain in this position until birth and then move farther down until they reach their adult position in the pelvis.

In the male, this early internal movement of the gonads is followed by the descent of the testes into the scrotal sac. As early as the third month preparations for this movement are underway. Sacs invade the scrotum in the seventh month and are usually followed by the testes within the next month or so (*see* Figure 2.19). After the testes are in place, the passage above them closes.

Two problems may arise during this process. First, one or both of the testes may fail to descend into the scrotum before birth (as happens in about 2 percent of the males born). In most such cases the testes do descend by puberty. If they do not, hormone treatments or surgery may be necessary in order to prevent sterility. If both testes remain undescended, the higher temperature of the abdominal cavity will interfere with the production of healthy sperm.

The second problem arises when the passage through which the testes descended does not close or reopens when the tissues become slack in old age. If such abnormal passage is created, loops of the intestine may find their way into the scrotal sac causing a condition known as **inguinal hernia,** or **rupture.** This too can easily be corrected by surgery.

Differentiation of the Genital Ducts

In the early stages of development the gonad has two ducts: the **mesonephric,** or **Wolffian** (the potential male ducts), and the **paramesonephric,** or **Müllerian** (the potential female) (*see* Figure 2.17). The Wolffian duct is the main genital duct in males. Its upper portion becomes the convoluted epididymis, and the lower part evolves into the vas deferens and ejaculatory duct. Parts of the Wolffian duct that do not become part of the reproductive system either degenerate or become blind tubules of no significance. Most of the Wolffian system in the female degenerates, leaving only a few blind canals that also are of no significance.

The genital passages of the female develop from the Müllerian duct system. The process is relatively simple, beginning with two sets of tubes. The upper portions remain independent and eventually develop into the two fallopian tubes. The middle and lower portions fuse to form, respectively, the uterus and the upper vagina (the rest of the vagina develops from other tissue). The Müllerian ducts in the male degenerate in the third month, although some fragments remain. In rare cases the Müllerian ducts do not degenerate and an otherwise perfectly normal male is born with a uterus.

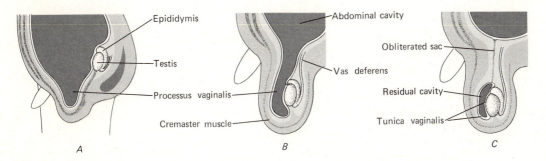

Figure 2.19 Descent of the human testis and its subsequent relations shown in diagrammatic hemisections. From Arey, *Developmental Anatomy,* 7th ed. (Philadelphia: Saunders, 1965), p. 333. Reprinted by permission.

Differentiation of the External Gonads

The external, like the internal, genitals are also quite similar in the early stages of development (*see* Figure 2.18). As mentioned earlier, by the sixth week, the sex of the embryo can usually be determined by means of a microscopic study of the gonads. Several more weeks of development are necessary before the external sex organs are easily visible, and by the fourth month the sex of the fetus is unmistakable. The developmental process of the external genitals is seen in Figure 2.18. This process usually proceeds in a predictable and orderly manner, though in rare cases there may be developmental problems (*see* Chapter 4).

SUMMARY

1. Anatomy is the study of the structure of organs and organisms. In this chapter we have looked at the anatomy of the male and female sex organs and have seen how they differ in structure but are complementary and similar in many ways. In addition to being capable of giving and receiving sexual pleasure, the sex organs are the reproductive tools of the species. When the male and female sex organs are joined during coitus (and no method of birth control is used) reproduction is made possible through the union of the germ cells produced by each sex.

2. The sex organs of both males and females are located inside and outside the body cavity. The internal organs are protected by and supported within the pelvic cavity. The external sex organs of the male are the penis and scrotum. The penis is divided into three sections—the root, the body, and the highly sensitive glans. Internally, the penis consists of three parallel cylinders of spongy tissue, two of which are attached to the pelvis. The urethra, which carries both urine and sperm out of the body, runs through the third cylinder. The scrotum is the multilayered pouch that hangs beneath the penis and houses the testicles.

3. The penis, the male organ of copulation, is capable of erection. When stimulated it grows in length, becomes hard, and stands erect. Erection is possible because the cylinders of the penis are wrapped in tough fibrous coats. When the spongy tissues of the penis are engorged with blood, they are constricted within their fibrous coats, and the resulting pressure produces the characteristic stiffness of the erect penis.

4. The internal sex organs of the male are the testes, in which sperm (and male hormones) are produced, and a system of tubes and ducts for the storage and transport of sperm. Each testicle is divided into cone-shaped lobes, within which are located the seminiferous tubules. It is in these tubules that spermatogenesis takes place. From there the sperm begin their long and tortuous journey out of the body—through the epididymis, the vas deferens, the ejaculatory duct, and the urethra—exiting through the meatus at the tip of the glans.

5. The prostate gland, seminal vesicles, and bulbourethral glands are also involved in the male reproductive system. They are primarily involved in the production of fluids that make up the semen. Among other things, this fluid aids the sperm in their movement. The fluid of the bulbourethral glands may play a role in neutralizing the acid condition of the urethra in preparation for the passage of sperm. Because these fluids sometimes contain sperm, pregnancies can result even if ejaculation has not occurred.

6. The female sex organs, like those of the male, are internal and external and have three main functions: the production and transport of germ cells and the reception of semen. In addition, the female sex organs provide a place for the fertilization of the egg and for the development of the fetus.

7. The external sex organs of the female include the mons pubis, the major and minor lips, the clitoris, and the vaginal opening. The mons is the soft, rounded mound of fatty tissue that covers the pubic symphysis. The major lips are two folds of skin that are usually close together, giving the female genitals an appearance of being closed. Between them are the minor lips, hairless folds of skin that enclose the clitoris (a highly sensitive erectile organ), the opening of the urethra, the opening of the vagina, and the openings of the two Bartholin's glands.

8. The internal sex organs of the female are the paired ovaries and the fallopian tubes, the uterus, and the vagina, along with some accessory organs. The ovaries produce eggs and female hormones. Approximately each month one of numerous follicles in the ovary matures, ruptures, and releases an egg. Ova break through the surface of the ovary and become caught in the fringed end of the fallopian tube. They are propelled through this tube (in which fertilization takes place) to the uterus, a hollow, muscular tube in which the fertilized egg, or embryo, develops until birth. The uterus opens into the vagina, the female organ of copulation. The vagina opens onto the vestibule between the minor lips. This opening is flanked by erectile tissue and encircled by muscles. The two Bartholin's glands open into the lower half of the vestibule.

9. Breasts are characteristic of mammals, the class of animals that suckle their young. They are not part of the reproductive system, but the female breasts have a high degree of erotic significance in our culture. The breasts contain fibrous and fatty tissue and milk-producing glands that open at the nipple, the prominent tip of the breast. The nipple consists of muscle tissue that can contract to make it stand erect. The nipple also contains many nerve endings that make it a highly sensitive and important area of sexual arousal.

10. The male and female sex organs develop along similar lines. Five or six weeks after fertilization the reproductive system makes its appearance in the form of a pair of gonads and two sets of ducts. The gonads will develop into either testes or ovaries (depending on the makeup of the sperm), and one set of ducts will develop into the tubes and ducts of the reproductive system. The male and female external organs also develop along similar lines, but by the fourth month the sex of the fetus is unmistakable.

SUGGESTED READING

Anatomy

Dickinson, R. L. *Human Sex Anatomy,* 2d ed. Baltimore: Williams & Wilkins, 1970.
One of the most detailed set of line drawings depicting parts of the reproductive system. Quite technical.

Dienhart, C. M. *Basic Human Anatomy and Physiology,* 2d ed. Philadelphia: W. B. Saunders, 1973.
An introductory level text which describes the anatomy of the reproductive system in simple terms.

Gray's Anatomy, 35th ed. R. Warwick and P. L. Williams (Eds). Philadelphia: W. B. Saunders, 1973.
One of the classical definitive texts on human anatomy. Medical school level complexity.

Netter, F. H. *The Ciba Collection of Medical Illustrations, Vol. 2, The Reproductive System.* New York: Ciba Pharmaceutical Company, 1965.
Excellent colored illustrations. Text is compact and moderately difficult.

Developmental Anatomy

Arey, L. B. *Developmental Anatomy,* 7th edition, rev. Philadelphia: W. B. Saunders, 1974.
One of the definitive texts on the subject. Medical school level complexity.

Tuchmann-Duplessis, H., and Haegel, P. (Translated by L. S. Hurley.) *Illustrated Human Embryology, Vol. 2. Organogenesis.* London: Chapman and Hall, 1972.
Simply written and clearly illustrated description of the development of the reproductive system.

The Physiology of Sexual Functions

chapter 3

Did You Know That . . .

sexual fantasy is the most common erotic stimulant?

during sexual arousal the scrotum thickens and loses its baggy appearance, and that male orgasm is possible only once the testes are fully elevated within the scrotum?

the sensations of orgasm are linked to ejaculation in males, but not in females because they do not ejaculate?

physiologically, males have one basic type of orgasmic response, but Masters and Johnson identified three different patterns for females?

some women can have multiple orgasms, or orgasms in rapid succession; and there is evidence that men can learn to have multiple orgasms?

during orgasm the clitoris is retracted under its hood and almost disappears from view until excitement lets up?

even though age brings about some changes in the sexual response cycle, there are many individuals who keep up active and fulfilling sex lives well into old age?

INTRODUCTION

"Whatever the poetry and romance of sex and whatever the moral and social significance of human sexual behavior, sexual responses involve real and material changes of the physiologic functioning of an animal," wrote Alfred C. Kinsey in 1953. For the past twenty-five years, Kinsey has probably been the best-known name in sex research. In the 1940s and 1950s he and his colleagues produced what were at the time the most thorough (and practically the only) studies of normal, healthy sexual behavior. Today there are hundreds of serious sex researchers (the best known of whom are probably Masters and Johnson), and their work is providing us with an explosion of knowledge, much of it dealing with the physiology of the sex organs and the human sexual response cycle.

Physiology is the study of the functions and activities of organs and organisms. In Chapter 2 we described the anatomy of the sex organs. In this chapter we will look at their physiology—how they work. An understanding of the physiology of the male and female sex organs lets us know what to expect of our bodies as well as of those of our partners during sexual activity.

SEXUAL STIMULATION

Sexual activity begins with erotic stimulation. All healthy humans have the ability to respond to sexual stimulation, and the types of stimuli to which they respond are many—kisses, caresses, pictures, stories, thoughts, and so on. The basic physiological response of the body to sexual stimulation is always the same, but the intensity of sexual arousal that each person experiences during a lifetime can vary from one sexual experience to another. Sometimes sexual excitement reaches a climax in the response known as orgasm. Sometimes it progresses no further than lingering thoughts or vague feelings.

What triggers such responses? It depends on the person: For some, almost anything and everything; for others, very few things. The stimuli may be "sexual" in the ordinary sense of the word, or they may involve factors that have no erotic interest for most people. Young boys, for instance, have been known to have erections in response to a wide variety of athletic activities (swimming, boxing, riding, skating), emotionally charged events (coming home late, receiving report cards, being chased by police), and even sitting in church or hearing the national anthem. (Unfortunately, no comparable information exists for young girls.) Nonsexual sources of erotic stimulation, however, are not as random as these findings might suggest. They generally involve activities and situations that are highly emotional.

As children grow older, sexual or erotic responses tend to become more specific. By the late teens, sexual response is usually limited to direct stimulation of the genitals or to obviously erotic situations. In later years, sexual stimulation is even more dependent on actual physical stimulation.

Stimulation through Touch

Tactile, or touch, stimulation is one of the most important methods of sexual arousal in humans. It is, in fact, the only type of stimulation to which the body can respond reflexively—without thinking. (See Chapter 7 for further discussion of the importance of tactile stimulation.) Even a man who is unconscious or whose spinal cord is injured at a point that prevents impulses from reaching the brain (but leaves sexual coordinating centers in the lower spine undamaged) can have an erection when his genitals or inner thighs are caressed.

Nerve endings in the skin and deeper tissues allow us to feel tactile stimulation. But because the nerve endings are distributed unevenly, some parts of the body (fingertips) are more sensitive than others (the back). It is the areas of the body with the most nerve endings that have the greatest potential for stimulation.

In addition to the distribution of nerve endings, other differences also play important roles in determining the sensitivity of certain areas of the body. In one study, for instance, researchers measured breast sensitivity in young men and women and in boys and girls who had not yet reached puberty. Before puberty there were no differences between the sexes with regard to breast sensitivity. After puberty, the tactile sensitivity of the women's breasts was much greater than that of the men's breasts. The researchers also found that the degree of sensitivity of a woman's breasts changes, not only at puberty, but during the monthly menstrual cycle and shortly after giving birth. Maximum sensitivity occurred at midcycle (when the egg leaves the ovary) and again at menstruation. (The midcycle peak was absent in women who were taking oral contraceptives; *see* Chapter 6.) The most dramatic change, however, occurred within twenty-four hours of giving birth—when there was a great increase in breast sensitivity. At all of these times (puberty, during certain stages of the menstrual cycle, and after giving birth) there are hormonal changes in women that appear to play a role in breast sensitivity.

In addition to the female breast, there are many areas of the body that are especially susceptible to tactile stimulation. They are called **erogenous zones** (Eros was the Greek god of love—also known as Cupid). Erogenous zones include the genitalia (particularly the corona and the underside of the glans in men, and the clitoris, the minor lips, and the space they enclose in women), the area between the anus and the genitals, the anus itself, the breasts and nipples (as already mentioned), the mouth (lips, tongue, and the whole interior), the ears (especially the lobes), the buttocks, and the inner surfaces of the thighs.

Although it is these areas that are most often involved in sexual arousal, they are by no means the only erogenous zones. The neck (throat and nape), the palms and fingertips, the soles and toes, the abdomen, the groin, the center of the lower back, or any other part of the body may well be erotically sensitive to touch. Some women have reportedly reached orgasm when their eyelashes were stroked or when pressure was applied to their teeth.

A knowledge of erogenous zones can enhance one's effectiveness as a lover, but these zones are often indistinct and do not correspond to a specific pattern of nerve endings. In addition, previous learning experiences can affect one's interpretation of stimuli. A specific erogenous zone may thus be quite insensitive in one person, or it may be sensitive to the point of pain. Someone who expects to be an effective lover will not, therefore, approach another person in a mechanical, push-button manner and expect to produce automatic sexual arousal. Instead, a good lover will seek to learn the unique erogenous map of his or her partner.

Stimulation through Other Senses

Sight, sound, smell, and taste can be (depending on the person) almost as important in sexual stimulation as is touch—with one major difference. Our responses to certain types of tactile stimulation, such as genital stimulation, are based on natural reflexive reactions (modified by learning). Our responses to stimulation that comes through the other senses are probably all learned. Almost everyone, for instance, can respond sexually to stimulation of the genitals. Responses to various sights, sounds, smells, and tastes, however, differ far more because of previous learning experiences. And because sexual experiences differ from person to person and from time to time, the sights, sounds, smells, and tastes we learn to associate with sex will vary greatly from person to person and from time to time.

After touch, sight is probably the most important form of sexual stimulation. The sight of genitals of the opposite sex, for instance, is a very common source of sexual arousal, even though there appear to be some differences between males and females in this regard (as we will see later in this chapter).

The effect of sound is less obvious than that of sight but can be as significant a sexual stimulant. The tone and softness of voices as well as certain types of music (with pulsating rhythms or repeated languorous sequences) can serve as erotic stimuli. However, responses to such things are learned, so what stimulates one person may only distract or annoy another.

The importance of the sense of smell is not as important in humans as it probably once was. Nevertheless, the use of scents in many cultures, as well as an interest in body odors, suggests that the sense of smell still has considerable influence on us.

In addition to our learned responses to certain odors, it has been suggested that there may be naturally occurring body odors that are involved in sexual arousal. This suggestion is based on observations and studies of animals that have built-in mechanisms for signaling sexual arousal and for attracting mates. In addition to the plumage of some birds, the specific movements of certain fish, the brightly colored genital areas of some monkeys, and the mating calls of frogs, there is the powerful effect of smell, as seen for instance, in dogs, cats, and hogs, and in the almost imperceptible odors of chemicals produced by insects.

If there is a naturally occurring, sexually stimulating odor produced by humans, we would expect it to be associated with vaginal secretions or semen, or with the odor of the genital areas and perhaps the armpits. Some researchers claim to have found evidence for the existence of human **pheromones** (chemicals produced by one individual that affect the behavior of another), but the evidence is not conclusive.

Emotional Stimulation

As important as physical stimulation is, the key to understanding human sexual arousal lies in our internal processes, especially our emotional processes. Animals have to rely on primarily physical, external stimuli, but humans, with their more highly developed nervous systems and brains, can also react sexually to purely internal, mental images—which makes sexual fantasy the most common erotic stimulant. Sexual arousal is influenced greatly by emotional states. Even reflexive reactions are usually influenced by the emotions. Stimulation through any or all of the senses will result in sexual arousal if and only if accompanied by appropriate emotional conditions. Feelings like affection and trust will enhance, others like anxiety and fear will inhibit, or hold back, erotic responses in most cases. Our responsiveness, therefore, is not based solely on the physical situation, but includes the entire store of memory from past experiences as well as thoughts projected into the future. What arouses us sexually is the combination of all these influences—the physical situation, our fantasies, our emotional state, and the context in which these influences act on us.

As human beings, we all share to some extent a common history as well as a common biology. For example, we are all cared for as infants by older persons who become the first and most important influences in our lives. But we are also unique in many ways. Therefore, the earlier remarks about learning experiences and erogenous zones can be applied even more strongly to our psychological, or inner, reactions. Just as most of us are likely to respond to gentle caressing on the inside of our thighs, we are also likely to respond positively to another person's expression of sexual interest in us. In both cases, however, the response will depend on the person involved as well as on external and highly personal internal (subjective) factors—and is hardly an automatic reaction.

Gender Differences in Sexual Arousal

Do men and women react differently to sexual stimuli? Are men or women "turned on" more easily? Are such differences, if they exist, the result of biological differences between the sexes or of differences between learning experiences and cultural expectations? These questions have been asked many times, and the answers, along with our culture, seem to be changing. In the 1950s Kinsey reported that more men than women are stimulated by viewing sexually explicit materials (such as pictures of nudes, genitals, or sexual scenes), but that women are as likely to be stimulated as men by viewing motion pictures and reading literary material with romantic content. At the time, Kinsey's results seemed quite reasonable. The readership of "girlie" magazines, the collectors of "dirty pictures," and the audiences at stag films and burlesque shows were predominantly male. Although this pattern still exists, it seems that the times are changing. *Playboy* now also publishes *Playgirl,* and women are likely to be seen sitting with men watching erotic films.

Experimental methods and results are changing also. Kinsey asked people what aroused them. Today researchers attempt to make actual measurements of sexual arousal. In a study reported in 1970, for instance, fifty male and fifty female students at Hamburg University were shown sexually explicit pictures under experimental conditions. In general, the men did find the pictures with frankly sexual themes more stimulating, but when the scene had a relational component or affectionate theme (a couple kissing) women were equally if not more responsive.

When looking at these pictures, the most frequent physiological reactions of women were genital sensations (warmth, itching, pulsations), and about a fifth of the women reported vaginal moistening. The men usually responded with an erection.

Slightly more men than women (forty men and thirty-five women, out of fifty in each group) reported these reactions. Differences in the sexual aftereffects of the experiment were also slight. About half the subjects in each group reported increased sexual activity during the next twenty-four hours, involving masturbation, petting, or coitus.

In a companion study a larger sample (128 males and 128 females) were shown films featuring masturbation, petting, and coitus. Once again, men responded more readily, but the difference between the sexes was slight. Among the women, 65 percent experienced genital sensations—28 percent felt vaginal moistening and 9 percent had sensations in their breasts. Among men, 91 percent had full, and 55 percent had partial, erections.

About one in five men and women reported some masturbatory activity while viewing the film, and in four cases, all of them male, this was carried to the point of orgasm.

More-recent studies, using more-precise measures of sexual arousal, found even fewer differences between men and women. Instead of relying solely on an individual's report of genital sensations, researchers can now gauge the extent of sexual arousal with instruments designed to measure certain physiological changes. One such instrument is the penile strain gauge, a flexible device about the thickness of a rubber band that fits around the base of the penis. It measures blood volume and the pressure of the pulse in the penis—both good indicators of the exact degree of arousal. The first sign of sexual arousal in males—an erection—is usually quite obvious, but the penile strain gauge measures the firmness and extent of the erection. The first sign of sexual arousal in females—vaginal moistening—is not always obvious. It is a lot harder to feel a few tingles and moistenings in the vagina than it is to feel a penis growing erect. So some women, unless they know what subtle signs to look for, may not notice when they are having a sexual response. An instrument has been designed, however, that can detect even low levels of arousal in women. It is called a photoplethysmograph, and when positioned just inside the vagina it indicates the degree of arousal by measuring the pulse pressure and blood volume in the vagina.

In a study published in 1975, these instruments were used to compare sexual responses to erotic and to romantic tape recordings. It was found that explicit sex, not romance, is what turns people on—women as well as men. Women, in fact, rated the erotic tapes as more arousing than did the men.

Another recent study, this one of women only, suggests that women may be even more interested in films depicting explicit sexual activity (and thus more like men) than was previously thought. The women were given a number of short stories to read, and it was found that the "hard-core" stories produced significantly greater arousal on the vaginal pressure pulse measure (but not on the vaginal blood volume measure).

While these and other studies suggest that women today are much more like men with regard to sexual arousal than was previously assumed, there are still differences between the sexes. These differences, however, are probably due to a great extent to social and cultural expectations rather than to biology. Traditionally, in our society, women have been taught that they are not supposed to react as openly as men do to explicit sexual material. This teaching is often enough to inhibit their responses. In some instances women may not be aware that they are becoming sexually excited, and even if they are aroused, they may keep quiet about their true feelings and thus appear to be unaffected by sexual stimuli.

Another factor that confuses the measurement of differences between the sexes is the selection of erotic stimuli. Most erotic art, for instance, is produced by men. So when male-produced and male-preferred stimuli are used, we would not expect women to become as aroused as men. Furthermore, sex on television, in movies, and in advertising is almost always directed at men, and in these and hundreds of other instances society teaches males (but less often females) to respond to sexual stimuli.

The fact that some of the differences between men and women may be due to cultural expectations does not mean that those differences do not exist. It does mean that those differences are learned, rather than biologically built in—and behaviors that have been learned (including sexual inhibitions and response patterns) can usually be modified.

Currently, women are becoming more willing to reveal their sexual preferences and to oppose the expectations of the traditionally male-dominated society. It is already possible to see males and females becoming more and more alike in sexual response patterns as stereotyped views of sex-linked differences are overturned. As these changes become more widespread, it will be easier to see exactly what biological differences do exist between the sexes that pertain to cues that elicit sexual arousal.

Although many of the apparent differences between men and women may prove to be the result of "sexist" bias, there may be biologically based differences as well. Nevertheless, whatever differences do exist between men and women, they are not as great as the differences that exist among the members of either sex. In other words, there are many women who will be less responsive to erotic stimuli than is the "average" man. But there are also many women who will be more responsive than the "average" man. It is likely that there are a variety of responses that men and women share in varying degrees, but none of which is exclusive or characteristic of either sex.

Even though we have emphasized in this section the question of erotic response to visual stimuli, it should be remembered that sight is only one aspect of the many complex (internal and external) processes involved in sexual arousal. All of the other senses are involved. Hormones, too, play important roles in sexual arousal (as we will see in Chapter 4), and there are many behavioral patterns ("body language") as well as quite obvious and extremely subtle verbal and nonverbal methods of communicating sexual interest. A great deal of such communication is so subtle that it is barely recognized consciously—even by the person manifesting it. In the final analysis, sexual arousal must be understood in the broad interpersonal and psychosocial context in which it occurs. It should also be remembered that arousing sexual interest goes far deeper than mere sexual coquetry or teasing. It is the first step in the reproductive effort by which a species maintains itself.

SEXUAL RESPONSE: GENERAL CHARACTERISTICS

What comes after sexual stimulation? If the stimulation is effective, it leads to sexual arousal. If effective stimulation goes on long enough, it can eventually lead to orgasm. Most of us have some idea of what sexual arousal and orgasm are, but not everyone has experienced these responses and even for those who have, they are difficult to describe. For one thing, there is far too much variation among individuals for us to generalize from our own experiences. For another thing, most of us are in no mood for scientific observation at the height of sexual arousal, and we may not be aware of everything that we are experiencing. In fact, there is some blurring of our perceptual abilities during sexual arousal, as a result of which we are not quite fully aware of our own sensations and physiological reactions.

In this section we will describe the general behavioral characteristics of sexual response patterns, and then we will deal with the physiological changes seen in the sex organs and the rest of the body. The descriptions will be of ordinary patterns of human sexual response, but these are not meant to be taken as standards of "normal" or "healthy" behavior. There are many variations on these patterns that are also perfectly normal and healthy.

Approach to Orgasm

Whenever we are effectively sexually stimulated, a sensation of heightened arousal develops. Our thoughts and attentions turn to the sexual activity at hand, and we become less and less aware of whatever else may be going on around us. Anxiety or strong distractions might shut down sexual arousal in the early stages, and it is even possible to suppress excitement or ward it off by directing attention to other matters, but if the stimulation, the time, and the circumstances are favorable, erotic stirrings will be difficult to ignore. As the level of tension rises, external distractions become less effective, and orgasm (meaning "to swell" or "to be lustful") becomes more likely.

Sexual excitement can intensify at different rates—rapidly and relentlessly in younger persons, more gradually in older persons. It has also been assumed that men respond more rapidly to sexual stimulation and are capable of reaching orgasm more rapidly than women. A great deal of advice in marriage manuals revolves around this very point: Because women supposedly respond

more slowly, they must be stimulated for longer periods if they are to reach a climax. This belief may have some validity, for it is women more often than men who complain of being "left behind" by their partners. Even so, there is no known physiological basis for this claimed difference, and females can respond more or less as quickly as males do to effective stimulation. The average female, for example, takes somewhat less than four minutes to reach orgasm during masturbation, whereas the average male needs between two and four minutes. Some women, however, may achieve climax in as little as fifteen to thirty seconds. The difference between the sexes in achieving orgasm during intercourse therefore does not seem to be related to basic physiological differences between the sexes but rather to psychological factors and to the effectiveness of stimulation. Some women, for instance (and some men), may not know what type of stimulation is effective for them. Even if they do know, they may be inhibited about telling their partners what to do.

When sexual arousal is achieved, reactions may differ greatly from person to person. The response to effective sexual stimulation, however, does have some general characteristics. The person in the grip of sexual excitement appears tense from head to toe. Muscular tensions and movements gradually take on a rhythmic pattern best exemplified by pelvic thrusts—the major characteristic of mammalian coitus. Other reactions include flushed skin, increased salivation, pounding of the heart, and heavy breathing. These and other reactions may be dramatic in some cases, subtle in others. Thrusting, for instance, may involve only the buttocks and be barely noticeable. No matter how mild the response, however, there will always be distinct physiological changes—otherwise the person simply is not fully aroused.

For some people, orgasm is the most important part of sex, but the period leading up to orgasm can be quite satisfying and pleasant in itself. It is even possible to prolong the buildup by dwelling on its pleasant aspects. In fact, following a period of sustained sexual excitement, some people voluntarily forgo the climax. Lingering tensions, however, sometimes lead to irritability and restlessness if unrelieved by orgasm.

Orgasm

Orgasm is a very intense and satisfying experience. In physiological terms, it is the explosive discharge of accumulated neuromuscular (relating to both nerves and muscles) tensions. Its subjective counterpart is a state of altered consciousness characterized by intense pleasure, which is experienced with considerable variation from one instance to another.

The patterns of response during orgasm vary among individuals and according to age, fatigue, time since last orgasm, and so on, but there is some evidence that each person has a fairly characteristic set of responses. On strictly biological grounds, there is no reason why men and women should react differently during orgasm. However, psychological factors and cultural expectations can play roles in altering the behavior of the two sexes. Differences in orgasmic response can also arise from physical considerations, such as whether the person is experiencing orgasm during oral-genital stimulation, while lying down or standing up, and so on.

At one extreme, the signs of orgasm may be so subdued that an observer would hardly notice them; on the other hand, the experience may be like an explosive convulsion. Most commonly, there is a visible combination of genital and total body responses: sustained tension or mild twitching of the arms and legs while the rest of the body becomes rigid, a grimace or muffled cry, and rhythmic throbbing of the sex organs and pelvic musculature before relaxation sets in. Less often, reactions are restricted to the genitals alone. The pelvic thrusts are followed by subdued throbbings, and the general body response seems minimal. At the peak of sexual excitement, one may bite and scratch with only a vague realization of doing so. Vision, hearing, taste, and smell—all sensations—become partly numbed; the person may even lose consciousness for a few seconds. At the climax, the person may moan, groan, scream, or utter fragmented and meaningless phrases. In more extreme reactions there may be uncontrollable laughing, talking, crying, or frenzied movement.

Male Orgasm

In adult males the sensations of orgasm are linked to ejaculation, but orgasm and ejaculation are two separate processes. Orgasm is the release of neuromuscular tensions. Ejaculation is the sudden discharge of semen through the urethra. It is experienced only by males past the age of puberty, when the prostate and accessory glands become functional. Although the fluid that lubricates the vagina is produced during arousal, females do not ejaculate as some people have mistakenly concluded.

Ejaculation occurs in two stages. First, there is a sense that ejaculation is imminent, or "coming," and that one can do nothing to stop it. Second, there is a distinct awareness of the rhythmically contracting urethra, followed by fluid moving out under pressure.

Female Orgasm

In the female, orgasm starts with what some women have described as a feeling of momentary suspension followed by a peak of intense sensation in the clitoris. This sensation then spreads through the pelvis. This stage varies in intensity and may involve sensations of "falling," "opening up," or even emitting fluid. Some women compare this stage of orgasm to mild labor pains. It is followed by a feeling of warmth spreading from the pelvis through the rest of the body. The experience ends with characteristic throbbing sensations in the pelvis. The female orgasm, unlike that of the male, can be interrupted.

Are all orgasms the same? The question is impossible to answer with any certainty. In one sense, no two experiences are ever the same because each of us is unique, and even the same person is different in some ways at different times. In addition to these variations, there is the possibility that women experience different types of orgasm, involving different physiological mechanisms.

Sigmund Freud proposed that females experience two types of orgasm: clitoral and vaginal. A **clitoral orgasm** is one that is achieved through direct stimulation of the clitoris. A **vaginal orgasm** is achieved through stimulation of the vagina. Freud's concept of dual orgasm assumes that in young girls the clitoris is at first the primary site of sexual excitement. With maturity the sexual focus is said to shift from the clitoris to the vagina. Should this transfer not occur, according to Freud, the woman remains incapable of experiencing the fully mature vaginal orgasm and is restricted to the "immature" and presumably less-fulfilling clitoral orgasm.

Kinsey and his associates raised doubts about the concept of dual orgasm. They pointed out that the vagina is an insensitive organ. During pelvic examinations many women simply cannot tell when the vaginal wall is being gently touched. In surgery the vagina has been found to be rather insensitive to pain, and microscopic studies fail to reveal nerve endings of touch in the vaginal walls of most women.

The research of Masters and Johnson supports the Kinsey point of view: Physiologically there is one and only one type of orgasm, regardless of whether the clitoris, the vagina, or for that matter neither one is directly involved (as when orgasm occurs after breast manipulation only). It may also be that women vary in clitoral and vaginal sensitivity. For some women the tug of the penis on the labia, and hence on the clitoris, that occurs during intercourse is not sufficient stimulation to bring about orgasm. Such women may require additional clitoral stimulation if they are to achieve orgasm during intercourse. For other women intercourse without direct clitoral stimulation is enough to result in orgasm.

The question of dual orgasm has not been resolved to everyone's satisfaction, and researchers are still trying to answer it one way or the other; however, even if there is only one type of orgasm, this does not mean that the subjective experience of orgasm (brought about by whatever means) is always the same. The subjective experience of orgasm resulting from masturbation, oral-genital stimulation, coitus, or from coitus in a given position or with a specific person can certainly vary tremendously. But the basis of these differences is primarily psychological and subjective, as can be seen in the following descriptions of orgasm.

Descriptions of Female Orgasm from The Hite Report

There are a few faint sparks, coming up to orgasm, and then I suddenly realize that it is going to catch fire, and then I concentrate all my energies, both physical and mental, to quickly bring on the climax—which turns out to be a moment suspended in time, a hot rush—a sudden breath-taking dousing of all the nerves of my body in Pleasure—I try to make the moment last—disappointment when it doesn't.

Before, I feel a tremendous surge of tension and a kind of delicious feeling I can't describe. Then orgasm is like the excitement and stimulation I have been feeling, increased, for an *instant*, a hundred-fold.

It starts down deep, somewhere in the "core," gets bigger, stronger, better, and more beautiful, until I'm just four square inches of ecstatic crotch area!!

The physical sensation is beautifully excruciating. It begins in the clitoris, and also surges into my whole vaginal area.

It's a peak of almost, almost, ALMOST, ALMOSTTTT. The only way I can describe it is to say it is like riding the "Tilt-a-Whirl."

Just before orgasm, the area around my clitoris suddenly comes alive and, I can't think of any better description, seems to sparkle and send bright dancing sensations all around. Then it becomes focused like a point of intense light. Like a bright blip on a radar screen, and that's the orgasm.

There is an almost frantic itch-pain-pleasure in my vagina and clitoral area that seems almost insatiable, it is also extremely hot and I lose control of everything, then there is an explosion of unbelievable warmth and relief to the itch-pain-pleasure! It is really indescribable and what I've just written doesn't explain it at all!!! WORDS!

I can't answer this question. The charm of an orgasm is that, when it's there, all your concentration is on it, until the feeling of intense relief encompasses your whole body and mind—then when it's over, it's impossible to describe it accurately or catch any remnant of the feeling. So you go at it again and it seems all fresh and new again, but then the moment it's over it's as elusive as ever: pure *amnesia* seems to set in the minute you try to explain it.

Descriptions of Male Orgasm
from Beyond the Male Myth

Not too much different. Each orgasm is usually emphatic. [Improved] by more response and passion from the woman and oral sex by the woman and lip caressing on my back, behind my ears, tongue in my ears, etc.

Feel very relieved (tension)—satisfied. I do not delay them—no will power.

I try to delay orgasm to get the full effect. Half the fun is in the buildup.

My orgasms differ. Exactly how goes by how I feel at the time and the amount of stimuli affecting me.

I think my orgasm can be improved by understanding my partner and teaching her what stimulates me.

Some are more intense. With my wife they are better than with other girls. When I am more unaware of the pleasure I'm going to receive because of the desire to give pleasure, they are better.

Foreplay is very important. I enjoy the feeling that I get when I make my partner very excited and I enjoy making her have an orgasm or more than one if possible. It is very important that my partner be satisfied.

I feel like I have had a beautiful high. No, there is no delay, whenever it comes, it comes, and I let go.

It's extremely important to "feel" your partner out occasionally. I think touching, kissing, hugging, sucking, etc., is a very emotional response which displays a great deal of consideration and love. I enjoy any and all of the above. I think consideration is extremely important in pleasing my sexual partner.

They differ in intensity. The more prolonged the sex act the better and more intense the orgasm.

Orgasms come very quickly each time. Could be improved with more "practice."

They differ from time to time—different positions with the unnormal time element causes them to be better.

It depends on the mood of the partner. By having plenty of time and not be in a hurry to get through.

Foreplay is as important as climax and I use it extensively preceding and following!

If I have a lot on my mind or am very nervous for one reason or another my orgasms are less intense—if I have one at all. My orgasms could be improved if I were more relaxed.

Better when I'm not tired or something on my mind.

Depending on the physical condition of my body. It could be improved if my body has had the proper rest.

Aftereffects of Orgasm

The period leading up to orgasm is quite distinct, but that following it is more ambiguous. In general, the changes gone through after orgasm are the opposite of those leading to orgasm. The rhythmic throbs of the genitals and the convulsions of the body become less intense and less frequent. Neuromuscular tension gives way to profound relaxation, and the entire musculature of the body relaxes. Immediately following orgasm the person may feel an intense wish to rest. The pounding heart and accelerated breathing return to normal. Congested and swollen tissues and organs resume their usual colors and sizes. As the body rests, the mind reawakens, and the various senses gradually regain their full alertness. For most persons, the predominant feeling is one of peace and satisfaction.

The descent from the peak of orgasm may occur in a steep step or more gradually. Particularly at night the feeling of relaxation contributes to natural weariness, and the person may fall asleep. Others feel relaxed but perfectly alert or even exhilarated.

It is not unusual to feel thirsty or hungry following orgasm. A smoker may crave a cigarette, and often there is a need to urinate, sometimes to move the bowels. In addition, there are numerous reactions that may differ from person to person. Some people feel numb or itch, some want more physical contact, and some want to be left alone. It is difficult, however, to separate the purely physiologically determined reaction from the psychological, or learned, patterns of behavior in this area.

Regardless of the immediate postorgasmic response, most people recover fully from the aftereffects of orgasm in a short time. Prolonged fatigue following orgasm is usually the result of activities that may have preceded or accompanied sex (drinking, lack of sleep), rather than of orgasm itself. When a person is in poor health, however, the experience itself may be taxing.

THE SEXUAL RESPONSE CYCLE

In the fourth century B.C. Aristotle, the Greek philosopher, observed that the testes are lifted within the scrotal sac during sexual excitement. More than twenty centuries passed before his observation was scientifically confirmed under laboratory conditions, and so far there has been only one major investigation of the physiology of orgasm—the one conducted by William H. Masters and Virginia E. Johnson.

A total of 694 normally functioning men and women were volunteers in the Masters and Johnson study. The subjects, 382 women and 312 men, were between the ages of 18 and 89 years. Most were married, and many were from a university community in St. Louis, Missouri. All were closely screened, and only those who were physically normal and emotionally stable were chosen. They were not selected for their sexual attributes, but it was required that they be able to experience orgasm under laboratory conditions.

The research involved observation, monitoring, and sometimes filming the responses

of the body as a whole and the sex organs in particular during sexual stimulation and orgasm. Both masturbation and coitus were included in the experiments. In order to observe the vagina, a special penis-shaped instrument made of clear plastic was used that allowed direct observation and filming of the inside of the vagina.

The laboratory in which the research took place was a plain, windowless room containing a bed and monitoring and recording equipment. The subjects were first left alone to engage in sex and only when they felt comfortable in this setting were they asked to perform in the presence of the investigators and the technicians who operated the equipment (recording heart rates, blood pressure, brain waves, and so on).

Even though effort was made to ensure that the subjects were comfortable in the laboratory surroundings, questions have been raised about the conditions under which the study was conducted: Do people respond in the same way, even physiologically, in the laboratory as they do in the privacy of their homes? This question has not been finally answered, and no one has attempted to repeat the Masters and Johnson study, but the scientific validity of their findings has been widely accepted.

During almost a decade, beginning in 1954, about ten thousand orgasms were investigated. Because more of the subjects were women, and because women, much more so than men (as we will see later in this chapter), can experience several orgasms in a short period of time, about three-fourths of these orgasms were experienced by females.

The sexual response patterns shown in Figures 3.1 and 3.2 summarize the observations of Masters and Johnson. They represent general patterns, rather than consistent reactions of individuals. But as might be expected, there were many variations on the typical pattern. These differences were in the length and intensity of the phases, not in the order in which they followed.

The sexual response pattern for males (see Figure 3.1) and the three patterns for females (see Figure 3.2) include the same four phases: excitement, plateau, orgasm, and resolution.

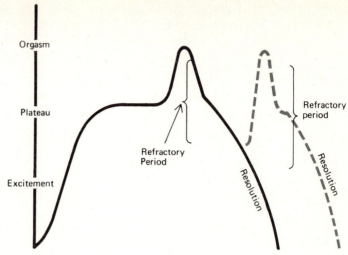

Figure 3.1 The male sexual response cycle.

From Masters and Johnson, *Human Sexual Response* (Boston: Little, Brown and Company, 1966), p. 5. Reprinted by permission.

The plateau phase is actually an advanced stage of sexual excitement in which high tensions are maintained for a while before the climax. This stage is often difficult to distinguish from the excitement phase, and many people do not recognize it as a separate phase.

The basic response patterns tend to be the same, no matter what type of stimulation or sexual activity produces them. In other words, the physiology of orgasm is the same whether it is brought about by masturbation, oral-genital contact, coitus, or some other activity. Differences in the type of stimulation,

however, can affect the intensity of the response.

The basic pattern of response in males and females is similar. Excitement mounts in response to effective stimulation, which may be psychogenic (erotic thoughts and feelings) or somatic (physical stimulation), but usually involves both. Excitement may rise rapidly or slowly, depending on the situation and the individual. If stimulation continues, the level of excitement becomes stabilized at a high point, the plateau phase. Excitement does not always lead to a climax, but if stimulation con-

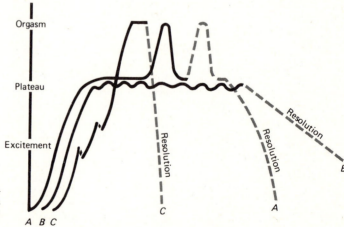

Figure 3.2 The female sexual response cycle.

From Masters and Johnson, *Human Sexual Response* (Boston: Little, Brown and Company, 1966), p. 5. Reprinted by permission.

tinues, a point of no return will be reached and orgasm will follow. This abrupt release is then followed by a leveling off of excitement in the resolution phase.

The lengths of the phases vary greatly, but the excitement and resolution phases are usually the longest. The plateau phase is relatively short, and orgasm usually lasts only about ten seconds or less. The overall time for one complete coital cycle can range from a few minutes to much longer.

The physiological response to orgasm is similar in males and females, but differences do exist. Some result from obvious anatomical, or physical, differences between the sexes, and others may be due to differences in nervous-system organization. The first major difference is in the range of possible variations. As can be seen in Figures 3.1 and 3.2, a single sequence characterizes the male pattern, while the Masters and Johnson research identified three alternatives for females. Even these diagrams do not show fully the much richer variety of female responses.

The most common response pattern in females (Figure 3.2 line A) is similar to that of males. In the other two patterns for females (lines B and C) the plateau phase as such is absent. In line B, excitement mounts and immediately breaks into a series of rapid orgasms, which the woman experiences as a sustained climax followed by a prolonged resolution phase. Line C is characterized by more abrupt increases in excitement, ending in a single sustained climax, followed by a sharp drop into the resolution phase. Both of these responses are more intense than is the more common response.

The second difference between male and female responses involves a refractory period in the male cycle. (Cells, tissues, and organs do not respond to a second stimulation until a certain period of time has passed since the first stimulus. This period is known as a "refractory period.") As can be seen in Figure 3.1, the refractory period comes immediately after orgasm and extends into the resolution phase. During this period the male is incapable of physical sexual response, regardless of the type and intensity of sexual stimu-

lation. He cannot regain full erection nor have another orgasm until after the refractory period, the duration of which varies but has not yet been precisely determined. It is very brief for some men (especially younger men) and longer for others.

Females do not have refractory periods. Even in the pattern closest to that of the male (line A), as soon as the orgasm is over the level of excitement can mount immediately to another climax. Some women can thus have multiple orgasms, or orgasms in rapid succession. However, the ability of some women to have multiple orgasms does not mean that they always want to go on for extra orgasms when they make love. Some women prefer to have more than one orgasm, whereas others prefer one orgasm in an episode.

Reports of multiple orgasm in men have been rare, but there is recent evidence (reported by Jensen and Robbins) that men can learn to have multiple orgasms, the first one or several including all of the physiological reactions of orgasm except ejaculation. Men who are capable of experiencing several such orgasms in a series report that the sensations are the same as when they do ejaculate. Laboratory studies of such men found the physiological response of nonejaculatory orgasm to be the same as those of orgasm with ejaculation—increased breathing and heart rate, muscular tension, and urethral and anal contractions. The erection lessens slightly after each orgasm, then builds up to another orgasm. These men, the researchers say, apparently inhibit or control ejaculation until the final orgasm of a series, which they describe as being the most intense. After this final orgasm with ejaculation they experience complete loss of erection and the usual refractory period.

Physiological Mechanisms of Sexual Arousal

The body goes through a great many complex changes during sexual arousal, but most of these changes are the result of two basic processes: **vasocongestion** and **myotonia**.

Vasocongestion is the engorgement, or excessive filling, of the blood vessels and increased flow of blood into body tissues. The erection of the penis and the swelling of the female genitals are the most obvious examples of vasocongestion. Ordinarily the flow of blood through the arteries into various organs is matched by the outflow through the veins, and a fluctuating balance is maintained. Under some conditions, however, blood will flow into an area faster than the veins are able to drain that area, and vasocongestion results.

Blood flow is controlled primarily by the smaller arteries (arterioles), whose muscular walls dilate and constrict in response to impulses from the nerves. When the arteries dilate, the blood rushes in and the tissues become swollen, red, and warm. The cause may be physical, such as when the skin turns red due to heat, or psychological, as during blushing. Sexual arousal is always accompanied by widespread vasocongestion.

Myotonia is increased muscle tension. Even when you are relaxed or asleep, your muscles maintain a certain firmness or "muscle tone." From this base level, muscle firmness increases during voluntary flexing or during certain involuntary contractions, including those of orgasm. Myotonia is present from the start of sexual arousal and becomes widespread, but it tends to lag behind vasocongestion.

Reactions of the Male Sexual Organs

The Penis

Of all the sex organs, the penis undergoes the most dramatic changes during sexual excitement. Erection (**tumescence**) can occur reflexively without erotic feelings, but usually it is positive evidence of sexual arousal.

Erection is experienced on many occasions by practically all males—from infancy to old age, while awake and while asleep. It occurs more rapidly in younger men, and there are many gradations between the totally flaccid penis and the maximally congested organ just before orgasm. A penis that can be inserted into a normally responsive vagina is considered to be fully erect.

During the four phases of the sexual response cycle, the penis goes through several changes. Erection, for instance, may come and go several times during the excitement phase, the varying firmness of the penis indicating varying degrees of sexual excitement and desire. During this time a man is quite vulnerable to loss of erection. Even if stimulation continues, distractions can cause partial or total **detumescence** (loss of erection).

Once a man moves into the plateau phase, erection is more stable. The man may even turn his attention away from the sexual activity for a short while and the penis will remain tumescent. During the plateau phase the penis undergoes two changes. Vasocongestion causes further engorgement, primarily in the corona of the glans, as well as occasionally a deepening of the reddish purple color of the glans.

During orgasm rhythmic contractions begin in the prostate, seminal vesicles, and vas, but very soon extend to the penis itself (*see* Figure 3.3). These orgasmic contractions involve the length of the penile urethra and the muscles around the root of the penis. They begin regularly at intervals of approximately 0.8 seconds, but after the first several strong contractions they become weak, irregular, and less frequent.

Ejaculation ("throwing out") is the forcible ejection of spermatic fluid through the urethra. The fluid, which flows in various amounts (usually about 3 cubic centimeters, or a teaspoonful), is known as semen, seminal fluid, or spermatic fluid. It consists of sperm (only a small part of the total volume) and the products of the prostate mainly and to a much lesser extent the seminal vesicles.

Ejaculation happens in two stages. During the first phase (emission, or first-stage orgasm) the prostate, seminal vesicles, and vas deferens pour their contents into the dilated urethral bulb, and the man feels the inevitability of ejaculation. In the second phase (ejaculation proper, or second-stage orgasm) the semen is forced out by strong contractions of the muscles surrounding the root of the penis and by contractions of the various genital ducts. At this point the man feels intense pleasure associated with orgasmic throbs and the sensation of spermatic flow.

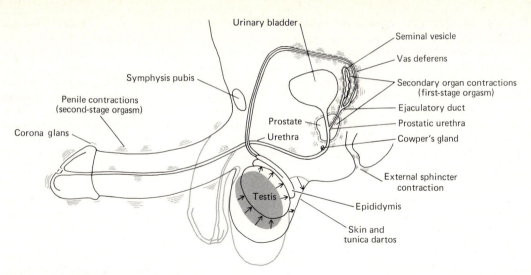

Figure 3.3   The male pelvis: orgasmic phase.

From Masters and Johnson, *Human Sexual Response* (Boston: Little, Brown and Company, 1966), p. 184.
Reprinted by permission.

The first vigorous thrust during orgasm propels the semen out with some force. The fluid can sometimes be projected a distance of several feet, but usually it goes barely beyond the tip of the penis. After this first ejaculation, the remaining semen flows out in gentle spurts. In successive orgasms, the volume of fluid will be less.

In the resolution phase the changes of the first three phases are reversed, and erection is lost, but the penis does not become flaccid all at once. Detumescence occurs in two stages. First, there is the relatively rapid loss of stiffness to a semierect state. Then there is a more gradual decongestion as the penis returns to its unstimulated size. Usually, the longer the excitement and plateau phases have been (and the more complete vasocongestion has been), the longer the first stage of detumescence will be, which delays the second stage.

If sexual stimulation continues after ejaculation (if the penis stays in the vagina or even if the man stays near his sexual partner), the penis stays hard longer. If, on the other hand, he withdraws, is distracted, or attempts to urinate, loss of erection will be more rapid. (Actually, a man cannot urinate with a fully erect penis because the urinary sphincter—

see Chapter 2—closes reflexively during full erection in order to prevent the mixing of urine and semen.)

The Scrotum

Changes in the scrotal sac are distinct but not as dramatic as those of the penis. During the excitement phase the skin of the scrotum contracts, thickens, and loses its baggy appearance (as it does in response to cold, fear, or anger). If the excitement phase is prolonged, the scrotum may relax, even though the sexual cycle is not yet completed. There are no further changes during the plateau and orgasmic phases, and there is usually a rapid loss of the thickening of the scrotal sac during the resolution phase. The scrotum shows no color changes.

The Testes

The changes undergone by the testes are also distinct. During the excitement phase both testes are lifted up within the scrotum (*see* Figure 3.3), mainly as a result of the shortening of the spermatic cords and the contraction of the scrotal sac. During the plateau phase this elevation progresses further until the organs are actually pressed against the body wall. Full elevation of the testes is necessary for orgasm and always precedes it.

The testes also undergo a marked increase in size (about 50 percent in most cases) because of vasocongestion. There are no further changes during orgasm, and in the resolution phase the size and position of the testes return to normal. The process may be rapid or slow (and is usually the same for one person), but the longer the plateau phase, the longer is the process of detumescence.

Cowper's Glands

In some mammals, such as stallions, rams, bears, and goats, the Cowper's glands secrete a great deal of fluid during sexual arousal. In men these glands are almost inactive. If sexual excitement is sustained, a drop or so of clear fluid, produced by these glands, appears at the tip of the penis. Most men produce only several drops or none at all, but some produce enough to wet the glans or even to dribble freely. As mentioned earlier, this fluid may help neutralize the acidity of the urethra.

The Prostate and Seminal Vesicles

Changes in the prostate and seminal vesicles take place only during the orgasmic phase (*see* Figure 3.3). Ejaculation begins as these structures pour their secretions into the expanded urethra. The mixing of sperm from the throbbing vas with the secretions of the seminal vesicles (whose walls also pulsate spasmodically) takes place in the ejaculatory duct. Sperm that may have been stored in the seminal vesicles, along with those coming from the vas, are propelled through the duct into the urethra. The prostate and seminal vesicles participate in the rhythmic convulsions of orgasm, and their contractions, along with the filling of the urethra, are responsible for the sensation that orgasm is near.

Reactions of the Female Sex Organs

The Vagina

The warm, moist vagina, like the erect penis, is a good indication of sexual excitement and desire. In fact, moistness of the va-

ginal walls is the first sign of sexual response in women and usually occurs within ten to thirty seconds after erotic stimulation. Just as the penis becomes erect in order to enter the vagina, the vagina becomes moist and lubricates itself in order to more easily receive the penis. The clear, slippery, and mildly scented vaginal fluid not only lubricates the vagina, it also helps neutralize the vaginal canal (which tends to be acidic) in preparation for the semen.

Vaginal fluid oozes directly from the walls of the vagina. The secreting mechanism is not fully understood (the vaginal wall has no glands that secrete), but it probably is related to vasocongestion of the walls. The Bartholin's glands do produce a fluid, but like that of the Cowper's glands in males, it tends to be scanty, erratic, and probably of little or no lubricating value.

The vagina shows two other changes during the excitement phase: expansion of its inner two-thirds and color change. The ordinarily collapsed interior vaginal walls lengthen, expand, and create a space where semen will be deposited. The ordinarily purple red vaginal walls will take on a darker hue in response to stimulation. This coloring begins in patches, then spreads over the entire vaginal surface, reflecting the progressive vasocongestion of the vagina.

During the plateau phase the focus of change shifts from the inner two-thirds to the outer one-third of the vagina. This area may have dilated somewhat during the excitement phase, but in the plateau phase it becomes congested with blood and the vaginal opening becomes at least a third narrower. The congested walls of the outer third of the vagina are called the **orgasmic platform.** It is there that the rhythmic contractions of orgasm are most apparent. During the plateau phase the "tenting effect" of the inner end of the vagina continues, and full vaginal expansion is achieved. Vaginal lubrication tends to decrease at this stage, and if the excitement phase has been long, lubrication may cease altogether in the plateau phase.

Observations of the vagina during orgasm confirm that it is much more than just a passive receptacle for the penis. It is an active participant in coitus, and capable of enveloping and stimulating the penis to a climax. During orgasm (*see* Figure 3.4), the most visible effects occur in the orgasmic platform. This area contracts rhythmically (initially at approximately 0.8-second intervals) from three to fifteen times. After the first three to six contractions, the movements become weaker and more widely spaced. This pattern varies from person to person and from time to time, but the more frequent and intense the contractions of the orgasmic platform, the more intense is the subjective experience of climax. At high levels of excitement the rhythmic contractions are preceded by spastic (non-rhythmic) contractions of the orgasmic platform that last two to four seconds. The inner portion of the vagina does not contract but continues its "tenting."

During the resolution phase the orgasmic platform subsides rapidly, whereas the inner walls return much more slowly to their usual condition. With decongestion the color of the vaginal walls lightens during a period of ten to fifteen minutes. If the process of lubrication has continued into this phase, it indicates lingering or rekindled sexual tension. With sufficient stimulation, a second orgasm may follow rapidly.

The Clitoris

The clitoris is an exclusively sexual organ. It plays no direct part in reproduction. In response to sexual excitement the clitoris becomes tumescent through vasocongestion, but its overhanging prepuce prevents it from standing erect as the penis does.

Although slower to respond to stimulation than the penis, the clitoris is a highly sensitive organ. Practically all women can feel tactile stimulation in this area, and most women respond erotically to such touches. In examinations conducted for the Kinsey study, 98 percent of the women were able to detect tactile stimulation of the clitoris, while fewer than 14 percent could detect being touched in the interior of the vagina.

During the excitement phase the clitoris becomes congested, though in the majority of females the change is so small that a microscope is needed to detect it. Tumescence of the glands of the clitoris coincides with vasocongestive response of the minor lips and comes quite late in the excitement phase (when the penis has been erect for some time and the vagina is fully lubricated). This response will be more rapid and more obvious if the clitoris and adjoining areas of the mons are stimulated directly. The sequence of changes, how-

Figure 3.4 The female pelvis: orgasmic phase.
From Masters and Johnson, *Human Sexual Response* (Boston: Little, Brown and Company, 1966), p. 77. Reprinted by permission.

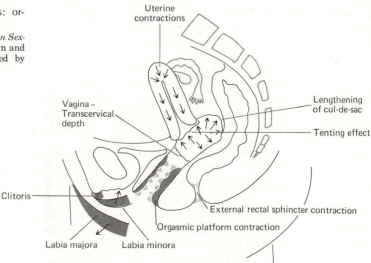

Uterine contractions

Vagina – Transcervical depth

Lengthening of cul-de-sac

Tenting effect

Clitoris

External rectal sphincter contraction

Orgasmic platform contraction

Labia majora

Labia minora

ever, is not related to the method of stimulation. Once tumescent, the glans of the clitoris remains so throughout the sexual cycle.

During the plateau phase the entire clitoris is retracted under the clitoral hood, or prepuce, and almost disappears from view. This reaction is particularly rapid and striking in response to direct stimulation and may result in the clitoris receding to half its unstimulated length. Because the initial enlargement of the clitoris indicates sexual excitement, an uninformed male who is attempting to stimulate his partner's clitoris may misinterpret this reaction as a loss of sexual tension. When excitement does let up, the clitoris reemerges from under the hood. And during a long plateau phase there may be several repetitions of this in-out sequence.

During orgasm the clitoris remains hidden from view. And following orgasm it promptly (in five to ten seconds) reemerges. The rapidity and timing of this response are similar to the first-stage loss of penile erection. Final detumescence of the clitoris (like the second-stage loss of erection) may take five to ten minutes but sometimes as long as half an hour. When orgasm has not occurred, however, the engorgement of the clitoris may last for hours and cause discomfort.

The Major Lips

Both the major and minor lips, or labia, undergo changes due to vasocongestion during sexual arousal, but there are differences between the changes seen in the labia of women who have not given birth (nulliparous) and those who have (parous). This is because the pressure of childbirth may cause permanently distended (varicose) veins in the tissues of the labia.

During the excitement phase, nulliparous major lips become flattened, thinned, and more widely separated, "opening" and slightly exposing the external genitals and their congested moist tissues. During the plateau and orgasmic phases, nulliparous lips show no further changes, and at resolution they return to their decongested size and shape and resume midline contact. If orgasm does not occur, resolution proceeds rapidly. Otherwise the changes brought about during excitement last longer, sometimes up to several hours after all sexual stimulation has ceased.

Parous major lips (those of women who have given birth) are larger and more pendulous than those of nulliparous women. Instead of flattening, they become markedly engorged and may double or triple in size during arousal, while still exposing the entrance to the vagina. There are no other changes during the next two phases, and the speed of resolution depends on how distended the veins may have become and how effectively they can be drained.

The Minor Lips

The changes in the minor lips during the sexual cycle are quite impressive and remarkably consistent. As excitement progresses to plateau, the minor lips become engorged and double or even triple in size in both parous and nulliparous women. These tumescent lips project between the overlaying major lips and become quite apparent, which may explain the parting of the major lips during excitement.

Color changes in the minor lips are also the result of vasocongestion and are therefore related to the condition of the veins in parous women. During the plateau phase the minor lips become progressively pink or even a bright red in light-skinned women. In women who have had children the resulting color may be a more intense red or a deeper wine color.

The vivid coloring of the inner lips at the height of arousal is so closely associated with sexual arousal that these lips have been called the "sex skin" of the sexually excited women. If erotic stimulation continues beyond this point, orgasm is inevitable; but if stimulation is interrupted, orgasm will not occur. In fact, orgasm will not occur unless congestion of the minor lips reaches this peak. In this sense the "sex skin" is similar to full testicular elevation in men; both are preconditions and good indications that orgasm is coming.

In the resolution phase the coloring of the minor lips returns to normal in two steps: Within the first ten to fifteen seconds after orgasm the deep red color gives way to a pinkish tone; following that, there is a slower and less-regular return to the unstimulated pale appearance.

Bartholin's Glands

Bartholin's glands secrete a few drops of clear, slippery fluid rather late in the excitement phase or even in the plateau phase. They appear to be most effectively stimulated by the action of the copulating penis during a long period of time. The contribution of these glands to vaginal lubrication and neutralization is relatively minor.

The Uterus

Despite being hidden from view the uterus has long been known to participate actively in the changes of the sexual response cycle. Elevation from its usual position is the first response of the uterus to sexual excitement. This reaction pulls the cervix up and contributes to the tenting effect in the vagina. Full uterine elevation is achieved during the plateau phase and is maintained until resolution. Then it returns to its usual position within five to ten minutes.

In addition, vasocongestion causes a distinct increase in the size of the uterus during the early phases. Myotonia is evident in the activity of the muscles of the uterus, resulting in distinct contractions. These contractions start in the fundus and spread downward. They occur simultaneously with those of the orgasmic platform but are less distinct and more irregular.

The cervix shows no specific change until the resolution phase. Then its external opening may dilate slightly immediately after orgasm. The more intense the orgasm, the greater the likelihood of this reaction. Because of changes in the cervix during childbirth this reaction is best seen in women who have not had children.

Sexual excitement centers on the genitals, but the entire body is involved in the responses of the sexual cycle.

The Breasts

Even though the male breasts do respond to sexual excitement, changes during the response cycle are far more striking in the female breasts. Erection of the nipple is the first response. It occurs during the excitement phase as a result of contractions of "involuntary" muscle fibers rather than of vasocongestion. Engorgement of the blood vessels is responsible for the enlargement of the breasts as a whole, including the areolae. Nipple erection in the male occurs, if at all, in the late excitement and plateau phases.

In the plateau phase engorgement of the areolae is more marked, making the nipples appear relatively smaller. The breast as a whole expands farther during this period, particularly if the woman has not nursed a child (it may increase as much as one-fourth of its unstimulated size). A breast that has been suckled may change little in size or not at all. During orgasm the breasts show no further changes. In the resolution phase, along with the rapidly disappearing sexual flush, the areolae become detumescent and the nipples regain this fully erect appearance ("false erection"). Gradually the breasts and nipples return to normal size.

The Skin

The significance of skin changes accompanying emotional states is well known. We blush in embarrassment, flush in anger, turn pale in fear. These surface reflections of inner feelings result from either the infusion of blood (blush) or the draining of blood (pale) from the vessels in the skin. Not surprisingly, sexual activity also results in definite skin reactions, including flushing, temperature change, and perspiration.

The flushing response is more common in women. It appears as a color change with the appearance of a rash, in the center of the lower chest as a woman moves into the plateau phase. It then spreads to the breasts, the rest of the chest, and the neck. This sexual flush reaches its peak in the late plateau phase and is an important part of the excited, straining, and uniquely expressive physiology of the person about to experience the release of orgasm. During the resolution phase the sexual flush fades very quickly—in reverse order, with color leaving the chest last.

People often refer to sexual excitement as a sort of "glow," "fire," or "fever," but the temperature of the body does not change much during the sexual response cycle. Vasocongestion of the skin is the likely explanation for the feeling of warmth that people sometimes feel after orgasm.

Perspiration is one of the ways in which the overheated body cools itself, and apart from the perspiration caused by physical exertion, it is a fairly common response during the resolution phase. Among men this response is less consistent and may involve only the palms of the hands and the soles of the feet.

The Cardiovascular System

The heart races and pounds during fear, anger, and excitement, and it does the same in response to sexual excitement. This reaction is not always immediate, and mild erotic thoughts may not change the heart rate. But high levels of sexual arousal and certainly orgasm do not occur without some increase in heart rate. In the plateau phase the heart rate rises from the normal 60 to 80 beats per minute to 100 to 160 beats per minute. Blood pressure also shows a definite increase at this time. These changes are similar to those seen in athletes exerting maximum effort or in persons engaged in heavy labor. The resulting strain on the cardiovascular system is easily handled most of the time, but persons with heart disease require medical guidance in this regard.

The Respiratory System

Changes in breathing, or respiratory rate may lag behind those in heart rate but al-

ways accompany them. Flaring nostrils, a heaving chest, and a gasping mouth are well-known signs of sexual excitement. Faster and deeper breathing becomes apparent during the plateau phase, and during orgasm the respiratory rate may go as high as forty a minute (normal is about fifteen a minute, with inhalation and exhalation counting as one). Breathing becomes irregular during orgasm—some people momentarily hold their breath and then breathe rapidly. Following orgasm some people take a deep long breath or sigh as they sink into the resolution phase.

The Digestive System

The response of the digestive tract to sexual stimulation can best be seen at its beginning and at its end: the mouth and the anus. During sexual arousal the secretion of saliva increases and some people actually water at the mouth. Some may drool or even spray saliva, and during intense erotic kissing or mouth-genital contact, increased salivation is very apparent.

At the other end of the digestive tract is the anus, a very sensitive area. Not only is it quite close to the genitals, it is intimately involved in both causing and responding to sexual stimuli. Although some people are indifferent to, turned off, or disgusted by anal stimulation, others react erotically and anal stimulation is common in male homosexual and in some heterosexual relationships. Stimulation of the anus or rhythmic contractions of the anus along with flexing of the buttocks can bring on sexual tension, and some individuals are able to reach orgasm through this maneuver alone.

Not only does stimulation of the anus contribute to sexual arousal, sexual arousal causes anal responses. During the excitement and plateau phases, the rectal sphincter contracts irregularly in response to direct stimulation. More striking reactions occur during orgasm, when involuntary contractions can be seen to occur at approximately the same 0.8-second intervals as the throbs of the penile urethra and the orgasmic platform. Anal contractions do not always occur, however, and usually involve only two to four spasms. The anal sphincter then relaxes while the other signs of orgasm are still in progress.

The Urinary System

The male urethra is part of the penis, and its changes during the sexual response cycle have already been mentioned. The female urethra is independent of the reproductive system, but in some women it does undergo a few irregular contractions during orgasm. Unlike the anal spasms these contractions are quite feeble. In some women urination may be frequent and uncomfortable after prolonged intercourse because of irritation to the urinary bladder. This condition is sometimes known as "honeymoon cystitis."

The urinary meatus (the opening of the urethra to the outside) is quite sensitive in both sexes, and stimulation of it is sexually arousing for some people. Masturbation may sometimes involve manipulation and insertion of various objects like hair pins into the urethra. Occasionally, especially in women, these objects slip into the urinary bladder and must be removed surgically.

Reactions in Older People

Sexuality and sexual activity are not reserved for the young (even though our culture sometimes seems to assume so). People do tend to lose sexual ability and interest gradually as they grow older, but this need not be the case. There are many individuals who keep up an active sex life well past the age of 60 and on into old age. What accounts for the sexual vigor of such people is not clear, but in addition to many important biological and psychological factors, it seems that past behavior may play a role. Individuals who have led active sex lives in their youth and throughout adulthood appear to continue this pattern well into old age. Time does, however, bring about changes in sexual responsiveness. In general, there is a slowing and lessening of body responses in both sexes. This does not mean that older people react in a different or abnormal manner. Some reac-

tions continue the same as always, others are only modified or limited, and some cease altogether. Basically older men and women respond as before and continue to be capable of orgasm (even if they do not achieve it as often). Studies of these and other changes that come with age are important because in the past people did not understand these changes, and this often led to needless sexual problems and unnecessary cessation of sexual activity.

For older men the major problem is potency—the ability to have and to keep an erection, a process that slows with age. Instead of the several seconds required in the prime of youth, an older man needs more time to achieve an erection, no matter how exciting the stimulation.

Once an erection has been achieved, however, it can usually be maintained longer, perhaps because of better control based on experience or because of physiological changes. Although erection can be maintained throughout the excitement and plateau phases, it is not sustained at its maximum—which is only achieved just before orgasm. Should an older man lose his erection before orgasm he will probably have greater difficulty regaining it. During orgasm contractions start at the same 0.8-second intervals but die out after a few throbs. Ejaculation is no longer so vigorous as in youth, and in very old age the semen just seeps out.

The responses of other male organs are also diminished. Scrotal changes may not occur at all, testicular elevation is limited, and after the age of 55 the testicles may not increase in size during the sexual response cycle. Regardless of these changes, psychological enjoyment remains possible.

During the resolution phase whatever physical changes may have occurred disappear with dramatic speed. In fact, some disappear even before they can be detected. Loss of erection occurs in a matter of seconds, rather than in a lingering two-stage process. Few older men seek multiple orgasm and even fewer achieve them, but given a chance to recover during a longer refractory period, some men can and do go on to have additional orgasms.

The impact of age on the female sex organs is more pronounced in some ways. After menopause, hormonal loss (*see* Chapter 4) causes progressive and marked physical changes. The walls of the vagina lose their thick, wrinkled texture, their purplish color, and their elasticity. They appear thin and pale. Vaginal lubrication takes longer (several minutes) and is less abundant; the tenting effect is limited and delayed; and the orgasmic platform does not develop fully.

In the orgasmic and resolution phases, the older vagina is similar to the older penis. Orgasmic contractions are fewer and less intense, and resolution is rapid.

Thinner vaginal walls, delayed or inadequate lubrication, and the loss of tissue flexibility may result in painful intercourse for older women. These problems usually can be remedied medically or by the use of lubricants.

The uterus also undergoes great changes. Within ten years after menopause, its body will have returned to its preadolescent size, about the size of the cervix. Uterine elevation during the sexual response cycle is less marked and occurs later, and no vasocongestive swelling of the uterus is seen in postmenopausal women. Some older women report uterine spasms that can be quite painful, similar to labor pains. This reaction in some cases discourages an older woman from seeking sexual gratification.

The responses of the labia also change considerably with advancing age, with the major changes taking place with menopause. The major lips lose their fatty deposits under the skin and appear thin and show no visible response to sexual stimulation (particularly if the woman has not borne a child). The minor lips continue to show a vasocongestive response, but swelling is less and color change is limited or absent. The response of the clitoris is relatively unchanged even in very old age, and resolution is unusually rapid.

The responses of the rest of the body in both sexes decline in varying degrees. The heart and respiratory reactions, for instance, continue and are even more taxing. The breasts continue to respond with nipple erection, but vasocongestion of the female breasts is greatly reduced.

A problem sometimes faced by older women is a burning sensation during urination following intercourse. It is similar to that of "honeymoon cystitis" and is caused by irritation of the bladder and urethra by the penis, but in older women this is because the thinner vaginal walls give inadequate protection. The discomfort may last for several days following coitus, but it does not follow orgasm through masturbation.

It appears that men and women are affected to some extent by the inevitable physical changes of old age. Men are less virile and must save their strength. Women are more sensitive to pain and discomfort. These problems, however, can be overcome in many instances, often with little more than patience and artificial lubrication. Physiologically, older men and women remain sexually capable. As they adjust to other physical limitations, they can adjust to sexual ones. Aging need not quench sexual desire or its fulfillment. Sex in old age need not be thought of as worse than earlier but merely different.

Overview of Physiological Responses

A great many things seem to be happening all at once during sexual arousal and orgasm. Tables 3.1 and 3.2 will help provide an overview of the events taking place during each phase of the sexual response cycle.

THE NEUROPHYSIOLOGICAL BASIS OF SEXUAL FUNCTIONS

Sometimes sex seems as simple as A, B, C. Even though our reactions may be many and varied, there are times when we move through the phases of the sexual cycle with the greatest of ease. However, as natural and straightforward as sex may sometimes seem, it is made so by a set of highly complex mechanisms of control. Some of these mechanisms

Male	Female
EXCITEMENT PHASE	
Penile erection (within 3–8 seconds)	Vaginal lubrication (within 10–30 seconds)
As phase is prolonged:	*As phase is prolonged:*
Thickening, flattening, and elevation of scrotal sac	Thickening of vaginal walls and labia
As phase is prolonged:	*As phase is prolonged:*
Partial testicular elevation and size increase	Expansion of inner $\frac{2}{3}$ of vagina and elevation of cervix and corpus
	As phase is prolonged:
	Tumescence of clitoris
PLATEAU PHASE	
Increase in penile coronal circumference and testicular tumescence (50–100% enlarged)	Orgasmic platform in outer $\frac{1}{3}$ of vagina
Full testicular elevation and rotation (orgasm inevitable)	Full expansion of $\frac{2}{3}$ of vagina, uterine and cervical elevation
Purple hue on corona of penis (inconsistent, even if orgasm is to ensue)	"Sex-skin": discoloration of minor labia (constant, if orgasm is to ensue)
Mucoid secretion from Cowper's gland	Mucoid secretion from Bartholin's gland
	Withdrawal of clitoris
ORGASMIC PHASE	
Ejaculation	*Pelvic response (no ejaculation)*
Contractions of accessory organs of reproduction: vas deferens, seminal vesicles, ejaculatory duct, prostate	Contractions of uterus from fundus toward lower uterine segment
Relaxation of external bladder sphincter	Minimal relaxation of external cervical opening
Contractions of penile urethra at 0.8-second intervals for 3–4 contractions (slowing thereafter for 2–4 more contractions)	Contractions of orgasmic platform at 0.8-second intervals for 5–12 contractions (slowing thereafter for 3–6 more contractions)
Anal sphincter contractions (2–4 contractions at 0.8-second intervals)	External rectal sphincter contractions (2–4 contractions at 0.8-second intervals)
	External urethral sphincter contractions (2–3 contractions at irregular intervals, 10–15% of subjects)
RESOLUTION PHASE	
Refractory period with rapid loss of pelvic vasocongestion	Ready return to orgasm with retarded loss of pelvic vasocongestion
Loss of penile erection in primary (rapid) and secondary (slow) stages	Loss of "sex-skin" color and orgasmic platform in primary (rapid) stage
	Remainder of pelvic vasocongestion as secondary (slow) stage
	Loss of clitoral tumescence and return to position

Table 3.2 **GENERAL BODY REACTIONS DURING THE SEXUAL RESPONSE CYCLE**

Male	Female
EXCITEMENT PHASE	
Nipple erection (30%)	Nipple erection (consistent)
	Sex-tension flush (25%)
PLATEAU PHASE	
Sex-tension flush (25%)	Sex-tension flush (75%)
Carpopedal spasm	Carpopedal spasm
Generalized skeletal muscle tension	Generalized skeletal muscle tension
Hyperventilation	Hyperventilation
Tachycardia (100–160 beats per minute)	Tachycardia (100–160 beats per minute)
ORGASMIC PHASE	
Specific skeletal muscle contractions	Specific skeletal muscle contractions
Hyperventilation	Hyperventilation
Tachycardia (100–180 beats per minute)	Tachycardia (110–180 beats per minute)
RESOLUTION PHASE	
Sweating reaction (30–40%)	Sweating reaction (30–40%)
Hyperventilation	Hyperventilation
Tachycardia (150–80 beats per minute)	Tachycardia (150–80 beats per minute)

are hormonal (and will be described in Chapter 4). Others involve the nervous system and the brain. A brief look at the neurophysiology of sex can add to our appreciation of the extreme delicacy of the sexual experience.

The Mechanism of Arousal

A caress of the genitals can bring about almost instant sexual arousal, but the mechanism of response is not completely contained in the genital area. The nervous system and the brain are always involved. The fact that memory and imagination can initiate sexual arousal further emphasizes the role of the brain in sexual response.

When the genitals are caressed, or when some other form of physical stimulation is applied, nerve endings in the skin of the stimulated area detect the stimulation and send a message to the spinal cord and brain. Specialized nerve endings respond to touch, cold, warmth, pain, and so on, but none respond specifically to "sexual stimulation." It is up to the brain to interpret a touch as a lover's ca-

ress. When the brain receives a message from the senses, it interprets it and sends back an answer telling the body how to respond.

The Mechanism of Erection

In males, a sensual caress usually brings about an **erection.** This reaction is triggered by a nervous reflex, which is a three-part response. First the "receptors," or sense organs, detect the stimulus and send it to centers in the spinal cord and brain. These centers, "transmitters," interpret the signal and send the appropriate response to the end organs, "effectors," completing what is known as a reflex arc. A good example is the quick withdrawal of your hand after you touch a hot object. The response is immediate and involuntary. All reflexes, including erection, are involuntary; the response is automatic and does not require a decision by the brain. The brain, however, is conscious of such responses and can, in some cases, inhibit them.

A reflex arc links the genital organs and adjoining areas (like the insides of the thighs) to an "erection center" in the lowest (sacral) portion of the spinal cord. From there impulses are carried to the blood vessels that supply the spongy tissue of the penis. Ordinarily the cavernous and spongy bodies receive only modest amounts of blood from the arteries and are drained by the veins. After effective tactile stimulation, like stroking the insides of the thighs or the glans penis, nerve impulses are sent to the spinal erection center. This center then activates nerve fibers connected to the muscular coating of the arterial walls. There are two sets of such fibers. One set (the parasympathetic system) causes the walls of the arteries to relax and expand their openings. The other set (the sympathetic system) causes them to contract and narrow. Sexual stimulation activates the parasympathetic system and inhibits the sympathetic fibers, which immediately results in expansion of the arterial walls and a rush of blood into the cavernous and spongy tissues of the penis.

The veins, hampered by their valves and by compression of their thin walls by the swelling of the organ, cannot handle the outflow of blood. As a result, the penis is rapidly engorged so that it stiffens and stands erect. Loss of erection is due to a reversal of this process. Sympathetic nerve fibers constrict the arteries, cutting down the inflow of blood, and drainage through the veins increases until the penis returns to its flaccid condition.

The part of the process described so far is purely reflexive and can occur without assistance from the brain. As mentioned earlier, a man whose spinal cord has been cut above the erection reflex center (so that messages from the genitals cannot reach the brain) may still be capable of erection. He will not "feel" the stimulus of his penis, but it will respond.

The independence of the reflex centers does not, however, mean that they cannot be influenced by the brain. You can, for instance, keep your hand from reflexively withdrawing from a hot object. Likewise, a man can inhibit erection despite continued physical stimulation. Usually the brain and the reflex center, which are connected by an intricate nerve network, work together. Erotic thoughts can encourage a man to stimulate his genitals, or conversely, physical stimulation can inspire erotic thoughts.

The instances in which erection seems to be nonerotic in origin involve tension of the pelvic muscles (as when lifting a heavy weight or when straining while moving the bowels). Irritation of the glans or a full bladder may have the same effect. Erections that occur during infancy are explained on a reflex basis also.

Erection is the most delicate of the male sexual responses. Frequent failure to achieve erection is known as **impotence,** and it can take many forms. A man may be unable to achieve erection under any circumstances, or he may be impotent only during some sexual activities or with some partners. Failure may also be partial, as when the penis, though erect, is not firm enough to permit sexual intercourse, or when a man is unable to maintain an erection long enough to participate in intercourse satisfactorily.

At one time or another every man experiences some loss of potency, but fluctuations and occasional failures do not constitute impotence. It is only when the problem is persistent that it is considered a malfunction (*see* Chapter 11).

The opposite of impotence is a rare condition known as **priapism**—constant erection. This condition is not a sign of virility but instead is usually related to some medical problem or disease (tumor, infection, and so on) that triggers and maintains the mechanism of erection. Such erections are not usually accompanied by sexual desire and may be quite painful. They can also cause permanent damage to the penis and result in impotence.

The Mechanism of Ejaculation

Ejaculation, like erection, is reflexive, but it is much more independent of the brain than is erection. Once ejaculation has been triggered it cannot be stopped until it is finished. The ejaculation control center is in the lumbar portion of the spinal cord, somewhat higher than the erection center. The impulses that trigger ejaculation travel to the genital area through the sympathetic nerves.

Apart from premature ejaculation, disturbances of this process are very rare. Occasionally a man with a normal erection will fail to ejaculate no matter how hard he tries. Sometimes the ejaculation reflex is triggered, but the fluid, instead of flowing out normally, empties into the urinary bladder (**retrograde ejaculation**). The sensation of orgasm when this happens is unchanged, but the man may be alarmed by the absence of semen. This condition occurs in certain illnesses and occasionally after the use of some common tranquilizers. When use of the drug is discontinued, the usual flow of semen is reestablished.

Some men have reportedly developed the ability to produce retrograde ejaculation as a means of birth control. The physiological explanation of this involves the two urethral sphincters. Normally the internal sphincter (which guards the entrance to the bladder) closes during ejaculation, and the external sphincter (which is located below the point of entry of the ejaculatory ducts) opens. In retrograde ejaculation the external urethral sphincter closes and the internal sphincter opens, permitting semen to back up into the bladder.

The ability to delay ejaculation voluntarily is one of the most admired attributes of male virility. It enables a man to provide protracted sexual gratification for his partner, as well as to prolong his own enjoyment. Techniques for delaying ejaculation will be discussed later, but the basic idea is to control excitement while maintaining erection, rather than allow excitement to build up relentlessly. Mental distraction (thinking about a neutral or even unpleasant topic) and muscular relaxation (slowing pelvic thrusts or stopping all movement) are among the methods of control.

Coitus reservatus (known as *karezza* in India) is the ultimate in control of ejaculation. Men trained in this practice are able to approach ejaculation repeatedly without completing it. They claim they thus achieve the equivalent of multiple orgasms.

Reflexive Mechanisms in Women

It is generally assumed that there are spinal centers in women that correspond to the erection and ejaculatory centers in men. Strictly speaking, women neither have erections nor ejaculate, but the vasocongestive response that causes male erection results in similar tumescent changes in the clitoris and the rest of the genital tissues. The orgasmic response is also similar, except for some important differences already mentioned.

The reaction of the reflexive centers in the spinal cords of women is not well understood in part because the outward signs of vasocongestion and orgasm are relatively more difficult to detect in female animals in experimental settings. In addition, our knowledge of neurophysiology is so limited that broad generalizations about definite similarities and differences between the sexes cannot be made at this time. As research continues, however, it may be possible to pinpoint and to better understand the similarities and differences that exist between the male and female nervous system and brain.

Brain Mechanisms

It has often been said that the brain is the most important erogenous zone, and realizing the importance of the brain in almost all human behavior, few would disagree with that statement. Until recently, however, little was actually known of the neurophysiological role of the brain in sexual functioning. During the past several decades, many researchers have been investigating the neurophysiology of animals. These studies are contributing to our knowledge of how the brain influences human sexual functioning.

One area of the brain, the limbic system, has been found to be especially important in emotional and sexual behavior. The limbic system (from the Latin word for "fringe" or "border") forms a border at the internal edges of the two halves of the brain and surrounds the brain stem, the continuation of the spinal cord into the brain. The limbic system is not a single entity but consists of a number of separate components with numerous pathways to other centers in the brain.

One of the ways researchers study the limbic system is by electrically stimulating it. Stimulation of various parts of the limbic system suggests that it is involved in some of the most basic of behaviors—alimentary (feeding), aggressive, defensive, and sexual. Stimulation of one small area, for instance, results in penile erection and other sex-related activities in male animals. The limbic system, however, is not the only part of the brain involved in sexual behavior. Stimulation of other areas (for instance, the thalamus) results in ejaculation.

In addition to locating an area of the brain that appears to be involved in sexual behavior, these studies also suggest associations between parts of the brain involved in sex and others involved in olfaction (smell) and aggression. This may explain the well-known relationship between sexual and olfactory functions in animals and possibly in humans. It also provides clues to the relationship between sex and aggression as seen in various behaviors, including competition for mates.

Another set of experiments has led to the location of what have been called "pleasure centers" in the brain. Electrodes were implanted in the brain of a rat and attached to a circuit allowing the animal to stimulate itself by pressing a pedal or lever. Ordinarily, rats in such experimental setups will spontane-

ously press the lever several times an hour. But when the electrodes were placed in certain areas of the brain, the rat would go on pressing the pedal as often as 5000 times an hour, and would do this despite hunger and thirst. Since the stimulation of these locations seemed to be so rewarding, they were called "pleasure centers."

There have also been cases in which electrodes were implanted in humans (for medical reasons). The areas that yielded pleasure when stimulated were found to be in roughly the same areas as in the animal brains. In humans the pleasure was clearly of a sexual nature when certain parts of the limbic system were stimulated. In addition, changes in brain waves were noted in the same areas when the patients were sexually aroused.

These "pleasure centers" in humans are in areas that lie close to the regions where stimulation leads to erection in animals. They are also connected to areas that receive sensory input from the body surface (tactile stimulation). As more pieces of this puzzle are discovered, we will eventually have a map of the brain that shows how incoming erotic tactile stimuli activate sexual behavior and reinforce it with pleasurable feelings. As more and more of the brain is mapped and its functions understood, we will begin to appreciate more fully the complex and intricate physiology that underlies the poetry and romance of sex.

SUMMARY

1. Sexual activity begins with stimulation, either physical or mental, and tactile stimulation is one of the most important methods of sexual arousal in humans. Our bodies respond to it reflexively. Areas of the body that are especially susceptible to tactile stimulation are known as erogenous zones. Many of these zones are the same in all individuals, but through different experiences people learn to like or dislike certain types of tactile stimulation. The other senses, sight, sound, smell, and taste, can be almost as important in sexual stimulation as is touch, but our reactions to these senses are mainly learned rather than reflexive.

2. In addition to physical stimulation, humans can react to purely mental stimulation, and sexual fantasy is the most common erotic stimulant. Sexual arousal is also influenced strongly by emotional states, and arousal will occur if accompanied by appropriate emotional states.

3. In the past it has been assumed that men are more easily sexually aroused than are women, but many of the observed differences are probably due to cultural and learning experiences rather than to biological differences. Recent research, conducted with precise methods of measuring arousal, suggests that women and men are much more alike in this regard than was believed. Changing cultural attitudes may bring about further changes in behavior, making it easier to detect purely physiological differences between the sexes.

4. Effective sexual stimulation can set off a chain of events that leads to orgasm—an explosive release of neuromuscular tension. Men and women can respond at about the same rate and in much the same manner to sexual arousal, but there can be great variation from person to person and from time to time. In general, the body tenses from head to toe, and involuntary muscular twitches gradually take on a rhythmic pattern. The skin becomes flushed, salivation increases, the nostrils flare, the heart pounds, breathing grows heavy, and the face becomes contorted. Reactions during orgasm also vary but the most common responses include sustained tension or mild twitching of the arms and legs while the rest of the body becomes rigid, a grimace or muffled cry, and rhythmic throbbing of the sex organs and pelvic muscles before relaxation sets in.

5. In males the sensations of orgasm are linked to ejaculation, which occurs in two stages. First is the feeling that orgasm is imminent, or coming. Second is the feeling of fluid moving out under pressure. In females orgasm starts with a feeling of momentary suspension followed by a peak of intense sensation in the clitoris. This feeling then spreads through the pelvis. The aftereffects of orgasm differ among individuals, but in general there is a relaxation of the body and a feeling of peace and satisfaction.

6. The first and only major investigation of the physiology of the human sexual response cycle was conducted by Masters and Johnson. They outlined four basic responses: excitement, plateau, orgasm, and resolution. In women two additional responses are possible. In both, the plateau phase is absent and the sensations of orgasm are more intense. In men there is a refractory period following orgasm during which a man cannot have another orgasm.

7. Vasocongestion and myotonia are the two processes responsible for most of the physiological responses of the sex cycle. In males the most obvious response is seen in the penis. During excitement it becomes erect but may fluctuate in firmness, and an erection can easily be lost due to distraction. During the plateau phase erection becomes fuller and more permanent, and the glans may deepen in color. During orgasm the urethra and muscles at the base of the penis contract, at first irregularly then at approximately 0.8-second intervals. Ejaculation occurs in two stages: first when the prostate, vas, and seminal vesicles pour their fluid into the urethra, then when the fluid is forced out. Resolution also occurs in two stages: the penis becomes semierect shortly after orgasm; then it gradually returns to its flaccid state.

8.   During the excitement phase the scrotal sac becomes thicker and the testes are lifted up within the scrotum. During the plateau phase the testicles increase in size and are further lifted up against the body wall just before orgasm. The Cowper's glands may secrete a drop or more of fluid during the late excitement phase. The prostate and seminal vesicles pulsate and pour out their fluids during orgasm. All return to normal during resolution.

9.   The vagina exhibits three changes during the excitement phase: lubrication, expansion of its inner two-thirds, and a change to a deeper color. During the plateau phase the outer third of the vagina narrows to form the orgasmic platform. During orgasm this platform contracts at approximately 0.8-second intervals. During resolution the orgasmic platform relaxes, and the rest of the vagina returns to its normal size and color in ten to fifteen minutes.

10.   The clitoris is a highly sensitive, exclusively sexual organ. It becomes engorged during the excitement phase and then is retracted under the clitoral hood during the plateau phase. It remains hidden from view during orgasm but reemerges quickly following orgasm.

11.   The major lips become flattened, thinner, and more widely separated during excitement, with those of women who have given birth becoming even more engorged (due to distended veins). The inner lips become engorged and may double or triple in size by the time of the plateau. They also become progressively pink or bright red in light-skinned women. During resolution they return to normal size and color, with color loss occurring in two steps. The Bartholin's glands may secrete slightly during the excitement phase. The uterus responds to excitement by elevation from its usual position, pulling the cervix up and contributing to the tenting effect in the vagina. Orgasmic contractions occur in the uterus simultaneously with those of the orgasmic platform.

12.   Breast reactions are most prominent in women. The nipple becomes erect due to muscle contractions, and the areola and breast itself become engorged. Skin changes include a spreading, rashlike coloration beginning at the lower chest (especially in women), a feeling of body warmth due to vasocongestion of the skin, and perspiration. Heart and breathing rate also increase during excitement and reach a peak at orgasm. Salivation also increases, and the anus may contract at the start of orgasm. The male urethra contracts during orgasm, but the female urethra may contract only a few times if at all.

13.   The ability to enjoy sexual relations and to experience orgasm continues into old age, but the aging process usually does limit sexual activity. Loss of potency is the major problem in men as the

ability to achieve and sustain erection decreases with age. The responses of the female sex organs are similarly limited. The vagina becomes thinner and less responsive, and lubrication is slowed. Orgasmic contractions in both sexes are fewer and less intense.

14.   The neurophysiological mechanism of arousal consists of nerve links between the genitals and the spinal cord and the brain. The mechanism of erection is controlled by a reflex arc: stimulation of the genitals sends a message to the spinal control center, which sends messages to the muscular walls of the blood vessels of the penis. The arteries dilate and let in blood, which cannot be effectively drained by the veins. The process is mainly reflexive, but the brain has some control over it. Ejaculation is even more independent of the brain, and once it has started it cannot be stopped. It is assumed that the neurophysiological mechanisms of women are similar to those of men, but they have yet to be thoroughly studied.

15.   The role of the brain in the sexual response cycle is not fully understood, but recent research has added some interesting pieces to this puzzle. Certain areas of the brain have been found to be closely associated with sexual activity and with pleasure. As more is found out about these and other areas of the brain we will begin to understand more fully just how important a role the brain plays in our sex lives.

SUGGESTED READING

Brecher, R., and Brecher, E. *An Analysis of Human Sexual Response.* New York: New American Library. 1966.
An abbreviated and simplified account of the Masters and Johnson work.

Kaplan, H. S. *The New Sex Therapy.* New York: Brunner/Mazel, 1974.
Chapters 1 and 2 provide a good overview of the physiology of sexual response and of the brain mechanisms controlling them.

MacLean, P. D., "Brain Mechanisms of Elemental Sexual Functions," in Sadock, B. J., Kaplan, J. I., and Freedman, A. K. (Eds.). *The Sexual Experience.* Baltimore: Williams & Wilkins, 1976.
A fairly complex discussion of the neurophysiology of sex based on the author's work.

Masters, W. H., and Johnson, V. E. *Human Sexual Response.* Boston: Little, Brown, 1966.
The original and still the most extensive source of information on the physiology of the sexual response cycle.

Olds, J. "Pleasure centers in the brain," *Scientific American, 193* (1956): 105–116.

Sex Hormones and the Reproductive Period

chapter 4

Did You Know That . . .

a young woman's first menstrual period usually occurs at around 12 or 13 years of age, but one hundred years ago women did not begin menstruating until they were 16 or 17 years old?

the fact that a 13-year-old male can ejaculate does not mean that he is fertile?

emotional factors (such as fear of being pregnant) and possibly even the odors of other women can influence the timing of a woman's menstrual cycle?

uterine contractions experienced during orgasm may increase the rate of menstrual flow, and some women have reported that this helps relieve some of the painful symptoms of menstruation?

menopause comes at an earlier age in women who smoke than in nonsmokers?

castration of a male does not necessarily render him impotent?

puberty begins later and lasts longer in males than in females, but it is triggered by the same hormones in both sexes?

a true hermaphrodite is an individual who has both ovarian and testicular tissues, but in the entire world medical literature of the twentieth century only sixty cases of true hermaphroditism have been reported?

INTRODUCTION

Do humans have a sex drive? Is there some internal mechanism that urges us to make love and reproduce? If we consider the importance of sex in the reproduction of the species, it is logical to assume that our bodies are programmed in some way to ensure that we reproduce. If we consider the success humans have had in populating the earth, it is hard to believe that we do not have an inborn or instinctive sex drive. Nevertheless, that does seem to be the case. If by instinct we mean innate, unlearned patterns of sexual behavior specific to human beings, the evidence seems to be against it. Humans are thinkers. Most of our behaviors are the result of mental activity rather than of purely biological or chemical activity. Learning has a powerful influence on almost all human behavior and is much more important an influence on sexual behavior than are inborn needs or drives.

Many of the lower animals (such as fish and birds) have courtship and mating behaviors that are always the same within a species and thus seem obviously the result of inborn sex drives or instincts. No such instincts have been proved to exist in humans. As powerful and as otherwise unexplainable as our sexual urges may seem at times, and as natural and unlearned as our sexual attitudes and behaviors may feel, it is probable that most of our sexual behaviors are the result of learning experiences rather than of inborn drives.

The term "sex drive" may not explain human sexual behavior, but the notion of a sex drive as an internal state of tension influenced by various external stimuli and relieved by a particular sort of experience may have some validity in describing (but not necessarily explaining) human sexual behavior. An erotic film, for instance, can set up a sort of internal tension that we feel urged or driven to relieve through sexual activity, but the same movie may turn some people off or just bore them. So, what seems like a natural sexual urge in one person may be completely absent in another person under the same circumstances—or it may be even stronger in a third person.

Although there is no inborn mechanism that controls human sexual behavior and makes us want to have sex at certain times of the month or year (as with some animals), there are chemicals that play extremely important roles in many aspects of our reproductive and sex lives. These chemicals are produced by the sex glands and are known as **sex hormones**. Reproduction would not occur were it not for the sex hormones. Development of the anatomical equipment and the physiological processes described in Chapters 2 and 3 depend on sex hormones, and even though human behavior is so profoundly influenced by learning experiences that it is difficult to sort out the effects of sex hormones on the sex drive, there is evidence that sex hormones can influence our sexual urges, drives, and behaviors. The effects are much more clear cut in animals than in humans, but it appears that administration of female sex hormones to males tends to diminish the sex drive in some instances. Administration of male sex hormones to females seems to enhance sex drive in some cases.

In this chapter we will examine the hormonal processes that occur during the reproductive years—the period beginning with puberty and ending in the female with menopause.

BASIC ENDOCRINOLOGY

What are sex hormones, and how do they influence our lives? **Endocrinology,** the study of the secretions of the endocrine (**ductless**) glands, attempts to answer these questions.

The **endocrine glands,** unlike the salivary and some other glands, secrete their products directly into the bloodstream. These products are hormones, and they have dramatic effects on specific tissues or organs to which they travel through the bloodstream. The endocrine glands include such structures as the thyroid, parathyroid, and adrenal glands. We will look specifically at the sex glands, the ovaries and testes) and at the **pituitary** gland, which controls the secretions of the other endocrine glands.

The Pituitary

The pituitary is the most complex of all the endocrine glands. It is a pea-sized structure located at the base of the brain and connected to the brain by a system of microscopic blood vessels and nerve fibers (see Figure 4.1). The pituitary is often called the "master gland" because it secretes hormones that travel through the bloodstream and stimulate other endocrine glands to produce their specific hormones.

The two pituitary hormones that stimulate the gonads are called **gonadotrophins.** One is the **follicle-stimulating hormone** (FSH). The other is the **luteinizing hormone** (LH). A third pituitary hormone, **prolactin,** stimulates milk production in the female breast (see Chapter 5).

In the female, FSH and LH stimulate the ovaries to manufacture and secrete the female sex hormones, **estrogen** and **progesterone.** In the male, LH stimulates the interstitial cells of the testes (see Chapter 2) to secrete the male hormone, **testosterone.** In the male LH is usually called **interstitial-cell-stimulating hormone** (ICSH). The sex hormones, estrogen, progesterone, and testosterone, belong to a group of chemical substances called **steroids.** Steroid hormones are widely used in medicine, and birth-control pills consist of mixtures of synthetic female sex steroids.

The early history of endocrinology included some fascinating experiments that demonstrated the effects of steroid hormones. Castration (removal of the testicles) of a rooster, for instance, was shown to prevent growth of the cock's comb. In 1849 it was shown that this effect could be reversed by transplanting testes from another rooster to a castrated one. These dramatic effects encouraged some researchers to treat themselves with sex hormones. Extract of testicles was claimed to increase a man's potency. This and various other highly publicized dramatic effects (longevity, youthful appearance, energy, and virility) attributed to extracts of the sex glands gave endocrinology a bad reputation among the more conservative members of the medical profession.

In recent years there has been a regrowth of interest in the sex hormones, especially in the way the brain can influence the timing and extent of hormone secretions. The study of these brain mechanisms is a separate field called **neuroendocrinology.** The focus of this field is on two adjacent sites in the brain, the pituitary gland and the **hypothalamus.**

At first a rather straightforward system was thought to control the release of sex hormones. The pituitary is divided in two sections, the **posterior** (rear) and the **anterior** (front). Since the sex gland stimulating hormones (**gonadotrophins**) are known to be produced by cells in the anterior pituitary, it seemed that a simple feedback system could explain how the pituitary and the sex glands worked together to control the level of sex hormones: Gonadotrophins are released by the pituitary, causing the production of hormones by the sex glands. When the amount of sex hormones in the bloodstream reaches a certain level, they "turn off" secretion of gonadotrophins by the pituitary. When the level of sex hormones goes down, the pituitary is turned back on. The system works like a thermostat, with the pituitary monitoring the level of sex hormones passing through it in the bloodstream just as a thermostat monitors the temperature in a house and turns off the furnace when the temperature reaches the thermostat setting. Experiments with animals tended to confirm this model. When animals are given injections of sex hormones, gonadotrophin production by the pituitary decreases. When the level of sex hormones is decreased (for example, by castration), gonadotrophin output increases.

Although this model does help explain how the level of sex hormones is controlled, it does not explain the entire system.

The pituitary does not always turn on and off strictly in relation to the level of sex hormones in the blood. The changes in secretions of hormones during a woman's menstrual cycle, for instance, suggest that there are regular, monthly variations in the messages sent from the pituitary to the ovaries. Furthermore, physical and psychological stress is known to have an effect on pituitary-controlled events, such as menstruation and testosterone production. So it appears that the pituitary is subject to regulation by the brain, just as a thermostat is subject to outside control. You can turn your home thermostat up or down, depending on the weather; the brain can turn the pituitary up or down, depending on various factors.

The Hypothalamus

Brain researchers have now shown that the hypothalamus is the portion of the brain that regulates the pituitary. Researchers have found that destruction of certain cells of the hypothalamus of animals can cause changes in estrus cycles (the regular times at which a female animal is interested in sexual activity and capable of conceiving, also known as "heat"), in lactation (milk production), and in a number of other bodily functions, such as temperature regulation, growth, and sleep.

The hypothalamus weighs about 5 grams, only 1/300 of the whole brain, but as small as it is in relation to the rest of the brain, it is known to receive inputs from almost every part of the central nervous system and to produce extremely potent chemicals. These chemicals travel through the system of blood vessels that links the hypothalamus to the pituitary (*see* Figure 4.1). The two chemical factors secreted by the hypothalamus that are of greatest importance to reproductive functions are the **follicle-stimulating, hormone-releasing factor** (FSH-RF) and the **luteinizing hormone-releasing factor** (LH-RF). These brain-generated chemicals, as their names imply, stimulate the release of FSH and LH from the pituitary gland. A third hypothalamic factor, **prolactin-inhibiting factor** (PIF), controls milk production by preventing prolactin secretion except after childbirth.

Although we now understand many of the relationships of the secretions of the hypothalamus, pituitary, and sex glands, there are still unanswered questions. The changes in physical appearance at puberty, for instance, clearly result from dramatic increases in the production of stimulating hormones by the pituitary, but what triggers the pituitary to pour out these hormones? It may be that some sort of "biological clock" in the brain, possibly in the hypothalamus, triggers the pituitary at a certain stage of maturity. The final answers, however, may be slow in coming because the hypothalamus is so small and because the chemicals it produces are present in only small amounts.

FEMALE REPRODUCTIVE ENDOCRINOLOGY

Puberty

Some of the most obvious effects of the secretions of the sex glands can be seen in the physical changes that occur during puberty. Puberty begins sometime between the ages of 9 and 12 years for most girls. A girl's first menstrual period (**menarche**) usually occurs between the ages of 11 and 14, several years after the beginning of the physical changes that define puberty.

External Changes

As a girl goes through puberty her body gradually takes on the rounded contours that distinguish the adult female profile from that of the male. These external changes are set in motion by an increase of FSH production by the pituitary gland.

FSH stimulates the ovaries to produce estrogen (a collective noun referring to a group of chemically related female sex hormones produced by the ovaries), which travels

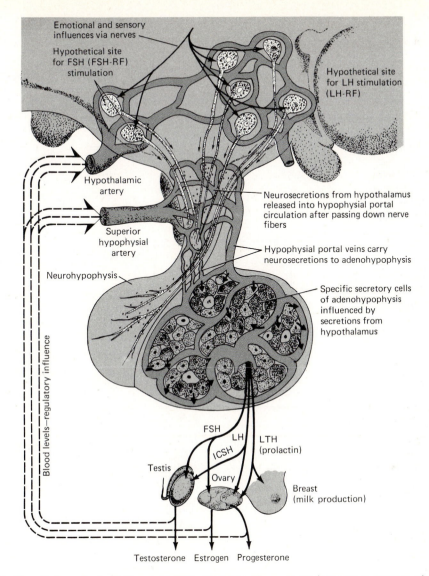

Figure 4.1 The pituitary gland. © Copyright 1953, 1972 CIBA Pharmaceutical Company, Division of CIBA–GEIGY Corporation.

through the bloodstream to the breasts, where it stimulates growth of breast tissue (*see* Figure 4.2). The darker area around the nipples becomes elevated, and the breasts begin to swell as a result of development of ducts in the nipple area and an increase in fatty tissue, connective tissue, and blood vessels. The milk-producing part of the breast (**mammary gland**) does not develop completely during puberty and does not become fully mature and functional until after childbirth.

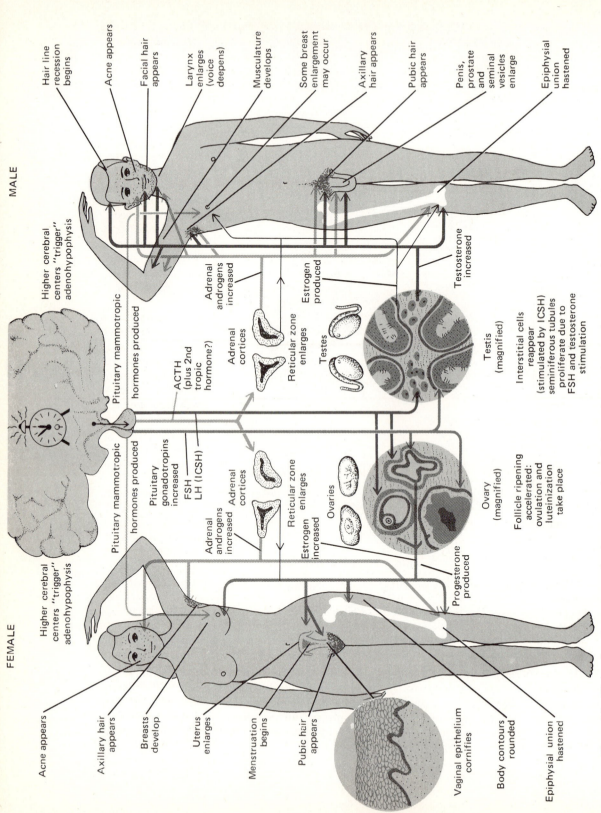

MALE

- Hair line recession begins
- Acne appears
- Facial hair appears
- Larynx enlarges (voice deepens)
- Musculature develops
- Some breast enlargement may occur
- Axillary hair appears
- Pubic hair appears
- Penis, prostate and seminal vesicles enlarge
- Epiphysial union hastened

Higher cerebral centers "trigger" adenohypophysis

Pituitary mammotropic hormones produced

Adrenal androgens increased

Adrenal cortices

Reticular zone enlarges

Estrogen produced

Testes

Testis (magnified)

Interstitial cells reappear (stimulated by ICSH) seminiferous tubules proliferate due to FSH and testosterone stimulation

Testosterone increased

ACTH (plus 2nd tropic hormone?)

Pituitary gonadotropins increased

FSH
LH (ICSH)

Adrenal androgens increased

Adrenal cortices

Reticular zone enlarges

Estrogen increased

Ovaries

Ovary (magnified)

Follicle ripening accelerated; ovulation and luteinization take place

Progesterone produced

FEMALE

- Acne appears
- Axillary hair appears
- Breasts develop
- Uterus enlarges
- Menstruation begins
- Pubic hair appears
- Vaginal epithelium cornifies
- Body contours rounded
- Epiphysial union hastened

Higher cerebral centers "trigger" adenohypophysis

Pituitary mammotropic hormones produced

Figure 4.2 Effects of sex hormones on development at puberty. © Copyright 1965 by CIBA Pharmaceutical Company, Division of CIBA−GEIGY Corporation. Reproduced with permission, from The Ciba Collection of Medical Illustrations by Frank H. Netter, M.D. All rights reserved.

At the same time that estrogen is bringing about the development of fatty and supporting tissue in the breasts of a young girl, a similar process is taking place in the hips and buttocks.

Another visible change at puberty is the appearance of **pubic** and **axillary** (underarm) **hair**. This hair is usually thicker and has more coloring than that of the scalp. Its growth is stimulated partly by estrogen and partly by hormones secreted by the adrenal glands in response to another stimulating hormone (**adrenocorticotrophic hormone, or ACTH**) from the pituitary.

The adrenal glands are paired glands located above each kidney. In females they produce small amounts of **androgens** (male sex hormones) that stimulate pubic and axillary hair growth and are perhaps related to the female sex drive (as we will see later in this chapter). The adrenal glands also produce cortisone, adrenalin, and other substances.

In addition to the rounding out of the body and the growth of pubic hair, another (sometimes embarrassing) change that often comes with puberty is the appearance of facial **acne**. This problem is usually temporary and seems to be related to changes in hormones. It tends to be most severe in young women whose menstrual cycles are highly irregular. Although acne usually is nothing worse than a cosmetic problem, it can sometimes be severe and require medical treatment, especially if it is accompanied by skin infections that can lead to permanent scars. Plastic-surgery techniques, when performed by a competent physician, can sometimes satisfactorily remove such scars.

Estrogen also causes speeded-up growth of the external sex organs at puberty, including enlargement of the labia. Androgens from the adrenal gland stimulate enlargement of the clitoris, and at the same time there is a noticeable increase in skeletal size, stimulated by the increased secretion of growth hormone by the pituitary.

Internal Changes

While the external changes of puberty are taking place, estrogen is also stimulating growth of the internal sex organs and some other structures. Estrogen specifically stimulates growth of the uterus and vagina during puberty. The muscular wall of the uterus enlarges, and its glandular lining develops. The lining of the vagina is extremely sensitive to estrogen, and its thickness is directly related to the amount of this hormone present in the bloodstream at any given time. Examination of cells from the vaginal walls is even used as a simple test by doctors to determine how much estrogen is present. Another change has to do with the acidity of the vagina. As the vaginal walls mature, the pH of the secretions that moisten its surface changes from alkaline to acid. (The pH scale is a commonly used index of acidity and alkalinity. The scale runs from 0 to 14. The neutral point is 7. Values from 0 to 7 indicate an acid state, from 7 to 14 an alkaline state.)

The bone structure of the female also changes at puberty under the influence of estrogen. The female pelvis enlarges and takes on a shape different from that of the male. Finally, estrogens also prevent further growth of the long bones of the skeleton (counteracting the effects of the growth hormone), and usually no further increase in height occurs after about the age of 17 in girls. Although many other factors contribute to height, a deficiency of estrogen in late puberty can lead to great height in a young woman.

Estrogen secretion not only increases in quantity during puberty (bringing about the various external and internal changes just described), it also takes on a cyclical pattern. An obvious sign of this is the monthly menstrual cycle. For the first few years after the menarche (which may come as a shock to a young woman who has not been prepared for it), the menstrual periods tend to be irregular, and ovulation does not occur in each cycle. For some time after her first period, then, a young woman will be relatively infertile, but she can still become pregnant.

In American culture, unlike some other societies, puberty does not mark one's entrance into adulthood, but the timing of the physical changes that come with puberty can have important effects on a young woman's psychological development. Studies have shown that females who mature later tend to be more popular and better liked by their age mates. This involves not only how they view themselves but how they behave toward others.

One interesting but unexplained fact is that the average age of menarche has been declining in Western countries. In 1860, a woman usually had her first period between 16 and 17 years of age. In 1960 it occurred between 12 and 13. Better nutrition may be the cause of this phenomenon, but other factors are probably also involved.

In very rare cases diseases can upset the timing of menarche. A tumor in the hypothalamic region of the brain, for example, can cause the pituitary to stimulate the ovaries prematurely. Tumors of the ovaries also can result in the premature outpouring of estrogen. Girls with such disorders may be capable of becoming pregnant at a very early age. The youngest documented pregnancy occurred in Peru in the widely publicized case of Lina Medina. When this girl was 5 years and 7 months old in 1939 she gave birth to a 6.5-pound (2.4-kilogram) baby boy by cesarean section. The girl had menstruated regularly since the age of 3 and had become pregnant at 4 years and 10 months.

The Menstrual Cycle

Every month, approximately, a woman's reproductive organs prepare for pregnancy. An egg is released from the ovary, and the uterus develops a thick lining in preparation for housing and nourishing the fertilized egg. However, fertilization may occur only a few times, if ever, in a woman's life. So every month the tissues that built up in the uterus in preparation for the embryo are shed, and a new cycle begins.

Menstruation (from the Latin word for "monthly") is the periodic uterine bleeding that accompanies the ovarian cycle and the shedding of the lining of the uterus. Menstruation is regulated by hormones and is seen only in female humans, apes, and some monkeys. An ovarian, or estrus, cycle occurs in other mammals but is not accompanied by bleeding. The length of the ovarian cycle is specific for each species. It is approximately twenty-eight days in the human, thirty-six days in the chimpanzee, twenty days in the cow, sixteen days in sheep, and five days in mice. Dogs and cats usually ovulate only twice a year.

For the first few years after menarche a young woman's menstrual cycles may be very irregular in length, but by the age of 18 or 20 years her periods usually take on a certain rhythm. Although there may be considerable variation among mature women in the frequency of menstrual periods, most cycles fall into the range of twenty-six to thirty-four days, but some women have even shorter or longer cycles. The duration of menstrual bleeding varies between three and seven days in most women.

The occurrence of irregular menstrual cycles in women after the age of 20 could be related to many factors, some of which are not well understood. Psychological states certainly play a role, particularly prolonged or severe emotional stress. Some young women cease menstruating or menstruate irregularly while at college but have regular cycles when they are home for summer and in a different emotional atmosphere. An unmarried woman who has had intercourse and fears pregnancy may have a late period due to her emotional state. In such cases it is also possible that the woman did become pregnant but spontaneously aborted the fetus at a very early stage of development without even being aware of it.

Preovulatory Phase

Menstruation can be seen as a four-stage process: the preovulatory phase, ovulation, the secretory phase, and menses. During the preovulatory phase the lining of the uterus (the **endometrium**) shed during the preceding menstruation is reconstructed. This stage usually lasts about fourteen days in a twenty-eight-day cycle (*see* Figure 4.3). During this time the pituitary gland secretes FSH, which

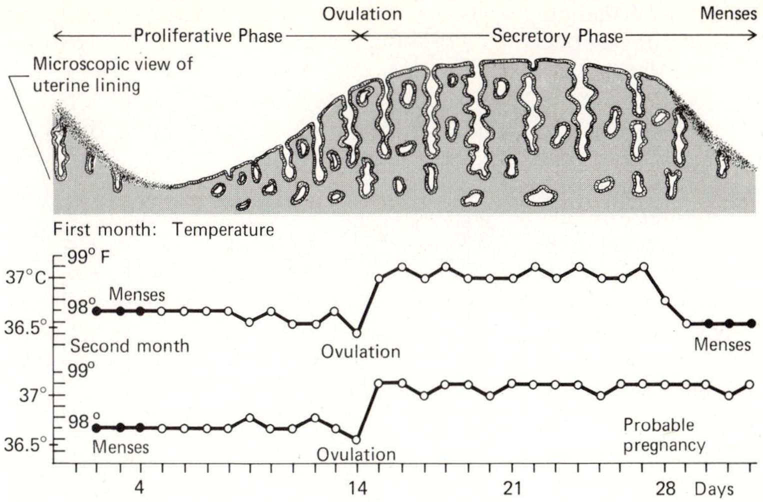

Proliferative Phase ——→|←— Ovulation —→|←——— Secretory Phase ———→|←— Menses —→

Microscopic view of
uterine lining

First month: Temperature

37°C
98° Menses
36.5°

Second month
37°
98° Menses
36.5°

Ovulation

Menses

Ovulation

Probable
pregnancy

4   14   21   28 Days

Figure 4.3 The phases of the
menstrual cycle.

From Benson, *Handbook of
Obstetrics and Gynecology,* 3d
ed. (Los Altos, Calif.: Lange
Medical Publications, 1968),
p. 26. Reprinted by permission.

brings about an increase in estrogen production by the ovaries. The estrogen is responsible for the regrowth of the endometrium, and the FSH stimulates one of the egg-carrying follicles to mature (*see* Figure 4.4). This follicle will eventually rupture during ovulation in response to the stimulus of increased production of LH by the pituitary gland.

With estrogen stimulation, the glandular surface of the endometrium grows to a thick-

ness of about 3.5 millimeters. Estrogen also brings about an increase in the size and productivity of the cervix. Cervical mucus produced under estrogen stimulation is plentiful, thin, and highly viscous (sticky). It has an alkaline pH and contains nutrients that can be used by the sperm. (One of the effects of birth-control pills is to change the makeup of the cervical mucus, creating a more hostile environment for the sperm.) As previously men-

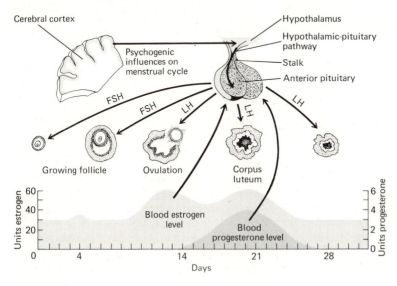

Figure 4.4 Ovulation during
the menstrual cycle.

From Benson, *Handbook of
Obstetrics and Gynecology,* 3d
ed. ·(Los Altos, Calif.: Lange
Medical Publications, 1968),
p. 26. Reprinted by permission.

tioned, rising estrogen levels also stimulate growth of the lining of the vagina so that maximum thickness is reached at ovulation.

Ovulation

During the preovulatory phase the amount of fluid inside the maturing follicle builds up until at ovulation the follicle ruptures and the egg is released into the fallopian tube. This process occurs about fourteen days before menstruation, but not always fourteen days after the start of the preovulatory phase. In a twenty-eight-day cycle ovulation would occur on the fourteenth day, but in a thirty-four-day cycle it would occur on the twentieth day (or fourteen days before menstruation). These schedules have obvious significance for women who want to get pregnant or for women who are using the "rhythm method" of birth control. The rhythm method depends on abstaining from intercourse during the presumed fertile days just before and after ovulation (*see* Chapter 6).

Postovulatory Phase

The period after ovulation is called the **secretory,** or postovulatory, **phase** of the menstrual cycle. During this phase the pituitary gland responds to the increased levels of estrogen in the bloodstream by producing more LH, which in turn stimulates the remaining cells of the recently ruptured ovarian follicle to develop into a small structure called the **corpus luteum.** Continued LH stimulation of the corpus luteum causes it to produce progesterone and a good deal of estrogen. (This new source of estrogen accounts for the second peak in estrogen level seen in Figure 4.4. Figure 4.5 shows FSH and LH levels.) Under the combined influence of estrogen and progesterone, the glands of the endometrium that have developed during the preovulatory phase become functional and begin to produce nutrient fluid by the eighteenth day of a twenty-eight-day cycle. This corresponds with the time the ovum is free within the uterine cavity and dependent on the secretions of the uterus for nourishment. There is also a buildup of blood vessels within the uterus at this time. The cervical fluid, which under es-

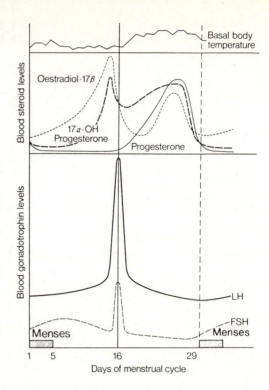

Figure 4.5 Hormone changes in the human menstrual cycle.

trogen stimulation was plentiful and hospitable to sperm during the preovulatory phase, becomes dryer and less hospitable to sperm under progesterone stimulation in the postovulatory phase.

Throughout these phases of the cycle, hormones stimulate the release of a number of fluids, many of which bear odors that can be detected by humans. Because vaginal odors in some animals communicate information about the estrous cycle (such as time of ovulation), it has been suggested that human vaginal odors may also contribute to communicating information about the estrous cycle and may even influence sexual behavior. A highly pleasant odor around the time of ovulation, for instance, might encourage sexual activity at a time when fertilization is most likely, but experimental procedures designed to test such suggestions have failed to find any evidence that humans can use vaginal odors to determine the time of ovulation.

If fertilization does not occur, the pituitary gland responds to increased blood levels of estrogen and progesterone and shuts off production of FSH and LH. Without these chemicals, the corpus luteum ceases production of estrogen and progesterone and then withers away.

Menstruation

The final stage of the menstrual cycle is menstruation, or *menses,* the shedding of the endometrium through the cervix and the vagina. The trigger for menstruation appears to be the drop in estrogen level.

The menstrual discharge consists primarily of blood, mucus, and fragments of endometrial tissue. About 60 milliliters (2 ounces) of blood are lost in an average menstrual period. This loss of blood should cause no problem for a woman on an adequate diet, but a heavy menstrual flow can lead to anemia in a woman on an iron-deficient diet. The duration of menstrual bleeding is usually from three to seven days, and periods longer than one week usually indicate some problem.

Traditionally, women have used externally worn sanitary napkins to absorb the menstrual discharge, but the trend now is toward internally worn tampons—cylinders of absorbent cotton that are inserted into the vagina and removed by an attached string. When tampons were first introduced in 1933, the public and some church leaders became very concerned about possible abuses of the tampon and claimed for some years that it was an instrument of contraception, masturbation, or defloration. It is now realized that these claims are all untrue, and tampons are becoming increasingly popular. Tampons can be used whether or not a woman has had intercourse, since most hymens will easily allow their insertion.

As the estrogen level continues to fall during the final stage of the cycle, the pituitary again responds and turns on its secretion of FSH, initiating the proliferative phase of the next cycle. However, the timing of the menstrual cycle is not determined by hormones alone. Women who room together in college and close friends tend to menstruate on a similar schedule in some cases. Although the rea-sons for this are not understood fully, it is possible that pheromones (scent signals) are involved. It has been shown that bodily odors produced by one woman during her cycle can influence the cycles of women around her, bringing their cycles closer together.

Symptoms and Syndromes

Considering the number of changes that a woman's body goes through each month, it is not surprising that problems sometimes accompany these changes. The most common symptom related to the menstrual cycle is painful menstruation (**dysmenorrhea**). Almost all women at one time or another experience discomfort in the pelvic area during a menstrual period, and for some women the pain can be frequent and severe. Some women have no symptoms, others continue their normal activities with little more than the help of aspirin, and still others may be forced to stay in bed for a day or two during each menstrual period. The basic complaint of women with this condition is cramps in the pelvic area, but there may also be headaches, backaches, nausea, and general discomfort. In women for whom dysmenorrhea is a monthly problem, it usually begins at an early age; it is relatively uncommon for a women to have her first painful menstrual period after the age of 20. Those women who do suffer from menstrual cramps often notice a great improvement after childbirth, but the reason for this "cure" is unknown.

The cause of menstrual cramps seems to be related to uterine spasms. It may be that these spasms are caused by chemicals in the menstrual fluid known as **prostaglandins** (*see* Chapter 6). Some women's health centers treat women with painful or difficult periods by removing these chemicals and other fluids through a method known as **menstrual extraction**. The menstrual tissue and fluid are removed shortly after the start of the menstrual flow by means of a flexible plastic tube and a suction device. There are some indications that this so-called five-minute period may be dangerous for women with a history of uterine infections, tumors, or a number of other conditions. Masters and

Johnson reported that some women also use orgasm as a means of helping relieve dysmenorrhea. The contractions of orgasm increase the rate of menstrual flow, and some women have reported that orgasm experienced shortly after the onset of menstruation not only increases the rate of flow but reduces pelvic cramping when present and frequently relieves menstrually associated backaches.

In addition to pelvic pains, some women experience other problems with their periods. **Menstrual migraines** are migraine headaches that occur just before or during menstruation. **Mastalgia** is a painful swelling of the breasts that is related to cyclic hormone changes and to the buildup of fluid in the body. **Mittelschmerz** is an unexplained phenomenon that occurs during ovulation and is most common in young women. It consists of intermittent cramping pains on one or both sides of the lower abdomen lasting for about a day. The reasons for these symptoms related to menstruation are not fully explained, but there is evidence that psychological factors may be involved. Cultures that treat women as if they were sick or undesirable during menstruation tend to condition women to find menstruation painful, depressing, and so on.

During the four to seven days preceding menstruation most women experience symptoms that make them aware of their coming period. When these symptoms are particularly severe they are known as **premenstrual tension**. Fatigue, irritability, headache, pain in the lower back, sensations of heaviness in the pelvic region, and a weight gain of as much as several pounds (due to retention of fluids) are among the symptoms. For some women these problems can contribute to emotional and psychological upset at this time.

Related Considerations

There is no medical reason why a woman should refrain from intercourse while she is menstruating. Nevertheless, many societies strictly prohibit this practice and consider women "unclean" during menstruation. The Old Testament, the Koran, and Hindu law books all specifically prohibit such intercourse on the grounds that women are polluted and dangerous at this time and will defile anyone who has contact with the menstrual discharge. Certain societies impose other restrictions on women during their periods. They may have to follow diets and may be forbidden to participate in certain activities. There may also be special rules about bathing at this time, as in orthodox Judaism.

Several South American and African tribes believe that a man would become physically ill if he had sexual relations with a menstruating partner. Some nomads of northeast Asia believe that a woman would become sick and eventually sterile if she copulated while bleeding. Other tribes believe that a menstruating woman who had any physical contact with a man could cause him to lose his virility and his hunting ability. In such societies women are physically isolated from their communities during menstruation.

Today, modern societies understand menstruation for what it is (the sloughing off of part of the uterine wall) and realize that it does not have any mystical, magical, or negative implications.

Menopause

The end of a woman's reproductive period comes at **menopause**—the cessation of menstruation due to physiological changes associated with aging. Menopause usually occurs between the ages of 46 and 50, but just prior to and following menopause various changes take place in connection with the altered functioning of the ovaries. This period, from about the age of 45 to 60 years, is known as the **climacteric** ("critical period") or the "change of life." The mechanism of menopause, unlike that of puberty, is not related to the pituitary gland. It continues to produce FSH, but the ovaries gradually fail to respond and very little estrogen is produced.

Menstrual periods usually become very irregular several years before menopause, and this period of time is one of relative infertility (as is the time just after menarche). Pregnancy beyond the age of 47 years is rare, but it has been medically documented as late as age 61. It has been suggested that long-term use of birth-control pills may prolong a woman's reproductive period and delay menopause, but as yet there is no evidence to support this idea. There is, however, evidence that menopause comes at an earlier age in women who smoke than in nonsmokers. In a study of 3500 women in seven countries researchers found that at ages 48 to 49, a woman who smokes a pack a day or more is nearly twice as likely to be past menopause as is a woman who has never smoked. The researchers suggest that nicotine may have an effect on the secretion of the hormones involved in menopause or on the way the body handles sex hormones.

The symptoms of the climacteric are well known, and they affect almost all women to some degree, but as with dysmenorrhea it is not clear how much of the symptoms of the climacteric are biologically or culturally induced. Some cultures view menopause as a disability, and such strong cultural biases can affect a person's behavior. Only about 10 percent of women are obviously inconvenienced by the changes of the climacteric, and the only consistent symptom is the **hot flash,** or **flush,** a feeling of waves of heat spreading over the face and the upper half of the body. This feeling may be followed by perspiration or chills and may last for only a few seconds or much longer. Other symptoms (which may be due to psychological factors rather than to hormonal or biological changes) include headaches, dizziness, heart palpitations, and pains in the joints. Doctors have prescribed estrogens to relieve these symptoms, but in 1976 the U.S. Food and Drug Administration warned that women who take female hormones to relieve menopause symptoms run a "marked increase" in the risk of cancer of the womb. The agency cautioned that women should be given the lowest possible doses for the shortest possible time. However, the fact that estrogen treatment does not always relieve the symptoms only strengthens the idea that the symptoms are due more to psychological than biological causes.

Along with the changes already mentioned, there are certain changes in the genitals during the years after menopause. These changes include gradual shrinking of the uterus and of the lining of the vagina. It has also been found that some women experience a new awakening of sexual desire after menopause, perhaps because they no longer need to worry about pregnancy.

MALE REPRODUCTIVE ENDOCRINOLOGY

Puberty

Puberty begins somewhat later (and lasts longer) in boys than it does in girls—as is quite obvious if you look at a class of sixth graders. The girls tend to be taller and look more mature than boys of the same age. Puberty begins at about age 10 or 11 in boys and is triggered by the same pituitary hormones that trigger puberty in girls, FSH and LH. (As mentioned earlier, LH is called ICSH in males because of the site of its action—the interstitial cells.)

ICSH reaches the interstitial cells of the testes through the bloodstream and stimulates them to start the process of puberty. Few changes are seen at first, but the interstitial cells gradually begin producing testosterone, the primary male sex hormone, or androgen. Testosterone is responsible for all the physical changes, including development of the **secondary sex characteristics,** that occur during puberty (*see* Figure 4.4).

External Changes

Enlargement of the testes and penis and the appearance of fine, straight hair at the base of the penis are the first changes brought about by testosterone. At first the penis increases in circumference more than in length, and by age 12 it is still, on the average, about 1.5 inches (3.8 centimeters) long in the relaxed state and less than 3 inches (7.6 centimeters) long when erect.

As the testes enlarge, their ability to produce testosterone increases, and at age 13 or 14 rapid growth of the penis, testes, and pubic hair begins. By this age most girls will have had their first menstrual period but probably will not be ovulating yet.

Underarm, or axillary, hair does not appear until about age 15 in most boys, and at the same time some fuzz appears on the upper lip. Adult beards do not appear for two or three more years, and by age 17 about 50 percent of the boys in the United States have not yet shaved and many others shave only infrequently. Development of facial and chest hair continues with androgen stimulation beyond the age of 20 in many young men, while the hair on the scalp begins to recede (*see* Figure 4.6).

Another very noticeable change that occurs during puberty is the deepening of the voice. This happens as hormones stimulate growth of the larnyx (voice box). The deepening of the voice may be gradual or fairly abrupt, but it usually occurs by the age of 14 or 15.

Two sources of possible embarrassment are also brought on by puberty at age 15 or 16 — acne and **gynecomastia,** a temporary enlargement of the breasts. This breast enlargement is seen in about 80 percent of pubertal boys and is probably related to small amounts of female hormones produced by the testes.

Other external changes include overall changes in both height and weight during puberty. While women develop fat deposits in their breasts and hips at this time, young men gain weight in the form of increased muscle mass, resulting in a quite different physique from that of women. (The use of extra androgens to increase muscle mass in Olympic athletes and professional football players has become a common but controversial treatment in recent years.) Also adding to the differences between male and female bodies is the expansion that occurs in the rib cages and shoulders of males at this time, while the female pelvis is undergoing enlargement. Finally, there is a definite increase in height at puberty. This process continues until age 20 or 21, when the male hormones put a stop to further growth of the long bones of the skeleton. As mentioned earlier, female hormones put a stop to growth more rapidly, which partially accounts for the generally smaller height of women, but this does not mean that tall girls have a deficiency of female sex hormones or that tall boys have a deficiency of male sex hormones. Other factors, including heredity and nutrition, influence height, and until recently, Americans of both sexes have been growing progressively taller with each successive generation.

Some, but not all, of the physical differ-

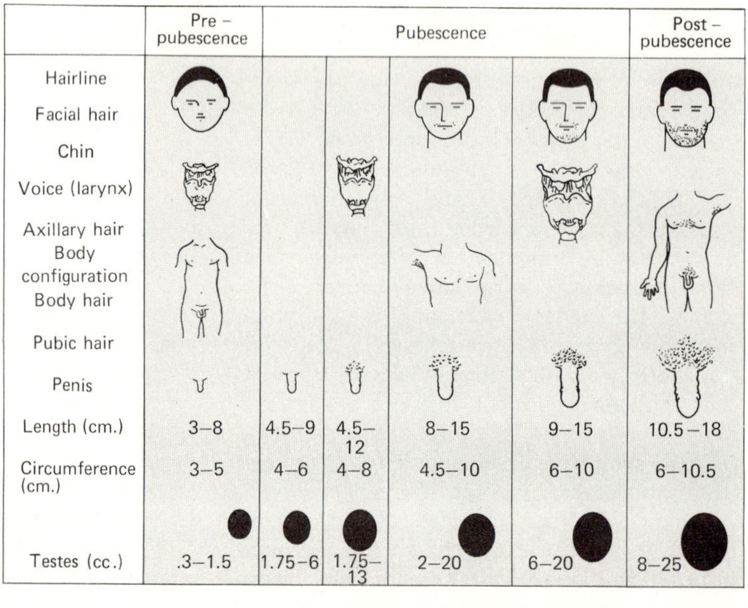

Figure 4.6 Development of some secondary sex characteristics in men.

From Wilkins, L., Blizzard, R., and Migeon, C., *The Diagnosis and Treatment of Endocrine Disorders in Childhood and Adolescence,* 3d ed. (Springfield, Ill.: Charles C Thomas, 1965), p. 200. Reprinted by permission.

	Pre-pubescence	Pubescence			Post-pubescence
Hairline, Facial hair, Chin, Voice (larynx), Axillary hair, Body configuration, Body hair, Pubic hair, Penis					
Length (cm.)	3–8	4.5–9	4.5–12	8–15	9–15	10.5–18
Circumference (cm.)	3–5	4–6	4–8	4.5–10	6–10	6–10.5
Testes (cc.)	.3–1.5	1.75–6	1.75–13	2–20	6–20	8–25

ences between the sexes are the result of hormonal influences. The difference in strength displayed by preadolescent youngsters, for instance, is also influenced by cultural expectations and socialization patterns that encourage activity in young males and passivity in young females. In fact, 12-year-old girls could be stronger than boys of the same age because they are generally taller and heavier at that time. However, after the hormonal influences of puberty begin, males put on muscle mass at a rate approximately two times that of females. So if a male and female do exactly the same exercise for the same amount of time, the male will gain approximately two times the muscle mass that the female gains. Nevertheless, muscle mass is not everything. In endurance sports, like long-distance swimming, women hold many of the records. It may be that the true physiological differences between the sexes cannot yet be determined. It is only recently in our society that women have begun to take part in sports and athletic training to the same degree that men have—with the result that women are proving to be much more like men in more physical abilities than was previously believed. Recent studies even suggest that women may have the same potential for strength development as men do.

Internal Changes

A mustache, broad shoulders, and a deep voice may give the appearance of physical maturity to a growing boy, but some important internal changes must take place before reproductive maturity is actually reached.

FSH, which stimulates the ova to mature in the female, is also necessary for the production of mature sperm in the male. With the increase in production of FSH by the pituitary during puberty, germ cells in the lining of the seminiferous tubules of the testes (see Chapter 2) begin to develop into mature sperm. Mature sperm are first seen in the ejaculatory fluid at age 15, on the average, but may be found as early as age 11 or as late as age 17.

FSH is necessary but not sufficient for the production of mature sperm. Other hormones,

particularly thyroid hormone, must also be present. In addition, mature sperm can only be produced in an environment with a temperature lower than normal body temperature. In undescended testes, which are still in the abdominal cavity, mature sperm cannot be produced because of the warmth of their environment.

The prostate gland is particularly sensitive to the stimulation of testosterone. It and other organs that supply fluid for the semen enlarge during puberty, and by the age of 13 or 14 years, the prostate is producing fluid that can be ejaculated during orgasm. At about this same age a boy will begin to have "wet dreams", or **nocturnal emissions** of seminal fluid (see Chapter 8), but this fluid probably will not contain mature sperm at so early an age. Just as menarche does not mean that a girl has ovulated, the ability to ejaculate does not mean that a boy is fertile.

All of these changes will, of course, have some psychological effects on young men. Like young women, young men are sensitive to the changes taking place in themselves and in their friends of the same age during puberty, but unlike the case with females, early-maturing males appear to have a social advantage over late-maturing males. Early-maturing males usually have greater prestige among their friends and are most often ranked as leaders among males of pubertal age. It has been found, however, that in adulthood the late maturers are often more adventurous, flexible, and assertive than are early maturers.

Aging in the Male

There is no precise male equivalent of the menopause, though there may be gradual declines in the rates of testosterone secretion and sperm production. The ovaries cease to function at a fairly specific time in a woman's life, but the testes continue to function indefinitely. There are well-documented reports of men of 90 years of age having fathered children, and living sperm have been found in the ejaculations of men even older.

Although the effects of age on hormone

production are not as dramatic in men as they are in women, there are certain changes that occur in men in their 40s and 50s and later that are believed to be related to changes in hormone levels. The most common is enlargement of the prostate gland, which occurs in 10 percent of men by age 40 and in 50 percent of men by age 80. This enlargement interferes with control of urination and causes frequent nightly urination, but it can usually be corrected (*see* Chapter 2).

Depression, irritability, and other symptoms similar to those of menopause may occur with increasing frequency in men, but such symptoms are not known to be related to any specific hormonal changes. And, as explained in Chapter 3, there is no change related to hormone levels that need interfere with sexual activities in men or women as they grow older. Both men and women can continue to have fulfilling sex lives well into old age.

HORMONES AND SEXUAL BEHAVIOR

Female mammals come into "heat"—that is, they become receptive to the sexual advances of males at specific points in their estrus cycles. These points coincide with maximum levels of female hormones and with ovulation, so mating at this time enhances the probability of fertilization and successful reproduction. In fact, there is usually no sexual activity in lower mammals except when females are fertile and likely to conceive.

The human female is quite different in this respect. Women are fertile for only a few days during their cycle, but human sexual activity is not limited to specific periods of the estrus cycle, nor is it regulated by hormone levels. The same is true of men. Their sexual activity is not directly controlled by hormone levels, and because men have no estrus cycle they are fertile at all times (unless there is a medical or health problem). Sperm are normally produced throughout the reproductive years, and the secretion of testosterone is fairly constant, in contrast to the cyclic secretion of sex hormones in the female.

Although testosterone secretion and spermatogenesis are relatively constant, variations do occur in certain situations. Severe emotional shock, for instance, has been known to cause temporary cessation of sperm production in some men. Studies of soldiers in combat show that testosterone levels rise and fall in response to the degree of stress to which they are exposed. Studies have also shown that intercourse is followed by an increase in testosterone in males.

Other factors can also affect fertility in men, either temporarily or permanently. Certain drugs can cause temporary sterility. A prolonged exposure to high temperature (an illness involving high fever, frequent and prolonged hot baths) may inhibit sperm production. Mumps, as mentioned in Chapter 2, can cause permanent sterility. And prolonged or severe exposure to radiation can cause sterility or the production of abnormal sperm.

Except for these special instances, men are always fertile and women are always able to have sex, regardless of the fluctuations of hormones. There is evidence, however, that fluctuations in hormones can influence (in subtle ways) just how receptive a man or a woman will be to sexual activity. Studies have shown that there are certain times during the menstrual cycle at which women are more likely to have intercourse and to have orgasm. The peak times for both are at midcycle (ovulation) and just before menstruation. Other studies have shown a similar pattern among women in their self-ratings of sexual arousal.

It may be that androgens (male sex hormones) secreted by the adrenal glands of women play a role in the female sex drive. Surgical removal of the adrenal glands, for example, is more likely to reduce a woman's sex drive than is removal of the ovaries. Women who are given androgens for medical reasons sometimes report dramatic increases in sexual desire. There are several possible reasons for this: Androgens make women more sensitive to both mental and physical stimulation, androgens produce increased sensitivity of the genitals, or androgens induce greater intensity of sexual gratification (orgasm). Or it may be that androgens simply affect metabolism (rather than sex drive), making a woman more responsive in general, and this could carry over to her sex life.

The effect of the primary androgens, like testosterone, can perhaps be seen in the sexual behavior of married couples. One recent study has found that testosterone levels vary greatly among women, with some producing ten times as much as others—but all within the normal range and all showing peak testosterone production at ovulation. The women who produced the highest levels of testosterone were the ones who reported the greatest sexual satisfaction. And it was also found that in some married couples the husband's testosterone level peaks on a regular schedule with the wife's testosterone level at ovulation—when the greatest sexual frequency also occurs. A second peak of both male and female testosterone levels occurred on the seventh day following ovulation, approximately. So it may be that testosterone is related to sexual drive, frequency, and responsivity in both men and women. This and the fact that some husbands and wives have testosterone peaks at the same time suggest that there may be some form of chemical or biological communication (possibly pheromones) that encourages sexual activity at a time when a woman is fertile. This does not mean that biological or chemical processes are more important than social or psychological processes in influencing human sexual behavior; when our testosterone levels are at their peak, we may be for a variety of reasons completely uninterested in sexual matters.

HORMONAL ABNORMALITIES

The delicate balance of hormone levels, as we have seen, influences our physical development and reproductive functioning in many ways, and as would be expected, an imbalance of hormones can also have dramatic effects. Examples of this are seen in the effects of castration and in the conditions known as hermaphroditism and pseudohermaphroditism.

Just as removal of the testicles of a rooster prevents development of the cock's comb, removal of the testicles of a young boy prevents development of the secondary sex characteristics of that boy. **Castration,** the removal of the male sex glands, has been practiced in many cultures. It was most common in the Near East and probably was performed first in ancient Egypt, where hundreds of young boys would be castrated in a single religious ceremony and their genitals offered to the gods.

Males were not castrated only for religious reasons. Many were castrated for musical reasons. If a young boy's testicles are removed before puberty, he will no longer produce the testosterone necessary to bring about growth of the voice box. Consequently he will keep his high-pitched singing voice, which some claim has purer tonal qualities than that of the mature female voice.

Males have also been castrated in order to keep them from being sexually active, though this tactic probably was not always successful. **Eunuchs** (from the Greek for "guardian of the bed") were castrated men who were supposedly incapable of having sex and could therefore be trusted as guards of a harem, but the sex drive probably varied greatly among these men. Even prepubescent males with their low levels of androgens are capable of erection and orgasm. So if castration was performed after puberty, the penis was of adult size and possibly capable of erection; and although deprived of androgen from the testes, the castrated male still produced some androgen in his adrenal glands and might very well have been capable of having sex. It is now known that the effects of male hormones on sexual behavior are very complex. Removal of the testes does not automatically eliminate sexual activity, and administration of androgens to men who have lost their testicles does not automatically restore sexual potency if it has been lost.

Another type of hormonal abnormality is seen in **hermaphrodites,** individuals who exhibit external genital characteristics of both sexes. In medical terminology a true hermaphrodite is someone who has both ovarian and testicular tissue (and therefore both male and female hormones). The condition is extremely rare, however, and only sixty cases have been reported in the entire world medical literature in the twentieth century. A hermaphrodite may have one ovary and one testicle or sex glands that contain mixtures of ovarian and testicular tissues. This combination of tissues and hormones is usually accompanied by a mixture of masculine and feminine characteristics, but hermaphrodites usually have masculine genitals and feminine breasts. There often is some sort of vaginal opening beneath the penis, and many hermaphrodites menstruate. Development of the uterus is often incomplete with, for instance, only one fallopian tube present.

The development of both male and female sex organs is caused by the presence, in significant amounts, of male and female hormones during embryological development (*see* Chapter 2) and at puberty. Since male hormones can be produced by the adrenal glands,

a defect in the adrenal glands can result in the production of large amounts of androgens. If this happens in a female the result can be **pseudohermaphroditism.** Such a woman may have normal internal female organs, including ovaries, but her clitoris will usually be enlarged and resemble a penis. In addition, the folds of the labia may be fused in such a manner as to resemble a scrotum—with the result that such a female may be reared as a male. In the male, this condition may lead to premature development of adult male characteristics.

Pseudohermaphroditism can be corrected by a combination of hormonal and surgical techniques, but it is important that the correct diagnosis be made early in life. Psychological problems are quite common in individuals who have lived for several years or more with ambiguous sexual identity, or who have lived with a mistaken identity for a number of years before the condition is recognized.

SUMMARY

1. Humans do not have an inborn sex drive in the sense that animals do, but certain chemicals (sex hormones) play important roles in human reproduction processes and in sexual development, and they can influence our sexual behavior. Sex hormones are secreted directly into the bloodstream by the ductless endocrine glands. The pituitary is the master endocrine gland. Its secretions stimulate the sex glands to produce sex hormones—estrogen and progesterone in the female and testosterone in the male.

2. Two pituitary hormones, the gonadotrophins, stimulate the sex glands to produce hormones. One is the follicle-stimulating hormone (FSH). The other is the luteinizing hormone (LH), which is called interstititial-cell stimulating hormone (ICSH) in males because of the site of its activity. Release of the gonadotrophins by the pituitary is controlled in two ways. One is a simple feedback mechanism that works like a thermostat—when the level of sex hormones in the bloodstream decreases to a certain level, gonadotrophins are released that stimulate production of more sex hormones; when the level of sex hormones increases past a certain level, gonadotrophin production is shut off. Pituitary secretions are also controlled by messages from another part of the brain—the hypothalamus. It secretes chemical factors called the follicle-stimulating, hormone-releasing factor (FSH-RF) and the luteinizing hormone-releasing factor (LH-RF).

3.   The physical changes that define puberty are the most obvious effects of sex hormones. In girls, puberty begins between the ages of 9 and 12, with the first menstrual period usually occurring between the ages of 11 and 14. At the time of puberty in females, FSH stimulates the ovaries to produce female sex hormones (estrogens), which in turn stimulate the growth of breast tissue and the rounding out of the hips and buttocks. Estrogen and hormones from the adrenal glands stimulate the growth of pubic and axillary hair. Other external changes include speeded-up growth of the genitals and an increase in skeletal size.

4.   Internal changes in the female during puberty include growth of the uterus and vagina as well as of their linings. Estrogen also stimulates enlargement of the pelvis and puts a stop to skeletal growth by about the age of 17. Estrogen production not only increases at puberty, but it takes on the cyclic pattern responsible for the monthly menstrual cycle of women.

5.   Menstruation is the periodic bleeding from the uterus that accompanies the estrus cycle. The average menstrual cycle lasts twenty-eight days, but it may be as short as twenty-six days in some women or as long as thirty-four days. Hormones control menstruation, but psychological factors (such as stress) can also affect it.

6.   Menstruation is a four-stage process. During the preovulatory phase, which lasts about fourteen days in a twenty-eight-day cycle, the lining of the uterus grows thicker under estrogen stimulation. The FSH that stimulates production of estrogen also stimulates one of the follicles to mature. At ovulation this follicle will rupture and release an egg in response to the stimulus of increased LH production. Ovulation usually occurs about fourteen days before menstrual bleeding begins. During the postovulatory, or secretory, phase, LH stimulates the ruptured follicle to develop into a structure called the corpus luteum, which produces progesterone and some estrogen. These hormones influence the endometrium (lining of the uterus) to become functional by about the eighteenth day of the cycle, at which time the egg will be free in the uterus and dependent on secretions of the endometrium. If fertilization does not occur, the pituitary responds to the buildup of estrogen by shutting off production of FSH and LH. This shuts off production of the female sex hormones and leads to the shedding of the tissues, mucus, and blood of the endometrium through the cervix and vagina. Menses (monthly bleeding) usually lasts from three to seven days, and as the estrogen level continues to drop, the pituitary again responds by producing FSH — starting a new cycle.

7.   Menstruation is sometimes accompanied by discomfort, and for some women the pain can be severe. The basic complaint is cramps in the pelvic area (related to spasms of the uterus), but there also may be headaches, backaches, nausea, and general discomfort. Women who suffer painful menstruation often notice a great improvement after childbirth. During the four to seven days preceding menstruation, some women expe-

rience premenstrual tension—fatigue, irritability, headaches, pain in the lower back, sensations of heaviness in the pelvic region, and weight gain due to retention of fluids.

8. Menopause, the end of a woman's reproductive period, usually occurs between the ages of 46 and 50. The period just prior to and following menopause is called the climacteric or change of life. It is during this time that certain hormonal changes take place as the ovaries gradually fail to respond to FSH and cease production of estrogen. Menstrual periods usually become irregular several years before menopause, and during the change of life some women suffer discomfort, including hot flashes, headaches, dizziness, heart palpitations, and pains in the joints. Shrinkage of the uterus and of the lining of the vagina also occur during this time.

9. Puberty begins later in boys than in girls and lasts longer. It begins at about the age of 10 or 11 when FSH and ICSH from the pituitary stimulate the production of testosterone in the testes. Testosterone is responsible for the secondary sex changes seen in males during puberty. These changes include enlargement of the penis and testes, the appearance of pubic, axillary, and facial and chest hair, deepening of the voice, expansion of the chest and rib cage, and changes in body weight and height. The weight changes are due to increased muscle mass. Height may continue to increase until the age of 20 or 21.

10. Reproductive maturity in the male also occurs during puberty when FSH and other hormones stimulate the development of mature sperm. The prostate and other glands that contribute fluid to the semen enlarge by puberty, and by 13 or 14 years of age a boy will usually be able to ejaculate—though he may not produce mature sperm for several more years.

11. There is no male equivalent of menopause, though there may be gradual declines in sperm production and testosterone secretion with age. Enlargement of the prostate often occurs with age, and men may show signs of depression, irritability, and other symptoms similar to those of menopause. These symptoms probably are not related to hormonal changes.

12. In addition to the physical changes brought about by hormones, there may be some human behaviors that are influenced by hormones, especially by testosterone. Men and women can have sex at any time during the estrus cycle, but studies suggest that women are more likely to have sex and to have orgasm when their testosterone levels are highest (especially at ovulation when a woman is fertile). Studies have also found that married men tend to have peaks in testosterone levels at the same time their wives do, suggesting some sort of biological or chemical communication between the sexes (possibly pheromones) that encourages sexual activity during a woman's fertile period.

13. 91

Sex
Hormones
and the
Reproductive
Period

The effects of castration and condi-
tions known as hermaphroditism and pseudohermaphroditism are examples of
severe malfunctions in hormone production. Castration, removal of the testicles,
will prevent development of secondary sex characteristics (enlargement of penis,
testes, shoulders, voice box, and so on) if performed before puberty. Hermaphroditism is an extremely rare condition in which an individual has both male and
female sex glands (and, therefore, male and female hormones). One cause of
pseudohermaphroditism is malfunction of the adrenal glands and resulting over-
production of testosterone—leading to development of male characteristics in
the female and premature puberty in the male.

SUGGESTED READING

Tepperman, J. *Metabolic and Endocrine Physiology,* 3rd ed. Chicago: Year Book
Medical Publishers, 1973.
An excellent, relatively concise text on all human hormones, including sex hor-
mones.

Reichlin, S., Elden, R., Baldessarini, J., and Martin, J. B. (Eds.). *The Hypothalamus,* New York: Association for Research in Nervous and Mental Disease,
Research Publication Volume 56, 1978.
The latest research on the interaction between the brain, particularly the hypothalamus, and hormone functioning.

Sandler, M., and Gessa, G. L. (Eds.). *Sexual Behavior: Pharmacology and Bio-
chemistry.* New York: Raven Press, 1975.
A collection of a variety of research reports on sex hormones, drugs, and behavior, both animal and human studies.

Katchadourian, H., *The Biology of Adolescence.* San Francisco: Freeman, 1977.
A concise, up-to-date coverage of the role of sex hormones in the regulation of
puberty, as well as other hormonal influences in adolescents.

Chapter 5 Conception, Pregnancy, and Birth

Did You Know That . . .

human sperm were not actually discovered until 300 years ago, and human eggs only 150 years ago?

enough sperm to populate the world would fit into a space the size of an aspirin?

heavy alcohol consumption during pregnancy contributes to birth defects?

menstruation may not resume for several months after childbirth in nursing women, but ovulation may occur and a woman can become pregnant during this time?

except in certain cases where there may be medical problems, there is no reason why sexual activity, including intercourse, must be avoided during pregnancy?

a woman's ovaries may contain as many as 400,000 immature ova at birth, but only about 400 eggs are actually released from the ovaries during her reproductive lifetime?

a six-week-old human embryo has a prominent "tail"?

INTRODUCTION

For centuries the "miracle of birth" must have seemed just that—a miracle. No one could fully explain how it happened, and in some societies people did not even make the connection between sexual intercourse and pregnancy. Two South Pacific tribes, the Arunta and the Trobrianders, believed that intercourse was purely a source of pleasure unrelated to pregnancy. Natives of these tribes believed that conception occurred when a spirit embryo entered the body of a woman. The spirit was believed to enter the uterus either through the vagina or through the head. In the latter instance, it was thought to travel through the bloodstream to the uterus.

Other people, though recognizing that intercourse is essential to conception, believed that supernatural powers determined whether or not specific acts of intercourse would cause pregnancy. The Jivaro tribesmen in the Amazon region believed that women were particularly fertile during the phase of the new moon. Perhaps this belief reflects association of the lunar cycle with the menstrual cycle, both of which are about the same length.

A few tribes, like the Kiwai of New Guinea and the Baiga of India, believed that a woman could become pregnant from something that she had eaten, implying that a substance taken in through the mouth may have been contaminated with semen, which then found its way to the uterus.

Today we know that it is the union of sperm and egg that results in conception, pregnancy, and the birth of a child. Even though there are still aspects of these processes that have yet to be fully explained, the miracle of birth is no longer quite as mysterious as it once must have seemed.

CONCEPTION

The moment when sperm and egg unite is the moment of conception. In order to understand exactly what this means, it is necessary to have some basic knowledge of the cells involved—sperm and ova.

Sperm

The persistence of myths and misconceptions about conception is understandable when we realize that sperm were not discovered until three hundred years ago, and even then there was little agreement on what sperm were. The discovery was made in the laboratory of Anton van Leeuwenhoek (1632–1723), a Dutchman who did some of the first scientific investigations of life forms with a microscope. He noted that sperm resembled other microscopic organisms he had seen swimming about in pond water, and he named them **spermatozoa** ("seed animals"). Van Leeuwenhoek was convinced that sperm were involved in human reproduction, but others at the time thought that sperm were only miscellaneous organisms contaminating the seminal fluid. It was not until the twentieth century that it was finally proved that the sperm cell actually fuses with the egg at the time of conception.

From the union of male and female germ cells one new cell is formed. It divides into two cells, then into four cells, then into eight cells, and so on. If all goes according to plan, the result after approximately nine months is a fully formed human infant. The process of cell division is called **mitosis.** The information that guides cells in their division and multiplication is contained in the **chromosomes,** threadlike bits of material in the nucleus of each cell.

Human body cells contain forty-six chromosomes, twenty-two pairs and two "sex chromosomes" that determine the sex of an individual (*see* Figure 5.1). Females have two X chromosomes, and males have one X and a smaller Y chromosome. Human germ cells (sperm and egg) are different from other cells. Instead of containing the usual forty-six

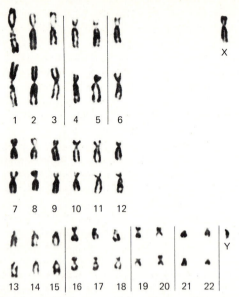

Figure 5.1 The human chromosomes (autosomes 1–22, sex chromosomes X and Y) from a male cell in culture. The forty-six chromosomes are from a photomicrographic print (cut single) arranged in pairs, and grouped according to sizes and relative lengths of the arms.

From Tjio and Puck, *P.N.A.S.* 44 (1958), 1232.

chromosomes, they contain only twenty-three. Thus, when sperm meets egg and their chromosomes combine, the result is one cell with the usual forty-six chromosomes. Germ cells have only half the normal number of chromosomes because they go through a special type of reduction division called **meiosis** (from the Greek word for "less").

Sperm Production

Sperm are produced in the seminiferous tubules of the testes, and they go through several stages of development beginning with cells called **spermatogonia** that lie along the internal linings of the tubules. The spermatogonia divide into **spermatocytes,** which in turn undergo reduction division, so that the resulting **spermatids** have only twenty-three chromosomes. Because this process begins with normal male cells (having both an X and a Y chromosome), half of the spermatids will

have an X and half will have a Y chromosome after meiosis. In females there are two X chromosomes in each cell. So, when meiosis occurs during the maturation of eggs, each egg ends up with one X chromosome.

It is the spermatid that eventually becomes a mature sperm. Its head is pear-shaped, and it has a cone-shaped **middlepiece** and a tail that enables it to swim (*see* Figure 5.2). The head of the sperm is about 5 microns long, the middlepiece another 5 microns, and the tail 30 to 50 microns (1 micron equals 0.000039 inches or 0.001 millimeters). Enough sperm to repopulate the world would fit into a space the size of an aspirin tablet.

As these tiny sperm cells are produced they move up the seminiferous tubules to the epididymis (*see* Figure 2.7) and are stored there until they are ejaculated. If ejaculation does not occur within thirty to sixty days, the sperm degenerate and are replaced by the new ones that are being produced all the time.

The Journey of the Sperm

Billions of sperm are ejaculated by most men during their lifetimes, but few sperm ever unite with an egg. Most sperm die. This is due to the use of contraceptives as well as to the fact that intercourse frequently occurs when the woman is not fertile. However, even if coitus has occurred during a fertile period, there are still many obstacles on the sperm's journey to meet the egg.

If ejaculation has occurred during intercourse, the sperm will be deposited in the woman's vagina and will begin to make their way to the uterus. One of the first obstacles they face is the force of gravity. If intercourse has taken place while the woman was lying on her back, and if she has remained in that position for sometime afterward, there is a greater chance that some of the sperm will travel toward the cervix and on into the uterus. But if the woman has been in an upright position during intercourse or if she has arisen immediately afterward, the force of gravity will cause the sperm to flow away from the uterus. Even when the woman lies on her back, sperm may be lost through the

ficial insemination may be used to impregnate the woman. In this process the male ejaculates into a container to which a chemical preservative (glycerine) has been added. This fluid is then injected into the vagina or directly into the uterus. Sperm can also be quick frozen in a glycerine solution and stored for later use.

If the sperm does reach the area of the cervix and is allowed to remain there, it still has another problem to face—acidity. As mentioned in Chapter 4, the pH of cervical secretions varies, and sperm are extremely sensitive to acidity. If the secretions of the cervix and vagina are strongly acidic, the sperm are destroyed quickly. (This is why for contraceptive purposes a vinegar or acetic acid douche is sometimes used to wash out the vagina after intercourse—*see* Chapter 6). Even in a mildly acidic environment (a pH of 6.0, for instance) the movement of sperm ceases. The best pH for sperm survival and movement is between 8.5 and 9.0 (alkaline). In such an environment the natural tendency of sperm is to swim toward the cervix against the flow of the fluid coming from the cervix.

Sperm swim at a rate of 1 to 2 centimeters an hour (about 1 inch), but once they are through the cervix and inside the uterus they may be aided in their journey by muscular contractions of the wall of the uterus. Women's orgasms are known to contribute to these contractions, so it may be that if a woman has an orgasm at or near the time of her partner's orgasm there is a greater chance that the sperm will reach the fallopian tubes.

Once through the uterus and into the fallopian tube, the sperm complete the final 2 inches or so of their journey by swimming against the current generated by small, waving, hairlike structures (cilia) that line the tube. Even if the woman has ovulated, only about half of the sperm that make it through the uterus end up in the fallopian tube that contains the egg (except on rare occasions when a woman ovulates from both ovaries at the same time.)

If one considers all the obstacles that sperm face on their journey it is not surpris-

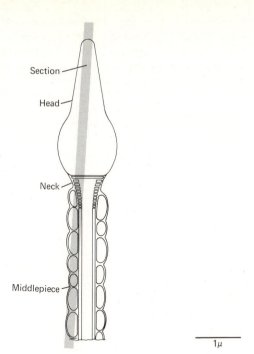

Figure 5.2 A human sperm. Electronmicrograph of a somewhat tangential "longitudinal" section through head and middlepiece. Diagram shows approximate plane of section.

Diagram from Lord Rothschild, *British Medical Journal,* 1 (1958), p. 301.

vaginal opening, especially if this opening has been widened during childbirth. However, as explained in Chapter 3, the engorgement of the blood vessels around the vaginal opening during sexual arousal creates a temporary orgasmic platform that helps keep seminal fluid in the vagina.

The position and structure of the penis may also affect the journey of the sperm. Continued in-and-out thrusting of the penis after ejaculation, for instance, tends to disperse the sperm and hinder them on their journey. The semen also may fail to reach the cervix because of incomplete penetration of the vagina by the penis. This may be unavoidable in the case of extreme obesity or because of a condition known as **hypospadias,** in which the opening of the urethra is located under rather than at the tip of the glans. In such cases arti-

ing that of the several hundred million sperm in the original ejaculation only about two thousand reach the tube that has the egg. And then only one actually unites with the egg.

Ova (Eggs)

The discovery of the human **ovum,** or egg, did not come until 150 years after the discovery of sperm. In 1827 Karl Ernst von Baer (1792–1876), the founder of modern embryology, published a book in which he described his research with pregnant dogs and his discovery of minute specks of matter in the fallopian tubes. The small objects proved to be eggs, the actual germ material essential for reproduction. Later studies of humans confirmed these findings, and the human egg has since been studied in detail.

The egg is much larger than the sperm and much larger than the other cells of the body, but it still is quite small—scarcely visible to the naked eye. The egg is a spherical cell about 130 or 140 microns wide (about 1/175 inch, or approximately the size of the period at the end of this sentence) and weighs about 0.0015 milligram or approximately one-twenty-millionth of an ounce.

Although only about 400 eggs are actually discharged from the ovaries during a woman's reproductive lifetime, the ovaries contain about 400,000 immature ova (**primary oocytes**) at birth. It is believed that no new egg cells are produced by the female after birth. It would seem that this vast quantity of eggs would help insure a woman's reproductive ability, but "aging" of the eggs and exposure to radiation or to certain drugs can alter all the germ cells at once and do permanent damage. Possibly related to such "aging" of eggs is the increased incidence of certain defects, particularly Down's Syndrome, in children born to older women. A woman in her forties is a hundred times more likely to have a Down's child than is a woman of twenty. This finding has been clearly correlated with the mother's age, although it is not known what causes chromosome defects as

women grow older. For these and other reasons, the age at which it is best for a woman to have a child, biologically speaking, is usually said to be between 20 and 35 years.

Egg Maturation

Eggs begin to mature while still in the ovary, encased in a larger spherical structure known as a **graafian follicle** (*see* Figure 5.3). The first division of the egg is mitotic and yields a **secondary oocyte** and a much smaller **polar body,** each containing forty-six chromosomes. The polar body disintegrates, though it may divide once more before doing so. The secondary oocyte undergoes meiosis, or reduction division, usually after leaving the ovary, and this division produces another polar body (which also disintegrates) and a mature egg with only twenty-three chromosomes.

In addition to chromosomes, the mature egg contains fat droplets, proteins, and nutrient fluid. It is surrounded by a gelatinous capsule (the **zona pellucida**), the final obstacle to the sperm.

Migration of the Egg

The egg, like the sperm, must travel through the reproductive system to the site of fertilization. This journey begins when the egg is expelled from the ovary at the time of ovulation. By this time hormonal influences will have caused the graafian follicle to grow to 10 or 15 millimeters in diameter, and it will protrude from the surface of the ovary (*see* Chapter 4). The follicle will be filled with fluid, and its wall will have become very thin. The egg floats free in the fluid until the thinnest part of the follicle wall bursts and the egg is carried out with the fluid. This process of ovulation is less like the explosion of a balloon and more like the leakage of water from a punctured sack.

If, as occasionally happens, a follicle fails to rupture, the result is a **follicle (retention) cyst,** one of the most common forms of **ovarian cysts** (fluid-filled sacs in the ovary). Such cysts vary in size from microscopic to 1 or 2 inches (2.5 or 5.1 centimeters) in diame-

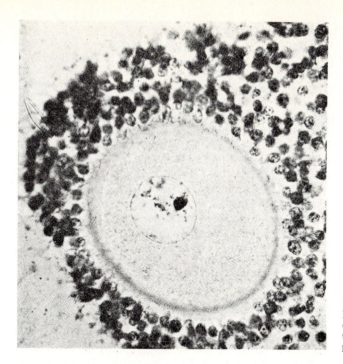

Figure 5.3 Human egg from a large graafian follicle (×480).

From Eastman and Hellman, *Williams Obstetrics,* 13th ed. (New York: Appleton-Century-Crofts, 1966), p. 60. Reprinted by permission.

ter. If they are large they can cause discomfort in the pelvic area and can make intercourse painful, but cysts of this kind rarely cause serious problems, and they usually disappear within sixty days.

Once out of the ovary, the egg must find its way to the fallopian tube. The process by which it does so is one of the mysteries of conception yet to be solved. The fringed end of the fallopian tube is near the ovary, but there is no direct connection to insure that the egg does not fall into the body cavity (*see* Figure 2.13). Once the egg has entered the tube (and most do), it begins a slow journey to the uterus, taking about three days to move only 3 to 5 inches (7.6 to 12.7 centimeters). Unlike the sperm, the egg does not move on its own. Instead, it is carried along by the movement of the cilia that line the tube. Contractions of the walls of the tube may also contribute to the movement of the egg.

If fertilization does not occur during this journey through the fallopian tube, the egg disintegrates.

Fertilization

If sperm and egg successfully complete their journeys, they will meet and unite in the fallopian tube. Each germ cell brings twenty-three chromosomes to this union, and the combination of these chromosomes results in one fertile human cell with forty-six chromosomes—and the potential to develop into a human being. However, the timing must be just right.

Intercourse must take place within one or two days before or after ovulation if the sperm and egg are to meet while both are capable of uniting and forming a fertile cell. If intercourse has occurred within thirty-six hours before ovulation, living sperm may be swimming about in the fallopian tube when the egg arrives on the scene. If fertilization does not occur within twenty-four to forty-eight hours of ovulation, conception will be impossible because the egg will no longer have the ability to become a fertile cell.

Sperm swim right up to the egg, and many

may surround it at the time of fertilization. But only one sperm actually unites with the egg. After a successful union of sperm and egg, a mechanism not fully understood prevents another sperm from entering the egg. This insures that the twenty-three chromosomes of the sperm and the twenty-three chromosomes of the egg—and no more—combine to provide the forty-six chromosomes necessary for a human being. These chromosomes, half from the mother and half from the father, determine the sex as well as many other characteristics of the child. If the sperm carries an X chromosome, the child will be a girl (XX). If it carries a Y, the child will be a boy (XY).

Attempts to predetermine the sex of a child are at least as old as recorded history. Aristotle suggested having sex in a north wind if a boy was desired, in a south wind for a girl. Researchers with more information available to them than Aristotle had have since come up with more scientific suggestions. One recent example calls for an acid douche (such as vinegar) prior to intercourse if a girl is desired and an alkaline douche (baking soda) for a boy. Acid destroys many of the sperm, especially the smaller Y sperm, but some of the more hearty X sperm may survive and travel on to the egg. In an alkaline environment the smaller, faster Y sperm are likely to reach the egg sooner than the X sperm. Still, the success rate of producing a child of the desired sex by this method is not very high.

Amniocentesis

The most accurate method for finding out the sex of an unborn child is **amniocentesis,** but this procedure usually is not performed until the fourteenth or sixteenth week after the last menstrual period. Although amniocentesis can be used to find out the sex of a fetus, it is most often used to test the chromosome makeup of the fetus when some abnormality is suspected.

The procedure of amniocentesis is simple. First, sound waves are used to make a picture (an ultrasonic scan) of the fetus in the womb. Once the position of the fetus is known, it is possible to insert a hollow needle through the abdominal wall into the pregnant uterus without harming the fetus. Some of the amniotic fluid that surrounds the fetus (and contains cells of the fetus) is then removed and analyzed. The condition and number of the chromosomes as well as the presence of either an X or Y chromosome can be determined with a high degree of accuracy.

Amniocentesis is a relatively safe procedure for both mother and fetus. In a study sponsored by the National Institutes of Health of more than one thousand amniocenteses there were no major complications. Only three sex determinations and six diagnoses of chromosomal abnormalities were incorrect. About 5 percent of all infants born live have some sort of recognizable defects, many of which are minor. Among the serious abnormalities that can be detected by amniocentesis are Down's syndrome (mongolism), sickle-cell trait, Tay-Sachs disease, cystic fibrosis, and Rh incompatibility. When chromosomal abnormalities are diagnosed, women can legally choose to have an abortion—though by the time the chromosome analysis is complete (the twentieth to twenty-fourth week of pregnancy) abortion is no longer a simple, risk-free operation (*see* Chapter 6).

Because a woman in her forties is one hundred times more likely than a woman in her twenties to have eggs with abnormal chromosomes, amniocentesis is currently recommended for all women who become pregnant after the age of 35. It is also recommended for women who have previously had a child with a chromosome abnormality or with some other problem that can be detected by analysis of fetal cells.

Infertility

Most couples are fertile and have no trouble producing children. Others (from 10 to 15 percent of married couples in the United States) are infertile and can have no children because either the male (in about 40 percent of the cases), the female, or both are sterile.

One of the most common causes of infertility in males is low sperm count. An ejaculation that contains fewer than 35 million sperm per cubic centimeter (fewer than 100 million to 150 million sperm per ejaculation) will almost never result in conception. Frequent ejaculation (one or more times a day for several days in a row) is one cause of low sperm count, but this deficiency, obviously, is easily remedied. Usually low sperm count has more serious causes, several of which have been mentioned already: undescended testes, physical damage to the testes, radiation, and infections that affect the testes. Infections of the prostate gland can also affect fertility, as can certain hormone disorders (such as hypothyroidism and diabetes).

Hormone problems can sometimes be treated successfully with hormone injections. Another solution to infertility in men with low sperm counts is AIH (artificial insemination with the husband's sperm). This consists of collecting and storing a series of ejaculations and injecting them into the woman's vagina or uterus when enough sperm have been collected. When the man produces no sperm at all, artificial insemination with donated sperm (AID) is sometimes performed.

The most common cause of infertility in women is failure to ovulate. This may be related to hormonal deficiencies or to other factors, such as vitamin deficiency, anemia, malnutrition, or psychological stress. If a woman does not ovulate there are several possible solutions. One is the drug *clomiphene,* which stimulates ovulation by causing the release of gonadotrophins from the pituitary. Clomiphene has also been used successfully, on an experimental basis, to treat men with low sperm counts. If a woman does not respond to clomiphene, it is sometimes possible to stimulate ovulation by hormone injections (FSH).

Overstimulation of the reproductive system with hormones or drugs, however, can result in undesirable side effects. Complications include blood clotting and accumulation of fluid in the abdomen. Another problem is multiple births. These occur because it is not always possible to calculate the exact dosage necessary to stimulate one (and only one) follicle. One study of women treated with clomiphene found that 10 percent of them had twins or other multiple births. There also have been cases in which women treated with

hormones had pregnancies with as many as fifteen fetuses. In such cases the risks of fetal death, miscarriage, and birth complications are extremely high. In at least one case, however, a woman has given birth to sextuplets. The six infants were born live, and the mother did well.

In addition to failure to ovulate, there are several other problems that can result in infertility. Infections of the vagina, cervix, uterus, tubes, or ovaries can cause infertility by preventing passage of the sperm or ova to the site of fertilization. Malformations of the reproductive tract, as well as tumors (particularly cervical or uterine), can also interfere with fertilization. There also are cases in which a woman may be preventing conception without knowing it by using certain commercial douches or vaginal deodorants containing chemicals that interfere with or destroy sperm.

Although there certainly are couples who cannot have children, research into fertility has found solutions to many fertility problems. The birth in 1978 of a so-called "test tube baby" to a woman with blocked fallopian tubes is an example. Human eggs can now be surgically removed from the ovary, fertilized outside the woman's body, and then inserted into the uterus so that a normal pregnancy results. Whenever a man and woman who wish to have children have been unsuccessful for about a year, they should consult a physician. There are numerous tests that can pinpoint fertility problems, and either the man or the woman or both may have treatable disorders.

PREGNANCY

The news that a woman has missed her period is rarely met with indifference. For a man and a woman who have been trying to have a child, a missed menstrual period will be joyful news. For a couple who had no intention of producing a child, a missed period may lead to feelings of fear and guilt. Or the news may be met with mixed feelings, as when a couple wants children "but not just yet." The news of a missed period causes such reactions, obviously, because it is one of the first indications that a **pregnancy** is under-way. The average duration of human preg-nancy is 266 days, or approximately nine months. Pregnancy is often described in terms of three-month periods called *tri-mesters*.

The First Trimester

First Signs of Pregnancy

A missed period is among the first signs of pregnancy, but it does not always indicate pregnancy. Women who are near the begin-ning or the end of their reproductive years and those who have recently experienced an emotional upset or illness may fail to men-struate (as explained in Chapter 4). Also, a woman who has recently had a child, partic-ularly if she is still nursing, may not men-struate for five or six months or more. Missed periods under these circumstances usually do not indicate pregnancy, but contrary to what some people believe, a woman can become pregnant during this time without having had a menstrual cycle since her previous pregnancy. She need only have ovulated.

On the other hand, a woman who is preg-nant may continue to have cyclic bleeding, though in smaller quantities and for shorter periods than usual. Such bleeding, which may be confusing to a woman who believes she is pregnant, is called "spotting." It occurs in about 20 percent of pregnant women, and it is particularly common in those who have al-ready had children. Spotting usually does not indicate a problem, but in some cases it may be an indication of miscarriage.

Another early sign of pregnancy is en-largement and tenderness of the breasts. When hormonal stimulation of the mammary glands begins after conception (*see* Chapter 4) a woman usually will become aware of sensa-tions of fullness in her breasts. The nipples in particular become quite sensitive to tactile stimulation early in pregnancy.

Many women also experience so-called morning sickness during the first six to eight weeks of pregnancy. This sickness usually consists of queasy feelings upon awakening, accompanied by an aversion to food or even to odors of certain foods. The nausea may be ac-companied by vomiting and great reluctance to be near food. Morning sickness is also expe-rienced by some women in the evenings, but about 25 percent of women never experience morning sickness, and only about one in two hundred pregnant women in the United States has to be hospitalized because of severe vomiting, which can have serious con-sequences (including malnutrition) if not treated. In rare cases a therapeutic abortion may be required in order to save the life of the woman.

A phenomenon known as "sympathetic pregnancy" is sometimes seen in the hus-bands of pregnant women. These husbands become nauseated and vomit along with their wives. The cause of this condition is implied in its name.

Frequent urination is another common early sign of pregnancy. It is caused by in-creased pressure on the bladder by the swell-ing uterus. This symptom usually goes away as the uterus enlarges and rises up into the abdomen, but frequent urination may again become a problem toward the end of the preg-nancy when the fetal head descends into the pelvis and puts pressure on the bladder.

Fatigue and the need for more sleep, also indications of pregnancy, are often quite obvi-ous during early pregnancy and may be quite puzzling to a woman who is usually very en-ergetic.

Early Diagnosis of Pregnancy

A sexually active woman who has missed her period and is experiencing any or all of the above symptoms may have good reason to believe that she is pregnant. If she wants to make sure, she can see a physician for a preg-nancy test. There are many such tests, but none is 100 percent accurate early in preg-nancy.

The first time that pregnancy can be de-tected by physical examination is usually in the sixth week of pregnancy (about four weeks after a missed period). By this time certain changes in the cervix and uterus can be detected during a pelvic examination. One particularly good indicator of pregnancy is **Hegar's sign,** softening of an area between the cervix and the body of the uterus. An experienced physician will be able to detect this softening by the sixth week. The examination is performed by placing one hand on the abdomen and two fingers of the other hand in the vagina (*see* Figure 5.4).

Various laboratory tests can also be performed to detect pregnancy in its early stages. If performed correctly these tests are 95 to 98 percent accurate. The most often used such tests are based on the presence of HCG (a hormone produced only by pregnant women). These tests are relatively simple and inexpensive. The woman's blood or urine sample is put into a test tube or in a small dish with specific chemicals. If HCG is present, it can be detected within minutes, even in very small amounts. These tests are highly accurate, sometimes as early as two weeks after conception. A relatively inexpensive version of the HCG test is also available for home use. If used correctly, it can detect HCG

in the urine of a pregnant woman as early as nine days after a missed period, but not enough data are presently available on these home-use kits to say how accurate they are.

False Pregnancy Occasionally a woman may become convinced that she is pregnant despite evidence to the contrary. About 0.1 percent of all women who consult obstetricians fall into this category. Usually they are young women who intensely desire children, but some are women near menopause.

Women suffering false pregnancy often experience the symptoms of pregnancy, including morning sickness, breast tenderness, a sense of fullness in the pelvis, and the sensation of fetal movements in the abdomen. They often cease to menstruate, and physicians may observe contractions of the abdominal muscles that resemble fetal movements. Even though pregnancy tests are negative, a woman suffering from a severe mental illness like schizophrenia may persist in her delusion for years.

Determining Date of Birth

Once pregnancy has been confirmed, the next question usually is, "When is the baby due?" The expected delivery date can be calculated by a simple formula: Add one week to the first day of the last menstrual period, subtract three months, then add one year. For example, if the last menstrual period began on January 8, 1980, adding one week (to January 15), subtracting three months (to October 15), and adding one year gives an expected delivery date of October 15, 1980. Only about 4 percent of births occur on dates predicted by this formula, but 60 percent occur within five days of the predicted date.

Sexual Activity during the First Trimester

There is no reason why early pregnancy or the suspicion of pregnancy should interfere with a healthy woman's sexual activities. Morning sickness in the early part of the day, fatigue in the evening, and other physiological changes may cause some inconvenience, but most couples find satisfactory occasions for continued sexual relations.

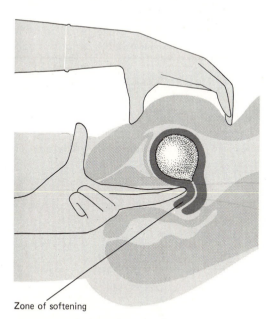

Zone of softening

Figure 5.4 Hegar's sign.

From Benson, *Handbook of Obstetrics and Gynecology,* 3d ed. Los Altos, Calif.: Lange Medical Publications, 1968, p. 42. Reprinted by permission.

Decreased sexual interest was reported by about one-fourth of the pregnant women in a recent study, but the frequency of sexual activity did not change much compared with frequency prior to pregnancy (*see* Table 5.1).

Intrauterine Events of the First Trimester

Once fertilization has taken place, the fertilized cell begins to divide into multiple cells as it moves down the fallopian tube (*see* Figure 5.5). There is no significant change in size during the first few days, but the original cell becomes a round mass of smaller cells called a **morula** (from the Latin word for "mulberry"). During the third to fifth day after ovulation, the cells of the morula arrange themselves in a spherical shape, leaving a fluid-filled cavity in the center. This structure, called a **blastocyst,** floats about in the uterine cavity. Between the fifth and seventh days after ovulation it attaches itself to the lining of the uterus and burrows in, permitting it to reach the blood vessels and nutrients below. By the tenth to twelfth day after ovulation the blastocyst is firmly implanted in the wall of the uterus, but the woman will still not know that she is pregnant because her menstrual period is not due for several more days.

The blastocyst, which has embedded itself in the lining of the uterus, will develop from a tiny ball of cells into an easily recognizable human fetus during the first trimester. In the early stages of development a disk-shaped layer of cells forms across the center of the blastocyst. It is from this **embryonic disk**

that the fetus grows. The remaining cells develop into the **placenta,** the membranes that will contain the fetus and the **amniotic fluid,** and the **yolk sac** (which has no significant function in humans).

Development of the Placenta Enclosed in the womb, the growing fetus is dependent on its mother for nutrients and for the disposal of waste material. The placenta is the organ through which such materials are exchanged. It grows from both fetal and maternal cells, and during the first trimester it develops into a bluish red, round, flat organ about 7 inches (17.8 centimeters) in diameter and 1 inch (2.5 centimeters) thick. It weighs about 1 pound (0.4 kilograms) and, along with the fetal membranes, makes up the "afterbirth."

The blood vessels of the placenta are connected to the circulatory system of the mother through the wall of the uterus. The circulatory system of the fetus is connected to that of the placenta by the blood vessels in the umbilical cord, which is attached to the placenta. Oxygen and nutrients reach the fetus through the umbilical vein, and waste products from the fetus reach the maternal system through the umbilical arteries.

The placenta also functions as an endocrine gland, secreting hormones essential to maintaining pregnancy. HCG (**human chorionic gonadotrophin**), the hormone measured in pregnancy tests, is produced by the placenta. It stimulates the production of

Table 5.1 **PERCENT OF WOMEN HAVING VARIOUS FREQUENCIES OF COITUS AT DIFFERENT STAGES OF PREGNANCY**

Number of acts of coitus per week	Baseline (1 year before conception)	1st trimester	2d trimester	7th month	8th month	9th month
None	0%	2%	2%	11%	23%	59%
1	7%	11%	16%	23%	29%	19%
2–5	81%	78%	77%	63%	46%	23%
6 or more	12%	9%	5%	2%	2%	1%

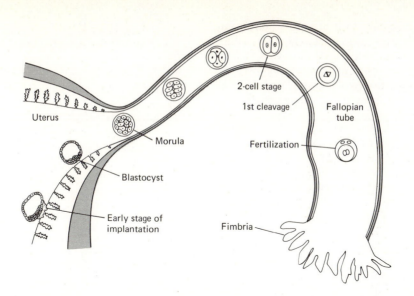

Figure 5.5 Fertilization to implantation of the human embryo.

From Tuchmann-Duplessis and Haegel, *Illustrated Human Embryology*, Vol. I (New York: Springer-Verlag; London: Chapman and Hall; Paris: Masson et Cie, 1971). Reprinted by permission.

progesterone by the corpus luteum during the first one or two months of pregnancy until gradually the placenta itself begins to produce large amounts of progesterone and estrogen. It appears that the labor process is triggered when the placenta stops producing these hormones just before delivery.

Transmission of Drugs and Diseases through the Placenta The fetus receives its nourishment through the placenta, but it is very important to realize that other substances—some of them quite harmful to the fetus, particularly during the first trimester—can also reach the fetus through the placenta. One of the most obvious examples of this was seen in the 1960s when the effects of the sedative thalidomide were widely publicized. Thalidomide causes abnormal development of the arms and legs of the fetus. Children whose mothers took thalidomide while pregnant were born with their hands and feet attached to their bodies by short stumps rather than by normal arms and legs.

Alcohol is another drug that can cause birth defects. Researchers have found that fa-cial, limb, and heart defects are more common among children of women who drink heavily during pregnancy than among those of women who do not drink. Three ounces (93.3 grams) of alcohol a day or one big binge may be enough to cause damage.

Addictive drugs like heroin and morphine can also pass through the placenta to the fetus and addict the unborn child to the drug. When such an infant is born it must be given further doses of the drug to prevent withdrawal symptoms that can be fatal.

Certain viruses can also reach the fetus and have damaging effects on development during the first trimester. One is **rubella,** or German measles, virus. If a woman has rubella during the first month of pregnancy, there is a 50 percent chance that her infant will be born with cataracts, heart disease, deafness, or mental deficiency. In the third month of pregnancy the risk of such abnormalities decreases to 10 percent. About 85 percent of the adult women in the United States are immune to rubella because they had the disease as children, but if a woman is in doubt about her immunity, she can be tested and vaccinated if necessary. A woman should not receive rubella vaccine if she is already pregnant, and she should avoid conception for two months after vaccination because the vaccine contains live rubella virus that can cause the disease it is supposed to prevent.

Another complication is Rh incompatibility, a disorder than can cause serious and even fatal anemia in the fetus. In this disorder, antibodies of the mother travel across the placenta and attack the red blood cells of the fetus. The antibodies occur when the mother's blood is Rh negative and the father is Rh positive. If the mother is Rh negative and the father is Rh positive (as in about 10 percent of the marriages in the United States), Rh incompatibility can develop. This happens in about 1 of every 200 pregnancies. In most cases the serious results of this disorder (death or brain damage) can be avoided by early detection (blood tests and amniocentesis) and treatment (blood transfusion of the newborn infant).

Development of the Fetus During the first trimester, there is relatively little change in size of the embryo, but its rather simple structure is transformed into a very complete organism called the fetus. (In medical terms the ovum becomes an **embryo** one week after fertilization. The embryo becomes a **fetus** after the eighth week of pregnancy.) By the second week after fertilization, the embryonic disk has become elongated (about 1.5 millimeters long) and oval-shaped. The actual sizes of the embryo during the first seven weeks of pregnancy are shown in Figure 5.6.

During the third week growth is most obvious at the two ends of the embryo. A prominent "tail" is seen at one end of the embryo, but it will be almost gone by the eighth week. In rare instances the tail fails to regress, and there are documented cases of human infants born with tails. The tails are usually removed surgically at an early age, but in one case reported in the medical literature a 12-year-old boy had a tail 9 inches (22.9 centimeters) long.

At the other end the head is beginning

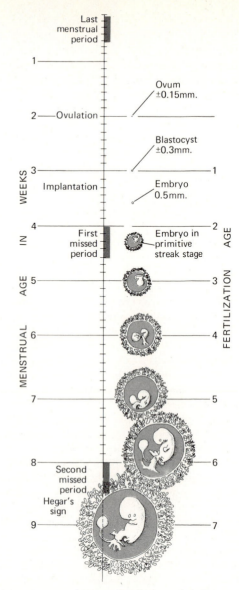

Figure 5.6 Actual sizes of embryos and their membranes in relation to a time scale based on the mother's menstrual history.

From B.M. Patten, *Human Embryology,* 3d ed., p. 145. Copyright © 1968 by McGraw-Hill, Inc. Used with permission of McGraw-Hill Book Company.

to take on a definite shape. By the end of the third week or the beginning of the fourth, eyes and ears become visible. In addition, the brain and other parts of the central nervous system are beginning to form. By the end of the fourth week two bulges appear on the front side of the trunk. The upper bulge represents the developing heart and is called the **cardiac prominence.** The lower one is the **hepatic prominence,** caused by the growing liver (*see* Figure 5.7).

Between the fourth and eighth weeks the facial features—eyes, ears, nose, and mouth—become clearly recognizable (*see* Figure 5.8). Fingers and toes begin to appear between the sixth and eighth weeks. Bones begin to ossify (harden) and the intestines are forming (*see* Figure 5.9). By the seventh week the gonads are present but still cannot be easily distinguished as male or female. The external genitals cannot be identified as male or female until about the third month (*see* Chapter 2).

Between the eighth and twelfth weeks the fetus increases in length from about 1.5 to 4 inches (3.8 to 10.2 centimeters), and in weight from about 2 to 19 grams (about $\frac{1}{15}$ to $\frac{2}{3}$ ounce). Although still very small, the fetus at twelve weeks has a human appearance. From this point on, development consists primarily of enlargement of the structures already present.

Complications of the First Trimester

One of the most common problems during the first trimester of pregnancy is the unwanted termination of pregnancy—miscarriage, or **spontaneous abortion.** Between 10 and 15 percent of all pregnancies end in spontaneous abortion. About 75 percent of these miscarriages occur before the sixth week of pregnancy, and most actually occur before the eighth week—long before the fetus or embryo has any chance of survival on its own. The first sign that a woman may miscarry is vaginal bleeding, or spotting. If the symptoms of pregnancy disappear and the woman develops cramps in the pelvic region, the fetus is usually expelled. About 15 percent of miscarriages are caused by illness, malnutrition, physical trauma (such as a fall), or other factors affecting the pregnant woman. In the remaining 85 percent the reasons are not apparent, but about 50 percent of

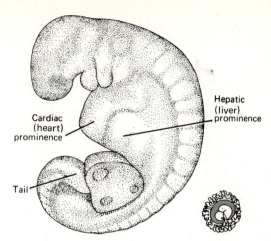

Figure 5.7 A human embryo about four weeks after fertilization (crown-rump length 3.9 millimeters). Retouched photograph (×20) of embryo 5923 in the Carnegie Collection. Sketch, lower right, shows actual size of embryo.

As modified by B.M. Patten for *Human Embryology*, 3d ed., p. 70, McGraw-Hill Book Company. With permission.

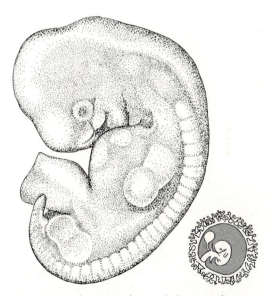

Figure 5.8 A human embryo a little more than six weeks after fertilization (crown-rump length 14 millimeters). Retouched photograph (×8) of embryo 1267A in the Carnegie Collection.

From B.M. Patten, *Human Embryology*, 3d ed., p. 74. Copyright © 1968 by McGraw-Hill, Inc. Used with permission of McGraw-Hill Book Company.

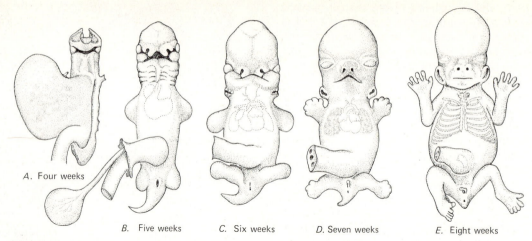

A. Four weeks

B. Five weeks   *C.* Six weeks   *D.* Seven weeks   *E.* Eight weeks

Figure 5.9 Frontal views of a series of human embryos, drawn as they would appear if the body curvatures had been straightened.

From B.M. Patten, *Human Embryology*, 3d ed., p. 146. Copyright © 1968 by McGraw-Hill, Inc. Used with permission of McGraw-Hill Book Company.

miscarried fetuses are clearly defective in some way.

Positive Diagnosis of Pregnancy

By the end of the first trimester a woman will almost always know that she is pregnant. However, for medical and legal purposes pregnancy can be established positively by one of three methods: identification of the fetal heartbeat, photographic demonstration of the fetal skeleton, or observation of fetal movements. Using a stethoscope, a physician can hear the fetal heart by the fifth month. The fetal heart rate is between 120 and 140 beats per minute and can be distinguished easily from that of the pregnant woman, which is usually between 70 and 80 beats per minute. A fetal pulse detector is also available that can detect the fetal heart as early as nine weeks. This device is based on ultrasonic technology. A sound wave of very high pitch is directed at the uterus and is reflected back to a receiver and amplified. Movements of the fetal heart will cause audible changes in the pitch of the reflected sound.

Variations in the echo from an ultrasonic pulse reflecting off the fetal skeleton can be converted into a photographic image that is more distinct than a conventional X ray (*see* Figure 5.10). Use of the ultrasonic procedure does not involve the radiation hazard to the fetus that X ray photography does.

The third way of positively determining pregnancy is by fetal movements, or **quickening,** which can usually be felt by the end of fifth month. Kicking movements of the fetus may be outwardly visible later, in the second trimester. Fetal movements not only confirm pregnancy but indicate that the fetus is alive.

The Second Trimester

Women generally consider the second trimester to be the most peaceful and pleasant time of pregnancy. The nausea and drowsiness of the first few months tend to go away, and worries about miscarriages are generally past. Fetal kicks and movements make the pregnant woman acutely aware of the living fetus she is carrying. Even women who did not want to become pregnant may come to accept the idea during this period.

A pregnant woman's condition becomes publicly recognizable during the second trimester. As the fetus grows, the woman's

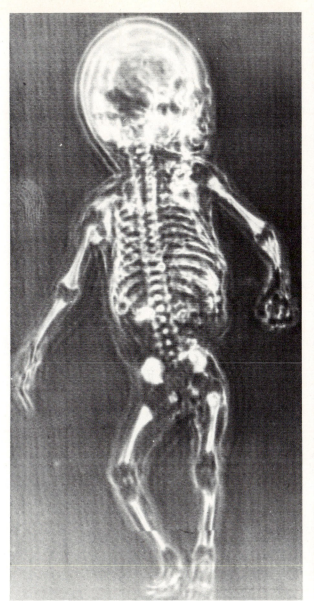
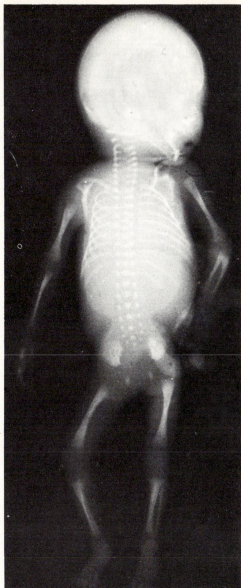

Figure 5.10 (*Left*) photographic image of fetal skeleton produced by ultrasonic technique; (*right*) conventional X ray of same skeleton.

Stanford Research Institute.

waistline begins to expand (particularly if she has already had a child), and her abdomen begins to protrude. If there are no complications or illnesses, the pregnant woman can continue to be quite active during this period. She can continue to work, do housework, travel, and participate in recreation and sports. Rather than forbid specific activities, most physicians urge "moderation in all things." Some employers discharge pregnant women or require them to take maternity leave (though court rulings are changing this situation).

Sexual Activity during the Second Trimester

The frequency of sexual intercourse usually does not decrease significantly during the second trimester (*see* Table 5.1). In fact, some women who experienced extreme nausea and fatigue during early pregnancy may experience renewed interest in sex as these symptoms disappear. There is usually an increase in vaginal lubrication from the second trimester on and less breast tenderness. Even if the frequency of intercourse does not change during this stage of pregnancy, the preferred positions of the male and female during intercourse may change because of the woman's growing abdomen. During the later stages of pregnancy the female-on-top, side-by-side,

and rear-entry positions are used more frequently than is the male-on-top position.

Development of the Fetus

After the twelfth week the fetus is clearly recognizable as a developing human (*see* Figures 5.11 and 5.12). It has a proportionately large head with eyes, ears, nose, and mouth. The arms and legs, which began as "limb buds" projecting from the trunk, now have hands and feet. The fingers and toes, which began as grooves at the ends of the limb buds, gradually appear (*see* Figure 5.13). At first the fingers and toes appear to be webbed, and in some children this webbing may remain after birth, but this can be easily corrected by surgery.

Very fine hair (called **lanugo**) appears on the scalp and above the eyes in the fifth or sixth month. The skin is quite thin at this time, and small blood vessels beneath the surface may show through. Beginning in the seventh month layers of fat build up beneath the

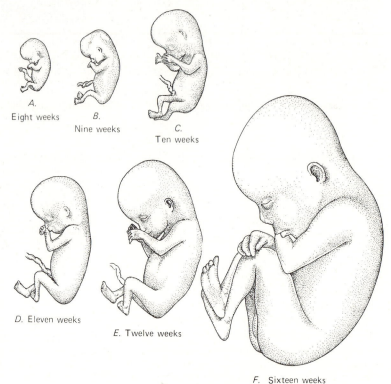

Figure 5.11 Human fetuses between eight and sixteen weeks, about one-half actual size.

A-D from photographs of embryos in University of Michigan Collection. *E* and *F* redrawn, with slight modification, from DeLee, "Obstetrics." From B.M. Patten, *Human Embryology,* 3d ed., p. 150. Copyright © by McGraw-Hill, Inc. Used with permission of McGraw-Hill Book Company.

A.
Eight weeks

B.
Nine weeks

C.
Ten weeks

D. Eleven weeks

E. Twelve weeks

F. Sixteen weeks

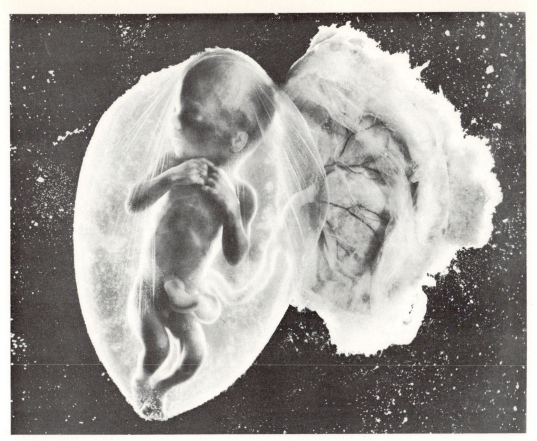

Figure 5.12 Fetus, about four months, 8 inches (20.3 centimeters) long.

From Nilsson *et al.*, *A Child Is Born* (Boston: Seymour Lawrence, Inc., 1965), pp. 116–117. Reprinted by permission.

skin, and the fetus takes on its characteristic chubbiness.

The internal organ systems continue to mature during the second trimester, and there is a substantial increase in the size of the fetus. At the end of the third month the fetus weighs about 1 ounce (31.1 grams) and is only about 3 or 4 inches (7.6 centimeters) long. At the end of the sixth month it weighs about 2 pounds (0.9 kilograms) and is about 14 inches (35.6 centimeters) long.

During the later stages of pregnancy the fetus alternates between wakefulness and sleep. Its eyes can open, and its arms and legs move, sometimes vigorously. These movements sometimes occur in response to what is happening outside the womb. The uterus provides a very sheltered environment for the fetus, but a loud noise near the uterus, a flash of high-intensity light, or a rapid change in the position of the woman can disturb the tranquillity of the womb and provoke vigorous movement by the fetus. Changes in temperature outside the womb are not noticed by the fetus, since the temperature of the uterus is maintained at a constant level slightly (0.9°F or 0.5°C) above that of the mother.

In rare cases a fetus may be delivered during the second trimester, but chances of survival at this stage of development are rare. Even with extraordinary efforts by hospital staff only 5 to 10 percent of infants weighing

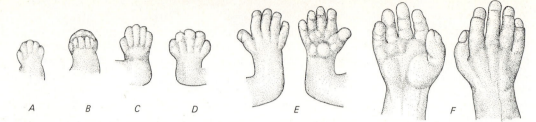

Figure 5.13 Stages in early development of the hand. *(A)* Anterior limb bud of an embryo 12 millimeters long; *(B)* anterior limb bud of an embryo 15 millimeters long; *(C)* anterior limb bud of an embryo 17 millimeters long; *(D)* hand and forearm of an embryo 20 millimeters long; *(E)* two views of the hand and forearm of an embryo 25 millimeters long; *(F)* two views of the hand of a fetus 52 millimeters long.

After Retzius, from Scammon, in Morris, *Human Anatomy.* From B.M. Patten, *Human Embryology,* 3d ed., p. 148. Copyright © 1968 by McGraw-Hill, Inc. Used with the permission of McGraw-Hill Book Company.

2 pounds (0.9 kilograms) survive. The smallest infant known to have survived weighed 400 grams at birth (less than 1 pound).

The Third Trimester

During the last three months of pregnancy the expectant mother becomes even more aware of the developing child she carries within her abdomen (*see* Figure 5.14). The kicking, tossing, and turning of the fetus may even keep the woman awake at night. The woman's weight may also become a problem at this time if she has gained excessively. According to the Committee on Maternal Malnutrition of the National Research Council, the desirable weight gain during pregnancy is 24 pounds (10.9 kilograms). The average infant at nine months weighs about 7.5 pounds (3.4 kilograms). The rest of the weight gain is accounted for by the placenta (about 1 pound [0.4 kilograms]), the amniotic fluid in the uterine cavity (2 pounds [0.9 kilograms]), the enlargement of the uterus (2 pounds [0.9 kilograms]), and enlargement of the breasts (1.5 pounds [0.7 kilograms]). The retained fluid and fat accumulated by the mother accounts for the rest.

Although both mother and fetus need a good diet, there are several reasons why women are warned against gaining too much weight during pregnancy. The most important is the higher incidence of medical complications, such as high blood pressure and heart strain. In addition, movement may become awkward for a woman who has gained as much as 40 pounds (18 kilograms) or more.

Prematurity

A major complication during the third trimester is premature labor and delivery. Since

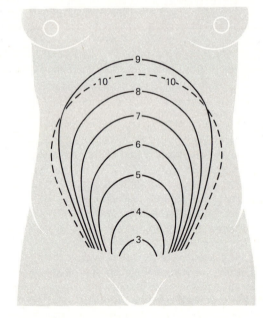

Figure 5.14 Relative height of the top of the uterus at the various months of pregnancy.

From Eastman and Hellman, *Williams Obstetrics,* 13th ed. (New York: Appleton-Century-Crofts, 1966), p. 263. Reprinted by permission.

the exact date of conception is not always known, prematurity is defined by weight rather than by age. An infant that weighs less than 2500 grams (5 pounds, 8 ounces) at birth is considered premature, and the smaller the infant, the poorer its chances of survival. Although an infant born in the seventh month or later can usually survive for a few hours without great difficulty, a premature infant may develop difficulty in breathing and die within forty-eight hours.

About 7 percent of all births in the United States are premature. This may be due to various maternal illnesses—such as high blood pressure, heart disease, or syphilis—or to factors such as cigarette smoking or multiple pregnancy. In at least 50 percent of the cases, however, the cause of prematurity is not known.

Complications During the Third Trimester

One of the most serious complications of pregnancy, if untreated, is a condition called **toxemia** (from the Latin word for "poison"). In fact, much modern prenatal care has been developed as a result of research done on the cause and treatment of toxemia. The cause of toxemia is still unknown, but it seems that a toxin, or poison, produced by the body causes the symptoms—high blood pressure, protein in the urine, and the retention of fluids by the body. This disease occurs only in pregnant women, usually in the last trimester, and if it is not treated successfully the result can be death for both the mother and the child. Uncontrolled toxemia is a major cause (along with hemorrhage and infection) of maternal mortality. Six to 7 percent of all pregnant women in the United States develop toxemia, and a small percentage of these die.

Sexual Activity during the Third Trimester

The frequency of sexual intercourse (and orgasm) declines with each successive month of the third trimester (*see* Table 5.1). The most common reasons given for this change are, in order of frequency, physical discomfort, fear of injury to the fetus, loss of sexual interest, awkwardness in having intercourse, recommendation of a physician, and feelings of loss of sexual attractiveness (as reported by the woman).

The basic medical reason for not having intercourse (or orgasm) during late pregnancy is the risk of causing premature labor. Orgasm in the third trimester is accompanied by strong contractions of the uterus, and in the ninth month the uterus may go into spasm for as long as a minute following orgasm. It is possible (though not conclusively proved) that orgasm during the final weeks of pregnancy could result in premature labor or rupture of the fetal membranes. (Rupture of the fetal membranes can lead to infection as well as to prematurity.) Women who have had a history of vaginal bleeding during pregnancy, ruptured membranes, or a prematurely "ripe" (soft) cervix are perhaps more likely to be at risk of premature labor due to orgasm. Women who have not experienced such complications and who are otherwise healthy can probably participate in sexual activity throughout the third trimester at no risk to themselves or the fetus. But because of possible dangers or discomfort, some couples prefer to practice intracrural (between the thighs) intercourse, oral-genital stimulation, or mutual masturbation during the last months.

Final Development of the Fetus

The last three months of pregnancy are a period of growth and development for the fetus. All of the essential organ systems have formed, and by the end of the seventh month the fetus is about 16 inches (40.6 centimeters) long and weighs about 3 pounds, 12 ounces (1.7 kilograms). If delivered at this time, the baby has about a 50-percent chance of survival.

In addition to the usual problems of prematurity, the position of the fetus can complicate birth at this early stage. The most common position for delivery, and the one that presents the fewest complications, is the **cephalic,** or head-down, **position.** When the fetus is situated in this position, the head appears at the cervix first during delivery. However, during the seventh month about 12 percent of fetuses are still upright in the womb (the **breech position**), and a few are positioned horizontally (**transverse position**), In addition to the baby's small size and immaturity, there is thus the added risk of a more complicated breech delivery early in the third trimester. At full term (nine months) only about 3 percent of babies are still in the breech position.

By the end of the eighth month the fetus is about 18 inches (45.7 centimeters) long and weighs about 5 pounds, 4 ounces (2.4 kilograms). If delivered at this time, it has a 90-to-95-percent chance of survival.

During the ninth month the fetus gains more than 2 pounds (0.9 kilograms), and organs like the lungs reach a state of maturity that will allow them to function in the outside world. In addition, less crucial details like hair and fingernails assume a normal appearance. At full term the average infant weighs 7.5 pounds (3.4 kilograms) and is 20 inches (50.8 centimeters) long—though the range of variation is wide. Newborn infants may be as small as 5 pounds (2.3 kilograms), and weights of 10 or 11 pounds (4.5 or 5 kilograms) are not uncommon. Ninety-nine percent of full-term infants born alive in the United States survive, and this figure could be improved if all expectant mothers and newborn babies received proper medical care.

CHILDBIRTH

By the ninth month of pregnancy a woman is usually anxious to "have it over with" and to "see what it is." Contractions of the uterus at irregular intervals are among the first signs that she will soon get her wish. An overanxious woman, especially one who has not previously had a child, may misinterpret these first contractions and rush to the hospital only to be told that she is experiencing **false labor.**

Before labor actually begins, several other events occur. Three or four weeks before delivery the fetus "drops" to a lower position in the abdomen. The next major step in preparation for delivery is the softening and dilation (opening) of the cervix. The woman may be unaware of this process, but usually just before labor begins there is a small, slightly bloody discharge that represents the plug of mucus that has been blocking the cervix. In a few cases (about 10 percent) the membranes that surround the fetus burst, and there is a gush of amniotic fluid down the woman's legs. Labor usually begins within twenty-four hours after such a rupture, but if it does not, there is a risk of infection and the mother should be hospitalized for observation.

Labor

Labor begins with regular uterine contractions that further dilate the cervix. The mechanism that triggers these contractions is not fully understood, but a number of hormones are known to be involved. The hormones produced by the placenta, for instance, are believed to inhibit uterine contractions, but the placenta stops producing these hormones just prior to the end of pregnancy. Other chemicals (**prostaglandins;** *see* Chapter 6) are known to stimulate the muscle of the uterus and may play a role in initiating labor. Finally, **oxytocin,** a hormone produced by the pituitary gland (*see* Figure 4.1), is released in the late stages of labor, and it causes the more powerful contractions necessary to expel the fetus.

Labor is divided into three stages, the first of which is the longest. It begins with the first contractions and lasts until the cervix is completely dilated (about 10 centimeters [4 inches] across). This stage lasts about fifteen hours in the first pregnancy and about eight hours in later ones. (Deliveries after the first are generally easier in all respects.) Uterine contractions begin at intervals as far apart as fifteen or twenty minutes, but they occur more frequently and with greater intensity and regularity as time passes. If the woman plans to have a regular hospital delivery, she will usually go to the hospital when the contractions are coming regularly four or five minutes apart. She will be admitted to a labor room (a regular hospital room) for the remainder of the first stage of labor. The expectant father is usually allowed to remain with her during this time.

The second stage begins when the cervix is completely dilated and ends with the delivery of the baby (*see* Figures 5.15 and 5.16). At the onset of the second stage the woman is taken to a delivery room (similar to a surgical operating room), and the father may or may not be allowed to stay with her. The current trend is to have the fathers involved in all stages of delivery whenever possible. Their presence during labor and at the delivery can be reassuring to a woman and can help diminish her stress as well as provide a sense of participation for the father.

The second stage may last from a few minutes to a few hours. If any anesthetic is used, it is usually given before the second

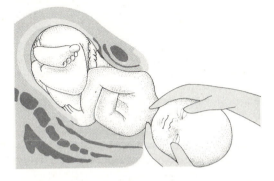

Figure 5.15 Gentle traction to bring about descent of anterior shoulder.

From Eastman and Hellman, *Williams Obstetrics,* 13th ed. (New York: Appleton-Century-Crofts, 1966), p. 423. Reprinted by permission.

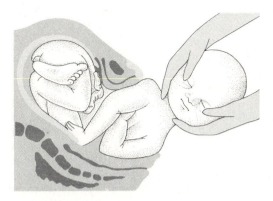

Figure 5.16 Delivery of anterior shoulder completed; gentle traction to deliver posterior shoulder.

From Eastman and Hellman, *Williams Obstetrics,* 13th ed. (New York: Appleton-Century-Crofts, 1966), p. 423. Reprinted by permission.

stage begins. General anesthesia (under which the woman is unconscious) is no longer used as often as it was earlier in this century. Its disadvantages include all the risks to the woman that general anesthesia usually includes plus a slowing effect on labor. It also includes risks to the infant, whose reactions (including breathing) are slowed by the anesthetic. A spinal anesthetic is currently considered to be preferable to general anesthetic. The spinal anesthetic is injected into the spinal canal, producing temporary loss of sensation (and paralysis) below the waist only. This allows the woman to remain alert during the delivery and protects the infant from the effects of anesthesia. However, the woman is unable to use the muscles of her lower body during delivery. Local anesthesia, which blocks the nerves in the vicinity of the vagina, is sufficient for a comfortable delivery for some women who desire a minimum of medical intervention at this stage. Some women prefer no anesthesia during delivery.

In the third stage the placenta separates from the wall of the uterus and is discharged along with the fetal membranes as **afterbirth.** The uterus contracts to a much smaller size during this stage, and there is some bleeding. The third stage of labor lasts about an hour, during which time the physician examines the mother and child carefully and sews up any tear that may have occurred in the **perineum** (the skin and deeper tissues between the openings of the vagina and anus). The **episiotomy** incision, if there has been one, is also sewn up at this time. An episiotomy is an incision of the perineum that is sometimes performed to ease the passage of the baby's head. These "stitches" may cause itching and discomfort for several days, but they usually heal with no complications.

Cesarean Section

If the infant's head is too large or the woman's pelvis too small to permit a regular delivery, a **cesarean section** may have to be performed. In this operation the infant is removed from the womb through an incision in the walls of the abdomen and uterus. About 10 percent of deliveries in the United States are performed by cesarean section, though the figure is increasing and may be as high as 22 percent in some hospitals. With modern surgical techniques the rate of complications in this type of delivery is no greater than in a vaginal delivery. And the incision can be placed just above the pubic hairline so that the woman can appear on a beach without her scar showing. It is possible to have several children by cesarean section, and it is also possible to have a normal vaginal delivery after a woman has had a cesarean delivery. The recovery period is somewhat longer after a cesarean section, and hospitalization usually lasts from seven to ten days.

(It is unlikely that Julius Caesar, for whom this operation was named, was actually delivered by cesarean section. Although it is known that the operation was performed in ancient times among both civilized and primitive peoples, it was almost always performed after the mother had died, and in hopes of saving the baby. Caesar's mother lived for many years after his birth. Cesarean section was definitely being performed on living women in the seventeenth century, but the operation at that time involved *removing* the uterus with the baby still inside and then sewing up the abdomen. The current practice of removing only the baby and leaving the uterus in place dates from 1882.)

Natural Childbirth

For as long as children have been being born, they have been born naturally. But because the birth of a child can be a painful experience, societies throughout history have developed numerous methods (rituals, prayers, potions, and medicines) to help ease the pain of the woman giving birth.

In Europe childbirth usually occured at home in familiar surroundings, and those who assisted were women (midwives) with special training and experience. Then about 300 years ago things began to change. Male physicians and surgeons began to replace midwives. Deliveries were moved from the home to lying-in hospitals in large cities. The forceps (invented about 1600) became popular as a tool for helping pull the infant from the womb. These and other changes were made as attempts to help women in labor, but many

women died of **childbirth (puerperal) fever** in the lying-in hospitals. The disease was spread by doctors who did not wash their hands after examining the pregnant women, so if one woman had the disease it would quickly spread through the ward. It was not until the mid-nineteenth century that Ignaz Semmelweis, a Hungarian physician, proved that the disease was contagious and instituted antiseptic practices to prevent it.

Chloroform anesthesia was introduced in the nineteenth century, and it became quite popular in England after Queen Victoria used it during the delivery of her eighth child in 1853. By the twentieth century even routine and uncomplicated deliveries were beginning to be treated as major surgical procedures. The woman was hospitalized, sterilized (in the antiseptic sense), anesthetized, and a variety of instruments were used in the delivery, which took place in a room resembling a surgical suite in appearance, facilities, and regulations (for example, fathers and other "nonparticipants" were excluded).

As childbirth became more and more mechanical, a growing number of people began to object. Some objected to the exclusion of the father, others to the domination of obstetrics by men (especially in the United States), and for some the most "unnatural" aspect of twentieth-century childbirth was the use of instruments and anesthetics.

The term "natural childbirth" was coined in 1932 by Grantly Dick-Read, an English physician. Dick-Read suggested that fear and the muscular tension it brings on are primarily responsible for the pain of childbirth. His still popular method of "natural childbirth" is described in his book *Childbirth without Fear*. It is based on the idea that fear can be eliminated through education about the birth process before delivery. A woman who is unafraid will be less tense, and if her muscles are relaxed she will be more likely to have a painless delivery.

A second type of "natural childbirth" originated in Russia but was popularized by Bernard Lamaze, a French physician. The Lamaze method is based on Pavlov's description of the conditioned reflex. Pavlov showed that many of our reflexive behaviors, including muscle contractions, are conditioned, or learned, responses. And many of these learned responses can be unlearned. The Lamaze method involves conditioning (teaching) the woman mentally to separate uterine contractions from the experience of pain by repeated reinforcement of the idea that such contractions are not painful. Certain exercises are also used to teach voluntary relaxation of the abdominal muscles. After having been successfully conditioned to experience uterine contractions without reflexive muscular contractions and pain, a woman may have a relaxed and painless delivery.

Another method of childbirth that has become popular in recent years was developed by French physician Frederick Leboyer. This method concentrates on protecting the infant from the pain and trauma of childbirth. In *Birth without Violence,* Leboyer describes what he believes to be the pain infants suffer being born and then goes on to describe a method of making birth less painful and shocking to the infant. It is a slow, quiet birth in which everything is done to protect the infant's delicate senses from shock. Lights are kept low, and unnecessary noises are avoided. When the infant's head appears the birth is eased along by the doctor's fingers under each of the infant's armpits. Supported so, the infant is gently settled onto the mother's abdomen. There, for several minutes, the child is allowed to adjust to its new environment while it continues to receive warmth and comfort from its mother as it did before birth. Instead of being held up and slapped (which helps the infant start breathing), the Leboyer method allows the child to lie quietly on its mother's abdomen with the umbilical cord still attached. The infant continues to receive oxygen from its mother in this way until it starts breathing on its own. Then the child is gently lowered into a warm bath where it will eventually open its eyes and begin to move its limbs freely. The result of such a nonviolent birth, according to Leboyer, is not a screaming, kicking, terrified infant, but a relaxed and even smiling child.

If a woman can give birth without surgical intervention or anesthesia, one might wonder why the birth need take place in a hospital. The primary medical justification for hospital delivery is the availability of backup personnel and equipment in the event of a sudden complication (for example, hemorrhaging). However, there is a growing interest in the United States in "alternative birth centers" (clinics that are less elaborate and expensive than hospitals) and in home deliveries. One reason for this interest is the rising costs of hospitalization. Another reason is the impersonal atmosphere of hospitals and restrictions that separate husbands from wives during childbirth and mothers from their babies in maternity wards. Increasingly, hospitals have been modifying their regulations to allow husbands to be present throughout labor and delivery and to allow "rooming-in," that is, keeping newborn babies in the same room with their mothers rather than in a separate nursery. This allows the mother to hold and feed her new baby when she wishes, rather than according to a fixed schedule.

The Leboyer method and other so-called methods of natural childbirth are becoming increasingly popular in the United States with expectant couples as well as with some obstetricians and in some hospitals. But the term "natural" does not mean that the more traditional type of hospital delivery is "unnatural." Many women and children are alive today thanks only to the extraordinary hospital care they received and to the techniques of modern obstetrics.

Multiple Births

The delivery of two or more infants is usually an event of great interest. Twins occur in 1 of 90 births in the United States, triplets in 1 of 9000, and quadruplets in about 1 of 500,000 births. Multiple births of more than four children are extremely rare (except, as mentioned, in connection with hormonal stimulation of ovulation). Because of their small sizes and usually premature delivery, the mortality rate among infants in a multiple birth is significantly higher than that of single births. Twins are born an average of twenty-two days before the usual expected date of delivery. Their mortality rate is two to three times that of single births.

There are two types of twins, identical and fraternal. Two out of three sets of twins are fraternal, developed from two eggs fertilized at the same time. Identical twins result from division of a single fertilized egg before implantation in the uterus. Identical twins usually share a placenta, and fraternal twins usually have separate placentas.

It is apparently biologically possible for twins to have different fathers. This phenomenon is called **superfecundation** and has been clearly documented in animal studies. Another bizarre occurence is **superfetation,** the fertilization and subsequent development of an egg when a fetus is already present in the uterus. There are a few such cases reported in the medical literature. In one instance, a woman gave birth to two normal children three months apart.

THE POSTPARTUM PERIOD

Three or four days after an uncomplicated delivery, a woman usually leaves the hospital—though the length of stay varies from place to place. With a first baby the first week at home may be a bit of turmoil for the new mother. She must cope with the needs of the baby (feeding, changing diapers, bathing) and the calls and visits of friends and relatives, and fatigue may be a major complaint along with a general "letdown" feeling.

About two-thirds of all women experience periods of sadness and crying some time during the first ten days after delivery. This phenomenon is known as the "postpartum blues." Doubts about their competence as mothers, fatigue, feelings of rejection or neglect by their husbands, and the drastic hormone changes that occur at this time are some of the factors involved in this syndrome.

Breast Feeding

Milk production (lactation) begins forty-eight to seventy-two hours after childbirth and "true milk" production is preceded by production of a yellowish substance called **co-lostrum,** which is rich in antibodies. Two pituitary hormones are involved in breast feeding: **prolactin** stimulates the production of milk by the mammary glands, and **oxytocin** causes the ejection of milk from the breast to the nipple. These hormones are produced in response to the stimulus provided by the sucking baby. So, if a woman does not breast feed or when she stops nursing, the production of prolactin and oxytocin, and therefore, lactation, ceases.

Along with the movement back to more natural child deliveries, breast feeding is currently becoming more popular in the United States than it was twenty years ago. Organizations such as the La Leche League provide information and encouragement to women who are interested in breast feeding. From the mother's standpoint, the experience of nursing can be emotionally satisfying, pleasurable, and even sensual. In fact, there is a positive relationship between nursing and sexual interest. From the standpoint of the baby there is no question of the superiority of human milk over cow's milk or commercial formulas. Human milk contains the ideal mixture of nutrients, it contains antibodies that protect the infant from certain diseases, it is free of bacteria, and it is always the right temperature.

In many countries cow's milk is neither hygienic nor cheap, and the water available for making formula may be contaminated. Nevertheless, the trend in many areas of the world has been to abandon the breast for the bottle. If this trend continues, the results could be nutritionally and economically disastrous. In the developing countries alone, the value of wasted human milk is estimated to exceed $750 million per year.

Resumption of Ovulation and Menstruation

There is a great deal of variation in the timing of the resumption of menstruation after childbirth. For about four weeks the woman will have a bloody vaginal discharge. Then one or two months later a woman who is not nursing may have a menstrual period. If the woman is nursing her child, her periods may not resume for as long as eighteen months, although five months is more usual. The first few periods may be irregular in length of flow, but women who have had painful periods before pregnancy often find that they suffer no such discomfort after childbirth.

Although menstruation may not occur while a woman is nursing, ovulation can occur during this time, and usually does before the first postpartum menstrual period. Consequently a woman can become pregnant without having had a period after the birth of her baby.

Sexual Activity during the Postpartum Period

Fatigue, physical discomfort, and the obstetrician's warnings play an important part in determining when a woman resumes sexual relations after childbirth. Doctors commonly advise women to refrain from intercourse for six weeks after delivery, but there is no reason why a healthy woman should not have vaginal intercourse as soon as the episiotomy or any tears of the perineum have healed and the vaginal discharge has ended. The only medical concern is the possibility of infection through the vagina.

PREGNANCY AND CHILDBIRTH IN OTHER SOCIETIES

Promitive people have developed various beliefs and practices in connection with pregnancy and childbirth. Many tribes believed that the fetus developed from a combination of male semen and menstrual blood. The Venda tribe of East Africa believed that "red elements" like muscle and blood were derived from the mother's menses (which ceased during pregnancy because the menstrual blood was being absorbed by the developing fetus). The "white elements"—like skin, bone, and nerves—were believed to develop from the father's semen.

Some societies imposed dietary restrictions on pregnant women, often from fear that the fetus might otherwise take on undesirable characteristics of food, plants, or animals. For example, if the mother ate rabbit, the child might have weak legs; if she ate trout, the child might exhibit characteristic quivering movements. In addition, Ashanti women were forbidden to look upon any deformed object or creature during pregnancy lest their children be born with similar deformities.

The majority of primitive tribes that have been studied prohibited sexual intercourse during the last month of pregnancy on the grounds that it might kill the child or cause premature delivery, an interesting observation considering the similar concern in modern societies and the absence so far of substantial medical evidence for or against this belief.

Abortions were performed in some primitive societies, particularly if the women were unmarried or pregnant as the result of adultery. Usually the fetuses were killed *in utero* by violent beating upon the abdomen, and this was followed by mechanical extraction of the fetus or spontaneous stillbirth.

Contrary to popular opinion, childbirth was not considered a routine and painless event by most primitive people. Among many tribes elaborate dietary and exercise regimens were practiced to prevent painful and difficult deliveries. Various rituals might be performed to insure easy delivery, and particular attention was paid to confession of sexual indiscretions at this time, for difficult deliveries were often attributed to violations of the tribal sexual codes.

Childbirth usually took place with the woman in a sitting or squatting position. Assistants were almost always present, usually older women designated as tribal midwives. Men were usually excluded from such scenes, though they might be assigned some rituals or tasks to perform away from the places where birth was taking place.

The placenta was almost always viewed as a potentially dangerous object and was carefully disposed of, usually by burying it in a special place. There was also usually a taboo on sexual intercourse for several weeks or more after delivery, another striking similarity to taboos in modern societies.

Deformed babies and multiple births were viewed with alarm in most primitive societies. Twins, triplets, and babies with congenital deformities were usually killed at birth. Twins were often believed to result from adultery or impregnation by an evil spirit. A more benign explanation was offered by the Kiwai tribesmen of New Guinea, who believed that a woman would give birth to twins if she ate bananas from a tree with two bunches!

SUMMARY

1. The moment when sperm and egg unite is the moment of conception. Each germ cells carries with it twenty-three chromosomes, and when they unite, they form one fertile human cell with forty-six chromosomes. This is the cell that will divide many times as it develops first into an embryo then into a fetus. However, before the egg and sperm can unite they must make difficult journeys through the reproductive systems.

2. Sperm are produced in the seminiferous tubules of the testes from cells called spermatogonia. These divide to produce spermatocytes, which in turn undergo meiosis to yield spermatids that have only twenty-three chromosomes, half with an X sex chromosome and half with a Y. Spermatids become mature sperm—each with a head, middlepiece, and long tail that enables it to swim. If sperm are not ejaculated within thirty to sixty days, they die and are replaced by new ones.

3. Billions of sperm are ejaculated by most men during their lifetimes, but few, if any, ever fertilize an egg. If they are deposited in the vagina, they will swim toward the uterus but must overcome the force of gravity as well as acidic conditions and the flow of fluids away from the uterus. If sperm succeed in reaching the fallopian tube, they have to swim against the current produced by the cilia that line it. Even then they may be in the wrong tube because women usually only ovulate from one ovary at a time. Of several hundred million sperm in an ejaculation only about two thousand reach the correct fallopian tube, and only one unites with the egg.

4. Each woman has about 400,000 immature ova at birth, and it is believed that no new ones are produced. Immature eggs undergo two divisions. The original cell, a primary oocyte, undergoes a mitotic division, yielding a secondary oocyte and a polar body. The second division of the oocyte is meiotic (reduction), yielding an egg with twenty-three chromosomes (including an X sex chromosome) and another polar body (which disintegrates). The eggs are released from the ovary when the graafian follicle that surrounds them fills with fluid and bursts. Once out of the ovary, the egg passes to the fallopian tube where it is propelled toward the uterus by the cilia and possibly by contractions of the walls of the tube. If fertilization does not occur during this journey, the egg disintegrates.

5. Fertilization occurs when sperm and egg meet and combine their chromosomes. Once a sperm enters the egg no other sperm can penetrate it. If the sperm carries an X sex chromosome the resulting child will be female; if it carries a Y, a male. Attempts to predetermine the sex of a child have not been overwhelmingly successful, but there are methods of finding out the sex of the fetus during pregnancy. One method is amniocentesis. It is a process by which amniotic fluid that surrounds the fetus is withdrawn from the womb and analyzed for fetal sex chromosomes as well as for chromosomal abnormalities.

6. If fertilization does occur, the new cell begins to divide as it moves down the fallopian tube. It becomes a round morula, then a spherical blastocyst before it becomes implanted in the lining of the uterus between the fifth and seventh day after ovulation. The primary reasons why fertilization does not occur are low sperm count in the male and failure to ovulate by the woman. In many cases, physical examination of both male and female can detect the cause of infertility and treat it. Artificial insemination is one method of helping men with low sperm counts. Drugs and hormone treatments can sometimes stimulate women to ovulate.

7. Pregnancy lasts for approximately 266 days, or about nine months. The first sign that a woman is pregnant is usually a missed period. Other signs include enlargement and tenderness of the breasts, morning sickness, more frequent urination, and fatigue. If a woman is experiencing the symptoms and wants confirmation of her pregnancy, there are several methods available. One is a physical examination of the cervix that can detect pregnancy as early as the sixth week (Hegar's sign). In addition, there are a number of laboratory tests that detect a hormone (HCG) present only in pregnant women. Some of these tests are fairly accurate as early as two to four weeks after conception.

8. During the first trimester (three months) of pregnancy the placenta develops and grows into an organ that provides the fetus with oxygen and nutrients as well as removes waste products. It also provides hormones necessary for maintaining pregnancy. Certain drugs (such as heroin and alcohol) can travel through the placenta and harm the fetus, especially during the first trimester. Certain diseases (rubella, Rh incompatibility) can also do great harm, but there are methods of preventing or treating these problems.

9. During the first trimester the blastocyst develops into an easily recognizable, if small, human fetus. By the twelfth week of pregnancy it is nearly 3 or 4 inches (6.6 or 10.2 centimeters) long and weighs about 20–30 grams (one ounce or less). A fetal heartbeat can be detected and ultrasonic equipment can be used to photograph the fetal skeleton. The major complication during the first trimester is miscarriage, or spontaneous abortion, which occurs in about 10 to 15 percent of all pregnancies. Studies have shown no decrease in sexual activity during this period, and there is no medical reason to restrict intercourse in the first trimester.

10.   The second trimester is usually considered the most peaceful and pleasant time of pregnancy. The fetus continues to grow and can be felt moving and kicking by the fifth month. Most women can continue to be active, sexually and otherwise, during this stage. During the third trimester the size and activity of the fetus becomes even more obvious, and some women have to guard against gaining too much weight. A major complication during the third trimester is prematurity. Infants born weighing less than 2500 grams (5.5 pounds) are considered premature, and the smaller they are, the less likely they are to survive. Another complication is breech delivery, which can occur if the infant is not in the head-down position at the time of delivery. At full term the average infant weighs 7.5 pounds (3.4 kilograms) and is 20 inches (50.8 centimeters) long. About 99 percent of all full-term babies born live in the United States survive.

11.   Labor occurs in three stages after the fetus has dropped to a lower position in the abdomen and after the cervix has begun to ripen, or soften. Labor begins with irregular contractions about fifteen or twenty minutes apart. This first stage lasts about fifteen hours with the first pregnancy (and about eight hours in later deliveries). By the end of the first stage the cervix is completely dilated and contractions are coming regularly at four- or five-minute intervals. The second stage may last for a few minutes or a few hours. It ends with the delivery of the baby. During the third stage the placenta and fetal membranes are expelled as afterbirth and the episiotomy (if there has been one) or any tears of the perineum are sewn up. In from 10 to 20 percent of births a cesarean section may be necessary. In this operation the infant is removed from the womb through an incision in the abdomen and the womb.

12.   In recent years there has been a trend toward more ''natural'' deliveries in which certain aspects of the typical hospital delivery are avoided, especially anesthesia that can affect the fetus and instruments like forceps. Natural childbirth methods attempt to teach women not to fear birth pains in the hope that the more relaxed a woman is, the easier her delivery will be. The Lamaze method uses conditioning techniques to teach women to dissociate pain from muscular contractions. The Leboyer method concentrates on avoiding as much as possible the pain an infant endures during the birth process.

13.   If there have been no complications, women usually leave the hospital within three or four days of giving birth. Milk production begins two or three days after childbirth and is maintained by hormones that are produced in response to stimulation of the breast by the sucking infant. Currently in the United States there is a movement back to breast feeding, which is superior to bottle feeding in many ways. Menstruation usually resumes about five months after delivery, but may begin as early as two months or as late as eighteen months if the woman is nursing. Even though she may not have had a period, a nursing mother can become pregnant is she has ovulated. The recommended time for resumption of sexual activity is usually six weeks, but there is no medical reason why a healthy woman should not have sexual intercourse as soon as the vaginal flow (which lasts for about four weeks after delivery) has ceased.

SUGGESTED READING

Nilsson, L. *A Child Is Born,* rev. ed. New York: Delacorte, 1977.
   A book about pregnancy which contains an incredible collection of black and white and color photographs of embryos and fetuses at various stages of development.

Guttmacher, A. F., M.D. *Pregnancy, Birth and Family Planning.* New York: New American Library, 1973.
   This book, available in paperback, is filled with practical information about problems and questions which arise in relation to pregnancy and childbirth. Written by one of the most noted obstetricians in the country.

The Boston Women's Health Collective. *Our Bodies, Ourselves,* 2nd ed. New York: Simon & Schuster, 1976.
   A well-written book by women with a feminist orientation. Contains much useful information about childbearing as well as information about health, nutrition, and birth control.

Raphael, D. *The Tender Gift: Breastfeeding,* New York: Schocken Books, 1976.
   An excellent book about the pleasures and problems of mothers with nursing infants. Includes interesting cross-cultural information and a foreword by Margaret Mead.

Pryor, K. *Nursing Your Baby,* new rev. ed. New York: Pocketbooks, 1973.
   This paperback book is a good practical guide to breastfeeding. It is recommended by La Leche League.

chapter 6 Contraception

Did You Know That . . .

after the Pill was introduced as a contraceptive method it became the most rapidly and widely accepted drug since penicillin?

for centuries Arab camel drivers have known that it is possible to keep a camel from getting pregnant by placing a small round stone in the uterus of the camel?

douching is one of the *least* effective methods of birth control because sperm can be on their way up the cervical canal and out of reach of the douche within moments of ejaculation?

a woman's body temperature goes up slightly at the time of ovulation?

vasectomy, the operation that sterilizes males, can be performed in a doctor's office in about fifteen minutes?

INTRODUCTION

As soon as it was realized that semen is in some way responsible for pregnancy, people probably began trying to avoid pregnancy by removing the semen from the vagina after intercourse. Some of the oldest documents to mention contraception (voluntary prevention of conception) date back nearly four thousand years to ancient Egypt. One method called for douching, or washing, the vagina after intercourse with a mixture of wine, garlic, and fennel. Other societies came up with even more complex methods. Soranus, a second-century Greek physician, recommended that:

the woman ought, in the moment during coitus when the man ejaculated his sperm, to hold her breath, draw her body back a little so that the semen cannot penetrate into the os uteri, then immediately get up and sit down with bent knees, and, in this position, provoke sneezes. She should then wipe out the vagina carefully or drink cold water in addition. (Himes, N. *Medical History of Contraception.* New York: Schocken Books, 1970)

Al-Razi, a Persian physician, suggested a similar procedure eight hundred years later: "First, immediately after ejaculation, let the two come apart and let the woman arise roughly, sneeze and blow her nose several times, and call out in a loud voice. She should jump violently backward seven to nine times." Seven and nine were magical numbers. Jumping backward was supposed to dislodge semen, and jumping forward was supposed to assure pregnancy.

Reliance on magic and on an incomplete knowledge of human physiology was not very effective in preventing pregnancy. In fact, until very recently there was only one sure method of avoiding pregnancy—avoiding intercourse. Today there are many methods of contraception, some extremely effective and a few that put the burden of contraception on the male, instead of on the female as has been the case traditionally.

Why would anyone want to prevent conception? The reasons are numerous and obvious in many instances. They include preventing the birth of a deformed or seriously ill child, preventing unwanted children, controlling population, avoiding the problems associated with pregnancy, and preserving the health of the woman (in the United States the death rate due to childbirth complications is approximately 14 deaths per 100,000 live births). In addition, there are numerous moral arguments, both for and against the use of **contraceptives** (*see* Chapter 12). But no matter what the arguments, contraception has already become a major force in our society and is influencing the history of the human race by its effect on population. In 1975, almost 80 percent of the married couples in the United States were using some method of contraception. In this chapter we will discuss the most-often-used methods of birth control as well as research trends that will affect the future of contraception.

THE PILL

No drug since penicillin has been as rapidly and as widely accepted as **the Pill,** the popular name for a number of commonly used oral contraceptives. The Pill was first put on the market in 1960, and by 1974, 50 million women around the world were using it.

History

Early in this century researchers discovered that ovulation does not occur during the luteal, or postovulatory, phase of the menstrual cycle (*see* Chapter 4) or during pregnancy. It was also discovered that those are the times at which the levels of progesterone (*see* Chapter 5) are highest. The connection seemed obvious—progesterone prevents ovulation. This conclusion was tested after progesterone was isolated and purified in the laboratory in 1934. When administered to rabbits, progesterone was shown to inhibit ovulation and to prevent pregnancy. Estrogen, another female sex hormone, was chemically isolated at about the same time, and by 1940 it was being used to treat certain menstrual disorders.

The next step in the development of an oral contraceptive was taken in 1954 when Carl Djerassi succeeded in synthesizing in the laboratory a group of steroid chemicals called **progestogens.** The term comes from the word "gestation" and refers to the ability of these synthetic compounds to bring about "pseudopregnancy," or fake pregnancy. The progestogens produce certain changes in the lining of the uterus (endometrium) and elsewhere in the reproductive system that are similar to changes seen during pregnancy. Once these changes have taken place a woman usually will not ovulate and cannot get pregnant. The synthetic compounds were found to be much stronger than natural hormones and could therefore be used in much smaller doses to prevent pregnancy.

The first large-scale test of a contraceptive pill for humans was undertaken in San Juan, Puerto Rico, in 1956 by Gregory Pincus (sometimes called "the father of the Pill"). The drug was highly effective in these first tests, and within a few years the era of "the Pill" had arrived.

Effects

Most contraceptive pills contain synthetic compounds resembling progesterone and estrogen. Studies of animals and humans have shown that progestogens tend to inhibit secretion of LH by the pituitary, while synthetic estrogens inhibit secretion of FSH. Both LH and FSH are essential to ovulation (*see* Chapter 4), and the Pill is believed to work primarily by preventing ovulation. The only sure way to find out if this is the case is by microscopic examination of the ovaries and fallopian tubes of a woman who has been taking the Pill. Such observations have been made during hysterectomies (surgical removal of

the uterus), and so far no eggs have been found in the tubes of women using the Pill. It is still possible, however, that the woman may have ovulated earlier in her period or that she would have done so later.

Even if the Pill does not prevent ovulation, it brings about other changes that can prevent pregnancy. There is some evidence, for instance, that the Pill has a direct effect on the ovarian follicles and prevents maturation of the ova. It is also possible that the Pill increases the rate at which the egg travels to the uterus, causing it to arrive there before it is sufficiently mature or before the lining of the uterus is ready to receive it.

A delicate balance of progesterone and estrogen is necessary if the lining of the uterus is to be receptive to implantation of the egg. However, changes in the endometrium have been seen in women taking the Pill, and these changes may contribute to temporary infertility. In addition, the cervical mucus is changed by the Pill (it becomes thicker and has a more acidic pH), and this may act as a barrier to the sperm on its way to the uterus.

Usage

The contraceptive pills commonly available (with a physician's prescription) contain a mixture of synthetic progestogens and estrogen compounds. Each pill contains from 0.5 to 10.0 milligrams of the progestogen (depending on the specific compound used and on the manufacturer) and a much smaller amount of estrogen, from 0.02 to 0.15 milligrams per pill. These pills are usually taken for twenty or twenty-one days of the cycle, beginning on the fifth day after the start of menstruation. If the pills are not begun until the sixth day, they are still effective, but if they are not started by the seventh or eighth day, there is a risk of failure.

After three weeks the pills are stopped. "Withdrawal bleeding" (considered by some not to be "true" menstruation because ovulation presumably has not occurred) usually begins three to four days after pill taking has stopped. The first day of withdrawal bleeding is considered the first day of the next cycle, and the pills are resumed on the fifth day thereafter. The most common brand names for the Pill are *Enovid, Ortho-Novum, Ovulen, Provest,* and *Norinyl.*

(Until 1976, a "sequential" pill was also marketed. These pills were taken on a twenty-day cycle, but the first fifteen pills contained only estrogen; the remaining five contained estrogen and progesterone. This was supposed to be more like the normal sequence of hormonal events during the menstrual cycle, but the sequential pills had several serious drawbacks. They were less effective and were possibly associated with a risk of blood clotting and cancer. When this was discovered, the sequential pills were removed from the market.)

In recent years the trend has been toward smaller doses of progestogen and estrogen in order to reduce side effects. The early birth-control pills contained 10.0 milligrams of progestogen, but manufacturers have since reduced this amount first to 5.0 milligrams, then to 2.5 or 1.0 milligrams. The first so-called mini-pill, containing only 0.35 milligrams of progestogen and no estrogen, came out in 1973. Its effectiveness is only slightly less than that of the other pills.

In order to make pill use less complicated, some manufacturers now recommend a 21:7 pill program. The pills are the same, but the woman takes twenty-one pills, then stops for seven days, then repeats the series again, regardless of when menstruation begins. The advantage of this is that the woman always starts taking pills on the same day of the week. Another way to help a woman remember to take the Pill is to have her take one every day—twenty-one hormone pills followed by seven placebo (inactive) pills packaged in such a way as to prevent her from taking the wrong pill on any given day.

Because most brands of birth-control pills are pretty much alike, manufacturers have used packaging as a selling point. Some pills come in plastic cases rather than in paper containers. Some packages have built-in calendars or other reminders; and some have dispensers indicating which pill is to be taken each day by date.

Effectiveness

There is no question that birth-control pills, when properly used, are the most effective contraceptive measure available today except for surgical sterilization. Taken as directed they are 100 percent effective in preventing pregnancy by the second month of usage. Effectiveness is slightly less than 100 percent during the first month. If a woman does become pregnant while using the Pill, it is probably because she failed to take it regularly. Forgetting one pill is not usually significant, provided that the woman takes two the next day, but there is a fair risk of failure if pills are skipped for two days or more. In order to minimize the risk of pregnancy in such cases, a woman who has missed two or more pills should rely on another form of contraception (such as condoms) for the remainder of the cycle.

Side Effects

The users of oral contraceptives are probably one of the largest and most closely-watched groups in the history of medical science. The reason for such close scrutiny is the large number of reports of side effects and possible side effects. The most common complaints of users of the Pill are nausea, weight gain, headaches, and vaginal discharge.

Nausea among users of the Pill is related to estrogen, and pills with smaller amounts of estrogen (or none at all) are sometimes recommended if the nausea persists. In many cases, however, nausea and other side effects diminish and then disappear after two or three months.

Weight gains occur in from 5 to 25 percent of users of the Pill, with high-dosage pills usually causing the greatest weight gains. Most weight gain is caused by the accumulation of fat, especially in the breasts and thighs. This weight gain occurs mainly during the first month of pill use and is related to increased appetite (similar to the increased appetite during pregnancy). Additional weight gain may be due to fluid retention caused by progestogens. Drugs (diuretics) can sometimes control this type of weight gain, or the woman can switch to a different birth-control preparation.

It is not clear why headaches are more common among users of the Pill, but there may be a connection with some of the known physiological side effects of the Pill: increased blood pressure, fluid retention, and changes in thyroid, adrenal, and blood-sugar control mechanisms.

The increased vaginal discharge and susceptibility to vaginal infections experienced by some women using the Pill are likely to be related to prolonged progesterone therapy, rather than to estrogens. Progesterone is known to change the chemical composition of cervical secretions and the composition of vaginal flora (the harmless microorganisms that usually inhabit the vagina). These changes make the vagina less resistant to fungus infections (*see* Chapter 11).

Breakthrough bleeding or minor "spotting" experienced while taking birth-control pills can usually be remedied by switching to a different prescription.

Acne sometimes improves with oral contraceptives, but coloration of the face (the so-called mask of pregnancy) and eczema can be undesirable side effects of prolonged pill usage.

Less-common side effects of the Pill include tenderness of the breasts, nervousness, depression, changes in sex drive, menstrual irregularities, and in some cases a general feeling of ill health.

Although the Pill is known to be responsible for certain side effects, there are indications that some of the side effects blamed on the Pill may be due to psychological rather than to physiological factors. In one study, for instance, the frequency of such complaints as dizziness, headache, nervousness, and depression was essentially the same for IUD users as for oral contraceptive users. In another study, women who thought they were receiving oral contraceptives but who were actually receiving placebos (inactive pills) reported a higher incidence of side effects, including decreased libido or sexual drive. And in a third study of women using oral contraceptives, the researcher changed the color of the pills every

six months and found a change in libido with each new pill color. Libido would gradually return to the previous level only to drop again with each color change.

Certain beneficial side effects of the Pill have also been found and have led to their prescription even when contraception is not the major goal. For example, the Pill can help relieve premenstrual tension and eliminate menstrual irregularity and pain, as well as other menstrual disorders. Pill use has also been linked with decreased incidence of ovarian cysts. In addition, some women report a general sense of well-being, as well as increased pleasure in sexual intercourse while using the Pill. This last effect is probably partially due to elimination of the fear of unwanted pregnancy. There is no evidence that fertility is either increased or decreased in healthy women who have taken the Pill for several years and then stopped.

When Not To Use the Pill

Recent research has shown that the Pill can have serious side effects that, while rare, can be fatal. Large-scale studies clearly indicate that there is a small, though statistically significant, increase in the incidence of blood clotting with subsequent complications in women who take the Pill. A blood clot (*thrombus*) may, for instance, form in one of the deep veins of the leg in association with a local inflammation (*thrombophlebitis*). The clot may then break loose (as an *embolus*) and travel toward the lungs, where it may block a major blood vessel (as a *pulmonary embolus*). The result can be fatal. There is also a slightly greater chance of a blood clot in the brain (*thrombotic stroke*) among users of the Pill. The risk of death from blood clots is between 1.5 and 4 per 100,000 users versus 0.4 per 100,000 among nonusers. The risk is greater with increasing age. Women with histories of difficulties with blood clots are advised not to use contraceptive pills. However, it should also be noted that the incidence of deaths associated with pregnancy and labor is about eighteen times greater than that associated with thromboembolic disease in users of the Pill.

So serious are some of the Pill's side effects that the Federal Food and Drug Administration now requires that each prescription for oral contraceptives contain a leaflet that describes the possible side effects as well as be labeled with a warning about smoking.

The warning about smoking is directed particularly at women 35 years of age and older. It is based on studies showing an increased risk of heart attack and other circulatory problems, such as stroke, for women who smoke while using oral contraceptives. Healthy women who do not smoke but who do use oral contraceptives double the risk of suffering a heart attack, compared with women who do not take the Pill. However, users of the Pill who also smoke, especially if they smoke fifteen or more cigarettes a day, are three times more likely to die of a heart attack or of other circulatory disease than are users of the Pill who do not smoke, and are ten times more likely to die of a heart attack or circulatory disease than are women who neither smoke nor use oral contraceptives. The risk of heart attack for women taking the Pill increases with the amount of smoking and with age, and is higher in women with other conditions that may lead to heart attack, such as high blood pressure, high serum cholesterol levels, obesity, and diabetes.

In addition to the warning about smoking, the leaflet that now comes with each prescription of contraceptive pills points out several other possible dangers associated with the Pill and makes the appropriate warnings:

Women who have had blood clotting disorders, cancer of the breast or sex organs, unexplained vaginal bleeding, a stroke, heart attack, or angina pectoris, or who suspect they may be pregnant should not take oral contraceptives.

Women with scanty or irregular periods (conditions that should be determined by a physician) are strongly advised to use another method of contraception, because if they use oral contraceptives they may have difficulty becoming pregnant or may fail to have menstrual periods after discontinuing the Pill.

Possibly fatal (though rare) side effects include blood clots in the legs, lungs, brain, heart or other organs, cerebral hemorrhage, liver tumors that may rupture and cause severe bleeding, birth defects (if the Pill is taken during pregnancy), high blood pressure, stroke, and gallbladder disease.

Estrogen, an ingredient in many oral contraceptives, causes cancer in certain animals and it may therefore also cause cancer in humans, though studies of women using the currently marketed pill do not confirm this. There is, however, evidence that estrogen use may increase the risk of cancer of the uterine lining in postmenopausal women (*see* Chapter 11).

Women who wish to become pregnant should stop using oral contraceptives and use a different method of birth control for a few months before attempting to become pregnant. This will help minimize the risk of birth defects associated with the use of sex hormones during pregnancy.

A woman should consult her physician before resuming use of the Pill after childbirth, especially if she intends to breast feed the baby, because hormones in the Pill may be transferred to the infant through the mother's milk or may decrease the flow of milk.

The brochure that comes with oral contraceptives concludes: "Oral contraceptives are the most effective method, except sterilization, for preventing pregnancy. Other methods, when used conscientiously, are also very effective and have fewer risks. The serious risks of oral contraceptives are uncommon [rare] and 'the Pill' is a very convenient method of preventing pregnancy."

INTRAUTERINE DEVICES

Another method of contraception that has proved to be highly effective is the **intrauterine device,** or **IUD.** Such devices have had a long history. Ancient Greek writings mention IUDs, and for centuries Arab camel drivers have used IUDs to keep their camels from becoming pregnant on long journeys. The camel drivers inserted a round stone in the uterus of each camel before a journey, and this practice is still used in some parts of the world.

Intrauterine devices for women have gone

in and out of favor several times during the late nineteenth and twentieth centuries. In 1930, E. Gräfenberg, a German physician, used a ring of coiled silver wire as an IUD. He inserted coils in 600 women and reported a failure rate of only 1.6 percent. A number of gynecologists at the time charged that the IUDs might lead to serious infection of the pelvic organs, and the devices were abandoned until 1959. In that year W. Oppenheimer, an Israeli who had worked with Gräfenberg, and A. Ishihama, a Japanese physician, published promising reports. Oppenheimer had used the Gräfenberg device in 1500 women over a period of thirty years with no serious complications and a failure rate of only 2.4 percent. Ishihama reported on the use of a ring developed by another Japanese physician, T. Ota, that had been used in 20,000 women with a failure rate of 2.3 percent and no complications. Ota was the first to use plastic instead of metal in an IUD. These two reports triggered a new enthusiasm for IUDs and within ten years nearly eight million were in use throughout the world.

Effects

IUDs, unlike oral contraceptives, do not change pituitary or sex-hormone secretions. Examinations of the ovaries and fallopian tubes of woman fitted with IUDs show these organs to be unaffected. The tissues and secretions of the cervix and vagina also appear to be normal, and eggs and sperm have been found in the tubes of women with IUDs. Except for temporary inflammation of the uterus for a few days after insertion, IUDs appear to cause no physiological changes—other than the prevention of pregnancy.

How do IUDs prevent pregnancy in humans? The answer is unknown at present, but it is likely that the devices interfere in some way with the implantation of the egg in the uterus.

Types of IUDs

IUDs come in a variety of shapes, sizes, and materials (*see* Figure 6.1). A metal ring

was the first widely used device, but the cervix must be dilated mechanically in order for the ring to be inserted. The same is true of the Ota ring, which is made of plastic and has been widely used in Japan and Taiwan. The Zipper ring, however, is made from coils of nylon thread and can be inserted through the cervix without prior mechanical dilation.

Most IUDs currently in use are made of flexible plastic. They can be straightened out for insertion, and once inside the womb they return to their original shape. The first such device was the Margulies spiral, introduced in 1959, which has the shape of a coil with a beaded tail.

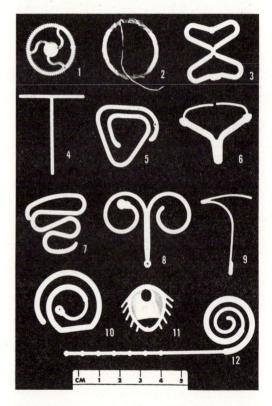

Figure 6.1 Common intrauterine devices: 1. Ota ring, 2. Zipper ring, 3. Birnberg bow, 4. "T" device, 5. Ahmed, 6. K.S. Wing, 7. Lippes Loop, 8. Saf-T-Coil, 9. Copper 7, 10. New Margulies spiral, 11. Dalkon Shield, and 12. Gynecoil.

From Rudel, Kincl, and Henz, *Birth Control: Contraception and Abortion,* Figure 4.1 (New York: The Macmillan Company, 1973), p. 158. Copyright © 1973 by Macmillan Publishing Co., Inc.

Shortly after the introduction of the Margulies spiral several other flexible devices — including the bow, the double spiral, and a stainless-steel spring — were introduced. These devices all have nylon threads that hang down through the cervical opening into the vagina, enabling the wearer to check that the device is in place. The threads usually do not interfere with intercourse. The newer plastic devices also contain small amounts of barium in the plastic so that they can be seen in X rays. One of the most popular of these flexible devices is the Lippes Loop. It comes in four sizes, ranging from 22.5 millimeters (0.9 inches) in diameter (for women who have not had children) to 30 millimeters (1.2 inches), with the larger sizes being the most effective. The loop is inserted by a physician, who straightens it and pushes it into the uterus through a plastic tube that is inserted in the cervical opening (*see* Figure 6.2). The loop returns to its original shape once inside the uterus.

Another relatively new device, the Copper 7, contains a small amount of copper that slowly dissolves in the uterus. (The amount of copper that dissolves daily is less than the amount recommended for a balanced diet and is therefore safe.) The Copper 7 is said to offer a higher rate of contraceptive protection than other IUDs, although how it does so is unknown. This device must be replaced every three years.

Finally, there is a recently developed IUD that contains progesterone, which is released at a slow, constant rate over a nine-month period. The small amount of progesterone (50–100 micrograms per day) does not inhibit ovulation but alters the lining of the uterus in a way that prevents implantation.

Effectiveness

Of every hundred women using IUDs, approximately two will become pregnant during the first year of use, and the failure rate tends to decline after the first year. In other words, IUDs are highly effective in preventing pregnancy. One reason they are usually more effective than some other contraceptive methods is that there is nothing either partner must remember to do to make it effective (although the woman must check periodically to see that the device has not been expelled).

Side Effects

The two most common side effects associated with IUDs are irregular bleeding and pelvic pain — seen in from 10 to 20 percent of the woman using IUDs. However, as with most of the minor side effects associated with the Pill, these problems tend to disappear after the first two or three months of use. Other side effects include bleeding, or "spotting," during the menstrual cycle and menstrual periods that may be heavier than usual after insertion of the IUD. Uterine cramps or general pelvic pain may also occur, and one study of 16,734 women reported that 833 had their IUDs removed for these reasons.

There are two rare but more serious complications, both related to insertion of the IUD: infection and perforation of the uterus. In the study previously mentioned, infection of the pelvic organs (uterus and tubes) was seen in 171 women. Hospital records showed, however, that half of these women had previous histories of such infections. Because insertion of an IUD seems to make such conditions worse, women who have recently (within the past few months) suffered pelvic infections are generally advised against using IUDs. If an IUD is inserted under antiseptic conditions and if a woman has no history of infection, there is very little chance of infection.

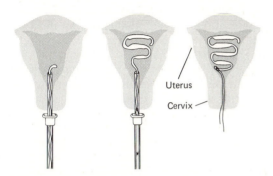

Uterus

Cervix

Figure 6.2 Insertion of the Lippes Loop.
Courtesy of Ortho Pharmaceutical Corporation.

Perforation of the uterus during IUD insertion is very rare (about 1 in 10,000), but it can be fatal. A 1967 survey of all gynecologists in the United States found four cases in which death appeared to have been caused by insertion of an IUD. Six other deaths were reported in which the relationship was unclear.

Spontaneous expulsion of IUDs can also be a problem, especially during the first year of use and especially with the smaller IUDs. In 1973 the FDA reported an overall expulsion rate of 10 percent during the first year after insertion. Expulsion occurs most often in younger women and in women who have had no children and is more likely to occur during menstruation. When expelled into the vagina, IUDs are sometimes discarded with tampons or sanitary napkins without the woman realizing it has been expelled. The various "tails" on IUDs enable women to check and verify that they are still in place.

There is no evidence so far that an IUD increases the risk of cancer of the cervix or uterus. Plastics of the type commonly used in IUDs have also been used extensively by surgeons for prosthetic devices in various parts of the body and have never been known to cause cancer.

Subsequent Fertility

IUDs appear to have no effect on subsequent fertility and can be easily removed when a woman wishes to become pregnant. Studies have shown that after removal of IUDs 60 percent of sexually active women become pregnant within three months and 90 percent within one year. These figures are similar to those for women who have never used any form of contraception.

OTHER METHODS

Since the 1960s the Pill and the IUD have been, by far, the most popular methods of contraception in the United States, but there are a number of other methods that are commonly used. Primarily because of the risks associated with the Pill and the IUD, it appears that increasing numbers of couples are deciding to use one or more of these birth-control methods. Some are highly effective, others almost ineffective.

The Diaphragm

One contraceptive method that has been staging a comeback in recent years is the **diaphragm,** a device designed to cover the cervix. The diaphragm is the modern equivalent of an old idea. The history of contraception includes many examples of women inserting gums, leaves, fruits, seed pods, sponges, and similar items into their vaginas in attempts to block the sperm. The women of Sumatra, for example, molded opium into a cuplike shape and inserted it into the vagina. The women of Hungary used beeswax melted into round disks. The modern diaphragm was invented by a German physician in 1882.

The principle of the diaphragm is straightforward. A thin rubber dome attached to a flexible, rubber-covered metal ring is inserted in the vagina and positioned over the cervix to prevent sperm from entering the cervical canal (*see* Figure 6.3). For added protection the inner surface of the diaphragm (the surface in contact with the cervix) and the rim are coated before insertion with a contraceptive jelly that destroys sperm.

Diaphragms are usually about 3 inches (7.6 centimeters) in diameter, but they come in various sizes and must be individually fitted. Following the birth of a child, an abortion, a change in weight of 10 or more pounds (4.5 or more kilograms), or any other circumstances that may have changed the size and shape of the vaginal canal, a woman must be refitted. When correctly fitted, the diaphragm is not uncomfortable.

If used with jelly, the diaphragm must be inserted no more than six hours before intercourse in order for the jelly to be effective. Thus, unless a woman knows in advance that she is going to have intercourse on a particular occasion she may have to stop and insert the diaphragm in the midst of lovemaking or risk pregnancy. During menstruation it is unlikely that a woman will become pregnant. Nevertheless, some women do use the dia-

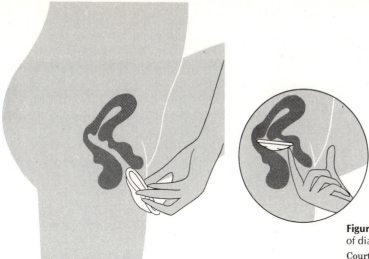

Figure 6.3 Insertion and placement of diaphragm.

Courtesy of Ortho Pharmaceutical Corporation.

phragm during menstruation to keep the lower portion of the vagina free of blood and to protect against the rare possibility of pregnancy.

When the diaphragm has been properly inserted, neither partner is aware of its presence during intercourse. After intercourse, the diaphragm should be left in place for at least six hours and can be left in for as long as sixteen hours. It should then be removed and washed, and additional jelly should be applied before reinsertion.

Effectiveness

In theory, the diaphragm when used with contraceptive jelly should be highly effective. This is particularly true if the device is unflawed, perfectly fitted, and used correctly during every act of intercourse. In practice, the failure rate for the diaphragm varies between 5 and 20 percent. Aside from failure to use the diaphragm during intercourse, the reasons for failure include improper insertion, wrong size, and displacement during coitus. Even if the diaphragm is in place before intercourse, it may have slipped by the time of ejaculation. Studies by Masters and his colleagues have also shown that the diaphragm can become dislodged during vigorous intercourse. This is especially true with multiple

withdrawals of the penis and when the woman is on top during intercourse.

The diaphragm is most effective when certain guidelines are followed:

The diaphragm must be inserted each time a woman has sexual intercourse, even during her period. Because ovulation can occur at irregular times during the cycle, a woman should not rely on the rhythm method to supplement use of the diaphragm.

The diaphragm can be inserted many hours before sexual intercourse; however, if a woman has intercourse more than six hours after insertion of the diaphragm she should insert an applicator full of spermicidal jelly. Additional cream or jelly should be inserted if intercourse is to be repeated before the diaphragm is to be removed.

The diaphragm should be refitted after childbirth and also one year after the start of intercourse on a regular basis.

Related Devices

Cervical caps are devices similar to diaphragms. Such caps have been popular in Europe for a long time but have not been widely used in the United States. The most popular version in Europe is shaped like a large thimble with a raised rim and is made of either rubber, plastic, or metal. It fits over the cervix in the same way that a thimble fits over the finger (*see* Figure 6.4). Cervical caps are more difficult to insert than diaphragms and not all women can wear them because of the sizes and shapes of their cervixes, but once in place the cap can be left in for days or weeks. The failure rate for cervical caps is about 8 percent.

Spermicides

Contraceptive jellies, like those used with diaphragms, are among several **spermicidal,** or sperm-killing, **substances** available. Various foams, creams, jellies, and vaginal suppositories that kill sperm on contact are available in drugstores without a prescription and are simple to use. A plastic applicator is usually supplied for inserting the substance in the vagina. Vaginal foam, actually a cream packaged in an aerosol can, provides the best distribution of the spermicide in the vagina. Of the currently available products, Delfen and Emko are among the best. Vaginal foams

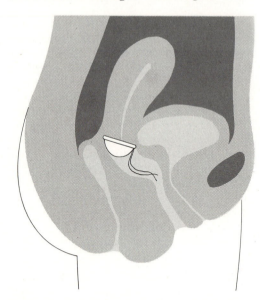

Figure 6.4   A cervical cap in position.

From *International Planned Parenthood Federation Medical Handbook,* p. 53. Reprinted by permission of the International Planned Parenthood Federation, 18–20 Lower Regent Street, London SW1, England.

are most effective when the following directions are followed:

Insert a *full* applicator of foam as soon before intercourse as possible, but no longer than fifteen minutes before intercourse.

Insert the spermicide while lying down and do not get up prior to intercourse.

Do not douche for at least eight hours after intercourse.

Use the preparation with every act of intercourse.

Use the preparation with a condom for a very safe method of contraception.

The least effective spermicides are the foaming vaginal tablets and suppositories that get distributed more unevenly in the vagina and depend partly on mixing with natural lubricants and dispersion during the movements of intercourse. If ejaculation occurs before sufficient lubrication, mixing, and dispersion have occurred, the spermicide will be of little benefit. Another drawback is that the foam tablets often cause temporary irritation of the vagina. The failure rates for foams, creams, and jellies is close to 20 percent, for tablets and suppositories closer to 30 percent, but with growing concern over the safety of oral contraceptives and IUDs, foams, jellies, and suppositories are assuming an increasingly important role in family planning. One contraceptive suppository, Encare Oval, appears to be quite effective when used consistently according to directions.

Douching

One of the oldest and *least* effective methods of contraception is **douching,** washing the sperm out of the vagina immediately after intercourse. This method is simple, requires only plain water, a douche bag, or a bidet (a basin-like fixture that makes douching easier). Various commercial products are available for douching, and vinegar, lemon juice, soap, or salt are sometimes added as spermicides. These substances, however, add little to the spermicidal properties of tap water and may irritate the vagina. The major disadvantage of douching as a contraceptive method is that it does not work very well. Within one or two minutes or less after ejaculation sperm can be in the cervical canal and out of reach of the douche. A woman must literally run from bed to bathroom if the douch is to be even mildly effective. The overall failure rate for the douche as a contraceptive method is between 30 and 35 percent.

Condoms

Another contraceptive device that has been making a comeback in recent years is the **condom** (*see* Figure 6.5). Condoms, also known as "rubbers," "prophylactics," "French letters," and "skins," are thin, flexible sheaths worn over the erect penis to prevent sperm from entering the vagina. They are the only mechanical birth-control device used by men. Condoms used to be kept hidden under the pharmacist's counter and sold rather quietly; now that they have become more popular, they are produced in bright colors and can be openly displayed in drugstores in most states. Approximately 750 million are sold in the United States each year.

Condoms are cylindrical sheaths with a ring of thick rubber at the open end. The thickness of the sheath is about 0.0025 inches (0.00635 centimeters). Each is packaged, rolled, and ready for use. Some condoms also come lubricated.

The advantages of condoms include their availability and the protection they offer against venereal diseases. One minor disadvantage is that they reduce sensation somewhat and thus may interfere with the sexual pleasure of the male or female. (To some men this slight decrease in sensation might be desirable if it allows them to prolong sexual intercourse.) Putting on the condom interrupts sexual activity after erection but before the penis is placed in the vagina. This may be distracting, but many couples learn to integrate it smoothly into their sexual activity. Condoms have been known to burst under the pressure of ejaculation, to leak, or to slip off during intercourse, but they are quite effective if used consistently. Failure rates range from 2.5 percent (with very consistent usage) to 15 percent. Using condoms with spermicidal cream or foam increases their effectiveness. Condoms are most effective when the following precautions are taken:

To avoid leakage the male should withdraw from the vagina soon after ejaculation — before detumesence — and should hold on to the rim of the rubber while removing it.

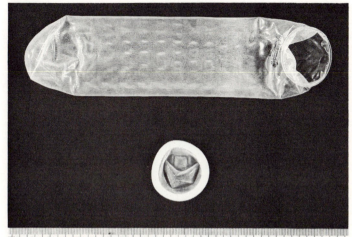

Figure 6.5 Condom, rolled and unrolled. Scale is in centimeters.

When putting the rubber on, leave about 0.5 inch (1.3 centimeters) at the end (if no reservoir is built in already) to allow space for the ejaculate so that it does not break the condom.

Do not use condoms with vaseline or any other petroleum-based product that can destroy rubber.

Always use new condoms because rubber deteriorates with age and heat.

Withdrawal

Withdrawal of the penis from the vagina just before ejaculation (**coitus interruptus**) is probably the oldest known method of birth control and is still commonly used throughout the world. The decline of the birthrate in western Europe from the late nineteenth century onward is believed to have been due to the popularity of this method.

The major problem with coitus interruptus is that it requires a great deal of motivation and will power just at the moment when a man is most likely to throw caution to the winds. Nevertheless, this method costs nothing, requires no devices, and has no physiological side effects—although some people find it psychologically unacceptable.

When withdrawal is the only contraceptive measure taken, failure rates range from 15 to 30 percent. This is partly because the male does not always withdraw quickly enough and partly because small amounts of semen may escape before ejaculation. The result is that withdrawal cannot be considered a very effective method of birth control.

The Rhythm Method

Women can become pregnant only during certain fertile days of the menstrual cycle, and it is possible to calculate when those days are and avoid pregnancy by avoiding intercourse during the fertile period. This method of **birth control,** known as the **rhythm method,** is especially unreliable for women whose menstrual cycles are irregular, but if a woman has kept track of her periods for ten or twelve months, she may be able to calculate her fertile period with some degree of accuracy (*see* Table 6.1). The safe period for intercourse includes only those days not included in the fertile period.

For women with a regular twenty-eight-day cycle the fertile period extends from day ten through day eighteen. For women with cycles ranging from twenty-four to thirty-two days the fertile period extends from the sixth through the twenty-second day. Some couples may see this as an unacceptably long time to abstain from intercourse. Even though the rhythm method is unreliable and requires a great deal of self-control, it is still used by many couples and is the only method of birth control currently approved by the Roman Catholic church.

Table 6.1 **THE FERTILE PERIOD**

Shortest Cycle (Days)	Day Fertile Period Begins
22	4
23	5
24	6
25	7
26	8
27	9
28	10
29	11
30	12
31	13
32	14
33	15
34	16

Longest Cycle (Days)	Day Fertile Period Ends
22	12
23	13
24	14
25	15
26	16
27	17
28	18
29	19
30	20
31	21
32	22
33	23
34	24

There are several ways of making the rhythm method more effective. One is based on changes in a woman's body temperature, which goes up slightly at the time of ovulation. In order to pinpoint the time of ovulation and fertility by this method a woman must take her temperature immediately upon awakening every morning before arising, moving about, eating, drinking, or smoking. An increase of 0.4°F (0.2°C) above the average temperature of the preceding five days indicates ovulation if the increase is sustained for three days. Minor illnesses, like colds and sore throats, however, can throw off the temperature curve.

A BBT (basal body temperature) chart does indicate when ovulation has occurred, but it is not helpful before ovulation. So if the BBT chart (*see* Figure 6.6) is to be used to determine the "safe period," a woman should abstain from intercourse from the end of her menstrual period until three days after the time of ovulation.

A device called the **ovutimer** has been developed by researchers at the Massachusetts Institute of Technology. It can be used to make the rhythm method more reliable and can also be used by couples who want to know when the fertile days are so they can try to conceive a child. The ovutimer is a 7-inch (17.8-centimeter) long plastic device that, when inserted into the vagina, determines the time of ovulation by measuring the stickiness of cervical mucus, which becomes thin and watery at the time of ovulation.

The ovutimer and the BBT method promise to make the rhythm method more reliable, but even when the time of ovulation is known, the success of the rhythm method depends on a couple's ability and motivation to follow directions exactly. Large-scale studies show failure rates ranging from 15 to 35 percent when the rhythm method is the only contraceptive method used.

Sterilization

Voluntary surgical sterilization has become increasingly popular in recent years among both men and women in the United States and in countries like India, where sterilization (especially for males) has been encouraged by the government. In fact, the acceptance rate of sterilization by people in the United States in the last half of their reproductive years (older than age 29) has increased significantly in recent years. It is estimated that more than one million surgical sterilizations are now being done in the United States each year.

Male Sterilization

The operation that sterilizes the male is the **vasectomy,** a simple procedure that can be done in a doctor's office in about fifteen minutes. A small amount of local anesthetic is injected into each side of the scrotum, and a small incision is made on each side in order to reach the vas deferens (*see* Chapter 2). Each vas is then tied in two places, and the segment between is removed in order to prevent the two cut ends from growing together again. After this operation sperm will no longer be able to travel through the vas from the testes.

No change in sexual functioning occurs as a result of vasectomy. The sex glands continue to function normally, secreting male sex hormones into the blood. Ejaculation still occurs because the seminal fluid contributed by

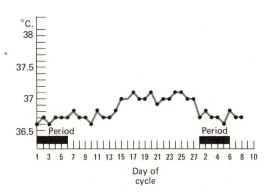

Figure 6.6 BBT chart showing ovulation about the thirteenth day (36°C=98°F).

From *International Planned Parenthood Federation Medical Handbook,* p. 62. Reprinted by permission of the International Planned Parenthood Federation, 18–20 Lower Regent Street, London SW1, England.

the testes through the vas only accounts for about 10 percent of the total volume. The only difference is that the semen will be free of sperm. Sperm may still be present two or three months after a vasectomy because they are stored in the reproductive system beyond the vas, but these sperm can be flushed out with water or with a sperm-immobilizing agent during the vasectomy. Once these remaining sperm are gone, vasectomy is 100 percent effective as a birth-control measure (assuming the procedure is performed correctly).

Vasectomy does not interfere physiologically with a man's sexuality. His sexual response and orgasm after vasectomy are the same as before. Some men feel a new sense of freedom after being sterilized, but others experience negative psychological effects—possibly because vasectomy is usually considered a permanent form of sterilization. However, improved surgical techniques are changing this, and vasectomy may eventually become a reversible or temporary form of sterilization. The reversal procedure is not simple, but the cut ends of the vas can be reunited surgically. Using pregnancy of partner as a measure of success, some surgeons report rates of reversal of vasectomy as low as 18 percent, others as high as 60 percent. Another method of making vasectomy reversible consists of inserting a small valve in the vas. The valve allows the flow of sperm to be turned on or off when desired. These valves are still in the experimental stage, and the truly reversible vasectomy is still in the future, but there are several reasons why some men request that their vasectomy be undone: remarriage after divorce or death of wife, death of one or more children, improved economic condition, and removal of negative psychological effects of vasectomy.

Female Sterilization

The most common surgical procedure for sterilizing women is often called "tying the tubes." Tying or cutting the fallopian tubes prevents eggs from reaching the uterus, just as cutting the vas prevents sperm from reaching the penis. Female sterilization used to be a major surgical procedure involving hospital-

ization, general anesthesia, and all the associated costs and risks. The search for simple, effective, and inexpensive sterilization procedures, however, has led to the development of more than one hundred techniques for cutting, closing, or tying the tubes.

There are still medical situations in which a major abdominal operation may be necessary for female sterilization, but the current trend is in the direction of an outpatient procedure performed under local anesthetic. It is possible to approach the fallopian tubes through the vagina rather than through the abdominal wall and to perform the sterilization with a **culdoscope.** This instrument is basically a metal tube with a self-contained optical system that allows the physician to see inside the abdominal cavity. Sterilization using the procedure called **culdoscopy** involves puncturing the closed end of the vagina and, after locating the tubes with the culdoscope, tying and cutting them.

In addition to the traditional methods of tying the tubes, a variety of clips, bands, and rings have been developed for blocking the tubes. Chemicals that solidify in the tubes, caps that cover the ends of the tubes, and lasers that heat and destroy a portion of the tubes are among the sterilization methods currently under investigation. Various plastic and ceramic plugs have also been designed for blocking the tubes, and one still-experimental plug appears to be both effective and removable—allowing for reversibility of sterilization.

Most methods currently being used to sterilize women are almost 100 percent effective, and like vasectomy, they have no physiological effect on sexual functioning.

In addition to sterilization by tying the tubes, many women have been sterilized by the surgical procedure known as **hysterectomy** (surgical removal of the uterus). It is estimated that one-third of all women in the United States have had a hysterectomy by age 65, but charges have been made that the operation is overused. The operation is performed in one of two ways: through an incision in the abdominal wall or through the vagina. The ovaries are left in place (unless there is some medical reason for their removal), so the secretion of female sex hormones remains normal. Hysterectomy is usually not performed solely as a means of sterilization, however, but is done because of some medical problem, such as tumor removal.

See Table 6.2 for a comparison of the contraceptive methods discussed in this chapter.

Abortion

Abortion has been used as a form of birth control for thousands of years in numerous cultures, whether or not the procedure was considered legal. In the United States in the 1800s, for instance, abortion was relatively common—it is estimated that there was one

Table 6.2 **SUMMARY OF CONTRACEPTIVE METHODS**

Method	User	Effec- tiveness Rating	Advantages	Disadvantages
Birth-control pills	Female	Excellent	Easy and aesthetic to use	Continual cost; side effects; requires daily attention
IUD	Female	Excellent	Requires little attention; no expense after initial insertion	Side effects, particularly increased bleeding; possible expulsion
Diaphragm with cream or jelly	Female	Very good	No side effects; minor continual cost of jelly and small initial cost of diaphragm	Repeated insertion and removal; possible aesthetic objections
Cervical cap	Female	Very good	Can be worn 2–3 weeks without removal; no cost except for initial fitting and purchase	Does not fit all women; potential difficulties with insertion
Condom	Male	Very good	Easy to use; helps to prevent venereal disease	Continual expense; interruption of sexual activity and possible impairment of gratification
Vaginal foam	Female	Good	Easy to use; no prescription required	Continual expense
Vaginal creams, jellies, tablets, and suppositories	Female	Fair to good	Easy to use; no prescription required	Continual expense; unattractive or irritating for some people
Withdrawal	Male	Fair	No cost or preparation	Frustration
Rhythm	Male and female	Poor to fair	No cost; acceptable to Roman Catholic church	Requires significant motivation, cooperation, and intelligence; useless with irregular cycles and during postpartum period
Douche	Female	Poor	Inexpensive	Inconvenient; possibly irritating
Abortion	Female	Excellent	Avoids unwanted pregnancies if other methods fail	Expensive; possible medical complications; psychologically or morally unacceptable to some
Sterilization	Male or female	Excellent	Permanent relief from contraceptive concerns	Possible surgical, medical, or psychological complications

abortion for every five or six live births. Abortionists advertised in newspapers and frequently sold drugs that were supposed to induce abortion. Laws were gradually enacted against abortion in the last century, but these laws were not always strictly enforced. Then, in 1973, abortion was legalized in the United States, and by 1975, legal abortions were estimated at more than 1 million per year. Meanwhile, illegal abortions declined from an estimated 530,000 in 1970 to 10,000 per year.

Even though legal, abortion has not become a primary means of birth control. As a back-up procedure when contraception fails, however, abortion is becoming increasingly popular, and although it remains a highly controversial issue on ethical and moral grounds (*see* Chapter 13), it is widely practiced in the Soviet Union, parts of eastern and central Europe, and Japan. It is less common in some of the Catholic countries of Europe and South America.

The method used for abortion in the United States is usually determined by the length of the pregnancy. During the first trimester, abortion is performed by mechanically removing the contents of the uterus through the cervix. Extraction is sometimes used as late as the twentieth week, but during the second trimester, abortion is usually performed by stimulating the uterus to expel its contents, in effect, inducing a miscarriage.

Vacuum Aspiration

One of the simplest methods of abortion is called **vacuum aspiration** (the use of suction to withdraw fluids and tissues from the uterus). As mentioned in Chapter 4, vacuum or suction techniques are used for "menstrual extraction." This same technique has become popular for first-trimester abortions. It can be performed in a doctor's office or clinic quickly and at a relatively low cost. Before the eighth week of pregnancy it can be performed with minimal or no anesthesia, and it is often unnecessary mechanically to dilate the cervix.

The instrument used to perform a vacuum abortion is a **suction curette,** a plastic tube with holes at each end and a hole on the side. One end is inserted into the uterus through the cervix (*see* Figure 6.7), and the other end is attached to a suction pump. The hole on the side can be covered and uncovered as required to increase or decrease the vacuum pressure within the uterus. The suction tip is rotated within the uterus until, on examination, all

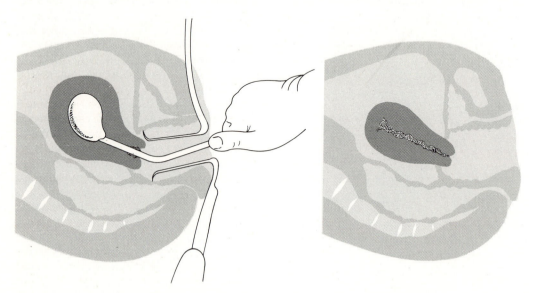

Figure 6.7 *(Left)* initial insertion of angled suction curette into the cervical canal; *(right)* uterus contracted after completion of evacuation of the uterus.

tissue related to conception has been removed. A uterus-contracting drug (such as oxytocin; *see* Chapter 5) may then be administered to minimize bleeding and to insure complete evacuation of the uterus. The entire procedure (not counting examination and preparation time) can usually be performed in less than two minutes.

Complications with vacuum aspiration are relatively rare but can include perforation of the uterus, hemorrhage, uterine infection, cervical damage, and drug reactions if anesthetics or other drugs are used. Although abortion does present risks, the overall death rate due to abortion is relatively low. The death rate for legal abortions performed during the first trimester is 1.7 deaths per 100,000 abortions. In the second trimester the figure increases to 12.2 per 100,000, but this is still lower than the death rate due to childbirth complications—14.1 per 100,000.

Dilation and Curettage (D and C)

Another method of abortion sometimes used during the first trimester is dilation of the cervix and curettage (scraping) of the uterus. The first step, **cervical dilation,** can be accomplished by passing a series of progressively larger metallic dilators (curved rods) through the cervical opening, but in recent years a less painful (if slower) method has become popular—**laminaria sticks.** These sticks, which are made from compressed seaweed, are inserted into the cervix. As they absorb cervical secretions they expand to five times their dry size in about twenty-four hours. When the cervix is enlarged sufficiently, a **curette** (a bluntly serrated metal instrument) is inserted and used to scrape the tissues off the inner walls of the uterus. In more advanced pregnancies dilation may have to be more extensive in order to allow passage of a forceps that can be used mechanically to grasp the fetal tissues for removal. The possible complications of an abortion by the D-and-C method are the same as those of vacuum aspiration.

Dilation and Extraction (D and E)

After the twelfth week of pregnancy, abortion becomes an increasingly serious proce-

dure, and the rate of complications increases. One abortion technique that is often used between the thirteenth and twentieth weeks of pregnancy is dilation and extraction. D and E is similar to D and C and the suction method, although the fetus is larger at this stage and not as easily removed as during the first trimester. Once dilation is achieved, suction, forceps, and curettage are used. D and E is considered to be a simple, effective, and relatively inexpensive procedure, and recent studies suggest that up to the twentieth week, D and E is as safe or safer than some of the other procedures that are commonly used during the second trimester.

Saline Abortions

During the second trimester, abortion is often induced by injection of a salt solution into the uterus. This method or any other method used during the second trimester is much more complicated than is abortion in the early weeks of pregnancy. The fourth month of pregnancy is a particularly difficult time for an abortion. The pregnancy is too far along for a safe, simple aspiration, but the uterus is not yet large enough to allow the physician easily to locate the proper place in the abdominal wall in which to insert a needle for a **saline abortion** (*see* Figure 5.14).

The method of inducing a saline abortion is simple, but exactly how it works is not well understood. After examination to verify the exact location of the uterus, a needle is inserted through the abdominal and uterine walls using local anesthesia. About 200 cubic centimeters (less than 7 ounces) of amniotic fluid is removed, and 200 cubic centimeters of a 20-percent salt solution is injected into the uterus. Contractions of the uterus usually begin within twelve to twenty-four hours, and most women deliver the fetus and placenta within forty-eight hours of the injection. Some take longer, and a second injection of saline solution or of oxytocin may be necessary to stimulate more vigorous contractions.

Uncommon but severe complications can occur with saline abortion. The most serious is "salt poisoning." Early symptoms of salt poisoning are abdominal pain, nausea, vomiting, and headache. If treatment is not administered promptly, this condition can result in high blood pressure, brain damage, and death. Other complications include intrauterine infection and hemorrhage. Delayed hemorrhage (days or weeks after the abortion) occurs in some cases in which the fetus has been aborted but part or all of the placenta has been retained. In such cases curettage and blood transfusion may be required. The risk of death from a saline abortion is close to the risk of death from carrying and delivering a child at full term.

Prostaglandin Abortions

More than forty-five years ago it was reported that injections of human semen into the uterus cause vigorous contractions of uterine muscles. By 1935 it was shown that the substance responsible for this action is produced by the prostate gland and seminal vesicles, and it was thus named **prostaglandin.** Later it was discovered that there are more than a dozen chemically related prostaglandins, and some of them can now be synthesized in the laboratory.

Because prostaglandins cause uterine contractions, they can be used to induce abortion. They are usually injected directly into the uterus but can also be injected into the bloodstream or into a muscle. Laminaria sticks are sometimes used with prostaglandins because by dilating the cervix they reduce the number of uterine contractions necessary to expel the fetus. This can hasten the abortion of the fetus and the placenta. Some success has also been reported in bringing about abortion after insertion of a prostaglandin suppository into the vagina. This procedure has been used to induce first- and second-trimester abortions, but in the United States, suction is still the primary procedure for first-trimester abortions.

Complications with prostaglandin abortion include nausea, vomiting, and headache, with at least 50 percent of women experiencing one or more of these side effects. These effects are temporary, rarely serious, and can be easily treated. Complications such as hemorrhage, infection, and uterine rupture (possible with all types of second-trimester abortion) are in-

frequent with prostaglandin abortion. One major drawback is that the proportion of live births is higher with prostaglandin than with saline abortion, especially after the twentieth week (45 live births out of 607 abortions, in one recent study). For this reason some physicians do not like to perform abortions after the twentieth week. When they do, they sometimes use saline, and some have reported success in using a combination of prostaglandin and urea. Urea can also be used alone to induce abortion. It has the same effects as saline but is slightly less effective than either saline or prostaglandin.

THE FUTURE OF CONTRACEPTION

As we have seen, contraceptive practices have been with us in many forms for a long time, but until recently there have been no absolutely foolproof, completely acceptable birth-control devices or methods. This situation has changed dramatically in recent years and is expected to continue to change as our knowledge of human reproduction grows.

A Morning-after Pill

A major drawback with most forms of contraception is that they require action prior to intercourse. The Pill must be taken every day, even if a woman is rarely sexually active. Condoms, diaphragms, and IUDs must be in place before intercourse if they are to be effective. However, research now suggests that it may be possible to take effective steps to prevent pregnancy after intercourse. Interestingly, most attention has focused on estrogens, progestogens, and IUDs—all of which are already in use as contraceptives.

The first "morning-after pill" was approved by the Food and Drug Administration in 1975 for use in emergency situations (rape, incest, or where, in the physician's judgment, the woman's physical or mental well-being is in danger). It contains a potent estrogen, diethylstilbestrol (DES) and is taken in a dosage of 25 milligrams twice a day for five days.

DES has not been approved for routine use because its safety has not been established. To be effective in preventing pregnancy, treatment must begin within seventy-two hours of unprotected intercourse and preferably within twenty-four hours. This is because estrogens apparently prevent pregnancy by interfering with implantation of the ovum, which reaches the uterus within four or five days of ovulation. The most common side effect of DES (seen in about 16 percent of users) is nausea and vomiting. Nevertheless, studies conducted so far suggest that it is highly effective as a morning-after pill.

Studies have also found that other estrogens, progestogens, and combinations of the two can be successful in preventing pregnancy when taken following intercourse. Researchers are working to determine the minimum effective dose and the best method of administering these preparations as morning-after contraceptives.

The copper IUD is also being used to prevent pregnancy in cases in which intercourse has taken place without any form of contraception. It is believed that the device prevents pregnancy by interfering with implantation, and when inserted shortly after intercourse, it appears to be highly effective in preventing pregnancy. The side effects associated with this procedure are the same as when the IUD is used as a contraceptive.

A Long-Acting Pill

Instead of taking a pill every day, it is possible that a safe, long-acting injection will be developed for contraceptive purposes. One such preparation is already being used in some parts of the world but has not been approved for use in the United States. Each dose of the preparation (brand name, Depo Provera) contains 150 milligrams of progesterone, enough to prevent ovulation for ninety days. Side effects include irregular menstrual bleeding and an unpredictable period of infertility following cessation of the shots. The FDA's primary reason for disapproval of this drug for long-term contraception is based on studies showing that it is related to an increased incidence of pre-

malignant breast tumors in dogs. The drug's effect on humans is still being investigated.

A Pill for Men

It has long been known that the male reproductive system is similar to that of the female in one important aspect—both are controlled by sex hormones. Because this is so, it should be as simple to regulate male fertility (sperm production) with hormones as it is to regulate female fertility (ovulation). Although this is the case, there has been a major problem in using hormones as male contraceptives—the same hormone treatment that decreases sperm production also decreases male sex desire. This is an unacceptable side effect for most men. Some recent developments suggest that this problem may be overcome in the near future. Danazol is a drug that cuts production of male hormones (and thus sperm production and sexual interest) when administered on a daily basis. The mechanism involves suppression of FSH and LH (ICSH) by the pituitary (see Chapter 4), but when men using this drug are given a monthly shot of testosterone, a healthy sex drive is maintained. The dosage of testosterone, however, must be carefully monitored because too much of it will stimulate sperm production and undo the contraceptive effects of the danazol.

Other Developments

The field of fertility research has been expanding rapidly, and scientists are optimistic that the developments of the near future will solve many of the problems of today's birth-control methods. Among the contraceptive methods that may soon be available are such things as hormone capsules that can be implanted under the skin and exert their effects for up to six years. A vaccine may also be developed that immunizes women against HCG, one of the hormones necessary for pregnancy. And finally, research at the molecular level is leading to development of chemicals that will control reproduction more subtly and with fewer side effects than current methods.

Promising reports, for instance, have been made concerning chemicals that can do such things as prevent implantation and sperm production without interfering with other physiological functions. These and similar lines of study, researchers hope, should soon lead to development of birth-control methods that are completely safe, easily administered, 100 percent effective, and always reversible.

SUMMARY

1. Contraceptive practices have been in use for centuries, but it is only in recent years that a number of truly effective birth-control methods have become available on a wide scale. Some of the primary reasons for using contraception include preserving the health of the woman, preventing the birth of a severely ill or deformed child, preventing unwanted children, and controlling population.

2. Since 1960, oral contraceptives—the Pill—have become one of the most popular methods of birth control. Oral contraceptives are made from synthetic female sex hormones (progestogens and estrogens) that prevent pregnancy by preventing ovulation. The Pill also affects the maturation rate of the egg, the speed at which the egg moves through the fallopian tubes, the ability of the egg to implant in the uterus, and the composition of cervical mucus—all of which act as barriers to conception.

3. The Pill is usually taken once a day for three weeks and then stopped. Within a few days "withdrawal bleeding" begins, and the pills are resumed on the fifth day thereafter. Because there is a risk of pregnancy if two or more pills are missed, manufacturers have devised various methods of helping users remember to take the pills. When correctly used, oral contraceptives are 100 percent effective by the end of the second month of use.

4. Oral contraceptives are known to cause undesirable side effects in some women. The most common complaints are nausea, weight gain, headaches, and vaginal discharge. These side effects may disappear after several months. Sometimes a prescription with a smaller dose of hormones relieves side effects. More-serious side effects are rare, but they are so potentially dangerous that the FDA requires that each prescription contain information on possible side effects as well as a warning about increased risk of heart attack for users of the pill who smoke.

5. Intrauterine devices have become increasingly popular since 1959. IUDs seem to work by causing changes in the lining of the uterus that prevent implantation of the fertilized egg. A variety of IUDs of different shapes and sizes are currently available. Most are made of flexible plastic (for easy insertion) and have a "tail" that allows the wearer to check that the device has not been expelled. Newer IUDs containing copper or progesterone are believed to be especially effective. Side effects include "spotting" and pelvic pain (in from 10 to 20 percent of users). Infection and perforation of the uterus are serious (but rare) complications related to insertion of IUDs.

6. Primarily because of side effects associated with the Pill and IUDs, a number of other contraceptive methods are becoming popular:

The diaphragm is a rubber, disklike device that fits over the cervix and prevents sperm from reaching the egg. It is highly effective when used consistently and when used with a spermicidal jelly.

Spermicides (foams, creams, jellies, and suppositories) prevent pregnancy by destroying sperm in the vagina. They are only effective if they are well dispersed in the vagina prior to ejaculation.

Douching, or washing, the vagina after intercourse is a very *ineffective* method of birth control because within seconds of intercourse sperm can be in the cervical canal and out of reach of the douche.

Condoms, rubber sheaths worn over the erect penis, prevent sperm from entering the vagina and are highly effective when used consistently.

Withdrawal of the penis just prior to ejaculation is effective in preventing pregnancy, but it requires a high degree of will power and motivation.

The rhythm method (avoiding intercourse on a woman's fertile days) is effective only if directions are followed. It is less effective for women with irregular periods.

7. Sterilization is the most effective method of birth control, and it is becoming increasingly popular. In a vasectomy, the operation that sterilizes the male, the vas deferens leading from each testicle is cut so that sperm can no longer travel out of the scrotum. The operation is simple, 100 percent effective, and sexual functioning is not affected. With extremely delicate surgical techniques vasectomy is sometimes reversible.

8. The most common technique for sterilizing women is often called "tying the tubes." This refers to the many procedures that can be used to tie, cut, block, or close the fallopian tubes and prevent ova from reaching the uterus. With the methods now available sterilization can be performed in a doctor's office. The procedure is 100 percent effective and has no effect on sexual functioning.

9. Abortion is not usually considered a primary method of contraception (in the United States), but when contraception fails or in emergencies, abortion is often used as a back-up procedure for avoiding pregnancy. The method of abortion is determined by the length of pregnancy — with the procedure becoming more dangerous later in pregnancy. In the first trimester, vacuum aspiration and D and C are simple and usually safe mechanical (suction or curette) methods of removing the contents of the uterus. In the second trimester, dilation and extraction (D and E) is sometimes used (up to the twentieth week), and saline injections and prostaglandins are the other two most often-used methods of inducing abortion.

10. As research on human reproduction progresses, contraception will become safer, more effective, and completely reversible. Recent progress has been reported in the development of a "morning-after pill," a vaccine against pregnancy, long-lasting injections and implants, and a pill for men.

SUGGESTED READING

The Boston Women's Health Collective. *Our Bodies, Ourselves,* 2nd ed. New York: Simon & Schuster, 1976.
See Chapter 5.

Callahan, D. *Abortion: Law, Choice and Morality.* New York: Macmillan, 1970.
A scholarly discussion of the psychological, legal, and moral issues relating to abortion. Attitudes and policy in the U.S. are compared with those of various other societies around the world.

Ehrlich, P. R. *The Population Bomb.* New York: Ballantine, 1968.
This book, now a classic, was responsible for sensitizing millions of people to the problems associated with unrestrained population growth.

Guttmacher, A. F., M.D. *Pregnancy, Birth and Family Planning.* New American Library, 1973.
See Chapter 5.

Rudel, H. W., *et al. Birth Control: Contraception and Abortion.* New York: Macmillan, 1973.
A well-written, comprehensive textbook covering the history, current usage, and effectiveness of all the various methods of contraception.

Westoff, L. A., and Westoff, C. F. *From Now to Zero: Fertility, Contraception and Abortion in America.* Boston: Little, Brown, 1971.
A detailed discussion of the sociology and demography of contraceptive usage in the United States and its implications for the future.

Behavior

PART TWO

Sexual Behavior and Development

chapter 7

Did You Know That . . .

there is not a single study of sexual behavior the results of which would be applicable to the general population?

the capacity for sexual response is present before puberty and some infants as young as five months of age are capable of having orgasms?

according to recent surveys, both married and single men and women rely on masturbation as a source of erotic pleasure more than in previous generations?

the most recent data indicate that premarital coitus is becoming increasingly common among the youth of this country?

anthropological surveys have found coital frequency to range from once a week in some cultures to ten times a night in others?

monkeys reared in social isolation do not learn adequate sexual behavior and in many cases are incapable of copulation?

INTRODUCTION

Sexuality is a lifelong phenomenon. It begins in infancy, develops through several stages, takes on an amazing variety, and is often an important part of our lives at all ages. So far in this book we have dealt mainly with the structure and function of the sex organs. Now we turn to people themselves to see how and why they behave sexually. In order to do this we must first understand what sexual behavior is and how sex researchers go about measuring it. After we have considered these important questions we will look at the origins of sexual behavior and see how it develops through childhood, adolescence, and adulthood. Finally, we will examine some of the experimental and research evidence that helps explain the various aspects of the development of sexual behavior.

WHAT SEXUAL BEHAVIOR IS

In the ordinary sense "behavior" is how we act—what can be witnessed by others, in contrast to our inner feelings and thoughts. This distinction between "inner" and "outer," is arbitrary, however, because we seldom act without thinking or feeling, and we rarely fail to reflect thought and emotion in our actions.

All behavior, including sexual behavior, has several main characteristics. First, it is integrated and indivisible. When we describe it as conscious, unconscious, or innately or socially determined, we refer simply to different components of behavior, not to different behaviors. Second, all behavior expresses the total organism, the personality as a whole. Third, all behavior is part of a lifelong developmental sequence and can be understood only as links in a chain of events. Finally, all behavior is determined by multiple forces. Each act has biological, psychological, and social determinants, which are themselves quite complex. We do not think, feel, or do anything for one single reason.

Range of Sexual Behavior

The question "What is sexual behavior?" sounds quite simple, but it is actually impossible to answer. Most people would agree that it involves more than just coitus, but how much more is another matter. A physiological definition based on tumescence of sex organs or on orgasm leaves out vast areas of activity that are commonly recognized as sexual. Furthermore, it would include certain behavior, like erections in very young boys, the sexual nature of which can be questioned.

Observations of human behavior reveal that any and all objects and activities can have sexual significance. The concept then becomes so nearly global that it cannot possibly be quantified for comparison and analysis. Confronted with these alternatives we must resort to working definitions that, though deficient in some respects, are at least operationally useful. For example, although we are aware of the many varieties of sexual expression, we shall deal primarily with those that culminate in orgasm. Just as with the physiology of sex, orgasm will serve as our unit of behavioral measurement.

In a sense this approach is regrettable, for it obscures the myriad nuances and the subtlety of sexuality in favor of a "mechanical" definition. Unfortunately, we have no alternative. If we are to discuss what people do, we must have a unit of measurement. We shall not stop there, however, but shall attempt also to capture some of the less quantifiable, more ephemeral, but no less important manifestations of human sexuality.

Even after such drastic concessions, we can still say relatively little in quantitative terms about how people actually live their sex lives. There are five or six general ways in which they can achieve orgasm, but how often do they use each, who prefers which, and how does it all add up? We do not really know except for select populations. But almost everyone seems to have known all along that we actually behave quite differently from the ways in which we are "assumed" to behave.

It was established in the Kinsey surveys that the vast majority of people of both sexes usually attain orgasm through one or more of six main methods: masturbation, nocturnal sex dreams, heterosexual petting, coitus, homosexual relations, and contacts with animals. Other activities like voyeurism, sadism, masochism, and fetishism are rare as exclusive means for achieving orgasm. They may, however, accompany any of the main six.

An important problem for sex research is the documentation of actual sexual behavior in large populations. Before we have such a global picture, to attempt to explain in depth any aspect of sexual activity is likely to be misleading. The study of a given individual must begin with the determination of that person's position in a relevant group; we therefore need to know how all kinds of people behave, not only those deemed well or ill, normal or abnormal.

There is still no definitive information on the sexual behavior of large communities anywhere in the world. We shall refer often to the distribution and frequencies of various types of sexual behavior. The presentation of such data in percentages and other mathematical forms tends to lend a certain scientific dignity and to imply accuracy. There is nothing in these pages, however, that can be taken to reflect accurately the behavior of whole nations or of all human beings. What we do have are fragments of information on some facets of sexual activity in some groups. The resulting picture is like the image in a broken mirror with many missing pieces. It is to be hoped that enough is reflected to suggest broader outlines.

Everything we know indicates that sexual behavior is extremely varied. Like the stars, individual patterns of activity are countless, but they cluster in definite constellations, some of which are apparent to anyone's eye and others only to trained observers.

This extreme variability is another reason for caution in drawing conclusions from information obtained from groups. Even when careful study has uncovered the patterns of behavior in a given community, this information cannot be automatically applied to any one member of that community. Averages tell us about groups but not individuals. Understanding each person requires a special study of each: There are no shortcuts. But such studies can yield more meaning if we know the averages and variations for the group.

Most of us behave most of the time in ways that allow a certain classification for sexual activities. Many similarities in sexual behavior depend on the fundamental biological unity (though not uniformity) of all living beings. Many of the differences arise from different modes of social adaptation and the complexity inherent in human societies. The more advanced a species is on the evolutionary scale, the more complex are the determinants of its sexual behavior.

Judgments of Sexual Behavior

Of all the varieties of human behavior sex is the most controversial, conflict-ridden, and subject to contradictory judgment. In dealing with the biology of sex we managed to skirt this issue, but now that we must deal with behavior we no longer can ignore such problems.

Assessments of behavior, sexual or otherwise, are generally made according to four criteria. First is the statistical norm: How common is the behavior? Second is the medical norm: Is the behavior healthy? Third is the ethical norm: Is the behavior moral? Fourth is the legal norm: Is the behavior legitimate?

It would be helpful if these four criteria were mutually reinforcing, or at least not contradictory. For instance, unprovoked murder during peacetime is infrequent, obviously unhealthy for the victim, morally inadmissible by almost everyone, and illegal in practically all societies. It would be difficult, however, to find other examples that are quite so clearcut. In actual practice we must judge behavior primarily according to one or another of these criteria, but there is a strong tendency to seek corroboration from the rest. In fact, one set of judgments is often predicated on another. For example, an act is considered immoral or illegal because it is unhealthy or offends the majority (or the reverse). In addition, we seek to strengthen arguments against behavior that we wish to suppress: An activity that we consider immoral seems worse if it is indulged in by only a few, is unhealthy, and is also illegal.

The application of such judgments to sexual behavior in heterogeneous and pluralistic societies has resulted in much confusion. The meaning of the statistical norm has been distorted, partly through ignorance and partly deliberately. Medical judgments have often lacked scientific support. Morality has been confused with tradition and the idiosyncrasies of those in power. Statutes and ordinances have frozen into law many dubious factual claims and moral conclusions. Not infrequently the original determination that an act is unhealthy or uncommon turns out to be incorrect or no longer applicable, but the moral and legal judgments based on it persist.

THE STUDY OF SEXUAL BEHAVIOR

The vast store of presently available information and misinformation on sex has been gathered largely through informal observation and inference. Only a small part of it is the result of careful, systematic study. As even the latter often has serious shortcomings, and because the notion of sex research itself raises certain pertinent questions, we shall briefly review those studies we have cited most often in this book.

The Kinsey Study

The one major, systematic attempt to study and classify human sexual behavior in the United States is that conducted by Alfred C. Kinsey and his colleagues. Because it remains the pre-eminent study in the field we have referred to it several times and will continue to refer to it throughout this book. Other studies of more modest scope will be discussed more briefly.

A primary goal of the Kinsey survey was to broaden our understanding of individual sexual behavior through examination of that behavior in relation to group behavior. In the 1940s and early 1950s Kinsey and his colleagues collected more than 16,000 histories from people across the United States. Kinsey himself collected 7,000 such histories—an average of two a day for ten years. He died in 1956, long before he could fulfill his goal of interviewing 100,000 individuals.

Probably no other book published in this field in the past several decades has had such a powerful impact as has the first Kinsey report on the sexual behavior of the human male. It brought the subject of sex into the open for the first time in the United States and prompted a great deal of thoughtful (and not so thoughtful) discussion and criticism.

The more relevant criticisms of the Kinsey study were aimed at the sampling and interviewing techniques. The men and women whose sexual histories provided Kinsey with his data were not statistically representative of the population as a whole. Even though the Kinsey sample involved forty times as many subjects as had been included in any previous study, it was hampered by Kinsey's reliance on volunteers. People who volunteer to tell a stranger about the most private aspects of their sex lives may not be representative of the general population. This was especially true thirty years ago, when sex was not discussed as openly as it is today. Kinsey, aware of this shortcoming, tried to minimize its effects, but considering the nature of his research and the numbers of subjects required he had to take all applicants.

The Kinsey sample—5,940 female and 5,300 male residents of the United States—included individuals from a wide variety of age, educational level, occupation, geographical location, and religious denominations. But these groups were not represented in the same proportions as they are found in the U.S. population. Lower educational levels and rural groups were underrepresented, and data from blacks and other nonwhites were so few that they were not included in the final reports. Because of these and other considerations the Kinsey data are, strictly speaking, applicable only to his sample and cannot be generalized to the country as a whole. If interpreted with care, however, they still yield the best clues we have to the patterns of sexual behavior in this country several decades ago.

In view of the obvious shortcomings of the Kinsey study, as well as the fact that the data were collected almost three decades ago, it would seem that we should not rely heavily on it. Unfortunately, we have nothing better. But if both the strengths and the weaknesses of the Kinsey survey are understood properly, it can continue to provide a useful reference in which to examine the broader aspects of human sexual behavior.

Considering the extraordinary interest generated by the Kinsey studies, one would have expected that during the past three decades additional investigations would have been conducted in attempts to prove, disprove, or add to the Kinsey findings. This has not been the case. The Masters and Johnson work dealt primarily with physiology rather than with behavior. A great number of books on sex and sexual behavior have been popular successes in recent years, but few can be called a scientific study of sexual behavior. The few attempts that have been made to examine sexual behavior scientifically have been either restricted in focus (such as investigations of premarital sex) or have been poorly carried out.

Recent Surveys

With all their shortcomings, the Kinsey surveys were monumental efforts by serious scientists. Virtually all large-scale studies of sexual behavior since then have been carried out through market research organizations, questionnaires published in magazines, or interviews by self-appointed experts on sexual behavior.

The population samples in these studies have been so highly self-selected that their findings cannot be generalized to the population as a whole. Therefore, these studies should be viewed as descriptions of the specific groups of people they deal with and no more.

The Playboy Foundation Survey

One relatively recent investigation was sponsored by the Playboy Foundation and carried out by The Research Guild, Inc., an independent market-survey and behavioral-research organization. The sample investigated in the Playboy survey consisted of 2,026 persons residing in 24 cities in the United States. This sample, 982 males and 1,044 females, reportedly paralleled closely the U.S. population of persons 18 years old and older. The data were gathered by means of an extensive self-administered questionnaire.

An additional sample of 200 individuals similar in characteristics to the survey sample was selected for more intensive investigation. This group of 100 men and 100 women was interviewed by Morton Hunt and Bernice Kohn, both professional writers. Preliminary reports from this survey appeared in five installments in *Playboy* magazine, and a more comprehensive presentation was offered in a book.

Despite attempts to be comprehensive and representational, this survey has a number of apparently serious shortcomings, including the lack of specific demographic details concerning the survey respondents. One does not know, for example, the exact age distribution of the sample. To be told that the "sample closely parallels the American population of persons 18 years old and over" is not sufficient. The same criticism applies to all of the other variables in question. Aside from these and other shortcomings, Hunt's analyses and interpretations are sensible. In subsequent chapters we will present some of these data while maintaining our reservations.

The Sorensen Study

The next survey to be considered was conducted by Robert C. Sorensen, a social psychologist and marketing and research executive. His work bears important similarities to the Playboy survey. The objective was to collect a comprehensive set of data on various forms of sexual behavior that would be generalizable to the population at large. The task of data collection was delegated to a commercial survey research organization (in this case the Response Analysis Corporation based in Princeton, New Jersey). The instrument used to gather the data was once again a self-administered questionnaire. The main difference between the two surveys is that whereas the Playboy investigation dealt with the adult population, Sorensen was interested in adolescent sexuality, and his sample was restricted to those between the ages of 13 and 19. Ideally these two investigations carried out within a year of each other using comparable methods should have yielded information that would have complemented each other. Unfortunately, Sorensen's sample is badly compromised and therefore not generalizable.

Of the original randomly selected adolescents eligible for the survey, less than half were actual respondents. We are confronted, therefore, with a serious problem of self-selection. The problem of self-selection was further compounded by the process of obtaining parental consent. As one would suspect, the more conservative parents would be more likely to deny their consent, and the examples of parental refusals which Sorensen duly reports confirm this. In other words, the sample used has a high probability of being weighted in favor of the sexually more permissive adolescents of sexually more liberal parents, rather than being a true national portrait.

The problem of how much one can learn through a self-administered questionnaire on such a complex behavioral matter as sex was already briefly dealt with; that problem obviously applies here as well. Additional shortcomings of the Sorensen report become dwarfed by these major considerations. Therefore, with reservations we will report some of the findings of this survey in subsequent chapters, since faulty data are perhaps better than no data at all as long as one is aware of their defects.

Kantner and Zelnik's Study

Another study that we will discuss presents a considerably brighter picture in methodology and reliability, but unfortunately it pertains to select areas of sexual behavior. This study, conducted by two highly qualified researchers, Kantner and Zelnik, deals with the coital experience of young unmarried women in the United States between the ages of 15 and 19. The primary focus of the investigation was therefore on contraception and pregnancy among the unmarried rather than on sexual behavior as such. It has nevertheless yielded some important information about the prevalence and demographic and social correlates of premarital intercourse.

The Redbook Report

The Redbook Report on female sexuality was compiled from responses to a questionnaire published in the October 1974 issue of *Redbook* magazine. Reportedly, 100,000 women responded, which is indeed an impressive number. But given the claim that approximately 10 million women read the magazine, the response rate is a miniscule 1 percent. Furthermore, the readers of any magazine obviously tend to be of a selected background rather than representative of the women in the country at large.

The Hite Report

The *Hite Report* was also primarily based on questionnaires that were initially distributed through "women's groups, including chapters of the National Organization of Women, abortion rights groups, university women's centers, and women's newsletters." Subsequently, attempts were made to broaden the study's representativeness by placing notices in various magazines and church newsletters, but the women who responded cannot be viewed as representative of the general population or even of some definable part of it. After all was said and done, only 3,000 persons responded of the 100,000 who had received the questionnaires—a response rate of only 3 percent.

Beyond the Male Myth

The last of these "nation-wide surveys" focused on men. As reported in *Beyond the Male Myth* by Pietropinto and Simenauer, some 4,066 men responded to the survey questionnaire administered by the staff of a private marketing research firm. The subjects were "approached primarily in shopping centers and malls, as well as office building complexes, tennis clubs, college campuses, airports, and bus depots." In attempting to get to the average person, the investigators seem to have literally gone to the proverbial "man in the street." The interviewers "estimated" that half of the men approached agreed to respond.

As scientific studies of sexual behavior, such studies are of no real value. But they are not totally worthless because they produce interesting revelations about individual lives. This is particularly true in the case of women who traditionally have had little occasion to report their sexual experiences. Thus, it is interesting and valuable to know what the 3,000 women in the Hite study had to say, regardless of how representative those women were. For this reason and because of the small amount of current information in this area, we shall occasionally refer to the findings of these studies.

DEVELOPMENT OF SEXUAL BEHAVIOR

Having looked briefly at how information on sexual behavior is gathered, we now consider how sexual behavior develops. Throughout this discussion keep in mind that there is great variety in all aspects of human sexual behavior. Although much information is available, most of it pertains to specific groups, and there is little that can be said about how "all" people develop or behave sexually. The information we have, however, can be useful in suggesting general patterns and trends.

Infant Sexuality

Sexuality begins in infancy. This fact has probably long been known to many parents and others who have had infants in their care, but it seems to have come as a surprise to much of the scientific world in 1905 when Sigmund Freud published his ideas on infant and childhood sexuality. Freud said, "The capacity for sensate experience develops very early in life, beginning prenatally. What the child lacks is opportunity, not capacity." In other words, Freud believed that even the youngest infants were capable of genital arousal. At the time he was saying this, many people held—and were unwilling to give up—the idea that human sexuality develops at around the time of adolescence. It was believed that sexual development progressed from a state of childhood innocence through a stage of adolescent sexual awakening to adult sexual behavior. Reproductive ability does mature along such lines, but the same is not true of sexual behavior.

The ability to respond sexually is present at birth—with newborn males capable of erection and infant females of vaginal lubrication. Spontaneous arousal, which is seen in many infants, is most likely to occur while infants are crying, during or following feeding, urination, or bowel movement, and during sleep. The evidence for sexual arousal in these cases is usually based on the presence of an erection. Because female arousal is less obvious it is more difficult to monitor. In addition, rhythmic mouth and tongue movements are often seen in association with what is believed to be infant sexual arousal.

Not only do infants show spontaneous sexual arousal from the first days of life, they respond to certain types of sexual stimulation in much the same way adults do. There is evidence, for instance, that genital stimulation provides pleasant sensations for even the youngest of infants and tends to soothe them when they are restless and crying. Stimulation of slightly older infants (three to four months) produces smiles and soft cooing sounds, and frequently erection. Orgasm (or a physiological response similar to adult orgasm) has been observed in infants as young as five months of age.

Since infants can't tell us what their subjective experiences are, there is no way of knowing exactly what their feelings are during arousal. It is quite probable that any sexual arousal at this early age is of a purely reflexive nature. That is, it is a physiological reaction controlled by networks of nerves in the spinal cord and is not dependent on the higher centers of the brain that deal with thoughts and emotions. Such arousal, therefore, is not likely to be related to adultlike erotic feelings. Even if it is of a reflexive nature and involves no erotic motivation, infants are still aware of the physical sensations involved. Some infantile behavior is so strikingly similar to that of sexually aroused adults that there can be little doubt that it is sexual in nature and that at least the basics of sexual responsiveness are present in infancy.

One reason that infant sexuality was not an easily accepted fact in Freud's time (and still today, in many cases) is that many people either fail to see or refuse to recognize sexual behavior at so young an age. In addition, because direct genital stimulation of infants is not a common practice, we often cannot tell whether a child would be sexually responsive. Aside from such considerations, we also know that sexual behavior emerges at different times in different individuals and that only some infants and children are sexually responsive at any given age. Most of us are born with the necessary biological potential for sexual arousal, but the rate of maturation of this potential can vary from one person to another. Some people are sensually responsive soon after birth, others have their first orgasms during puberty, and still others years later. In general, as with other bodily functions, more and more children attain their sexual capacities as they grow older.

Prepubescent Sexuality

Sexual arousal during infancy is usually spontaneous or accidental. Infants actively explore their bodies, and contact with their genitals, even when not deliberate, can lead to arousal. As children grow, self-exploration becomes more thorough, and though most infants do not appear to give special attention to their genitals, there are instances in which self-manipulation seems deliberate and clearly erotic (see Figure 7.1).

By the time children are 2 or 3 years old they have usually come into contact with other children, and if allowed they will continue their sexual explorations in such relationships. Much of this sexual activity among children takes the form of play. Adults may dismiss play as mere amusement, but it is in many ways a serious and necessary activity for children (as will be seen later in this chapter). During play children will investigate each other's genitals as well as exhibit their own. If permitted, children might carry on this sexual exploration with adults, but in most societies there are strict prohibitions of such activity. Such cultural attitudes begin to have an influence early in life and are an important part of the process of socialization.

Although some people claim to remember specific instances of sexual arousal and orgasm from as early as 3 years of age, it is only around the age of 5 that substantial numbers of children (about one in ten) appear to have their first sexual experiences other than self-exploration, according to the Kinsey studies (see Figures 7.2 and 7.3). Kinsey's data are based mainly on the recollections of adults about their own experiences (and such recollections are not always accurate), but some were also gathered directly from children. Comparison of Figures 7.2 and 7.3 shows that boys became considerably more active in sex play as age increased. Approximately 28 percent of the boys and 14 percent of the girls had engaged in some sort of sex play by the age of 9 years.

Figure 7.1 Infantile masturbation.

From *The Erotic Drawings of Mihály Zichy* (New York: Grove Press, 1969), plate #24. Copyright © 1969 by Grove Press, Inc.; reprinted by permission.

In the Kinsey study "sex play" meant actual genital play. It did not include casual physical contact between children in which the erotic intent was not obvious. This fact, as well as faulty memories and possible unwillingness to report childhood sex play, may have kept the reported figures low. Kinsey thought that his reported percentages were altogether too low and that nearly all boys (but only about one fifth of the girls) had engaged in sex play some time before reaching puberty.

These actual or estimated percentages do not mean that children are constantly involved in sex play. For most children it is only an occasional activity. For example, one out of four boys who had engaged in sex play had done so only during one year, and some had participated in such play just once before puberty. Only one in three boys had engaged in such play on and off for five or more years. Sex play was even more limited among prepubescent girls.

Finally, sex play did not increase with the approach of puberty. In fact, there was a slight but noticeable decline in sexual activity as puberty neared. This decline, however, does not appear to be related to biological factors. There is evidence that in some cultures there is no such "break" between childhood and adult sexuality. Studies of the most humanlike animals, monkeys and apes, suggest that the sexual activity of the young merges gradually with adult sexual behavior. Therefore, the decline in sexual activity reported by Kinsey in children prior to puberty may be due to cultural and social, rather than physiological, factors.

Types of Prepubescent Sex Play

Autoeroticism, or self-stimulation, is the most common form of prepubescent sex play. Children's curiosity eventually leads them to self-exploration and self-manipulation, with fondling of the penis and stimulation of the clitoris becoming the typical forms of autoeroticism. The erotic potential of rubbing against beds, furniture, toys, and the like, is easily discovered. Girls in particular are likely to stimulate themselves by rhythmic movements of the buttocks while lying down. Some children (especially boys) also learn to masturbate by seeing others do it or from actually being taught by others.

Next to autoerotic activities, the most common forms of prepubescent sex play are ex-

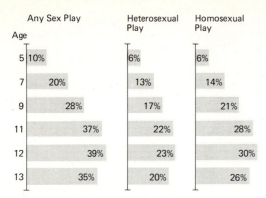

Figure 7.2 Percentages of prepubescent boys who had engaged in sociosexual play.

From A.C. Kinsey *et al., Sexual Behavior in the Human Male* (Philadelphia: Saunders, 1948), p. 162. Courtesy of the Institute for Sex Research.

hibiting and handling one's own genitals in the presence of companions. These types of sex play are the beginnings of sociosexual encounters. Figures 7.2 and 7.3 show the extent of such play Kinsey found at various ages as well as the sexes of the companions involved. As can be seen, sex play among members of the same sex tends to be more frequent than heterosexual play at these early ages, especially among boys. This is probably because young children more often associate with members of their own sex. Preteen-age boys, for instance, often become involved in groups

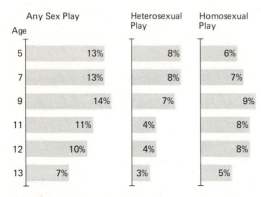

Figure 7.3 Percentages of prepubescent girls who had engaged in sociosexual play.

From A.C. Kinsey *et al., Sexual Behavior in the Human Female* (Philadelphia: Saunders, 1953), p. 129. Courtesy of the Institute for Sex Research.

or gangs of boys. Genital exhibition, demonstration of masturbation, group masturbation, and similar activities are quite common among groups of boys. It is believed that these activities satisfy social needs far broader than the mere release of sexual tension. Occasionally sex play in such situations appears to be more like adult homosexual behavior, with oral-genital contacts and attempts at anal intercourse.

What is the relation between preadolescent homosexual play and adult homosexual behavior? According to Kinsey's findings, fewer than half of all males who engaged in prepubertal homosexual activity continued it into adolescent and adult activity. At the lower educational levels the likelihood of continuing homosexual behavior into adulthood was greater (about one out of two) than among college-educated men (closer to one in four). Although homosexual play tends to stop at puberty, most adults who describe themselves as homosexual do trace their sexual preference to their childhood. In other words, prepubescent homosexual play does not necessarily lead to adult homosexuality, but adult homosexuality may have started with childhood homosexual activity.

Prepubescent girls in the Kinsey study were more likely to engage in mutual genital examination and vaginal insertions among themselves than with boys. In about one out of three instances such sexual activity did not go beyond genital exhibition and superficial exploration. Only 5 percent of girls with childhood homosexual experience reported continuing it into adolescence.

Heterosexual play experiences usually occur even earlier than homosexual activities for boys, and boys tend to be the instigators of heterosexual play. Approximately 40 percent of men and 30 percent of women recall having experienced such play before puberty, with showing and handling of the genitals being the most common activities. Finger insertions were often part of exploration but usually they did not go farther than the girl's introitus. Children also have games like "playing house," "mama and papa," and "doctor." The names may change, but the games are the same. During such games there may be a good deal of exploration and lying on top of one another, but even when the children occasionally undress, the activity does not usually proceed beyond placing the male and female genitals next to each other. In the Kinsey sample more than 10 percent of the boys and a smaller proportion of the girls were reported to have taken part in such "coital play."

Adult types of sexual activity during preadolescence are rare but are most likely to occur when one partner is older and more experienced. In the hands of an adult, a child can be trained to engage in practically all forms of sexual activity, including oral-genital contact and coitus.

Prepubescent Orgasm

Although females do not ejaculate with orgasm and males do not ejaculate until puberty when the prostate has developed, observations of sexually aroused children leave little doubt that even some very young children are capable of orgasm. In response to sexual stimulation, for instance, some male infants experience erection and other physiological changes that accompany arousal in adult males. Their muscles tense, and there are rhythmic pelvic thrusts that build up to distinct climaxes that include convulsive movements of the arms and legs. A child may cry at the height of this activity, but he soon grows quiet, loses his erection, and shows signs of relaxation similar to that of the postorgasmic phase in adults.

A more graphic description comes from a woman who watched her 3-year-old daughter masturbate:

Lying face down on the bed, with her knees drawn up, she started rhythmic pelvic thrusts, about one second or less apart. The thrusts were primarily pelvic, with the legs tensed in a fixed position. The forward components of the thrusts were in a smooth and perfect rhythm which was unbroken except for momentary pauses during which the genitalia were readjusted against the doll on which they were pressed; the return from each thrust was convulsive, jerky. There were 44 thrusts

in unbroken rhythm, a slight momentary pause, 87 thrusts followed by a slight momentary pause, then 10 thrusts, and then a cessation of all movement. There was marked concentration and intense breathing with abrupt jerks as orgasm approached. She was completely oblivious to everything during these later stages of the activity. Her eyes were glassy and fixed in a vacant stare. There was noticeable relief and relaxation after orgasm. A second series of reactions began two minutes later with a series of 48, 18, and 57 thrusts, with slight momentary pauses between each series. With the mounting tensions, there were audible gasps, but immediately following the cessation of pelvic thrusts there was complete relaxation and only desultory movements thereafter. (Kinsey, et al., 1953)

Such activity is not an everyday occurrence, but it is impossible to say exactly how many infants and children have such experiences or how often. Adults may tend to ignore or at least fail to recognize the sexual significance of such activity, and much of it goes unobserved. But as far as the ability to have orgasm is concerned, it has been reported in a five-month-old boy and in a four-month-old girl. Although sexual responsiveness develops at different rates, Kinsey estimated that more than half of all boys could achieve orgasm at 3 to 4 years of age and almost all could do so three to five years before reaching puberty. (No similar data are available for females, but there is no reason to believe that there are major differences between the sexes in this respect.)

The fact that children can become sexually aroused at such early ages does not mean that they should be stimulated; in fact, cultural attitudes prohibit such activity in most societies.

Prepubescent Sexual Contacts with Adults

Children of both sexes have been sexually exploited by adults probably in all cultures. Regardless of laws against such activity, some adults continue to approach children sexually. Exactly how often this happens we do not know, but in the Kinsey female sample about one out of four women had been sexually approached by someone five or more years older while she was still preadolescent. Most of these women (about 80 percent) had experienced such contacts only once, but about 5 percent had had such encounters nine or more times before adulthood. About half the time the adult was a stranger, but one third of the approaches involved friends and acquaintances. About one fifth involved relatives (uncles, fathers, brothers, and grandfathers — in order of decreasing frequency).

In about half the instances the approaches consisted of exhibition of the adult male genitals. Next came fondling the child without genital contact (about 30 percent) and genital manipulation (about 20 percent). Other forms of activity were less common. Coitus, for instance, was reported in only three out of one hundred instances of adult sexual approach (less than 1 percent of the entire Kinsey female sample). It was reported by 7 percent of the Playboy sample. Most of these girls were 10 years old or older (though still prepubescent), but a few were as young as 4 or 5 years old when these incidents occurred.

The adults who approached young boys sexually were most often males, but it is possible that adult females can more easily conceal their sexual motives and get away with sexual approaches to children than can men because we generally find it more "natural" that a woman be physically affectionate toward children, even if they are strangers.

The use of children as sexual objects is assumed to be more frequent in poorer neighborhoods where living conditions are crowded, but Hunt (who did not study lower-class populations) found incestuous acts to be more common among college-level males and females. In either case, such activity is severely condemned at all levels of society. It is condemned primarily because the impact of sexual stimulation on young children by adults is generally believed to be quite harmful. In cultures in which genital stimulation of children by adults is considered normal, children apparently do not develop psychological problems as a result of it. There are cases in our culture, however, in which adult psychological problems do seem to stem from such child-

hood experiences, especially from traumatic experiences (those involving high degrees of emotional stress or physical injury).

Significance of Prepubertal Sexuality

Because children are often unaware of the sexual significance of their behavior we should not attribute adult motives to them. The sexual play and activities of children are largely experimental, imitative, exploratory, and sexual only in a general sense (unless an older person is involved in stimulating the child for specifically adult sexual purposes). It is particularly important not to label the sex play of children as deviant or perverse, no matter what it involves. To do so would be like calling a child who believes in Santa Claus or in ghosts "delusional" or "mentally ill."

But how should we regard childhood sexuality? The sexual activity of children and their often unused sexual potential raise important developmental and social questions. In the West there is no general agreement on how we should regard or regulate the sex lives of children. The dominant traditional values have generally been restrictive: Sexual contact with adults has been strictly prohibited and sex play among children discouraged. Sexual instruction in any form has often been opposed as potentially stimulating and therefore harmful. There is now a growing concern that this area may be one of the most neglected in the upbringing of children and that a great deal of confusion and damage result when the children are left on their own to "sink or swim" in their sex lives. In certain countries (such as Sweden) there are already extensive sex-education programs in schools, but attitudes in the United States are still mixed. The issue still causes sharp disagreements among various segments of the population, but increasingly sex education is coming to be seen as an important and necessary part of one's schooling. In 1970, for instance, 65 percent of those questioned in a Gallup poll survey said that sex education should be taught in the schools. By 1977, the figure had risen to 77 percent. Acceptance of discussions of contraceptive practices in sex-education courses increased from 36 percent to 69 percent over the same time period, and in 1977, 56 percent of those polled were in favor of making birth-control devices available to teenagers. From these figures it would appear that attitudes toward sex education have changed greatly in recent years.

It is often suggested that children should be educated in sex at home, but many parents find the task bewildering—often because they lack adequate information themselves. When is one to begin such instructions; what does one say; how far does one go beyond stories of "birds and bees"? Even so-called sexually liberated parents may feel at a loss in trying to decide what to encourage and what to discourage in their children. Professional advice tends to be fragmentary and more often based on the adviser's "common sense" than on tested evidence, although such advice can still be useful (*see,* for example, *Baby and Child Care* by Benjamin Spock, 1976). As a result of confusion and uncertainty, most parents currently steer a middle-of-the-road course and neither give demonstrations of intercourse to their children nor punish children every time they touch their genitals. Instead, they try to respond to questions as they arise. But even this approach often involves considerable uncertainty and discomfort for all involved.

Adolescent Sexuality

Despite the importance of infant and childhood sexuality, adolescence and puberty remain the turning points in psychosexual development—the time when true adult sexuality emerges. **Adolescence** (from the Latin word meaning "to grow up") refers to the phase of psychological development that culminates in full genital and reproductive maturity. This period overlaps with but does not correspond exactly in time with the biological phase known as **puberty** (from the Latin word meaning "adulthood"). Puberty begins with the appearance of secondary sexual characteristics and lasts until the start of reproductive ability. The term **nubility** (from the Latin for "able to marry") refers to the fi-

nal stage of puberty during which full fertility is achieved. Puberty extends over three or four years in females and longer in males. Adolescence lasts even longer in both sexes.

As explained in Chapter 4, puberty begins at different times, not only for each sex but among members of the same sex. The changes in sexual behavior seen during puberty also tend to differ between the sexes. Partly because prepubescent sex play is more common among boys (despite the already mentioned decline in sexual activity prior to puberty) more of it actually continues into adolescence. Petting to orgasm, for example, was likely to continue during the transition into puberty and adolescence among 65 percent of the boys in the Kinsey study. Sexual activity between members of the same sex was the most likely sexual outlet to be interrupted at puberty. A year or so before the onset of puberty the relatively inactive period comes to an end, and boys show an upsurge in sexual activity that accelerates during puberty, with sporadic prepubescent sex play being replaced by steady levels of sexual activity. Within a few years most boys reach the highest levels of sexual activity they will achieve in their lives.

Although an adolescent boy may have already achieved orgasm, his first ejaculation is usually an impressive event. Among physiologically normal males in the Kinsey study the earliest first ejaculation remembered had occurred at about 8 years of age and the latest (also among apparently healthy males) at about 21 years of age. About 90 percent of all males had this experience between the ages of 11 and 15, with the average being close to 14 years of age. But even this purely biological phenomenon was influenced by social factors. Among the lowest educational group the average age of first ejaculation was almost one year later than in the most educated group. The differences among individuals, however, were greatest. Some boys in elementary school were more mature than others in college.

The first ejaculation resulted most often from masturbation (in about two out of three cases). It came as a result of nocturnal emissions, missions, or "wet dreams," in one out of eight cases, and during contacts with other males in about one out of twenty instances. The first ejaculation rarely occurred spontaneously (through fantasy alone without direct genital stimulation).

Spontaneous ejaculations, though rare, are of interest. The ability to have them is almost always lost after puberty, but they emphasize the high and indiscriminate level of excitability in younger males. This is also evident in frequent erections that reportedly occurred in response to various physical (but not genital) activities (chinning on bars, vibrations of a boat) and psychological stimulations (watching couples petting, milking a cow, reciting in front of a class). Some erections and ejaculations that appear to be spontaneous (as when climbing a tree) may in fact be caused by genital friction, even though the boy may have been, at least initially, quite innocent of sexual intent.

The sexual development of females contrasts with that of males in a number of ways. First, because prepubescent sex play was less common among females, the interruption in sexual activity prior to puberty appeared much more marked. The prepubescent girl had to begin all over, as it were. Furthermore, during female puberty there was no sudden upsurge in sexual activity similar to that seen in males. Instead, women showed slow but steady increases in sexual responsiveness that reached a peak between the middle twenties and early thirties. So to say that females in our culture mature more rapidly sexually is somewhat misleading, even though they do mature earlier in terms of reproductive ability. Cultural variables greatly influence the emergence of sexual responsiveness in the two genders. In other words, it may well be that our culture teaches females to repress their sexuality, more so than males.

There have been many studies of adolescent dating behavior but few specific investigations of adolescent sexual activities. Those that do exist, such as the study conducted by Robert C. Sorensen, do not accurately represent the U.S. population. They are, nevertheless, of some interest because they are current.

In Sorensen's sample of youth of both sexes between the ages of 13 and 19 years, 48 percent reportedly were virgins (55 percent of the girls and 41 percent of the boys), and 52 percent had had intercourse one or more times (45 percent of the girls and 59 percent of the boys). About one in five persons in the total sample was sexually inexperienced, not having engaged even in petting (girls 25 percent, boys 20 percent). An almost equal number had engaged in petting but not coitus (girls 19 percent, boys 14 percent). According to Zelnik and Kantner's 1971 findings, 30 percent of unmarried women between the ages of 15 and 19 years had experienced sexual intercourse. By 1976, the figure had risen to 40 percent.

The nonvirgins could be classified in several ways. About one in five (girls 28 percent, boys 15 percent) had had a sexual relationship with one person ("serial monogamist"). Fifteen percent of all adolescents were "sexual adventurers" who moved freely from one partner to another. The remaining nonvirgins were "inactive," having had no coitus for more than a year (or were classified in still other ways).

We will deal in more detail with specific sexual behaviors during adolescence, including masturbation and coitus, in later chapters. Petting, because it is a typically adolescent activity and one of the major contributors to the development of sociosexual relations, will be discussed here.

Petting

"Petting," or erotic caressing, is not an exclusively Western or even human practice. In one form or another petting is practiced all over the world, and among many mammals there is a good deal of sex play that does not lead to coitus. In the United States petting has been known by a variety of names ("bundling," "spooning," "smooching," "larking," "sparking," and so on), all of which now sound quaint and old-fashioned. The term "petting" itself also seems to be on the way out. One current replacement, "making out," is quite ambiguous in that it is also used to indicate sexual intercourse.

No matter what it is called, the techniques of petting (which are basically those of foreplay) are essentially the same. Petting may or may not lead to orgasm for either partner, but if it leads to coitus it is more accurately called "foreplay."

The relative popularity of petting at various periods provides interesting clues to changes in sexual patterns and attitudes. For example, it was shown in the Kinsey survey that successive generations of women in this country had engaged in petting in increasingly larger numbers. Of those born before 1900, 80 percent reported some premarital petting (about 15 percent to the point of orgasm). Of those born between 1900 and 1909, 91 percent reported such experiences (more than 30 percent to orgasm). Nearly 99 percent of those born between 1910 and 1929 reported petting, and about a third of these women had reached orgasm through petting at least once. No similar information was obtained for males.

Sorensen's sample suggests that about two out of three adolescents in this country currently have some petting experience. But both public and scientific interest have moved beyond this issue, and the fine distinctions between "necking," "petting," and "heavy petting" hardly seem worth mentioning. Today the question usually has to do with intercourse—whether or not to do it, with whom, and under what circumstances.

Even among those who stopped short of coitus, petting appears to involve fairly extensive mutual sexual exploration. In the group that stopped short of coitus (17 percent of the total sample) almost all girls have their breasts felt by boys and nearly half had their genitals touched by boys. About half of these girls had in turn felt the sex organs of boys. Among the boys, a third had their sex organs touched by girls, more than half had felt the genitals and almost all had touched the breasts of girls.

The most significant thing about petting, in terms of sexual development, is the role it plays in the development of sociosexual behavior. For many people petting provides the bridge from adolescent to adult sexual behavior. It is pleasurable as an end in itself, and for many people who do not choose to have intercourse (for whatever reason) it is an acceptable means of experiencing orgasm. Adolescents learn much about each other's bodies, sexual responses, and so on during petting. Through these encounters they also learn the social rules of sexual behavior. Petting also often goes beyond the specifically sexual and involves feelings of intimacy, tenderness, and love. Through these interactions adolescents learn about each other's emotions and thoughts. It is during this period that concepts of sex roles, notions of masculinity and femininity, and other aspects of sexual identity begin to mature.

Petting, of course, is not the only means of learning about adult sexual attitudes and behaviors. The same things can be learned with minimal or no sexual contact at all. Or, adolescents may proceed directly to full-fledged sexual activity without the benefit of these "trials." The outcome, in the nature and quality of adult sexual life, is thus not a result of how much sex or what sort of sex a person has during adolescence. Instead, a great many factors, sexual as well as nonsexual, interact to shape sexuality as a part of overall sexual development.

FREQUENCIES OF SEXUAL ACTIVITY

The shift from adolescence to adulthood is usually a subtle one that occurs gradually rather than at a specific point in time. As far as sexual activity is concerned, the change in status may have little or no effect. Many young men, as we shall see, will already have reached their sexual peak (as far as frequency is concerned) before they are legally considered adults at age 18 or sometimes as late as age 21. The same is not true for young women in our culture, many of whom may not reach their peak sexually active years until they are in their thirties. So even though it is possible to conduct surveys of adolescent sexual behavior, it is not always easy to distinguish between adolescent and adult sexual behavior. The major portions of the Kinsey survey, for example, concentrated on individuals between 15 and 85 years of age. One of the first questions addressed by this survey had to do with frequency. How much sex do people have?

When Kinsey set out to measure the frequency of sexual activity he had to use strict guidelines. Although a lot of sex goes on without orgasm, Kinsey counted as a person's "total sexual outlet" only the most obvious form of sexual outlet—orgasm, as achieved through the six main types of sexual activities mentioned earlier. To make his findings easier to understand and deal with, Kinsey measured frequency over specific periods of time. Since our lives are usually organized around weekly schedules, he used the week as a unit of measure. Since sexual frequency changes over the years, he examined it in five-year periods.

Frequency of Total Sexual Outlet among Adult Males

The average (mean) frequency of total sexual outlet for men between adolescence and

85 years of age in the Kinsey study was calculated to be nearly three orgasms per week. This, of course, does not mean that the "average man" necessarily had this many weekly orgasms nor that such frequencies are standards of normality, health, virility, and so on. The data show that there is extreme variation even among apparently healthy people living under similar conditions. One man in good health had had only one orgasm in 30 years. Another man, also apparently in good health, claimed to have averaged 30 orgasms per week for 30 years.

Much more meaningful than such single figures is the frequency pattern of the number of orgasms per week for the same men (*see* Figure 7.4). As can be seen, the highest percentages of men had about one orgasm per week, indicating that the three-per-week figure was inflated by the higher rates. What this means is that men cannot be easily grouped as typical or average on the basis of orgasm and that the range of normal variation is quite wide.

The most important factor related to frequency of outlet was age. Figure 7.5 shows how the mean, or average, number of orgasms per week was related to the age group of the individual. The first group consisted of boys 15 years old and younger (but past puberty), the next group of those between 16 and 20 years of age, and so on, in five-year spans.

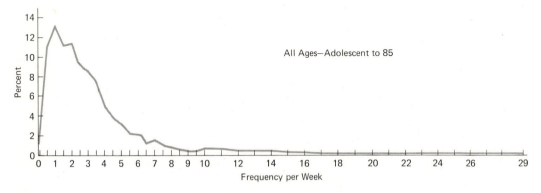

Figure 7.4 Individual variation in frequency of total sexual outlet among males.

From A. C. Kinsey *et al.*, *Sexual Behavior in the Human Male* (Philadelphia: Saunders, 1948), p. 198. Courtesy of the Institute for Sex Research.

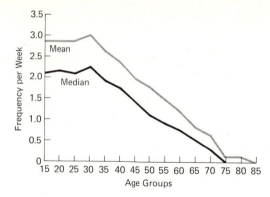

Figure 7.5 Frequency of total sexual outlet for males, by age groups.

From A.C. Kinsey *et al., Sexual Behavior in the Human Male* (Philadelphia: Saunders, 1948). p. 220. Courtesy of the Institute for Sex Research.

The most active groups appear to have been those younger than 30 years of age. After that age the frequency of orgasm steadily declined with advancing age.

When Hunt compared the weekly frequency of intercourse (as opposed to total sexual outlet) reported by married men in 1972 with Kinsey's data, he found an increase in coital frequency, especially in the men younger than 35 years of age, who had increased since Kinsey's time from twice a week to three or four times a week.

Frequency of Total Sexual Outlet among Females

Exact comparisons of male and female frequencies of total sexual outlet cannot be made easily. For one thing, female orgasm is more difficult to recognize and count than male orgasm because there is no ejaculation. Also, the sexual behavior of women (especially at the time of the Kinsey study) is more strictly controlled by social attitudes than is that of men. Therefore, women's behavior patterns are less likely than those of men to reflect natural tendencies. One way to cancel out at least some of the influence of social restrictions is to compare unmarried and married women. Social constraints regarding sexual activity are fewer for married women, so the

behavior of married women probably more closely reflects natural tendencies than does that of unmarried women.

In the Kinsey sample about a third of the single women in most age groups experienced an average of one orgasm every other week. A smaller proportion had one orgasm per week, and an even smaller number reported two or more orgasms per week.

Among married women between 21 and 25 years of age, about one third reported one or two orgasms per week. Another 5 percent or so averaged three orgasms per week, and about another 5 percent reached five to seven orgasms per week. Fewer than 20 percent had one or less orgasms every other week. In the 36-to-40 age group about a fourth of the women averaged one orgasm per week, and this percentage decreased with age. Between 51 and 55 almost two out of three women experienced fewer than one orgasm per week. About 20 percent still reached one or two weekly orgasms, but higher frequencies were rare. Among the married women in the Redbook survey (which counted frequency of sexual intercourse), the largest percentage (nearly 32 percent) reported having intercourse approximately two times per week.

The average number of orgasms per week (mean) and the number of orgasms per week of the "average" woman (median) in the Kinsey study are seen in Figure 7.6. When compared with the same number for men (*see* Figure 7.5), several differences appear. First, the frequencies of total sexual outlet for fe-

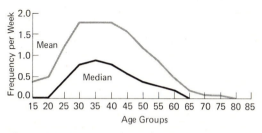

Figure 7.6 Frequency of total sexual outlet for females, by age groups.

From A.C. Kinsey *et al., Sexual Behavior in the Human Female* (Philadelphia: Saunders, 1953), p. 548. Courtesy of the Institute for Sex Research.

males were lower than for males in all age groups, even though women, probably more so than men, are capable of multiple orgasm (*see* Chapter 3). Almost 15 percent of the women in the Kinsey survey reported experiencing multiple orgasms, but Kinsey could not have expected his subjects to recall exactly how many orgasms they had during each past episode of sexual activity. Instead, he had to be satisfied with their memories of the number of sexual acts that included orgasm. The women actually may have had a higher number of orgasms than the data show. But even if multiple orgasms are not considered, the differences between the sexes are not great. The most active male group reported an average of three orgasms per week, and the most active female group reported nearly two (1.8) orgasms per week.

The difference in medians is somewhat larger. The average male in the peak group experienced slightly more than two weekly climaxes, while the average female had closer to one. The wider difference between means and medians among women indicates wider individual variability. The level of activity for some women was so much higher than that of the others that the mean values for the group as a whole were inflated.

Another, more intriguing sex difference is revealed in the shapes of these curves, which indicate quite different patterns with regard to age. Men had achieved high levels of sexual activity right after puberty and by the age of 15, but the youngest female group was quite inactive sexually (about one orgasm every three weeks). For males the highest level of outlet was during the years from 16 to 30. For females these years were a time of increasing (rather than peak) activity, with the highest levels of sexual outlet coming at around the age of 30 and continuing for another ten years. During the peak decade for women, males were beginning a period of steady decline. But because of the overall higher weekly rate for males, at no time was a given age group of females having more orgasms per week than were males in the same age group. Once the decline had begun, however, increasing age brought the two sexes progressively closer. The averages for males and females came closest in the age group of 41 to 45 years.

High and Low Levels of Sexual Activity

Although we have been dealing with average frequencies of sexual outlet, the Kinsey data make it quite clear that a wide range of variation is the norm. A great many healthy males and females have weekly rates of sexual outlet that are far above or far below the group average. More than 7 percent of the males in the Kinsey sample, for example, averaged seven orgasms a week. One in four of these men was younger than 30 years of age, and about a third of them were capable of having more than one orgasm during a single sexual episode. Women with high frequencies of sexual outlet were fewer in the Kinsey sample, but certainly many were as active as the most active males. And some may have been even more active. Some women attain multiple climaxes every time they have intercourse throughout long and active sexual lives; occasionally such a woman may reach a dozen or more climaxes in an hour, which probably no man is capable of doing.

Like "high frequency" individuals, sexual low-frequency people are distributed among the general population and by no means constitute a distinct or abnormal group. Sexual abstinence for days or weeks is quite common for both males and females. About one in ten males between puberty and 31 years of age in the Kinsey sample averaged only one orgasm every two weeks. About 3 percent of this same age group had about one orgasm each in ten weeks. The number of males with low outlets increases steadily after the age of 35.

In the Kinsey study the highest percentage of unmarried females (almost 80 percent) who engaged in no activity that led to orgasm were those younger than 15 years of age. As age increased, this percentage dropped, but even between the ages of 30 or so and 40, the peak years of female sexual activity, about a third of the unmarried women reported having had no orgasms. More than a fourth of all unmarried women reported never having had an orgasm.

Among married women the proportion that

had never experienced orgasm was smaller, but still considerable. In the younger age groups (16 to 20 years) about one in five had not reached orgasm. Between the ages of 21 and 25 this proportion dropped to about one in ten.

Extremely high and low levels of sexual activity are found in all segments of the population, in all ethnic, social, educational, and occupational groups, and in individuals who are ordinary in most other ways. Frequency of sexual outlet in itself is in no way an indication of normality or abnormality. There are instances in which physical or psychological problems affect sexual activity and in which sexual activity affects physical and psychological health. But each such case must be considered as a specific instance, and generalizations about "normality" should not be based on rates of sexual frequency.

VARIETIES OF SEXUAL EXPERIENCE

Throughout history men and women have resorted to every imaginable type of activity in the pursuit of sexual gratification. They have copulated with each other, with members of their own sexes, and with animals. They have used their bodies in solitude, in twosomes, in threesomes, and in greater numbers. Every orifice that can possibly be penetrated has been penetrated. Every inch of skin has been caressed, scratched, tickled, pinched, licked, and bitten for love. Orgasms have come amid murmurs of tender affection and screams of pain, in total awareness and while fast asleep. An important aspect of this diversity is the fact that some members of the population lead very restricted sex lives and there are some apparently healthy people who go through life without ever experiencing orgasm.

What accounts for this diversity? The two most obvious answers have to do with biological and cultural differences. Variation is the cardinal rule of all biological phenomena, and cultures are diverse by definition. The ranges of variation are quite narrow in some physiological matters (like the degree of heat that

sperm can tolerate) and much broader in others (like the ability to have multiple orgasms). Certain behaviors (such as incest) are strictly prohibited in most cultures, and other behaviors (premarital sex, homosexuality) are viewed with widely varying tolerance among cultures. Such real differences exist among individuals within groups as well as among groups of various sizes. Biological and cultural differences explain some if not all variations, but even without complete information on the causes of sexual behavior, we can examine the types and frequencies of the more common components of total sexual outlet.

The six types of sexual outlet found by Kinsey to account for practically all orgasms experienced by men and women were:

Masturbation—self-stimulation for sexual arousal and orgasm. It usually involves manipulation of the genitals, but can also be achieved through breast stimulation, rhythmic muscular contractions, and other activities.

"Sex dreams," or nocturnal orgasms—orgasms that occur during sleep (including those that occur during daytime sleep).

Heterosexual petting—any physical contact between members of opposite sexes that is undertaken for the purpose of sexual arousal but not including copulation of the vagina and the penis. Accidental contacts, even though sexually stimulating, are not considered petting. In the Kinsey study only petting that led to orgasms was counted.

Coitus—heterosexual intercourse involving coupling of the vagina and the penis. In most instances coitus is not an isolated act but comes as the culmination of petting, or foreplay. When foreplay precedes coitus, it is considered part of the act rather than as petting, although the activities involved—kissing, caressing, and so on—are identical to those of petting.

Homosexual relations—physical activity between members of the same sex for the purpose of erotic arousal and orgasm. Much homosexual activity consists of petting, though the term usually is not used in this context. Homosexual relations may also involve oral-genital contacts and anal intercourse—acts that are also performed in heterosexual relations. What makes an act homosexual is not the nature of the act but the fact that those involved are of the same sex.

Animal contacts—physical contact by a person of either sex with an animal of either sex deliberately undertaken for sexual gratification. These activities are similar to human petting and intercourse, but modified to allow for physical differences. The incidence of animal contact in the Kinsey study made it the least significant of the six sexual outlets.

That men and women engage in all these activities has been well known and documented throughout history. What has been unclear is the extent to which people rely on one means of gratification over another. In most Western societies coitus has traditionally been accepted as the only legitimate sexual outlet. Other forms of sexual expression have usually been condemned, with punishments ranging from mild disapproval to the death penalty—depending on the nature of the act and the identities of the participants.

Among the most important factors affecting types of sexual outlet among women in the Kinsey study was marriage. For single women in the under-15 age group, masturbation was the primary source of orgasm (almost 85 percent of the total). As age increased this proportion decreased, so that between the ages of 36 and 40 coitus and masturbation provided about equal proportions of orgasms (more than 35 percent for each). In the next two age groups masturbation increased, but only enough to account for slightly more than half of all orgasms in the 46-to-50 age group.

Nocturnal orgasms, or sex dreams, were a very minor source of orgasm for single women. Interestingly, they were most common (4 percent of total outlet) in the oldest age group, even though we tend to think of nocturnal orgasms as being more typical of adolescence.

Petting accounted for almost 20 percent of orgasms between the ages of 16 and 25 years and continued to be frequent even in the older age groups. Petting provided the same ratio (4 percent) of orgasms for adolescents younger than 16 years of age as it did for single women 41 to 45 years old. But it is likely that if all petting, not just petting to orgasm, were considered, teenagers would show a higher level of activity than would older women.

Coitus was the second most important source of orgasm for single women. Beginning with the youngest age group, in which premarital coitus accounted for 6 percent of orgasms, this outlet reached its peak between the ages of 41 and 45 years, when it provided 43 percent of total outlets.

Although there are still many restrictions against premarital sex, the more recent surveys suggest that premarital coitus is becoming more prevalent among the young. In the Playboy survey about 65 percent of the women between 25 and 35 years of age reported having had premarital intercourse, but more than 80 percent of those younger than 25 reported engaging in premarital coitus. The Redbook figures are even higher, with 96 percent of those younger than 20 reporting premarital coitus. The most reliable figures in this regard come from Kantner and Zelnik which show 40 percent of women between 15 and 19 to have had sexual intercourse.

Homosexual contacts provided a steadily increasing proportion of the orgasms of single women up to the age span of 36 to 40 years, when almost one out of five orgasms was achieved by this means.

When compared with single women, married women showed much more uniform sex lives. Through all age levels examined they reported an overwhelming reliance on coitus as a source of no fewer than four out of five orgasms. Some of these orgasms, however, occurred outside of marriage, with the rates of extramarital orgasm being the highest (slightly more than 10 percent) between the ages of 41 and 50.

Although coitus was the primary source of orgasm for married women in the Kinsey sample, it was not the only source. Masturbation provided a fairly steady proportion (about 10 percent) of total sexual outlet, and there was a slight increase with age. Kinsey reported that about 30 percent of married women in their late twenties and early thirties masturbated, the median rate being about ten times a year. More current findings suggest that masturbation is more common than it was in Kinsey's time. Hunt, for instance, reports that nearly 70 percent of married women masturbate, with the rate remaining at about ten times a year. Almost 75 percent of the married women in the Redbook survey reported masturbating, and the figure was as high as 82 percent in the Hite survey (which included both married and unmarried women). Nocturnal orgasms increased slightly with age, and homosexual contacts were a minor source of orgasm for married women.

Previously married women (those who were separated, divorced, or widowed) appeared to be closer in their sexual behavior to married than to single women: Coitus was the predominant source of orgasm, even though these women did rely more heavily on masturbation, nocturnal orgasms, and homosexual contacts than did married women.

Components of Total Sexual Outlet among Males

The Kinsey study of men considered age and marital status as well as educational level, and the data revealed important associations between educational level and the components of total sexual outlet. Among single males with elementary-school education (see Figure 7.7) masturbation accounted for a little more than half the total sexual outlets even at the youngest age levels. It became less significant with increasing age. Between 21 and 35 years of age masturbation accounted for only about a quarter of all orgasms. Starting at age 16, coitus was the primary outlet for this group, with these single men showing increasing reliance with age on prostitutes as sexual partners. Homosexual contacts also increased, so that between 31 and 35 years of age they accounted for one fourth of all orgasms. Nocturnal orgasms provided a small but steady outlet for these men, but petting contributed only slightly to total outlets.

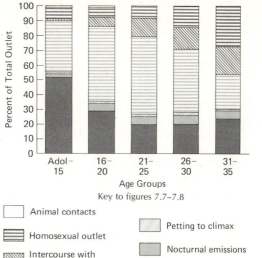

Key to figures 7.7–7.8

□ Animal contacts

▤ Homosexual outlet

▨ Intercourse with prostitutes

▦ Intercourse with companions

▧ Petting to climax

▒ Nocturnal emissions

■ Masturbation

Figure 7.7 Sources of orgasm for single males with elementary-school education, by age groups.

From A.C. Kinsey *et al., Sexual Behavior in the Human Male* (Philadelphia: Saunders, 1948), p. 490. Courtesy of the Institute for Sex Research.

In contrast, single males with some college education relied heavily on masturbation (*see* Figure 7.8). In the youngest age group it ac-

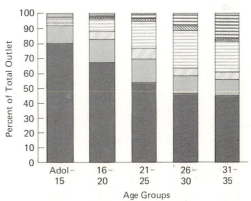

Figure 7.8 Sources of orgasm for single males with some college education, by age groups.

From A.C. Kinsey *et al., Sexual Behavior in the Human Male* (Philadelphia: Saunders, 1948), p. 491. Courtesy of the Institute for Sex Research.

counted for about four out of five orgasms. In successively higher age groups this figure declined, but not much below 50 percent. The better-educated single male's reliance on masturbation was at the expense of coitus, particularly with prostitutes. Petting and nocturnal emissions were more substantial outlets for this group, but homosexual contacts were less important than for less-educated males. There was however, a similar increase in reliance on such contacts with age.

In contrast to the patterns of single males, those of married males (like those of married females) were much more uniform. Marriage greatly narrowed the differences between the groups, with coitus being the primary sexual outlet. Even so, a few differences remained. Masturbation and nocturnal emissions were relatively more important sources for the better-educated group. More than 70 percent of the married men in the Playboy survey reported masturbating, with a median rate of 24 times a year. Also, the less-educated married male was shown to be more involved with extramarital coitus and homosexual contacts in his earlier years. The better-educated married male became more involved with these activities in his later years.

The data on males further illustrates the important associations of sexual behavior with various biological and social factors. For example, there are no biological differences between less- and more-educated males in general, so the important differences between these two groups must be explained in psychological and social terms. Education itself was not the key factor. These men were not behaving differently because of what they were taught in school. Instead, education was primarily an indicator of social class. Apparently it was social class that determined the lifestyles, values, and so on of these men. Similar associations could be shown, for example, between occupational choice and patterns of sexual behavior.

So far we have singled out a few important factors to illustrate their connection with sexual behavior. But other factors were also shown by the Kinsey study to be significantly related to both the frequency and the types of

sexual outlet. For example, the age at which a boy reached puberty was shown to be related to future sexual behavior. Those maturing earlier had higher total outlets. This relationship held true for those who married as well as for those who remained single, so it suggests the possibility of biological differences. The age of menarche did not appear to matter in this respect. Religious beliefs were also shown to be related to total sexual outlet. Among males, orthodox Jews were the least active, and nonpracticing Roman Catholics the most active sexually. In both sexes, those who took religion more seriously were less likely to engage in noncoital or extramarital sexual activities.

These observations are but a few that have emerged from the Kinsey study. Some of them were obvious and expected, others surprising and questionable. Some of these observations are probably valid today while others are not. What is more important is the indication that sexual behavior is highly varied and profoundly influenced by a great many biological and social factors, even though we do not fully understand the exact nature and size of these influences. The cross-cultural comparisons that follow will help emphasize these points.

Cross-Cultural Comparisons

There is a vast amount of information on sexual practices in various parts of the world, but description rather than quantification has been the traditional anthropological approach. Large-scale studies of populations on the order of the Kinsey investigations do not exist, but what is available gives a good idea of the variety of sexual behavior found around the world. Because all human beings share a common biological heritage, many of the differences seen in various cultures can almost certainly be attributed to cultural rather than biological factors.

In general, three types of societies have been identified: restrictive, semirestrictive, and permissive. But the United States appears to be in a transition between restrictive and semirestrictive. In almost all cultures there is a good deal of variation with regard to attitudes as well as to frequency and types of sexual outlet. A brief look at the frequencies observed in several cultures, however, will give us a good idea of just how important cultural effects are on our sex lives.

An extensive review (by Ford and Beach) of anthropological studies of almost 200 societies, for example, found tremendous variation among different peoples in the frequency of intercourse. Males of the Keraki (of New Guinea) generally had coitus once a week, of the Lesu (of New Ireland) once or twice a week, of the Chiricahua (of Arizona) two or three times a week, of the Hopi (Arizona) three or four times a week, of the Aranda (Australia) three to five times a night, and of the Chagga (Tanganyika) up to ten times a night.

The following passage about the Lepchas (of the Southeastern Himalayas) further illustrates the high frequency of sexual outlet common to some cultures:

In their youth and young manhood (the period Lepchas call *fleng*) Lepcha men would appear to be remarkably potent; trustworthy people said that when they were first married they would copulate with their wives five or six, and even eight or nine times in the course of the night, though they would then be tired the next day. I have got no comparable information from women but such statements were often made in mixed company without the women present making any comment or in any way expressing incredulity. This potency diminishes around the age of thirty, but copulation once nightly is still the general rule for married couples. Tafoor claimed that in his youth he was almost indefatigable, but says that now he only sleeps with his wife once every three or four nights; that is the reason why he is relatively fat, for chastity induces fatness. It is believed that people accustomed to regular copulation will feel extremely uncomfortable for the first few days if for any reason their partner is removed; but it is considered that people over thirty should be able to support long periods of chastity. (Gorer, 1938)

At the other end of the scale, in the re-pressive societies attitudes toward sexual behavior, especially in the young, are usually highly restrictive. For instance, both the Apinaye (a primitive, peaceful people in Brazil) and the Ashanti (a complex society in Guinea) expressly forbade children to masturbate from an early age. In New Guinea a Kwoma woman who saw a boy with an erection would strike his penis with a stick. Kwoma boys soon learned not to touch their penises even while urinating.

Restrictive attitudes toward children did not always mean that these cultures were sexually prohibitive in general. In some, once boys reached maturity (usually marked by some rite, or ceremony) they could immediately be permitted wide sexual freedom. Most of these cultures also enforced the double standard so well known in our society. Girls were almost always more strictly guarded, and coitus before menarche (or some other sign of puberty) was believed to be harmful.

While the restrictiveness of a society does not always show up in the frequency of sexual outlet among adults, the effects of restrictive attitudes can affect not only frequency but types of sexual outlet, among other behaviors. A detailed account of one unusually repressive island folk community in Ireland illustrates this. The community has been given the fictitious name of Inis Beag:

Both lack of sexual knowledge and misconceptions about sex among adults combine to brand Inis Beag as one of the most sexually naive of the world's societies. Sex never is discussed in the home when children are about; only three mothers admitted giving advice, briefly and incompletely, to their daughters. We were told that boys are better advised than girls, but that the former learn about sex informally from older boys and men and from observing animals. Most respondents who were questioned about sexual instructions given to youths expressed the belief that "after marriage nature takes its course," thus negating the need for anxiety-creating and embarrassing personal confrontation of parents and offspring. We were unable to discover any cases of childlessness based on sexual ignorance of spouses, as reported from other regions of peasant Ireland. Also, we were unable to discover knowledge of the sexual categories utilized by researchers in sex: insertion of tongue while kissing, male mouth on female breast, female hand on penis, cunnilingus, fellatio, femoral coitus, anal coitus, extramarital coitus, manifest homosexuality, sexual contact with animals, fetishism, and sado-masochistic behavior. Some of these activities may be practiced by particular individuals and couples; however, without a doubt they are deviant forms in Inis Beag, about which information is difficult to come by.

Menstruation and menopause arouse profound misgivings among women of the island, because few of them comprehend their physiological significance. My wife was called on to explain these processes more than any other phenomena related to sex. When they reach puberty, most girls are unprepared for the first menstrual flow and find the experience a traumatic one—especially when their mothers are unable to provide a satisfactory explanation for it. And it is commonly believed that the menopause can induce "madness"; in order to ward off this condition, some women have retired from life in their mid-forties and, in a few cases, have confined themselves to bed until death, years later. (Messenger in Marshall and Saggs, 1971)

Boys and girls in this community are segregated in school and even in church. There is no observed courting. Elders insist that it does not occur, but young males admit to it in rumor ("walking out"). Premarital coitus is unknown.

The development of sexual repression is described as follows:

The seeds of repression are planted early in childhood by parents and kin through instruction supplemented by rewards and punishments, conscious imitation, and unconscious internalization. Although mothers bestow considerable affection and attention on their offspring, especially on their sons, physical love as manifested in intimate handling and kissing is rare in Inis Beag. Even breast feeding is uncommon because of its sexual connotation, and verbal affection comes to replace contact affection by late infancy. Any form of direct or indirect sexual expression—such as masturbation, mutual exploration of bodies, use of either standard or slang words relating to sex, and open urination and defecation—is severely punished by word or deed. Care is taken to cover the bodies of infants in the presence of siblings and outsiders, and sex is never discussed before children. Several times my wife inadvertently inquired as to whether particular women were pregnant, using that word before youths, only to be "hushed" or to have the conversation postponed until the young people could be herded outside. The adults were so embarrassed by the term that they found it difficult to communicate with her after the children had departed. (Messenger in Marshall and Saggs, 1971)

As repressive as this Irish community may sound, it is possible that the situation has changed since 1959 when the researchers began their study there. In fact, it is possible that attitudes toward certain aspects of human sexuality are undergoing change in many parts of the world—if the United States is any example. As we have seen, current surveys, while not as reliable or comprehensive as Kinsey's, suggest an ongoing change in attitudes in the United States, especially with regard to such things as premarital sex, masturbation, and the concept of sex as pleasure rather than as a purely reproductive process. In this day of rapid, world-wide communications, it is probable that even communities like Inis Beag are being influenced by outside attitudes (although "pornographic" magazines like *Time* and *Life* mailed from relatives abroad have received spirited criticism from church leaders in that community).

Whether or not Inis Beag has changed, the point is that sexual attitudes and behaviors vary greatly around the world. When we make cross-cultural comparisons, several points must be kept in mind.

All attempts at using anthropological data must view each feature of a culture in its total context. The point in learning about other cultures is not to search for better models or to congratulate ourselves on how much more "civilized" we are. It is neither meaningful nor possible to import or export wholesale a given set of sexual practices. Such behavior makes sense only in its larger context, but if viewed in this manner, it provides insights into the workings of other cultures, thereby enhancing the understanding of our own. Ultimately our aim is to better comprehend the universals as well as the diversities in human behavior of which the sexual is only one component.

RESEARCH AND THEORY IN SEXUAL DEVELOPMENT

Statistics tell us how many people do what how often, but a thorough understanding of any behavior requires a knowledge of the causes of that behavior. Why does sexual behavior develop the way it does? Why do people do what they do? Why is it that even though we are all basically similar biologically we are all behaviorally different in our sex lives?

There are no simple answers to these questions, and there is no comprehensive, generally accepted theory of sexual development. We have many facts, but only a few can be explained; we have many explanations, but only a few can be supported by facts. Among the explanations that have been most influential in shaping our understanding of sexual development and behavior are psychoanalytic theory and learning theory.

Sigmund Freud (1856–1939), an Austrian physician, was the founder of **psychoanalytic theory,** an intellectual movement that helped shape twentieth-century thinking in the West, especially regarding human sexuality. Freud elaborated the concepts of the unconscious and of infantile sexuality in attempting to explain factors that shape the human personality and human sexuality. His followers have contributed to and updated many of his original ideas, but his basic scheme of sexual development remains the core of psychoanalytic theory.

All human behavior, according to Freud, is caused by psychodynamic forces, or "energies of the mind," that constantly direct behavior and shape the personality. A "sexual instinct," in particular, Freud said, influences or "drives" much of our behavior. Freud believed the sexual instinct to be based on a physiological process (as hunger is) with both physical and mental manifestations.

Another concept that can help explain the development of sexual behavior is **learning theory,** which is based more on social than on physiological processes. Children demonstrably learn certain behaviors at one stage, other behaviors at later stages, and gradually build up a set of complex behavioral patterns. Learning theory not only explains the development of behavior patterns, it can also be used to explain behavioral similarities and differences among human beings. We all learn that certain experiences can be rewarding, and we tend to repeat those experiences, so many behavior patterns will be the same from person to person. Many experiences will also differ from one person to another, so many of our behavior patterns will also differ. Theories of learning can thus explain many aspects of human sexual behavior, without recourse to some of the assumptions underlying psychoanalytic theory.

As important as psychoanalytic theory and learning theory have been in contributing to current concepts of sexual development and human behavior, the size and scope of this book do not allow for detailed consideration of them. Furthermore, almost every introductory psychology textbook can provide a discussion of these two areas. Instead, we will look at certain less widely known research and experimental evidence that bears directly on sexual development.

The Development of Affectional Systems

During the past two decades psychologists have been studying the development of affectional systems in monkeys, with fascinating results. The leader in this research has been Harry F. Harlow. Although the research is still in progress, enough has been learned to suggest certain general principles that appear to be quite pertinent to understanding human sexual behavior. Monkeys, of course, are not the same as people, and their interactions lack the enormous complexity of human relations. Yet the relative simplicity of their behavior patterns, coupled with the opportunities to manipulate them experimentally, make them excellent subjects for study.

Perhaps the most important result of this research so far is the confirmation of the notion that sex, even among nonhuman primates, involves complex behavior that can emerge effectively only when related developmental tasks have been properly met. Monkeys do not "automatically" copulate. Their ability to do so is dependent on a long sequence of interactions with caretaker adults, as well as with peers.

In this context "love" refers to affectional feelings for others. It consists of five basic kinds: maternal love, paternal love, infant-mother love, peer or age-mate love, and heterosexual love. These love systems, though discrete, are not necessarily temporally distinct. Each love system prepares the individual for the next phase, with which it overlaps, and problems in one are reflected in the experiencing of difficulties in the others.

These integrated and interdependent affectional systems have their "sexual" components. The infant monkey clings to its mother without an overt desire for coitus; but it is nevertheless manifesting a form of behavior that is a necessary precursor for more specifically sexual activities in the future. In this sense, the following discussions of love are not a digression from but an integral part of our discussion of sexuality.

Maternal Love

The love of the mother for the infant is as nearly universal an emotion as we could hope to find. We generally assume that maternal love is innate in females. Girls respond to babies differently than do boys long before they reach puberty. Although such differences between the sexes could reflect cultural influences, the coexistence of innate propensities is not ruled out.

The maternal-love system appears in several stages. First is the stage of care and comfort. As the very survival of the infant monkey depends on the feeding, care, and protection afforded by its mother, it spends a great deal of time being physically cradled or clinging to the mother and thus obtaining vital "contact comfort." It is in this early and intimate relationship that the infant establishes the basis for all its future associations, sexual and otherwise.

Maternal love is initially elicited by the mere presence of the baby, but if it is to be sustained, the baby in turn must respond. A monkey mother can even "adopt" a kitten as her own, but because the kitten cannot reciprocate by clinging as a monkey baby can, she will ultimately abandon it.

Among humans the life-sustaining functions of the mother can be adequately replaced with bottle feeding, for example. But close, physical, comforting contact with affectionate adult caretakers remains imperative.

The second, or transitional, stage in maternal love is characterized by ambivalence. As the infant must ultimately survive on its own, the monkey mother begins to encourage the development of independence by becoming less protective and even by rejecting and punishing at times. In sexual terms this emotional "weaning" is essential if the infant is going to be able to go out as an adult and relate to mates.

The third and final stage of maternal love is that of relative separation, which among monkeys gradually leads to the severance of the affectional bond between the mother and the maturing offspring. The arrival of a younger sibling accelerates this process.

Infant Love

The love of the infant for the mother is closely related to and reciprocal with maternal love. The two affectional systems are nevertheless distinct and can be studied separately. Unlike the mother, who develops emotional ties to the baby even while she is still pregnant, the newborn is at first quite indiscriminate in its feelings toward others. Among both human beings and other primates, the infant's earliest responses are reflexively determined. They include sucking responses, the rooting reflex (stimulation of the cheek elicits exploratory head movements that help to locate the nipple), groping, grasping, clinging, and so on. Such unlearned, species-specific behavior patterns among human infants have been called "instinctual response systems."

As these interactions between infant and mother are reflexive, the first stage in the development of the infant's affectional system is that of "organic affection." This stage is practically concurrent with the stage of comfort and attachment that, among monkeys, consists of actual bodily contact between infant and mother soon after birth. This stage includes both the cradling of a passive infant and active clinging by the infant to the mother. Such "contact comfort" seems to be more important than even nursing in the development of the monkey infant's attachment to the mother.

Next comes the stage of solace and security, in which the presence of the mother or mother surrogate enables the infant monkey (and the older human child) to wander beyond the mother's immediate vicinity to explore the environment. This initial effort is followed by greater detachment and environmental exploration, culminating in a stage of relative independence.

The parallels between the development of the maternal and infant love systems are quite clear. First, there is a phase of close and intense attachment, followed by progressive independence. When the infant's personal and social security are established, it can move out. Without this basic security, the infant is socially paralyzed. On the other hand, when the attachment to the mother persists in full force, the infant remains helplessly dependent on her. The primary function of the maternal and infant love systems is, then, to prepare the infant for the demands and satisfactions of the peer relations that must be developed next.

Paternal Love

Manifestations of paternal love among monkeys and apes are infrequent and inadequately studied. It has been hypothesized that innate, biologically determined affection for the infant is much less strong in the nonhuman primate male than in the female. Male monkeys do, however, learn to love and protect infants through imitation of the mother. Conversely, the infant's affectional ties to the male are far less apparent than are its attachment to the mother, although infants will occasionally seek out adult males for comfort when no females are available.

Among humans paternal love can be just as intense as maternal love, and, though in most cultures mothers perform the primary child-rearing functions, fathers can and occasionally do fulfill the same role. It is generally assumed that, ideally, maternal and paternal love must supplement each other in providing the infant with the full complement of love and emotional nurture during growth and development.

Age-mate or Peer Love

Research with monkeys indicates that the peer affectional system is probably the most important of all affectional systems in sociosexual development. The rudiments of peer love appear in early infancy and expand progressively throughout childhood, adolescence, and adulthood. The primary vehicle for the development and expression of peer love is play, through which earlier affectional systems are integrated and the love systems to follow are anticipated.

Attachment to peers begins as the infant becomes capable of wandering away from the mother briefly and is permitted and encouraged to do so. In human beings, affectional relations with peers are usually established at about age 3 years (four months for monkeys) but do not reach their peak until between the ages of 9 and 11 years. They gradually decline during adolescence as the heterosexual affectional system emerges.

If the child is to develop normal sexual responses, it must have been provided with and must have accepted a certain degree of physical contact very early. Such contact must have been pleasurable and comforting or the child will not seek it in play with peers. Contact comfort does not necessarily refer to specifically genital contact, but is based on general body contact. At the psychological level the child must also be able to transfer to peers the "basic trust" that has developed toward the adult caretaker.

Heterosexual Love

The heterosexual affectional system has its roots in the earlier love systems, but it emerges as a distinct entity at the time of puberty, matures during adolescence, and operates as the primary sociosexual affectional system for most adults.

The heterosexual love system in primates, including human beings, develops through three subsystems: mechanical, hormonal, romantic. The mechanical subsystem depends on the anatomical and physiological properties of the sexual organs, physiological reflexes, appropriate body postures and movements, and so on. As discussed in earlier chapters, some of these mechanical functions, like penile erection, are present at birth. Others, like ejaculation, develop at puberty. Some features of this mechanical subsystem (for example, sexually differentiated genitals or pelvic thrusting) are common to all primates. Others are peculiar to some. Monkeys, for example, have a basic adult sexual posture (*see* Figure 7.9), whereas human beings are far more versatile in this respect (*see* Figures 9.5 and 9.6). This basic adult monkey posture has been shown to arise out of three discrete responses during infant play: threat by the male, passivity (turning her back), and rigidity (supporting the male) by the female.

In Figure 7.10 we see the basic presexual play position adopted by a juvenile pair and in Figure 7.11 the first attempts at mounting. These monkeys are engaged in play, not in coitus, yet the female's passive position and willingness to support the male and the latter's grasping of her hindquarters and efforts at mounting have an unmistakable resemblance to the basic adult sexual posture (*see* Figure 7.9).

The second, or hormonal, subsystem has also been discussed as it operates in humans (*see* Chapter 4). The sexual behavior of nonhuman primates and of lower animals is much more firmly under hormonal control. Although much remains to be learned about the precise roles of sex hormones in human

Figure 7.9 Basic adult sexual posture.
Courtesy of Wisconsin Regional Primate Research Center.

physiology, their importance cannot be underestimated, particularly in relation to sexual growth and maturation.

The third component of the heterosexual love system is the romantic subsystem—among monkeys the subsystem of transient heterosexual attachments. Although we cannot attempt to do justice here to human romantic love, we should point out that in a general sense comparable attachments also characterize the relations of nonhuman primates. Their associations are characterized by the formation of pairs of compatible individuals.

Although each of these three subsystems can operate independently to some extent, full heterosexual expression requires their integrated and complementary functioning. These subsystems also vary in their vulnerability to disruption. For example, social isolation early in life does not disturb hormonal functioning but seriously disrupts some mechanical functions and has a disastrous effect upon the transient affectional, or romantic, subsystem. As studies of social isolation in infant monkeys conducted by Harlow and his

Figure 7.10 Basic presexual position.

Courtesy of Wisconsin Regional Primate Research Center.

associates have provided highly pertinent insights into sexual behavior, we shall briefly describe them here.

In these experiments male and female infant monkeys were reared in isolated wire-mesh cages and thus denied the opportunity to develop infant- and peer-love affectional systems. At puberty the socially deprived males showed every evidence of normal physical development. They also achieved erection and masturbated, sometimes to orgasm, at rates comparable to those of undeprived monkeys. Socially deprived females also behaved essentially in a fashion comparable to that of undeprived females, as far as hormonal functioning and autoerotic activities were concerned.

But the effect of social isolation in infancy on adult sociosexual behavior was calamitous. Deprived males would be visibly aroused in the presence of females, but would stand puzzled, not knowing what to do (*see* Figure 7.12). They would grope aimlessly and act clumsily with receptive females, or they would brutally assault them. The impact of social isolation on females was somewhat less damaging. Although they mistrusted physical contact and would flee or attack males, they

Figure 7.11 The first attempt at mounting.

Courtesy of Wisconsin Regional Primate Research Center.

Figure 7.12 Inappropriate response by socially deprived male to receptive female.

Courtesy of Wisconsin Regional Primate Research Center.

could be induced in time to endure at least partial sexual contact with undeprived males. Figure 7.13 shows the inadequate sexual posturing of a socially deprived female and the lack of sexual interest of a normal male in response to it.

These experiments leave no doubt that heterosexual activity cannot develop ade- quately in an affectional vacuum, and that even the coital postures have to develop in the context of infantile and peer interactions. Although we obviously cannot and should not attempt to replicate these findings in human beings, there is much in them that seems familiar to faulty human sexual development. Human interactions are infinitely more com-

Figure 7.13 Inadequate sexual presentation by socially deprived female.

Courtesy of Wisconsin Regional Primate Research Center.

plex, and the transition from peer love to the romantic subsystem involves transitional mechanisms of great intricacy, involving trust, acceptance of physical contact, and motivation for physical proximity and behavioral sex-role differentiation. As Harlow has put it: "Sex secretions may create sex sensations, but it is social sensitivity that produces sensational sex."

Gender Identity

As we have just seen, affectional systems and eventual adult sexual behavior are greatly influenced by social factors. An equally crucial question in the development of sexual behavior has to do with gender identity: How do we develop a self-concept of our own masculinity or femininity? Our own self-concepts obviously have a great deal to do with how we behave. As explained in Chapter 4, chromosomes and hormones determine biological sex—whether we are male or female. But this is not the same as gender identity, which develops gradually and carries with it an appropriate set of emotional, social, vocational, motivational, and sexual behaviors.

No serious investigator of psychosexual development now argues against the proposition that human gender identity can best be understood as the end product of the interaction between biological and social variables. But such an agreement, in the abstract, has not prevented serious controversy about the relative influences exerted by various factors in shaping sexual identity.

Traditionally, it was assumed that genetic sex determined at conception inexorably guided sexual development throughout the prenatal and postnatal life eventuating into full-fledged sexual adulthood. The effects of learning as well as deviations from the norm were recognized, but the major underlying differentiating force was assumed to be biological.

During the past two decades this model was challenged by a number of investigators who studied a group of hermaphrodites and showed that, in the majority of cases, these children grew up according to their assigned sex rather than genetic sex (see Chapter 4). Their conclusion was:

in place of a theory of instinctive masculinity or femininity which is innate, the evidence of hermaphroditism lends support to a conception that psychologically, sexuality is undifferentiated at birth and that it becomes differentiated as masculine or feminine in the course of the various experiences of growing up. (Money, et al., 1955)

This hypothesis of sexual neutrality at birth was quite influential, but did not go unchallenged. The major criticisms were that data from hermaphrodites may not be generalizable to the general population, and also that this approach failed to take into account other evidence that pointed to the existence of a distinct sexual orientation rather than sexual neutrality at birth.

More recently, Money and Ehrhardt have brought together a vast amount of information from numerous fields and have proposed an interactional model of psychosexual differentiation.

Money and Ehrhardt refer to their proposed scheme as a model of psychosexual or gender-identity differentiation (rather than psychosexual development), and consider the process as a continuous one starting with conception and culminating in the emergence of adult gender identity (see Figure 7.14). The process begins, as previously explained, with chromosomal and hormonal factors exerting their influences. Normally, the sequence of events leads to **genital dimorphism,** whereby genetic males and females are born with internal and external sex organs congruent with their chromosomal sex. To follow the left part of Figure 7.14 first, we next encounter the effects of "others' behavior" and "body image."

Up to this point social factors have had no direct bearing in sexual dimorphism. But the moment the baby's sex is identified at birth, social influences become enormously important. Cultures undoubtedly differ in this respect, but the infant's perceived or assigned sex will from here on constitute one of the key factors defining the person. The choice of pink or blue clothing often is the first step of iden-

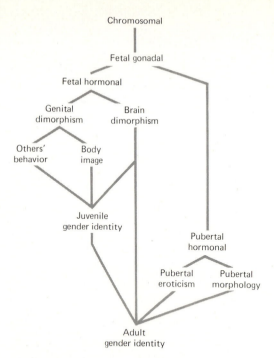

Figure 7.14 The sequential and interactional components of gender-identity differentiation.

Money, J., and A.A. Ehrhardt, *Man and Woman, Boy and Girl* (Baltimore: The Johns Hopkins University Press, 1972), p. 3. Reproduced by permission.

tification. Choice of name, pronomial use, legal statutes, social conventions, and a myriad other distinctions relentlessly remind and reinforce in the child's mind that he is a boy or she is a girl, and with a varying degree of clarity and consistency define what that means in behavioral terms.

Differential attitudes based on the sex of the child are pervasive and often barely conscious. But such attitudes are not all externally imposed. There are sex differences in behavior that appear very early and presumably spontaneously, which themselves elicit differences in response. The presence of cultural forces does not necessarily mean the absence of biologically determined influences in gender differentiation. These two sets of variables mutually reinforce each other, often creating "chicken-and-egg" sequences that cannot be readily disentangled.

Body image refers to the concept of our physical self or the way in which we visualize

our bodies. Sexuality is an important component of body image and includes at the most concrete level the knowledge of our gender, of which we become aware early in childhood. More involved are our notions of masculinity, femininity, and "sex appeal," which are far more ambiguously defined. All of these factors contribute to our eventual sexual definition of ourselves.

The impact of fetal hormones on **brain dimorphism** presents a far more complicated situation than the more obvious changes of genital dimorphism. As indicated earlier (*see* Chapter 3), there is as yet no direct evidence for sex differences in the human brain. But there is a wealth of positive information in this regard among animals and some inferential data on human beings, which allow the tentative assumption that the brain (particularly the hypothalamus) is prenatally influenced by fetal hormones and that it continues to exert a subtle influence on subsequent behavior.

Some of the indirect evidence of brain dimorphism is that genetic females who had been subjected to high levels of androgen before birth but who were treated early with corrective surgery and who looked and were reared as girls have been reported to show "tomboyish" behavior compared to a control group. These girls were more self-assertive, athletic, functional in dress, more interested in boys' games than doll play, more interested in achievement than they were romance- or marriage-oriented. Likewise, boys with the androgen-insensitivity syndrome revealed a picture the obverse of the above. But because of their female-looking genitalia, these boys had been reared as girls, so that in their cases the possible effects of prenatal hormones (or their lack) could not be separated from socially imposed role expectations.

These findings raise interesting conceptual and political problems. Who decides what is "tomboyish"? Have these traits naturally evolved or for various reasons been monopolized by males? Are we using a biological or a cultural yardstick?

There are no ready answers to these questions. Even serious textbooks contain many unsubstantiated claims about innate feminine psychology. One can make women or men adhere to a set of cultural expectations and then declare that to be the "natural" way, and we have certainly done a good deal of that. But then, to repeat, while the presence of bias in one area ought to make one suspicious, it does not preclude the truth of other and similar observations. It is difficult at this point reliably to separate what constitutes prenatally influenced predilections from culturally imposed guidelines which masquerade as such. The point to remember is that whatever the nature of brain dimorphism, its influence is subject to major modification as a result of learning and social forces.

The factors of the behavior of others, body image, and brain dimorphism lead to juvenile gender identity, which is further differentiated through identification and all of the learning devices that are theorized to be operative in shaping human behavior.

The last major developmental event in Figure 7.14 is puberty. The effects of pubertal hormones and their impact on sexual morphology and eroticism (discussed in detail in Chapter 4) combine with the gains of juvenile gender identity and culminate in adult gender identity.

Gender identity is linked to **gender role,** and the terms are defined as follows:

Gender Identity: The sameness, unity, and persistence of one's individuality as male, female, or ambivalent, in greater or lesser degree, especially as it is experienced in self-awareness and behavior; gender identity is the private experience of gender role, and gender role is the public expression of gender identity.

Gender Role: Everything that a person says and does, to indicate to others or to the self the degree that one is either male, or female, or ambivalent; it includes but is not restricted to sexual arousal and response; gender role is the public expression of gender identity, and gender identity is the private experience of gender role. (Money and Ehrhardt, 1972)

The model of psychosexual differentiation just outlined is unlikely to be the last word on this complex issue. Many pieces of the puzzle are still missing. Many of the conclusions are inferences and extrapolations from animal research or clinical work that need to be substantiated as to their applicability to normal human development. But this model adequately underscores the multifaceted complexity of the issues. Before closing this chapter we need to consider one last aspect of sexual development; namely, its relationship to the larger process of psychosocial development.

Psychosocial Development

Sexual behavior, as we have seen, does not develop in a vacuum. It is the product of a great many forces, some of which have been explained and some of which are not fully understood. Research like that done by Kinsey, Harlow, Money, and numerous others has filled in some gaps, but pieces of the puzzle are still missing. Without all the pieces, we cannot explain sexual behavior and its development completely, but a number of theories have been proposed that attempt to do so. Such theories, even when based on incomplete data, are a necessary part of the process. In addition to attempting to explain sexual development in the light of overall human development, they help point out gaps in our knowledge. As new information becomes available a theory can be modified or updated to give us an even better picture of human sexuality.

One theory that has been influential in recent years is that proposed by Erik Erikson, which explains sexual development as a part of the overall process of psychosocial development. In addition, it attempts to account for biological (genetic) as well as environmental (societal) factors.

In Erikson's scheme the life cycle — the entire lifespan from birth to death — is characterized by eight phases of psychosocial development. Each phase is defined by the primary accomplishment of a phase-specific task, even though the resolutions are generally prepared in preceding phases and worked out further in subsequent ones.

Each phase is defined as a crisis (in the sense of a critical period rather than of a threat of catastrophe) and labeled according to the extreme successful and unsuccessful solutions. The actual outcome for any given individual phase is, however, generally a balance between such extremes. For instance, we all emerge from Phase 1 with mixtures of trust and mistrust. Theoretically there are as many gradations between such extremes as there are people.

Identity formation is the concept for which Erikson is best known, and part of the process of identity formation is the formation of its sexual aspect. Biological features are the primary "givens," but they do not necessarily determine the individual's own definitions of himself or herself as masculine or feminine or the way that he or she is perceived by others. The components of such definitions and the sex-role expectations implied vary markedly from culture to culture, even though the basic biological givens remain constant. It is thus up to each individual to clarify and consolidate his or her own sexual character as part of the larger task of identity formation. Cultures that provide clear and consistent models and guidelines facilitate this task for their members.

Despite the upsurge in sexual activity during adolescence, only after identity formation has been fairly well consolidated does true intimacy with the opposite sex (or with anyone else) become possible. According to Erikson, adolescent sexuality is often experimental, part of the search for identity. People may marry in the hope of finding themselves through each other, but the need to fulfill defined roles as mates or parents often actually hampers this effort.

The task of intimacy versus isolation is specific to young adulthood. On the strength of the accomplishments of earlier phases, the young adult develops the capacity to establish a workable ratio between these two extremes. Intimacy requires expressing (and exposing) oneself, giving and sharing, and both sexual and more general union.

Isolation and loneliness ("distantiation") in appropriate amounts are also necessary. No matter how satisfying a relationship, both partners need some solitude. A certain distance in this sense helps them to keep each other in proper focus. When intimacy fails or is exploited, self-preservation is reliant on the ability and readiness to repudiate it, to isolate oneself, and, if necessary, to annul such destructive ties.

The similarities in the general conclusions we can draw from Harlow's experimental work and Erikson's clinical research are quite clear. Monkeys or humans cannot grow and function in isolation. Even though each individual is unique, each can be understood only in the context of relations with his or her fellow beings. Sex is a complex and pervasive force that has a biological basis but can function properly (or be understood adequately) only in the context of affectional networks and life as a whole.

Erikson has said:

As an animal, man is nothing. It is meaningless to speak of a human child as if it were an animal in the process of domestication; or of his instincts as set patterns encroached upon or molded by the autocratic environment. Man's "inborn instincts" are drive fragments to be assembled, given meaning, and organized during a prolonged childhood by methods of child training and schooling which vary from culture to culture and are determined by tradition. In this lies his chance as an organism, as a member of a society, as an individual. In this also lies his limitation. For while the animal survives where his segment of nature remains predictable enough to fit his inborn patterns of instinctive response or where these responses contain the elements for necessary mutation, man survives only where traditional child training provides him with a conscience which will guide him without crushing him and which is firm and flexible enough to fit the vicissitudes of his historical era. (Erikson, 1963)

1. Because almost any object or activity can have sexual significance, it is difficult to define sexual behavior in a way that does not omit many important aspects of human sexuality. In this chapter, however, our discussion of sexual behavior has been confined to the six general ways in which people achieve orgasm: masturbation, nocturnal sex dreams, heterosexual petting, coitus, homosexual relations, and contacts with animals.

2. The one major, systematic attempt to study and classify human sexual behavior is that conducted by Alfred Kinsey and colleagues in the 1940s and early 1950s. Despite certain shortcomings (it is almost three decades old and has been criticized for its sampling and interviewing techniques), the Kinsey data continue to provide a useful frame of reference for examining sexual behavior. More recent surveys of sexual behavior offer some valuable insights into current behavior, but most of them are smaller in scope and less reliable than the Kinsey study.

3. The ability to respond sexually is present at birth. Infants respond to genital stimulation and some are capable of orgasm by at least 5 months of age. Although infants are aware of the physical sensations involved during sexual arousal, their reactions are purely reflexive and are probably not related to adultlike erotic feelings.

4. Sex play, or genital play, is in many ways a serious and necessary activity for children. According to Kinsey's findings, nearly all boys and about one-fifth of girls had engaged in sex play before reaching puberty. Genital exploration often leads to self-stimulation, the most common form of prepubescent sex play, but as children grow older and come into contact with other children, they may continue sex play with others—the beginnings of sociosexual encounters. Because children are unaware of the sexual significance of such play we should not attribute adult motives to them.

5. Adolescence is the time during which true adult sexuality emerges. Petting, or erotic caressing, is a common form of sexual activity for most adolescents. It is a pleasurable activity, and for many it is an acceptable means of experiencing orgasm. During petting encounters many adolescents learn the social rules of sexual behavior as well as learn about each other's sexual responsiveness.

6. One important point made by the Kinsey survey is that there is great variety in human sexual experience. The average frequency of total sexual outlet for males in the study was three orgasms a week, with the largest percentage of men reporting only one orgasm a week and the most active men being younger than 30 years of age. However, the reported frequency ranged widely within the study population.

7. Exact comparisons of male and female frequencies are not easily made, but the differences between the sexes with regard to frequency are small. The most active male groups in the Kinsey study reported an average of three orgasms a week, and the most active females reported an average of almost two orgasms a week. The most obvious difference between the sexes had to do with age. Males achieved their highest levels of sexual activity shortly after puberty. For females the highest levels of sexual outlet were reached, on the average, at around age 30. This difference may well be culturally determined.

8.   Marriage was the most important factor affecting types of sexual activity among women in the Kinsey study. Among unmarried women masturbation was the primary source of orgasm for the younger age groups, with coitus becoming more important with age. Current findings suggest that premarital coitus is becoming much more common than in previous generations. Coitus was the primary source of orgasm for married women at all age levels, but recent surveys suggest that masturbation is perhaps more common among married women than it was at the time of the Kinsey study.

9.   Educational and social levels were important factors influencing the type of sexual outlet among unmarried males, with those having some college education relying more heavily on masturbation than those with elementary school education, for whom coitus was the primary outlet following age 16. Married men relied primarily on coitus, with masturbation and nocturnal orgasm remaining slightly more important sources for the more-educated men.

10.   Large-scale studies of sexual behavior in other cultures have not been conducted, but anthropological data suggest that there is extreme variation with regard to sexual frequency and variety around the world.

11.   Research into the origins and development of sexual behavior is contributing to a fuller understanding of that behavior. Animal research with monkeys has demonstrated that primate sexual behavior develops through stages and emerges effectively only when certain developmental tasks are met. The interlocking and overlapping stages of development of affectional systems and love among monkeys are maternal love, infant love, paternal love, peer love, and heterosexual love. Interference with this developmental process through social isolation has damaging effects on adult sexual behavior.

12.   Another area of research that is providing insights into human sexual behavior deals with the question of gender identity: How do we develop a concept of our own masculinity or femininity? Although all of the answers are not known, it is probable that both biological and social factors are involved. Chromosomes and hormones determine biological sex, but once we are born a host of social factors contributes to our eventual gender identity.

Kinsey A. C., Pomeroy, W. B., and Martin, C. E. *Sexual Behavior in the Human Male;* Kinsey, A. C., Pomeroy, W. B., Martin, C. E., and Gebhard, P. H. *Sexual Behavior in the Human Female.* Philadelphia: Saunders, 1948 and 1953.
The most extensive surveys of human sexual behavior. Despite a number of serious flaws, still the most useful source of its kind.

Hunt, M. *Sexual Behavior in the 1970s.* Chicago: Playboy Press, 1974; Sorensen, R. C. *Adolescent Sexuality in Contemporary America.* New York: World, 1973; Tavris, C., and Sadd, S. *The Redbook Report on Female Sexuality.* New York: Dell, 1978; Hite, S. *The Hite Report.* New York: Macmillan, 1976; Pietropinto, A., and Simenauer, J. *Beyond the Male Myth.* New York: Times Books, 1977.
Variously informative surveys of sexual behavior.

Zelnik, M., and Kantner, J. F. "First Pregnancies to Women Aged 15-19: 1976 and 1971," *Family Planning Perspectives,* **10** (1), Jan./Feb., 1978.
Most reliable source of information on premarital sex in the stated age group.

Money, J., and Ehrhardt, A. A. *Man and Woman, Boy and Girl.* Baltimore: Johns Hopkins University Press, 1972.
Clear and comprehensive discussion of differentiation of gender identity as the end product of interaction between biological and social variables.

Katchadourian, H. A. (Ed.). *Human Sexuality: A Comparative and Developmental Perspective.* Berkeley, Calif.: University of California Press, 1978.
Essays on sexual development with special emphasis on gender identity and sex roles by a multidisciplinary group.

chapter 8 Autoeroticism

Did You Know That . . .

erotic fantasy is probably the most common form of sexual experience?

everyone dreams every night, and most people have erotic dreams from time to time?

substantial numbers of people have had orgasms during their sleep, and a few do so on a regular basis?

masturbation is practiced by many species of animals and has most probably been engaged in by people of all cultures since the beginning of human history?

there is no general agreement as to what would constitute excessive masturbation?

some sex therapists now encourage certain clients to use masturbation as a way of finding out about their own sexuality?

INTRODUCTION

His

When I masturbate, I usually think about girls seducing me. These girls are usually older experienced women and are so used to having sex that they can pay attention to your satisfaction, rather than thinking about their own orgasms or satisfying themselves. Sex symbols do not turn me on at all; I usually think that they have no sexual organs. . . . The pictures that easily produce an erection are those of women in very natural unself-conscious poses, and the women are usually *not* endowed with silicone breasts, pink vulva lips and combed pubic hair. I often think of anal sex.

Hers

Masturbation is important to relieve tension, to indulge in fantasies, plus, I feel I owe it to myself, as a belated form of self-love. Until I was twenty-nine I never masturbated despite the fact that I was tempted to. As an adolescent, masturbation meant "self-abuse." After shyly joining the women's movement, however, feelings of worth and self-respect grew and I gradually dropped the mantle of "professional Martyr" which my husband, Church, and mother were only too willing to help me possess. A door mat feels she doesn't deserve the pleasure of masturbating. So masturbation had a symbolic meaning for me. It was one of my first overt expressions of self-love, of the dissolution of guilt and the beginning of self-confidence.

The above statements (His from *Beyond the Male Myth,* Hers from *The Hite Report*) deal with two common forms of sexual behavior—erotic fantasies and solitary sex play, or masturbation. These, along with erotic dreams, constitute an important type of sexual behavior known as **autoeroticism.**

We often think of sex as a social activity (involving two or more individuals), but it is not necessary to have a partner in order to enjoy sex. There are many times in our lives that sex is solitary—either of necessity or be-cause we chose to experience sexual pleasure while alone.

For centuries, traditional moral and religious thinking in the Western world held that the only legitimate purpose of sex was reproduction. Engaging in sex for any other reason was usually considered to be immoral. And autoeroticism, which has no direct reproductive function, was condemned. But attitudes about the purpose of sex are changing, as we mentioned in Chapter 1, and sex is no longer regarded as a purely reproductive behavior. Most people engage in sex because it is pleasurable, and autoerotic activities have come to be seen by many as acceptable and even beneficial ways of experiencing sexual pleasure. In this chapter we will discuss three types of autoerotic behavior: erotic fantasies, sexual dreams, and solitary sex play.

EROTIC FANTASIES

A whole world of sexual activity takes place in our minds. This mental activity, which moves in and out of our consciousness a good deal of the time, can take many forms— fleeting erotic images or thoughts, intricately woven fantasies, fading sexual memories, or fresh hopes for the future. Fantasies frequently are triggered by and lead up to other sexual outlets (thinking about tonight's date, for example), but more often they exist on their own. In their various forms, erotic thoughts are probably the most common type of sexual activity, and it is difficult to imagine anyone who has not had such thoughts at one time or another. Many adolescents, for instance, tend to spend a good deal of time daydreaming. In the private and safe theaters of their minds they endlessly rehearse their favorite fantasies—sometimes in the form of continuing stories, more often as variations on the same theme.

Although daydreaming and fantasizing may be more common during adolescence, such activity continues throughout the life span, as does all autoerotic activity. Single people as well as many happily married couples with satisfactory sex lives indulge in sexual fantasies. They may think about sexual experiences they have had or plan to have with each other, they may dwell on past experiences with others—particularly missed opportunities—or they may let their imaginations run freely through any and all forms of sexual activity.

The person doing the fantasizing is usually the central character in a fantasy. The other characters may change from one fantasy to the next, or the same characters may turn up again and again. They may be people the dreamer knows only from afar (movie stars, popular sex symbols), they may be fictitious figures with somewhat vague and occasionally changing features, they may be actual acquaintances, or they may be individuals out of the dreamer's past (*see* Figure 8.1). Memories of past loves may even take on a particularly persistent and haunting quality (*see* Figure 8.2).

Like the cast of characters in erotic fantasies, the kinds of imaginary activities that take place are countless and are usually determined by the dreamer's wishes. According to psychoanalytic theory, the fantasies may be related to wishes or desires the dreamer did not know existed. But in most cases it is only the extent of a person's imagination that limits the characters and content of erotic fantasies.

The degree of sexual arousal that accompanies fantasies varies as much as do the fantasies themselves. At one extreme a fleeting sexual image or thought may involve no arousal at all. At the other extreme the intensity of feeling may be overwhelming. But as exciting as a fantasy may be, only a few individuals, usually women, are apparently able to reach orgasm through fantasy alone. Some women are reportedly able to reach orgasm even in public simply by being in a sexually exciting situation or in the presence of a particularly attractive person.

Figure 8.1 *Young Man Fantasizing* (artist unknown).

Even though erotic fantasies can be enjoyable, there are times when they may not be pleasant experiences. Fantasies may include socially unacceptable themes that can cause the individual a great deal of embarrassment and guilt. And even if the subject matter is not troubling, the act of fantasizing itself may cause anxiety and guilt for someone who has been conditioned to feel that sexual thoughts are abnormal or wrong.

The Functions of Sexual Fantasies

Erotic fantasies fulfill at least three functions. First, they are a readily available source of pleasure that most people can enjoy and through which many people learn about and come to accept their own sexuality. For women who have difficulty achieving orgasm, for instance, sex therapists sometimes recom-

Figure 8.2 Rene Magritte, *Ready-made Bouquet.* Courtesy of Alexander Iolas Gallery.

mend fantasizing as a means of increasing sexual excitement.

Second, erotic fantasies are often good substitutes for the actual experience. They can provide temporary satisfaction while one awaits a more substantial encounter (such as an upcoming date or a honeymoon), or they can compensate for unattainable goals. Despite this apparent function as wish fulfillment, people often have fantasies they do not want to come true, no matter how exciting or arousing they may be. By allowing for expression of forbidden urges, fantasies thus compensate for an individual's inability or unwillingness to fulfill those urges. Even though fantasies do not yield full gratification of sexual desires, they can relieve sexual frustrations and ease the pain and pressure caused by unfulfilled wishes, making those wishes more bearable.

A third function of fantasies is that they play a role in preparing people for future sociosexual situations. Consider the question, "What might happen if we end up back at my place after the movie tonight?" Many answers may come to mind, and as people fantasize about what might happen, they can anticipate problems and mentally practice different plans of action. This sort of fantasizing helps control anxiety and prepares people to cope with novel situations. Thus there is a difference between fantasies that substitute for action and those that prepare for it.

Unhealthy Fantasies

Considering how common sexual fantasizing is, it must be assumed to be part of "normal," "healthy" mental life. But does fantasizing have unhealthy as well as healthy forms? This question can be answered in terms of the quantity as well as the quality of fantasies. Judging quantitatively, we may say that fantasizing beyond a certain point about sex or anything else can be a waste of time. Particularly during adolescence, erotic fantasies may become excessively time-consuming. If they interfere with necessary work or if they regularly take the place of satisfying interaction with others, they may cause problems in psychosocial development.

As to the quality or content of sexual fantasies, there is no simple answer. We have seen that sexual behavior takes various forms, and there is not complete agreement on the "normality" of many types of sex. To determine whether or not particular fantasies are normal or healthy is therefore difficult. Some people are disturbed by thoughts of very common activities, while others may be unaffected by even the most bizarre fantasies. But even though the question cannot be answered simply, certain factors should be considered if judgments of fantasies are to be made.

Thinking about socially unacceptable behavior is common. Sometimes the activity is merely silly and apparently senseless (like thinking about urinating on someone), but it can also involve highly disturbing and guilt-provoking behavior. Fantasies having to do with the use of force, for example, may result in a curious mixture of feelings of pleasure and distress, of excitement and disgust.

What do such thoughts mean, and how

should one deal with them? First, it must be remembered that most of these fantasies are never acted out. According to psychoanalytic theory, we all have deeply buried desires that occasionally surface in thinly disguised forms. But if such wishes are not acted upon, they do not "define" us as adults.

There is no easy way to deal with unpleasant or disturbing fantasies. Conscious attempts to get rid of them often simply cause us to focus on them more strongly. It is better to take them for what they are: isolated thoughts that do not mean very much. We are not, however, completely helpless in such matters, and it is usually possible to minimize opportunities for lengthy fantasies.

Only in rare instances does fantasizing become obviously harmful, and that is when it leads to antisocial or otherwise harmful activities. When individuals realize that they are losing control and that they are likely to commit a seriously antisocial act they should seek professional help (from a psychologist, psychiatrist, or counselor trained to deal with such problems). For most people, however, sexual fantasies are common, pleasant experiences.

SEXUAL DREAMS

Dreams have long been a subject of fascination and speculation. At various times throughout history dreams have been viewed as clues to an individual's past and even as keys to the future. The interpretation of dreams plays a key role in psychoanalytic theory and therapy. In the past two decades research has resulted in a growing understanding of the neurophysiology of sleep and dreams—and some of this research is particularly relevent to the study of human sexuality.

The Neurophysiology of Sleep and Dreaming

Sleep is not the simple state that it seems, nor are dreams the erratic and unpredictable events that they may seem. Instead, there is a definite, recurring sleep-dream cycle. Brain waves (electroencephalogram, or EEG, readings) show four distinct sleep patterns, one of which is characterized by bursts of rapid eye movements (REM). The eyes of sleepers can be seen to be moving under the eyelids during this type of sleep and people who are awakened during a REM phase almost always report that they have been experiencing vivid dreams. In other phases of sleep dreaming is apparently less common and less vivid.

During an ordinary night's sleep there are four or five dream periods, accounting for almost a quarter of the total sleeping time. The first occurs 60 to 90 minutes after one falls asleep, and the rest at approximately 90-minute intervals. These dream periods are usually quite regular, which means that we all dream every night, whether or not we remember the dreams in the morning.

These periods of active dreaming appear to be times of intense physiological activity, with rapid and irregular pulse and respiration. Among males, in a high number of cases (85–95 percent) partial or full erections have been observed during REM states, even among infants and elderly men. The occurrence of erections during REM sleep may explain why males sometimes have an erection when they wake up. The erections that occur during REM sleep are not necessarily accompanied by sexual dreams, and their full significance remains unclear. Evidence of sexual arousal in females (such as vaginal lubrication) is relatively less easy to detect during REM sleep; thus it has not been as convincingly demonstrated. There is no reason to expect that females should react any differently than males in this regard.

Sexual dreams, particularly those that result in orgasm, are intensely pleasant, but they can also be bewildering. Like all other dreams, sexual dreams are usually fragmentary and difficult to describe. Sometimes their sexual content is accompanied by erotic emotions, but often a person may dream of obvious sexual activity without being aroused. On the other hand, a person may feel intense excitement while dreaming of an apparently nonsexual, even improbable, situation like flying or falling.

Fantasies and dreams are closely related.

In both there is a temporary relaxation of conscious restraints, allowing a wide variety of wishes and desires to be expressed. Fantasies, however, are more subject to the rules of logic and reality. In dreams anything is possible, without regard for rhyme or reason. The meaning of dreams can thus vary from the obvious to the completely obscure. They may represent well-known or only thinly veiled wish fulfillments, or they may contain deeply concealed fears. Some women, for example, may have fearful fantasies that during intercourse their vaginas will be torn apart. Some men may fear that vaginas are full of razor blades or ground glass or are armed with teeth that will mutilate any penis that ventures in. Such perceived threats to the genitals suggest a mixture of aggressive and sexual impulses. Such fleeting thoughts are not uncommon and usually should not be taken seriously.

NOCTURNAL ORGASMS

Visitations by "the angel of the night" is what pioneer sexologist Pablo Mantegazza called nocturnal orgasms. The Babylonians believed in a "maid of the night" who visited men in their sleep and a "little night man" that sleeps with women. During medieval times demons (see Figure 8.3) rather than angels were accused of causing nocturnal orgasms. An incubus was the demon that would lie upon women, while a succubus would lie under men. The West African Yoruba tribe believed in a single being who could act either as male or female and visit members of either sex in their sleep.

Although orgasms during sleep (night or day) do not contribute greatly to total sexual outlets (2–3 percent for females, 2–8 percent for males depending on age, marital status, and other characteristics; see Chapter 7), they are an interesting phenomenon, and substantial numbers of people experience them. By age 45 almost 40 percent of females and more than 90 percent of males in the Kinsey study had such experiences at least once. Approximately 5 percent of men and 1 percent of

women averaged weekly orgasms through this means.

Nocturnal orgasms are generally accompanied by dreams. The content of the dreams may or may not be clearly erotic, but there is usually a sensation of sexual excitement. The dreamer often awakens in the process but may be hazy about what is happening. In some instances orgasm continues to completion after the dreamer has awakened, but the person may go back to sleep without having fully awakened. At other times the person may wake up startled, and if orgasm has not started it may be possible to avert it.

As with fantasies, the dream images that accompany nocturnal orgasms may cause distress because they may contain elements that are startling to the dreamer. The pleasure usually associated with nocturnal orgasms may, in such cases, be tinged with feelings of apprehension, remorse, or guilt. Occasionally, however, the person will sleep right through the experience and will have only vague recollections of the dream in the morning. With males, even if they do not remember the dream, they will have evidence that it took place. Because male orgasms are accompanied by ejaculation (which is why nocturnal orgasms among males are called **nocturnal emissions,** or **wet dreams**), there is little doubt that an orgasm has occurred. The fact that females do not have such tell-tale evidence may account in part for the fact that women report a lower incidence of nocturnal orgasm. Although nocturnal orgasms are usually pleasant, a young man may be upset by his first such experience if he does not know that orgasms can occur during sleep and that fluid is emitted during mature male orgasms.

Frequencies of nocturnal orgasms among males were found to be closely linked with educational level among Kinsey subjects. The highest frequency of nocturnal orgasms at one extreme was associated with the highest educational levels and was almost seven times greater than the frequency at the other extreme, representing the lowest educational levels. At all social levels frequencies were higher before marriage. Otherwise no differences were found between rural and urban groups, among various religious groups, or

Figure 8.3 Illustration by Frédéric Bouchot in *Diabolico Foutromanie*.

between those practicing and not practicing their religions. Among females any differences were even less obvious.

Health Aspects

Adolescents used to be advised to empty their bladders at bedtime, not to sleep in one position or another, not to wear tight nightclothes, and so on, in order to minimize the chances of so-called nighttime pollution. But because nocturnal orgasms are beyond the individual's control, moral attitudes concerning them have generally not been severe or critical. More commonly this sexual outlet has been regarded as nature's way of taking care of sexual needs in the absence of other outlets.

Do nocturnal orgasms actually compensate for the lack of other outlets? This possibility was tested on Kinsey's female sample. In about 14 percent of the women who refrained from other forms of sexual activity nocturnal orgasms became more frequent. Increased frequency occurred most often when sociosexual outlets—rather than masturbation—had been drastically reduced or completely eliminated, such as following the loss of a spouse.

Even when nocturnal orgasms did increase after a reduction in other outlets, the increase was not nearly as great as the decrease in other outlets. For example, a woman who lost her usual access to several coital orgasms a week might have had only a few more nocturnal orgasms a year. In some cases the relation between nocturnal orgasms and other outlets was reversed. In about 7 percent of the cases nocturnal orgasms became more frequent as other outlets increased. So the evidence, at least for females, does not clearly support the idea that nocturnal orgasms act as a "natural" safety valve.

MASTURBATION

Masturbation must be at least as old as the human race. It is practiced by various species of animals, including monkeys and apes, and was undoubtedly engaged in by human beings even in the earliest stages of evolution. Anthropological records indicate that masturbation is probably practiced in all cultures.

In the widest sense **masturbation** is self-stimulation for erotic pleasure. This includes manipulation of one's own genitals, but it can also include a wide variety of autoerotic activities. In a narrower sense masturbation includes only deliberate acts of self-arousal that result in orgasm. For our purposes when we refer to the Kinsey study we will consider only masturbation that leads to orgasm. Otherwise we will mean any erotic activity that involves voluntary self-stimulation for erotic pleasure. Most often this behavior occurs in private, but two or more people may masturbate together. Mutual stimulation, however, is not masturbation but is considered to be either petting, homosexual play, or foreplay. Masturbation thus involves a variety of sexual behaviors that overlap with other forms of sexual expression.

Techniques

The techniques of masturbation are generally similar to those of foreplay. Pre-

dictably, the highly sensitive external sex organs are the primary targets of stimulation. The physiological reactions of such stimulation are vasocongestion and muscular tension. The first is usually beyond voluntary control, but the second can be deliberately used to heighten sexual tension.

Because we are all pretty much the same physiologically, masturbation has certain common characteristics in both sexes. Physical differences between the sexes, however, as well as a great many social, cultural, and life-history differences among people lead to a great variety of techniques of masturbation. *The Hite Report*, for example, lists a number of basic types of female masturbation and describes variations within these types. Instead of discussing each form of masturbation, we will examine the more common ones, as well as a few of the more exotic variations that illustrate how far some people go in their autoerotic behavior.

Genital Manipulation

Manual techniques of masturbation are commonly used by both sexes, but particularly by males (*see* Figure 8.4). The most frequent form of male masturbation involves simply manipulating the penis by hand. This technique usually consists of gripping the shaft of the penis and moving the hand over it firmly to and fro or in a "milking" motion. The glans and frenulum may be lightly stroked in the earlier stages, but as tensions mount and movements become more vigorous direct contact with these areas is usually avoided because of their extreme sensitivity. It is possible, however, to continue stimulation of these parts by moving the frenulum over them.

Women also rely primarily on genital manipulation, though perhaps to a lesser extent than do males. In one fashion or another the clitoris and the labia minora are the structures most commonly involved (*see* Figure 8.5). They are stroked, pressed, and rhythmically stimulated. Because the clitoris and labia minora are the most sensitive parts of the female genitals, the motions are usually quite gentle and deliberate. Just as males

Figure 8.4 Boys masturbating.
From *The Erotic Drawings of Mihály Zichy* (New York: Grove Press, 1969), plate #30. Copyright © 1969 by Grove Press, Inc.; reprinted by permission.

avoid direct friction of the glans, females usually avoid the glans of the clitoris. Instead, they tend to concentrate on the shaft of the clitoris, which can be stimulated on either side. If too much pressure is applied or if manipulation is prolonged over an area, the site may become temporarily less sensitive. Switching hands or moving the fingers about is therefore quite common.

Although the clitoris is usually thought of

as the primary target of erotic manipulation, Masters and Johnson report that women usually manipulate the mons area as a whole. In this way they can prolong the buildup of tension and avoid potentially painful contact with the glans of the clitoris. Sometimes rhythmic or steady pressure over the mons is all that is necessary to bring about orgasm.

The vaginal introitus is quite sensitive and frequently is stimulated during masturba-

Autoeroticism

to females. About one in ten women in the Kinsey study manipulated her own breasts, often just the nipples, as part of her autoerotic activities. On rare occasions such manipulation alone may lead to orgasm.

Friction against Objects

Physiologically it does not make much difference whether the genitals are excited by the hand, the heels, or the back of a chair. But behaviorally such distinctions can be significant. When the hands are used there can be no mistake about the deliberate nature of the act, so out of shame or guilt some individuals may resort to indirect ways of achieving the same end. Adolescents may feel that they are thus obeying the rules against "playing with yourself." In many cases, however, people use different objects during masturbation because they find the practice heightens excitement or because they want some variety. The possibilities are many: a pillow, a towel, nightclothes tucked between the legs, a bed cover, or the mattress itself may provide a convenient surface to rub and press against, and orgasms can sometimes be achieved without even touching the genitals (*see* Figure 8.6).

Many adolescent girls actually discover the potential of self-stimulation through an activity like climbing a pole or riding a bicycle. The health manuals of some years ago devoted a good many pages to the design of bicycle seats that would minimize such an event.

Aside from its usefulness in disguising masturbation, using friction against objects also may seem more like actual intercourse and may make accompanying fantasies about intercourse seem more real.

Muscular Tensions

Even when the first two techniques of masturbation are used, muscular tension can also be employed to heighten sexual excitement. Occasionally a woman will achieve orgasm by using only muscular tension. She may, for example lie with her knees drawn up against her stomach and move her buttocks or press them together rhythmically. The movements

Figure 8.5 Illustration by Caylus in *Thérèse Philosophe.*

tion. The motions involved are similar—gentle stroking, steady or rhythmic pressure, and so on. Actually these movements usually merge into one another, and the fingers of one or both hands move from one structure to the other, perhaps pulling on the labia and stimulating the clitoris alternately with circular strokes to excite the introitus. The outer labia are less often involved.

In both male and female masturbation the buildup to orgasm follows the description given in Chapter 3. Slow and deliberate movements become progressively more intense. As a woman approaches orgasm she may require firm and forcible manipulation to bring herself to the peak of excitement.

Breast stimulation is confined essentially

Figure 8.6 Jean Honoré Fragonard, *Sleeping Girl*.

involved are similar to the pelvic thrusts during coitus. They must be performed with deliberate force and determination in order to bring about orgasm.

Thigh Pressure

Thigh pressure is an exclusively female method of masturbation. When a woman's legs are crossed or pressed together, steady rhythmic pressure can be applied to the whole genital area. This method combines the advantages of direct stimulation and muscular pressure. It can be indulged in practically anywhere the woman may be. One woman subject of *The Hite Report* explained: "I masturbate by rubbing my thighs together, usually lying down, but it can be done sitting up (in an office, on a bus, etc.). I rub them rhythmically, putting subtle pressure on the clitoris. The tension gradually builds to an orgasm."

Years ago, when people were more interested in preventing masturbation than they are today, they went to a great deal of trouble to uncover it. There are descriptions, for instance, of how in large French dress factories (equipped with treadle-operated sewing machines) shop stewards would listen for the occasional uncontrollable acceleration of a machine as its female operator went into the mounting excitement of orgasm.

Fantasy

Fantasy is often an important part of masturbation, and what we said about erotic fantasies also applies to masturbatory fantasies. Unlike pure erotic fantasies, however, fantasies associated with masturbation are accompanied by various forms of self-stimulation which frequently lead to orgasm.

The intensity and level of mental imagery

varies considerably from person to person during masturbation. Some may concentrate on the physiological sensations they are experiencing and have no erotic thoughts, but most people do fantasize while masturbating. In the Kinsey survey only 11 percent of the men and 36 percent of the women reported that they did not fantasize while masturbating. In Sorensen's survey of 13- to 19-year-olds, 20 percent of the males and only 10 percent of the females reported that they rarely or never fantasized while masturbating. On the other hand, as mentioned earlier, a few people, usually women, claim to be able to reach orgasm through fantasy alone (although subtle and hard-to-detect muscular tension may be involved).

Masturbatory fantasies often involve memories of past experiences, but erotic photographs or literature may also be used as sources of stimulation. In the Playboy Foundation survey, about half of the men and a third of the women indicated that exposure to erotic pictures or movies increased their desire to masturbate, and this was true for married as well as single persons. Reading erotic literature was found to be an even more potent stimulus than visual material, especially among women, more than half of whom reported such responses.

In the Playboy survey the most commonly mentioned type of fantasy involved sexual intercourse with a loved person (reported by three-quarters of all men and four-fifths of all women). But in the case of nearly half the males and more than a fifth of the females, masturbatory fantasies involved various acquaintances and individuals in a variety of sexual encounters. Among the other fantasies mentioned were intercourse with strangers (47 percent of males, 21 percent of females), sex with several persons of the opposite sex simultaneously (33 percent of males, 18 percent of females), being forced to have sex (10 percent of males, 19 percent of females), forcing someone to have sex (13 percent of males, 3 percent of females), and homosexual contacts (7 percent of males, 11 percent of females).

Masturbatory fantasies often provide safe expression of a wide variety of sexual interests that the fantasizer might find impossible or unacceptable in real life. Among the many purposes served, masturbatory fantasies are also used to test one's inclinations. For example, a 17-year-old woman who had fears about hidden Lesbian, or homosexual, tendencies was reassured of her heterosexuality by the fact that she could not reach orgasm while visualizing naked females.

Vaginal Insertions

Men are inclined to think that women usually insert their fingers or other objects into their vaginas when they masturbate, but only one in five women in the Kinsey study reported doing this, and often they may have meant merely slight penetrations of the sensitive introitus. When insertion does occur it is not usually an isolated activity but is accompanied by manipulation of adjoining genital structures. The inner vagina is poorly supplied with nerves, which probably explains why penetration is not used more often during masturbation. Some women, however, clearly enjoy deep penetration, perhaps because of its similarity to intercourse.

Fingers are most often used for insertion, but various common objects are also employed during autoerotic activities. Conveniently shaped objects like bananas, cucumbers, pencils, and candles have no doubt been used from time to time.

Special devices are also used as aids to masturbation. The most common are artificial penises (which are also used by male homosexuals). Although the frequency with which these objects are used may be exaggerated, there is evidence that they have been available in many parts of the world throughout history.

Artificial penises have been fashioned from gold, silver, ivory, ebony, horn, glass, wax, wood, and stuffed leather. They range from crude specimens to products of fine craftsmanship. Their most common name in English is **dildo** (from the Italian *diletto*). Dildos have sometimes been designed to permit the passage of warm liquid (usually milk) to simulate ejaculation. Modern versions have been further refined and can vibrate on battery power. Ten percent of the women in the Redbook survey reported using vibrators during masturbation.

Vibrators of various shapes and designs are available. Some are cylindrical dildos, others have vibrating rubber tips or can be attached to the back of the hand, through which they transmit their vibrations. Many of these gadgets are sold as "instruments of massage," or they are advertised as devices that "soothe the nerves" yet are "harmless to delicate tissues," and so on. In recent years vibrators have been found to be useful in connection with the treatment of orgasmic dysfunction.

In addition to artificial penises, artificial vaginas are available. The most common form is probably the masturbatory doll, an inflatable, life-size rubber or vinyl doll which comes equipped with an artificial vagina and sometimes an anus.

Another ingenious device for self-stimulation is the Japanese *rin-no-tama*. It consists of two hollow metal balls, one of which is empty and is inserted first into the vagina. The other contains a smaller metal ball, lead pellets, or mercury, and is inserted next. Both are held in place by a tampon. The slightest movement then makes the balls vibrate and send shocks of voluptuous sensations through the vagina. Some geishas reportedly swing in hammocks or rock in chairs while thus equipped.

Other Methods

Occasionally masturbation involves organs other than the genitals and unusual methods of stimulation. Some women, for instance, find that running a strong stream of water over the genitals is very exciting. Pulsating shower heads are sometimes used in this type of masturbation. Wearing tight clothing or any other practice that either creates friction or induces muscular tension may have the same effect.

Anal masturbation involves stimulation of the anus and penetration of the rectum (by fingers, dildos, and so on). It may occur independently or along with stimulation of the genitals. It is usually thought that homosexuals are more likely to use this method, but curiosity and the search for novel sensations may prompt others to try it.

Urethral insertions are rare. Women and children are more likely to attempt them, and for those to whom pain is erotically arousing this approach may be tempting. Surgeons have had to recover hairpins and other foreign objects from the urinary bladders of children or mentally incompetent women. Some women are able to suck their own nipples, and in some cases a man may be able to put his penis in his mouth (many try). Masturbation is clearly a versatile procedure.

Learning To Masturbate

As infants explore their bodies, sooner or later they learn that touching or stimulating their genitals can provide pleasure. Some infants and preadolescent children do masturbate, but deliberate masturbation does not usually become a common practice until the early teens. Most boys, for instance, are 10 to 12 years old when they begin. Most girls begin masturbation at a later age, as we shall see.

Boys in our society often learn to masturbate from one another—a fact that illustrates the importance of social learning, especially learning from peers. In the Kinsey sample nearly all males reported having heard about the practice before trying it themselves, and quite a few had watched companions doing it. Prepubescent boys appear to be much more communicative about their sexual activities than are girls, and are also bolder in seeking information. Fewer than one in three boys reported discovering this outlet by himself, and fewer than one in ten was led to it through homosexual contact.

Females learn to masturbate more often through individual discovery of the possibility (two out of three in the Kinsey sample), and some women learn it as late as in their thirties. Apparently females do not discuss their own sexual behavior as openly as males do. Some women who know of male masturbation are startled to discover that the practice also occurs among females. Some women may even masturbate for years before they realize the nature of their act—though such innocence was probably more common in the past.

Verbal and printed sources of information, though less important for females than for males, lead to masturbation (in more than 40 percent of the cases), and so does observation of others (11 percent). Slightly more than 10 percent of females are initiated into masturbation through petting (usually as a result of manipulation by the male). After achieving orgasm through petting or even through coitus a woman may then use the same methods autoerotically. Homosexual contacts account for very few initiations into masturbation for females.

Prevalence and Frequency

There is little doubt that masturbation is one of the most widespread sexual outlets. It is prevalent among males and much more common among females than is generally believed. Prevalence figures from different studies differ somewhat, but all have been high. In the Kinsey sample, 92 percent of males and 58 percent of females were found to have masturbated to orgasm at some time in their lives.

Figures 8.7 and 8.8 are known as accumu-

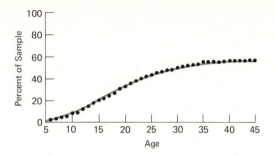

Figure 8.8 Accumulative incidence curve for masturbation to orgasm by females (curve for masturbation short of orgasm omitted).

From A.C. Kinsey *et al., Sexual Behavior in the Human Female* (Philadelphia: Saunders, 1953), p. 141. Courtesy of the Institute for Sex Research.

lative incidence curves. They answer the question: "How many people ever have such experiences in their lives?" The curves do not distinguish among the behavior of individuals, so a person who has masturbated only once and one who has done so many times are counted in the same way. In Figure 8.7 we see that only a small proportion of males had masturbated to orgasm by age 10 (even though the majority had attempted self-stimulation, stopping short of orgasm). Between the ages of 10 and 15 years the incidence curve climbed dramatically and then leveled off as it approached age 20. Practically every man who was ever going to masturbate had already done so by this age. The curve did not go beyond 92 percent, indicating that 8 out of every 100 males never masturbated to orgasm.

The female curve is quite different (*see* Figure 8.8). First, the curve never rose above 62 percent. Second, it climbed only gradually to this high point. Up to the age of 45 years, more and more women were still discovering this outlet by experiencing orgasm through masturbation for the first time.

What was the weekly frequency of masturbation among men? As with total sexual outlet, age and marital status made a great deal of difference. In boys from puberty to 15 years of age, among whom masturbation reached a peak, the mean, or average, frequency was about twice a week. If we exclude those who never masturbated, the weekly figure in-

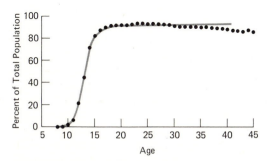

Figure 8.7 Accumulative incidence curve for masturbation by males (data corrected for U.S. population).

From A.C. Kinsey *et al., Sexual Behavior in the Human Male* (Philadelphia: Saunders, 1948), p. 502. Courtesy of the Institute for Sex Research.

creases to 2.4 times. Beyond age 15 the figures dropped steadily with age: In the total unmarried population the 46- to 50-year-old group averaged fewer than one orgasm every two weeks. Frequencies for married men were small, no more than once every two or three weeks.

These figures, of course, represent group averages, and as with most forms of sexual behavior there was a wide range of variation. There were men (apparently healthy) who never masturbated or did so only once or twice in their lives. Others may have averaged twenty or more such orgasms a week over many years.

The average (mean and median) frequencies for the active female sample were quite uniform at various age levels (up to the mid-fifties) and did not show the steady decline with age that was characteristic of males. The average unmarried woman, if she masturbated at all, did so about once every two or three weeks. For married women it was about once a month.

The range of variation in frequency in female masturbation was very wide. In addition to many who never masturbated, some masturbated yearly, monthly, weekly, or daily; and some reported reaching staggering numbers of orgasms in a single hour. These few individuals inflated the female means to two or three times the corresponding medians.

Recent Surveys

Changes in attitudes since the time of the Kinsey study appear to have resulted in changes in masturbatory behavior, particularly among women. Attitudes, though still ambivalent, have become more liberalized, and the prevalence of masturbation has increased. One of the most distinct changes is that both boys and girls appear to start masturbating at earlier ages. In the Kinsey sample the incidence of masturbation among 13-year-old boys was about 45 percent. In the Playboy survey the corresponding figure had increased to 65 percent. The rates for young girls increased from 15 to 40 percent.

The increase in prevalence rates of masturbation since the Kinsey study is not restricted to adolescents. The rates for single young males have gone up moderately, and those for young females even more so. Currently, 60 percent of women between the ages of 18 and 24 report some masturbatory experience, as opposed to a 25- to 35-percent rate for young women in the Kinsey study. More than 80 percent of the women in *The Hite Report* reported masturbating. Frequency rates have also increased. For young males the frequency has gone from 49 to 52 times a year, for young females from 21 to 37 times a year.

Biological, social, and situational factors affect masturbation as they do other types of sexual behavior. Among Kinsey subjects, for instance, males who reached puberty at a younger age were more likely to masturbate and to do so more frequently than boys who reached puberty later. (The same did not hold for females.) Social factors, as measured by educational and occupational status, also affect masturbation. The better-educated person (especially if female) is more likely to masturbate, but class-related differences appear to be less significant than in previous years.

Masturbation and Marriage

As mentioned in Chapter 7, masturbation accounted for far greater shares of total outlet among single people than among marrieds, but current data indicate an increase in the prevalence of masturbation among young married men and women. In the Kinsey study about 40 percent of the husbands in their late twenties and early thirties masturbated (about 6 times a year), now about 70 percent do so (about 24 times a year). For wives of corresponding ages the percentages have gone up from 30 to 70 percent, but the median rate has not changed (about 10 times a year).

Why would married people masturbate at all? The most recent data do not suggest that increased masturbation is in compensation for frustrations in marital coitus. As we will see in the next chapter, this is far from the case. Instead, modern married persons, especially those who are younger, appear relatively freer to rely on masturbation as an additional outlet for sexual pleasure and related needs.

The most common reason for masturbation by married men and women is the temporary unavailability of the spouse—through absence, illness, pregnancy, disinclination, and so on. Of all the alternatives to marital coitus (other than abstinence and nocturnal orgasm) masturbation is probably the least threatening to the marital relationship.

There are also instances in which masturbation is considered preferable to coitus. During masturbation people can give freer reign to their fantasies, and if they are simply after sexual pleasure masturbation allows both husband and wife to avoid the lengthy and sometimes tedious demands of the spouse. If a man has a potency problem, masturbation can save him repeated humiliations. If a woman finds coitus unfulfilling, she can attend to her own sexual needs through self-stimulation. As an autoerotic activity, masturbation provides a person with full and complete control without the obligations and restraints necessary when dealing with another person.

Masturbation and Religion

Both Jewish and Christian moral codes have traditionally condemned masturbation, and this condemnation has had some effect on behavior. But interestingly, men and women seem to have been influenced differently. The very high prevalence of masturbation among males indicates that religious belief has not had a significant effect. A man may feel less or more guilty about masturbating, but sooner or later more than nine out of ten indulge in the practice. There is a difference, however, in how often they do so. The more religious men (particularly Orthodox Jews and practicing Roman Catholics) in the Kinsey sample did masturbate somewhat less often. The highest frequencies were among religiously inactive Protestants.

Among women, masturbation was definitely less widespread among the more devout (41 percent) than the less devout (67 per-

cent), with the degree of devoutness seeming to be more important than the denomination. But unlike men, once a woman had engaged in masturbation she did not seem to be influenced by religious beliefs in how often she used it.

Even though the devout female was less likely to masturbate, this practice accounted for a higher proportion of her sexual outlet than it did for her nondevout counterpart. Apparently masturbation still provided a "lesser evil" in comparison with alternatives like premarital coitus.

The Playboy survey indicates that devoutness continues to have a significant influence on masturbation today: The nonreligious are more likely to masturbate, to start doing it at a younger age, and to continue it into adult life and also into marriage. These differences between the devout and nondevout are not as striking as at the time of the Kinsey study, but the effect of religion is generally much more marked among women than among men.

Cross-cultural Variations

Europeans are a "race of masturbators," said anthropologist Mantegazza (whose writings were popular in the 1930s). He reasoned that Western civilization simultaneously stimulates and represses sexuality and that restrictions on premarital coitus compel people to masturbate instead. European masturbation patterns seem very similar to those of the United States, but masturbation is not a predominantly Western practice. The anthropological record indicates that masturbation is prevalent in all cultures. Like all human behavior, however, it is subject to cultural variations.

Masturbation has been documented for many ancient cultures, including the Babylonian, Egyptian, Hebrew, Indian, and Greco-Roman. Greek and Roman mythology told of how the god Mercury invented masturbation to console Pan for the loss of his mistress Echo. Zeus himself was known to indulge occasionally. Classical writers, such as Aristophanes, Aristotle, Herondas, and Petronius, refer to masturbation, but attitudes seem to have been ambivalent. Demosthenes was condemned for the practice, whereas Diogenes was praised for doing it openly in the marketplace.

Condemnations by medieval theologians (as many as 50 days penance) acknowledge that masturbation was practiced then. Muslim theologians regarded it as a Christian vice and prayed for mercy for any of their own who fell into this error.

Masturbation has been reported for about 40 primitive cultures and is thought to be less prevalent in societies that are permissive toward nonmarital coitus and rare in many preliterate groups. Most groups seemed to disapprove of it for adults. For instance, Trukese men (monogamous fishermen of the Caroline Islands) were said to masturbate in secret while watching women bathe. Men of the Tikopia (Pacific island agriculturists) and of Dahomey (West African agriculturists and fishermen) masturbated occasionally, even though both cultures permitted polygamy.

Female masturbation was reported less frequently, and in most cultures it was disapproved. Vaginal insertions, rather than clitoral stimulation, were more common among some cultures: African Azande women used wooden dildos (and were severely beaten if caught by their husbands); the Chukchee of Siberia used the calf muscles of reindeer; Tikopia women relied on roots and bananas; Crow women used their fingers, and so did the Azanda of Australia.

Among the Lesu (polygamous peoples of New Ireland) female masturbation was an accepted practice, as one researcher reported:

Masturbation . . . is practiced frequently at Lesu and regarded as normal behavior. A woman will masturbate if she is sexually excited and there is no man to satisfy her. A couple may be having intercourse in the same house, or near enough for her to see them, and she may thus become aroused. She then sits down and bends her right leg so that her heel presses against her genitalia. Even young girls of about six years may do this quite casually as they sit on the ground. The women and men talk about it freely, and there is no shame attached to it. It is a cus-

tomary position for women to take, and they learn it in childhood. They never use their hands for manipulation. (Powdermaker, 1933, in Ford and Beach, 1951)

Masturbation and Health

Masturbation has been erroneously suggested at one time or another to be associated with insanity; epilepsy; various forms of headaches (in addition to "strange sensations at the top of the head"); numerous eye diseases (including dilated pupils, dark rings around the eyes, "eyes directed upward and sideways"); intermittent deafness; redness of the nose and nosebleeds; "morbid changes in the nose"; hypertrophy and tenderness of the breasts; afflictions of the ovaries, uterus, and vagina (including painful menstruation and "acidity of the vagina"); pains of various kinds, specifically "tenderness of the skin in the lower dorsal region"; asthma; heart murmurs ("masturbator's heart"); and skin ailments ranging from acne to wounds, pale and discolored skin, and "an undesirable odor of the skin in women."

There is absolutely no evidence to support claims that these or any other type of physical harm result from masturbation. Yet for more than 200 years (from the dawn of the Age of Enlightenment) and until recently these dire effects have held an unshakable place in the beliefs of the medical elite in the Western world.

From the time of Hippocrates physicians have expressed concern that overindulgence in sex might be bad for one's health. But only in the past 250 years has masturbation been singled out as a particularly harmful activity. Before the eighteenth century there were only occasional references to masturbation in medical texts. Then a book called *Onania, or the Heinous Sin of Self-Pollution* appeared in Europe. Its author was probably a clergyman turned quack who peddled a remedy along with the book. The book became popular in Europe but appears to have had no immediate impact on medical opinion.

In 1758, *Onania, or a Treatise upon the Disorders Produced by Masturbation* appeared. Written by a distinguished Swiss physician named Tissot, it amplified the claims of the earlier work. Tissot's views, coming from a respected authority, found ready acceptance. Despite rebuttals and accusations that he was exploiting his medical reputation to further his personal, moral points of view, the book became a standard reference. By the end of the eighteenth century the "masturbatory hypothesis" of mental disease and assorted ills was well established—and it has taken more than 100 years to discredit this view.

Currently, no informed person has any real concern about the physical effects of masturbation. Whatever concerns exist are based on psychological and moral issues. Psychological judgments of masturbation are based on the motives for the practice, the degree of dependence on masturbation, and the extent to which it substitutes for sociosexual relationships.

The most frequently mentioned motive for masturbation is the relief of sexual tension (claimed by four out of five men and two out of three women in the Playboy survey). The need for such release is often to compensate for the lack of a sexual partner or the temporary unavailability of one. As mentioned earlier, however, masturbation is often relied on as an additional source of gratification, by single as well as by happily married persons. The fantasy-gratification functions have also been mentioned. Other motivations are nonsexual. In the Playboy sample more than a quarter of the males and a third of the females reported that they masturbated to combat feelings of loneliness. People also rely on masturbation to release tensions caused by occupational or personal problems or simply to relax in order to get to sleep.

A listing of motives such as these does not in itself provide an adequate basis for making judgments. A proper evaluation of masturbatory behavior, as with any other type of behavior, can be made only in the context of the individual's overall life. Clearly, masturbation can become a liability if it is relied upon compulsively at the expense of ultimately more rewarding interpersonal encounters. In other words, it is a convenient shortcut that can have the potential of shortchanging a per-

son. The problem in such cases is not primarily the result of masturbation but rather of other, more fundamental psychological conflicts. In these cases masturbation is just one more facet of the general picture of poor adjustment. Even in these circumstances, though, masturbation may provide to the disturbed individual one of the few readily available forms of sexual release and psychological comfort.

Even when doctors condone masturbation, they often conclude that a person should not carry the practice to "excess." "Excess," however, is not defined, and the harm that will result is not specified. Such vagueness is a reflection of the discredited but not yet discarded notions of former times. Masturbation is still not quite "respectable." Ambivalence in this regard appears to characterize even modern youths who have been spared, for the most part, the horror stories of earlier periods. Sorensen reports, for example, that of all sexual practices, masturbation was the one about which 13- to 19-year-olds were most defensive and least willing to speak.

The problem was only partly one of guilt. Among the adolescents currently using masturbation as a sexual outlet, only 19 percent claimed never to have felt guilty (32 percent had guilt feelings only rarely, 32 percent sometimes, and 17 percent often). An element of shame was also associated with masturbation, since this form of sexual activity implied that one is not mature enough, attractive enough, or sophisticated enough to have a sexual partner. Yet masturbation was more common among those who were engaging in coitus than among those who were not. Similar attitudes have been reported from the Playboy survey. People tend to feel ashamed and secretive about the practice, and "almost no adults, not even the very liberated can bring themselves to tell friends, lovers, or mates that they still occasionally masturbate."

Though many people still believe masturbation is wrong, there is a clear connection between these attitudes and age. In the 55 and older age group, 29 percent of males and 36 percent of females agree that "masturbation is wrong." These percentages decrease with decreasing age, so that in the 18- to 24-year-old bracket only 15 percent of males and 14 percent of females agree with this statement. These figures indicate not only a relative change in attitudes with age but also the disappearance of differences between the sexes in such attitudes.

The general social acceptance of masturbation is also clearly on the rise, as can be judged by the explicit discussions of it in popular and literary works (such as *Portnoy's Complaint* by Philip Roth) and by the endorsement of the practice of popular sex manuals. Sex researchers, such as Masters and Johnson, encourage women who have never reached orgasms with partners to seek orgasm first through masturbation. The women's movement has also stressed the value of masturbation, especially for women who have difficulty in achieving orgasm. As one woman in *The Hite Report* put it: "I never masturbated when I was young, and when I found out about it, I was filled with a sense of power and liberation. Masturbating helped me learn a great deal about the changes my body goes through in achieving orgasm."

SUMMARY

1.   Autoerotic activities constitute a large and important type of sexual behavior. The most common forms of autoeroticism are sexual fantasies, erotic dreams, and masturbation. Moral and religious restrictions against such activities are no longer as strict as they once were, and autoeroticism has come to be accepted by many people as a legitimate and beneficial way of enjoying sex.

2.   Erotic fantasies take many forms—from fleeting erotic thoughts and images to intricately woven fantasies. They may be more common among adolescents than among adults, but erotic fantasies are an important form of autoeroticism throughout life for most people.

3.   While the person doing the fantasizing is usually the main character in erotic fantasies, the other characters and the content of the fantasies are limited only by the dreamer's imagination. The degree of arousal that accompanies these fantasies varies from no arousal in some cases to intense feelings of excitement in others. A few individuals, usually women, are reportedly able to reach orgasm through fantasy alone.

4.   Although erotic fantasies are usually pleasant experiences, they can also be a source of unpleasant feelings. Socially unacceptable fantasies can cause some people to feel guilt and embarrassment, and simply having erotic thoughts can result in guilt feelings on the part of persons who have been conditioned to believe that erotic thoughts are wrong. In general, erotic fantasies are not considered to be harmful unless they are particularly disturbing or lead to the acting out of antisocial thoughts.

5.   Erotic fantasies serve several functions. They are an easily available source of pleasure which most people can enjoy and through which some people learn about and come to accept their own sexuality. Fantasies are often a substitute for sexual experiences that are otherwise unavailable or unattainable. They also provide a sort of mental practice field for future sociosexual situations.

6. Neurophysiological studies indicate that everyone has regular periods of dreaming every night. These dream periods are accompanied by rapid eye movements (REM) and intense physiological activity, including erections in males in many instances. Sexual arousal during sleep is not always accompanied by erotic dreams, but most people have erotic dreams from time to time.

7. Nocturnal orgasms—often accompanied by erotic dreams—do not make up a large percentage of total sexual outlets, but many females and most males experience them. It was once thought that nocturnal orgasms provided a sort of sexual "safety" valve for individuals who did not have other avenues of sexual activity, but this does not appear to be the case. In some instances the rate of nocturnal orgasms has actually increased as other outlets increased.

8. The techniques of masturbation are numerous, but in general they are similar to those of foreplay and usually involve manipulation of the genitals with the hands. Muscular tension can also be used to heighten arousal during masturbation, and most people have erotic fantasies while masturbating. Vaginal insertions (fingers, dildos, vibrators, and other objects) and anal stimulation are among the less-common methods of masturbation; thigh pressure is an exclusively female technique.

9. Most young children learn that touching or stimulating their genitals can provide pleasure, but masturbation usually does not become a common practice until the early teens. Young boys often learn to masturbate through hearing about it from one another or from watching others do it. Females usually discover it for themselves, sometimes as late as in their thirties (although this was probably more common in former years).

10. Masturbation is one of the most common sexual outlets. According to the Kinsey survey, more than 90 percent of males and at least 60 percent females engage in it at some time or other. Although there is great variation in how often people masturbate, surveys indicate that young males average two to three times per week, with this figure tending to decrease with increasing age. Female averages are lower (about once every two or three weeks), but recent surveys suggest that both males and females are beginning to masturbate at an earlier age and are doing it more often than in previous generations.

11. Attitudes toward masturbation are changing from negative to positive. For one thing, there is no evidence whatsoever that masturbation is harmful, though even some sexually liberated people still occasionally have guilt feelings about it. Masturbation can sometimes be beneficial. Some sex therapists now encourage patients — especially women who have trouble achieving orgasm — to learn about their sexual responses through masturbation.

SUGGESTED READING

For more detailed information on the statistics of autoerotic behavior see the Kinsey surveys and the more recent studies of sexual behavior listed under the suggested reading section of Chapter 7.

Comfort, A. *The Anxiety Makers.* New York: Delta, 1967. An historical review of the irrational fears and absurd remedies perpetuated by physicians in earlier times.

Hare, E. H. "Masturbatory Insanity: The History of an Idea," *Journal of Mental Science,* **452** (1962): 2-25.
An historical account of how masturbation became a source of medical concern in the nineteenth century.

Friday, N. *My Secret Garden.* New York: Pocket Books, 1974.
Narrative accounts of women's fantasies.

The Hite Report and *Beyond the Male Myth* (referred to in Chapter 7 readings) also have accounts of female and male fantasies and masturbatory experiences.

chapter 9 Sexual Intercourse

Did You Know That . . .

some postures in sexual intercourse are more likely than others to result in pregnancy, but no posture is a reliable method of birth control?

many women find it easier to achieve orgasm during coitus in the woman-on-top position?

the face-to-face lateral position during sexual intercourse allows the male greater ejaculatory control and tends to make coitus more prolonged and leisurely?

there is no such thing as a true "aphrodisiac," and some of the substances that are currently used in attempts to enhance sexual potency can cause temporary impotence and produce dangerous side effects?

even though simultaneous orgasm has been praised by many as a way of enhancing pleasure, attempts to coordinate sexual excitement can distract from the enjoyment of the sexual experience for one or both partners?

INTRODUCTION

People enjoy sex in a great variety of ways, as we saw in Chapter 7, but for many adults sexual intercourse is what sex is all about. As we will see in this chapter, there are many ways people enjoy sexual intercourse—including the period leading up to intercourse, the act itself, and its aftermath.

At one level sexual intercourse is a purely physical activity, but centuries of human experience have endowed it with profound psychological and moral significance for people. Throughout this chapter it will be important to keep in mind that sexual intercourse is a complex interaction between two individuals, and it can be fully understood only within the overall context of such a relationship.

FOREPLAY

While some couples can proceed right to coitus after only a few simple caresses, sexual intercourse is almost always preceded by a lengthier period of sexually arousing activity called **foreplay.** The activities involved in foreplay are usually the same as those engaged in during petting except that they lead to sexual intercourse.

Although this book is not intended as a manual on the techniques of sexual arousal, instruction in erotic techniques may be useful for those of us who are anxious about sex and unsure of ourselves. Even when nothing new is said, the written text inspires confidence to do what we already know about. Those who wish to go beyond ordinary levels of sexual competence may also want to learn from the experiences of others who are more imaginative or resourceful.

Psychological Context

Nothing could be more appropriate than expressions of affection during foreplay, and few measures are more effective in arousing a partner. Most people require certain min-

imums of affection and trust before they can engage in satisfactory sexual encounters. Many even profess and some actually believe that unless they are "in love" they cannot engage in sex without cheapening the act. This issue has profound moral as well as psychological significance.

Discussions of sexual arousal and coitus must be understood within this larger emotional context. For a person who is deeply in love, the mere presence or the slightest touch of the beloved can be highly stimulating; for others love may exist without overt erotic content. Still others may achieve high levels of sexual gratification without benefit of such intense emotions. But even then there is usually some reaction to the partner as a person beyond physical sexual interest.

Even though expressions of affection are more meaningful when they are spontaneous, some people cannot help trying to extract such assurances at every turn; others are guilty of mouthing passionate endearments for pragmatic ends. There are many ways of expressing affection and all (not just the verbal forms) should be recognized.

The prelude to coitus may be as pleasurable as coitus itself. A certain mix of seriousness (but not heavy drama) and light-heartedness (but not comedy) is often the most effective mood. There is no absolute standard, and different occasions require different attitudes. Some couples enjoy chasing each other around, wrestling on the floor, and jumping into bed amid screams and giggles. Others prefer a more subdued mood, with voices gentle and hushed and movements restrained.

There are various ways of approaching sex, but it is perhaps best simply to "be oneself," though emphasizing one's assets. Yet it is difficult to drop all pretense without a feeling of mutual trust. To "be oneself" and to accept the other person as is, however, is only the beginning. As incompatibilities and differences are unavoidable, both partners must also be willing and able to accommodate to each other's needs—but only up to a point. Some relationships may be incompatible and are best abandoned. People may be so hopelessly dominated by conflicts that they need to mature or change before they can engage in sexual intercourse responsibly and satisfactorily.

Another way of looking at it is to consider one of the functions of sex as a form of adult play. Play is of crucial importance during childhood and ought to retain some of its usefulness in adulthood as well. In order for adults to play, it is necessary that they regain the carefree ability to pretend and play-act without losing touch with reality or becoming deceitful. Such play-acting revitalizes and makes sex more fun and allows our fantasies safe and partial fulfillment.

In sexual matters it is tempting to look for simple physical means to ecstasy, and we are annoyed when instead we are offered psychological generalities. Nevertheless, if one wants to become an accomplished lover, the simple-minded search for buttons and levers will have to be abandoned. There is no denying the importance of knowing where the nerve centers are, but the current that feeds those circuits is emotion.

Sex does not operate within a psychological vacuum, and the range of possible emotional reactions varies tremendously, depending on circumstances and the relations of the individuals. As we cannot possibly deal here with even a fraction of these variations, we shall assume in this chapter that we are dealing with physically healthy and affectionate couples engaging in sexual intercourse without conflict and with a clear conscience.

The following arousal techniques are not limited to foreplay and can continue while coitus is in progress. The male has traditionally taken the more active role in these activities, but there is no reason why women cannot be just as active. For mature people, making love is an interaction between equals.

Techniques of Arousal

At least some understanding of which parts of the body respond to which types of stimulation is necessary if one is to become a competent lover. The information on "erogenous zones" and the body's responses to sexual stimulation offered earlier (Chapter 3) is relevant here. Of the innumerable activities that may be included in foreplay, we shall single out a few that are generally found to be quite effective and are acceptable to most people.

Kissing

Erotic kissing is a common part of sex play in many, but not all, cultures. It is both an expression of sexual desire and an effective erotic stimulant. Although kissing takes several forms, it generally involves the tongue and the inside of the mouth. "A humid kiss," says an ancient Arabic proverb, "is better than a hurried coitus." Erotic kissing, like coitus, builds up gradually and requires sensitivity and timing.

Initially kissing involves mostly lip contact. A light, stroking motion may be used in alternation with tentative tongue caresses and gentle nibbling of the more accessible lower lip. Gradually, as the tongue becomes bolder, it can range freely in the mouth of the partner, who may suck on it. The use of the tongue in erotic kissing is sometimes referred to as "French kissing," but as Figure 9.1 illustrates, this is a common form of foreplay and unlikely to have originated in a single culture.

Kissing need not be restricted to the sexual partner's lips. Any part of the body may be similarly stimulated, although the neck, ear lobes, breasts, inside of the thighs, fingertips, palms of the hands, and, of course, the genitals have a higher erotic potential.

Oral-Genital Stimulation

An exceedingly effective (but for some a controversial) erotic stimulant is the "genital kiss," also known as **cunnilingus** ("to lick the vulva") and **fellatio** ("to suck") for the oral stimulation of female and male genitals respectively. It is a fairly widespread though unevenly distributed practice. The Playboy survey found that 80 percent of single males and females between the ages of 25 and 34 years had engaged in mouth-genital stimu-

Figure 9.1 Mochica pottery.

Courtesy of William Dellenback and the Institute for Sex Research.

lation. This suggests an increase in these activities over previous years. Among college-educated married males in the Kinsey sample 45 percent reported having orally stimulated the genitals of their wives. The corresponding percentage figure in the Playboy sample was 66 percent. College-educated married women in the Kinsey sample reported such experiences in 58 percent of cases. Currently, 72 percent of married women have had their genitalia orally stimulated by their husbands. The figure is even higher for younger women. And more than 40 percent of the women in *The Hite Report* said they usually had orgasms during oral stimulation. The increase in prevalence of cunnilingus among married couples is most impressive among lesser-educated males, where the practice appears to have lost some of its former unacceptability.

There are many types of genital kiss, including gentle caressing of the clitoris, the minor lips, and the area of the introitus with the tongue. In the male the glans is the primary focus of excitement; gentle stroking of the frenulum, with the tongue and lips mouthing and sucking the glans while firmly holding the penis, and grasping and pulling gently at the scrotal sac with the other hand are some of the means of stimulation. These activities must be conducted with tact and tenderness, since a person is not likely to appreciate a tooth-and-nail assault.

A couple may engage in mutual oral-genital contact ("sixty-nine") as a prelude to coitus or for its own sake (*see* Figure 9.2). It is not unusual for a woman to have one or more orgasms from genital stimulation before intercourse begins. The man thus need not fear leaving his partner unsatisfied during coitus and can time his own orgasm as he wishes.

Oral-genital stimulation may be repulsive to some people, but if the genitals are clean, objections are difficult to support on hygienic grounds. No one is obliged to perform or submit to such activity, of course, but to carry judgments beyond personal preference and to make legal or moral issues out of these acts is another matter.

Tactile Stimulation

Tactile stimulation is another important method of sexual arousal. Fondling and caressing are most common, but scratching and gentle pressure can also be effective. The areas to be stimulated are again the "erogenous zones," though, as we indicated earlier, each person has a unique erotogenic map.

Kissing and caressing operate on the same physiological principle: The object is to stimulate the sensory receptors on the surface of the skin. In fondling, deeper tissues are also stimulated and the erotic response is somewhat different. Actually these approaches are interchangeable. For example, the lips can be stimulated through gentle caressing by the fingertips, and the lips and tongue can be used in turn to caress some other part of the body.

Tactile stimulation can be greatly enhanced if surfaces are moist. The mouth has a

Figure 9.2 *Fantasy,* attributed to P. Breughel.

Tactile stimulation of the genitals is particularly exciting for most people. In the Kinsey sample 95 percent of males and 91 percent of females reported manually stimulating the genitals of their sexual partners. Males tended to be more active in this regard. Almost 20 percent of the men who responded in *Beyond the Male Myth* indicated a desire for more genital stimulation by their partners. For many women manual stimulation of the clitoris during foreplay (and during coitus) is much more exciting than coitus alone. The techniques of genital stimulation during foreplay are similar to those employed in autoerotic activities (*see* Chapter 8).

Some people also stimulate themselves during foreplay or even coitus. If they feel free enough, they can thus demonstrate to their partners how best to stimulate them. The more a couple is able to communicate, the less is the need for extraneous instruction.

Stroking the anal orifice and inserting fingers into the rectum are also appreciated by some and rejected by others on esthetic and other grounds, but recent surveys indicate that anal stimulation is more common than in previous years.

Since each person knows best what is exciting, personally, there is much that can be learned from masturbation that would be useful in foreplay. These can then be modified and supplemented with additional techniques of stimulation that become possible with the presence of a partner. Tactile stimulation of the inner thighs, buttocks, and genitals, for instance, can be most effectively combined with oral stimulation of these parts.

When natural vaginal lubrication is inadequate, it is necessary that the couple use saliva or a coital lubricant (for example, "K-Y jelly"). In these cases the jelly would be applied just prior to intromission or used much earlier during coital foreplay to enhance tactile stimulation of the clitoris and the adjoining structures. There is no reason why women with adequate natural vaginal lubrication cannot also use these jellies for their erotic enhancement.

Despite differences in individual responsiveness, some general principles are worth

natural advantage over the hands in this regard, but saliva can also be used quite effectively to moisten the area to be caressed. Even more effective is the use of lotions. Any hand lotion that has a pleasant scent for both partners will do. Apart from their physical effects, lotions provide additional advantages. Whereas ordinary caresses may be cursory and fleeting, when lotions are used, foreplay is prolonged, becomes more deliberate, and helps the participants to stimulate each other unabashedly rather than furtively.

The effectivenss of fondling female breasts is well known in many cultures. Breast stimulation can be enhanced by using both the mouth and hands. The nipples, though the most responsive parts, need not be the exclusive focus of attention. Most women also enjoy more general fondling, mouthing, and caressing of their breasts. The size of the breast has no relation to its sensitivity, and a small-breasted woman should not be assumed to be less sensitive in this area.

bearing in mind. Most people find it best to start slowly and with the less sensitive areas. Some do enjoy rough handling, but many others do not. As no one objects to tenderness, it would seem preferable to start gently and to become more forceful as appropriate, rather than to startle and offend at the beginning.

Sensitive surfaces respond best to gentle stimulation, whereas larger muscle masses require firmer handling. Once an area has been singled out for stimulation, it should be attended to long enough to elicit arousal. Frantic shifting from one part of the body to another can be as ineffective as monotonous and endless perseverance. If stimulation is to be effective, it should be steady and persistent. Its tempo and intensity may be modulated, but sexual tension should not be permitted to dissipate. Erotic arousal requires patience and may even be somewhat boring at times, but effective lovers usually manage to sustain a sense of novelty and a feeling of excitement.

Other Means

Several additional considerations are important. First is the matter of timing. The correct technique applied to the right place at the wrong time will fail to arouse. The same stimulus may be experienced as unpleasant or painful at one stage yet catapult a person to peak excitement at another. Correct timing in turn requires the ability to gauge excitement.

The necessity for effective communication is obvious to most people, but it is often difficult to achieve. Almost everyone will complain when in pain, but most of us are much more reluctant to ask for enhancement of pleasure for fear of seeming forward, lascivious, or perverted. Wishes are sometimes more easily communicated indirectly, such as by guiding the partner's hand.

Expression of emotion during lovemaking should cause no feeling of shame. It is a time to let oneself go. Furthermore, lovers who wish to enhance their partner's excitement and pleasure can most effectively do so by letting them know how they feel. The awareness of a woman's arousal fills a man with pride

and provides proof of his competence as a lover. The same is true of a woman. The sighs and moans, squeaks and squeals, grunts and groans of sex are also songs of love.

The erotic potential of pain is well known. Even ordinary versions of foreplay and coitus involve enough physical activity to result in some strain. Within limits and with certain partners mild pain from bites and scratches can be quite stimulating. It will be recalled from Chapter 3 that the threshold of pain is higher during sexual excitement, and this type of stimulation is usually attempted during advanced stages of lovemaking.

There are many additional techniques of stimulation, but a basic acceptance of oneself and one's partner as individuals, unabashed pride in the body and its sexual functions, the conviction that sex is moral and honorable, and some knowledge of the basic sexual functions are what generally count most in sex.

Amount of Foreplay

How long does foreplay usually last? Preferences seem to vary widely among individuals and cultures. The Playboy survey found the average amount of time spent on foreplay to be about 15 minutes, but it seems best to leave the length of foreplay to each couple to decide. Aside from preferences, different circumstances require different amounts of preparation. Physiologically, full erection and adequate vaginal lubrication indicate readiness. Emotionally, a couple is ready when both members feel a mutual urge for sexual union.

In attaining this physiological and emotional readiness for sexual intercourse the importance of psychological factors cannot be emphasized enough. All of the foreplay techniques in the world will lead nowhere if the person is not in the right frame of mind. The mental set that is conducive to making love is in turn influenced by a host of factors, including a reasonable conviction that one is doing the right thing, warmth and affection for the other, and a basic acceptance of one's own sexuality.

It is possible to debase and trivialize sexual intercourse so that affection, for instance, is replaced with disinterest or contempt for the other person. If this happens, intercourse becomes a parody.

In view of these possibilities the techniques for erotic arousal and those to be described for sexual intercourse must be understood in their psychological contexts. A few tender words felt and expressed convincingly and a gentle caress are likely to be far more effective stimulants than furious friction of some erogenous zone. This is not to depreciate the importance of the body but to properly appreciate the importance of the mind. As it has been said before, but cannot be repeated enough, sex is ultimately experienced in the head, not the groin.

INTERCOURSE

Making love has been compared to a game of chess: The moves are many, but the ending is the same. Coitus proper starts with the coupling of the penis and the vagina. It can be achieved from a variety of postures, and intercourse involves various types of movements. Even though there is more to making love than coital mechanics, understanding the physical basis of the act is helpful. The relationship between male and female sexual organs during face-to-face intercourse is illustrated in Figure 9.3; the theme was also treated by Leonardo da Vinci five centuries ago (*see* Figure 9.4). One important biological fact to remember is that except for very rare anomalies, all penises and vaginas are for all practical purposes perfectly adequate organs for providing sexual pleasure to the partner and oneself. Recent evidence suggests, however, that many women enjoy additional clitoral stimulation during coitus and some require such stimulation if they are to achieve orgasm.

Although discussions of the mechanics of coitus suggest that their main contribution is to enhance the physical aspects of intercourse, the benefits are in fact mostly psychological. Some of us approach sex with uncer-

tainty and a tendency to hurry. In experimenting with various approaches, we become more deliberate, controlled, and purposeful. This effort implies care and concern for the partner, so that intercourse literally fits the meaning of the term: an interaction between two people. Involving the female partner more actively can increase both the male's and female's enjoyment. When she takes some of the initiative, the male partner in turn is reassured that he is giving as much pleasure as he is feeling. Knowledge of and experimentation with sexual techniques can thus greatly enrich a sexual relationship.

A second advantage is obtained from the variety of possible postures. Married couples especially, sooner or later, begin to find sex a bit monotonous. "Marriage," Honoré de Balzac wrote, "must continually vanquish a monster that devours everything: the monster of habit." The imaginative use of different positions can be an antidote to habit, though sustaining real variety year after year is difficult to do.

Various coital positions also yield different physical sensations, and, though most of us are able to improvise, some of us need the inspiration and information that come from knowing about the experiences of others. Finally, it is important to know how conducive to impregnation a given position is likely to be. Such knowledge is helpful to a couple that is trying to conceive a child, but no posture is reliable as a contraceptive measure.

There is nothing mysterious or magical about coital positions. Experimentation shows one approach to be more exciting at one time and others under other circumstances. There is no "position to end all positions," and the search for mechanical perfection is endless and pointless.

A certain agility is indispensable to both partners if they wish to explore the limits of coital gratification, but sex should not become a series of gymnastic feats as in the story of the Oriental courtesan who had attained such perfect control that she could engage in coitus while holding a cup of tea on one uplifted foot. Another potential drawback is that reading about coital techniques can result in a "cook-

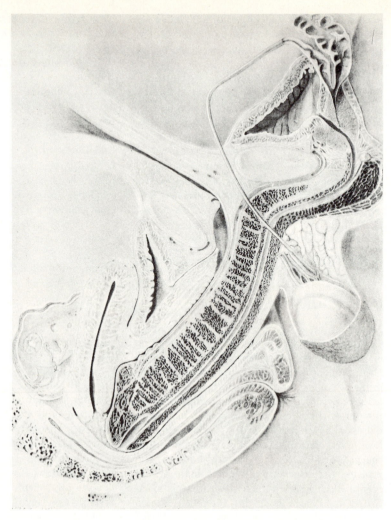

Figure 9.3 Male and female genitals in face-to-face coitus.

From Robert L. Dickinson, *Atlas of Human Sex Anatomy,* 2d ed. (Baltimore; Williams & Wilkins, 1949), figure 142. Copyright © 1949 by The Williams & Wilkins Co., and reprinted by permission.

book" approach to lovemaking, which robs the act of the spontaneity that ought to be its hallmark.

Many marriage manuals, both ancient and contemporary, give such detailed instructions that the reader becomes overwhelmed by the apparent complexity of the act and cannot help but wonder how millions of people ever manage to accomplish it all by themselves. Illustrations of coital postures are no less bewildering, particularly some of those from the Far East (*see* Figure 9.5). The complexity of Indian sexual practices prompted the six-

teenth-century Arab sage Sheikh Nefzawi to comment: "This position, as you can perceive, is very fatiguing and very difficult to attain. I even believe that the only realization of it consists in words and designs."

To speak of coital positions is thus misleading, for we are actually dealing with general approaches rather than specific postures. During face-to-face intercourse, for instance, a woman lying on her back will stretch her legs out, then pull them up halfway or bring her knees close to her chest for a while, then stretch them out again, and so on. Even when

Figure 9.4 Leonardo da Vinci, figures in coition.

more marked shifts in posture occur, one position flows into another, and, sexual activity never loses its fluid quality.

Approaches

Despite the innumerable erotic postures described in love manuals, the basic approaches to coitus are relatively few. The couple may stand, sit, or lie down; the two may face each other, or the woman can turn her back to the man; one person can be on top, or the couple can lie side by side.

Figure 9.6 illustrates some of the more common coital approaches. Instead of giving detailed descriptions we shall examine the

Figure 9.5 Pages from a nineteenth-century Orissan posture-book.

Reprinted by permission of G.P. Putnam's Sons and Weidenfeld & Nicholson Ltd., from *Erotic Art of the East,* Philip Rawson, ed., p. 43. Copyright © 1969 by Philip Rawson.

Figure 9.6 Four variations in coital position: (*top*) the so-called "missionary" position; (*middle left*) rear entry, which can be used with the couple either sitting or standing; (*middle right*) with the woman in the superior position, sitting; and (*bottom*) side entry.

relative advantages of these various alternatives.

Face-to-Face

The primary advantage of face-to-face approaches is the opportunity for direct interaction. The partners can kiss and gaze into each other's eyes, fully communicating their feelings through speech and facial expressions.

In the traditional and most commonly used approach in the Western world, the woman lies on her back with the man on top of her. Coitus in this position is the most likely to lead to pregnancy. The optimal pooling of the ejaculate in this approach has been described earlier (*see* Chapter 5). In order to maximize the chance of conception, the woman must maintain this posture for a while after coitus, and the man should not withdraw abruptly.

There are also several drawbacks to male-on-top positions. If they are used exclusively, sexual interest may eventually diminish. The man's weight can also be a problem: He can support himself, but a really heavy man will still be a considerable burden on the woman. Furthermore, in this position the man's hands will not be free to stimulate his partner.

A more serious problem is the restriction that such positions impose on the woman's movements. Although she can move her legs, her pelvis remains largely immobilized or can be moved only with considerable effort.

Just as many variations are possible if the woman lies or sits on top of the man. Her weight is usually less of a problem, and she has the opportunity to express herself fully by regulating the speed and vigor of her movements and the depth of penetration. Many women find it easier to achieve orgasm in this manner. Furthermore, a man is less likely to be bothered by her weight and is therefore less handicapped than she would be underneath.

A host of other alternatives is available to the partners when they lie on their sides. Penetration is somewhat more difficult in these positions and requires that the woman lift her upper leg. Partners may effect union in one of the other positions and then roll onto their sides. Masters and Johnson report that after couples try the lateral position they recommend for better ejaculatory control, they subsequently choose that position 75 percent of the time. And more than one half of those responding in the Playboy survey said they sometimes or often use the on-the-side position.

The primary advantage of this approach is the comfort it provides by eliminating weight on either partner. The participants lie side by side, with their legs intertwined in one of several ways. Penetration is, however, shallow and movements are restricted. Coitus tends to be prolonged and leisurely. Ovid commended this approach above others: "Of love's thousand ways, a simple way and with least labor, this is: to lie on the right side, and half supine."

The prone face-to-face approaches provide a rich variety of alternatives, allowing either partner to take the active role. Depending on excitement, fatigue, body build, and agility, each partner has the opportunity to give and obtain pleasure. An important advantage of all prone postures is that the postorgasmic lassitude can be accommodated effortlessly.

Sitting and kneeling positions involve deliberate attempts at variety, for couples cannot simply "roll" into these positions but must set them up.

In seated face-to-face intercourse the woman stands in front of the seated man and lowers herself onto his erect penis. By keeping her feet on the ground she can control her pelvic movements up and down. Or she may achieve deeper penetration by straddling him and perhaps locking her feet behind the chair. His pelvic movements are restricted, but his hands are entirely free.

In the kneeling position (the man on the floor beside the bed) he controls the pelvic thrusts. Being on solid ground gives him excellent leverage, which he cannot achieve lying down unless he pushes against the frame of the bed. Pushing the toes down into the bed is not very effective. The kneeling position is often recommended for a woman's first coitus. The superior control of the man, the angle of penetration, and the exposed position of the woman in combination are said to make the rupture of the hymen least painful for her and easier for him.

There is another, famous approach in this category: The woman straddles the man lying on his back and lowers herself onto the erect penis. She can then lean forward or backward. His legs may be extended or flexed enough to provide support for her back. As her feet rest firmly on the bed, her control of movement is excellent. The ancient Romans were reportedly fond of this position and women boasted of how they "rode" their partners (some writers used to call this position the "attitude of equitation"). Many experts consider it, of all possible approaches, to have the maximum voluptuous potential.

Penetration, when the couple is standing up face to face, is difficult. If, however, the woman can lift one leg high enough, it is possible. She may then wrap her legs around his waist while he supports her buttocks. Ancient manuals call this position "climbing the tree."

Rear Vaginal Entry

In the Kinsey sample, only about 15 percent reported having tried vaginal entry from the rear, but more current surveys (Playboy) indicate the figure to be at least 40 percent. In addition to the variety that they provide, the rear-entry positions make it easy for the man to fondle the woman's breasts and stimulate her genitals manually. This ability is of major importance when clitoral stimulation is desired by the woman to achieve orgasm. In some other positions, though manipulation of the clitoris is possible, it tends to be more difficult and interferes with full contact between the partners.

Rear-entry positions have no serious disadvantages. It is true that they somewhat isolate the partners, who cannot conveniently see each other. On the other hand, close and comfortable body contact is easy to achieve— no other position will allow a woman to curl up as snugly in a man's lap.

It was generally maintained until recently that the rear-entry approach bypassed the clitoris and left it unstimulated by the penis. Direct observations have now shown that the

movements of the clitoral hood during coitus stimulate the clitoris, no matter what the direction of entry (*see* Chapter 3). However, such contact may be inadequate, and more direct stimulation of the clitoris may be desired.

Rear entry is possible while lying down, sitting, or standing up. When a woman is lying on her face, penetration is not deep. Coitus in this manner may be impossible for obese people. If the two lie on their sides (usually on the left), however, intromission is easy even with a relatively weak erection. This method is very restful and is suitable for coitus during pregnancy or ill health, when exertion is better avoided. In the sitting versions the man is astride the woman's buttocks. Or the other position already described may be modified so that she has her back turned to him.

The rear approach allows many other variations in the woman's position. She can go down on all fours or even put her head down ("knee-chest position"). Penetration is easy, and the man's hands are free to roam over her buttocks, inside her thighs, on her genitals, over her breasts, and so on.

Movements

In contrast to emphasis on sexual approaches, the importance of coital movements has been generally neglected. Pelvic thrusts during coitus are a mammalian characteristic. Typically such thrusts start with penetration, build up momentum, and culminate in orgasm. Both male and female can control the depth of penetration, as well as the speed and vigor of coital thrusts, in order to prolong and intensify the pleasure of both partners.

The way in which penetration is performed sets the tone for the act. If the man is taking the initiative, the initial step calls for gentle firmness and confident deliberateness. Even when the vagina is properly lubricated, the introitus may still be tense. The glans must first be placed firmly against the introitus, but because the area is highly sensitive, a little patience may be required before the orifice relaxes. A skilled lover may not penetrate even then but may keep moving his glans in the introitus as well as in the clitoral region until the woman shows signs of wanting deeper penetration. When the woman initiates the penetration phase, she needs to ensure that her partner's erection is firm enough. Otherwise, as the penis bends and shifts away, her partner may feel embarrassed and experience further loss of erection.

Coital movements, like positions, have an almost infinite variety, often shading into one another. Generally the initial thrusts are slow, deliberate, and progressively deeper. Thrusts and counterthrusts may then follow various patterns. The man can thrust and withdraw; then the woman does the same. Or they may thrust and withdraw simultaneously. These movements may be rhythmic or not, fast or slow, with shallow or deep penetration, and so on. It is possible for a movement to be executed by only one person while the other remains relatively passive.

In all these movements, variation and steady work must be artfully combined with an element of surprise. Frantically rushing through pattern after pattern is as bad as monotonous concentration on one, unless both of the partners prefer it that way, in which case their choice should supersede the combined advice of all experts. As coitus progresses, the penis may be thrust completely into the vagina and be rotated inside.

The motions described are merely illustrations. These and other movements must be coordinated with the various approaches. Some movements are quite versatile; others can be used only with particular approaches. Perhaps the most important dictum in this connection is that control of coital movements should be as much a prerogative of the female as of the male. During sexual intercourse the genitals must cease to be the exclusive possessions of the male or female and must become instead shared organs.

Enhancement of Coital Pleasure

Are some orgasms "better" than others? Even in physiological terms, orgasm is not a uniform experience. The subjective perception of orgasm varies among individuals and in the same person at different times. Although we have no objective criteria with which to assess the psychological intensity of orgasm, experience would indicate that some orgasms are perceived as more pleasurable and gratifying than others. It is safe to assume that a host of psycho-physiological factors determine this. The identity of the partner and the circumstances under which coitus is taking place all contribute to the mood of the individual. But in addition, physical factors evidently play a role. These may include the time interval since the preceding orgasm, level of fatigue, length and nature of foreplay, and so on. While it is reasonable to assume that these factors are significant, we do not know as yet with sufficient certainty how and why they are important.

The central thrust of the sex literature aimed at the general reader involves the enhancement of coital pleasure. There are a number of widely shared presuppositions in this regard. One is the conviction that sex is good, but for most people it is not what it can and ought to be.

The majority of writers in this field and an increasing proportion of the population at large also believe that in striving for sexual enhancement an adult couple need not feel inhibited in doing anything so long as it is by mutual consent, pleasurable to both, injurious to neither, and out of sight and earshot of unwilling observers. One encounters a range of opinion whereby these interactions are viewed as legitimate only between loving married couples at one end or any consenting pair at the other with no further questions asked.

Enhancement of coital pleasure as such is a rather global and often ill-defined aim which comes to mean different things to different people. But there are also some aspects that are commonly held to be desirable, including prolongation of coitus.

A number of techniques have been evolved to extend the period of sexual intercourse on the premise that if sex that lasts half an hour is fun then that which lasts an hour should be twice as much fun. This is sound common sense in general, but nonsense as a blanket rule. There are brief but intense sexual encounters that will take your breath away, while protracted episodes may drag on tediously.

Given their capacity for multiple orgasms, some women may want to continue intercourse as long as the male is able to sustain an erection. Prolongation of coitus thus essentially becomes a function of the ability of the male to retain erection and delay ejaculation, but according to *The Hite Report,* most women are usually satisfied with one orgasm per sexual encounter.

Ejaculation may be delayed through mental distraction (thinking of something else or looking the other way) or through deliberate checks on the buildup of muscular tension (slowing coital movements, pausing entirely, consciously relaxing). It is also helpful to minimize friction, particularly on the glans. In short, when excitement seems to be mounting out of control, one follows the opposite of what we have described as effective methods of erotic stimulation. How long to sustain coitus is a matter of individual judgment. Sexual intercourse is not an endurance contest. The only criterion is optimal mutual gratification.

Another goal for some couples is mutual orgasm. There is something to be said for the simultaneous experience of orgasm, as long as it does not become the overriding criterion of a successful sexual encounter. The movements and stimulation that each partner enjoys during orgasm may not provide the best stimulation to the other partner. Also, trying to coordinate the sexual excitement of two people to make sure that their orgasms come at the same time can detract from the enjoyment of the sexual experience. Actually there is also some advantage to entering the climax separately. If the woman experiences orgasm several times, the last may be made to coincide with the male's ejaculation.

The enjoyment of coitus is in part dependent on the circumstances under which it takes place. There is a general human preference for privacy during coitus. Why is not clear. It is true that human beings are vulnerable to attack at such a time, but animals generally do not seem to mind copulating in front of one another. When two partners are bothered by a third animal, they will, of course, try to elude it.

In various cultures coitus occurs in or out of doors, depending on which affords more privacy. For the sake of novelty and additional excitement, some venturesome couples in various societies occasionally make love on the beach or in other natural settings. Sometimes simply using a room other than the bedroom fulfills the same function.

Bedrooms are usually furnished with some thought to romantic atmosphere. Most often, provisions are made for soft lighting; less often, mirrors are positioned strategically so that the partners can observe themselves. There is no end to the refinements that can be added—sound systems, erotic art, and so on.

The preferred times for coitus vary. Practical, as well as psychological, considerations play a role. Most couples make love at night because it is convenient within the routine of our everyday life. But it is unwise always to relegate coitus to the very last waking moments of the day, for a certain amount of stamina and alertness are essential for real pleasure. It is thus advisable occasionally to change the time for coitus to the morning or the middle of the day, simply for variety.

Should intercourse be planned or spontaneous? Some people claim that coitus requires preparation as does any other activity. Apart from practical considerations, they believe that anticipation heightens excitement. Others cannot even bring themselves to take contraceptive measures because they imply forethought.

Some of the most exciting sexual encounters may well occur at the spur of the moment and in the least likely places. Nevertheless, the realities usually require some advance planning if the act is to have more than ordinary significance. As in almost everything else in life, virtuosity in sex requires that natural gifts be supplemented by preparation and practice.

Preparation usually is not a matter involving elaborate arrangements and fine-tuning of exotic machinery. Sometimes it is simply a matter of brushing your teeth or taking a shower. A recurrent whiff of unpleasant odor is all it may take to ruin things for some. These are highly idiosyncratic matters culturally and individually.

Body odors can be stimulating if fresh. The smell of perspiration, semen, and vaginal fluid can be highly erotic, but not after bacteria have worked on them for a while. It is usually not very effective to try to mask these odors by artificial scents. But the use of perfumes, colognes, aftershave lotions, or burning incense can also be quite pleasant and provide an interesting variety of olfactory sensations which in turn impart novelty to the overall coital experience.

Attitudes toward coitus during menstruation vary. The matter is one of personal preference. There are no health considerations to worry about.

Other physical aspects that may cause discomfort are the unexpected sounds and smells that occasionally emanate from the digestive tract. Persistant rumbling or gurgling noises from the abdomen can be further distracting if one is tense. Passing flatus is potentially quite embarrassing. It is also not unusual for air to get sucked into the vagina during genital foreplay and then come out audibly. One can ignore these noises or laugh at them together, but if handled clumsily, they become more than mere nuisances.

Other Forms and Variations

More esoteric forms of lovemaking often rely on special equipment. These may be no more complicated than condoms of different colors and attachments to tickle and titillate the vagina (though they may be of little value since the inner walls of the vagina are relatively insensitive), or they may involve specially constructed chairs, beds fitted with vibrators, or water beds.

Combining sex and bathing is an ancient device. Soaping each other and making love while showering together can be quite pleasurable. Doing it in the bath tub is another variant, but this is harder on the man since erections are difficult to maintain in warm or cold water. This often necessitates that intromission precede submersion.

Erotic massage, especially with the use of lotions and scented ointments, adds many dimensions to coitus, as was indicated earlier in connection with foreplay. Unlike some of the mechanical devices, erotic massage blends far more naturally with the tender, caring aspects of making love while simultaneously stimulating the body.

Combining motion and sex offers other possibilities. One can use rocking chairs or swings. For intercourse, train berths speeding along with rhythmic noises and jerks are much recommended and so are ship cabins. Airplane bathrooms provide more cramped and hectic shelter. Where life comes cheap, cars and motorcycles may intrigue some people as sexual settings.

Some coital variants involve ejaculation at a point other than intravaginally. While hardly anyone practices withdrawal for fun, some do prefer a body orifice or the surface over the vagina as part of foreplay or as the end point of coitus. Any and all body surfaces and orifices that can be used have probably been used in this way at one time or another.

Anal intercourse is the most common choice in this category. According to the Playboy survey, almost half of married men and more than a quarter of married women between the ages of 18 and 34 have tried anal intercourse at least once. More than 40 percent of the women in the Redbook survey reported engaging in anal intercourse. Rates for singles and older married couples are lower. Doubtless, many more persons have thought about it but have never done it.

For most people anal intercourse is an experimental or occasional variant rather than a mainstay of their sexual lives. It is enthusiastically endorsed by some and thought to be vulgar and offensive by others. There is some risk of pain, especially when being initiated into the practice by a clumsy male; and there is a serious risk of infection if vaginal intercourse follows, without washing first. Anal intercourse carries horrendous penalties under sodomy laws in some states.

Aphrodisiacs

The search for substances that may increase sexual drive or potency is as old and, so far, as unsuccessful as is the search for the fountain of youth. "Erotic potions" are described in medical writings from ancient Egypt (c. 2000 B.C.). Among various societies since that time all the following and many more preparations have been recommended: pine nuts, the blood of bats mixed with donkey's milk, root of the valerian plant, dried salamander, cyclamen, menstrual fluid, tulip bulbs, fat of camel's hump, parsnips, salted crocodile, pollen of date palm, the powdered tooth of a corpse, wings of bees, jasmine, turtles' eggs, henna (externally applied), ground crickets, spiders or ants, the genitals of hedgehogs, rhinoceros horn, the blood of executed criminals, artichokes, honey compounded with camel's milk, swallows' hearts, vineyard snails, certain bones of the toad, sulfurous waters, and powdered stag's horn. We have already mentioned the role of androgens in human sexual arousal. When taken in excess of normal physiological doses, androgens have a number of side effects, particularly in women where beard growth, clitoral enlargement, and other indications of virilization will occur.

From time to time amphrodisiac properties are noted as side effects of drugs which have been developed for other medical purposes. One such drug is levodihydroxyphenylalanine (L-dopa). L-dopa has been widely used in human subjects as a treatment for a neurological disorder, Parkinson's disease, and a number of investigators have reported apparent sexual rejuvenation in male patients in their sixties and seventies as a result of taking the drug. Although informal reports of this phenomenon have had wide publicity, the evidence for renewed sexual vigor in males is not overwhelming at the present time.

Alcohol and marijuana are currently the most frequently used chemical substances in conjunction with sexual intercourse. What alcohol and marijuana in moderate amounts do for most people is in part to allay anxiety, counteract inhibitions, and give license to indulge in behaviors that would not be done otherwise. More specifically, the effects of marijuana are quite variable, ranging from no perceptible change to marked intensification of the erotic experience. Given the perceptual changes and alterations in time sense that occur under the effect of marijuana, it becomes difficult to judge whether sexual performance in fact improves or one merely perceives and recalls ordinary experience as extraordinary.

It is also important to be aware of the contrary effects of these substances. Tolerance to alcohol varies, but any one who drinks enough will eventually lose the ability to perform adequately.

Among the more potent illicit drugs heroin is known to decrease sexual desire and activity temporarily, whereas amphetamines and cocaine are reported to increase sexual desire initially, while continued usage significantly reduces the pleasure of intercourse because of the side effects of these drugs (dryness and inflammation of the vagina, feelings of nervousness, exhaustion, and paranoia). Psychedelic drugs, such as LSD, are not aphrodisiacs, but obviously alter the sensory experience of sex in ways that are often idiosyncratic to the user, the partner, and the setting in which the "trip" takes place.

Amyl nitrite ("poppers") is a highly volatile drug that, when inhaled from a small glass vial which is "popped" open for use, causes rapid dilation of the blood vessels. This pharmacologic action of amyl nitrite causes a drop in blood pressure and a feeling of giddiness. Historically, the drug has been used to relieve chest pains associated with heart conditions (angina pectoris), but in recent years it has been used in conjunction with sexual activity. Reports indicate that amyl nitrite is used much more frequently by men than women. It is claimed that inhaling a "popper" just prior to orgasm intensifies and prolongs the experience of orgasm. The most common side effect is a severe but usually brief headache.

Cantharides (Spanish fly) is a powder made from certain dried beetles (*Cantharis vesicatoria*) found in southern Europe. When taken internally it causes acute inflammation and irritation of the urinary tract and dilation of the blood vessels of the penis, producing, in some instances, prolonged erections. Spanish fly is a dangerous drug and can produce severe systemic illness. Legend has it that in sixteenth-century Provence cantharides was used to cure fever. One woman reported that after she gave the drug to her husband he had intercourse with her forty times in forty-eight hours and then died.

Yohimbine is an alkaloid chemical derived from the bark of the African yohimbe tree (*Pausinystalia yohimbe*). Its use was first observed by Europeans among natives in the nineteenth century. Samples were brought back to Germany for analysis. The drug stimulates the nervous system and is dangerous in large doses. It is available (by prescription) in the United States in capsule form in combination with *nux vomica* (also a nervous system stimulant) and testosterone.

A drug commonly thought to have antiaphrodisiac properties is *saltpeter* (potassium nitrate). Rumors occasionally circulate among boys in boarding school or men in prison that saltpeter is added to the food to eliminate the sex drive and sexual activity. Saltpeter tends to increase urine flow, but has no particular effect on sexual interest or potency.

The Aftermath

If the proof of the pudding is in the eating, then the quality of intercourse is best judged by the figurative taste it leaves in the mouth. This is why the postorgasmic phase or aftermath of coitus requires separate consideration here. Coitus does not end with orgasm. The final phase is one in which the physiological effects of excitement recede and the individuals regather their wits. The physical manifestations during this stage of detumescence and its behavioral components have been described earlier (*see* Chapter 3).

Marriage manuals devote considerable attention to this phase. Men are warned not to dismount abruptly and turn their backs or to go to sleep; rather, they are told to disengage themselves gradually with endearments and tender caresses. Such advice is predicated on the assumption that women are slower to become aroused, more difficult to satisfy, and require longer to return to a quiet state; it is thus the man's responsibility to see to it that the activities of foreplay, coitus, and afterplay are prolonged appropriately.

There is a good deal to be said for these admonitions, although the presumably gender-linked differences should not be exaggerated. A man needs and will want as much tenderness as a woman, unless he is made to feel "unmasculine" or "weak" if he should reveal such inclinations.

The aftermath of coitus is a time of reflection. Thoughts meander and earlier experiences, sexual or otherwise, float into consciousness. There must be room for parallel solitude as well as sharing, and the partners should not drift away emotionally.

One may share feelings and thoughts at this time with some discretion. If coitus was not all that it could have been, tenderness restores confidence and makes amends. But this is no time for clinical postmortems or statistical tallies. Even if orgasm has been highly pleasurable, the experience may be partially ruined if the feeling is conveyed that another notch was added to one's belt or that one came out "on top" and is gleefully chuckling over the victory. Likewise, a sinking feeling that one was seduced or manipulated against one's own interests can be quite disturbing.

These remarks presuppose that both partners have reached orgasm. But sometimes one partner, more often the woman, has not reached orgasm. Because the male is less frequently able to have multiple orgasms, it is generally preferable that the woman's climax comes first or simultaneously with his. When occasionally the man's climax precedes the woman's, and he feels unable or disinclined to have a second erection, the woman can, of course, reach climax by noncoital stimulation.

The aftermath of coitus may signify the end of an episode of sexual activity or it may simply be an interlude between two acts of intercourse, where afterplay imperceptibly merges into foreplay again. Even nonconsecutive acts of coitus are to some extent linked together through memory. In a letter to her husband Abelard, after years of enforced separation, Heloise writes:

Truly, those joys of love, which we experienced together, were so dear to my soul that I can never lose delight in them, nor can they vanish from the mirror of my remembrance. Wheresoe'er I turn, they arise before me and old desires awake. (Quoted by Van de Velde, 1965)

SUMMARY

1. Sexual intercourse is almost always preceded by a period of sexually arousing activity (psychological and physiological) called foreplay. This activity contributes to the physical and emotional readiness of the partners. An important aspect of foreplay is the psychological context within which it occurs, with expressions of affection and emotion being especially important.

2. Kissing, erotic touching, and oral-genital contacts are among the techniques most often used during foreplay. Fifteen minutes is reported to be the average amount of time devoted to foreplay, according to a recent survey, but different people and different situations call for different amounts of preparation.

3. Sexual intercourse begins with the coupling of the penis and vagina. There are many ways to approach this union, some of which may enhance the physical aspects of the act. Using different approaches also adds variety and keeps intercourse from becoming monotonous.

4. During sexual intercourse the traditional and most commonly used approach in the Western world is probably the face-to-face position with the woman lying on her back and the man on top. This approach allows for direct interaction (kissing, gazing into each other's eyes) between the partners and is the position most likely to lead to pregnancy.

5. The face-to-face position with the man on top may be most common, but it has several drawbacks—a man's weight can be a considerable burden to a woman, and the woman's movements are restricted. The face-to-face position with the woman above or the partners on their sides avoids these problems, helps the male control ejaculation, facilitates the woman's reaching orgasm, and makes sexual intercourse more prolonged and leisurely.

6. Pelvic thrusts are a characteristic of sexual intercourse, and these movements can vary greatly. They may be slow or rapid, and penile penetration of the vagina may be shallow or deep. The thrusting typically starts slowly and builds momentum culminating in orgasm.

7. Enhancement of pleasure during sexual intercourse is an often-stated goal. Although enhancement means different things to different people, prolongation of sexual intercourse is thought to be desirable by many. In most instances prolongation of intercourse depends on the male's ability to delay ejaculation. Mutual orgasm is another goal for some couples, but it is not always easy to achieve and may detract from the physical pleasure of one or both partners.

8. The circumstances under which coitus takes place, the time and the place, as well as other physical factors, can affect a person's perceptions of sexual intercourse as more or less enjoyable.

9. Aphrodisiacs are substances that are supposed to increase sexual potency, but so far none has proved to have the desired effect. Alcohol and marijuana tend to lessen inhibitions and may alter perceptions of an erotic experience, but it is difficult to determine whether or not they improve sexual performance. When used to excess these drugs, especially alcohol, can result in loss of potency. Other drugs are also available that are supposed to improve or intensify erotic experiences, but the effectiveness of these drugs has not been proved, and some of them have dangerous side effects.

10. Sexual intercourse does not end with orgasm. It continues into a postorgasmic phase during which the physiological effects of excitement recede and there is a return to an unexcited state. Both men and women usually desire tenderness at this time, and either or both may want some degree of solitude, or they may wish to share their feelings.

SUGGESTED READING

There are countless books that purport to instruct people in the art of love. Such books used to be called "marriage manuals" and now are referred to as "sex manuals." Among the ancient classics of this literature are *The Perfumed Garden* by Shaykh Nefzauri (New York: G. P. Putnam's Sons, 1964), and the *Kama Sutra* by Vatsyayana (New York: G. P. Putnam's Sons, 1963). Of current selections, Alex Comfort's *The Joy of Sex* and *More Joy of Sex* (New York: Crown, 1972 and 1975) are gracefully written and illustrated.

Variations and Deviations in Sexual Behavior

chapter 10

Did You Know That . . .

according to Kinsey's findings, by age 45, about 37 percent of men and 13 percent of women have had at least one homosexual encounter leading to orgasm?

there is no homosexual act that cannot be performed by a heterosexual couple?

incest is one sexual activity that has been condemned in nearly all societies?

true transsexuals sincerely believe, usually from a young age, that they are members of the opposite sex?

adults who molest children are, in most cases, relatives, friends, neighbors, or acquaintances of the child to whom they make sexual advances?

INTRODUCTION

Almost any object or activity can have sexual significance. Even though many people tend to think of heterosexual intercourse and the various autoerotic activities discussed in Chapter 8 as the usual methods of sexual expression, they are by no means the only methods. Many people engage in other varieties of sexual behavior at one time or another, and many do so exclusively. In this chapter we will discuss some of the variations on what are generally considered to be the usual forms of sexual expression.

Departures from standard coital practice have been called **sexual deviations,** but because this term implies some form of pathology, many people prefer the term **sexual variations.** This conflict over terminology reflects current uncertainties in the evaluation of such behavior. There is no serious disagreement when the activity is flagrantly bizarre or obviously harmful, such as necrophilia—"love of the dead"—or sex murder. The conflict centers instead on behavior such as homosexual contacts between consenting adults in private. Well-meaning people (as well as some bigots) disagree on questions of whether such behavior is "normal," morally right or wrong, or constitutes an illness in need of treatment.

Because there is a tendency to discuss sexual variations in the manner of a tour through a zoo, pointing out individuals with one characteristic or another, certain considerations must be emphasized. First, although it is convenient to call individuals "pedophiles," "voyeurs," and so on, it is much more useful to speak of pedophilic or voyeuristic behavior and of people who exhibit various degrees of such behavior. Human sex life does not consist of pure types of behaviors but of combinations of various activities at various times.

Second, many types of aberrant behavior exist in all shades and gradations and are exceedingly common (although we may not be conscious of them). Again, we are not mainly interested in the bizarre. Although few of us are necrophiliacs or child molesters, there is a range of voyeuristic-exhibitionistic and sadomasochistic activity, for instance, that is part of common heterosexual experience, and that we do not—and have no reason to—label as deviant or pathological.

Judgments of sexual behavior are just as appropriate as are judgments of other forms of human activity because not all sexual behavior is equally adaptive, healthy, socially desirable, moral, and so on. Such judgments, however, ought to be made with great care. Experience shows how arbitrary they can be and how easy it is to inflict unnecessary hardship on people whose main offenses may consist in being different.

Our approach in this chapter will be predominantly descriptive, and in view of the many types of behavior possible, it will have to be cursory.

CLASSIFICATION OF SEXUAL VARIATIONS AND DEVIATIONS

The first attempt at a comprehensive review of sexual deviations was undertaken by the Viennese psychiatrist Richard von Krafft-Ebing, who published his classic *Psychopathia Sexualis* in 1886. Freud's formulations, to be discussed here, appeared in 1905 in his *Three Essays on the Theory of Sexuality*.

Freud based his classification of sexual deviations on the assumption that among adults any form of sexual behavior that *takes precedence* over heterosexual intercourse represents a defect in psychosexual development. Freud labeled the person from whom sexual attraction emanates the "sexual object" and what one wishes to do with the object the "sexual aim." In a healthy, or mature, sexual relationship an adult of the opposite sex would thus be the sexual object and the wish for coitus the sexual aim. The use of the term "object" in this context is not intended to imply that people are or should be used as inanimate objects. Applied to persons, "objects" means individuals who fulfill essential functions in the gratification of others.

It then follows that deviations from this pattern can take one of two forms: deviations in the *choice of sexual object* and deviations in the *choice of sexual aim*. In the first instance the alternative object could be an adult of the same sex (as in homosexuality), a child (as in pedophilia), a close relative (as in incest), an animal (as in zoophilia), an inanimate object (as in fetishism), or even a dead body (as in necrophilia). In the second instance, instead of seeking (and when permissible engaging in) coitus, the individual would prefer to watch others having coitus (voyeurism), to expose his or her own genitals (exhibitionism), to inflict pain (sadism) or to suffer pain (masochism). When the activity involves choice both of object and of sexual aim, it is usually designated by the choice of object.

VARIATIONS AND DEVIATIONS IN OBJECT CHOICE

Homosexual Behavior

Of all the possible variations and deviations, homosexual behavior is the most common, as well as the most controversial. Much of the controversy, however, is based on various myths about persons who engage in homosexual behavior. There are, for instance, no data to support the idea that a homosexual teacher is any more likely than a heterosexual teacher to molest a child.

The term **homosexual** is derived from the Greek *hom*, "the same," rather than from the Latin root *homo*, "man." The term "homosexual" can be applied correctly to either sex, but in common usage it is usually applied to males, while **lesbianism** is applied to sexual activity between females.

One source we will cite is the recently pub-

lished study from the Institute for Sex Research (The "Kinsey Institute"). The subjects in this study included 1,057 U.S. male homosexuals and, for cross-cultural comparisons, 1,077 Dutch and 303 Danish homosexuals. Although large in numbers, the U.S. sample was by no means representative of all elements of the society. About half were from two states, New York and California. Ninety-six percent were white; 82 percent had some college education; and most lived in large cities. Comparisons within the United States were made utilizing a sample of 3,101 men drawn from the general adult male population.

There are no comparable studies of lesbians yet available, and our statements regarding lesbianism are therefore more tentative. These observations are made now so as to avoid the tediousness of qualifying remarks in conjunction with every declarative statement in the ensuing discussion.

Attitudes toward Homosexuality

Neither the American Psychiatric Association nor the American Psychological Association classifies homosexuality as a psychiatric disorder or as an illness. However, 71 percent of the respondents in a public-opinion survey viewed homosexuality as an illness. In the same study the remaining 29 percent were almost evenly divided in viewing homosexuality either as a crime, a sin, or a preference. Another survey indicates that two thirds of the adult U.S. population considers homosexuality to be "obscene and vulgar," but the majority also consider it a "curable illness."

About three fourths of adolescents consider homosexual acts abnormal or unnatural, yet they hold a more tolerant view than their parents, with 40 percent agreeing that: "If two boys/girls want to have sex together, it's all right so long as they both want to do it."

Not surprisingly, the vast majority of homosexuals do not subscribe to the "illness" viewpoint, but about 11 percent do. The majority of homosexuals believe that being a homosexual is something that is "completely beyond one's control." However, there is wide disagreement among homosexuals (and others) on the issue of whether or not one is "born" homosexual or heterosexual. These issues are important because they relate to questions of moral and legal responsibility for one's behavior, as well as to issues of illness and treatment.

As a Way of Life

Homosexuals, like heterosexuals, have not one but many life styles. Some are conventionally married men and women who occasionally indulge in furtive homosexual affairs; others live openly as homosexual couples.

Homosexuals are widely distributed throughout the country and are found in all socioeconomic strata. After all, among males only, we are dealing with at least 2 million people (2 percent of the male population) who indulge in exclusively homosexual behavior, and an even larger group for whom homosexual acts constitute one of several sexual outlets.

In our brief review we shall touch only on the more salient aspects of life in the homosexual or "gay" community. This community represents a subculture in our society, one in which the life style encompasses many activities beyond sexual ones. Because of certain important differences, we shall discuss the life styles of male and female homosexuals separately.

Among Males

The behavioral characteristics of male homosexuals are highly influenced by their vulnerability to harassment, censure, and persecution by society. Since it is only in certain areas of large cities that homosexuals can be observed behaving in relative freedom, we cannot speak with confidence of how homosexuals would behave if they were left alone. At present, many homosexuals are psychologically isolated from society, dependent on other homosexuals for sexual expression, and ruled by a concealed but complex system of social relations and reciprocal obligations, even though this pattern may be changing rapidly in some parts of the country.

The first criterion for differentiating among homosexual life styles is whether a man is a covert or an overt homosexual. Covert homosexuals are to be found within the full range of occupations in our society. They "pass" for heterosexuals in most of their business and social relationships. They may even be married, be parents, and in most other respects remain indistinguishable from the rest of the population. They may lead "double lives," or restrict their homosexual behavior to periods when they are away from home, as men do who participate in extramarital heterosexual affairs.

Overt homosexuals constitute a smaller group than covert homosexuals. They have given up all pretense and openly rely on the homosexual community for gratification of their sexual needs. These men work in professions in which they are either tolerated or in which there are no penalties (and perhaps even some advantages) for being homosexual. They tend to be defiant of the heterosexual world and willing to face it only on their own terms.

Overt and covert homosexuals tend to shun each other. The former consider the latter hypocrites; and the latter shun the former to protect themselves. If a person does not blatantly display his homosexual way of life, can he be identified through physique, dress, mannerisms, and so on? The answer is generally "no." Probably the most common misunderstanding of male homosexuals is reflected in stereotypes that portray them as "effeminate," "swishy," "faggots," or "fairies." There are individuals who fit these stereotypes, to be sure, and within the gay community they are known as "queens." But these men represent only a very small proportion of the homosexual population and are by no means appreciated by the rest. Some gay bars will actually refuse admission to "queens in drag"; that is, men dressed in flagrantly effeminate fashion.

At the other extreme, there are homosexuals who make a point of looking and acting extremely "masculine." Some may be bodybuilding enthusiasts, with formidably muscular torsos. Others may be military career officers with all the trappings of power and authority.

Most ordinary homosexuals look and act as ordinary people do. Homosexuals can, however, effectively identify one another. People who must communicate covertly develop systems of cues involving dress, mannerisms, and so on. Male homosexuals tend to be more innovative in and conscious of dress, and the heterosexual population often unwittingly adopts their styles. The homosexual significance of the style then becomes completely lost. Similarly, just as most homosexuals are neither effeminate nor unusually masculine, not all men who have limp wrists or speak in high-pitched, lisping voices or are physical-culture enthusiasts are homosexual. Guessing games about sexual behavior based on such superficial traits are quite futile and misleading. Masculinity and femininity are culturally defined attributes (and not clear ones at that) and they have no demonstrable correlation with sexual orientation.

Most male homosexuals tend to have a series of brief relationships, though some ties may be very intense. Most homosexuals live alone, and approximately two thirds have never had an exclusive relationship for more than a year. Whatever the explanation, these facts have an important bearing on the life style of the homosexual—as can be seen in a study released in 1978. The study was conducted by the Institute for Sex Research in 1970 and is based on interviews with nearly 1,000 male and female homosexuals who were living in the San Francisco Bay area. The researchers found that homosexual men, in general, differed little from heterosexuals in feelings of happiness and good physical health, but the gays did express more feelings of loneliness, depression, and lack of self-acceptance. A significantly larger percentage of homosexual men than heterosexual men had attempted or had contemplated suicide.

The researchers (psychologist Alan Bell and sociologist Martin Weinberg) classified homosexuals in five categories, or "homosexualities." They found that the happiest and

best-adjusted gays are those living in a "close coupled" relationship, the equivalent of a happy heterosexual marriage. Those homosexuals classified as "functional" (self-assured, unattached "swinging singles") and as "open coupled" (living together but tending to seek fulfillment outside the home) were also found to be relatively happy and well adjusted. A minority of homosexuals were found to have emotional and psychological problems. They were classified as "dysfunctionals" and "asexuals." Dysfunctionals—13 percent of gay males and 5 percent of gay females—were those who were sexually active but who felt guilty and confused about their homosexuality and had sexual problems. The asexuals were those who regretted their homosexuality, who were less sexually active and less exclusively homosexual. (About 30 percent of the homosexuals in the study did not fit into any of the five categories.)

Psychological problems, such as self-acceptance, may not be the only problems faced by the male homosexual. As his affairs tend to be short, he frequently needs to find new partners. To find them, many homosexuals go "cruising" in search of "tricks" or "pickups." Of course, heterosexuals "cruise" "singles bars" in a similar fashion, with concerns over rejection but less concern over social disapproval. Every major city has its known homosexual hangouts. Some are public places like parks, bus depots, and men's rooms. Others are special "gay bars," or "clubs," or "baths."

Important as life around certain bars is for some homosexuals, such behavior is not unique to them. Female prostitutes and heterosexuals of both sexes looking for "one-night stands" operate in much the same way. The actual approaches used are also quite similar: The prospective partner is spotted, subtle and less subtle cues are exchanged, and the couple may have a drink or two; they become progressively intimate and leave the bar together or arrange to meet somewhere.

For those ignorant of homosexual ways, it is difficult to understand such relationships. It is easier if we forget for a moment that an encounter of this kind is between members of the same sex and simply try to reconstruct what would transpire in a comparable situation between a man and a woman. Homosexuals, like heterosexuals, may be shy and inhibited or forward and aggressive. Witty homosexuals tell witty jokes, and uncouth homosexuals tell vulgar jokes; some are subtle in their approaches, others clumsy; and so on.

Even more mystifying to many people is what homosexuals actually do when they are together. The answer is that they do what is physically possible, including everything that heterosexuals do except vaginal intercourse. Kissing and petting are the usual preliminaries, followed by mutual genital stimulation. The three primary activities leading to orgasm are oral-genital contact (singly or mutually), mutual masturbation, and, less frequently, anal intercourse. (With practice and the use of lubricants the anus can readily admit an erect penis).

There is no "homosexual act" that cannot be performed by a heterosexual couple. By the same token, homosexuals claim that anal intercourse is just as "real" and satisfying as is vaginal coitus. Whatever its rewards, anal intercourse also carries some of the same penalties as does vaginal intercourse. Veneral disease, for instance, is readily transmitted in this way, and homosexuals who have numerous sexual partners have some of the highest rates of such disease in the country.

To counteract what they consider distorted images of homosexuals, various private groups have been organized. The best-known, until recently, was the Mattachine Society (named after medieval court jesters, who were fearlessly outspoken), a national organization with chapters in many major cities and a predominantly but not exclusively homosexual membership. The purpose of such groups is to promote fair and equal treatment for homosexuals and to protest the oppression and abuse to which they have been subjected, as have other minorities. The Mattachine Society holds meetings, arranges lectures, and issues several publications (for example, *Homosexual Citizen* and *Mattachine Newsletter*).

More recently important changes are taking place in the homosexual world as part of the "gay liberation movement." Organizations like the Gay Liberation Front and the Gay Activist Alliance are much more open and forcible in their efforts to acquaint the public with their cause. Despite the common name, these organizations vary widely, from moderately conservative to very radical in orientation.

Despite these differences there is generally far greater readiness among homosexuals in these groups to come out into the open. On a number of college campuses, for example, there are semiformal homosexual organizations that make no effort to conceal their identities. At least among younger homosexuals there is now a tendency to shun gay bars and other traditional hangouts in favor of dances and a variety of social and political functions. There are also gay communes, "consciousness-raising groups," and various alliances with other "liberation movements" in pursuit of common goals.

These often dramatic changes in attitudes both inside and outside the homosexual community are not uniform throughout the country. In some cities police officers participate in encounter sessions with homosexuals in an effort to further mutual understanding. In others, homosexuals continue to live in constant fear of the police. In view of these disparities it is impossible to describe general patterns of homosexual life. Much of what is said in this chapter, for example, may be applicable to some parts of the country but out of date in others, or true of some subgroups but not at all of others.

Among Females

The majority of lesbians, like their male counterparts, are indistinguishable from the general population in physique, dress, and mannerisms. Despite the points of contrast to be discussed, much of what we have said about male homosexuals also applies to females. Some of the differences between the life styles of female and male homosexuals simply reflect traditional expectations for men and women in general—as in vocational opportunities, for example. Other distinctions are less specific: Lesbians tend to form more lasting ties, operate in less differentiated subcultures, and are generally far less often detected and harassed.

Lesbians generally have far fewer sexual partners than do male homosexuals, and there is a much greater tendency among lesbians, as compared to male homosexuals, to pair off and to live as couples in relatively stable relationships. Such relationships are sometimes "marriages," and may be sealed by exchanges of wedding rings. Roles are somewhat more clearly defined in lesbian relationships, and one partner may take the role as "head of the family" with protective responsibilities. This form of relationship is most clearly visible between the "butch" and "femme" (or "fem"). The extreme butch (or "dike," sometimes spelled dyke) is in a sense the counterpart of the male queen. She wears masculine pants and shirts, cuts her hair very short, and may even be employed in some predominantly male occupation. Although she is quite aggressive and masculine in appearance and manner, such a woman can still pass in the straight world as simply a "masculine woman." It has been less common in our society to suspect or to identify lesbianism, whereas there is widespread suspicion of effeminate males. The "femme" or feminine member of the couple is typically feminine in dress, mannerisms, and general appearance. Not surprisingly, younger lesbians are more likely to reject these stereotypes, which are less common today than they once were.

When it comes to sexual activities, the distinctions between butch and femme tend to blur, though some lesbian couples do preserve particular roles in lovemaking.

A common type of lesbian relationship involves two women who live together in a close and mutually dependent relationship, but not as butch and femme. Although the initial meeting may have occurred in a lesbian bar or club, more often the two have met at work, school, or through mutual friends. Two women may live together for many years and never arouse the suspicions of their neighbors or families, much less of casual acquaintances,

which is not as true for men in a similar situation. Consequently the lesbian is subject to relatively little harassment or social pressure, except for the occasional well-meaning friend or relative who insists on arranging heterosexual dates for her. The lesbian couple tends to lead a self-contained social life, going to the movies, the beach, the theater, or shopping together and occasionally entertaining gay (male or female) or straight couples. Women friends may also live together and participate in all these activities without being lesbians.

Lesbian sexual activities consist primarily of kissing, caressing, fondling and oral stimulation of the breasts, mutual masturbation, and oral-genital contacts. **Tribadism** is an exclusively lesbian but not particularly common practice, in which the genitals are mutually stimulated as one woman lies on top of the other and simulates coitus.

Lesbians with heterosexual experience claim that orgasms achieved through homosexual activities are incomparably more satisfying. The Kinsey study did in fact reveal a higher incidence of orgasm among lesbians than among heterosexual women. One explanation is that lesbians have a natural advantage over male partners, who often have foggy notions of female anatomy and sexual functioning.

The literature on lesbianism, though less extensive than that dealing with male homosexuality, is nevertheless still quite large. Lesbian organizations are more recent in origin and remain less prominent than their male counterparts. The best known has been The Daughters of Bilitis (founded in 1956), which draws its name from a book of prose poems by Pierre Louys, which appeared in 1894 and purported to be a translation from the Greek of Sappho's love poems to a courtesan named Bilitis. The general aims and functions of this society are comparable to those of male homosexual organizations. These women, however, claim double social disadvantages, being both female and homosexual. *The Ladder: A Lesbian Review* is the society's official publication. Changes similar to those affecting male homosexuals are also currently affecting lesbian groups. Liberation movements among women, however, tend to be primarily concerned with the protection of women's rights in general rather than of lesbians' rights in particular.

The Incidence of Homosexual Behavior

There had been surveys of male homosexuality before the Kinsey study, but it was that study which brought to light how widespread the use of this sexual outlet was. In fact, the findings about homosexuality and premarital sex caused the most furor when Kinsey's work was published. His data are still rejected by some people, even though his challengers have no quantitative information of their own. One criticism is that because of Kinsey's tolerant view of homosexuality a disproportionate number volunteered as subjects for his study, thus swelling the figures. At any rate, it should be recalled that even under the best of circumstances Kinsey's findings cannot be taken as representative of the country as a whole, nor are they current. But they are still the most extensive data available and therefore will be outlined here.

The Kinsey volumes on the male and the female contain exhaustive tables and graphs on various facets of homosexual contacts. We can present only two of these. Excluding homosexual activity before puberty (which about 60 percent of males had experienced), Kinsey found that by age 45 about 37 percent of males had had at least one homosexual encounter leading to orgasm. For females this figure was 13 percent. Such activity was much more common among single people of both sexes (at age 45 about 50 percent of single males and 26 percent of females) than among married people (by age 45 about 10 percent of married males and 3 percent of females).

The extent to which these people participated in homosexual activities varied greatly. Kinsey never said nor implied that every second male was a practicing homosexual. Actually he avoided calling anyone "homosexual," preferring to describe variable frequencies of homosexual contact, with or without other sexual outlets.

The only reasonable way that Kinsey thought this data could be conceptualized was by placing everyone on a heterosexual-homosexual behavior rating scale (*see* Figure 10.1). People in categories 0 and 6 were *exclusively* heterosexual (0) or homosexual (6) in both their physical contacts and erotic interests. Those in categories 1 and 5 had *predominant* heterosexual (1) or homosexual (5) orientations, with only incidental interest in the other sex. Categories 2 and 4 included those in whom a *clear preference* for one sex coexisted with a lesser but still active interest in the other. Finally, people with *approximately equal* heterosexual and homosexual interests constituted category 3. In computing these ratios Kinsey departed from his own definition of sexual outlets (activities leading to orgasm) and considered as relevant all erotic responses, physical as well as psychic, whether they had culminated in orgasm or not.

This rating scale indicates not the amount of sexual activity but only the ratio between two sexual orientations. A person with a hundred heterosexual and ten homosexual experiences would be placed closer to the heterosexual end of the scale than would someone with ten heterosexual and five homosexual contacts during a comparable period of time. The man with ten homosexual contacts would thus be "less homosexual" than would the man with only five homosexual contacts.

Individuals were found to be unevenly distributed within these seven categories. The whole notion of such categories is itself artificial: The categories in fact overlap very much, so that we are actually dealing with a continuum rather than with discrete entities. The figures in Table 10.1 must be understood in that sense. The ranges of percentages resulted from different ratios in various subgroups. With the exception of the exclusive categories (0 and 6), the percentages in Table 10.1 are not for discrete groups but for ranges of behavior. Categories 1–6 thus include those who have exhibited some homosexual behavior, as well as more extensive contacts all the way to the exclusively homosexual.

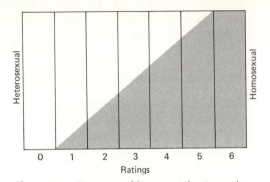

Figure 10.1 Heterosexual-homosexual rating scale.

From A. C. Kinsey *et al., Sexual Behavior in the Human Female* (Philadelphia: Saunders, 1953), p. 470. Courtesy of the Institute for Sex Research.

These figures are rather startling both because of the absolute numbers involved and because of the implications for large segments of the population that would like to think of themselves as exclusively heterosexual (a claim that only 50 percent of males in the Kinsey sample could make). These considerations moved Kinsey to write:

Males do not represent two discrete populations, heterosexual and homosexual. The world is not to be divided into sheep and goats. Not all things are black nor all things white. It is a fundamental of taxonomy that nature rarely deals with discrete categories. Only the human mind invents categories and tries to force facts into separated pigeon-holes. The living world is a continuum in each and every one of its aspects. The sooner we learn this concerning human sexual behavior the sooner we shall reach a sound understanding of the realities of sex. (Kinsey, 1948)

The findings from other studies in the United States and other countries (like Sweden and Germany) come close to the Kinsey figures for exclusive homosexuals: 2–4 percent of the adult male population.

Exclusively homosexual men and women regard themselves, and are regarded by others, as true homosexuals. For the rest of the population the question of who is and who is not homosexual is impossible to answer (and,

according to Kinsey, unnecessary to pose). The law condemns a man for a single homosexual offense. Some men with high rates of homosexual activity disclaim the label for one reason or another. A working compromise among some clinicians and social scientists is to define homosexuals as people whose primary source of sexual gratification is through this outlet, and to discount those with sporadic and transient homosexual involvements.

Adolescent Homosexuality

About 9 percent of young people in the United States have one or more homosexual experiences between the ages of 13 and 19. As with adults, the incidence is higher among males (11 percent) than females (6 percent). The likelihood of homosexual activities in adolescence is significantly greater among those who have had homosexual experiences prior to adolescence.

Table 10.1 **HETEROSEXUAL-HOMOSEXUAL RATINGS (AGES 20–35)***

Category	In Females (percent)	In Males (percent)
0 Entirely heterosexual experience		
Single	61–72	53–78
Married	89–90	90–92
Previously married	75–80	
1–6 At least some homosexual experience	11–20	18–42
2–6 More than incidental homosexual experience	6–14	13–38
3–6 as much or more homosexual experience than heterosexual experience	4–11	9–32
4–6 Mostly homosexual experience	3–8	7–26
5–6 Almost exclusively homosexual experience	2–6	5–22
6 Exclusively homosexual experience	1–3	3–16

*From data in Kinsey *et al.* (1953), p. 488.

Contrary to popular myths that portray adult homosexuals as preying on the young and innocent, *most adolescents have their first homosexual experience with another adolescent.* Thirty-seven percent of boys and 14 percent of girls report someone making homosexual advances to them on at least one occasion, but most adolescents apparently turn away such approaches without trauma or serious emotional upset. Among the minority who have homosexual experiences during adolescence, the frequency of such activity appears to be low, and in many instances is motivated by curiosity or factors other than a love relationship.

Bisexuals

The two terms **bisexual** and **transsexual** are often mistakenly applied to homosexuals. "Bisexual" applies to people who engage in both homosexual and heterosexual activities. They would be classified in the middle range of Kinsey's homosexual-heterosexual scale. These people claim, however, that they are not "basically" one way or the other and do not simply alternate sexual objects occasionally. Rather, they claim a permanent need for relations with both sexes, to enjoy the best of two worlds, as it were. Other people may view them as standard homosexuals who are simply rationalizing their activities. Because of their dual orientations they are sometimes called "AC-DC" (for "alternating" and "direct" current), and they may exhibit conflicts over their ambivalent sexuality.

Transsexuals

Transsexuals are different from homosexuals in important ways, even though they are often lumped together on the basis of behavioral similarities. The transsexual is a person (usually a male) who wishes to be, or sincerely believes that he is, a member of the opposite sex. Some males say that they have always felt themselves to be "women in male bodies" and trace such feelings to their childhoods. Although the transsexual often engages in homosexual (as well as heterosexual) relations, these activities are not homosexual in their view. After all, if a man feels himself to be a woman, he will view sex with a man from a different perspective.

In contrast to the hostility toward women that some male homosexuals express, the transsexual male claims to like women and would prefer to be a full-fledged woman himself. He does everything possible to attain this end, with occasionally astounding results. The ultimate aim for many of these biological males is a "sex change" operation, in which the penis and the testes are removed and an artificial "vagina" is created through reconstruction of pelvic tissues. The individual thus altered can have "vaginal" coitus. Contrary to occasional newspaper reports, however, pregnancy is absolutely impossible. A full transplant of ovaries and uterus has never been attempted, though it is not beyond the realm of possibility.

Most sex-change operations involve changing males to females, and some make international news. James Morris, for instance, a well-known British journalist and father of four, underwent a sex-change operation in 1972 and wrote the book *Conundrum* (under the name of Jan Morris) about the experience. Sex-change operations are now performed in a few medical centers in this country. Applicants are carefully screened to eliminate those with serious mental derangements and those who might have second thoughts after the surgery. If the applicant has not already had hormone treatments, he must undergo them first. The resulting changes are marked but reversible, so that the patient's reactions can be further evaluated before the irrevocable step of surgery is taken. Even then, some transsexuals, much to their own chagrin, may be disillusioned with the results of surgery, and severe psychological repercussions may occur.

The very concept of a sex-change operation raises numerous moral and medicolegal problems. For instance, the surgeon may be prosecuted under "bodily mayhem" laws, though such charges are unlikely to be pressed. Or a judge may refuse to grant changes in legal status (because the person remains genetically male), thus condemning newly made "women" to live under men's names.

Homosexual behavior has existed at all times in all parts of the world. But what such behavior has meant in any given culture is more difficult to assess. The Old Testament is explicit in its condemnations. The prevalence of homosexuality (particularly among males) in classical antiquity has been much belabored, often as justification for later behavior. The tutorial relationships between older and younger Greek men did have a sexual component. Some Greek cities had regiments of lovers fighting side by side. Homosexual behavior was also, however, subject to censure and penalties in classical Greece, depending on the ranks and relationships of the men involved. Greek democracy was not free from the all-too-universal proclivity for letting some people, but not others, indulge in certain kinds of behavior.

The same generalization applies to homosexual behavior among primitive peoples: It is apparently universal but varies widely in prevalence, acceptance, and significance. Of seventy-six societies surveyed by Ford and Beach about a third disapproved of homosexual behavior; and such activity was reported as absent, rare, or covert. Penalties ranged from derision to death. The balance (64 percent) approved some forms of homosexuality.

There is relatively scant reference in either the historical or anthropological records to female homosexuality. One exception is the work of Sappho, who lived on the Greek island of Lesbos (from which comes the term "lesbianism") in the sixth century B.C. Sappho's poems extolled the virtues of the love of women for each other. Sappho was also a proponent of women's rights and had a school for young women in which poetry, dancing, music, and art were taught.

Most primitive societies do not have terms in their languages for such women. A few, however, accept female homosexual activities as normal, particularly mutual masturbation and the use of artificial penises. Among the Dahomean tribe of Africa frigidity in a married woman was attributed to lesbian activities, and a similar belief was held in Haiti.

Cross-cultural data, fragmentary as they may be, generally contradict simple explanations of homosexual behavior as arising only when heterosexual outlets are unavailable or blocked by inhibitions and restrictions. The historical emergence and functional explanations of homosexual behavior remain generally obscure.

Changing Sexual Preference

For those who view homosexuality as a pathological condition, improvement or "cure" means changing the individual's orientation to a heterosexual one. Relatively few such "cures" have been reported for several reasons.

First, most homosexuals do not consider themselves abnormal or sick and thus do not seek treatment. When they come to psychiatrists for problems of anxiety or depression what they want is relief of their symptoms. Whether or not homosexuals are more prone to such symptoms because of something inherent in homosexuality, or because of the pressures that they experience as members of an "outlawed" minority, is open to question. Certainly some homosexuals develop problems of anxiety, depression, and so on, for the same reasons that heterosexuals do, but many others are happy with their sexual orientation.

A small percentage of homosexuals is apprehended and forced to undergo treatment by court order, either in state institutions or as a condition of probation. As we might suspect, such individuals are little motivated to change and will usually "play along" in therapy in order to satisfy the law.

There are, finally, some individuals who seek psychiatric treatment of their own volition, who are genuinely eager to change their sexual orientations. The results of treatment in such situations is determined by several variables; for example, how long the patients have been homosexual and whether or not they have had heterosexual experiences. Many psychiatrists believe that changing the sexual orientation of homosexuals is either unnecessary or unrealistic, and consequently gear their treatment to helping individuals become "better adjusted" homosexuals so that

235

Variations
and
Deviations
in Sexual
Behavior

they will no longer be dissatisfied with their orientations.

Pedophilia

The **pedophile** (from the Greek, "lover of children") is someone who uses children for sexual gratification. The definition of a pedophile depends on the definition of a child. The laws of many states define "child molesting" and related offenses like "statutory rape" to include victims up to the ages of 16, 18, or even 21. Sexual involvement with even a postpubescent 15-year-old girl, however, is usually a different sort of activity from what we describe here as pedophilia. In the former the "victim" may actually have been the seducer, and the "offender" may have misjudged the age of his sexual partner because of her physical appearance or because she lied about her age. Gebhard *et al.* (1965) define a child as younger than 12 years old, a minor as between 13 and 15 years old, and an adult as more than 16 years old. These age limits correspond well with stages in biological maturation. All statistical references in the rest of this chapter are from this work, unless otherwise specified. Pedophilia is a serious legal offense; almost all pedophiles who are arrested are male. They may be interested in either prepubescent males or prepubescent females, but usually not in both.

The heterosexual pedophile is usually mistakenly pictured as a stranger who lurks about the school playground, abducts an unsuspecting little girl, takes her by force to some secret place, and ravishes her. The facts rarely fit this stereotype. Studies have shown that in about 85 percent of such incidents the pedophile is either a relative, a family friend, a neighbor, or an acquaintance. He makes advances to the child either in her home, where he is visiting or living (as an uncle, stepfather, grandfather, or someone renting a room) or in his own home, where she is used to visiting or is enticed by promises of candy or other treats. (Seventy-nine percent of such contacts occur in homes, 13 percent in public places, and 8 percent in cars.) Physical damage to the child occurs in only 2 percent of the instances, though threats of force or some degree of physical restraint is present in about one third of instances in which arrests and convictions follow. Psychological harm depends in large extent on how the parents handle the situation. At least one session with a counselor or therapist is advisable.

The entire pedophiliac episode is often quite brief, and, though there may be a series of such episodes before the child reports them to her parents, it is unusual for a prolonged or intimate relationship to develop. (In this sense the story of Vladimir Nabokov's *Lolita* is atypical.)

Actual sexual contact most often consists of the man's taking the child on his lap and fondling her external genitals. *Intercourse is rarely attempted* because, among other factors, these men are often impotent. (Coitus is attempted in about 6 percent of instances, but intromission is achieved in only about 2 percent.)

Individuals involved with little girls (heterosexual offenders against children) tend to be older than any other group of sex offenders, with the exception of those involved in incest. The average age at conviction is 35, and 25 percent of these offenders are over 45. About 5 percent are actually senile individuals whose judgment is impaired through mental deterioration; 15–20 percent of offenders are mentally retarded, and their behavior can be considered as attempts to socialize with girls at similar mental levels. Treatment of such men is obviously difficult, for it is rather unlikely that a man with a child's mentality can establish a satisfactory relationship with an adult woman. Through the use of aversive conditioning techniques, however, he can sometimes be trained to stay away from children.

The majority of heterosexual offenders with children are, however, neither senile nor mentally defective; 70–80 percent have been married at some time in their lives. They tend to be conservative and moralistic, and some require alcohol before they can commit their offenses. They usually do not have criminal records, with the exception of possible previous convictions for molesting children.

The homosexual pedophile obtains sexual gratification through the use of young boys as sexual objects. Although this activity is viewed by some people as a variation of adult homosexuality, it is uncommon and scorned by the vast majority of homosexuals. Most homosexuals confine their sexual activities to other adults.

Homosexual pedophiles also do not usually molest strangers, and the boys with whom they become involved are most often relatives or the sons of acquaintances. In addition, contacts are sometimes made through youth organizations. The popular notion that better police surveillance will prevent such crimes is thus difficult to justify.

Sexual activities with a young boy may include fondling and masturbation of the boy, mutual masturbation, fellatio, and **pederasty** (anal intercourse with a child).

Homosexual offenders against children generally show deficiencies in socialization and interpersonal relationships. They often say that they prefer the company of boys because they feel uneasy around adults. Their average age when they commit their offenses is 30.6 years, and only 16 percent are married at this time. Their sexual experiences have usually been predominantly but not exclusively homosexual.

The child molester, especially when he uses force, arouses strong aversion and anger in the community. Even in jail he is so poorly tolerated that he must be isolated from other inmates.

Incest

Incest is quite rare but of great social significance. It is one sexual offense that is universally condemned, but it does occur, and historical and literary records include some well-known examples. The story of Lot and his daughters is told in Genesis 19 and that of Oedipus in the Greek tragedy *Oedipus Rex* by Sophocles. The circumstances in both stories are extraordinary. Lot and his daughters are the only survivors of the cataclysmic destruction of Sodom and Gomorrah, and the apparent motivation of Lot's daughters in intoxicating and seducing their father is to insure the continuity of their family line. Oedipus is not even aware that the queen

whom he has married is his own mother.

The term **incest** (from the Latin for "impure," or "soiled") is commonly used for sexual relations between parents and offspring. In this sense it is much more common between fathers and daughters than between mothers and sons. Actually incest includes all sexual relations between a person and close relatives (for example, siblings, grandparents, uncles, and aunts). The taboo is extended to cousins in some but not in all groups. (The Roman Catholic and Greek Orthodox churches prohibit marriage between first cousins, but such marriages are permitted by many Protestant churches, as well as by Judaism and Islam.)

The incest taboo is generally assumed to have evolved very early in human history in an attempt to safeguard the integrity of the family unit, for sexual competition within the family would be highly disruptive (as it is when incest does occur). Furthermore, mating outside the family has been important in the formation of larger social units held together by kinship ties. The proposition that the incest taboo arose from recognition of the genetic dangers of inbreeding (through concentration of disease-carrying recessive genes) is much less plausible.

Whatever their precise origins, prohibitions against incest are now universal. Ford and Beach came to the conclusion that:

Among all peoples both partners in a mateship are forbidden to form sexual liaison with their own offspring. This prohibition characterizes every human culture. This generalization excludes instances in which mothers or fathers are permitted to masturbate or in some other sexual manner to stimulate their very young children. A second exception is represented by the very rare cases in which a society expects a few individuals of special social rank to cohabit with their immediate descendants. The Azande of Africa, for example, insist that the highest chiefs enter into sexual partnership with their own daughters. In no society, however, are such matings permitted to the general populations. (Ford and Beach, 1951)

Similar exceptions for intermarriage between siblings were also made among the

Incas and the ancient Egyptian pharaohs (Cleopatra was the offspring of and herself a partner in such matings). Incidentally, 72 percent of the societies surveyed by Ford and Beach were found to have more extensive incest prohibitions than is common in the West. Sometimes they were broad enough to exclude half the population as potential sex mates for a given individual.

The only data on offenders of incest laws available from the Gebhard study is on father-daughter relationships. The ages of the daughters at the time of the offenses were correlated with some characteristics of the fathers. Fathers who became sexually involved with prepubertal daughters tended to be passive, ineffectual men who drank excessively. The sexual contacts involved either fondling the external genitals or oral-genital contacts.

Offenders against teenage daughters tended to be religious, moralistic, and often active in fundamentalist sects. (They were rated as the most religious of all the groups of sex offenders studied by Gebhard and his colleagues.) They were poorly educated and had a median age of 46 at the time of the offense. Activity culminated in coitus in 91 percent of instances, and in only 8 percent did the daughters clearly resist the advances of their fathers, whereas 58 percent participated either encouragingly or passively.

Charges of incest are usually pressed by wives, but sometimes the daughters go directly to the police. Often the incestuous relationship has been continuing for some time and then is suddenly discovered by the wife or is reported by the daughter because she is angry at her father for some unrelated reason. Also, the daughter may not report incest because of fear or lack of understanding as to what is happening or what to do.

Animal Contacts

Sexual contacts with animals (**zoophilia, or bestiality**) were by far the least prevalent of the six components of total sexual outlet studied by Kinsey. Even though 8 percent of adult males and 3 percent of females reported such contacts with animals, their activities

accounted for a fraction of 1 percent of the total outlets. In some groups, however, such behavior was relatively common: Among boys reared on farms as many as 17 percent had had at least one orgasm through animal contact after puberty.

The human race has a long history of intimate associations with animals in many aspects of life, including sexual ones (*see* Figure 10.2). This theme has been an important source of fantasy and an inspiration for many works of art. Classical mythology abounds with tales of sexual contacts between the gods disguised as beasts and apparently unsuspecting goddesses and mortals. Zeus, for instance, approached Europa as a bull, Leda as a swan (*see* Figure 10.3), and Persephone as a serpent. From such unions issued the many half-man, half-beast denizens of the mythological woods: satyrs (half-goats), centaurs (half-horses), and minotaurs (half-bulls), to name only the most familiar.

Historical references are also plentiful. The historian Herodotus mentions the goats of the Egyptian temple at Mendes, which were specially trained for copulating with human beings. More often, we find references to animals as sexual objects framed as prohibitions. The Hittite code, the Old Testament, and the Talmud specifically prohibit such

Figure 10.2 Petroglyph in a cave in northern Italy.

From E. Anati, *Camonica Valley* (New York: Alfred A. Knopf, 1961), p. 128. Reprinted by permission.

239

Variations
and
Deviations
in Sexual
Behavior

Figure 10.3 *Leda and the Swan* (after Michelangelo).
Courtesy of The National Gallery, London.

contacts for males; and the Talmud extends the prohibition to females. The prescribed penalties for animal sexual contacts tended to be severe (death for both human and animal participants; *see* Leviticus 20). Such sanctions remained in effect in Europe throughout the Middle Ages and, indeed, until fairly recently. In 1468 one Jean Beisse was convicted of copulating with a cow and a goat. Jean, the cow, and the goat were all burned at the stake. Sixteen-year-old Claudine de Culam was convicted of copulating with a dog in 1601. Both were hanged, and their bodies burned. In 1944 an American soldier was convicted at a general court-martial of sodomy with a cow and sentenced to a dishonorable discharge and three years at hard labor.

The animals and the specific activities in-

volved in these sexual encounters vary widely. Copulation with dogs is well documented, but other purported combinations strain our credulity. Some Indian illustrations, for instance, may have been intended symbolically rather than literally. Common sense suggests that the animals most often used would be those found on farms and in homes and that the most common activity would be some form of masturbation or intercourse.

In the Kinsey sample general body contact with animals was more often reported by women, whereas men were more likely to have masturbated the animals. Oral-genital contacts involving the animals' mouths and the human genitals were reported by both sexes, but coitus with animals was more common among men and very rare among women.

We hear and read about "sex dogs" that are specially trained and sold for purposes of zoophilia, but such tales are difficult to document. There are, however, establishments that feature exhibitions of coitus between prostitutes and dogs (or even donkeys). These activities fascinate men more than they do women.

Group Sex

Many people are attracted by the idea of having sex with more than one other person at a time. Illustrations of such activities are plentiful in the erotic art of classical Greece (*see* Figure 10.4) and in that of the Far East. The theme has also been much exploited in erotic literature.

Although sex orgies are not new, they have in all likelihood been indulged in only by occasional men of wealth or by small and special groups. Recently it has been claimed that group sex is quite common among less exclusive segments of the general population. Although it no doubt occurs among "swingers," there is no way of quantifying the actual prevalence of such practices. At the level of fantasy many people are no doubt intrigued by the notion, and pornographic films exploit the theme frequently.

The participation of several couples in simultaneous coitus does not meet the definition of a deviation, for neither choice of object nor means is necessarily aberrant. The practice does raise questions of exhibitionism and voyeurism, however, for sex is ordinarily conducted in private.

Among animals the sight of copulation is

Figure 10.4 Love play, painting on an Attic red-figure Stamnos, fifth century B.C.

Louvre, Paris

sometimes quite arousing to nonparticipants. When "public" sexual activity breaks out in an animal group, it may lead to violent conflict. It has been suggested that prohibition of public sex among human beings arose from fears that it would excite bystanders and result in uncontrollable sexual activity and disruption of the group.

When one person takes more than one partner at a time, the definition of deviation seems applicable. When three people are involved (one male and two females or the opposite), the practice is known as **troilism.** As simultaneous coitus is impossible in the first instance and highly impractical in the second, usually some combination of coitus with oral-genital stimulation is adopted. All other versions of "group sex" are variations of this theme. Group sex may be exclusively heterosexual, homosexual, or mixed. It may also include homosexual behavior that would otherwise be unacceptable: Two males who would otherwise not touch each other may do so in the process of sex play with the same woman. Or two men having coitus with the same woman successively may be striving to achieve physical contact between their own genitals, as it were, by placing their penises in the same vagina in rapid succession. Overt homosexual contact during group sex is rare in males, but common in females.

Fetishism and Transvestism

In **fetishism** the sexual object is an inanimate article. The word "fetish" means an artificial, or fake, object. Anthropologists apply it to objects that are believed by primitive peoples to have magical power. In a more general sense it includes any article that is valued beyond its intrinsic worth because of superstitious or other meanings ascribed to it. Most often it is a piece of clothing or footwear, but parts of the body may also take on fetishistic significance. The boundary between normally erotogenic objects or parts of the body and fetishes is frequently quite nebulous. Many heterosexual males, for instance, are aroused by the sight of female underwear. Each man is also partial to particular por-

tions of the female anatomy besides the genitals. There is an intermediary group in whom such partiality becomes quite pronounced. For example, a man may become so preoccupied with the shape of a woman's legs or her provocative stockings and garters that he loses sight of the woman as a whole. It is only when a man becomes clearly focused on these paraphernalia or body parts to the exclusion of everything else, however, that we can speak of true fetishism.

This deviation, at least in the sense in which the term is generally used, is an almost exclusively male one. The attachment of women to jewelry or furs, for instance, is excluded because women obtain no conscious sexual gratification from these objects.

In principle, any article or body part can become endowed with fetishistic meaning, but some objects are more commonly chosen than others. The attraction may arise from the shape, texture, color, or smell of the article, or from a combination of these features. Most fetishes fall into two categories: "feminine" objects that are soft, furry, lacy, pastel-colored (like pink panties with frilly edges); and "masculine" objects that are smooth, harsh, or black (like chains and leather garments). The latter category is more often associated with sadomasochistic fantasies and practices.

What do fetishists do with these objects? Most incorporate them into masturbation sequences. Some may actually ejaculate into or over their fetishes. A fetish can also become associated with some other deviant practice, as we have noted. For example, a masochist may require that he be whipped by a woman wearing spike-heeled shoes, black garters, and so on.

Some fetishes may be so disguised or so far removed from actual sexual objects that the source of their erotic significance is hardly apparent, even to the fetishist himself. Outward circumstances can be quite misleading, however. For instance, a man may masturbate with female underwear because he has no access to a woman and the feminine garment helps him in his fantasies. In this sense the underwear is more a masturbation aid than a fetish. The key criterion, as for most deviations, is whether the choice of object is "voluntary" or resorted to only in the absence of feminine company.

Fetishism is explained by two processes: learning by association and symbolism. In the former a person "eroticizes" certain nonsexual objects because of their frequent associations with actual sexual parts and functions or because of chance associations under emotionally charged conditions. For example, when a boy has his first glimpse of the female genitals in conjunction with other sights, sounds, and activities, some of the latter may become indelibly impressed on his mind, even to the extent of overshadowing the primary stimulus. We also learn to value certain parts of the body over others simply by growing up in given cultures.

Objects like feces and urine may also be involved in fetishism, although human responses to body smells and products vary widely. Most people learn to find such odors and sights offensive and sexually repellent (except that vaginal secretions during excitement are frequently stimulating to men). Occasionally, however, the opposite occurs, and a person becomes highly aroused by filth ("mysophilia"), feces ("coprophilia"), and urine ("urophilia"). The sound of a woman urinating is intriguing to many males, but the deviant may be exclusively preoccupied with such elimination functions. It is said that in some exclusive Continental brothels a man could, for a fee, watch women defecate into transparent toilet bowls.

Transvestism, though a separate variation is closely linked to fetishism, for the transvestite (also usually a man) achieves sexual gratification through wearing the clothing of the opposite sex. Again appearances can be quite misleading. Some "transvestites" are actually transsexuals. As far as they are concerned, they are wearing the clothes of their own sex. Others are homosexuals using female clothing to attract other homosexuals. Then there are socially accepted instances in which men dress as women, as in amateur burlesque skits or Japanese Kabuki plays.

Very few transvestites in the Kinsey data were overt homosexuals or even consciously inclined toward homosexuality. These apparently heterosexual men claimed simply to enjoy wearing women's clothing, and it was not unusual for their mothers to have dressed them as girls in childhood.

Others

A number of additional deviations in object choice deserve brief mention. **Necrophilia** is the sexual use of corpses. It is exceedingly rare and usually involves psychotic men. Literary and artistic references to love and death are sometimes interpreted as suggestions of necrophiliac fantasies, as in Edgar Allan Poe's:

> I could not love except where death
> was mingling his with beauty's breath.

Practices like kleptomania and pyromania are much more common and may involve unresolved sexual conflicts. The first involves compulsive stealing without much interest in the nature and intrinsic value of the objects stolen. The pyromaniac suffers from irresistible impulses to set fires. In both instances the deviant may actually experience sexual arousal during the activity.

VARIATIONS AND DEVIATIONS IN SEXUAL AIM

The deviations in object choice discussed in the preceding section involve relatively distinct entities: Children, animals, and inanimate articles are distinct and mutually exclusive classes of objects. Abberations in aim are far more difficult to characterize, for differences between the "normal" and the "deviant" are more quantitative than qualitative.

The activities to be considered next are described as they occur in the context of adult heterosexual relationships. When they coexist with deviations in object choice, they are classified according to the latter. Deviations in sexual aims are rare in their "pure" forms and are most common among men.

Voyeurism

Leofric, Lord of Coventry in the eleventh century, agreed to remit an oppressive tax if his wife, the Lady Godiva, would ride through the town naked on a white horse. The lady, a benefactress of monasteries and a friend of the poor, consented. Out of respect and gratitude everyone in town stayed behind closed doors and shuttered windows during her ride—everyone, that is, except Tom the tailor, who peeped and went blind. At least, that is the way the legend goes.

Only the very naïve would be surprised to hear that men are usually erotically aroused at the sight of uncovered female bodies. When such exposure is accompanied by movements, it can be even more exciting. Male interests are widely indulged through "girl watching," attending "topless" shows, and so on. Such behavior is often loosely called "voyeuristic," but it does not constitite a deviation. Women, at least according to current studies, are less interested than men in viewing members of the opposite sex nude.

Strictly speaking **voyeurism** is viewed as a deviation when it is preferred to coitus or indulged in at a serious risk. It is socially unacceptable when the person is observed without her knowledge and would be offended if she became aware of it.

The typical voyeur is not interested in ogling his own wife or female friend. In 95 percent of incidents he observes strangers. What draws him to peep through her windows is in large measure the danger and excitement involved. The practice is culturally widespread (*see* Figures 10.5 and 10.6).

Voyeurs tend to be young men (the average age at first conviction is 23.8 years). Two thirds of them are unmarried; one fourth are married; and the rest are either divorced, widowed, or separated. Very few show evidence of serious mental disorders, and alcohol or drugs

Figure 10.5 Erotic scene, c. 1780, by an anonymous French artist.

Figure 10.6 Chinese bathing scene (eighteenth century?). Artist unknown.

are usually not involved in their deviant behavior (only 16 percent of Gebhard's sample was drunk at the time of offense, and none was under the influence of drugs). They frequently masturbate while watching or immediately thereafter. The voyeur usually takes great care not to be seen by the object of his attentions, and most voyeurs are reported to the police by passersby or neighbors rather than by the women being looked at. Voyeurs are also known to have fallen off window ledges or been shot as burglars.

In intelligence, occupational choice, and family background "peepers" tend to be a heterogeneous group. They are, however, more likely to be the youngest children in their families. The single most common characteristic of this group of sex offenders is a history of grossly deficient (both in quantity and in quality) heterosexual relationships. Most voyeurs do not have serious criminal records, but many have histories of minor offenses (misdemeanors). As a rule they do not molest their victims physically or have any contact with them.

Exhibitionism

The word "exhibitionist" is a good example of the arbitrariness and confusion with which certain terms, and the concepts that they embody, have come to be used. The drunken man who fleetingly exposes his genitals to a woman passing by while he is urinating in a dark alley is an exhibitionist (for practical purposes, only if she takes offense). A woman who spends hours on end undressing herself to musical accompaniment or displays herself naked on a stage in front of a paying audience is "exhibitionistic" in her behavior but is not an "exhibitionist" (*see* Figure 10.7).

The male behavior carries a stiff prison sentence; the woman is permitted to make her living this way. However badly females may fare in other areas of sexual behavior, where voyeurism and exhibitionism are concerned, the law is on their side. A woman undresses in front of an open window, and a man looks up at her: He is a voyeur. The roles are reversed: Now he is an exhibitionist.

The mating behavior of animals, as well as of humans, includes a great deal of "exhibitionistic" activity. Society has permitted and expected a certain amount of enticement by women, from coquettish exposure of an ankle to unceremonious baring of her buttocks; and, depending on the time and the place, either may still be appropriate.

Exhibitionism is a deviation when an adult male obtains sexual gratification from exposing his genitals to women or children who are involuntary observers, usually complete strangers. In a typical sequence the exhibitionist drives or walks in front of a woman with his genitals exposed. He usually, but not always, has an erection. Most often, as soon as she has seen him, he flees. Sometimes he wears a coat and exposes himself periodically while riding on a subway or bus. Or he may stand in a park and pretend that he is urinating.

The exhibitionist, in common with the voyeur, does not usually attack or molest his "victim." His gratification comes from observing her reaction, which is predictable surprise, fear, disgust, and so on. Women who keep their calm foil his attempt. (For the same reason, a nudist camp, where he would hardly be noticed, does not attract this type of deviant.) Some men ejaculate at the scene of exposure; others experience a subjective thrill; still others become highly aroused and masturbate right afterward.

The average age of the exhibitionist ("the flag-waver" in prison slang; "the flasher" is another term) at conviction is 30 years. About 30 percent of arrested exhibitionists are married; another 30 percent are separated, divorced, or widowed; and 40 percent have never been married. The exhibitionist often describes a compulsive quality in his own behavior, triggered by feelings of excitement, fear, restlessness, and sexual arousal. Once in this state he feels "driven" to find relief. Despite previous arrests and convictions, he tends to repeat his behavior. One-third of the offenders in this category in the Gebhard study had had four to six previous convictions, and 10 percent had been convicted seven or more times.

Figure 10.7 Thomas Rowlandson, *Untitled*.

The exhibitionist seems to need to display and reaffirm his masculinity, and sometimes an element of sexual solicitation (rarely realized) is present as well. Exhibitionists do not usually show signs of severe mental disorder, and alcohol and drugs are involved only in rare instances.

Although usually not classified with exhibitionism, the practice of making obscene telephone calls is similar in some ways. The caller is usually a sexually inadequate person, who can have sexual interchanges with the opposite sex through this apparently safe (though progressively less so as detection mechanisms are improved) method. His pleasure is also derived from eliciting embarrassment and intense emotion. Telephone companies recommend that the recipient of an obscene call remain calm and either hang up immediately or alert the operator by means of a second telephone to trace the call to its source and have the caller arrested.

Sadomasochism

Even though our individual and collective security depends on understanding and defending ourselves against aggression, we know relatively little about it. To what extent is it an inborn drive? If it is learned, how is it learned? There is a vast literature on the topic, but few conclusions have been generally accepted. This uncertainty applies also to the interrelation of sex and aggression.

The sex act entails a certain degree of force. In the animal world sexual encounters include varying amounts of force. Nips and bites are often inflicted (usually by the male) during copulation; among skunks and minks such biting may be savage. Most sexually active people make judicious use of force in lovemaking, but rarely to the point of causing pain. Scratching and "love bites" do occur between ardent lovers, but they are inflicted in the heat of passion and are not calculated to make the partner suffer. As noted earlier, the threshold of pain perception is raised during sexual excitement, so that one is less aware of pain.

Aggressive fantasies are also quite common. They may take the form of dreams, daydreams, or fleeting thoughts (see Chapter 8). A man may harbor such thoughts about a variety of women, and the imagined responses may range from playful resistance to humiliating submission. Women, too, may have such fantasies, often mixed with fear.

Although the term is often used loosely, **sadism** as applied to sexual deviation is restricted to instances in which the individual needs to inflict pain in order to achieve sexual satisfaction. **Masochism,** also frequently used loosely, is applied to instances in which the individual must be subjected to pain in order to achieve such satisfaction. These terms are derived from the names of two historical figures who wrote on these respective themes. The first was the eighteenth-century French nobleman Donatien-Alphonse-François, Marquis de Sade; the second was the Austrian Leopold von Sacher-Masoch (1836–1905), also a nobleman of rather involved ancestry. The works, as well as the biographies, of both men are widely known. Sadism and masochism will be discussed jointly, for they are mirror images of the same phenomenon. Although occasionally innocent people are harmed by sadists or inadvertently satisfy the masochis-

tic needs of others, in general, sadists and masochists use each other as partners.

As sexual deviations, sadism and masochism tend to be discrete. That is, a sadist does not wish alternately to whip someone and then to be whipped (see Figure 10.8). However, the conflicts and experiences that result in one or the other of these impulses may be quite similar. It is therefore common to define **sadomasochism** as a form of behavior in which sex and pain become pathologically attached.

It is neither possible nor necessary to catalogue the infinite variety of obvious, as well as startling, devices that have been imagined and sometimes (though very rarely) actually used in sadomasochistic sexual encounters. We shall therefore briefly describe only those sadomasochistic practices that are still fairly commonly encountered.

Both in this country and abroad a person can pay to be whipped. In the sadomasochistic subculture this practice is referred to as "Discipline." This type of service is usually provided by specialized prostitutes and is more likely to be found in large cities. It is far more difficult to find someone who will submit to such treatment for money, for there are certainly easier ways to earn a living.

The majority of sadomasochistically oriented people tend to restrict their activities to reading special magazines that feature either cartoons or photographs of women dressed in leather and spike-heeled shoes trying to look menacing as they gag, bind, chain, whip, and variously "torture" their victims. Sadomasochistic sexual practices may include "bondage," which consists of tying down the sexual partner prior to sexual stimulation, but they stop short of physical harm to the partner.

Sadists who are more apt to act out their impulses are another matter. At their mildest, sadistic men merely soil women ("saliromania") or cut their hair off. At their worst they may rape, mutilate, and kill.

Psychiatric and forensic writings are replete with case histories of sadomasochism, but literature conveys the atmosphere of such activities better, as illustrated in the following parody from *Myra Breckenridge.* The narrator is Letitia Van Allen:

247

Variations
and
Deviations
in Sexual
Behavior

Figure 10.8 Mauron, *The Cully Flaug'd* (eighteenth-century illustration for *Fanny Hill*).

It began upstairs when he tore my clothes off in the closet. Then he raped me standing up with a metal clothes hanger twisted around my neck, choking me. I could hardly breathe. It was exquisite! Then one thing led to another. Those small attentions a girl like me cherishes . . . a lighted cigarette stubbed out on my derriere, a complete beating with his great thick heavy leather belt, a series of ravenous bites up and down the inner thighs, drawing blood. All the usual fun things, except that this time he went beyond anything he had tried before. This time he dragged me to the head of the stairs and raped me from behind, all the while beating me with his boot. Then, just as I was about to reach the big O, shrieking with pleasure, he hurled me down the stairs, so that my orgasm and the fi-

nal crash with the banister occurred simultaneously. I fainted with joy! Without a doubt, it was the completion of my life.

Rape

Rape refers to the use of force or threat of force in conjunction with sexual gratification at the expense of an unwilling victim. The victim is usually a woman, but men are sometimes raped by other men in prison, and there are occasional instances of women "raping" adolescent boys through a combination of force and seduction.

To the woman being raped, the experience can be extremely frightening and traumatic. Not only is she forced to engage in a sexual act, she has no way of knowing how much force the rapist would actually use if she did not submit. She cannot judge whether his intent is to rape her or to rape, beat, and murder her.

The rapist is usually aware that his behavior is illegal, antisocial, and deviant, although rapists are well known for their rationalizations and ability to deceive. Eldridge Cleaver wrote of himself:

Rape was an insurrectionary act. It delighted me that I was defying and trampling upon the white man's law, upon his system of values, and that I was defiling his women. . . . After I returned to prison, I took a long look at myself and, for the first time in my life, admitted that I was wrong, and I had gone astray—astray not so much from the white man's law as from being human, civilized—for I could not approve the act of rape. (Cleaver, 1968)

Some rapists use force only to achieve their sexual aims (usually coitus). They are not interested in otherwise hurting the woman. Other rapists use considerably more force than necessary, and in such cases it seems that the primary purpose of the attack is aggressive. Even though there is usually a sadistic element in rape, rapists may be differentiated from sadists. Most sadists rely on masochists or prostitutes, whereas rapists assault unwilling victims. Also the rapist usually has overt sexual aims (most often coitus or oral-genital contact), whereas the sadist may be content with the pleasure obtained from inflicting pain with or without genital involvement. Rapists are generally younger men (the average age is 24.5 years at the time of first offense); and their victims are young women (the average age is 24 years, but 3 percent are 50 years old or older). In the United States rapes occur most often in homes and apartments. Other common sites include public buildings, automobiles, and outdoors. The rapist in about 50 percent of cases meets his victim on the streets, but he takes her to his residence to complete the crime. Rape occurs more frequently at night, on weekends, and during the warmer spring and summer months in the United States. Al-

Figure 10.9 Franz Masareel, *Sex Murder.* Book illustration, *Ginzberg L'Enfer,* p. 185.

though the majority of rape offenses occur between strangers, in at least 40 percent of cases the rapist is a casual acquaintance, friend, relative, employer, or is otherwise known to the victim.

Group or "gang" rapes are not uncommon and tend to involve younger males who are members of a street gang or club which indulges in a variety of antisocial activities.

The sex murderer is a dangerous and terrifying person (*see* Figure 10.9). He usually tortures and sexually assaults his victim before killing her. Such men, who are very seriously deranged (often psychotic) may also mutilate the corpses or have further sexual contact with them. Every decade brings a few of these "lust murderers," who keep entire cities in chilling terror until apprehended.

What is it that drives people to violent sexual activities with unwilling partners? Unfortunately most answers are only conjectural.

The personality and family profiles drawn by Gebhard and his associates are revealing but do not permit conclusions about causation. For instance, heterosexual aggressors against children tend to be intellectually dull and the victims of broken and unhappy homes. They have few and poor relationships with adult females and rely heavily on prostitutes for sexual partners. They tend to use alcohol excessively. Offenders against minors (12–15 years old) have equally unfortunate home backgrounds, and many have criminal records. They are usually amoral, aggressive young men who seek whatever immediate gratification they can find, regardless of the ultimate consequences. Aggressors against adults are similar in their unconcern about the welfare and rights of others. They violate women in the same way that they help themselves to other people's property, and use whatever force is necessary to do so. Some are flagrantly disturbed, but a few are ordinary people who occasionally act impulsively or misjudge situations.

To understand sexual violence, we must therefore understand the overall problem of antisocial behavior and criminality, and the mixture of sex and aggression is but one facet of this problem.

SUMMARY

1. Heterosexual intercourse and auto-erotic activities represent only the most common forms of sexual behavior. There are numerous variations that can be classified in two general ways: variations in choice of sexual object and variations in choice of sexual aim.

2. Homosexual behavior is the most common variation in choice of sexual object. Homosexual behavior is seen in all parts of the country and at all social and economic levels. There are at least two million men who engage exclusively in homosexual acts and a larger number for whom homosexual acts constitute one of several sexual outlets. No similar data are available for females.

3. For all practical purposes no distinctions other than choice of sexual object can be made between people who engage in homosexual behavior and those who engage in heterosexual behavior. Because of the often negative attitudes and myths about people who engage in homosexual behavior, some such people prefer to keep their sexual orientation private. Others prefer to express their sexual orientation openly.

4. Homosexual behavior among men consists of everything that takes place in heterosexual relationships except vaginal intercourse. Homosexual activity among women consists primarily of kissing, caressing, fondling and oral stimulation of the breasts, mutual masturbation, and oral-genital contacts.

5. Kinsey's investigations found the incidence of homosexual behavior to be much higher than many people had supposed. By age 45, about 37 percent of men and 13 percent of women reportedly had had at least one homosexual encounter leading to orgasm. Kinsey's data further

suggest that exclusively homosexual behavior is rare, with many people falling on a scale somewhere between the two extremes.

6. Bisexuality and transvestism are two other variations in choice of sexual object. "Bisexual" is the term used to describe people who engage in both homosexual and heterosexual activity. "Transsexual" refers to people (usually males) who sincerely believe they are members of the opposite sex. With hormone treatments and sex-change surgery some of these individuals can (in all except chromosomal terms) effectively change their sex.

7. Pedophilia—the use of children as sex objects—is a variation of choice of sex object that is also a serious legal offense. Almost all pedophiles arrested are males. They may be interested in either prepubescent males or females, but usually not in both. Intercourse in such cases is rare, and actual contact usually consists of fondling the child's external genitals.

8. Incest—sexual intercourse between close relatives—is quite rare and is prohibited in all cultures, but it does occur. Sexual contact between humans and animals is also quite rare, but it has a long and widespread history.

9. In fetishism the sexual object is an inanimate object. Some people employ certain objects to increase sexual excitement; others focus on such objects exclusively. Transvestism is similar to fetishism in that the transvestite (usually a male) achieves sexual gratification by wearing the clothing of the opposite sex.

10. Voyeurism, exhibitionism, and sadomasochism are among the most common variations in sexual aim. Voyeurism involves achieving sexual gratification through secretly observing others naked or engaged in sex. Exhibitionism involves exposing one's genitals to an unwilling observer. Sadists need to inflict pain and masochists need to be subjected to pain in order to achieve sexual satisfaction.

11. Rape is the use of force or threat of force in order to achieve sexual satisfaction from an unwilling victim. Most rapists are young men and their victims are usually young women, though men are sometimes raped by other men (especially in prison), and women can use force against men or other women. The causes of this violent antisocial behavior are not well understood.

SUGGESTED READING

Bell, A. P., and Weinberg, M. S. *Homosexualities.* New York: Simon & Schuster, 1978.
The most recent and thorough study to date of life styles and activities of U.S. homosexuals. This is the Kinsey Institute study that is referred to in this chapter.

Ford, C. S., and Beach, F. A. *Patterns of Sexual Behavior*. New York: Harper & Row, 1951.

A cross-cultural study of sexual behavior, with emphasis on primitive societies.

Weinberg, S., and Williams, J. *Male Homosexuals: Their Problems and Adaptations*. New York: Oxford University Press, 1974.

A cross-cultural study comparing the life styles and problems of male homosexuals in the United States, the Netherlands, and Denmark.

Martin, D., and Lyon, P. *Lesbian/Woman*. San Francisco: Glide Publications, 1972.

A book about the myths and realities of lesbian life in the United States by the two women who founded the lesbian organization The Daughters of Bilitis.

Gebhard, P. H., *et al. Sex Offenders*. New York: Harper & Row, 1965.

The most thorough study of sex offenders of all sorts ever undertaken in the United States. It was conducted by the staff of the Institute for Sex Research — the Kinsey Institute.

Brownmiller, S. *Against Our Will: Men, Women and Rape*. New York: Simon & Schuster, 1975.

An historical analysis of rape in our society and a provocative discussion about the significance of rape and the threat of rape in defining male and female relationships.

CHAPTER 11 Sexual Disorders

Did You Know That . . .

it is currently estimated that 50 percent of all young people in the United States contract either syphilis or gonorrhea by the age of 25?

there is a widespread strain of gonorrhea called super clap that is resistant to penicillin?

cancer of the breast is the most common form of cancer in women, and cancer of the prostate is the most common form of cancer in men?

the vast majority of sexual malfunctioning in both sexes results from psychological causes?

one veneral disease, a viral infection called Herpes Simplex Virus Type 2, is twice as common as syphilis and almost as widespread as gonorrhea?

INTRODUCTION

Everyone experiences physical ill health or mental turmoil at one time or another, so it is realistic to view a certain amount of illness as a natural part of life—including our sex lives. In addition to the ordinary wear and tear on our bodies and minds, we are all subject to certain common ailments, as well as to some less common and more serious disorders. Some knowledge of these matters is helpful in reducing worry and discomfort, as well as in alerting us to the presence of possible danger signals.

A great number of disorders can affect the sex organs and sexual functioning, and several medical specialties are involved in the treatment of these various disorders. **Gynecologists,** for example, deal with disorders of the female reproductive system. Most male sexual disorders are treated by **urologists.** Because many sexual malfunctions have no obvious physical cause and are believed to be the result of psychological conflicts, psychiatrists, psychologists, and various types of counselors often treat them.

SEXUAL HYGIENE

Any person who practices regular cleaning of the genitals and related areas is less likely to be afflicted with some of the infectious diseases we will describe. Therefore, before discussing specific disorders of the reproductive system, we will mention some general principles for the cleaning and care of the genitals and related areas.

As has already been noted in Chapter 9, one's attractiveness as a sexual partner may be enhanced by specific attention to matters of sexual hygiene. It is not by any means necessary to equate hygiene with the elimination or covering up of natural odors, but a large-scale advertising campaign in recent years has attempted to convince people that deodorant sprays and similar products are a necessity for sexual hygiene. Actually, some of these products have been found to contain chemical irritants, and there may also be allergic reactions associated with their use in some people. Some evidence exists that natural odors, such as those produced by pheromones, play a role in sexual attraction and arousal. There is a difference, however, from both hygienic and esthetic viewpoints, between the causes and effects of fresh and stale odors. The fresh and often attractive odor of someone who bathes regularly is related to a combination of the secretions of various glands located on and around the genitalia and, perhaps, a slight residue of unscented or mildly scented soap. The stale and often offensive odor of someone who bathes infrequently or does not wash the genital region carefully is related to the action of skin bacteria and other microorganisms on accumulated body secretions and, on occasion, remnants of fecal material as well. A lengthy delay in changing tampons or externally worn absorbent pads during menstruation can produce similar results, but this is a less common occurrence.

Most of the skin is smooth, relatively hairless, and relatively devoid of glands other than sweat glands. Both the male and female genitalia, on the other hand, are wrinkled (the labia in the female, the scrotum and foreskin in the male), surrounded by hair, and rich in various glands (*see* Chapter 2). These three factors contribute to the likelihood of unpleasant odors in this area. (The next most likely source of strong odor is under the arms, where similar conditions exist, except that there are not as many crevices that can be overlooked.) The primary means of preventing these adverse health and esthetic consequences is simple: regular, careful washing of the genital region with soap and water. Regular means several times a week or more, at least as frequently as one has sexual intercourse. Careful means somewhat methodical coverage of the genitals with a washcloth; a simple shower is less than satisfactory for cleansing this area.

Although the vagina is a self-cleansing organ, some women do find it desirable to cleanse the vagina by douching. This is not usually necessary for hygienic purposes, but the insertion of creams, foams, gels, lubricants, and so forth, results in residues which may necessitate douching for some of the women who use them. Others prefer to douche at least once a month at the end of their menstrual periods (*see* Chapter 4 for the physiology of menstruation and related aspects). Plain tap water or a mildly acidic solution (for example, two tablespoons of vinegar in a quart of water) is preferable to most commercial douching preparations. Regular, alkaline (soda) douches should be avoided because they interfere with the normal chemical balance and flora of the vagina.

With these general principles in mind, let us move to a discussion of the causes, treatment, and prevention of various sexual disorders.

MINOR DISORDERS

The most common minor disorder of the female reproductive organs is **leukorrhea,** characterized by a whitish vaginal discharge, which almost every woman experiences at some time in her life. Leukorrhea is not a discrete disease entity but rather a condition that has multiple causes. Infectious organisms commonly cause it; a protozoan called *Trichomonas vaginalis* accounts for about one third of these conditions. A man may harbor this organism in the urethra or prostate gland without symptoms, and it is therefore customary to treat sexual partners simultaneously with a drug called metronidazole (*Flagyl*) to prevent reinfection.

A yeast-like organism called *Candida albicans* is another frequent cause of vaginal irritation and discharge. This organism is normally present in the vagina, but it produces symptoms only when it multiplies excessively. **Candida infections** are most commonly seen in women using oral contraceptives, diabetic women, and during the course of pregnancy or prolonged antibiotic therapy for some other condition. Although not usually serious, yeast vaginitis can be rather annoying, especially when it involves itching skin on the thighs. This condition is sometimes difficult to cure, but usually responds to treatment with mystatin (*Mycostatin*) suppositories. Although much less common in males, candida infections can occur, particularly under the foreskin of the penis.

Leukorrhea may also be related to alterations in hormone balance (during pregnancy or menopause) or to irritation from foreign bodies (like a contraceptive device). Irritating chemicals in commercial douche preparations may also cause vaginal discharges. For that matter, frequent douching of any sort is likely to increase the production of vaginal mucus.

There is no male counterpart to leukorrhea. Urethral discharges in males almost always result from venereal disease. Frequent urination and difficulty initiating urination may be psychologically caused, but if they persist, a physician should be consulted.

VENEREAL DISEASES

The term "venereal" comes from the Latin *venereus,* "pertaining to Venus," the goddess of love. Venereal diseases are propagated through sexual intercourse. Our discussion will focus first on **gonorrhea** and **syphilis.** Other venereal diseases are discussed later in this chapter.

Although syphilis and gonorrhea are readily curable with penicillin or other antibiotics, the incidence of gonorrhea and syphilis is rising in the United States. Most cases occur in the 15–29 age group; it is currently estimated that 50 percent of American young people contract syphilis or gonorrhea by age 25. It is not an overstatement to describe the present situation in the United States as an epidemic. In recent years gonorrhea has been the most prevalent disease of those reported to the U.S. Public Health Service, and syphilis ranks fourth. Gonorrhea is more common today than measles, mumps, or tuberculosis. Of all the contagious diseases, VD is second in prevalence only to the common cold. Although public-health codes require physicians to report all cases of venereal disease to public-health authorities, in actual practice probably less than 25 percent of the cases are reported. The purpose in reporting cases of venereal disease is to enable public-health workers to locate sexual "contacts" of contagious individuals and to treat them. This method has been successful in virtually eliminating epidemics of other infectious diseases. But many people are unwilling to disclose names and addresses of sexual contacts for a variety of reasons, ranging from embarrassment to fear of more serious consequences including self-incrimination and incrimination of past or present lovers. In many states intercourse with someone other than a spouse is a criminal offense. Homosexual acts are also crimes in most states. Although such information cannot legally be used as a basis for criminal prosecution, it is not difficult to understand the reluctance of someone who, by revealing the identity of a sexual partner, is revealing the identity of a partner in crime.

Fear of repercussion is only one factor in the current epidemic situation. The one to which we address ourselves in this chapter is ignorance. Some people are unaware of symptoms of venereal disease and many do not realize that venereal disease is not limited to the genitalia.

Gonorrhea

Gonorrhea is an infection caused by the bacterium *Neisseria gonorrhoeae* and can affect a variety of mucous-membrane tissues. This microorganism does not survive without the living conditions (temperature, moisture, and so on) provided by the human body, and is transmitted from human being to human being during contact with infected mucous membranes of the genitalia, throat, or rectum.

Ancient Chinese and Egyptian manuscripts refer to a contagious urethral discharge that was probably gonorrhea. The ancient Jews and Greeks thought that the discharge represented an involuntary loss of semen. The Greek physician Galen (A.D. 130–201) is credited with having coined the term "gonorrhea" from the Greek words for "seed" and "to flow." For centuries gonorrhea and syphilis were believed to be the same disease, but by the nineteenth century a series of experiments had demonstrated that they were two separate diseases. In 1879 A.L.S. Neisser identified the bacterium that causes gonorrhea and now bears his name (*see* earlier).

Symptoms in Males

In males the primary symptom of gonorrhea (known also as the "clap" or "strain") is a purulent, yellowish urethral discharge. The usual site of infection is the urethra, and the condition is called **gonorrheal urethritis.** The discharge from the tip of the penis appears within three to ten days after contraction of the disease and is usually accompanied by burning during urination and a sensation of itching within the urethra. The inflammation may subside within two or three weeks without treatment, or it may persist in chronic form. The infection may spread up the genitourinary tract to involve the prostate gland, seminal vesicles, bladder, and kidneys. In 1 percent of cases the disease spreads to the joints of the knees, ankles, wrists, or elbows, causing gonorrheal arthritis, a very painful condition.

More than 90 percent of cases clear up immediately with prompt penicillin treatment. For persons allergic to penicillin, tetracycline or erythromycin may be used. The discharge often disappears within twelve hours after treatment, though a thin flow persists for a few days in 10–15 percent of patients.

Although penicillin has been effective in treating gonorrhea since the 1940s, there is now a strain of gonorrhea that is resistant to penicillin. This so-called **"super clap"** first appeared in the United States in 1976 and has spread worldwide. Public-health officials hope to stop the spread of this strain of gonorrhea through early identification and treatment (with spectinomycin), but as with any venereal disease, it is often difficult to get patients to identify those with whom they have had sex.

Gonorrheal urethritis can usually be prevented by one of two methods: use of a condom and thorough washing of the sex organs and genital area with bactericidal soap or solution after sexual exposure, or a single dose of penicillin or other appropriate antibiotic within a few hours after exposure.

Pharyngeal gonorrhea is an infection of the throat which is transmitted during fellatio. The primary symptom is sore throat, but there may also be fever and enlarged lymph nodes in the neck. Kissing or cunnilingus apparently do not provide sufficient contact to transmit gonorrhea.

Rectal gonorrhea is an infection of the rectum transmitted during anal intercourse. The primary symptom is itching associated with a rectal discharge. Many cases are mild or asymptomatic, however. Treatment of rectal or pharyngeal gonorrhea is the same as for gonorrheal urethritis.

Symptoms in Females

In females the symptoms of gonorrhea may be mild or absent in the early stages. In fact, 80 percent of women with gonorrhea (and at least 10 percent of men) are essentially without symptoms, a major factor in the unwitting spread of the disease and a reason that public-health officials are now calling for screening of all men and women who may have come in contact with gonorrhea, whether or not they have any symptoms. The primary site of infection is usually the cervix, which becomes inflamed. The only early symptom may be a yellowish vaginal discharge. Not all such discharges are gonorrheal, however. Microscopic examination and bacterial culture of the discharge are required for definitive diagnosis. Unfortunately, there is no routine blood test that will detect gonorrhea. This is a major reason why identification of asymptomatic gonorrhea has been much less successful than identification of asymptomatic

syphilis. Treatment with antibiotics is usually effective if the disease is recognized and treated promptly.

If left untreated, however, the infection may spread upward through the uterus to involve the fallopian tubes and other pelvic organs. Often this spread occurs during menstruation, when the uterine cavity is more susceptible to gonorrheal invasion. Acute symptoms—severe pelvic pain, abdominal distension and tenderness, vomiting, and fever—may then appear during or just after menstruation. Again, treatment with antibiotics usually brings about a complete cure, but if the disease is not treated or is inadequately treated, a chronic inflammation of the uterine tubes ensues. This condition is accompanied by formation of scar tissue and obstruction of the tubes and constitutes a common cause of infertility in females, particularly those who frequently contract gonorrhea—for example, prostitutes.

Until recently a common cause of blindness in children was *ophthalmia neonatorum*, a gonorrheal infection of the eyes acquired during passage through infected birth canals. Instilling penicillin ointment or silver nitrate drops into the eyes of all newborn babies is now compulsory and has helped to eradicate this disease.

Syphilis

It is commonly believed, though the belief has not been thoroughly substantiated, that syphilis was brought to Europe by Columbus and his crew after their first voyage to the West Indies. It is true that, within a few years after Columbus' return in 1493 from his first voyage to the New World, epidemics of syphilis spread across Europe with devastating effects. History suggests that the Spaniards introduced the disease to the Italians while fighting beside the troops of Alfonso II of Naples. Then in 1495 an army of mercenaries fighting for Charles VIII of France conquered Naples. As they returned home through France, Germany, Switzerland, Austria, and England, they took the disease along with an excess of celebration. By 1496 syphilis was rampant in Paris, leading to the passage of strict laws banishing from the city anyone suffering from it. In 1497 all syphilitics in Edinburgh were banished to an island near Leith. In 1498 Vasco da Gama and his Portugese crew carried the disease to India, and from there it spread to China; the first epidemic in that country was reported in 1505. Outbreaks of syphilis in Japan later followed the visits of European vessels.

The term "syphilis" was introduced in 1530 by the Italian physician Girolamo Fracastoro, who wrote a poem in Latin about a shepherd boy named Syphilus (from the Greek *siphlos,* meaning "crippled" or "maimed") who caught the disease as a punishment from the gods for having insulted Apollo.

Various historical figures have been afflicted by syphilis, as is indicated by records of their physical appearances and symptoms. Columbus himself died in 1506 with symptoms typical of advanced syphilis, involving the heart, extremities, and brain. It is generally accepted that the first four children of Catherine of Aragon, first wife of Henry VIII of England, all died of congenital syphilis, leaving only one survivor, the future "Bloody Mary." (Mary died at age 42 of complications of congenital syphilis, it appears.) Henry's disappointment over not having a male heir undoubtedly played a role in his insistence on legalizing his second and subsequent marriages, which led to the break between England and Rome.

It was not until 1905 that the microorganism that causes syphilis was identified. A German investigator, Fritz Richard Schaudinn, identified and named **Spirochaeta pallidum,** describing it as a "slender, very pale, corkscrewlike object" (*see* Figure 11.1).

Symptoms

In its late stages syphilis can involve virtually any organ or tissue of the body, producing myriad symptoms similar to those of other diseases, which led the famous physician Sir William Osler to call it the "Great Imitator." The early stage, however, is marked by a primary skin lesion at the site of

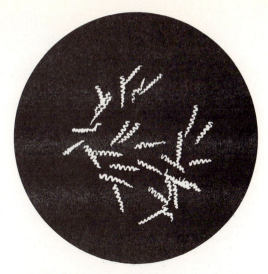

FIGURE 11.1 Typical organisms of *Treponema pallidum* from tissue fluid in a dark field. The length of each is about 10 microns.

From Jawetz *et al., Review of Medical Microbiology,* 9th ed. (Los Altos, Calif.: Lange Medical Publications, 1970, p. 220. Reprinted by permission.

contact and known as a **chancre.** The chancre (pronounced "shank-er") is a hard, round ulcer with raised edges, and is usually painless. In the male it commonly appears somewhere on the penis, on the scrotum, or in the pubic area (*see* Figure 11.2). In the female it usually appears on the external genitals (*see* Figure 11.3), but it may appear in the vagina or on the cervix and thus escape detection. It may also appear on the mouth, in the rectum, on the nipple, or elsewhere on the skin.

Because syphilitic infections in men may begin at sites other than the penis, condoms do not necessarily provide protection against them. As it is usually not apparent that someone is a carrier of syphilis, the only sure way to avoid the disease is to know before sexual contact whether or not the anticipated partner has had a negative blood test for syphilis—an unlikely question to ask as a prelude to making love. The point, is, however, that casual sexual contacts are more likely to expose one to syphilis (or other venereal disease), for statistically the greater the number of sexual partners, the greater the probability of encountering someone who is a carrier.

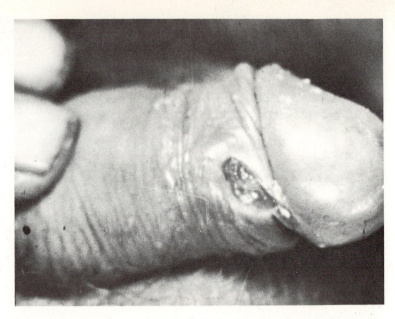

FIGURE 11.2 A chancre of the penis. Note the raised hard appearance of the ulcer.

From Dodson and Hill, *Synopsis of Genitourinary Disease,* 7th ed. (St. Louis, Mo.: The C.V. Mosby Co., 1962), p. 201. Reprinted by permission.

Syphilis (and gonorrhea) are transmitted *only* by intimate contact with another human being. The most infectious times are when a chancre is present or during the second stage of the disease when skin lesions are present (particularly lesions in moist areas of the body, such as the mouth). Thus, syphilis can be caught through kissing if the chancre is on the lips or if the lesions are on the mouth. Explanations involving contact with contaminated toilet seats, wet towels, chairs, drinking glasses, swimming pools, or domestic animals may save face but are pure myth and/or self-deception.

The chancre appears two to four weeks after contraction of the disease and, if not treated, usually disappears in several weeks, leading to the illusion that the individual has recovered. Actually this chancre is usually only the first stage in the development of a chronic illness that may ultimately be fatal. Treatment with penicillin or other antibiotics when the chancre occurs cures most cases, and relapses after proper treatment are rare.

Secondary and Tertiary Syphilis

When syphilis is untreated, the "secondary stage" becomes manifest anywhere from several weeks to several months after the healing of the chancre. There is usually a generalized skin rash, which is temporary and may or may not be accompanied by such vague symptoms as headache, fever, indigestion, sore throat, and muscle or joint pain. Many people do not associate these symptoms with the primary chancre.

After the secondary stage all symptoms disappear, and the so-called latent period begins. During this period, which may last for years, the spirochetes burrow into various tissues, particularly blood vessels, the central nervous system (brain and spinal cord), and bones.

About 50 percent of untreated cases reach the final, or "tertiary," stage of syphilis, in which heart failure, ruptured major blood vessels, loss of muscular control and sense of balance, blindness, deafness, and severe mental disturbances can occur. Ultimately the disease can be fatal, but treatment with penicillin even at late stages may be beneficial, depending on the extent to which vital organs have already been damaged.

Syphilis can be transmitted to the fetus through the placenta; hence the mandatory blood tests to identify untreated cases of the disease before marriage and before the birth of a child. Treatment with penicillin during

nongonococcal urethritis (NGU). This disease is most often seen among white and affluent patients and is probably the most common form of urethritis seen in student health centers and in the offices of private physicians. NGU is transmitted sexually (the organism involved is frequently, but not always, *Chalmydia trachomatis*), and although it causes urethritis in males (with a urethral discharge as in gonorrhea), it may be asymptomatic in females. A woman who gives birth while infected runs the risk of transmitting the disease to her newborn infant, and the child may develop a form of conjunctivitis (a serious infection of the eyes).

Because NGU was only recently identified as a sexually transmitted disease and because it is sometimes asymptomatic, many cases have gone undiagnosed and mistreated. The result is that this disease is becoming more and more widespread. NGU can be effectively treated with tetracycline and usually clears up within five days of treatment.

Other Venereal Diseases

Chancroid ("soft chancre") is caused by a bacillus known as *Hemophilus ducreyi* (the "bacillus of Ducrey"). The primary lesion of this veneral disease is a chancre which resembles the syphilitic chancre in appearance, but, in contrast to the syphilitic lesion, is quite painful. Diagnosis is based on microscopic examination or culture of the bacillus. Treatment with sulfa drugs is quite effective.

Lymphogranuloma venereum ("tropical bubo," LGV) is caused by a microorganism which is neither a bacteria nor a virus, though it has some of the properties of each. Although the site of entry is usually the penis, vulva, or cervix, the first obvious manifestation of the disease is usually enlarged, tender lymph glands in the groin accompanied by fever, chills, and headache. Treatment consists of sulfa or broad-spectrum antibiotics such as chlortetracycline. LGV is most common in the tropics and subtropics. In the United States it is seen most frequently in the South.

Granuloma inguinale ("chronic venereal sore") is caused by an infectious agent known

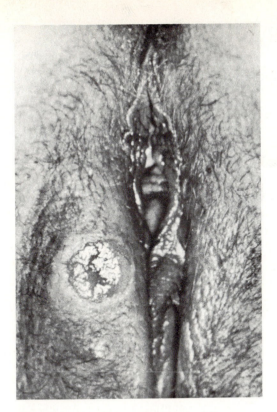

FIGURE 11.3 A large chancre on the labia majora. Primary syphilis in the female is not usually this obvious.

From Weiss and Joseph, *Syphilis* (Baltimore: Williams & Wilkins, 1951), p. 73. Copyright © 1951 by The Williams & Wilkins Co.; reprinted by permission.

the first half of pregnancy can prevent congenital syphilis in the child. Nine out of ten pregnant women who have untreated syphilis either miscarry or bear stillborn children or give birth to living children with congenital syphilis.

Children with congenital syphilis are prone to impaired vision and hearing, as well as to certain deformities of the bones and teeth. Treatment with penicillin can alleviate many of the manifestations of congenital syphilis if it is initiated early in infancy.

Nongonococcal Urethritis

A form of urethritis that is perhaps more common than that caused by gonorrhea is

as *Donovanian granulomatis,* or the "Donovan body," after its discoverer. Like LGV, it is most common in warm climates. The disease is characterized by ulcerated, painless, progressively spreading skin lesions. The most common sites of infection are the skin and mucous membranes of the genitalia, but the disease may also involve the rectum, buttocks, or mouth. The most effective antibiotics for treatment are tetracycline and streptomycin.

Viral Infections

Viral infections (genital warts and herpes) can also be the result of venereal transmission, though this is not their only mode of transmission. **Genital warts** are similar to common plantar warts. They appear most often in women on the vulva, vagina, and, less frequently, the cervix; in males, on the surface of the glans and below the rim of the corona. They have also been known to develop in and around the anus, particularly in male homosexuals. Traditionally, physicians have treated genital, or "venereal," warts in several ways: surgically, with electrodes, with cryosurgery (freezing), or with various drugs. A vaccine made from the patient's own wart tissue has also been shown to be effective in fighting the virus and in getting rid of the warts. One reason it is important to have these warts treated is that the virus which causes them can be transferred from an infected woman to her newborn child at the time of birth. The virus is believed to be responsible for tumors of the larynx in infants. For this reason some physicians advocate cesarean delivery if the mother has an active case of warts at the end of pregnancy.

The other viral infection of the genitals is **Herpes Simplex Virus Type 2** (HSV-2), which is now recognized as the second most common venereal disease in the United States. It is twice as common as syphilis and almost as widespread as gonorrhea. (HSV-2 should not be confused with HSV-1, which causes "cold sores," eye infections, and skin conditions above the waist.)

The HSV-2 infection results in the appearance of small vesicles (fluid-filled pockets or blisters) surrounded by inflamed tissue. The most common sites of herpes infections in females include the surface of the cervix, the clitoral prepuce, and the major and minor lips; in males, the foreskin and glans. When the blisters are internal, such as on the cervix, the condition may go undetected because the cervix is insensitive to pain. The usual mode of transmission of HSV-2 is sexual intercourse; therefore it is best to avoid sex when herpes blisters or ulcers are present. One reason that the disease has spread so rapidly, however, is that people often do not recognize it or know that they have it.

In most cases herpes causes burning and itching sensations, and when the blisters break open they may become infected with bacteria from the skin. A pregnant woman who is infected runs a risk (one in four) that her newborn child will be seriously injured or die of the virus. There is also the possibility that HSV-2 can cause cancer. Approximately 6 percent of women who have HSV-2 develop cervical cancer, so it is recommended that women who have had herpes get two Pap smear tests a year to check for cancer.

There is no completely effective treatment for herpes. Even though the blisters usually clear up after a few weeks, the virus may remain in the body for years, and the infection can recur cyclically.

Pubic Lice

Pediculosis pubis (pubic lice, "crabs") is an infestation of the pubic hair which is usually sexually transmitted. However, it is occasionally acquired from contact with infested bedding, towels, or toilet seats. The primary symptom of pubic lice is intense itching, which results from bites (the lice feed on blood like mosquitoes). Adult lice are visible to the naked eye, but just barely. They are bluish gray and about the size of a pinhead. Cream, lotion, or shampoo preparations of gamma benzene hexachloride (*Kwell*) are very effective in eliminating both adult lice and their eggs ("nits").

CYSTITIS

Cystitis is an infection or inflammation of the bladder. It is not a venereal disease, but its occurrence in women is sometimes associated with sexual activity. (It is so common among newlywed women, for instance, that the term "honeymoon cystitis" has been used to describe it.)

The bacteria that invade the bladder through the urethra are not usually caught from the sexual partner, but are normally present on the genital skin of the infected person. Women are more prone to cystitis because of their significantly shorter urethras, compared to those of males. The primary symptom of cystitis is frequent and painful ("burning") urination. It may subside spontaneously in a few days, but it is advisable to receive proper antibiotic treatment because untreated infections may spread from the bladder to the kidneys, causing a much more serious condition called **pyelonephritis.**

CANCER OF THE SEX ORGANS

The most common cancers in both sexes involve organs of the reproductive system.

Of the Breast

Cancer of the breast is the most common form of cancer in women. It is rare in women under age 25, but increases steadily in each decade thereafter. Ultimately, more than 5 percent of all women develop cancer of the breast. The cause of this disease is unknown, but it is clear that many breast cancers respond to sex hormones. The spread of this cancer is thus accelerated by increased hormone secretion during pregnancy. Some investigators feel that the long-term ingestion of hormones in birth-control pills may stimulate the growth of breast cancer, but a definitive answer to this question will not be available until sufficient women have taken the pills for twenty years, permitting follow-up studies in the 1980s.

Removal of the ovaries is often beneficial in the treatment of breast cancer, as is treatment with the male sex hormone testosterone. The primary treatment is surgical removal of the breast (**mastectomy**).

Cancer of the breast can be fatal, but with early diagnosis and treatment the prognosis is much more favorable. About 45 percent of patients with cancer of the breast are still alive five years after the initial diagnosis, and about 30 percent survive ten years or more. Early diagnosis and treatment are often missed because cancer of the breast begins with a painless lump in the breast, which may go unnoticed for a long time, until spread of the disease produces other symptoms. Hence the need for breast examinations at regular intervals and surgical biopsy of any questionable lump.

New techniques for diagnosis of breast cancer include special X rays (**mammograms**) and infrared scanning devices which can detect the slight increase in heat that is usually produced by cancer tissue. These and other devices for detecting breast cancer have been credited with saving the lives of many women, but questions have been raised about the safety of X-ray mammograms. Because X-rays may actually cause cancer, some scientists suggest that the technique not be used on a routine basis but only when a woman is at high risk for breast cancer.

When breast cancer is detected and breast removal recommended, one of the most difficult problems the woman faces is the disfigurement caused by the mastectomy. But this situation is changing. Breast-reconstruction techniques have become so sophisticated in recent years that women no longer need fear loss of self-image and confidence as a result of the operation. Plastic surgeons not only can reconstruct the breast contours (using silicone gel implants), they can also reconstruct the nipple and areola from the intact nipple.

Of the Cervix

Cancer of the cervix is the second most common type of cancer in women. About 2 percent of all women ultimately develop it. It is very rare before age 20, but the incidence rises over the next several decades. The average age of women with cancer of the cervix is 45. This disease is more common in women who have had large numbers of sexual contacts and who have borne children.

Cancer of the cervix may present no symptoms for five or ten years, and during this period treatment is extremely successful. The well-publicized Pap smear test (which women usually are recommended to have annually) is the best means now available for identifying cancer of the cervix in the early stages (when it is most susceptible to treatment). From the patient's point of view the Pap smear is an extremely simple test. The physician simply takes a specimen of cervical mucus with a cotton-tipped swab and makes a "smear" of this material on a glass slide. The procedure is quick, simple, and painless. The smear is then stained and examined under a laboratory microscope for the presence of cancerous cells.

As cancer of the cervix begins to invade surrounding tissues, irregular vaginal bleeding or a chronic bloody vaginal discharge develops. Treatment is less successful when the cancer has reached this stage. If treatment (surgery, radiation, or both) is instituted before the cancer spreads beyond the cervix, the five-year survival rate is about 80 percent, but it drops precipitately as the disease reaches other organs in the pelvis. The overall five-year survival rate for cancer of the cervix (including all stages of the disease) is about 35 percent. The comparable figure for ten years is about 26 percent.

One possible cause of cancer of the cervix is the drug DES (diethylstilbestrol, a synthetic estrogen). Between 1940 and 1970, DES was given to many pregnant women who had a history of bleeding, repeated miscarriage, or long periods of infertility. DES was of dubious value in preventing miscarriages, and a greater than usual risk of cancer of the cervix or vagina has been found in daughters of women who took the drug while pregnant. It is recommended that women find out if their mothers took DES and if so inform their doctors so they can be checked for vaginal cancer.

Of the Endometrium

Cancer of the endometrium (the lining of the uterus) has also been linked to the use of estrogens. Estrogens have proved to be effective in treating certain symptoms of menopause (*see* Chapter 4), but some evidence suggests that the risks of this treatment may outweigh the benefits, especially in postmenopausal women who were given estrogens over a prolonged period of time. The Federal Drug Administration now suggests that if estrogen therapy is employed, it be used cyclically in the lowest effective dose for the shortest possible time with appropriate monitoring for endometrial cancer. There is some recent evidence that the addition of progesterone to the estrogen therapy may decrease the risk of endometrial cancer.

Of the Prostate

Cancer of the prostate is the most common form of cancer in men. Nevertheless, cancer of the prostate has never been a significant cause of death, although the mortality rate is rising as the life expectancy has risen. Historically, cancer of the prostate has had a low mortality rate for two reasons: First, it is rare before age 50 and uncommon before age 60. About 70–80 percent of cases occur between the ages of 60 and 80, and about 25 percent of men in the ninth decade of life have cancer of the prostate. By that time they are likely to die of other causes, like heart disease, rather than of cancer. Second, most cancers of the prostate are relatively small and grow very slowly. Only a minority spread rapidly to other organs.

Cancer of the prostate, like cancer of the

breast, is responsive to sex hormones. Androgens stimulate its growth, and surgical castration (removal of the testicles) is thus part of the treatment for this disease. Furthermore, estrogens slow the growth of prostatic cancer and are often given as part of the treatment, again highlighting the physiological antagonism between estrogen and androgen (compare the use of testosterone in treatment of cancer of the breast). Whereas administration of androgen to women causes "masculinization" (beard growth, deepening of the voice, enlargement of the clitoris) and increases the sex drive, administration of estrogen to men may cause "feminization" (enlargement of the breasts), impotence, and loss of libido.

The initial symptoms of prostatic cancer are similar to those in benign enlargement of the prostate (*see* Chapter 4). They include frequent urination, particularly at night; difficulties initiating urination; and difficulties emptying the bladder. These symptoms largely result from partial obstruction of the urethra by the malignant growth. Early in the course of the disease libido may increase, and frequent erections (related to increased androgen secretion?) may occur. Later on, however, there is usually a loss of sexual functioning. A tentative diagnosis of cancer of the prostate can usually be made on the basis of a rectal examination (palpation of the prostate through the rectum), the history of symptoms, and certain laboratory tests. A prostate examination should certainly be part of an annual physical checkup for any man over 50, for, as with other cancers, the prognosis is much more optimistic when it is diagnosed and treated early. The cause of prostatic cancer remains unknown despite efforts to link it with hormonal factors, infectious agents, excessive sexual activity, and sexual frustration.

Of the Penis

Cancer of the penis is rare in the United States, accounting for about 2 percent of all cancer in males. It is interesting, however, because of its apparent relation to circumcision. Cancer of the penis almost never occurs among Jews, who undergo circumcision within the first two weeks of life, as do most male infants in this country. This disease is also rare, though somewhat less so, among Muslim men, who usually undergo circumcision before puberty. Yet in areas of the world where circumcision is not common cancer of the penis is much more prevalent. It accounts for about 18 percent of all malignancies in Far Eastern countries, for instance. The usual explanation, though it has not been confirmed, is that circumcision prevents accumulation of potentially carcinogenic secretions, or possibly a virus, around the tip of the penis (the usual site of this type of tumor).

SEXUAL MALFUNCTIONING

Competence in sexual intercourse is not an all-or-none phenomenon, and there is no absolute scale on which to evaluate it. No one is expected to be able to copulate at will with anyone, anywhere, anytime. Considerable fluctuation is normal in sexual desire, and it is expected that performance will occasionally falter. Beyond a certain ill-defined boundary, however, the extent or frequency of failure—whether at the level of desire, performance, or gratification—must be considered malfunction.

Types of Sexual Malfunctioning

Difficulties in sexual intercourse are not easy to define, even though the specific labels attached to some of them may give that impression. Rather, they belong on a continuum in which physical, psychological, and social influences interact. Problems of men and women should also be viewed jointly, for many difficulties in sexual intercourse are caused by interpersonal difficulties.

The signs of sexual apathy and lack of gratification in coitus are similar in the two sexes, but the difficulties in actual performance differ because of the peculiarities of the sexual apparatus of each sex. Among men the primary problems are inability to achieve and sustain an erection and inability to delay ejaculation. If an erection is achieved and sustained, there is very rarely any difficulty in achieving orgasm, and pain is almost never an issue. For women the main difficulties are failure to attain orgasms and painful intercourse.

Apathy

It is expected of healthy men and women that they will wish to engage in sexual intercourse with someone, sometime, someplace, even though they may elect not to carry out this wish or may be prevented from doing so. Beyond this stipulation, judgments of the intensity of sexual desire are arbitrary.

A most important factor in sustaining sexual desire is the satisfaction gained from coitus itself. If, for whatever reason, a person finds the experience distasteful, painful, or merely tedious, the incentive to join in it is much weakened.

In its mildest form sexual apathy is simple indifference. A person forgoes sexual intercourse for extended periods because he or she does not feel like having it, despite acceptable circumstances and willing partners. Sometimes the person is so preoccupied with other events and activities that sex is understandably set aside for a while. But it is also possible that these other activities are at least unconsciously aimed at avoiding sex. In treating sexual difficulties it is necessary to determine when a person is making unreasonable demands on a harassed marital partner and when a sexually apathetic partner is deliberately becoming exhausted before bedtime in order to have an excuse to avoid sex.

Sexual apathy can be part of a general listlessness, perhaps resulting from concrete external causes or from a general depression reflecting internal conflicts. Sexual apathy is not restricted to mere listlessness, however. A person may feel consciously uneasy about coitus and may actively seek to avoid it. Perhaps the experience has been uncomfortable and unsatisfying, or feelings of guilt and shame may have overbalanced the pleasure and joy in the act. Some people actually dread coitus, out of disgust or fear.

Coital Inadequacy in Males

Disturbances in male performance are generally called **impotence** or **erectile dysfunction.** In addition to the simple inability to have an erection, the term covers partial or weak erections, inability to sustain an erection long enough to penetrate, and orgasm before or right after entry (**premature ejaculation**), as well as the more rare condition in which an erect penis fails to ejaculate (**ejaculatory impotence**). The last two conditions can be appropriately considered as disturbances of ejaculation. Men who are potent in autoerotic or other noncoital activities but unable to consummate coitus are also considered impotent. It is customary to separate primary from secondary impotence, though such distinctions are not always consistent. The most common one is between men who have never been able to have an erection that would permit coitus (primary impotence) and those who are impotent only in some situations. For clinical purposes a man may be considered secondarily impotent if his attempts at coitus fail in one out of four instances.

Again there is no absolute scale against which to evaluate male performance. Obviously a man must keep his erection long enough to penetrate and reach a climax. Beyond such minimal criteria, judgments can be only relative. A male may perform inadequately in one instance but adequately in a better-lubricated vagina, a relaxed introitus, a more accessible position, and so on.

The length of intercourse preceding orgasm is not always related to the gratification obtained by either partner. Generally, the longer a man can delay ejaculation, the greater is the opportunity for the woman to achieve orgasm. But, again, some women may be gratified very quickly, whereas others would not respond, no matter how long the man could continue. Judgments of male adequacy must, therefore, be based on performance with a hypothetical woman of average receptivity and ordinary responsiveness. The more practical question in sexual conflicts is not whether a man is sufficiently potent in the abstract but whether he is potent enough to satisfy his partner.

In view of these ambiguities, accurate assessment of the prevalence of impotence is impossible. Most figures quoted in surveys include only individuals with long-standing and nearly complete impotence.

Erectile dysfunction affects about one of every hundred males under 35 years of age, but the inadequacy is chronic and totally incapacitating in only some of them. At 70 years of age about one in four males is impotent. The progressive decline of potency with age is fairly general, though some men retain their potency into old age. Failure to ejaculate is very rare and affects no more than one in seven hundred men of all ages.

Impotence resulting from aging or from actual physiological disturbance tends to be generalized. Impotence resulting from psychological causes may also be general, or it may be specific to certain situations and interactions. Some men are impotent only during coitus with their wives, with women other than their wives, or with women with certain types of physical appearance or personality. Sometimes it is the inhibitions that are specific, but, conversely, sometimes erection is possible only if equally special conditions are fulfilled. These conditions may be relatively simple (total darkness) or may revolve around such intricate rituals as the woman's wearing black stockings fastened to a special type of garter, and so on.

Erectile potency and sexual desire usually go together. The problem is worse when desire persists despite physical failure. In the rare condition known as "priapism" (see Chapter 3) the opposite is true—erections do not reflect sexual desire and may actually be painful.

Premature ejaculation, which may or may not be associated with failures of erection, is the other major disturbance of male sexual functioning. Attempts to define this condition have generally been based on the amount of time between vaginal insertion and ejaculation, with some authors defining prematurity as the occurrence of orgasm 30 seconds or less after insertion. Others define prematurity as the occurrence of orgasm prior to one and one-half or two minutes after insertion. Masters and Johnson diagnose a man as a premature ejaculator if he reaches orgasm before his partner does more than 50 percent of the time. Another definition comes from sex therapist Helen Singer Kaplan, who says premature ejaculation is probably best defined as "a condition wherein a man is unable to exert voluntary control over his ejaculatory reflex, with the result that once he is aroused, he reaches orgasm very quickly." Armed with the finding that three out of four men reach orgasm within two minutes of intromission, and that most male animals do so even sooner, the Kinsey group made light of premature ejaculation as a form of sexual malfunctioning.

Although it may be impossible to set exact time limits to define normal functioning, there is no mistaking the fact that a significant number of men (and their partners) complain of inability to delay ejaculation until some measure of deliberate mutual enjoyment has been obtained. It is small comfort to them to realize that subhuman primates ejaculate even sooner. Especially when their own orgasms may even precede penetration, the whole point of sexual intercourse may seem lost.

Coital Inadequacy in Females

The main disturbances in female sexual response are failure to reach orgasm and unresponsiveness. Painful intercourse is also a problem but to a lesser degree. The problems can be either general or restricted to specific situations, partners, and so on. Women, however, have felt less pressure to achieve orgasm at coitus as frequently as men do, partly because coitus can take place when a female is unresponsive but not when the male is, and also because women traditionally have been sexually subservient. This situation is changing rapidly, however.

Even though definitive current data are lacking, the available evidence indicates that the problem of female coital inadequacy is receding significantly. In the Playboy survey 53 percent of women who had been married for fifteen years reported that they always or nearly always reached orgasm in coitus. The corresponding figure in the Kinsey survey was 45 percent. Likewise, the proportion of wives who never reached orgasm had gone down from 28 percent in the Kinsey sample to 15 percent in the Playboy sample.

As we discussed in Chapter 3, there is still considerable confusion about the nature of female orgasm. Besides, orgasm and sexual gratification are not synonymous. Despite the substantial numbers of women who are not regularly orgasmic, nine out of ten of the wives in the Playboy sample reported that their marital coitus in the past year had been "generally pleasurable or very pleasurable." Likewise, in over 4 percent of "extremely happy marriages" the wives reportedly never experienced orgasm in marital coitus. The inference to be drawn from these findings is not that since women can be happy without orgasm they should forget about orgasm if they cannot attain it. Rather, these data point out the greater complexity in evaluating female sexual malfunction compared to that in the male.

In the more usual cases of **orgasmic unresponsiveness** a woman may become aroused sexually yet not attain orgasm. Or, less commonly, she may go through the motions of sexual intercourse but "feel nothing." To placate and satisfy her partner, she may actually be quite active sexually, and she may attain considerable gratification from expressions of affection, from body contact, and from other aspects of lovemaking, even though erotic pleasure as such is absent. More likely, the experience leaves her frustrated and angry.

Pelvic pain is a common complaint among women, and sometimes it causes problems in coitus. It may be experienced at penetration, during intercourse, or afterward. Pain and fear of pain may be indistinguishable, partic-

ularly in the first instance. When pain occurs only during intercourse, it is less likely to be confused with fear of pain. Pain after coitus usually takes the form of a dull ache associated with irritability. When pain is felt or anticipated, a certain amount of muscular tension is inevitable. As the pelvic muscles surrounding the introitus become spastic, penetration becomes difficult and sometimes (as in vaginismus) impossible.

Achievement of coital orgasm was correlated with various factors (age, age at marriage, length of marriage, frequency and technique of coitus) in the Kinsey sample. The likelihood that a woman would reach orgasm during sexual intercourse seemed unrelated to techniques of foreplay and coitus. Religious background also made no difference, nor did the age at which adolescence had begun.

There was some positive correlation with age and social class. Older (up to middle age) women, more educated women, and women whose parents were in higher occupational classes were all more likely to attain orgasm. Marrying young seemed to be a deterrent: The group that had married by 20 years of age least frequently responded with orgasms. There was also a marked positive correlation with the length of marriage. Only half had experienced coital orgasm within the first month of marriage. But this percentage rose steadily with time: 63 percent in the first year, 71 percent in the fifth year, and 85 percent by the twentieth year of marriage.

The likelihood of orgasm during marital coitus also appeared to be markedly correlated with premarital experience of orgasm through either masturbation, petting, or coitus. Also the incidence of coital orgasm was shown to have steadily increased in the younger generation.

Failure in Coital Gratification

How do we determine whether or not an act of intercourse with orgasm has been satisfactory? The question is not rhetorical, even though it may be impossible to answer. Any experienced person can testify that not all coital orgasms are the same; and some may complain that, though they are potent or responsive, they are not enjoying sexual intercourse enough.

Enhancing coital gratification is an ancient quest, and we have described some ways in which it can be accomplished. As the only criterion is subjective experience, however, complaints cannot easily be evaluated as symptoms of sexual malfunctioning. Sometimes the problem is one of unrealistic expectations.

In the current preoccupation with sex and its exploitation for commercial purposes, some men and women have come to expect of every orgasm an earth-shaking experience. Ordinary and otherwise perfectly acceptable levels of gratification leave them disappointed. The only cure for this problem is to recognize that the body cannot necessarily deliver everything that the imagination calls for.

Sometimes orgasm is experienced with markedly diminished pleasure. The problem may be fear of experiencing strong emotion and resulting loss of emotional control. It is also possible that genuine neurophysiological disturbances may be present, even though we are as yet unable to identify them.

Causes of Sexual Malfunctioning

Sexual functioning is vulnerable to disruption from biological, psychological, and cultural causes. At least in theory the interaction of forces from all three areas can occur. In practice, however, we identify the disorder according to the dominant cause only. The causes of sexual malfunctioning can thus be subsumed under several categories: organic, psychogenic (intrapsychic or interpersonal), and cultural.

Organic Causes

Sexual inadequacy is known to arise from physical causes. In these instances psychological factors may contribute or be present as secondary reactions to the malfunction itself, but they are not the primary causes. Organic causes may be natural or pathological. A

prime example of the former is the aging process. Organic causes other than aging account for only a minority of instances of sexual malfunctioning.

The effect of aging on sexual function has recently become a topic of considerable interest as a result of more objective and enlightened views. The prevalent professional opinion is that older individuals are capable of far more satisfying sexual lives than they often realize or than society is willing to allow them, especially those who are institutionalized.

The effects of aging on the physiological aspects of the orgasmic response cycle were discussed in Chapter 3. The relationship between age and sexuality has also been examined. Our concern here will be to deal briefly with the impact of aging on the adequacy of sexual function.

By the time a man reaches middle age his sexual responses have undergone discernible changes. There is reduction in the frequency of orgasm and lengthening of the refractory period. Orgasm is also usually less intense. Psychological stimuli remain important but often insufficient to bring about erection without direct, physical stimulation.

Although there is considerable variation in this regard, middle-aged and older men who are still perfectly capable of sexual functioning find it more difficult to have successive orgasms. Masters and Johnson found that many among those over 50 were unable to attain erection for twelve to twenty-four hours following ejaculation. They also observed that if during extended foreplay the older man lost his erection, he was often unable to regain it for a while, just as if he had experienced orgasm.

Age-related changes in female sexual functions are more difficult to evaluate because of greater individual variation. The major physiological changes in adult women occur around the menopause. The anatomical changes and modifications in the sexual response cycle that follow were discussed in Chapters 3 and 4. Yet, in terms of sexual desire and responsiveness, middle-aged women do not generally show a decline. The depression and irritability that may occur in menopause will tend to decrease sexual interest, but this is an indirect effect.

Actually, on hormonal grounds one would expect an increase in erotic drive in middle-aged women because of the heightened effects of androgen due to the reduction of estrogen levels. On physiological grounds the natural course of events should produce an enhancement, not a reduction, of female sexuality in the postmenopausal woman, and this is in fact what many women experience. Furthermore, unlike men, elderly women do not lose their ability for multiple orgasmic response.

The biological effects of aging on sexual function are very real, but they do not tell the whole story. It is quite likely that more of the decline in sexuality in later life is due to psychological and socially generated reactions to aging than to the physical process of aging itself.

So far as we know, the majority of cases of sexual malfunction result from psychogenic and not organic causes. However, in a significant number of persons there may well be a physical basis underlying the sexual disorder. It is therefore essential that all cases of sexual malfunction (especially where pain is present) be seriously evaluated for the presence of organic illness by a physician.

There are a large number of medical conditions that can result in sexual disturbance. A detailed consideration of these conditions is impossible in the present context. We will therefore briefly consider some illustrative examples.

Sexual functions in both sexes can suffer as a result of chronic debilitating illnesses such as cancer, degenerative diseases, severe infections, or systemic disorders involving the renal, cardiovascular, and pulmonary systems. Certain liver diseases (for example, hepatitis, cirrhosis) and endocrine disorders (for example, hypothyroidism, hypopituitarism, diabetes) are also likely to interfere with sexual performance.

Diseases specifically affecting the genitalia will obviously cause problems. Among males

there are conditions that cause pain during intercourse (for example, inflammations, Peyronie's disease), interfere with penetration (for example, congenital anomalies), or affect testicular function (for example, estrogen-producing tumors). Among females there are even more common causes for pain during coitus (for example, inflammations, clitoral adhesions, deep pelvic infections, various forms of vaginitis, allergic reactions to deodorants).

Various surgical conditions that can be at fault include procedures that damage the genitals and their nerve supply (for example, some types of prostatectomy, lumbar sympathectomy). Castration will also often (but not always) result in loss of libido and impotence. Likewise, surgical procedures among women which damage the sexual organs (for example, obstetrical trauma, poorly repaired episiotomies) will often cause pain during coitus. Conditions that interfere with the blood supply to the genitals (for example, thrombosis) will also cause difficulty, among males in particular.

Finally, there are neurological disorders that may seriously influence sexual functions in both sexes. These include diseases of the frontal and temporal lobes of the brain (for example, tumor, epilepsy, vascular damage, trauma) or disturbances of the spinal cord (for example, congenital anomalies, degenerative conditions, trauma).

Drugs are another important source of sexual difficulty that could be subsumed under organic causes. One category of drugs with deleterious effects acts on the brain. These include sedatives, like alcohol and barbiturates, and narcotics, such as heroin, morphine, codeine, and methadone. The effects of these drugs are usually confined to the period of their use, but more permanent effects on sexual function are also possible.

Other drugs act peripherally—for example, by blocking the nervous impulses controlling the blood vessels and nerves of the genitalia. Anticholinergic drugs, such as atropine, may cause impotence by their effects on the parasympathetic nervous system, and antiadrenergic drugs interfere with the sympathetic system and cause ejaculatory problems.

The main thing to remember in this connection is that whenever a person is using a drug—any drug—and develops sexual problems, the drug must be evaluated as possible cause of the problem. This is especially true for tranquilizers and all other compounds that act on the central nervous system.

Intrapsychic Causes

The vast majority of sexual malfunctions in both sexes result from psychological problems, internal conflicts primarily related to past experiences. When these conflicts dominate a person's sex life to the extent that inadequate performance is the rule, then the causes can be considered primarily intrapsychic. On the other hand, when the sexual problem seems to be part of a larger conflict between two specific people, it is more convenient to label it interpersonal. This distinction, though arbitrary, has practical merit in treatment. Intrapsychic causes must be dealt with as such. As veterans of successive divorces discover, when marital partners change, the conflicts may remain the same. Interpersonal conflicts also ultimately result from intrapsychic problems, but the latter may be more circumscribed and require no special attention. Treatment may then be focused on the relationship between two individuals rather than on the individuals themselves.

The psychological causes of sexual malfunctioning are innumerable and not specific to types of disturbances. The same conflict may cause sexual apathy in one man, impotence in another, and premature ejaculation in a third. The same lack of specificity is characteristic of women.

It is generally agreed that anxiety and depression are detrimental to sexual functioning. But how such emotional disturbances are generated and what constitutes sufficient psychological cause are matters of controversy. It would be impossible to review here all the possible intrapsychic causes of sexual malfunctioning, even according to only one school of psychological thought. The following discussion therefore offers only a series of illustrations that may convey some idea of the range of significant intrapsychic problems.

First, it is important to distinguish between anxiety and depression in response to external reality and in response to no such apparent cause. The damaging effects of fear—of discovery, of pregnancy, of venereal disease, or of injury during rape—are obvious. Other fears may be more subtle. A woman visiting her family or in-laws may be uneasy or apprehensive about engaging in sex with her husband if there is any chance that they will be overheard. The same may be true of a man. Loss of sexual interest in response to personal or community tragedies, financial and other worries, sickness in the family, and so on, is also quite understandable.

Most sexual problems arising from reality factors tend to disappear when the problems are resolved or when the person adapts to them. Sometimes, however, sexual inadequacy outlasts the original cause and becomes entangled with other internal conflicts.

In most established patterns of malfunctioning, specific external causes are difficult to identify (and there are also many instances in which such circumstances cause no sexual disturbance). Some therapists attribute these disorders to the influence of forgotten events from the past operating as repressed conflicts or as faulty learning.

Learning theorists have proposed a variety of models to explain the genesis of sexual malfunctions. Central to many is the mechanism of conditioning, in which the effect associated with an experience determines one's future reactions to similar situations. Sometimes the antecedents of the experience are easy to trace. A sexually adequate man suffers a mild heart attack during coitus; thereafter the very thought of sex makes him anxious. Another man develops a prostate infection, and sexual intercourse becomes painful; gradually his sexual adequacy declines, even though his infection is cured and he experiences no further pain.

More often malfunctioning results from a

complex series of learning experiences. The transmission of certain sexual attitudes and values to children—like teaching that sex is dirty or dangerous—is one example. The adult may have forgotten specific or implied parental admonitions and punishments, but their damaging effects on his or her sexual performance persist.

Psychoanalysts offer extensive explanations of the intricate intrapsychic conflicts behind sexual malfunctioning. In contrast to the view that the key lies in faulty learning, psychoanalytic interpretations emphasize unconscious conflicts that influence behavior. For instance, conflicts arising from unresolved oedipal wishes may be major causes of difficulties in both sexes. Castration anxiety is a common explanation for failures of potency among males.

When a man's inadequacy applies to coitus with his wife but not with a prostitute, he may unconsciously be equating the former with his mother and therefore failing. Men who distinguish between "respectable" women (to be loved and respected) and "degraded" women (to be enjoyed sexually) are said to have a "madonna-prostitute complex."

The female counterpart to this conflict, according to psychoanalytic theory, involves the father. As all men or certain types of men (defined by marital status, body build, or any of innumerable other characteristics) may be unconsciously identified with the father, the result may be to avoid coitus with any man, or at least to feel no pleasure in it. When no emotional involvement occurs, the woman is less likely to feel guilty about her incestuous conflict.

Finally, there is the threat of loss of control. As orgasm implies a certain abandonment of self-control, some men and women fear that other dangerous impulses will also be released. At times this fear is experienced consciously as a fear that the vagina will be torn or that the penis will be "trapped" by the vagina (*penis captivus*). Usually the apprehension is vague, not even consciously felt; the man simply fails to have an erection; and the woman fails to reach orgasm.

Some sexual difficulties result from fundamentally nonsexual conflicts. Some people experience primitive fears, for instance, of being engulfed, of losing their boundaries as individuals. Sexual penetration and the feeling of dissolution during orgasm may evoke such fears and can therefore be exceedingly threatening.

Interpersonal Conflict

It takes two to make love. Apart from moral considerations, an irreducible minimum of affection and intimacy is required if any mutual gratification is to emanate from intercourse. Some people insist that anything short of deep love cheapens the act; others find this view utopian or naïve.

Interpersonal conflicts are extensions of intrapsychic problems, but sometimes the pathology takes the form of a particular type of relationship. There is no end to the kinds of interpersonal conflicts that interfere with sex. Some people even claim that the quality of sexual intercourse is the best indicator of the nature of the overall relationship.

Intense disappointment, muted hostility, or overt anger will obviously poison sexual interaction. Subtle insults are just as detrimental. Women, for instance, are quite sensitive about being "used." If a man seems to be interested predominantly in a woman's body and neglects her thoughts and feelings, she will feel that she is being degraded to the level of an inanimate object.

Some women associate coitus with being exploited, subjugated, and degraded. It is natural for a woman who feels this way to rebel by failing to respond.

Men and women have deeply ingrained needs for love and security that are often obtained through sex. But traditionally women have had much more at risk because of pregnancy in fulfilling these needs. Consequently, any male behavior before or during intercourse that even remotely implies unconcern and insensitivity may make a woman reluctant to respond, even though she deprives herself of pleasure as well.

The attitudes most detrimental to the male's enjoyment are lack of feminine response, nagging criticism, and open or covert derision. A man who feels overburdened by a dependent wife may also react negatively if her sexual requirements appear to be endless as well. Women have sometimes used sexual apathy vindictively, or have used it to obtain what they want. These weapons, though effective, are double-edged swords.

Cultural Causes

Even though the blessings and burdens of a culture are unevenly distributed among its people, no one is entirely exempt from cultural influences. But, though it would be foolish to deny the impact of prevalent sexual mores on individual functioning, particularly on the development of sexual attitudes in childhood, sweeping indictments of the mores of particular cultures are difficult to substantiate and reflect the absence of a true cross-cultural perspective.

In this country, for instance, a great deal has been made of the damaging effects of Victorian attitudes, especially on female sexuality. The demands and anxieties of the modern world and the hectic pace of living are also blamed for sapping men's virility.

There is currently a growing literature linking sexual problems among males to the more radical attitudes and demands of feminists. Although one encounters terms like "the new impotence" and "sexual suicide," referring to this phenomenon, these are as yet speculative notions. On the other hand, many female sexual problems may be caused by inconsiderate, selfish males who view women as mere bodies to ejaculate into and who do not care if the woman enjoys the sexual encounter.

Although the detrimental effects of such forces on sexual functioning may seem obvious enough to some people, it is nevertheless preferable to have more evidence before stating the causal relations categorically. What is most misleading is the common implication that at other times or in other places conditions have been better. Eastern cultures in particular are held up to us these days as models of sexual good sense. It is perhaps helpful to realize that the average Indian has never heard of the *Kama Sutra* and that knowledge of Persian love manuals is re-

stricted primarily to scholars of Islamic literature (many of whom happen to be Westerners). Nor have the Eastern peoples simply lost the precepts embodied in these works, for only an aristocratic minority ever had the opportunity to enjoy them.

Not that various doctrines have not warped Western sexual attitudes in the past and do not continue to do so at present. Our public attitudes toward sex are indeed often ignorant, bigoted, and hypocritical. Some people think that we have recently become tasteless and shameless as well.

Guilt certainly interferes with sexual functioning, but is guilt always and necessarily bad? Goethe at least did not think so. Once, when he attempted to make love to a willing maid at an inn, his potency failed him, and he wrote and told his wife about it, apparently grateful that he had been prevented from being unfaithful.

Nevertheless, those who mistake their sexual weaknesses for strength of moral fiber ought to be aware that neurotic conflicts may lurk behind their scruples. Religions may be sexually restrictive, but none frowns on sexual enjoyment under the proper circumstances. What sometimes appears as fear of God is simply plain old fear of sex.

In our progressively secular society it is claimed that shame is replacing guilt as the primary social inhibitor. Some people argue that in Western society the premium on competence and success, combined with an overemphasis on sex, creates a formidable hurdle to enjoyment. Orgasm becomes a challenge, rather than the natural climax of coitus. Inability to achieve it, or failure to reach a certain intensity, become not only signals of sexual incompetence but also reflections of personal inadequacy.

Ironically, as we become freer about sex, new problems are beginning to arise related to excessive demands for performance or pleasing the partner. These become linked to fear of failure and a tendency to be a spectator of one's own actions. Such attitudes greatly detract from the joy and spontaneity of sex, and may well cause all manner of sexual dysfunction in the future.

Sexual malfunctioning may be mild and transient or may present formidable challenges to treatment. The remedies for sexual inadequacies that can be treated range from fairly simple educational programs and self-help to highly specialized, intensive, lengthy therapy. Although, for purposes of clarity, we shall describe various methods of treatment as separate entities, in practice these approaches are deliberately and inadvertently combined. Our discussion is aimed at treatment methods that deal with sexual malfunction. Some of these methods, such as psychotherapy or behavior therapy, are also the primary means of treatment for those variations and deviations of sexual behavior that are considered problematic enough to require therapy (*see* Chapter 10).

Sex Education

Even though instruction should ideally precede and prevent the formation of erroneous sexual notions and warped attitudes, most of us do remain educable to the end of our lives. In the treatment of sexual malfunctioning, the educational approach has two main goals: imparting information and changing attitudes.

Information may consist of basic data on anatomy, sexual functioning, coital techniques, methods of enhancing pleasure, and other topics such as those presented in this book. Or it may consist of "do's" and "don'ts," as encountered in popular sex manuals. Provided such information is accurate and the advice based on it consistent with good sense, such sources can be quite useful. The rate at which popular books sell in this field is obviously one indication of the need for information of this sort.

Sometimes knowledge of even the simplest kind can be very helpful. Consider, for instance, a young and rather unexperienced couple. They are fond of each other, eager for sexual intercourse, but for some reason she does not respond with adequate vaginal lubrication during foreplay. He attempts intromission; she tenses up. He pushes harder; she complains or asks him to be gentle. (He thinks he is being gentle.) All that may be required in such a frustrating situation is the simple expedient of some artificial lubricant (preferably a water-based lubricant) or saliva.

Let us take a more complex situation. A married couple has enjoyed a satisfactory sexual life over many years. The man reaches middle age and is not as ardent and responsive as before. Whereas earlier the sight of his wife in bed was enough to arouse him, now it is not sufficient to elicit an erection. They both feel distressed, but being "reasonable" people they ascribe his problem to the "natural" effect of aging, and gradually abandon sex. If they are made aware of the fact that he is far from being finished sexually, but that at his age he requires more direct physical stimulation, then the problem may be resolved. Or in a comparable situation, the menopausal wife may convey to the husband the idea that her days as a sexually active person are over, without this actually being the case.

Some people feel that sex is a "natural" act and needs no instruction. In fact, there are those who do very well indeed without benefit of formal instruction, but they are fortunate enough to respond uninhibitedly, to communicate freely, to figure out what to do intuitively, to experiment, and to learn from experience. That is all well and good, but not everyone is like that. Therefore, the first approach to sexual problems must be the easiest; namely, some measure of sexual education.

Sexual Counseling

Education is part of any therapeutic program, whether or not it is labeled as such. But it may not be enough: Where the problem is attitudinal or characterological rather than one of mere ignorance, superficial exposure to information will usually be inadequate.

When sexual difficulties arise in a casual relationship, the most common remedy is simply to forget about the other person and look for a new partner. It is almost always married couples who come for joint assistance because of what is at stake in their relationship. Hence the term "marital counseling" is sometimes used instead of **sexual counseling.**

The counselor is most often a clinical psychologist or a psychiatric social worker. General practitioners and clergymen also do a great deal of sexual counseling, though they may call it something else. Psychiatrists and gynecologists often offer sexual advice to their patients, as divorce lawyers do to their clients. In addition—particularly in certain family-oriented cultures—older, respected members of the community may be called on for guidance. Although issues more general than sexual incompatibility may be involved, the sexual aspects of the relationship also come under scrutiny.

Systematic counseling involves much more than information and advice. The whole relationship between the couple becomes the focus of attention. The sexual histories of the individuals are examined. The genesis of the sexual incompatibility is carefully uncovered, and its corollaries are separated. As the partners come to understand the basis of their sexual difficulties, they may gradually gain control of the negative factors and make the necessary adjustments. When sexual difficulties are secondary to other conflicts, they may receive only brief attention, but otherwise they are a primary focus. It is important that the counselor make this distinction clear as early as possible so that everyone involved is working toward the same goal.

Perhaps the single most important key to the solution of interpersonal sexual difficulties is to prevent the bedroom from becoming a battleground. The couple must learn that, though the tendency to carry other conflicts into the sexual realm is very tempting, it must be resisted. When people feel angry and hurt, they naturally do not want to engage in sex; these feelings cannot be helped. But often one or the other partner deliberately and consciously retaliates by depriving the mate sexually or by simply going through the motions apathetically. This tactic is classic. Indeed, in cultures in which wives are to-

tally dependent on their husbands, it may be their only effective weapon against them. But otherwise there is less justification for its use.

In addition to the various types of therapy, several couples may be treated together in group therapy, in encounter groups, in marathons, and so on. To a great extent the value of such methods depends on the skills of the particular group leader and the motivations of the participants.

Psychotherapy

Broadly defined, psychotherapy includes all methods of psychological treatment that do not involve drugs or other physical means. There are many types of psychotherapy, involving differing theoretical assumptions and clinical techniques.

In **supportive psychotherapy** the aim is to provide patients with an opportunity to express themselves, to share their feelings, and to ventilate their resentments within a secure and positive relationship with the therapist. Although the patient may reveal a great deal, no effort is made to link this information with forgotten childhood experiences. Rather, the therapist concentrates on the current and the conscious. Therapists often come to represent a respected and loved figure to the patient, and are sometimes able to alleviate guilt, shame, and suffering merely by accepting the patient as he or she is. In this context a great deal of relearning can also occur.

In **insight-oriented psychotherapy,** the most intense form of which is **psychoanalysis,** the goals of treatment are much more ambitious. The sexual complaint is considered merely a symptom. Its elimination, though important, may be considered secondary to achieving basic understanding and reorganization of the personality structure.

Psychoanalysis involves intricate, detailed, and lengthy exploration and analysis of the patient's past, psychological defenses, repressed conflicts, dreams, and relationship with the analyst (transference) in order to help the patient gain insight into the unconscious roots of any conflicts and sexual symptoms.

Behavior Therapy

This approach is based on the principles of theories of learning and the concept of conditioning in particular. In **behavior therapy** sexual problems are not viewed as symptoms of illness but rather as the result of faulty learning and therefore subject to the same mechanisms that are involved in the learning of normal behavior. Traditionally, behavior therapy has been the province of psychologists, but currently increasing numbers of psychiatrists are also utilizing these methods.

The primary aim of behavior therapy is not insight but modification of behavior. This is done through a variety of techniques which include extinction, aversive learning, positive reinforcement, and imitation of models.

An important therapeutic approach is **desensitization,** which is based on the fact that certain emotional states are antithetical and mutually exclusive: One is not simultaneously sad and glad or relaxed and anxious. Thus, a person who is anxious in sexual situations, and therefore fails to perform adequately, can be helped if the anxiety is inhibited through relaxation.

To achieve this, anxiety-provoking stimuli for the person in question are listed hierarchically. The patient is then trained in the techniques of deep-muscle relaxation. Desensitization proceeds in this way: When the person is in a state of relaxation, he or she is asked to fantasize the least potent of the anxiety-provoking stimuli on the list. If the patient gets anxious, the therapist asks him or her to switch back to the relaxation routine. This procedure is repeated until the person can cope with the anxiety-provoking scene without discomfort. At this point the patient moves up to the next item on the list and the process is repeated. Eventually the patient is able to confront mentally the main problem situation without anxiety.

The expectation, which is often fulfilled, is that when the person attains mastery over the anxiety-provoking situation in thought or fantasy, this ability will transfer to real-life situations. The approach has been used a great deal and works best with phobias. It can be helpful in cases of vaginismus that involve a phobic element. Or a man who fears or is repulsed by the female genitals can be desensitized, thus eliminating one source of anxiety interfering with his sexual performance.

Techniques of behavior modification are often useful in and of themselves. They can also be helpful as part of a larger treatment program. For example, simply overcoming fear of female genitalia may not be enough to cure a patient such as in the example just given of his impotence, but as long as the patient has such fears, other approaches would be seriously handicapped.

Physical Therapies and Mechanical Aids

All the methods of treatment described so far are slow, complex, often expensive, and not always effective. It would be so much easier if sexual disorders could be dealt with by simple methods, but no such methods are yet generally available.

The treatment of physical defects and other organic causes of sexual malfunction is primarily a medical matter. Some of these problems (like pain from infections) are simple to treat, whereas others are incurable. In dealing with sexual disorders, sex hormones, except in rare instances, are useless. Aphrodisiacs and "nerve tonics" are generally worthless and may even be harmful.

Tranquilizers may be helpful in allaying overt anxiety, but they do nothing for the sexually unresponsive woman or for the man with erectile difficulties. Alcohol, in moderate amounts, may help to relieve anxiety and to loosen inhibitions, but beyond a certain limit even the most virile man will have trouble having an erection under its influence.

Many other physical and mechanical methods have been used with varying degrees of success. Men prone to premature ejaculation, for instance, sometimes use condoms to reduce the sensitivity of the glans, and thus to retard excitement and orgasm. An alternative is the application of a local-anesthetic ointment to the glans about half an hour or so before intercourse. These methods, however, may not help improve ejaculatory control. They can impair erotic pleasure and delay the onset of arousal but do not improve control once arousal is achieved. In fact, Kaplan says such methods may be antitherapeutic because the aim of treatment is not to delay arousal but to enable the patient to tolerate prolonged periods of intense pleasurable arousal before ejaculation.

Finally, there are extreme measures that provide men with mechanical supports so that they can achieve penetration: splints that can be attached to the penis to carry the flaccid organ into the vagina, or silicone prostheses can actually be implanted in the penis. These permit a couple to carry on a semblance of intercourse, and sometimes, after using splints, a man gains enough confidence and potency to dispense with artificial aids (they are therefore sometimes called "coitus-training apparatus").

A man who has lost his penis through trauma or surgery may have recourse to a penile prosthesis—actually a dildo—which he attaches. Before cringing at the thought of such devices, it is well to contemplate the despair of men in this type of predicament.

Orgasmically unresponsive women may be brought to orgasm with mechanical vibrators, or they may be encouraged to learn to masturbate to orgasm. Again, the hope is that once they become conditioned to experiencing orgasm, they will be able to transfer this ability to sexual intercourse.

Some years ago, the gynecologist A.H. Kegel devised a set of pelvic exercises to help patients control the leakage of urine that sometimes follows childbirth ("stress incontinence"). His patients spontaneously reported that their sexual functioning had also improved. These Kegel exercises are quite effective in strengthening the muscles around the vaginal orifice, thus facilitating orgasm. The simplest way for a woman to learn the exercises is first to identify the main muscle involved, by voluntarily interrupting the flow of urine a few times. The exercises consist simply of flexing this same muscle ten times in a row six times a day at the beginning, and working up to longer periods. The objective, as in all other forms of exercise, is to strengthen the muscles through repeated use.

A "timeless" remedy that combines many aspects of these various therapies is to put the sexually inadequate person in the hands of an experienced lover. Moral considerations aside, some men and women are driven to this alternative, first to find out whether or not the failures are really their own, and then perhaps to learn from the experience. The proverbial knowing woman who seduces the tremulous young man, and the older man who initiates the virgin are well-known literary and folk figures. Some sex therapists hire women who assist in the treatment of impotent men in this way.

The Reproductive Biology Research Foundation Program

The therapeutic approaches described so far have been used by many clinicians in a generally unsystematic fashion, and the results have been often poor or poorly evaluated. The first effort at developing a major treatment program for dealing with sexual inadequacy was initiated by Masters and Johnson at the Reproductive Biology Research Foundation. Their approach combines well-tried methods with certain novelties. It has the outstanding merits of brevity (two weeks) and generally good rates of success. The results have ranged from the spectacular (100 percent cure for vaginismus) to the somewhat disappointing (40 percent failure for primary impotence, which is most difficult to treat). This program is based on the conviction that there is no such thing as an uninvolved sexual partner. Treatment therefore always and necessarily involves a pair and never a single individual. Furthermore, a therapeutic team composed of a man and a woman conducts the treatment. The procedure requires that the problem couple move from home to live near the treatment center for the duration of the treatment under as pleasant and relaxed circumstances as possible.

The first step is to take a detailed history from each partner. Then the partners are instructed (never commanded) to explore a little at a time their latent erotic capabilities: to disrobe in the privacy of their bedroom, to caress and explore each other's bodies in a gentle and pleasurable manner. Gradually, over the two-week period, interactions become more intimate, and eventually they culminate in intercourse. These physical activities in private alternate with detailed discussion with the therapist team. Successes and failures are analyzed with candor, in a nonthreatening, nonjudgmental manner. Ultimate success comes when it does. There is no fixed schedule, no pressure to perform.

The key tasks are to convince the couple that sex is a natural function that requires no heroic effort, but only a relaxed, accepting attitude. No one is at fault, and there is no uninvolved partner. Each must learn to give, as well as to receive, to involve himself or herself in sex rather than to remain an observer. Orgasm will come in time; there is no need to seek it anxiously. These and similar

attitudes are conveyed, along with an objective, factual approach to the sex organs and their functions.

Within this psychological framework the problem couple is instructed in specific physical techniques. As was already indicated, the first task is to learn to stimulate the partner effectively, as well as to be able to respond to such stimulation. The use of lotions has been found very useful in this respect. Interestingly enough, those who were repelled by the use of such lotions (ordinary products like hand lotions) were more likely not to respond to treatment.

After the couple has become adept at general body stimulation, they gradually engage in active genital play. When the presenting problem is premature ejaculation, it is recommended that the woman sit comfortably and that the man lie on his back facing her. This position provides her with easy and full access to his genitals (*see* Figure 11.4). After appropriate stimulation, when the man achieves full erection and is about to ejacu-

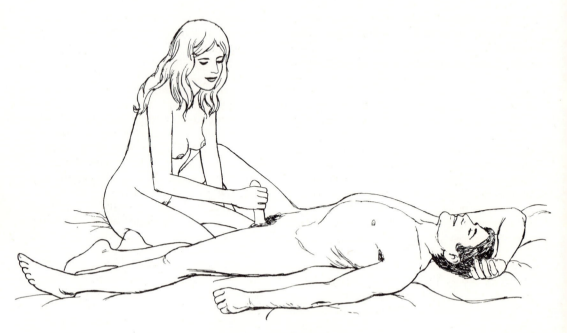

Figure 11.4   The training position for the treatment of male sexual dysfunction.

late, the woman holds the glans between her thumb and two fingers and squeezes it firmly for several seconds (*see* Figure 11.5). The woman then resumes genital stimulation, and the procedure is repeated. Gradually the man is able to maintain increasingly longer periods of erection. Next the woman straddles him and gently lowers herself onto his erect penis (*see* Figure 11.6). After penetration she remains motionless in order to minimize stimulation. If the man nevertheless feels the urge to ejaculate she withdraws and averts orgasm by the squeeze technique; then she reinserts the penis. By this method the man is able to maintain his erection intravaginally without premature ejaculation. The basic procedure in this approach was reported by Semans three decades ago, but hardly anyone took note of it until Masters and Johnson made it part of their overall therapeutic program.

The treatment for impotence follows the same general pattern. The first task is to bring the man to erection. He is encouraged

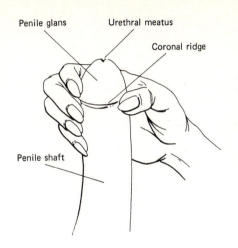

Figure 11.5 The "squeeze technique."

to communicate to the woman specifically what he finds arousing. When he has achieved erection the couple is discouraged from attempting coitus at first; instead, they continue to engage in relaxed and pleasurable

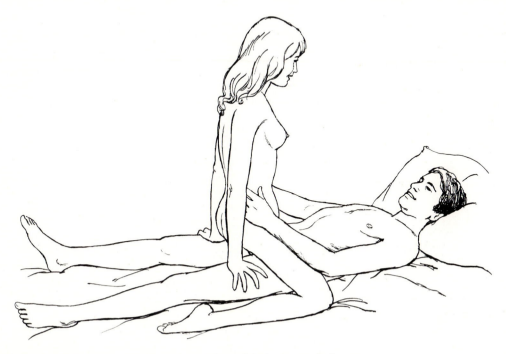

Figure 11.6 Coital position for the treatment of sexual dysfunction in both sexes.

foreplay. Only after sufficient confidence has been attained is penetration attempted in the same position described for treating premature ejaculation.

When the presenting symptom is orgasmic dysfunction or sexual unresponsiveness in the woman, the couple goes through the same preliminaries, but then the male becomes more active in stimulating his partner. A suitable position is with the man comfortably seated on the bed and the woman between his legs with her back turned to him, thus providing him with ready access to both her breasts and her genitals (*see* Figure 11.7). During coitus, however, the partners resume exactly the same approach as for male inadequacy. In both instances the woman takes the initiative and the more "active" role in coitus. The use of the lateral position for coitus is recommended after the female is comfortable having the penis inserted when she is in the female superior position.

Masters and Johnson are clinicians and not theorists. Therefore, they themselves have not offered explanations of how and why their approach works. Others can see in the Masters and Johnson procedure confirmation of their own theoretical tenets. For example, psychoanalysts may see in the kind and prestigious personalities of William Masters and Virginia Johnson parental figures listening with compassion, condoning the experience and expression of sexual pleasure, and through the transference relationship freeing people of their sexual blocks. Behavior therapists can just as easily point out that the procedures involved are clearly those of behavior modification.

The likelihood is that many of these elements do in fact contribute to the success of the Masters and Johnson approach. For practical purposes, what is more important is that this program can be fairly readily taught to other therapists. There are now many professional couples doing this type of work, and success rates are high in treating many forms of sexual dysfunction. If one is careful in selecting therapists (check their qualifications, references, and so on), there is a good chance that the therapy will be successful.

Figure 11.7   The training position for the treatment of female sexual dysfunction.

1. Numerous disorders and infections can affect the sex organs and sexual functioning. Gynecologists and urologists treat many of the disorders that have obvious physical causes. Regular cleaning of the genitals and related areas is one safeguard against infectious diseases. Psychologists, psychiatrists, and various types of counselors treat sexual malfunctions that appear to be the result of psychological conflicts.

2. The most common disorder of the female reproductive organs is leukorrhea, characterized by a whitish vaginal discharge. A yeastlike organism normally present in the vagina is another frequent cause of vaginal irritation and discharge. There is no male counterpart to leukorrhea. Urethral discharges in males are almost always the result of venereal disease.

3. Gonorrhea and syphilis are among the most common forms of venereal disease in the United States. Gonorrhea affects mucous-membrane tissue and is caused by an organism that survives only under living conditions provided by the human body. In males the usual site of infection is the urethra, and the primary symptom is a yellowish urethral discharge that appears within three to ten days after contraction of the disease. The infection usually causes a burning sensation during urination and itching sensations in the urethra. Most cases clear up with penicillin treatment, although a new strain of gonorrhea called super clap appears to be resistant to penicillin. In females the symptoms are less severe and may even be absent, but if left untreated the infection can spread to the pelvic organs, resulting in chronic inflammation of the uterine tubes.

4. Syphilis is a three-stage venereal disease that can eventually involve almost any organ or tissue of the body. It is transmitted only by intimate contact with another human being. During the first stage of the disease a chancre appears, usually on the external genitals, two to four weeks after the disease is contracted. The chancre disappears within several weeks, but if the disease goes untreated it develops into secondary syphilis, the major symptom of which is a generalized skin rash. After the secondary stage, all symptoms disappear, sometimes for years, but the disease organisms continue to burrow into various tissues and organs. The third-stage symptoms of syphilis can include heart failure, ruptured blood vessels, loss of muscular control and sense of balance, blindness, deafness, and severe mental disturbances. The disease can be fatal, but it can be effectively treated with penicillin even at the late stages. Because syphilis can be transmitted to a fetus through the placenta, blood tests to detect the disease are required before marriage and before the birth of a child.

5. Other venereal diseases include nongonococcal urethritis (NGU), a form of urethritis that may be even more prevalent than gonorrhea; chancroid, or soft chancre, which resembles the syphilis chancre but is more painful, tropical bubo, or LGV, which causes enlargement of the lymph glands in the groin, fever, chills, and headache, and is most common in the tropics; chronic venereal sore, which is characterized by lesions of the skin and mucous membranes of the genitalia; and viral infections, such as genital warts and herpes. For most of these diseases, though not for herpes (HSV-2), there are effective treatments.

6. Other conditions that can affect the genitals are pubic lice (crabs), cystitis, and cancer of the sex organs. Cancer of the breast is the most common form of cancer in women. Cancer of the cervix is the second most common form. Both have been linked, but not conclusively, with use of sex hormones. Cancer of the prostate is the most common form of cancer in men.

7. The primary problems of sexual malfunctioning in men are inability to achieve and sustain an erection and inability to delay ejaculation. For women the main difficulties are failure to reach orgasm and painful intercourse. The causes of these problems can be biological, psychological, or cultural, or they can be the result of an interaction of all three forces.

8. Organic causes of sexual malfunctioning can be natural (as in aging) or pathological. The most obvious effect of aging is a general slowing of sexual reactions. Although these effects are quite real, it is likely that the decline in sexuality in later life is due to psychological and social reactions to aging (many people don't expect older persons to be sexually active). In addition to natural causes, a number of medical conditions can interfere with sexual functioning. They range from chronic debilitating diseases to specific diseases of the genitalia to various surgical conditions, neurological disorders, and drug side effects.

9. The vast majority of sexual malfunctions in both sexes result from psychological problems and internal conflicts related to past experiences. When these conflicts interfere with sexual functioning they are said to be intrapsychic. When they stem from conflict between two people they are said to be interpersonal. The psychological causes of sexual malfunctioning are innumerable and not related to specific types of disturbances, but it is generally agreed that anxiety and depression can interfere with sexual performance.

10. The treatment of sexual inadequacies can range from fairly simple educational programs and self-help to highly specialized, intensive, lengthy therapy. The goals of sex education in such cases are to impart information and to change attitudes. When education is not sufficient, counseling by specialists may be called for.

11. There are many types of psychotherapy that are supplied to sexual problems, including supportive therapy and insight-oriented therapy. The therapist's aim in supportive therapy is to alleviate guilt, shame, and suffering by accepting the patient as he or she is. In insight-oriented therapy, or psychoanalysis, the sexual complaint is considered merely a symptom of a more deep-rooted problem. The goal of this therapy is to achieve a basic understanding of the personality and the cause of the symptom.

12.   The primary aim of behavior therapy is not insight but modification of one's behavior, which is achieved through a variety of techniques. A patient who is anxious in sexual situations, for example, might go through training to gradually learn to relax in sexual situations. If the training is successful in the therapeutic setting, patients often are able to transfer the ability to relax to real-life situations.

13.   The first systematic effort to develop a major treatment program to deal with sexual inadequacy was started by Masters and Johnson. Their approach combines old and new methods in a two-week therapy course that has had considerable success. A therapy team, composed of a man and a woman, conducts the therapy. Their key task is to convince the patients that sex is a natural function which requires no heroic effort, only a relaxed, accepting attitude.

SUGGESTED READING

Venereal Disease

Chiappa, J. A., and Forish, J. J. *The V. D. Book.* New York: Holt, Rinehart and Winston, 1976.
A concise book about all of the common forms of venereal disease. It is written in nontechnical language and can be easily understood with no background in medical terminology required.

Millar, J. D. *Epidemic Venereal Disease: Proceedings of the Second International Symposium on Venereal Disease.* St. Louis: American Social Health Association and Pfizer Laboratories Division, Pfizer, Inc., 1972.
A collection of somewhat technical research papers on various aspects of venereal disease in the United States and other countries.

Brown, W. J., *et al. Syphilis and Other Venereal Diseases.* Cambridge, Mass.: Harvard University Press, 1970.
A medical textbook on venereal disease.

Sexual Malfunction

Masters, W. H., and Johnson, V. E. *Human Sexual Inadequacy.* Boston: Little Brown, 1970.
The major work and original source of much of modern sex therapy. Fairly technical. For an abbreviated and simplified popularization of this work, see Belliveau, F. and Richter, L. *Understanding Human Sexual Inadequacy.* New York: Bantam, 1970.

Kaplan, H. S. *The New Sex Therapy.* New York: Brunner Mazel, 1974.
A comprehensive presentation of the causes, manifestations, and treatment of sexual disfunction.

LoPiccolo, J. and LoPiccolo, L. (Eds.). *Handbook of Sex Therapy.* New York: Plenum Press, 1978.
Contributions by a group of experts covering a broad range of therapeutic approaches to the treatment of sexual malfunction.

CHAPTER 12 SEX, MORALITY, AND THE LAW

Did You Know That . . .

until about 100 years ago some philosophers of the Catholic Church taught that abortion was permissible until the fortieth or eightieth day of pregnancy?

during the Victorian era the spillage of semen— even by married men—was considered a grievous and potentially lethal waste of a vital substance?

sexual intercourse between consenting, unmarried adults in private is considered a crime in most states?

almost all sexual activity that may occur between a husband and wife—except for kissing, caressing, and vaginal intercourse—is defined as criminal behavior in most states?

homosexuality as such is legal, but many sexual acts performed between members of the same sex are defined as criminal?

INTRODUCTION

Throughout this book we have confined ourselves mainly to discussions of such things as the structure and function of the sex organs and descriptions of how people behave sexually. Now we turn to the equally important questions of sexual morality and legality: How *should* people behave sexually? How do federal and state laws relate to sexual behavior? It is one thing to discuss how a contraceptive method works but quite another to consider whether or not one should use contraception or whether or not its use should be limited to those who are married, whose lives would be endangered by pregnancy or childbirth, or who already have "too many" children. Morality involves value judgments and questions of right and wrong that must be answered by every thinking person. Legality has to do with the state's formalized attempt to decide questions of right and wrong. Both morality and legality influence our sexual behavior in important ways.

In this chapter we will examine the historical development of Jewish and Christian ethics and how they bear on sexual and related behavior. Then we will provide an overview of laws governing sexual behavior in the United States. It is not our aim to support one set of values over another but rather to describe the kind of reasoning that results in development of a widely held moral principle.

THE HISTORY OF WESTERN SEXUAL MORALITY

The Jewish Tradition

Attitudes toward Marriage and Family

A high regard for marriage and children is a prominent theme in early Hebraic teachings. In particular, the notion that procreation is a primary obligation of human beings is fundamental to the Old Testament and the Talmud, and this notion has been preserved

to the present day by the Roman Catholic Church. Probably no other single doctrine has had as great an effect on sexual behavior as has the doctrine that the purpose of sex and marriage is reproduction. In the very first chapter of the first book of the Old Testament it is written:

So God created man in his own image, in the image of God he created him; male and female he created them. And God blessed them, and God said to them, "Be fruitful and multiply, and fill the earth and subdue it; and have dominion over the fish of the sea and over the birds of the air and over every living thing that moves upon the earth."

The belief among the ancient Jews that they in particular should multiply in order to propagate God's chosen people is repeatedly mentioned in the Old Testament. For example, God tells Abraham, "I will indeed bless you, and I will multiply your descendants as the stars of the heavens and as the sand which is on the seashore." Similar promises were made to Abraham's son Isaac and to Isaac's son Jacob.

The Talmud stresses the religious obligation to marry and to raise a family. The unmarried person was at best pitied, and for a man to remain single indefinitely was considered unnatural and immoral. A Jewish woman was expected to bear children, and, indeed, if she failed to do so after ten years of marriage she could be divorced on those grounds alone. Furthermore, a man had an obligation to see that the family name was carried on.

Marriage was to be entered into early but not lightly. Eighteen was the recommended age for males, shortly after age 12 (at which age minority status ended) for girls. Jews had a particularly high regard for the institution of marriage (and still do, if judged by the low divorce rate among Jews compared to that among adherents of other faiths, especially

Protestants). They were encouraged to be cautious and to give a great deal of thought to the selection of marriage partners. In contrast to the prearranged marriages, often with partners never seen as in some Oriental cultures, rabbinic law stated: "A man is forbidden to take a woman to wife without having first seen her, lest he afterwards perceive in her something objectionable and she becomes repulsive to him." Furthermore, marriages were believed to be divinely arranged and sanctioned.

The Jews were apparently very supportive of newlyweds and favored a sort of extended honeymoon. "When a man is newly married, he shall not go out with the army or be charged with any business; he shall be free at home one year, to be happy with his wife whom he has taken."

Attitudes toward Women

Although Jewish women were accorded great respect in their roles as wives and mothers, males had the upper hand in property rights and divorce. A woman could be divorced by her husband without her consent on the grounds that he found something "unseemly" or "indecent" about her, but a woman could not divorce her husband without his consent. There was a division of opinion on the interpretation of this law, and by the first century A.D. there were two fully developed schools of thought. The School of Shammai took the view that the law applied only in instances of adultery by the woman, but the School of Hillel took a much broader view, which encompassed such grounds as poor cooking and less beauty than that of another woman. Gradually, however, Jewish women were accorded equal rights under Jewish law regarding divorce and property ownership.

Boys were clearly preferred to girls as offspring, but feelings of tenderness and responsibility toward all children prevailed, as did a belief that all children were truly gifts from God.

Rules Governing Sexual Morality

Sexual behavior was strictly regulated by Jewish laws, and the penalties for infractions could be quite severe. Adultery, incest, homosexuality, and bestiality were forbidden, and punishments ranged from social ostracism to death. The early Jews were absolutely opposed to abortion and considered it an abomination. Contraceptive practices were totally forbidden for men and generally for women as well, though some exceptions were made for the latter: "A minor lest pregnancy prove fatal, a pregnant woman lest abortion result, and a nursing mother lest she becomes pregnant and prematurely wean the child so that it dies."

There seemed to be a very positive feeling among Jews about sexual intercourse, within the confines of marriage at least, which contrasts rather sharply with the attitude prevalent in the early Christian Church. This is the attitude that sex as such is intrinsically evil and tinged with guilt, and it has persisted to some extent until very recent times.

The Christian Tradition

Origins

Jesus and his twelve disciples were all Jewish, so it might seem reasonable to assume that Jewish sexual traditions were largely shared by them. But because Jesus radically departed from some of the major religious tenets and practices of his contemporaries, we cannot carry this assumption very far. We shall restrict ourselves to inferences from the biblical record.

Jesus was chaste and celibate, yet he did not shun the company of women from any walk of life, even in a culture in which heterosexual contacts were more or less restricted to members of one's own family. Because of the special circumstances of his life, we cannot assume that he necessarily intended his celibate existence to serve as a model, nor did he ever indicate that he meant it so.

What did Jesus say about sex specifically? We have only a fragmentary record of his teachings, and there is relatively little on this subject. His most restrictive statements are those in the Sermon on the Mount:

You have heard that it was said, "You shall not commit adultery." But I say to you that every one who looks at a woman lustfully has already committed adultery with her in his heart. If your right eye causes you to sin, pluck it out and throw it away: it is better that you lose one of your members than that your whole body be thrown into hell. And if your right hand causes you to sin, cut it off and throw it away: it is better that you lose one of your members than that your whole body go into hell.

What did Jesus actually mean by these remarks? It is highly unlikely that he was suggesting that one literally blind oneself rather than cast adulterous glances. Such a prescription simply does not fit the overall context and meaning of his sayings. Earlier in the same sermon Jesus equally condemned the nursing of anger, but surely no human being can avoid feeling angry at one time or another. Therefore it may be that Jesus was using these examples not as actual standards of behavior but rather as illustrations of how wretched and helpless human beings are apart from God. A minor yet significant point is that Jesus was speaking in a language and idiom that happen to be rich in metaphor.

As far as we know, Jesus made no statements extolling the virtues of sex. In view of the fragmentary record, however, such negative evidence is inconclusive. He did deal with a woman caught in adultery (the Mosaic penalty for which was death by stoning), and he said to her accusers: "He that is without sin among you, let him first cast a stone at her." Jesus was criticized by his pious detractors for consorting with sinners, including prostitutes, yet it is interesting that none of the three great temptations of Jesus was related to sex.

From this fragmentary record theologians, as well as other believers and nonbelievers, have reached any number of conclusions, casting Jesus in roles ranging from stern ascetic to proponent of free love to "Jesus Christ Superstar."

Christianity was based on the teachings of Jesus, but did not limit itself to them. Even in the early Church a variety of interpretations and points of view on all matters began to be incorporated into Christian doctrine.

Greek and Roman Influences

285

Sex,
Morality,
and the
Law

Very early in the history of the Church (the first century A.D.), and particularly under the influence of St. Peter and St. Paul, gentiles (non-Jews, especially Greeks and Romans) were incorporated into the Church. They brought with them the thinking of Greek and Roman culture about sexuality and morality. On one basic premise the Greeks, Romans, and Jews were agreed, however: that the purpose of marriage was to produce legitimate offspring (the Greeks and Romans on behalf of the state, the Jews on behalf of God).

Both the Greeks and the Romans held women to be inferior and subservient to men. In the early days of the Roman Empire women were treated with perhaps more respect than Greek women had been, but they remained subservient and dependent on their fathers until they married, after which time they were legally subject to their husbands. By the second century A.D. a gradual lessening of the husband's authority over his wife had occurred, but, rather than improving the quality of married life, it seems simply to have reflected the general breakdown of social life during the period just before the ultimate downfall of the Empire. Divorce rates and hedonism greatly increased, and family life degenerated. Abortion was practiced by both Greeks and Romans, especially the upper classes, and in both cultures the double standard was traditional. Men participated in extramarital sexual liaisons (both heterosexual and homosexual, especially among the Greeks), and prostitution was condoned.

Although hedonism prevailed in the gentile world at the time of Christ (at least in the large cities of Greece and Rome; the outlying provinces tended to be more conservative) there were schools of thought that condemned the common sexual practices of the time and extolled the virtues of asceticism. Particularly in Greece, the Cynics and the Stoics alike tended to renounce the world—including material possessions and marital and sexual relationships—in favor of purity (poverty and chastity, according to some). This ascetic tradition, rather than the hedonistic one, was quite influential in the thinking of the early Christians, as we shall see.

The Teachings of St. Paul

St. Paul was the first important Christian teacher on issues of sexual behavior. As discussed earlier, Jesus himself had had relatively little to say on such issues, although we have the distinct impression that he was quite understanding toward those who had been condemned or ostracized for offenses like adultery and prostitution. St. Paul, on the other hand, appears to have considered marriage and sexuality inferior to chastity and celibacy. Defenders of St. Paul point out that he wrote in the belief that the world would end within his lifetime. If the Kingdom of God was at hand, why worry about marriage and family when one should be preparing for the end? Nevertheless, for whatever reasons, St. Paul clearly elevated the single, celibate state to a status of greater purity than that of the married or sexually active state. This elavation was the beginning of a tradition that became influential in Christian thought over the centuries. St. Paul saw marriage as a relationship to be entered into in order to avoid the sin of fornication, and thus appropriate only for those too morally weak to resist venereal temptations. In one of his best-known statements on this subject he said: "To the unmarried and the widows I say that it is well for them to remain single as I do. But if they cannot exercise self-control, they should marry. For it is better to marry than to be aflame with passion."

Regardless of St. Paul's motives, the important point is that he provided a basis for future elaboration of the notion that sex is to be avoided, that abstaining from sexual activity *of any kind* leads to a higher moral state, and that marriage is a concession to the body that should be made only by those deficient in will power. St. Paul suggested that celibacy is not only more pleasing to God but also less anxiety-provoking:

I want you to be free from anxieties. The unmarried man is anxious about the affairs of the Lord, how to please the Lord; but the mar-

ried man is anxious about worldly affairs, how to please his wife, and his interests are divided.

St. Paul advised those who did marry: "Wives be subject to your husbands, as to the Lord. For the husband is the head of the wife as Christ is the head of the Church. . . . Husbands, love your wives, as Christ loved the Church."

The Patristic Period of the Church: St. Augustine

Theologians call the several centuries following the time of St. Paul and extending through the fall of the Roman Empire the patristic age because in that period formulation of the doctrines of the new religion was dominated by a small group of men who are known as the Fathers of the Church. Included in this group were St. Ambrose, St. Jerome, and St. Gregory (the Great), but the one who most influenced Christian doctrine on human sexuality was St. Augustine.

St. Augustine's personal struggle with his own sexual nature is recorded in his *Confessions.* In brief he had "sowed his wild oats" during the first thirty years of his life; then he had been converted to Christianity and had, in effect, renounced all sexual activity. We find a similar pattern in the lives of St. Jerome and the theologian Tertullian, but the contrast between "before" and "after" is not nearly as striking as in the life of St. Augustine. He was born in A.D. 354 of a Christian mother and a non-Christian father. While still a minor he fathered a child and began a thirteen-year sexual liaison with the mother of his son Adeodatus ("by God given"). During this time Augustine was involved in turn with Manichaeanism (which took a dim view of marriage and even of sexual intercourse), then with Skepticism, and, just before his conversion to Christianity, with Neo-Platonism. Having reached the conclusion that he could not successfully control his own sexual desires, St. Augustine decided to enter a legitimate marriage, and his mistress of many years was exiled to Africa in order to avoid complications. Even while betrothed and awaiting his marriage, however, he found himself taking another mistress to satisfy what seemed to him base but uncontrollable instincts. His conflict during this period is reflected in the oft-repeated prayer of his younger years: "Give me chastity—but not yet."

The turning point in St. Augustine's life came in his thirty-second year, when he read the writing of St. Paul, which convinced him that the highest calling in life was celibacy and total abstinence from sexual activity. He broke his engagement, renounced his mistresses, and was baptized into the Christian Church, much to the delight of his mother with whom he had been living.

Following his conversion, St. Augustine quickly became an influential member and ultimately a bishop of the Roman Catholic Church. Later in his life, beginning three years after Rome had been sacked by the Vandals in A.D. 410, St. Augustine spent thirteen years writing his monumental *The City of God.* Whereas his autobiographical *Confessions,* in the words of Lord Byron, "make the reader envy his transgressions," St. Augustine associates guilt rather than pleasure with sexuality in *The City of God.* He acknowledges that coitus is essential to the propagation of humanity, but argues that the act itself is tainted with guilt because of the sin of Adam and Eve. Sexual intercourse was thus transformed from something pure and innocent to something shameful—"lust" —by the original sin of Adam and Eve, which was passed on from generation to generation.

If lust is involved in all sexual acts because of Original Sin, it follows that chastity is a higher moral state than is marriage—and is certainly a prerequisite for priests and nuns. This view is being seriously questioned today by certain members of the Roman Catholic Church, as it was by Martin Luther during the Reformation. St. Paul had viewed the married state as inferior to celibacy on the grounds that it was distracting for those who truly wanted to dedicate themselves to God, but St. Augustine went a step farther and labeled intercourse, even within marriage, as sinful. Although he recognized that the act of copulation is essential for procreation—the subject of a divine commandment—he believed that the behavior and emotions that accompany intercourse make it shameful. Such behavior and emotions he took to be signs of human degradation since the Fall. Although one could minimize the sinfulness of coitus by performing it only as part of fulfilling one's *duty* to have children, one could not totally ignore the fact that a child conceived under these circumstances is the product of an act of sexual lust. Hence the need for infant baptism in order to wash away the guilt of lust as well as of Original Sin. The fact that an aborted fetus usually dies before it can be baptized and is therefore condemned was at one time a major argument against abortion.

The Middle Ages: St. Thomas Aquinas

The early centuries of the medieval period were the Dark Ages as far as significant new thoughts about sexual ethics are concerned. But as the Church ultimately assumed jurisdiction over marriage and divorce, previously a function of civil authorities, there ensued a lengthy controversy over the conditions, if any, under which divorce and remarriage could be allowed. Church authorities in Rome held that a lawful, consummated marriage could not be dissolved under any circumstances. Elsewhere, particularly in England, divorce was allowed to Roman Catholics for adultery, and remarriage was allowed when a husband had died or was presumed dead in battle.

By the twelfth century, however, the Roman Catholic Church had clarified and consolidated the official view that it still takes today—that marriages are final. There were a few loopholes, however. A Christian spouse could obtain a divorce from a non-Christian on the grounds that the latter would not convert: the so-called Pauline privilege, based on St. Paul's statement, "If the unbelieving partner desires to separate, let it be so, in such cases the brother or sister is not bound." Also, in practice, marriages outside the Church did not have quite the same binding force as did marriages performed within the Church. Another loophole involved "consummation" of the marriage; that is, sexual intercourse. Although a marriage was formed by mutual consent as expressed in the marriage vows, it did not become indissoluble until the couple had had intercourse. Consequently, if both parties wanted "out" of a Roman Catholic marriage they could (and still can) seek an annulment on grounds that it had never been "consummated."

By far the most influential writer in the Church during the Middle Ages was the thirteenth-century scholar and theologian St. Thomas Aquinas. An unusually systematic thinker and author, Aquinas spelled out the position of the Roman Catholic Church on questions of sex and morality in such minute detail that essentially nothing new has had to be added since. There is virtually no form of sexual behavior to which Aquinas did not address himself. In his massive work *Summa Theologica* he has included dissertations on touching, kissing, fondling, seduction, intercourse, adultery, fornication, marriage, virginity, homosexuality, incest, rape, bestiality, prostitution, and related topics.

Some of Aquinas' arguments are quite compatible with modern professional thinking. Consider, for instance, the argument against coitus by an unmarried couple. In essence, Aquinas argued that offspring should have both mother and father for optimal upbringing and that, as fornication involves the possibility that a child will be born without defined parents to care for it, fornication is morally wrong *because of the potential deleterious effects upon the child* who may be conceived. Many recent studies have shown higher rates of juvenile delinquency, emotional disturbance, and suicide among young people who have grown up in "broken homes"; that is, in homes from which one or both parents are absent because of divorce, death, separation, or other reasons.

One might think that the current availability of reliable contraceptives would have nullified the argument against fornication, but the Catholic Church has remained firmly opposed to all forms of birth control (except the "rhythm method"). Pope Paul VI, in 1968, addressed this issue with the following admonitions:

Not much experience is needed in order to know human weakness, and to understand that men—especially the young, who are so vulnerable on this point—have need of encouragement to be faithful to the moral law, so that they must not be offered some easy means of eluding its observance. It is also to be feared that the man, growing used to the employment of anticonceptive practices, may finally lose respect for the woman and, no longer caring for her physical and psychological equilibrium, may come to the point of considering her as a mere instrument of selfish enjoyment, and no longer as his respected and beloved companion.

This position was reaffirmed in 1976. In a document called a "Declaration on Certain Questions Concerning Sexual Ethics," prepared under a mandate from Pope Paul VI, it was stated that all forms of premarital sex, homosexual activity, and masturbation are contrary to Church teaching.

The question of abortion was also addressed by Aquinas. From the earliest days of the Catholic Church abortion at any stage of pregnancy was equated with murder. But Aquinas and other Church philosophers of the Middle Ages held that abortion was permissible in the early stages of pregnancy. Aquinas reasoned that the fetus was not "formed" and was not "infused" with a soul until the time of quickening—around the end of the fifth month of pregnancy. Others argued that the fetus was fully formed by the fortieth or eightieth day of pregnancy, and only abortions performed after that time were murder. In 1588, Pope Sixtus V declared that all abortions were a form of murder, but in 1591, Pope Gregory XVI reversed that and allowed abortions up to the fortieth day. That position held until about 100 years ago. In 1869, Pope Pius IX again declared that abortion at any stage is murder—a position that is still held today by the Catholic Church, with two exceptions. Abortions are allowed by the Catholic Church in the case of an ectopic pregnancy and when the pregnant woman has cancer of the uterus. The justification in these situations is that an operation performed to save the life of the pregnant woman is morally correct because the death of the fetus is an unintended, unavoidable, indirect result of the procedure.

Attempts to suppress sexual activity have not been entirely negative in their approach. Throughout the Middle Ages a positive virtue was ascribed to chastity; that is, total abstinence from sexual activity. The chaste person was often characterized as happy, content, and someone to be envied rather than pitied. It is somewhat difficult to appreciate today how widespread this view has been for many centuries, not only in the Christian world but also in other developed cultures and in some primitive societies. The glorification of virginity, as in the cult of the Virgin Mary, was long a popular subject for both secular and religious writers.

Havelock Ellis has written an interesting history of the "chastity movement" during the Christian era from the beginnings of the Church to the twentieth century. Ellis has pointed out that the romantic aspects of chastity were not as mysterious as might appear at first glance—underlying this movement was an element of female protest against subjugation in the traditional marriage arrangements of the times. He has noted that chastity was advocated not simply as a source of rewards after death or "because the virgin who devotes herself to it secures in Christ an ever-young lover," but also because "its chief charm is represented as lying in its own joy and freedom and the security it involves from all the troubles, inconveniences, and bondages of matrimony."

The Reformation

Ellis has perhaps exaggerated somewhat in his statement that "the Reformation movement was in considerable part a revolt against compulsory celibacy." Nevertheless, both Luther and Calvin, from the earliest stages of their revolt within the Church, attacked the prevailing notions of chastity, celibacy, and marriage. One of Calvin's arguments sounds not at all dissimilar to those being put forward by certain Roman Catholic priests today:

Both under the apostles, and for several ages after, bishops were at liberty to have wives: that the apostles themselves, and other pastors of primitive authority who succeeded them, had no difficulty in using this liberty, and that the example of the primitive Church ought justly to have more weight than allow us to think that what was then received and used with commendation is either illicit or unbecoming.

Luther's arguments against celibacy were somewhat different from those of Calvin. Luther seems to have drawn from his own emotional experiences in formulating his doctrines, as had St. Augustine. Luther's childhood in Germany had been filled with visions of demons and witches and with severe beatings for the most minor offenses. In 1505, caught in a terrible thunderstorm, he vowed to St. Ann that he would become a monk if his life were spared. He entered an Augustinian monastery and reflected on his sins. But, in contrast to St. Augustine, he came to the conclusion that the desires of the flesh could be neither conquered nor atoned for by good works, penances, and the like. On the specific issue of celibacy Luther argued, in the style of Aristotle and Aquinas, that celibacy is not a natural state and, indeed, that those who are prone to practice it are inclined to be peculiar. Luther viewed marriage not only as normal but also as a secular arrangement that should fall under the jurisdiction of civil authorities rather than of the Church. Luther himself set an example by being married in his home rather than in a church. He felt strongly that marriage is not a specifically Christian sacrament but rather an institution established long before the founding of the Christian Church. Although this notion ultimately led to more flexible divorce laws in Protestant countries, Luther himself did not condone divorce and remarriage except in instances of adultery or "desertion" (the latter term came to be interpreted more and more broadly with time).

The Reformers were influential not only in elevating the status of marriage but also to some extent in removing the onus of sin from sexual intercourse. Calvin departed farther from tradition than did Luther. Whereas Luther viewed the sexual appetite as natural, on the order of hunger and thirst, he still shared some of St. Augustine's feeling that sexual behavior has a certain intrinsic shamefulness. Calvin, on the other hand, viewed sex as something holy and honorable, at least within the confines of marriage. He also challenged the long-standing notion that the purpose of marriage is procreation and put forth the idea that marriage should be a social relationship, in which the wife provides companionship for her husband rather than serving simply as the mother of his children and as a source of relief for his sexual tensions. Nevertheless, both Luther and Calvin held the notion that women should be subject to male authority, within both marriage and the Church. Underlying this teaching was a belief that women are the inferior of the two sexes. This was hardly a uniquely Christian, or even religious, doctrine. It is seen in Aristotle's description of women as "deficient males" and various other secular writings that preceded the Christian religion.

The Reformation was an extraordinary challenge to established belief and traditions. Yet exceedingly important changes were actually being brought about throughout the Renaissance as well. This transitional period between medieval and modern times began in Italy in the fourteenth century, spread to other parts of Europe, and continued into the seventeenth century. It was characterized by the revival of classical influences and humanistic attitudes, expressed through an unprecedented outpouring of the arts and literature. Medieval asceticism was rejected in favor of full expressions of romantic and physical love, and the human body was glorified. It was also a period of considerable confusion in sexual morals and of sharp contrasts even in the behavior of the popes. Alexander VI (1492–1503), for example, was well known for his worldly interests and illegitimate children. Yet fifty years later Pope Paul IV judged Michelangelo's nude frescoes in the Sistine Chapel indecent and had clothes painted over the figures in the *Last Judgment*.

It would be impossible to trace here all further developments of sexual morality during succeeding centuries. However, two movements will be discussed briefly because of their direct bearing on present-day beliefs.

Puritanism

The Puritan movement for religious reform began early in the reign of Queen Elizabeth of England in the sixteenth century. Calvinist in theology, the early Puritans felt that the Church of England was too political and too Catholic. During the intermittent periods of persecution throughout the next two centuries large numbers of Puritans emigrated to New England in search of religious freedom.

To the Puritan, the human race was by nature weak and sinful and therefore in need of constant self-examination, unremitting self-discipline, and hard work. The Puritan sexual ethic, although severe and uncompromising, was primarily concerned with regulating behavior that threatened the stability of the family unit. Apart from their biblical faith, as newcomers to a harsh land the Puritans were concerned with survival, and protecting the integrity of the family as the basic social unit was felt to be vital to that end. Therefore, the Puritans were unforgiving of adulterers and quite concerned about sex that might lead to the birth of illegitimate children.

In their eagerness to discourage sexual laxity the Puritans imposed rigid codes of dress and behavior. Activities appealing to the senses were frowned upon. Women accused of witchcraft or of partaking in sexual orgies with Satan faced torture and sometimes death. However, despite these excesses, sexual activity within marriage was not strictly regulated. The Puritans were therefore not "antisexual" in principle but rather were opposed to sexual behavior outside the bonds they believed to have been ordained by God and society.

The Victorian Era

The reign of another English queen, Alexandrina Victoria (1819–1901), is referred to as the Victorian period. During the two centuries separating the reign of Victoria from that of Elizabeth important changes seem to have taken place in sexual attitudes. For instance, whereas the Puritans were content with restricting sex to marriage, Victorians attempted to restrict sexual behavior within marriage as well. Even the stated basis for the restrictions had changed. The Puritans were concerned with piety: Adultery was a sin against God and a violation of community trust. The Victorians were concerned with "character," health, and how best to harness sex and rechannel it to loftier ends.

How did this remarkable change come about? Since Victorian society was considerably more secular than Puritan communities, religion can hardly be responsible for it. There is some evidence that the more indiscriminate antisexuality within Victorian morality was based on the erroneous medical and scientific beliefs of the time.

Victorian sexual ideology revolved around a theory in which semen was viewed as a vital substance and its spillage a grievous and potentially lethal waste. In principle, it mattered little if a man ejaculated into his wife or into some other woman, although procreative necessities required that some concessions be made in this regard.

This semen theory did not originate in the Victorian period. Such notions were current long before the nineteenth century. But from this starting point Victorian morality evolved into a code of sexual behavior as well as a theory of human sexuality. In this scheme, men were the sexual beings who victimized women and were in turn victimized by them. In the first instance, men imposed their "beastly" sexual urges on innocent women who were "pure," asexual beings. In the second case sexually provocative women lured men into wasting their seed. A "moral" man abstained from sex outside marriage and was highly selective and considerate in sexual expression within marriage. "Moral" women endured these sporadic ordeals and did nothing to encourage them. Pleasure was not an appropriate goal for either sex, but especially not for women.

So far as noncoital sex was concerned, the ideas of Victorian morality should be predictable. Since these acts served no procreative purpose, they were without any redeeming value whatsoever. Masturbation was particularly bad since it involved the young and, being unrestrained by the need for a partner, most readily led to excessive indulgence.

The semen theory of human sexuality has not been entirely abandoned, even today. It is impossible to say, however, to what extent such attitudes rule people's sexual lives. Even during the Victorian period countless thousands undoubtedly paid no heed. Some people today see the shadow of "Puritanism" or "Victorianism" behind any attempt to regulate private or public sexual behavior. Others pine for bygone days when men were gentlemen, women "pure," and so on, with total disregard for the realities of those periods.

Modern concepts of sexual morality, which allow that pleasure is a legitimate sexual goal, probably date back most immediately to the post-World War I era (and may, in fact, have been influenced by it). We shall next examine some of the important changes that have been occurring since then.

THE TWENTIETH CENTURY AND SITUATION ETHICS

Theoretical Background

Rather than attempt to review contemporary scholarly thinking in sexual ethics, we shall concentrate on examining some of the forces that have helped shape present-day morality and will discuss the works of a few writers who have reached a wide readership, particularly among the young.

At least two major forces have had profound influence on Western ethics in the twentieth century: science and technology, and World War II.

What can serve as foundation for ethics in an age dominated by an ethically neutral discipline, science? The belief that truth is to be found by means of the scientific method is widespread; and belief in the discovery of truth, moral or otherwise, through divine revelation combined with "right reason," in the tradition of Aquinas and other theologians, has apparently waned as modern society has glorified the scientific method and the products of technology. Only recently have significant numbers of scientists (still only a minority) voiced the notion that we have expected more from science than it can offer. Technology can produce internal-combustion engines, but it cannot tell us whether or not the benefits of their availability and use outweigh the harm of the air pollution they produce. Scientists have given us the power to build nuclear weapons, but have not provided guidance in using them. In fact, there are moral problems inherent in the decision even to build them. Yet the scientific community has usually remained aloof from, or above, involvement in such value judgments. The scientist frequently attacks a problem because it is there, as the mountain climber scales Mount Everest simply because it is there.

There has been some attempt to use scientific observations (broadly defined) in arriving at moral judgments; that is, in deciding what is right and wrong. In relation to human sexuality we can cite an example. In 1929, Margaret Mead published her anthropological study of adolescence and sex in primitive society, *Coming of Age in Samoa*. She drew certain implications from her study of sexual-behavior patterns in another culture: A nonpunitive attitude toward sexual experimentation (premarital intercourse) among adolescents leads to happier and healthier acceptance of sexuality in the culture as a whole; as happiness and health are legitimate goals for any society, we should adopt such standards in our own culture.

The second major force that caused twentieth-century societies to rethink traditional morality was World War II. Death camps, atomic bombs, and the Nuremberg trials raised anew many moral questions that are still unresolved. At what point do responsibility and loyalty to the law and the state end, and at what point does one choose other, higher standards? Conventional religious principles were found wanting, and one response was the notion of **situation ethics.**

To put it briefly, the notion of a moral rule book that one can follow to the letter, rather than simply conforming to its spirit, may lead to immoral behavior, in the view of many modern theologians. The Ten Commandments say, "Thou shalt not kill" and "Thou shalt not bear false witness [lie]," yet there are specific *situations* in which strict obedience to these principles seems likely to lead to evil consequences, as in the Resistance during World War II. The Vietnam war and, more recently, the "Watergate era" raised similar dilemmas for many people—for instance, the problems of violating a confidence or disobeying a lawful order in order to attain some presumably higher ethical goal. Should rules be discarded, so that each individual can be free to decide what is right or wrong each time the situation calls for a moral decision? Opinion is divided on this point. No ethical system, no matter how complete, can possibly cover every situation. Because every individual human being is in a sense unique, each will be confronted sooner or later with a situation that does not fit the rules or in which the rules conflict. For instance, should an unmarried college woman who is pregnant and plans to have an abortion tell the truth to her overprotective father, who has just had a major heart attack, knowing that the news might kill him? According to the Danish Christian existentialist Sören Kierkegaard, certain special situations call for "suspension of the ethical"; that is, a break with the usual universal ethical principles; but such variations, he advises, should be made with "Fear and Trembling" (the title of his essay on the subject). The latter advice seems well founded, especially when we look at the consequences of the flexible approach as put forth in a different way by Friedrich Nietzsche. Conventional moral rules can be put aside by the superior individual (Superman) when it is necessary to advance his own power, said Nietzsche—and Hitler took that seriously.

Twentieth-century situation ethics is the first attempt in a long time to rethink our approach to ethical questions, particularly those relating to human sexuality. We have chosen to focus on situation (or contextual) ethics here, and particularly on the writings of Joseph Fletcher, for several reasons. Situation ethics appears to be a logical outgrowth of the life and experience of the twentieth century, and consequently has achieved, in a relatively short period of time, widespread popularity and acceptance (uncritical acceptance, some thinkers say). In addition, Fletcher, the principal popular spokesperson for situation ethics, addresses himself particularly to questions of human sexuality. (For instance, four of the eight chapters on "Situations for Ethical Decision" in his book *Moral Responsibility* deal with problems related to sexuality.)

Situation ethics appears deceptively simple—undoubtedly another reason for its popularity. There is only one fundamental principle: "whatever is the most loving thing in the situation is the right and good thing." Fletcher sees right and wrong in terms of its effects on interpersonal relationships and love as the one and only guiding principle for moral decisions. "Christian situation ethics reduces law from a statutory system of rules to the love canon alone." That is, one's *attitude* or *intentions* in a given situation determine whether or not behavior in that situation will be right or wrong. Behavior should be motivated by love of a particular kind (the Greeks distinguished several different kinds)—not *eros,* the passionate love, or desire, commonly associated with sexuality; not *philia,* the brotherly sort of love between friends, which is also emotional to some extent; but *agape,* the spiritual love which is manifested by an attitude of concern for one's fellow human beings with no expectation of receiving something in return. The person who is motivated by *agape* can do no wrong, and therefore has no need of rules or laws. Fletcher believes that this teaching is the essence of Christianity. Whether or not it is so is a question for theologians to debate. We shall consider here how this approach works in practice.

First, in situation or contextual ethics *any means* is justified by the end (love). According to this approach, even killing may conceivably be the most loving thing to do in a given situation—for instance, killing a baby whose crying endangers the lives of an entire party traveling through hostile territory and facing certain death if discovered. Presumably, then, there are also instances when almost any form of sexual behavior is justified. Fletcher (1966) has declared:

Whether any form of sex (hetero, homo, or auto) is good or evil depends on whether love is fully served. The Christian ethic is not interested in reluctant virgins and technical chastity. What sex probably needs more than anything is a good airing, demythologizing it and getting rid of its mystique-laden and occult accretions, which come from romanticism on the one hand and puritanism on the other.

The second general consideration has to do with the inherent difficulties in applying situation ethics:

A common objection to situation ethics is that it calls for more critical intelligence, more factual information, and more self-starting commitment to righteousness than most people can bring to bear. We all know the army veteran who "wishes the war was back" because he could tell the good guys from the bad guys by the uniforms they wore. There are those who say situationism ignores the reality of human sin or egocentricity, and fails to appreciate the finitude of human reason.

The demands that situation ethics places on the individual are tremendous and, perhaps, unrealistic when applied to the general population. This point seems particularly valid in connection with sexual behavior, because situation ethics calls for rational, unemotional appraisal of each situation and its short- and long-term ramifications. This is a prodigious accomplishment for those who are, by definition, involved in extremely emotional situations. That is, we suggest that even two people who are not in bed may have some difficulty in achieving *agape* while discussing whether or not they *should* go to bed together. Fletcher has cited the following instance:

A young unmarried couple might decide, if they make their decision Christianly, to have intercourse (e.g., by getting pregnant to force a selfish parent to relent his overbearing resistance to their marriage). But as Christians they would never merely say, "It's all right if we *like* each other!" Loving concern can make it all right, but mere liking cannot.

Sexuality involves powerful emotions—not only love (*eros*) but also feelings of guilt. The former tends to predominate before and during the sexual encounter, it seems. When a question of morality is involved, however, feelings of guilt tend to appear the following day or even months or years later. Guilt feelings may be regarded as the "voice of conscience," but actually their origins are extremely complex and may be totally unconscious and irrational. Again, we shall leave debates over whether or not conscience is a God-given faculty to the theologians, but we cannot deny the reality of guilt feelings. Situation ethics emphasizes the processes that occur before an act. That the individuals believe *at the time* that what they are about to do is right is the important variable. But what of the potentially painful aftermath of guilt feelings, irrational as they may be?

It seems that the current generation of young people is living in a transitional period, in which there is an overlap between two phenomena. One is the belief that guilt feelings associated with sex are a heritage from past generations and are acquired in childhood; the other is the new morality, intellectual acceptance of the premise that sex in the proper context is good and should not be associated with feelings of guilt. Those who find it difficult to shake their feelings of guilt sometimes seek psychotherapy, implying that the feelings of guilt, rather than the behavior that engendered them, are bad and must be dispelled so that these people will be free to act according to their reason.

The Roman Catholic Church has its own method for dealing with guilt—the confessional. It may work as well as psychother-apy in relieving guilt feelings, but the underlying assumptions are quite different. Take, for instance, the devout woman, who, after due consideration, participates in sexual intercourse with a young man whom she deeply loves and plans to marry. She goes to confession, and the priest, if he is true to the tradition of the Church (as he may not be nowadays), acknowledges that the woman has committed a wrongful act (fornication, which is always wrong in the Roman Catholic view, regardless of the situation) but offers absolution in exchange for a specific penance.

One thing that can be said about the Roman Catholic confessional and any other "legalistic" system of ethics, secular or religious, is that the individual always knows where he or she stands in terms of right and wrong. There is no need for the element of "fear and trembling" that Kierkegaard describes, and there are those who argue that the average person either does not want or cannot cope with the vagaries of an unstructured approach like situation ethics. It is an age-old problem, the responsibility that accompanies freedom of choice. The more rules or laws there are to follow, the less freedom we enjoy—but the lighter is our burden of responsibility.

SEX AND THE LAW

Now that we have seen something of the Judeo-Christian tradition of sexual ethics and the traditions leading to present-day concepts of morality, we are better prepared to understand the precepts embodied in the laws that treat sexual behavior in our society. It will become apparent as we describe specific statutes in a typical U.S. penal code that the laws pertaining to sexual behavior are, for the most part, not directed toward "the preservation of public order" as most criminal laws are. Rather, they embody a particular ethical point of view of sexual behavior: that the sole purpose of sexual activity is reproduction. When we recognize that a majority of legislators held this point of view when these laws were written, it is not difficult to understand how such activities as masturbation and homosexuality came to be designated as criminal offenses. Other notions arising from the particular ethical and religious backgrounds of the founders of Anglo-American society are also embodied in law, including the opinion that sex in general is evil and the belief that having more than one spouse at a time is wrong.

A distinction can be made among three general categories of sexual behavior, all of which are subject to criminal sanctions in the majority of the fifty states at the present time. The first includes the sexual behavior of consenting adults in private. Many, if not the vast majority of, authorities on criminal law believe that such activities should be legalized. The second category includes offenses involving force or violence (for instance, rape), offenses against children ("child molesting"), and offenses that present a public nuisance (for instance, exhibitionism). Legal opinion is almost unanimous that such offenses should remain under criminal sanctions. No one, obviously, favors the legalizing of forcible rape (though some revision of the laws pertaining to statutory rape may be in order in some states). The third category of offenses is the most controversial at the present time; it includes those offenses that involve commercial exploitation of sex (prostitution and the sale of pornography).

We shall discuss some of the specific offenses included in each of these three categories and compare existing U.S. statutes with those of the American Law Institute's *Model Penal Code* and with some codes from other countries. We shall attempt to describe how existing laws are usually enforced and shall present arguments for and against their retention in our society.

Laws Pertaining to Consenting Adults

In 1962, Illinois became the first state to revise its criminal code along the lines suggested in the *Model Penal Code*. Specifically, oral-genital contacts and anal intercourse between consenting adults (of the same or opposite sex) in private are no longer criminal offenses. More recently, Connecticut, Colorado, Oregon, Hawaii, Delaware, Ohio, California, North Dakota, South Dakota, Washington, New Mexico, Maine, and Arkansas have made similar revisions. Other states—including New York, Kansas, Minnesota, and Utah—have not legalized all consensual sex acts between adults but have reduced such offenses to misdemeanor status. Not all states are moving in this direction. In 1970 Georgia revised its penal code and *doubled* the maximum penalty for consensual sodomy (from ten years to twenty years).

Fornication

On June 13, 1969, a jury in Paterson, New Jersey, found a man and a woman guilty on three counts of **fornication;** that is, the defendants were convicted of a crime of sexual intercourse between consenting unmarried adults. According to Municipal Judge Ervan F. Jushner: "I saw a crime being committed when an unmarried woman walked into my courtroom pregnant." There were three counts of fornication in the indictment, for the woman had already borne three illegitimate children. The couple was convicted under Section 2:133-1 of the *New Jersey Statutes,* which reads:

Any person who shall commit fornication shall be guilty of a misdemeanor, and be punished by a fine not exceeding $50, or imprisonment not exceeding six months, or both.

The defense attorneys argued that this couple was being prosecuted not for fornication but because they were poor and sought welfare for the support of the children. It certainly seems likely that the prosecution in this case, as in so many others involving sex offenses, was not directed toward eliminating the behavior specified in the charges. The intention was most likely to punish this couple for having had illegitimate children whom it could not support adequately.

Intercourse between unmarried adults is prohibited in most of the fifty states. Obviously there are millions of offenses under these laws annually. Prosecution, however, tends to be quite selective. One survey of 426 prosecutors indicated a tendency to prosecute welfare recipients, as in the case just cited. The same survey described one admittedly unusual Midwestern district attorney who had tried 266 fornication cases from 1968 through 1972; 260 of these cases involved persons from racial minorities.

In those states where fornication is prohibited by law, the offense is usually a misdemeanor punishable by a fine, which may be as small as $10 (Rhode Island) or as large as $1,000 (Georgia). In Arizona the statute defines fornication as a felony punishable by imprisonment for not more than three years. The offense is defined as "living in a state of open and notorious *cohabitation*," one of several variations among state statutes defining fornication. In some states, for instance, a single act of intercourse between two unmarried adults is an offense. In other states there must be evidence of repetition or of cohabitation. In such a state a couple living in a stable relationship may be penalized, but the promiscuous individual has not violated the law.

An interesting aspect of some fornication laws is the differences in application to males and females. A married woman who has intercourse with a single man is more likely to be charged with adultery if she is prosecuted. On the other hand, a married man who has intercourse with a single woman is likely to be charged with fornication, a lesser crime in most states and no crime at all in some states. The rationale behind this form of discrimination dates back to Roman law. It reflects concern for property rights; the illicit sexual activities of a married woman were viewed as more serious because they raised the possibility of the introduction of a fraudulent heir into the family. A man might then end up unwittingly supporting a child that was not his own.

The difference between fornication and **statutory rape** is based on the age of the girl. When the girl is under a certain age (varying from 14 to 21, depending on the state), the crime is defined as statutory rape rather than as fornication; only the male is

then considered guilty of the offense, even if the girl has been a willing partner.

Our society is unique in many aspects of its sex laws, particularly those defining sexual intercourse between unmarried consenting adults as *criminal* behavior. Other societies may condemn such activity as immoral; some may set certain limits on it; and others may encourage it; yet most of our states define it as a crime. As we have noted earlier, the majority of men and women in our society do engage in sexual intercourse before marriage.

The American Law Institute has not included a fornication statute in the *Model Penal Code.*

Marital Sexual Activities

Most people assume that whatever varieties of sexual activities a married couple engages in at home in private are legal. This assumption is incorrect. Almost all sexual activity that may occur between husband and wife—with the exception of kissing, caressing, and vaginal intercourse—is defined as criminal in most states of the union. Oral-genital contacts (cunnilingus and fellatio) and anal intercourse (sodomy), in particular, are so defined. In most states they are felonies and carry severe penalties.

In some states oral-genital contacts, anal intercourse, and intercourse with animals are all included under single sodomy laws and are labeled crimes against nature. The rationale for these laws is based on the notion that the natural purpose of sex is reproduction, and therefore any sex act that does not include the potential for conception is a sin (crime) against the laws of nature. A few states even include mutual masturbation or sex with dead bodies under sodomy, presumably for the same reason.

We have already presented data from the Kinsey and other studies to show that many married couples do practice forms of sexual expression other than vaginal intercourse. It is unlikely that the average married man suspects that his marital sexual activity will ever be held against him. Even if he knows that a certain behavior is illegal, as long as he and his wife perform it in private, who can substantiate any charge? It turns out, however, that a wife can offer such evidence in order to win a divorce on grounds of cruelty. Or she may simply be angry at her husband and looking for vengeance. In 1965 a woman in Indiana had a major quarrel with her husband of ten years. In the heat of anger she filed a complaint of sodomy against him. She did not accuse him of having used force. Before the case came to trial the woman changed her mind and sought to withdraw the charge. She was not allowed to do so because sodomy is an offense against the state, and the state proceeded to prosecute. The husband, stunned by the whole affair, was convicted and sentenced to a term of from two to fourteen years in state prison. After serving three years of his sentence he was released when the U.S. Seventh Circuit Court of Appeals overturned the conviction on a technicality in the proceedings. The law itself was not challenged. So far the only landmark decision involving the constitutionality of laws governing the activities of married couples has been the 1965 decision by the U.S. Supreme Court in the case of Griswold v. Connecticut. The Court ruled that a law prohibiting the use of birth-control devices by married couples was unconstitutional on the grounds that the right to marital privacy excludes such prohibitions. The *Model Penal Code* recommends the legalizing of all private consensual marital relations.

The law also deals with the frequency of intercourse between a married couple. For example, if no intercourse at all has occurred the law provides for annulment of the marriage on these grounds. A man's impotence or a woman's refusal to engage in sexual intercourse with her husband has long been held sufficient grounds for divorce or annulment, though the historical reasoning is somewhat different in the two instances. The impotent male's inability to have intercourse has been held to nullify the reproductive purpose of marriage. To some extent the same notion applies to the unwilling female, but there is also

an additional reason. Wives have been viewed traditionally as a "remedy for the concupiscence" of her husband. This concept is reflected in the specific exclusion of rapes of wives from the rape laws. Even though the husband may have used force and the wife may have been an unwilling partner on a given occasion, legally, rape has not been committed (although the husband can be charged with assault and battery in some instances).

Perhaps one indication of the changing view of women's rights is the increasing number of divorces granted to women in the last several decades on the grounds that their husbands' demands for frequent intercourse are unreasonable and constitute cruelty. Judges seem to follow highly personal standards in rendering opinions on the "normal" frequency of intercourse for a married couple. For instance, Kinsey described an opinion upheld by the Supreme Court of Minnesota, in which it was ruled that intercourse on the average of three to four times a week represented an "uncontrollable craving for sexual intercourse" on the part of the husband!

Abortion and Sterilization

Because U.S. laws reflect a particular point of view about the purpose of sex and marriage, it is not surprising that the right *not* to have children has been limited, until recently, by statute.

In the late 1960s a number of states modified their abortion laws to provide for abortions when there was a risk that continuation of the pregnancy would impair the physical or mental health of the women, or when the pregnancy was a result of incest or rape. Many legal abortions were done in these states in the ensuing years, almost all of them under the "mental health" provisions of these statutes. Psychiatrists were often put in the uncomfortable position of certifying that continuation of the pregnancy posed a risk to the mental health of the woman (who was usually said to be depressed and likely to commit suicide if the abortion were not granted) when, in fact, there was little, if any, evidence to substantiate the claim. In actual practice the real concerns of the physicians were often overpopulation, the dismal prospects for an unwanted child, and the belief that women have the right not to bear children regardless of the circumstances under which they become pregnant.

In July 1970, a New York abortion law went into effect which removed all restrictions except the requirement that abortions must be performed within twenty-four weeks of conception (that is, before the third trimester of pregnancy). On January 22, 1973, the U.S. Supreme Court declared unconstitutional all state laws which prohibited or restricted abortions during the first trimester of pregnancy. The Court also limited state intervention in second-trimester abortions to the regulation of medical practices involved (certification of hospitals, licensing of physicians, and so forth) insofar as they affect the woman's health. The Court left the prohibition of third-trimester abortions to the separate states; and several other issues, most notably the right of minors to abortions without parental consent and the right to abortion without consent of the husband, were also left to the discretion of the states. In 1974, the Massachusetts Supreme Court ruled that a husband does not have the right to prevent his wife from having an abortion. The Attorney General of California, also in 1974, issued an opinion that an unmarried minor girl (under 18) does not need her parent's consent to have an abortion, provided she is sufficiently mature to give an informed consent herself.

Although women may now legally seek an abortion anywhere in the United States, in many states only a very few hospitals perform abortions, and there are areas of the country in which the lack of inexpensive clinics may make it financially difficult to obtain an abortion. Many counties, for instance, do not have a single facility that provides abortions, and the large-scale providers are overwhelmingly concentrated in large cities on the East and West coasts. Furthermore, physicians and nurses are not required to perform abortions "on demand" if this action would violate their personal moral or religious principles. Legal abortions for all women who want them were by no means guaranteed by the U.S. Supreme Court decision of 1973. The abortions still have to be paid for, and in 1977 the Supreme Court ruled that state and local governments can decide whether or not to finance the abortions of needy women. This ruling removed any doubt about the decisions of fifteen states to deny payment to Medicaid patients for nontherapeutic abortions. The result is that poor women may not be able to pay for legal abortions, but abortions will still be available to those with sufficient funds, just as they were available when abortions were illegal in the United States and a woman with money could fly to Sweden or Japan for an abortion.

Regardless of the law, the question of abortion is still alive. There have been attacks on abortion clinics in some parts of the country, and there are also efforts underway to amend the U.S. Constitution in such a way as to either greatly restrict or prohibit abortions. The most common legal doctrine in the numerous constitutional amendments that have been proposed (thirty-three thus far) is the doctrine that the constitutional rights to due process and equal protection should apply to fetuses. Supporters of these measures are most often motivated by moral and religious concerns.

Sterilization for birth-control purposes is now, like abortion, legal in the United States within broad limits. Unlike abortion, there is no Supreme Court ruling which defines the limits for state laws on the subject of sterilization. Thus, some states (Utah) expressly forbid the sterilization of someone who is mentally incompetent to give consent, whereas other states (California) have laws which expressly allow for *involuntary* sterilization of the mentally retarded and mentally ill.

Sterilization, except for reasons of medical necessity, has been illegal until recently for a variety of reasons. Under English law male sterilization was considered a crime of *mayhem,* a category which included any "maiming" of the body which would (allegedly) render a man unfit to fight for the king. In the

United States until the last decade there was concern about *underpopulation*. As recently as 1950 the Attorney General of California declared that sterilization operations were "violative of the state's social interest in the maintenance of the birth rate." In addition, there was the horror of selective sterilization of Jews and mental defectives during World War II, which added an understandable emotional element to the subject of sterilization. Ironically, it was groups such as the Human Betterment Association of America which advanced the cause of legalized sterilization for reasons such as the presence of known hereditary disease or "physical, mental or emotional defect which may seriously impair the patient's functioning as an adequate parent and/or which causes the physician to conclude that parenthood, at any future time, would be hazardous."

In 1969, California's Third District Court of Appeals ruled, in Jessin *v.* Shasta County, that "California has no public policy prohibiting consensual sterilization operations and . . . that non-therapeutic sterilization operations are legal in this state where competent consent has been given." This was the first occasion on which an appellate court in the United States had ruled specifically on the legality of nontherapeutic surgical sterilization.

Divorce Laws

Everyone is undoubtedly aware of the high and steadily increasing divorce rate—more than 25 percent nationwide and as high as 50 percent or more in some regions. Some jurists blame the high divorce rate on the fact that "our marriage laws and administrative procedures make it far too easy for the immature, the mentally and physically unfit, and the legally disqualified to become married." Some states recognize **common-law marriages,** which do not require licenses or ceremonies. Under English common law (still applicable in some states) a boy over 14 years and a girl over 12 years have only to agree that they take each other as husband and wife. Some states require that they live together a certain length of time or require parental consent for marriage if the male is under 21 or

the female under 18. If the partners falsify their ages and manage to obtain a license and marry, however, there is usually nothing that the parents can do to annul the marriage.

Obtaining a divorce is usually far more difficult. Most of the fifty states require proof of a "marital offense," resulting in the usually unrealistic findings that one party (most often the woman) is not at fault and that one party is "guilty" of the offense, which provides both grounds for the divorce and a basis for awarding property to the "innocent" party. The first exception was California, where the law (effective January 1, 1970) provides for dissolution of a marriage on the basis of irreconcilable differences. There are no "guilty" and "innocent" parties, and the property must be divided evenly. This law provides for divorce by consent of both partners, a concept that goes back to Roman law but was abolished when marriage came under the jurisdiction of the Roman Catholic Church. Colorado, Connecticut, Iowa, Michigan, North Dakota, Florida, and New Jersey have also adopted **no-fault divorce** laws recently. Texas has an optional no-fault divorce procedure.

The most common offenses acceptable as grounds for divorce are adultery, insanity, conviction of a felony, conviction of a sex crime, imprisonment, alcoholism, drug addiction, desertion, nonsupport, impotence, general cruelty, physical cruelty, and mental cruelty. Residence requrements vary from six weeks (Nevada) to five years (Massachusetts, though only three years are required if the person suing was a state resident when he or she married). Many states have restrictions on remarriage, particularly for the "guilty" party. South Dakota, for instance, prohibits the remarriage of an adulterer during the lifetime of the ex-spouse. Such restrictions can be evaded by remarrying in another state and then returning home, for the courts recognize a marriage as valid as long as it is valid in the state where it was performed.

Adultery

Our laws on sexual offenses reflect several sources, but the Judeo-Christian tradition is most prominent. In particular, the early

American settlers brought with them the traditions of the English courts, which had a long history of attempting to regulate sexual behavior. From the thirteenth century until the time of Oliver Cromwell and the Puritan Revolution (1640), sexual offenses were handled by the English ecclesiastical courts. Although they condemned all imaginable forms of "illicit" sexual behavior and punished offenders with fines or jail sentences, the ecclesiastical courts were notably ineffective in modifying the sexual activities of the general population. (They did not always receive support from royalty either, for at times the kings and their courtiers were the most notorious offenders.) The English Puritans abolished the ecclesiastical courts and made sexual offenses like adultery and incest capital crimes punishable by death in the common-law courts (adultery had not previously been a common-law offense). The Puritans of the Massachusetts Bay Colony also made adultery a crime punishable by death, but as the limited colonial population might have been nearly decimated by enforcement of this law, it was rarely invoked; in 1694 the death penalty was replaced by public whipping and the enforced wearing of the letter "A," a punishment immortalized by Nathaniel Hawthorne in *The Scarlet Letter.* Connecticut went a litter farther and prescribed that adulterers should have the letter "A" branded on their foreheads with a hot iron. Pennsylvania took a middle course, providing for branding only after the third conviction (prison sentences of one year or more were prescribed for the first and second offenses).

The penalties have diminished over time, but adultery is still a criminal offense in most states. It is a misdemeanor punishable only by fines in some states, but elsewhere it is a felony punishable by lengthy prison terms varying from one to five years. The penalties for adultery tend to be more serious than those for fornication, presumably because of the threat to the family that extramarital affairs pose. Adultery is also the only offense that is considered sufficient grounds for divorce in every state in the union where an offense is required.

We have already noted that under Roman law (and also under English common law) adultery was defined only as intercourse with a married woman. A married man who had intercourse with a single woman was not guilty of adultery. U.S. courts have tended to hold the view adopted by the English ecclesiastical courts that either a married man or a married woman having intercourse with someone other than his or her spouse is guilty of adultery. At least this definition is applied in divorce cases. But paradoxically, perhaps, this law is almost never applied to prostitution. A married man having intercourse with a prostitute is rarely prosecuted for adultery.

The *Model Penal Code* does not include adultery as a criminal offense, though certain extramarital contacts involving minors (under 16 years old) or seduction ("a promise of marriage which the actor does not mean to perform") are still included as offenses.

Homosexuality

Homosexuality as such is legal in all the states. It is only specific homosexual *acts* that are defined as crimes. It is no crime to be sexually attracted and oriented toward members of the same sex. In fact, the laws defining various common homosexual acts (oral-genital contacts, anal intercourse, mutual masturbation) as crimes do not specify the sexes of the participants. These acts, as we have already noted, are crimes under the laws of most states. As recently as 1976, the U.S. Supreme Court upheld Virginia's law against sodomy. Like most sodomy laws, that one specifically prohibits not only anal intercourse but oral-genital contact—no matter the sex of those engaged in the acts.

The penalties for these offenses can be quite severe, but in practice relatively few homosexuals are arrested and convicted under these laws because most homosexual acts are performed in private and are thus protected by the search-and-seizure provisions of the U.S. Constitution. When an arrest is made for a specific homosexual act, the latter usually has occurred in a public place (restroom, park, automobile, theater); and in about 90 percent of instances the act is oral-genital contact. Although this offense is often defined as a felony, judges in some states (for instance, California) have the discretionary power to reduce the charge to a misdemeanor (and in California they usually do). Judges do not have this prerogative when the offense is anal intercourse. In general, and for a first offense in particular, the individual convicted of a homosexual act is fined, given a suspended jail sentence, and placed on probation. As Hoffman has noted (in reference to California): "The judges realize that putting a homosexual into prison is like trying to cure obesity by incarceration in a candy shop."

But only a minority of homosexual arrests are made for specific sexual acts; the majority are for solicitation or loitering in public places. The pertinent California statute reads:

647. *Disorderly Conduct Defined—Misdemeanor.*—Every person who solicits anyone to engage in or who engages in lewd or dissolute conduct in any public place or in any place open to the public or exposed to public view . . . is guilty of a misdemeanor.

One survey conducted in the Los Angeles area indicated that 90–95 percent of all homosexual arrests were for violations of section 647(a) of the California Penal Code. The most controversial aspect of the majority of these arrests is the use of policemen as "decoys." Usually a young police officer dressed in casual clothes loiters in a public restroom or similar location for the express purpose of enticing homosexuals to solicit "a lewd or lascivious" act. The arrest is usually made by a second police officer stationed nearby. The decoy then serves as witness against the defendant. The controversy revolves around the accusation that police decoys are involved in *entrapment*—that they induce people to commit illegal acts that they would not otherwise commit. Certainly most homosexuals would not knowingly solicit police officers, but that point is irrelevant under the law. If an individual has a predisposition to commit a particular offense, it is not illegal for a police officer to *entice* that person to commit the offense.

In addition to the issue of enticement versus entrapment, there is the question of whether or not police decoys serve a useful function and represent a worthwhile investment of police manpower. As most homosexual soliciting that does occur in public places is quite subtle it seems unlikely that such behavior constitutes a significant enough offense to the public decency to justify such measures. Hoffman, in fact, has argued "that putting out as decoys police officers who are young, attractive, and seductively dressed, and who engage in enticing conversations with homosexuals is itself an outrage to public decency." We can argue that the use of police decoys serves to deter public homosexual soliciting, but the argument is unconvincing because the express purpose of using decoys is to promote such behavior in order to achieve arrest, rather than to prevent the behavior.

So far we have been discussing only homosexual activities between males, because female homosexuals are not usually subject to the same sanctions. With only a few exceptions (Georgia, Kentucky, South Carolina, and Wisconsin), the laws do not distinguish between male and female homosexuals, but in actual practice females are almost never arrested or prosecuted for homosexual activities. The Kinsey study reviewed all the sodomy convictions in the United States from 1696 to 1952 and failed to find a single one involving lesbians. In a review of all the arrests in New York City over a period of ten years the Kinsey researchers found "tens of thousands" of arrests and convictions of male homosexuals, but only three arrests of females for homosexual offenses; all three cases had been dismissed. Many factors contribute to this difference in treatment. Lesbians tend to engage in less public sexual behavior; lesbian activities are not considered as "sinful" as are male homosexual activities; and the law in general tends to be more protective of female sexual activities (with the exception of prostitution).

For poorly substantiated reasons, male homosexuals are regarded as more threatening to society than are lesbians. Police officers seem to think that homosexuals are more likely to commit crimes of violence and crimes against children than are other individuals. Although massive studies, like that conducted by Gebhard and his associates at the Institute for Sex Research, have not confirmed this belief, it is still commonly held. One result is the practice of requiring the registration of convicted homosexual offenders.

This requirement renders the convicted homosexual susceptible to being "picked up for questioning" whenever a "sex crime" is committed in the area in which he is living. Identified homosexuals are also subject to "purges," like that in the U.S. State Department and other government agencies in the 1950s. In 1978, an attempt was made in California to keep homosexuals from teaching in public schools, but the proposal was defeated by the voters. Homosexuals are generally prohibited from holding jobs that require security clearance or involve the handling of "sensitive information." This requirement is based not simply on the idea that "perverts" are unreliable but also on the belief that homosexuals are more vulnerable to extortion and blackmail. Legalizing homosexual acts between consenting adults would not necessarily change this situation. Homosexuals would probably still be vulnerable to blackmail because of the probable effects of public disclosure of their activities: Whether criminal or not, homosexuality is still widely condemned in our society. This point was made quite clearly in 1977 when the residents of Dade County, Florida—after a nationally publicized and highly emotional crusade by singer Anita Bryant—voted to repeal an ordinance outlawing discrimination against homosexuals in housing, employment, and public accommodations.

Consensual Sex Laws in Other Countries

Kinsey once remarked: "There is no aspect of American sex law which surprises visitors from other countries as much as this legal attempt to penalize pre-marital activity to which both of the participating parties have consented and in which no force has been involved."

The Napoleonic Code, adopted in France in 1810, contains no criminal laws relating to sexual intercourse or homosexual activities between consenting adults in private. Spain, Portugal, and Italy adopted similar codes long ago, as did Belgium (1867) and the Netherlands (1886). In the twentieth century Denmark legalized consensual adult sex in 1930, Switzerland in 1937, Sweden in 1944, Hungary and Czechoslovakia in 1962, England and Wales in 1967, East Germany in 1968, West Germany and Canada in 1969, Finland in 1970, Austria in 1971, and Norway in 1972.

These same sexual acts constitute crimes in the Soviet Union, Rumania, Bulgaria, Yugoslavia, Ireland, and Scotland. Of all the countries of Europe and North America, the United States has the most severe penalties for proscribed consensual sex acts. Even in the Soviet Union, considered by many to be equally as repressive as the United States in its sex laws, the maximum penalties for consensual sodomy are considerably less (five years versus ten to twenty years in prison in some states of the United States).

Public Nuisance Offenses

Those acts subsumed under the general category of public nuisances include exhibitionism, voyeurism, and transvestism. They do not involve physical contact with victims, and indeed the victims of voyeurism may be totally unaware of the crimes and of the people committing them. These acts are viewed as criminal on the grounds that they offend public decency, disturb the peace, and tend to subvert and corrupt the morals of the people. The greatest controversy over this general category of offenses involves exhibitionism.

Various problems in the wording of nuisance laws are apparent. One is that a person can be convicted of indecent exposure for an offense that occurs in comparative privacy, as long as someone present claims to have been offended. There have also been instances in which no one present was offended, yet the person or persons involved were convicted of "indecent exposure." These cases have usually involved people bathing in the nude at nudist camps or sunbathing in their own backyards.

There has also been some controversy in the courts over what portions of the anatomy constitute "private parts." Most courts draw an absolute line at the limits of pubic hair (which has led some "bottomless" dancers in California to shave their pubic hair in an effort to circumvent this definition). Traditionally a woman's breasts, with the exception of the nipples, have not been considered "private parts" under the law; hence the use of "pasties" by strip teasers. Recent court decisions in several states, however, have declared that the breasts, including the nipples, do not constitute "private parts," thus affirming the legality of "topless" dancers in certain jurisdictions.

The *Model Penal Code* does not differ significantly from present laws, except that the word "genitals" is substituted for "private parts."

Crimes against Children

Sexual offenses involving minors are subject to severe sanctions in every state, though prosecution is often difficult because the only witnesses are children, who are not always able to provide the reliable, consistent evidence necessary for conviction.

The definition of a child or minor in these statutes varies somewhat from state to state. The American Law Institute proposes that minority be defined as being less than 16 years, provided that the offender is at least four years older than the other person.

Although child molesters are almost always males, the children involved may be either male or female, depending on the orientation of the pedophiliac. The behavior involved most often consists of fondling the genitals, but may also include mutual masturbation, oral-genital contacts, intercourse, or pederasty (*see* Chapter 10).

A special type of sexual offense against a minor is incest. The law usually treats incest in special statutes prohibiting marriage or sexual activity between immediate family members and relatives of varying degrees of blood relationship. The offense is a felony and punishable by as much as fifty years in prison in some states. Of all *reported* sex offenses incest is probably the least common, accounting for 3–6 percent of the total reported sex offenses in various jurisdictions. The actual incidence is probably significantly higher, however, at least among certain segments of the population. In one study of delinquent adolescent girls, the incidence of sexual relations with fathers or stepfathers was found to be 15 percent. For obvious reasons, people are more reluctant to report family members than strangers to the police, particularly if they are the primary or sole source of support for the family. (The most common type of incest in the United States is between father and daughter; the next most common is between brother and sister; and the least common is between mother and son.)

Rape and Related Offenses

Sexual intercourse with a woman other than a spouse under conditions of force or threat of violence is considered the most serious of all sexual offenses under the criminal law. It is also the sex crime that has been subject to the most serious charges of racism and sexism, particularly in regard to procedures and penalties. Federal courts finally recognized the racial discrimination involved in the administration of the death penalty for this crime when it was pointed out in a series of cases in the late 1960s that of the 455 persons executed in the United States for rape between 1930 and 1964, 405 were blacks.

Discrimination against men in general is said to exist in the sense that the courts have rather consistently held that a man who is subjected to forcible anal intercourse in prison, for instance, has not been raped. Rape laws were written solely to "protect" women; but many people, as we shall discuss later, would take issue with this facile declaration.

Although attention has been focused primarily on procedures and penalties, there are difficult problems as well in the rape statutes, particularly in the legal definition of rape.

One difficulty involves the question of consent by the female. Whereas a woman who has been rendered unconscious by a drug or a blow on the head or who is mentally retarded or seriously ill mentally may be clearly incapable of having given responsible consent, the issue is not usually that clear. A man may have intercourse with a woman whom he has met at a party at which both have been drinking heavily. That the man was drunk at the time is no defense, yet the woman can claim that, because she was drunk (even though voluntarily), she was incapable of giving responsible consent, though she offered no resistance.

Certain rapes are viewed by some police authorities as "victim-precipitated." These include cases in which a woman initially consents to intercourse and then retracts her consent prior to the act, and other instances in which a woman places herself in a "vulnerable" situation (for example, hitchhiking or walking alone at night in an isolated area or a "rough" neighborhood). There is an obvious difference in the perception of some men and most women with regard to the kind of behavior that constitutes sexual "solicitation." Some men delude themselves into thinking that the woman who hitchhikes or is out jogging alone is "asking for it," but women are rightfully offended by this interpretation of such behavior. It is ironic that present attitudes toward rape make it such that women, the victims, are the ones who must restrict their behavior and thus limit their freedom to be in certain places at certain times.

A classic example of the attitudes of some males toward women in the area of rape was seen in one recent rape case in Madison, Wisconsin. A 15-year-old male was convicted of raping a high school girl in the high school stairwell, but the judge let him off with a probation sentence. The male judge said: "Whether women like it or not they are sex objects. Are we supposed to take an impressionable person 15 or 16 years of age and punish that person severely because they react to it normally?" Apparently not everyone agreed with the judge's attitude. He was voted out in a recall election and replaced by a woman.

Another unresolved issue in rape cases involves the weight to be given as to how much, if any, resistance was shown by the victim. The rules of evidence vary under the laws of the different states. Some courts require evidence of considerable physical resistance, but others do not on the grounds that a woman may have been paralyzed by fear or may have realized that resistance was useless and might even have brought greater injury to herself.

The areas where there is the greatest need (and hope) for change in the prosecution of rape cases are procedural. It is estimated that 50 percent or more rapes go unreported, in part, at least, because of the humiliating and accusatory sort of interrogation procedure that women have come to expect at the hands of the police. This problem can perhaps be remedied by the establishment of rape investigation units staffed by women who are trained in counseling rape victims, as well as obtaining the evidence which is necessary for apprehension, trial, and conviction of the offender.

The presentation of the victim's sexual history in detail in open court is usually just as traumatic as the investigation. Courts have traditionally considered such inquiry proper on the rather questionable grounds that a history of prior "fornication" (most rape victims are unmarried women) is relevant to the question of her likelihood of consenting to intercourse. The federal government and several states have now adopted a rule proposed by the rape task force of the National Organization for Women (NOW) that excludes all evidence of prior sexual activity except with the accused (if relevant). Some states have also dropped the former requirement that a corroborating witness—other than the defendant or victim—testify as to the fact of rape.

Serious disagreements exist over the appropriate penalty for rape. Some jurists believe that lighter sentences will increase the conviction rate for rapists, since juries may be reluctant to convict if the penalty is severe (for example, life imprisonment). Other jurists favor stiffer sentences—mandatory prison terms or restoration of the death penalty for rape. The least promising alternative of those currently under discussion is castration, since, as we have already noted (*see* Chapter 4), removal of the testicles in adulthood may have no effect on sex drive or potency.

Statutory Rape

The crime of statutory rape includes any act of intercourse with any female under the specified "age of consent" in a given state. For reasons that are not obvious the age of consent has been repeatedly raised in some jurisdictions. For instance, in California it was raised from 10 to 14 years in 1889, to 16 years in 1897, and to 18 years in 1913. This paternalistic protection of the law means that no female under this age is capable of consenting to intercourse, and consent, if given, is rendered meaningless for legal purposes.

The age of consent varies from state to state, but 16 and 18 are most common. In Tennessee the age of consent in this connection is 21, yet a girl can obtain a marriage license when she is 16. If a married woman under 21 has an affair with a man not her husband, he may be prosecuted for rape rather than for adultery. (There are such cases on record.) The law often fails to recognize that a girl of 17 or even younger may be quite experienced and motivated to make sexual contacts. She may even lie about her age and say that she is 18, especially if she also looks much older than she is. None of these factors can be used as a defense against a charge of statutory rape in most states. In a few states, however, a girl's promiscuity or the fact that she is a prostitute may be used as a defense against such a charge.

The American Law Institute recommends that the age for statutory rape be less than 10 years. A male who had intercourse with a girl under 16 would be guilty of the lesser offense of "corruption of minors," provided that he were at least four years older than the girl. These recommendations would eliminate the present possibility that a boy involved in an adolescent love affair could be convicted of a felony and sentenced to a long prison term.

COMMERCIAL EXPLOITATION OF SEX

Prostitution

The only sexual offense for which women are prosecuted to any significant extent is prostitution. In itself this phenomenon is interesting, for **prostitution,** as we shall define it for purposes of this discussion, is a profession of women who perform sexual acts with men who pay for them—and for the most part men write and administer the law in our society. Prostitution can exist only because of the demand for such services by men; and its extent is obviously correlated with the size of the male population without other readily available sexual outlets, as is attested to by the large numbers of prostitutes near military bases.

The history of prostitution has been the subject of many volumes, and we shall not attempt to cover it here. Suffice it to say that prostitution has always existed, despite repeated attempts to eliminate it. In various ancient cultures prostitution was associated with religious rites—so-called sacred or temple prostitution. Commercialized prostitution, as we know it today, goes back at least to ancient Greece.

Despite various dissenting voices, the prevailing opinion in our society is still that prostitution is a social and moral evil and should be subject to criminal sanctions, especially when young women and men are involved. In recent years a wave of child prostitution—involving both girls and boys, some as young as 12 years of age—has struck large cities and even small towns across the United States. New York City police estimated in 1977 that as many as 20,000 runaway youngsters were on the streets of that city, many of them available for commercial sex. There are no simple remedies for this situation, but the usual response has been to stiffen the penalties, especially against the pimps.

The laws dealing with prostitution are many and encompass various types of behavior and many individuals connected with organized prostitution beside the "solo practitioner." The most common form of prosecution by far, however, is for the offense of soliciting. Most arrests are made when prostitutes solicit customers or plainclothes police officers on streets or in public places like bars or hotels. The experienced prostitute is very careful in the wording of her offer in order to avoid arrest. She will mention no sexual activity at all but will speak vaguely of "wanting to have a good time," "some fun," or "having a date." She will also be wary of speaking directly of fees for services to be rendered. Instead, she may mention that she needs a certain amount of money for some new clothes or to support her sick mother. These ploys are not always successful, and courts have sustained convictions when there was sufficient reason to believe, on the basis of circumstances and general behavior, that the woman had been soliciting, regardless of whether or not she specifically "offered her body for hire." Usually a convicted prostitute is fined and then released to resume her occupation. This system obviously does not deter the prostitute much. Instead it functions as a sort of excise tax, the cost of which is passed on to the customer.

It has often been suggested that the customer should be arrested along with the prostitute as an accomplice to an illegal act. Customers are rarely arrested, however; in most states using the services of a prostitute is not a specific crime, though it may fall under the provisions of more general statutes covering fornication or adultery, for example.

Besides the prostitute and her customer others are usually involved in the enterprise of prostitution. They are often the ones who profit most from the business and are usually viewed as the major exploiters of prostitutes. They include procurers, pimps, operators, and "facilitators" of houses of prostitution and those who "traffic in women." The activities of all these individuals are generally prohibited by either state or federal law.

The procurer, or panderer, coerces women into houses of prostitution or otherwise entices them into becoming prostitutes. The coercion need not be physical but must involve some element of intimidation or fraud, to distinguish it from pimping, which involves soliciting customers for a prostitute or receiving her earnings. The relationship between the prostitute and the pimp is superficially voluntary, but the prostitute who attempts to sever the relationship is apt to be threatened or intimidated to such an extent that she quickly changes her mind.

Those who operate houses of prostitution or in any way contribute to the running of such enterprises are subject to prosecution in most jurisdictions. This category may include madams or business managers, landlords, taxicab drivers on commission to transport customers, and any other employees of such operations. Enforcement of these laws has led to an apparent decline in the number of brothels in the United States in recent years, but many continue to operate under the guise of massage parlors, "nude photography" studios, "nude counseling" centers, escort services, sex-therapy clinics, and other seemingly legitimate businesses. (Not all massage parlors, escort services, and so on, are fronts for prostitution. Some are strictly legitimate, and others offer these services only to selected customers who request them.) In addition, there has been an apparent increase in the number of call girls operating out of apartments "by appointment only," available at higher prices than those of "streetwalkers" who "turn tricks" in motel rooms, cars, or less private places.

Bringing women into the country or transporting them across state lines for the purpose of prostitution is now a federal offense under certain provisions of the Immigration and Nationality Act and the Mann Act (also known as the Federal White Slave Act). The Mann Act (U.S. Annotated Code, 1925, Title 18, Section 398) defines as a felony any act of transporting or aiding in transportation (for example, furnishing travel tickets or means of transportation) of a female for prostitution "or for any other immoral purpose." The latter clause provides for prosecution when no prostitution is involved. Men have been convicted under the Mann Act for crossing state lines with women friends and then having intercourse. Lovers who live near state borders are obviously particularly susceptible to such offenses.

There are those who argue that criminal sanctions against prostitution have obviously not eliminated it any more than Prohibition eliminated the consumption of alcohol, that the law has simply forced prostitution underground and into the hands of gangsters and the criminal underworld. It can also be argued that, if prostitution were legal, there could be regular medical supervision and licensing of prostitutes, leading to lower venereal-disease rates. The difficulty with any system of periodic medical examination is that a woman can be free of infection on examination and can then contract syphilis or gonorrhea from her very next customer and pass it on to all subsequent customers until the time of the next medical examination. (Contact with a prostitute is still the usual source of venereal infection among military personnel, but not among the civilian population.)

Among the male civilian population, contacts with prostitutes account for a relatively small percentage of total sexual outlet. Kinsey found that only 3.5–4.0 percent of the total sexual outlet of his male sample involved sexual relations with prostitutes. About 69 percent of the white male sample in the Kinsey study had had contact at some time or other with prostitutes, but these were often only isolated experiences. About 15–20 percent had had relations with prostitutes more than a few times a year during a period of up to five years at some time in their lives.

But even though prostitutes represented only a small *percentage* of the total sexual activity of the population, the *absolute number* of contacts with prostitutes was enormous. Kinsey estimated a total of 1,659,000 such contacts per year per million population in the United States. Put in terms of a community of 500,000 people, this figure comes to about 16,000 acts of prostitution a *week*. The magnitude of the problem that these figures present for law-enforcement officials is staggering. Full-scale enforcement of the laws governing prostitution is obviously doomed to failure, yet it seems unlikely that any major change will be made in the direction of more enforceable laws. In general, The American Law Institute recommends maintenance of the status quo. The *Model Penal Code* supports the concept that prostitution, whether carried on in private or in public, is criminal. It also appears to reaffirm the concept of prostitution as a "status crime"; that is, one in which the individual does not have to commit an act of prostitution to be guilty of an offense but has only to be identified as a prostitute to be considered guilty.

Pornography

Whereas relatively little public sentiment on regulating prostitution is apparent today, the public concern about pornography and pornography laws, both pro and con, is considerable. This is particularly true when pornography involves the use of children ("kiddie porn"), a phenomenon that has grown recently along with child prostitution. Pornography laws have a relatively short history, dating back only to the nineteenth century. The concern of the law with obscenity seems to be correlated with the development of mass communications, widespread literacy and availability of books, and the invention of the camera. In the United States the single most significant law designed to prevent the dissemination of pornographic materials is Section 1461, Title 18, of the U.S. Code, adopted in 1873. This law has been named for its primary advocate, Anthony Comstock, then Secretary of the New York Society for the Suppression of Vice. Under the Comstock Act it is a felony knowingly to deposit in the U.S. mail any obscene, lewd, or lascivious book, pamphlet, picture, writing, paper, or other publication of an "indecent character." Enforcement of this act comes under the Inspection Service of the U.S. Post Office Department. There is particular concern about material sent by mail because it is believed that this provides the "smut peddlers" with easy access to children.

In all the rhetoric on pornography it is not always clear exactly what sort of material people are including under the term. In the history of American literature we can note that Hawthorne's *The Scarlet Letter,* Mark Twain's *Huckleberry Finn,* and Henry Miller's *Tropic of Cancer* were all condemned as obscene at the time of their publication. Furthermore, some people distinguish between erotic works of art, literature, and the cinema that have potential cultural merit and those produced purely for commercial exploitation and "utterly without redeeming social value" (sometimes called "hard-core pornography"). These and other issues led the U.S. Supreme Court to provide a new definition of obscenity in the landmark case of Roth *v.* United States. The Roth case also addressed itself to the question of whether or not the Comstock Act violates the First Amendment provision that "Congress shall make no law . . . abridging the freedom of speech, or of the press." On the constitutional question, the Court clearly stated that "obscenity is *not* within the area of constitutionally protected speech or press."

In defining obscenity the Court laid down four essential elements: First, the material must be viewed in terms of its potential appeal to *the average person* (a modification of earlier definitions that included material which admittedly might affect only certain "suceptible" individuals). Second, *contemporary community standards* are to be applied. (The court acknowledged that standards vary from generation to generation.) Third, *the dominant theme* of the material and the content must be *taken as a whole,* rather than out of context. (It had previously been customary simply to present isolated "vulgar" quotes or pictures from a book, for example, without reference to the overall theme; under such a rule the Bible itself could be found obscene because of its descriptions of women's breasts, as in "The Song of Solomon," and of episodes of adultery, like that of King David. Pictures of nudes in a

magazine extolling the virtues of nudism for health purposes have become legal under this new definition.)

Fourth, the *appeal* must be *to prurient interest.* (This requirement is applicable to content as well as to the *intentions* of authors, publisher, and so on.) A typical obscenity statute—that of California—written since the Roth case defines "prurient interest" as "a shameful or morbid interest in nudity, sex, or excretion, which goes beyond customary limits of candor in description or representation of such matters and is matter which is utterly without redeeming social importance." Publishing, distributing, selling, and various related offenses are also considered crimes if the material involved is judged to be obscene by these standards.

The justifications for obscenity laws are generally three. Legislators and judges declare that pornography is damaging to children, causes increases in the numbers of sex crimes, and has deleterious effects on the morals of the population by causing sexual arousal in otherwise normal people. We shall comment briefly on each of these three issues.

There are no significant scientific data that either prove or disprove the notion of possible damage to children from pictures or books portraying or describing sexual activities. Although few argue seriously in favor of distributing "hard-core pornography" to children, the question of the benefits and dangers of early exposure to material dealing with sexual functioning, anatomy, reproduction, and so on, in sex-education classes at the elementary-school level is one that must, for the present at least, be settled by common sense. There are no reliable empirical data on this subject.

There is a substantial body of knowledge on the relation of pornography to sex crimes, particularly as reported in the Gebhard study, which has confirmed the reports of police officers and other law-enforcement officials that sex offenders often have pornography in their possession or admit to having seen pornographic materials. The cause-and-effect relation that so many have assumed, however, has not been established. In the

Gebhard study the use of pornography by sex offenders was compared to the experiences of a normal control group and to those of a group of prisoners who were not sex offenders. There were *no differences* among the three groups in use of, possession of, or exposure to pornography. Within each group variations in use and exposure to pornography were related primarily to age, socioeconomic class, and educational level. A further important finding was that sex offenders were not prone to greater sexual arousal from viewing pornography than were other groups of males.

This point leads us to the third and final issue: How susceptible are normal individuals to sexual arousal from various forms of erotica, and is such arousal an evil that should be prohibited by law? There is no doubt that viewing or reading erotic materials is sexually arousing for a significant percentage of the population. The Kinsey data on this subject are typical of the findings of other investigators (*see* Table 12.1). Should this fact be a source of concern for those responsible for criminal law? It has been the source of

such concern because of the assumption that sexual stimulation may lead normal individuals to commit illegal sex acts. But there is no particular reason to believe that sexual stimulation of a normal individual will lead to anything other than fantasies and normal sexual activity. If we accept the notion that there is nothing inherently wrong or criminal in the expression of human sexuality, then this argument is without substance.

Children are continually exposed to the graphic details of fighting, violence, and killing on television and in other media. It is paradoxical that our laws seem to be more preoccupied with prohibiting the stimulation of sexual activity than with prohibiting the stimulation of aggressive or violent behavior.

MORALITY, THE LAW, AND CHANGE

In recent years we have heard much about the "sexual revolution" and the "new morality," and the general impression is that there

Table 12.1 **SEXUAL RESPONSE IN NORMAL SUBJECTS TO VARIOUS FORMS OF EROTICA**

		Definite or frequent	Sometimes	Never	Number of subjects in study
Viewing portrayals of nudes	Male	18%	36%	46%	4,191
	Female	3%	9%	88%	5,698
Viewing commercial films	Male	6%	30%	64%	3,231
	Female	9%	39%	52%	5,411
Viewing burlesques and erotic floor shows	Male	28%	34%	38%	3,377
	Female	4%	10%	86%	2,550
Observing portrayals of sex acts	Male	42%	35%	23%	3,868
	Female	14%	18%	68%	2,242
Reading literary materials (for example, romantic novels)	Male	21%	38%	41%	3,952
	Female	16%	44%	40%	5,699
Reading erotic materials (for example, specifically sexual stories)	Male	16%	31%	53%	4,202
	Female	2%	12%	86%	5,523

Source: Compiled from data in Kinsey *et al.* (1953), Chapter 16.

has been a significant change in attitudes toward sexual morality. A poll conducted in 1977 (by Yankelovich, Skelly & White for TIME magazine) found, for instance, that up to 70 percent of Americans favor the right of homosexuals to live wherever they want, run for elective office, or serve in the army. A majority (64 percent) believe that regardless of morality, a woman should be legally free to have an abortion. Seventy percent feel that no laws, either federal or state, should regulate sexual practice. Similar data are available or could be obtained to tell us what the prevailing current attitudes are toward every aspect of human sexuality. We could base a set of moral principles on such data if we were willing to subscribe to the notion that what is right is defined by what most people believe is right—just as some social scientists define "normal" sexual behavior by the behavior patterns of the majority of people. But even in a democratic society majority opinion is not always right in the moral and ethical sense. There are standards, to which we all refer at some time or other, that go beyond the consensus and reflect belief in certain principles or moral guidelines, whether the specific issue is sexual behavior, business practices, or war. It appears that these standards and principles have remained fairly solid, even in the face of the so-called sexual revolution.

Although the TIME survey did find evidence of changing values, it seems that the sexual revolution is not as revolutionary as it once seemed, and the new morality is not as widespread as some would like to believe. There appears to be greater frankness, greater tolerance, and greater willingness to experiment in sexual matters, but basic values—especially regarding the institutions of marriage and the family—have not changed much in recent years. More than 75 percent of the men and women polled agreed that it is morally wrong for a husband or wife to be unfaithful. More than 60 percent said that it is wrong for teenagers to have sexual relationships. Seventy percent disapproved of having children without formal marriage.

The TIME survey further suggests that people are getting more conservative about pornography: 64 percent said that pornographic movies are morally wrong, and 59 percent said the same for advertisements promoting X-rated films. No less than 74 percent supported the view that the government should crack down more on pornography in movies, books, and nightclubs. Of these, 54 percent felt this strongly. When a similar question was asked in 1974, only 42 percent favored a government crackdown.

The existence of a real sexual revolution can be debated, but what cannot be debated is the fact that individuals and institutions do change their moral views with time. These changes will have to be incorporated in future moral choices. There is no doubt, for example, that the availability of reliable and reasonably safe contraceptives has already had a major influence on sexual behavior, primarily because most moral and legal codes of sexual behavior probably originated in response to concern about illegitimate offspring. The integrity of the family unit has had to be fiercely protected, because no culture can trifle with the upbringing of its progeny and hope to survive for long. It is possible, however, that such worries have now become less realistic and that certain traditional values, like reproductive fertility, are beginning to be viewed negatively in a rapidly overcrowded world.

Because changes in deep-rooted sexual mores tend to be slow—no matter how dizzying they may appear on the surface—we have yet to experience the full impact of the new separation of sex from reproduction. When it comes we will indeed have experienced a sexual revolution.

Certain taboos may well remain with us for a long time, but the reasons for observing them may change. For example, adultery may be disapproved not because it violates a religious commandment but because it violates a relationship based on trust. Sex with a teenage prostitute may be disapproved not because of a concern about venereal disease but because of a concern about exploitation. Most people, we believe, will make decisions about their sexual behavior for reasons beyond their immediate sense of pleasure or discomfort. The moral quality of behavior cannot be dissociated from motives, regardless of the consequences. As T. S. Eliot (1935) said:

The last temptation is the great treason:
To do the right deed for the wrong reason.

There is one further danger inherent in the new morality—that we may too readily justify doing the wrong thing for the right reason.

SUMMARY

1.   Probably no single doctrine has had as great an effect on sexual behavior as the doctrine which declares that the main purpose of sex and marriage is reproduction. This notion dates back to early Jewish and Christian traditions and has affected present-day moral attitudes and legal codes.

2.   St. Paul was the first important Christian teacher on issues of sexual behavior. He was in favor of the single, celibate state and taught that abstaining from all sexual activity would lead to a higher moral state. The Fathers of the Church, especially St. Augustine, carried on Paul's ideas and introduced the idea that sex, even within marriage, was shameful.

3.   In the Middle Ages St. Thomas Aquinas formalized the position of the Catholic Church with regard to sexual behavior. Premarital sex was considered sinful because it could lead to the birth of a child who might have to grow up with only one parent. The Catholic Church still forbids premarital sex. The position of the Church on abortion, however, has changed. Aquinas and others held that abortion was permissible during the early stages of pregnancy, but in 1869 the Church came out firmly against all abortions.

4.   Both Calvin and Luther, during the period known as the Reformation, helped change Christianity's views of sex and marriage. Calvin challenged the idea that the purpose of marriage and sex is procreation and viewed sex as something honorable rather than sinful. Calvin and Luther argued that priests should be allowed to marry, and Luther thought that marriage should be a civil, rather than a religious, institution. This led to more flexible divorce laws in Protestant countries.

5.   During the Renaissance (fifteenth and sixteenth centuries) romantic and physical love were glorified, but the Puritan movement (seventeenth and eighteenth centuries) restricted sex to marriage, and the Victorian era (nineteenth century) put even further restrictions on sex. It was not until the beginning of the twentieth century that pleasure came to be seen as a legitimate goal of sexual behavior. Since then, such things as the growth of science and technology and the horrors and immorality of World War II have

forced a rethinking of traditional moral values—leading to what is known as situation ethics. This approach to morality says, basically, that questions of right and wrong in any situation depend on a person's intentions and attitudes. No act is considered wrong if it is done out of love for one's fellow humans. Situation ethics may seem a simple solution to complex problems, but it puts a heavy load of responsibility on the individual.

6.   The American legal code reflects, to a great extent, traditional moral values and the notion that reproduction is the sole purpose of sex. This attitude is seen in the three general categories of laws pertaining to sexual behavior: the behavior of consenting adults in private, offenses involving force or violence or that present a public nuisance, and offenses that involve commercial exploitation of sex.

7.   Although oral-genital contacts and anal intercourse between consenting adults of the same or opposite sex in private are no longer criminal offenses in some states, most states have not legalized all consensual, private acts between adults. Fornication, adultery, certain sexual acts performed by married couples, and certain sexual acts performed by members of the same sex are illegal in most states. Abortion and sterilization for the purpose of birth control are now legal, but there are still many people who feel that abortion is morally wrong.

8.   Public nuisance offenses, such as exhibitionism, voyeurism, and transvestism, are defined as crimes on the grounds that they offend public decency, disturb the peace, and tend to corrupt morals. Sexual offenses against children are outlawed in every state, but the definition of a child, or minor, differs from state to state. The American Law Institute's *Model Penal Code* suggests that minority be defined as 16 years of age, provided the offender is at least four years older than the other person.

9.   Rape, sexual intercourse under conditions of force or the threat of violence, is considered the most serious of sexual offenses. There are, however, problems with the definition of rape (What constitutes consent? How much resistance must be shown by the victim?) and with sexist attitudes and the legal procedures involved in proving rape.

10.   Prostitution is illegal, and the general attitude in our society is that it is a social and moral evil. Criminal sanctions against prostitution have not been effective in eliminating it, but the *Model Penal Code* supports the concept that prostitution is criminal.

11.   Although there is no particular reason to believe that sexual stimulation of a normal person through pornography will lead to anything other than fantasies and normal sexual activity, pornography is still regarded as immoral by many people and is considered criminal in some instances.

It has been suggested that we have **313**
gone through a sexual revolution in recent years, but whether or not this is the
case—and some indications are that if there has been a revolution it has not
been as revolutionary as it may have appeared at first glance—the fact remains
that individuals and institutions do change with time. Any changes that do occur
will have to be incorporated in future moral choices.

SUGGESTED READING

Barnett, W. *Sexual Freedom and the Constitution.* Albuquerque: University of
New Mexico Press, 1973.
A legal and historical analysis of sex laws in the United States, particularly
those that apply to the sexual behavior of consenting adults.

Dienes, C. T. *Law, Politics and Birth Control.* Chicago: University of Illinois Press,
1972.
A detailed history of the evolution of laws governing birth control and abortion
in the United States.

The Report of the Commission on Obscenity and Pornography. New York: Bantam
Books, 1970.
A detailed review of research, legal history, and political opinion about the
effects of pornography and efforts to control it in the United States.

Cohen, A. *Everyman's Talmud.* New York: Dutton, 1949.
A summary of traditional Jewish law and moral principles regarding sex, marriage, and the family, as well as other areas.

Fletcher, J. *Moral Responsibility: Situation Ethics at Work.* Philadelphia: Westminster Press, 1967.
A discussion of situation ethics, with particular emphasis on sexual morality,
written by a Protestant theologian.

Thomas, J. L., S.J. *Catholic Viewpoint on Marriage and the Family.* New York:
Doubleday Image Books, 1965.
A concise discussion of the Roman Catholic viewpoint on moral issues involving
sex, marriage, and reproduction.

abortion Termination of pregnancy, usually during the first 12 weeks, by expulsion of the fetus.

adrenocorticotrophic hormone Pituitary hormone that stimulates secretion of hormones by the adrenal glands.

afterbirth The discharge of the placenta, along with the fetal membranes, during the third stage of labor.

amniocentesis Procedure for testing the chromosomal makeup of the fetus when an abnormality is suspected or for determining the sex of an unborn child.

ampulla In the female, the second portion of the fallopian tubes located between the infundibulum and the isthmus. In the male, the terminal enlargement of the vas deferens before it joins the ejaculatory duct.

anal intercourse Intromission of the penis into the anus.

androgens Male sex hormones produced by the adrenal glands in both males and females and by the testes in the male; may be related to the female sex drive.

anterior pituitary The front portion of the pituitary gland.

anus The opening of the alimentary canal located between the buttocks.

aphrodisiacs Substances believed to enhance sexual drive or potency.

areola The area surrounding the nipple.

autoeroticism Solitary sexual behavior consisting of erotic fantasies, masturbation, and erotic dreams.

axillary hair Underarm hair which appears at puberty; a secondary sex characteristic.

Bartholin's glands Two small glands located behind the vestibular bulbs which are the female counterpart of the male Cowper's glands; also called bulbourethal glands.

behavior therapy Approach to the treatment of emotional problems, including sexual dysfunctions, based on the principles of learning theories.

bestiality See **zoophilia.**

birth control Prevention of pregnancy by artificial or voluntary means.

bisexual Term applied to individuals who engage in both homosexual and heterosexual activities.

blastocyst The fluid-filled structure that develops about five days after fertilization of the egg cell and that attaches itself to the lining of the uterus, eventually to become a fetus.

body of the uterus The main part of the uterus.

bulb of the penis The expanded inner end of the corpus spongiosum, or spongy body, of the penis; with the crura makes up the root of the penis.

bulbocavernosus A muscle surrounding the bulb of the penis which aids in ejecting urine and semen through the urethra; see also **ischiocavernosus.**

cardiac prominence By the end of the fourth week in the development of the embryo the upper bulge on the front side of the trunk representing the developing heart.

castration Removal of the testes, which in a young boy prevents the development of secondary sex characteristics. The term is also used to mean amputation of the penis.

cephalic position The head-down position

of the fetus in the final trimester of pregnancy, the most common position for delivery.

cervical caps Contraceptive devices similar to diaphragms, popular in Europe.

cervical dilation The first step in a method of abortion used in the first trimester of pregnancy involving the expansion of the cervix and the scraping of the uterus.

cervix The lower part of the uterus which projects into the vagina.

cesarean section Surgical operation through the walls of the abdomen and uterus for the purpose of delivering the baby.

chancre The hard, round ulcer at the site of sexual contact that characterizes the early stages of syphilis.

chancroid Venereal disease marked by a soft, painful chancre.

childbirth (puerperal) fever A contagious disease which spreads among pregnant women unless antiseptic practices are instituted to prevent it.

chromosomes Rodlike bits of material in the nucleus of each cell which are the site of genes and which provide information to guide cells in their division and multiplication.

cilia Tiny hairlike structures that line the fallopian tubes.

circumcision The surgical cutting off of part of the foreskin of the penis, leaving the glans exposed.

climacteric The period, usually between the ages of 46 and 50, during which women experience the physiological changes associated with menopause.

clitoral orgasm Culmination of sexual excitement achieved through direct stimulation of the clitoris.

clitoridectomy Removal of the clitoris.

clitoris A small, highly sensitive organ within the minor lips of the female; the developmental counterpart of the penis.

coitus Heterosexual intercourse, or copulation; the coupling of the penis and the vagina.

coitus interruptus The birth-control measure involving withdrawal of the penis from the vagina just before ejaculation.

coitus reservatus Coitus without ejaculation.

common-law marriages Marriages effected by agreement between couples without licenses or ceremonies.

condom Thin, flexible sheath worn over the erect penis to prevent sperm from entering the vagina.

contraceptive Device or drug to prevent pregnancy.

corona The extremely sensitive rim, or crown, of the glans penis.

corpora cavernosa The cavernous bodies, two of the three cylinders of spongy tissue which make up the penis.

corpus luteum Small structure that develops out of the ruptured ovarian follicle during the secretory phase of the menstrual cycle.

corpus spongiosum The spongy body, one of the three cylinders of spongy tissue which make up the penis.

Cowper's glands Glands which secrete a sticky, alkaline fluid that appears on the glans penis during sexual arousal.

crura The inner tips of the corpora cavernosa, or cavernous bodies, of the penis which are attached to the pubic bones; with the bulb make up the root of the penis.

culdoscope Instrument used by physicians to see inside the abdominal cavity.

culdoscopy A method for sterilization of the female involving locating the fallopian tubes through a puncture in the closed end of the vagina.

cunnilingus Oral stimulation of the female genitals.

curette In abortions involving cervical dilation, the metal instrument used to scrape the tissue off the inner walls of the uterus.

cystitis Infection or inflammation of the bladder.

desensitization Therapeutic approach to emotional problems, including sexual dysfunctions, based on gradually leading patients to confront their problem situations without anxiety.

detumescence Partial or total loss of erection of the penis.

diaphragm A thin rubber dome positioned over the cervix to prevent sperm from entering the cervical canal.

dildo Artificial penis used for sexual stimulation.

douching Washing out of the vagina.

ductus deferens See **vas deferens.**

dysmenorrhea Painful menstruation.

ectopic pregnancy Implantation of the fertilized ovum in the wall of the fallopian tube, a condition resulting in the death of the fetus and sometimes the rupturing of the tube.

ejaculation The ejection of semen in male orgasm.

ejaculatory impotence Failure of the erect penis to ejaculate.

embryo The organism resulting from the fertilized ovum approximately one week after fertilization; after the eighth week of pregnancy is termed the fetus.

embryonic disk Early in pregnancy a disk-shaped layer of cells which forms across the center of the blastocyst and from which the fetus grows.

endocrine glands Glands, including the thyroid, parathyroid, pituitary, and adrenal glands, that secrete hormones into the bloodstream.

endocrinology The study of the secretions of the endocrine glands.

endometrium The lining of the uterus shed during menstruation. See **mucosa.**

epididymis Mass of ducts at the back of the testes through which sperm first pass on leaving the seminiferous tubules.

episiotomy An incision of the perineum that is sometimes performed to ease the passage of the baby's head at birth.

erectile dysfunction See **impotence.**

erection The state in which the penis is engorged with blood and becomes firm and erect.

erogenous zones Areas of the body that are particularly sensitive to erotic tactile stimulation.

erotic fantasies Daydreams with a sexual focus that may be accompanied by sexual arousal; see **autoeroticism.**

estrogen Female sex hormone produced by the ovaries.

eunuchs Castrated males.

exhibitionism Male sexual deviation involving the exposure of the genitals to involuntary observers.

fallopian tubes The tubes through which ova are transported from the ovaries to the uterus; also called uterine tubes.

false labor Contractions of the uterus at irregular intervals in the ninth month of pregnancy which are sometimes taken as the beginning of actual labor.

fellatio Oral stimulation of the male genitals.

fetishism A sexual variation in which the sexual object is an inanimate article, such as a piece of clothing.

fetus A developing human being in the uterus from about eight weeks after conception until birth.

fimbriae Projections fringing the infundibulum of the fallopian tube.

flush See **hot flash.**

follicle (retention) cyst A common form of ovarian cyst resulting from failure of the graafian follicle to rupture.

follicles The many capsules, each containing an ovum in various stages of development, embedded in the tissues of the ovaries.

follicle-stimulating hormone One of the two pituitary hormones that stimulate the gonads.

follicle-stimulating releasing factor Chemical factor secreted by the hypothalamus which has a reproductive function.

foreplay Period of sexually arousing activity preceding coitus.

foreskin The skin covering part of the glans penis; see also **prepuce.**

fornication Sexual intercourse other than between husband and wife.

frenulum In the male, the thin strip of skin on the underside of the glans penis stretching from the glans to the body of the penis. In the female, the fold of skin beneath the clitoris formed by the lower portions of the minor lips.

fundus The rounded part of the uterus which is located above the fallopian tubes.

gender identity The recognition of one's individuality as male or female as experienced through self-awareness and behavior; see also **gender role.**

gender role All that one says and does to indicate to the self and others that one is male, female, or ambivalent; see also **gender identity.**

glans penis The smooth, rounded tip of the penis.

gonadotrophins The two pituitary hormones (follicle-stimulating hormone and luteinizing hormone) that stimulate the gonads.

gonads The paired reproductive glands; testes in the male and ovaries in the female.

gonorrhea A contagious venereal disease caused by a bacterial infection which affects mucous membrane tissues.

graafian follicle The spherical structure encasing the egg within the ovary.

Granuloma inguinale Venereal disease marked by spreading lesions.

gynecomastia Temporary enlargement of the breasts in males during puberty.

Hegar's sign The softening of an area between the cervix and the body of the uterus; a good indicator of pregnancy.

hepatic prominence By the end of the fourth week in the development of the embryo the lower bulge on the front side of the trunk representing the growing liver.

hermaphrodites Individuals with the gonadal and genital characteristics of both sexes.

Herpes Simplex Virus Type 2 Common viral infection characterized by blisters in the genital area.

hot flash Symptom of the climacteric characterized by the sensation of waves of heat spreading over the face and upper half of the body; also called **flush.**

homosexual An individual who engages in sexual activity with members of the same sex; the term is usually applied to males.

human chorionic gonadotrophin (HCG) The hormone measured in pregnancy tests which is produced by the placenta.

hypospadias Condition in which the opening of the urethra is located under rather than at the tip of the glans penis.

hypothalamus Site in the brain that regulates the pituitary gland; secretes the chemical factors follicle-stimulating hormone releasing factor and luteinizing hormone-releasing factor, among others.

hysterectomy The surgical removal of the uterus resulting in sterilization.

impotence Failure of the male to achieve erection during sexual activity.

incest Sexual relations between an individual and close relatives.

infundibulum The fringed, ovarian end of the fallopian tubes.

inguinal hernia A condition in males in which loops of the intestine make their way into the scrotal sac; also called **rupture.**

intercourse. See **coitus.**

interstitial-cell-stimulating hormone Term for the luteinizing hormone in the male.

intrauterine device (IUD) A device, usually plastic, inserted into the uterus by a physician in order to prevent pregnancy.

introitus The opening of the vagina within the minor lips.

ischiocavernosus A muscle attached to the bulb of the penis which aids in ejecting urine and semen through the urethra; see also **bulbocavernosus.**

isthmus of the fallopian tubes The third segment of the fallopian tubes located between the ampulla and the uterine border.

laminaria sticks Sticks made from compressed seaweed which when inserted into the cervix expand to cause cervical dilation, the first step in a method of abortion; see **cervical dilation.**

lanugo Fine hair that appears on the scalp and above the eyes in the developing fetus during the fifth or sixth month.

larynx The voice box, which in males enlarges as a secondary sex characteristic.

lesbianism Female homosexuality.

luteinizing hormone One of the two pituitary hormones that stimulate the ovaries.

luteinizing hormone-releasing factor Chemical factor secreted by the hypothalamus which has reproductive function.

Lymphogranuloma venereum Venereal disease characterized by tenderness of the lymph glands.

major lips (labia majora) Two elongated folds of skin that run down and back from the mons pubis and constitute the outermost portion of the female genitalia.

mammary gland The milk-producing part of the breast.

mammograms Special X-rays for diagnosing breast cancer.

masochism Sexual deviation in which an individual must experience pain in order to achieve sexual gratification.

mastalgia In females painful swelling of the breasts associated with cyclical hormone changes and the buildup of body fluid.

mastectomy Surgical removal of the breast.

masturbation Self-stimulation for sexual pleasure usually involving genital manipulation.

meiosis The process of reduction division by which male and female germ cells each end up with 23 chromosomes, or half the normal number.

menarche The first menstruation.

menopause In females the end of the reproductive period characterized by various physiological changes.

menstrual extraction Suction method of removing menstrual tissue and fluids to alleviate painful menstruation.

menstrual migraines Headaches associated with menstruation.

menstruation In females the periodic uterine bleeding that accompanies the ovarian cycle and involves the shedding of the lining of the uterus.

mesonephric duct One of paired ducts present in the early stages of development of the reproductive system from which develop the genital ducts in males. Also called **Wolffian duct.**

middlepiece The cone-shaped portion of the sperm lying between the head and the tail.

minor lips (labia minora) In the female two hairless folds of skin located between the major lips.

miscarriage The termination of pregnancy by natural causes.

mitosis The process of cell division.

mittelschmerz Unexplained intermittent cramps in the lower abdomen that sometimes occur during ovulation.

mons pubis The soft, rounded mound of fatty tissue that covers the female pubic symphysis; also called the **mons veneris.**

mons veneris See **mons pubis.**

morula A round mass of smaller cells, resulting a few days after fertilization, from the original fertilized egg cell.

Müllerian ducts See **paramesonephric duct.**

mutual orgasm The simultaneous experiencing by a couple of the sexual climax during intercourse.

myometrium The second, muscular layer of the uterus which gives it elasticity and strength.

myotonia The increased muscle tension that accompanies sexual arousal.

necrophilia Sexual deviation involving the sexual use of corpses.

neuroendocrinology The study of the role of the brain in hormone secretion.

nipple The prominent pigmented tip of the breast.

nocturnal emissions Nocturnal orgasms, or those that take place during sleep, among males; also called **wet dreams.**

nocturnal orgasms Orgasms that take place during sleep, usually accompanied by dreams; see also **nocturnal emissions.**

no-fault divorce Divorce by consent of both partners with property divided evenly.

nongonococcal urethritis A venereal disease that may result in infections of the eyes in infants of women so affected; in males causes inflammation of the urethra.

nubility The final stage of puberty, during

which full fertility is achieved.

ophthalmia neonatorum A gonorrheal infection, acquired by infants during passage through infected birth canals, which can cause blindness.

orgasm The climax of sexual arousal consisting of the discharge of neuromuscular tension accompanied by feelings of intense pleasure.

orgasmic platform The congestion of the walls of the outer third of the vagina which appears during the plateau phase of the sexual response cycle.

orgasmic unresponsiveness In females repeated failure to attain orgasm.

ova Germ cells, or eggs, produced by the ovaries (Singular, "ovum")

ovarian cortex The surface of the ovary.

ovarian cysts Fluid-filled sacs in the ovaries.

ovarian ligaments Bands of tissue that attach the ovaries to the sides of the uterus.

ovarian medulla The central portion of the ovaries, rich in blood vessels.

ovaries The pair of reproductive glands, or gonads, of the females that produce ova (eggs) and the sex hormones estrogen and progesterone.

ovum The egg, the germ cell produced in the ovaries.

ovutimer A device that when inserted into the vagina determines the time of ovulation by measuring the stickiness of cervical mucus.

oxytocin A pituitary hormone which in the late stages of labor causes contractions that expel the fetus and which also causes the ejection of milk from the breast to the nipple during breast feeding.

paramesonephric duct One of the paired ducts present in the early stages of development of the reproductive system; from which develop the female genital passages. Also called **Müllerian ducts.**

pedephile Individual who uses children for sexual gratification.

pederasty A sexual deviation involving anal intercourse with a child.

Pediculosis pubis Infestation of the pubic hair by lice, usually sexually transmitted.

pelvis The basin-shaped bony structure made up of the sacrum and the two hip bones which contains and protects the internal sex organs.

penis The external male sex organ for copulation and urination.

perimetrium The external third layer of the uterus; also called the **serosa.**

perineum The skin and deeper tissues between the openings of the vagina and anus which is sometimes torn or cut purposefully during childbirth.

petting Erotic caressing, basically similar to foreplay, but not leading to coitus.

phallus The Greek name for "penis".

pharyngeal gonorrhea A form of gonorrhea characterized by an infection of the throat transmitted during fellatio.

Pill, the Popular name for a number of commonly used oral contraceptives.

pituitary gland Complex endocrine gland located at the base of the brain.

placenta The organ through which nutrients are passed from the mother to the fetus growing in the womb.

polar body The result of the first, mitotic division of the egg, containing 46 chromosomes, which later disentegrates.

posterior pituitary The rear portion of the pituitary gland.

pregnancy The state of carrying a developing child in the womb.

premature ejaculation In males orgasm before or right after vaginal entry.

premenstrual tension Fatigue, irritability, and other discomforts that signal the onset of menstruation.

prepuce In the male the skin covering part of the glans penis; see also **foreskin.** In the female the single fold of skin covering the clitoris.

priapism A rare condition in males marked by persistent erection.

primary oocytes The several hundred thousand immature ova contained in the ovaries at birth.

progesterone A female sex hormone produced in the ovaries.

progestogens A group of synthetic compounds, which because of their ability to inhibit ovulation, are used as a contraceptive drug.

prolactin Pituitary hormone that stimulates milk production.

prolactin-inhibiting factor Secretion of the hypothalamus that controls milk production by preventing prolactin production except after childbirth.

prostaglandins Chemicals known to stimulate the muscles of the uterus as well as muscles of the gastrointestinal tract.

prostitution The performance of sexual acts by women with men who pay for them.

prostate gland A glandular body at the bottom of the bladder that contributes most of the fluid to the ejaculate.

pseudohermaphroditism In females the enlargement of external sex organs caused by a defect in the functioning of the adrenal glands.

puberty The biological stage of development that begins with the appearance of secondary sexual characteristics and lasts until the start of reproductive ability.

pubic hair Hair that appears at puberty in the pubic area of the lower abdomen; a secondary sex characteristic.

pubic symphysis The point in the lower abdomen at which the hip bones of the pelvis are attached to each other.

quickening Fetal movements, a positive determinant of pregnancy, which usually appear by the end of the fifth month.

rape The use of force on an unwilling victim to achieve sexual gratification.

rectal gonorrhea A gonorrheal infection of the rectum transmitted during anal intercourse.

retrograde ejaculation A condition in which the semen is ejaculated into the urinary bladder rather than flowing out normally.

rhythm method Method of birth control based on avoidance of intercourse during a woman's fertile period.

rubella German measles virus.

rupture See **inguinal hernia.**

sacrum The end of the spinal column which forms a part of the pelvis.

sadism Sexual deviation in which sexual gratification is derived by inflicting pain.

sadomasochism A form of behavior in which sex and pain are pathologically linked.

saline abortions Abortions induced by injection of a salt solution into the uterus; used during the second trimester of pregnancy.

scrotum The external sac that contains the testes.

secondary oocyte The result of the first, mitotic division of the egg, containing 46 chromosomes.

secondary sex characteristics The physiological changes that accompany genital and reproductive maturity.

secretory phase In the menstrual cycle the period after ovulation.

semen The whitish fluid which contains the sperm. Also called ejaculate.

seminal vesicle Paired sacs in the male reproductive tract which are believed to contribute fluids that activate the movement of sperm.

seminiferous tubules The tubes within the testes that are the site of sperm production.

serosa See **perimetrium.**

sex hormones Chemicals produced by the sex glands that play a role in reproduction and sexual behavior.

sexual deviations Departures from standard coital practice; also called **sexual variations.**

sexual variations See **sexual deviations.**

situation ethics Approach to ethical decisions in which the individual determines what is right or wrong on the basis of the situation itself rather than in terms of a universal moral law.

smegma The cheesy substance secreted between the glans penis and the foreskin.

spermatids The cells resulting from reduction division, or meiosis, of the spermatocytes, that eventually become mature sperm.

spermatocytes The second stage of development of sperm cells.

spermatogenesis The process of sperm formation which takes place within the seminiferous tubules of the testes.

spermatogonia Cells that lie along the internal linings of the seminiferous tubules; the first stage of development of the sperm.

spermatozoa The male germ cells produced in the testes; often shortened to sperm.

spermicidal substances Contraceptive jellies, foams, creams, and suppositories which are inserted into the vagina to kill sperm on contact.

sphincters Muscular rings that surround body openings, for example, the vaginal sphincter and the anal sphincter.

Spirochaeta pallidum The microorganism that causes syphilis.

spontaneous abortion Miscarriage, or the unwanted termination of pregnancy.

statutory rape The crime of intercourse with a girl under a certain age, varying from 14 to 21, depending on the state.

steroids Group of chemical substances including the sex hormones estrogen, progesterone, and testosterone.

suction curette The instrument used to perform a vacuum aspiration, or abortion.

"Super clap" A relatively recent strain of gonorrhea that is resistant to penicillin treatment.

superfecundation The biological phenomenon in which twins have different fathers.

superfetation The rare occurrence of the fertilization and development of an egg when a fetus is already present in the uterus.

syphilis An infectious venereal disease characterized by lesions in various parts of the body.

testes The pair of external reproductive glands, or gonads, of the male which produce testosterone and sperm; the singular is "testicle."

testicle See **testes.**

toxemia A condition that occurs only in pregnant women in which a poison produced by the body can, if uncontrolled, lead to infection, hemorrhaging, and death.

transsexual Term applied to individuals—usually males—who wish to be members of the opposite sex.

transvestism Sexual variation in which sexual gratification is obtained through wearing the clothing of the opposite sex.

tribadism A lesbian practice in which the genitals are mutually stimulated while one woman lies on top of the other and simulates coitus.

troilism Sexual relations among three people, one of whom is of the opposite sex.

tubal ligation For sterilization of females the procedure that involves tying or cutting the fallopian tubes.

urethra The tube running through the corpus spongiosum of the penis that carries both urine and semen out of the body. In the female the urethra, the opening of which is located just to the rear of the clitoris, carries only urine.

urethral meatus The opening of the urethra to the outside.

urethral sphincter Mass of muscle fibers that make possible the voluntary control of urination.

uterine mucosa The inner layer of the uterus consisting of numerous glands and blood vessels; also called the **endometrium.**

uterus The womb, the organ in which the developing organism is sustained until birth.

vacuum aspiration A simple method of abortion involving the use of suction to withdraw fluids and tissues from the uterus.

vagina The copulatory organ of the female.

vaginal orgasm Orgasm reached through stimulation of the vagina.

vas deferens Duct which conveys sperm from the epididymis to the ejaculatory duct.

vasectomy The surgical cutting of the vas deferens in the scrotal sac which results in male sterilization.

vasocongestion During sexual arousal the overfilling of the blood vessels and the increased flow of blood into body tissues; for example, the erection of the penis.

vestibular bulbs   Masses of erectile tissue which surround the vaginal opening.

voyeurism   A sexual variation that focuses on seeing, or "peeping" at a naked person without the person's knowledge.

vulva   The external female sex organs.

wet dreams   See **nocturnal emissions.**

Wolffian duct   See **mesonephric duct.**

womb   See **uterus.**

zona pellucida   The gelatinous capsule surrounding the mature egg.

zoophilia   Sexual deviation involving sexual contacts between humans and animals; also called **bestiality.**

A research questionnaire on sex. *Psychology Today,* 3, no. 2 (July 1969), 64–87.

A research questionnaire on sex. *Psychology Today,* 6, no. 2 (July 1972), 55–87.

Abraham, K. *Selected papers of Karl Abraham.* London: Hogarth Press and Institute of Psychoanalysis, 1948.

Advisory Committee on Obstetrics and Gynecology, Food and Drug Administration. *Report on the oral contraceptives.* Washington, D.C.: Government Printing Office, 1966.

——. *Report on intrauterine contraceptive devices.* Washington, D.C.: Government Printing Office, 1968.

——. *Second report on the oral contraceptives.* Washington, D.C.: Government Printing Office, 1969.

Ainsworth, M. *The effects of maternal deprivation: A review of findings and controversy in the context of research strategy.* World Health Organization, Public Health Paper no. 14. Geneva: WHO, 1962.

Allen, C. *A textbook of psychosexual disorders.* 2nd ed. London: Oxford University Press, 1969.

Amelar, R.D. *Infertility in men.* Philadelphia: F.A. Davis Co., 1966.

American Law Institute. *Model penal code: Tentative draft no. 4.* Philadelphia, 1955.

——. *Model penal code: Proposed official draft.* Philadelphia, 1962.

American Psychiatric Association. *Diagnostic and statistical manual of mental disorders.* 2nd ed. Washington, D.C.: APA, 1968.

Amir, M. *Patterns of forcible rape.* Chicago: University of Chicago Press, 1971.

Amos, S. *Laws for the regulation of vice.* London: Stevens & Sons, 1877.

Anati, E. *Camonica Valley.* New York: Alfred A. Knopf, 1961.

Anderson, G.G., and L. Speroff. Prostaglandins. *Science* 171:502–504.

Aquinas, St. Thomas. *The summa theologica.* Fathers of the English Dominican Province, trs. New York: Benziger Bros., 1911–1925.

Ard, B.N. Percentage of women who experience orgasm. *Medical Aspects of Human Sexuality* (April 1974), 35–39.

Arey, L.B. *Developmental anatomy.* 7th ed. Philadelphia: W.B. Saunders Co., 1965.

Arnstein, R.L. Virgin men. *Medical Aspects of Human Sexuality,* 7, no. 1 (January 1974), 113–125.

Athanasiou, R. A review of public attitudes on sexual issues. In *Contemporary Sexual Behavior: Critical Issues in the 1970's,* Joseph Zubin and John Money, eds. Baltimore: Johns Hopkins University Press, 1973, Ch. 19.

Augustine, St. *The city of God, book XIV.* J. Healey, trs., E. Baker, intro. London and Toronto: J.M. Dent & Sons, Ltd.; New York: E.P. Dutton & Co., 1934.

——. *Treatises on marriage and other subjects.* C. Wilcox *et al.,* trs., R.J. Deferrari, ed. New York: Fathers of the Church, Inc., 1955.

Austin, C.R., and R.V. Short. *Reproduction in Mammals.* Vol. 1: *Germ cells and fertilization.* Vol. 2: *Embryonic and fetal development.* Vol. 3: *Hormones in reproduction.* Vol 4: *Reproductive patterns.* Vol. 5: *Artificial control of reproduction.* London: Cambridge University Press, 1972.

Bailey, S. *Sexual relation in Christian thought.* New York: Harper & Row, 1959.

——. *Sexual ethics: A Christian view.* New York: Macmillan Co., 1963.

Bāṇa (Banabhatta). *Kādambarī.* C.M. Ridding, trs. Bombay: Jaico Publishing House, 1956.

Bandura, A., and R.H. Walters. *Social learning and personality development.* New York: Holt, Rinehart and Winston, 1963.

Bardwick, J. *Psychology of women.* New York: Harper & Row, 1971.

Barnett, W. *Sexual freedom and the constitution.* Albuquerque: University of New Mexico Press, 1973.

Bartell, G.D. *Group sex.* New York: Peter H. Wyden, 1971.

Bates, M. *Gluttons and libertines.* New York: Vintage Books, 1967.

Baudelaire, C. *Les fleurs du mal.* Paris: Société des belles lettres, 1952.

Beach, F. A review of physiological and psychological studies of sexual behavior in mammals. *Physiological Review* 27, no. 2 (1947), 240–305.

Beach, F.A., ed. *Sex and behavior.* New York: John Wiley & Sons, 1965.

Beckett, S. *Malone dies.* London: Penguin Books, 1962.

Bell, R.R., and M. Gordon, eds. *The social dimension of human sexuality.* Boston: Little, Brown and Company, 1972.

Belliveau, F., and L. Richter. *Understanding human sexual inadequacy.* New York: Bantam Books, 1970.

Belt, B.G. Some organic causes of impotence. *Medical Aspects of Human Sexuality.* New York: Hospital Publications, Inc. VII, no. 1 (January 1973), 152–161.

Benedek, T. The functions of the sexual apparatus and their disturbances. In *Psychosomatic medicine,* F. Alexander, ed. New York: W.W. Norton & Co., 1950, 216–262.

——. *Psychosexual functions in women.* New York: Ronald Press, 1952.

Benson, R.C. *Handbook of obstetrics and gynecology.* 3rd ed. Los Altos, Calif.: Lange Medical Publications, 1968.

Berelson, B. Beyond family planning. *Science* 163(1969): 533–543.

Bergstrom, S., M. Bygdeman, B. Samuelsson, and N. Wiqvist. The prostaglandins and human reproduction. *Hospital Practice* 6 (February 1971) 51–57.

Bieber, I., *et al. Homosexuality—A psychoanalytic study.* New York: Basic Books, 1962. (Paperback edition entitled *Homosexuality:* New York: Random House, Vintage paperback).

Bishop, N. The great Oneida love-in. *American Heritage* (February 1969) 20: 14–17, 86–92.

Boccaccio, G. *The decameron.* John Payne, trs. New York: The Modern Library, n.d.

Bohannan, P. *Love, sex and being human: A book about the human condition for young people.* Garden City, N.Y.: Doubleday & Co., 1969.

Bonaparte, M. *Female sexuality.* New York: International Universities Press, 1953.

Borell, U. Contraceptive methods—their safety, efficacy, and acceptability. *Acta Obstet. et Gynecolog. Scand.* 45, Suppl. 1 (1966): 9–45.

Bowlby, J. *Maternal care and mental health.* World Health Organization Monograph Series no. 2. Geneva: WHO, 1951.

——. *Attachment. Attachment and loss,* vol. 1. New York: Basic Books, 1969.

——. *Separation. Attachment and loss,* vol. 11. New York: Basic Books, Inc., 1973.

Brecher, E.M. *The sex researchers.* Boston: Little, Brown & Co., 1969.

Brecher, R., and E. Brecher. *An analysis of human sexual response.* New York: New American Library, 1966.

Brenner, C. *An elementary textbook of psychoanalysis.* Garden City, N.Y.: Doubleday & Co., 1957.

Brod, M. *Franz Kafka: Eine biographie.* New York: Schocken, 1946.

Broderick, C.B., and J. Bernard. *The individual, sex, and society: A SIECUS handbook for teachers and counselors.* Baltimore: The Johns Hopkins Press, 1969.

Brodie, H.K. *et al.* Plasma testosterone levels in heterosexual and homosexual men. *American Journal of Psychiatry* (1974), 131, 82–83.

Brown, W.J. *et al. Syphilis and other venereal diseases.* Cambridge: Harvard University Press, 1970.

Brunner, H.E. *The divine imperative.* O. Wyon, trs. Philadelphia: Westminster Press, 1947.

Burgoyne, D.S. Factors affecting coital frequency, *Medical aspects of human sexuality* 8, no. 4 (April 1974): 143–156.

Burroughs, W. *Naked lunch.* New York: Grove Press, 1959.

——. *The ticket that exploded.* New York: Grove Press, 1968.

Burton, R. *The anatomy of melancholy*. London: J.M. Dent & Sons, 1932.

Burton, R.F., trs. *The thousand and one nights*. n.d. Luristan, ed. n.p.: "Printed by the Burton Club for subscribers only."

Byron (George Gordon, Lord Byron). *The poetical works of Lord Byron*. London: Oxford University Press, 1912.

Cairns, R.B., J.C. Paul, and J. Wishner. Sex censorship: The assumptions of antiobscenity laws and the empirical evidence. *Minnesota Law Review* 46(1962): 1008–1041.

Calder-Marshall, A. *The sage of sex*. New York: G.P. Putnam's Sons, 1959.

Calderone, M.S., ed. *Manual of contraceptive practice*. 2nd ed. Baltimore: Williams & Wilkins Co., 1970.

Callahan, D. *Abortion: law, choice and morality*. New York: Macmillan Co., 1970.

Calverton, V.F., and S.D. Schmalhausen. *Sex in civilization*. New York: Citadel Press, 1929.

Calvin, J. *Institutes of the Christian religion*. J.T. McNeill, ed. London: S.C.M. Press, 1960.

Caprio, F., and D. Brenner. *Sexual behavior: Psycholegal aspects*. New York: Citadel Press, 1961.

Casanova de Seingalt, G.G. *Memoires*. Paris: Gallimard, 1958–1960.

Chall, L.P. The reception of the Kinsey report in the periodicals of the United States: 1947–1949. In *Sexual behavior in American society*, J. Himelhoch and S.F. Fava, eds. New York: W.W. Norton & Co., 1955, 364–378.

Chamove, A., H.F. Harlow, and G. Mitchell. Sex differences in the infant-directed behavior of preadolescent rhesus monkeys. *Child Development* 38(1967): 329–335.

Changing morality: The two Americas, a *Time*-Louis Harris poll. *Time* (June 6, 1969): 26–27.

Chertok, L. Psychosomatic methods of preparation for childbirth. *American Journal of Obstetrics and Gynecology* 98(1967): 698–707.

Christenson, C.V. *Kinsey: A biography*. Bloomington: Indiana University Press, 1971.

Churchill, W. *Homosexual behavior among males*. New York: Hawthorn Books, 1967.

Clark, L. "Is there a difference between a clitoral and a vaginal orgasm?" *Journal of Sex Research* 6, no. 1 (February 1970): 25–28.

Cleaver, E. *Soul on ice*. New York: Dell Publishing Co., 1968.

Cleland, J. *Memoirs of a woman of pleasure*. New York: G.P. Putnam's Sons, 1963.

Cochran, W.G., F. Mosteller, and J.W. Tukey. *Statistical problems of the Kinsey report of sexual behavior in the human male*. Washington, D.C.: American Statistical Association, 1954.

Cohen, A. *Everyman's Talmud*. New York: E.P. Dutton & Co., 1949.

Colby, K.M. *A primer for psychotherapists*. New York: Ronald Press, 1951.

Colette, S.G. *Claudine à l'école*. Paris: Le Fleuron, 1948–1950.

Collis, J.S. *Havelock Ellis: Artist of life*. New York: William Sloane Associates, 1959.

Comfort, A. *The anxiety makers*. New York: Delta Publishing Co., 1967.

Comfort, A. *The joy of sex*. New York: Crown Publishers, 1972.

Comfort A. *Likelihood of human pheromones*. *Nature*, 230(1971): 432–433.

Comfort, A. *More Joy*. New York: Crown Publishers, 1974.

Cory, D.W. *The lesbian in America*. New York: Citadel Press, 1964.

Crawley, L.Q., J.L. Malfetti, E.I. Stewart, and N. Vas Dias. *Reproduction, sex, and preparation for marriage*. Englewood Cliffs, N.J.: Prentice-Hall, 1964.

Curtis, Helena. *Biology: The science of life*. New York: Worth Publishers, 1968.

Daly, C.B. *Morals, law and life*. Chicago, Dublin, London: Scepter Publishers, 1966.

Danté Alighieri. *The inferno*. J. Ciardi, trs. New York: American Library, 1954.

De Beauvoir, S. *The second sex*. New York: Alfred A. Knopf, 1952.

Defoe, D. *The fortunes and misfortunes of the amorous Moll Flanders*. New York: The Modern Library, 1926.

Dement, W. An essay on dreams. In *New directions in psychology II*. New York: Holt, Rinehart and Winston (1965): 135–257.

Dengrove, E. The mecanotherapy of sexual disorders. *The Journal of Sex Research*, 7, no. 1 (February 1971): 1–12.

De Rougemont, D. *Love in the western world*. New York: Pantheon Books, 1956.

Deutsch, H. *The psychology of women.* 2 vols. New York: Grune & Stratton, 1944–1945.

——. *The psychology of women.* Vol. 1. *Girlhood.* New York: Bantam Books, 1973. (First published in 1944.)

Devereux, G. Institutionalized homosexuality of the Mohave Indians. In *Human biology,* 9. Detroit: Wayne State University Press (1937): 498–527.

DeVore, I., ed. *Primate behavior: Field studies of monkeys and apes.* New York: Holt, Rinehart and Winston, 1965.

DeWald, P.A. *Psychotherapy: A dynamic approach.* 2nd ed. New York: Basic Books, 1971.

Dewey, J. *Theory of the moral life.* New York: Holt, Rinehart and Winston, 1964.

Diamond, M., ed. *Perspectives in reproduction and sexual behavior.* Bloomington: Indiana University Press, 1968.

Dickinson, R.L. *Atlas of human sex anatomy.* 2nd ed. Baltimore: Williams & Wilkins Co., 1949.

Dienes, C.T. *Law, politics, and birth control.* Chicago: University of Illinois Press, 1972.

Dienhart, C.M. *Basic human anatomy and physiology.* Philadelphia: W.B. Saunders Co., 1967.

Djerassi, C. Birth control after 1984. *Science* 169(1970): 941–951.

Dmowski, W.P., Manuel Luna, and Antonio Scommegna. Hormonal aspects of female sexual response. *Medical Aspects of Human Sexuality,* 8, no. 6 (June 1974): 92–113.

Do marriage manuals do more harm than good? *Medical Aspects of Human Sexuality* 4, no. 10 (October 1970): 50–63.

Dodson, A.I., and J.E. Hill. *Synopsis of genitourinary disease.* 7th ed. St. Louis: C.V. Mosby Co., 1962.

Don Leon/Leon to Annabella: An epistle from Lord Byron to Lady Byron (Attributed to Byron). London: The Fortune Press, n.d.

Donnelly, R.C., and W.L. Ferber. The legal and medical aspects of vasectomy. *Journal of Urology,* 81(1959): 259–263.

Doshay, L.J. *The boy sex offender and his later career.* 2nd ed. Mount Prospect, Ill.: Patterson Smith, 1969.

Dostoyevsky, F. *The brothers Karamozov.* Constance Garnett, trs. New York: Random House, 1950.

Dumas, A. *La dame aux camélias.* Paris: Calmann-Levy, 1956.

Eastman, N.J., and L.M. Hellman. *Williams obstetrics.* 13th ed. New York: Appleton-Century-Crofts, 1966.

Edwards, J.N., ed. *Sex and society.* Chicago: Markham Publishing Company, 1972.

Egerton, C., trs. *The golden lotus (Chin p'ing mei).* London: Routledge & Kegan Paul, 1939.

Ehrhardt, A.A., and J. Money. Progestin-induced hermaphroditism: I.Q. and psychosexual identity in a study of ten girls. *Journal of Sex 'Research* 3(1967): 83–100.

Ehrlich, P., and A. Ehrlich. *Population, resources, environment.* 2nd ed. San Francisco: W.H. Freeman & Co., 1972.

Ehrlich, P.R. *The population bomb.* New York: Ballantine Books, 1968.

Eichenlaub, J.E. *The marriage art.* New York: Dell Publishing Co., 1961.

Eliot, T.S. *Murder in the cathedral.* New York: Harcourt Brace Jovanovich, 1935.

Ellis, A. *The art and science of love.* New York: Dell Publishing Co., 1965.

——. Healthy and disturbed reasons for having extramarital relations. In *Extramarital relations,* G. Neubeck, ed. Englewood Cliffs, N.J.: Prentice-Hall (1969): 153–161.

Ellis, A., and A. Abarbanel, eds. *The encyclopedia of sexual behavior.* New York: Hawthorn Books, 1967.

Ellis, H. *My life.* Boston: Houghton Mifflin Co., 1939.

——. *Studies in the psychology of sex.* 2 vols. New York: Random House, 1942. (Originally published in 7 volumes, 1896–1928.)

Engel, G.L. *Psychological development in health and disease.* Philadelphia: W.B. Saunders Co., 1962.

Epstein, L.M. *Sex laws and customs in Judaism.* Rev. ed. New York: Ktav Publishing House, 1968.

Erikson, E.H. Identity and the life cycle. *Psychological issues.* 1, no. 1. New York: International Universities Press, 1959.

——. *Childhood and society.* New York: W.W. Norton & Co., 1963.

——. *Identity: Youth and crisis.* New York: W.W. Norton & Co., 1968.

Eroticism: The disease of our age. *Films and Filming* (January 1961).

Eysenck, H.J., ed. *Behavior therapy and the neuroses.* New York: Pergammon Press, 1960.

Farnsworth, D.L., and G.B. Blaine, Jr., eds. *Counsel-*

ing the college student. Boston: Little, Brown & Co., 1970.

Fenichel, O. *The psychoanalytic theory of neurosis.* New York: W.W. Norton & Co., 1945.

Ferenczi, S. Male and female: Psychoanalytic reflections on the "theory of genitality," and on secondary and tertiary sex differences. *Psychoanalytic Quarterly* 5(1936): 249–260.

——. *Sex in psychoanalysis.* New York: Basic Books, 1950.

Fink, P.J. Dyspareunia: Current concepts. *Medical Aspects of Human Sexuality, VI,* no. 12 (December 1972): 28–47.

Finkle, A.L., *et al.* How important is simultaneous orgasm? *Medical Aspects of Human Sexuality* 3, no. 7 (July): 86–93, 1969.

Finler, J.W. *Stroheim.* Berkeley, Calif.: University of California Press, 1968.

Fisher, S. *The Female Orgasm.* New York: Basic Books, 1973.

Fisher, C., *et al.* Cycle of penile erection synchronous with dreaming (REM) sleep. *Archives of General Psychiatry* 12(1965): 29–45.

Fiumara, N.J. Gonococcal pharyngitis. *Medical Aspects of Human Sexuality* 5, no. 5 (May 1971): 195–209.

Fletcher, J. *Situation ethics: The new morality.* Philadelphia: Westminster Press, 1966.

——. *Moral responsibility: Situation ethics at work.* Philadelphia: Westminster Press, 1967.

Fleuret, F., and L. Perceau, eds. *Le cabinet satyrique.* Paris: J. Fort, 1924.

Ford, C.S. *A comparative study of human reproduction.* Yale University Publications in Anthropology no. 32, 1964. (Reprinted: New York: Taplinger Publishing Co., 1964).

Ford, C.S., and F.A. Beach. *Patterns of sexual behavior.* New York: Harper & Row, 1951.

Foster, J.H. *Sex variant women in literature.* Chicago: Muller, 1958.

Fox, C.A., and B. Fox. Blood pressure and respiratory patterns during human coitus. *Journal of Reproduction and Fertility* 19, no. 3 (August 1969): 405–415.

Fox, C.A., and B. Fox. Uterine suction during orgasm. *British Medical Journal* 1 (February 4, 1967): 300.

Fox, C.A., A. Ismail, *et al.* Studies on the relationship between plasma testosterone levels and human sexual activity. *Journal of Endocrinology,* 52(1972): 51–58.

Fox, C.A., H.S. Wolff, and J.A. Baker. Measurement of intra-vaginal and intrauterine pressures during human coitus by radio-telemetry. *Journal of Reproduction and Fertility* 22, no. 1 (June 1970): 243–251.

Fraiberg, S.H. *The magic years.* New York: Charles Scribner's Sons, 1959.

Frank, Gerald. *The Boston strangler.* New York: The New American Library, 1966. (Also available as a Signet paperback.)

Franklin, J. *Classics of the silent screen.* New York: Citadel Press, 1959.

Frazer, J.G., trs. *Pausanias's description of Greece.* New York: Macmillan, 1898.

Freeman, L. *Before I kill more.* New York: Crown Publishers, 1955. (Also available as a Pocket Books paperback.)

Freud, S. Letter to an American mother. *American Journal of Psychiatry* 107(1951): 787.

——. *The standard edition of the complete psychological works of Sigmund Freud,* James Strachey, ed. London: Hogarth Press and Institute of Psychoanalysis, 1957–1964.

Fromm, E. *The art of loving.* New York: Harper & Row, 1956.

Gagnon, J.H., and W. Simon, eds. *The sexual scene.* Chicago: Aldine Publishing Co., 1970.

Gagnon, J.H., and W. Simon. *Sexual conduct: The social sources of human sexuality.* Chicago: Aldine Publishing Co., 1973.

Gandy, P., and R. Deisher. Young male prostitutes. *Journal of the American Medical Association,* 212(1970): 1661–1666.

Gebhard, P.H. Factors in marital orgasm. *Medical Aspects of Human Sexuality* 2, no. 7 (July): 22–25.

Gebhard, P.H., J.H. Gagnon, W.B. Pomeroy, and C.V. Christenson. *Sex offenders.* New York: Harper & Row, 1965.

George Washington University Population Report. *Oral contraceptives.* Series A, no. 1 (April). Washington, D.C.: George Washington University Medical Center, 1974.

Gerassi, J. *Boys of Boise.* New York: Macmillan Co., 1967.

Gessa, B.L., *et al.* Aphrodisiac effect of p-chlorophenylalanine. *Science* 171(1971): 706.

Gilder, G.F. *Sexual suicide.* New York: Quadrangle/ The New York Times Book Co., 1973.

Ginsberg, G. L., *et al.* The new impotence. *Archives of General Psychology* 28(1972): 218.

Girodias, M., ed. *The Olympia reader.* New York: Grove Press, 1965.

Goldberg, I. *Havelock Ellis.* New York: Simon & Schuster, 1926.

Goodall, J. *See* Van Lawick.

Goodlin, R.C. Routine ultrasonic examinations in obstetrics. *Lancet* (September 11, 1971): 604–605.

Goodlin, R.C., *et al.* Orgasm during late pregnancy— possible deleterious effects. *Obstetrical Gynecology,* 38(1971): 916.

Gorer, G. *Himalayan village.* London: Michael Joseph Ltd., 1938.

Goy, R.W. Organizing effects of androgen on the behaviour of Rhesus monkeys. In *Endocrinology and human behavior,* R. Michael, ed. London: Oxford University Press, 1968: 12–31.

Grabstald, H., and W.E. Goodwin. Devices and surgical procedures in the treatment of organic impotence. *Medical Aspects of Human Sexuality.* 7, no. 12 (December 1973): 113–120.

Graves, R. *The Greek myths.* New York: George Braziller, 1959, 2 vols.

Greenblatt, R., E. Jungck, and H. Blum. Endocrinology of sexual behavior, *Medical Aspects of Human Sexuality* 6, no. 1 (January 1972): 110–131.

Greene, F.T., R.M. Kirk, and I.M. Thompson. Retrograde ejaculation. *Medical Aspects of Human Sexuality,* 4, no. 12 (December 1970): 59–65.

Gulevich, G., and V. Zarcone. Nocturnal erection and dreams. *Medical Aspects of Human Sexuality* 3, no. 4 (April 1969): 105–109.

Guttmacher, A.F. *Pregnancy and birth: A book for expectant parents.* New York: Viking Press, 1962.

Guttmacher, A.F., W. Best, and F.S. Jaffe. *Planning your family.* New York: Macmillan Co., 1964.

Hall, R. *The well of loneliness.* New York: Covici Friede, 1928.

Hamburg, D.A., and D.T. Lunde. Sex hormones in the development of sex differences in human behavior. In *The Development of Sex Differences,* E. Maccoby, ed. Stanford, Calif.: Stanford University Press, 1966: 1–24.

Hare, E.H. Masturbatory insanity: The history of an idea. *Journal of Mental Science* 452(1962): 2–25.

Harkel, R.L. *The picture book of sexual love.* New York: Cybertype Corp., 1969.

Harlow, H.F., J.L. McGaugh, and R.F. Thompson. *Psychology.* San Francisco: Albion Publishing Co., 1971.

Harris, F. *My life and loves.* New York: Grove Press, 1963.

Hastings, D.W. *A doctor speaks on sexual expression in marriage.* Boston: Little, Brown & Co., 1966.

Heath, R.G. Pleasure and brain activity in man. *Journal of Nervous and Mental Disease* 154, no. 1 (January 1972): 3–18.

Henriques, F. *Prostitution and society: A survey.* Vol. 1: *Primitive, classical, oriental.* Vol. 2: *Prostitution in Europe and the New World.* Vol. 3: *Modern sexuality.* London: MacGibbon & Kee, 1962– 1968.

Henry, G.W. *All the sexes.* New York: Holt, Rinehart and Winston, 1955.

Hewes, G.W. Communication of sexual interest: An anthropological view. *Medical Aspects of Human Sexuality* 7, no. 1 (January 1973): 66–92.

Hilgard, E.R. *Theories of learning.* New York: Appleton-Century-Crofts, 1956.

Hilgard, E.R., R.C. Atkinson, and R.L. Atkinson. *Introduction to psychology.* New York: Harcourt Brace Jovanovich, 1971.

Hill, A.B. *Principles of medical statistics.* London: Oxford University Press, 1966.

Hiltner, S. *Sex ethics and the Kinsey reports.* New York: American Book-Stratford Press, 1953.

Hinde, R.A. *Animal behavior: A synthesis of ethology and comparative psychology.* New York: McGraw-Hill, 1970.

Hobsbawm, E.J. Revolution is puritan. In *The new eroticism,* P. Nobile, ed. New York: Random House, 1970: 36–40.

Hoffman, M. *The gay world: Male homosexuality and the social creation of evil.* New York: Basic Books, 1968.

Hollister, L. Popularity of amyl nitrite as sexual stimulant. *Medical Aspects of Human Sexuality,* 8, no. 4 (April 1974): 112.

Hooker, E. An empirical study of some relations between sexual patterns and gender identity in male homosexuals. In *Sex research—new developments,* J. Money, ed. New York: Holt, Rinehart and Winston, 1965: 24–25.

Houston, P. *The contemporary cinema*. London: Penguin Books, 1963.

How does premarital sex affect marriage, *Medical Aspects of Human Sexuality,* 2, no. 11 (November 1968): 14–21.

How frequently is sex an important factor in divorce? *Medical Aspects of Human Sexuality,* 4, no. 6 (June 1970): 24–37.

Hunt, M. *Sexual behavior in the 1970's.* Chicago: Playboy Press, 1974.

——. Sexual behavior in the 1970's. *Playboy.* 20, no. 10 (October 1973): 84–88, 194–207.

——. Sexual behavior in the 1970's. *Playboy.* 20, no. 11 (November 1973): 74–75.

——. Sexual behavior in the 1970's. *Playboy.* 20, no. 12 (December 1973): 90–91, 256.

——. Sexual behavior in the 1970's. *Playboy.* 21, no. 1 (January 1974): 60–61, 286–287.

——. Sexual behavior in the 1970's. *Playboy.* 21, no. 2 (February 1974): 54–55, 176–177.

Hyde, H.M. *A history of pornography.* New York: Dell Books, 1966.

Inkeles, G., and M. Todris. *The art of sensual massage.* San Francisco: Straight Arrow Books, 1972.

International Planned Parenthood Federation medical handbook. London: IPPF, 1968.

Israel, S.L. *Menstrual disorders and sterility.* New York: Harper & Row, 1967.

"J." *The sensuous woman.* New York: Lyle Stuart, 1969.

Jackson, H. *Antifertility compounds in the male and female.* Springfield, Ill.: Charles C Thomas, 1966.

James, A.G. *Cancer prognosis manual.* 2nd ed. New York: American Cancer Society, 1966.

Janis, I.L., G.F. Mahl, J. Kagan, and R.R. Holt. *Personality: Dynamics, development and assessment.* New York: Harcourt Brace Jovanovich, 1969.

Jawetz, E., J.L. Melnick, and E.A. Adelberg. *Review of medical microbiology.* 9th ed. Los Altos, Calif.: Lange Medical Publications, 1970.

Jay, P.C., ed. *Primates: Studies in adaptation and variability.* New York: Holt, Rinehart and Winston, 1968.

Jones, E. *The life and work of Sigmund Freud.* 3 vols. New York: Basic Books, 1953.

Jones, E. *On the nightmare.* London: Hogarth Press, 1949.

Jones, H.W., Jr., and W. Scott. *Hermaphroditism, genital anomalies and related endocrine disorders.* Baltimore: Williams & Wilkins Co., 1958.

Jong, E. *Fear of Flying.* New York: Holt, Rinehart and Winston, 1973.

Joyce, J. *Ulysses.* New York: Random House, 1934.

Juhasz, A.M., ed. *Sexual development and behavior: Selected readings.* Homewood, Ill.: The Dorsey Press, 1973.

Jung, C.G. General aspects of dream analysis. *Structure and dynamics of the psyche,* Vol. 8. R.F.C. Hull, trs. New York: Pantheon Books, 1960.

Juvenal (Decimus Junius Juvenalis). *Satires.* G.G. Ramsay, trs. London: William Heinemann, 1961.

Kallmann, F.J. A comparative twin study on the genetic aspects of male homosexuality. *Journal of Nervous and Mental Disease* 115(1952): 283–298.

Kameny, F.E. Gay liberation and psychiatry. *Psychiatric Opinion* (February 1971): 18–27.

Kantner, J.F. Teens and sex: A national portrait? *Family Planning Perspectives,* 5, no. 2 (Spring 1973): 124–125.

Kantner, J.F., and M. Zelnik. Contraception and pregnancy: Experience of young unmarried women in the United States. *Family Planning Perspectives,* 5, no. 1 (Winter 1973): 21–35.

——. Sexual experience of young unmarried women in the United States. *Family Planning Perspectives,* 4, no. 4 (October 1972): 9–18.

Kaplan, H.S. *The New Sex Therapy.* New York: Brunner/Mazel, 1974.

Karim, S.M.M., and G.M. Filshie. Therapeutic abortion using prostaglandin $F_{2\alpha}$. *Lancet* 1(1970): 157–159.

Karlen, A. *Sexuality and homosexuality.* New York: Norton, 1971.

Karpman, B. *The sexual offender and his offenses.* New York: Julian Press, 1954.

Kaufman, I.C., and L.A. Rosenblum. The waning of the mother-infant bond in the species of macaque. *Determinants of infant behavior,* Vol. IV. B.M. Foss, ed. London: Methuen & Co., 1969: 41–59.

Keeton, W.T. *Biological science.* New York: Norton, 1967.

Kepecs, J. Sex and tickling. *Medical Aspects of Human Sexuality* 3, no. 8 (August 1969): 58–65.

Kessel, J. *Belle de jour*. Paris: Geoffrey Wagner, trs. New York: Dell Books, 1967.

Kessler, S., and R. Moos. The XYY karyotype and criminality: A review. *Journal of Psychiatric Research*, 7(1970): 153–170.

Kilpatrick, J.J. *The smut peddlers*. Garden City, N.Y.: Doubleday & Co., 1960.

Kinsey, A.C., W.B. Pomeroy, and C.E. Martin. *Sexual behavior in the human male*. Philadelphia: W.B. Saunders Co., 1948.

Kinsey, A.C., W.B. Pomeroy, C.E. Martin, and P.H. Gebhard. *Sexual behavior in the human female*. Philadelphia: W.B. Saunders Co., 1953.

Kleitman, N. *Sleep and wakefulness*. Chicago: University of Chicago Press, 1963.

Knight, A., and H. Alpert. The history of sex in cinema. *Playboy*. I. The original sin (April 1965); II. Compounding the sin (May 1965); III. The twenties: Hollywood's flaming youth (June 1965); IV. The twenties: Europe's decade of decadence (August 1965); V. Sex stars of the twenties (September 1965); VI. Censorship and the Depression (November 1965); VII. The thirties: Europe's decade of unbuttoned erotica (February 1966); VIII. Sex stars of the thirties (April 1966); IX. The forties: War and peace in Hollywood (August 1966). X. The forties: War and peace in Europe (September 1966); XI. Sex stars of the forties (October 1966); XII. The fifties: Hollywood grows up (November 1966); XIII. The fifties: Sex goes international (December 1966); XIV. Sex stars of the fifties (January 1967); XV. Experimental films (April 1967); XVI. The nudies (June 1967); XVII. The stag film (November 1967); XVIII. The sixties: Hollywood unbuttons (April 1968); XIX. The sixties: Eros unbound in foreign films (July 1968); XX. Sex stars of the sixties (January 1969).

Knight, R.P. Functional disturbances in the sexual life of women: Frigidity and related disorders. *Bulletin of the Menninger Clinic* 7(1943): 25–35.

Kolodny, R., W. Masters, *et al.* Depression of plasma testosterone levels after chronic intensive marijuana use. *New England Journal of Medicine*. 290, no. 16 (April 18, 1974): 872–874.

Kracauer, S. *From Caligari to Hitler: A psychological history of the German film*. Princeton, N.J.: Princeton University Press, 1966.

Kronhausen, E., and P. Kronhausen. *Pornography and the law*. New York: Ballantine Books, 1964.

Kuchera, L.K. Stilbestol as a "morning-after" pill. *Medical Aspects of Human Sexuality* 6, no. 10 (October 1972): 168–177.

Kyrou, A. *Amour, érotisme, et cinéma*. Paris: Le Terrain Vague, 1957.

Landtman, G. *The Kiwai Papuans of British New Guinea*. London: Macmillan, 1927.

Laub, D.R., and P. Gandy, eds. Proceedings of the second interdisciplinary symposium on gender dysphoria syndrome (February 2–4, 1973).

Lawder, S.D. Film: Art of the twentieth century. *Yale Alumni Magazine* (May 1968).

Lawrence, D.H. *The tales of D.H. Lawrence*. London: William Heinemann, 1948.

———. *Lady Chatterly's lover*. New York: Grove Press, 1957.

Legman, G. *Love and death: A study in censorship*. New York: Hacker Art Books, 1963.

———. *The horn book: Studies in erotic folklore and bibliography*. New York: University Books, 1963.

LeGrand, C.E. Rape and rape laws: Sexism in society and law. *California Law Review* 61(1973): 919–941.

Lehfeldt, H. Coitus interruptus. *Medical Aspects of Human Sexuality* 2, no. 11 (November 1968): 29–31.

Levinger, G. Husbands' and wives' estimates of coital frequency. *Medical Aspects of Human Sexuality* 4, no. 9 (September 1970): 42–57.

Lewinsohn, R. *A history of sexual customs*. New York: Harper & Row, 1958.

Liddon, S.C., and D.R. Hawkins. Sex and nightmares. *Medical Aspects of Human Sexuality*. 7, no. 1 (January 1972): 58–65.

Li Yü. *Jou-p'u-t'uan (The prayer mat of flesh)*. H. Lowe-Porter, trs. London: Penguin Books, 1955.

Lloyd, C.W. *Human reproduction and sexual behavior*. Philadelphia: Lea & Febiger, 1964.

Loth, D. *The erotic in literature*. New York: Macfadden, 1962.

Lunde, D.T., and D.A. Hamburg. Techniques for assessing the effects of sex hormones on affect, arousal and aggression in humans. *Recent Progress in Hormone Research* 28: 627–663.

"M." *The sensuous man*. New York: Lyle Stuart, 1971.

Maccoby, E., ed. *The development of sex differences*.

Stanford, Calif.: Stanford University Press, 1966.

McConnell, J.V. *Understanding human behavior*. New York: Holt, Rinehart and Winston, 1974.

Macdonald, D. *On movies*. Englewood Cliffs, N.J.: Prentice-Hall, 1969.

Macdonald, J.M. *Rape: Offenders and their victims*. Springfield, Ill.: Charles C Thomas, 1971.

Malinowski, B. *The sexual life of savages in north-western Melanesia*. New York: Harcourt Brace Jovanovich, 1929.

Malla, K. *The ananga ranga*. R.F. Burton and F.F. Arbuthnot, trs. New York: G.P. Putnam's Sons, 1964 ed.

Mann, T. *Death in Venice*. H. Lowe-Porter, trs. London: Penguin Books, 1955.

Manvell, R. *New cinema in Europe*. London: Studio Vista, 1966.

Marcus, S. *The other Victorians*. New York: Basic Books, 1966.

Marmor, J. Some considerations concerning orgasm in the female. *Psychosomatic Medicine* 16, no. 3 (1954): 240–245.

Marmor, J., ed. *Modern psychoanalysis: New directions and perspectives*. New York: Basic Books, 1968.

——, ed. *Sexual inversion: The multiple roots of homosexuality*. New York: Basic Books, 1965.

Marshall, D.S., and R.C. Suggs, eds. *Human sexual behavior*. Englewood Cliffs, N.J.: Prentice-Hall, 1971.

Martial (Marcus Valerius Martialis). *The epigrams*. Loeb Library trs. London: William Heinemann, 1920.

Martin, D., and P. Lyon. *Lesbian/Woman*. San Francisco: Glibe Publications, 1972.

Marx, J.L. Birth control: Current technology, future prospects. *Science,* 179(1974): 1222–1224.

Masters, W.H., and V.E. Johnson. *Human sexual inadequacy*. Boston: Little, Brown & Co., 1970.

——. *Human sexual response*. Boston: Little, Brown & Co., 1966.

May, R. *Love and will*. New York: Norton, 1969.

Mayo, J. The new black feminism: A minority report. *Contemporary Sexual Behavior: Critical Issues in the 1970's,* J. Zubin and J. Money, eds. Baltimore: Johns Hopkins University Press, 1973, Ch. 9.

McClintock, M. Menstrual synchrony and suppression. *Nature*. 229(1971): 244–245.

McGaugh, J.L., N.M. Weinberger, and R.E. Whalen. *Psychobiology*—The biological bases of behavior, readings from Scientific American. San Francisco: W.H. Freeman and Co., book published in 1966.

Mead, M. *Coming of age in Samoa*. New York: William Morrow & Co., 1929.

——. *Male and female*. New York: William Morrow & Co., 1949.

——. *Sex and temperament in three primitive societies*. New York: William Morrow & Co., 1935.

Meleager, Strato of Sardis, *et al. The Greek anthology*. W.R. Paton, trs. London: William Heinemann, 1918.

Menninger, K. *Whatever became of sin?* New York: Hawthorn Books, 1973.

Michael, R.P., and E.B. Keverne. Pheromones in the communication of sexual status in primates. *Nature,* 218(1968): 746–749.

Millar, J.D. The national venereal disease problem. *Epidemic Venereal Disease: Proceedings of the Second International Symposium on Venereal Disease*. St. Louis: American Social Health Association and Pfizer Laboratories Division, Pfizer, Inc. (1972): 10–13.

Miller, A. *The renewal of man*. Garden City, N.Y.: Doubleday & Co., 1955.

Miller, H. *Tropic of cancer*. New York: Grove Press, 1961.

Miller, W.B. Sexuality, contraception and pregnancy in a high-school population. *California Medicine,* 119(1973): 14–21.

Millett, K. *Sexual politics*. Garden City, N.Y.: Doubleday & Co., 1970.

Mirbeau, O. *Le jardin des supplices*. Paris: Les Editions Nationales, 1935.

Mittwoch, U. *Genetics of sex differentiation*. New York: Academic Press, 1973.

Money, J. *Sex errors of the body*. Baltimore: The Johns Hopkins Press, 1968.

Money, J., ed. *Sex research: New developments*. New York: Holt, Rinehart and Winston, 1965.

Money, J., J.C. Hampson, and J.L. Hampson. An examination of some basic sexual concepts: The evidence of human hermaphroditism. *Bulletin of Johns Hopkins Hospital* 97(1955): 301–319.

Montagu, A. *Life before birth*. New York: New American Library, 1964.

———. *Sex, man and society.* New York: Tower Publications, 1969.

Moos, R., D.T. Lunde, *et al.* Fluctuations in symptoms and moods during the menstrual cycle. *Journal of Psychosomatic Research,* 13(1969): 37–44.

Morin, E. *The stars.* Richard Howard, trs. New York: Grove Press, 1960.

Morris, D. *The human zoo.* New York: McGraw-Hill, 1969.

Morris, J. *Conundrum.* New York: Harcourt Brace Jovanovich, 1974.

Morrison, E.S., and V. Borosage, eds. *Human sexuality: Contemporary perspectives.* Palo Alto, Calif.: National Press Books, 1973.

Mostofi, F.K. Carcinoma of the prostate. *Modern Trends in Urology,* Sir Eric Riches, ed. New York: Appleton-Century-Crofts, 231–263 , 1970.

Murdock, G.P. *Social structure.* New York: Macmillan Co., 1949.

My secret life. New York: Grove Press, 1966.

Nabokov, V. *Lolita.* Greenwich, Conn.: Fawcett Books, 1959.

Nefzawi. *The perfumed garden.* R.F. Burton, trs. New York: G.P. Putnam's Sons, 1964 ed. (London: Neville Spearman Ltd., 1963.)

Netter, F.H. *Endocrine system.* The Ciba Collection of Medical Illustrations, Vol. 4. Summit, N.J.: Ciba, 1965.

———. *Reproductive system.* The Ciba Collection of Medical Illustrations, Vol. 2. Summit, N.J.: Ciba, 1965.

Neubardt, S., and H. Schulman. *Techniques of abortion.* Boston: Little, Brown, 1972.

Neubeck. G., ed. *Extramarital relations.* Englewood Cliffs, N.J.: Prentice-Hall, 1969.

Newton, N. Interrelationships between sexual responsiveness, birth, and breast feeding. *Contemporary Sexual Behavior: Critical Issues in the 1970's.* J. Zubin and J. Money, eds. Baltimore: Johns Hopkins University Press, 1973: 77–98.

Nilsson, A.L., *et al. A child is born.* Boston: Seymour Lawrence, Inc., 1965.

Noonan, J.T., Jr. *Contraception: A history of its treatment by the Catholic theologians and canonists.* New York: New American Library, 1967.

Novak, E.R., *et al. Novak's Textbook of Gynecology,* 8th ed. Baltimore: The Williams & Wilkins Co., 1970.

Novak, E.R., and G.S. Jones. *Novak's textbook of gynecology.* Baltimore: Williams & Wilkins Co., 1961.

Nunberg, H. *Principles of psychoanalysis: Their application to the neuroses.* New York: International Universities Press, 1969.

Olds, J. Pleasure centers in the brain. *Scientific American* 193(1956): 105–116.

Oliven, J.F. *Clinical sexuality.* Philadelphia: J.B. Lippincott Co., 1974.

O'Neill, N., and G. O'Neill. *Open marriage.* New York: M. Evans and Co., 1972.

O'Neil, R.P., and M.A. Donovan. *Sexuality and moral responsibility.* Washington and Cleveland: Corpus Publications, 1968.

Opler, M.K. Cross-cultural aspects of kissing. *Medical Aspects of Human Sexuality* 3, no. 2 (February 1969): 11–21.

Ovid (Publius Ovidius Naso). *Heroides and Amores,* G. Showerman, trs. London: William Heinemann, 1914.

Packer, H.L. *The limits of the criminal sanction.* Stanford, Calif.: Stanford University Press, 1968.

Parke, J.R. *Human sexuality.* Philadelphia: Professional Publishing Company, 1906.

Parker, E. *The seven ages of woman.* Baltimore: The Johns Hopkins Press, 1960.

Parran, T. *Shadow on the land—syphilis.* New York: Reynal & Hitchcock, 1937.

Patten, B.M. *Human embryology.* 3rd ed. New York: McGraw-Hill, 1968.

Paul, G.L. Outcome of systematic desensitization. C.M. Franks, ed. *Behavior therapy: Appraisal and status.* New York: McGraw-Hill, 1969.

Pavlov, I.P. *Conditioned reflexes: An investigation of the physiological activity of the cerebral cortex.* London: Oxford University Press, 1927.

Peterson, H. *Havelock Ellis, philosopher of love.* Boston: Houghton Mifflin Co., 1928.

Pfeiffer, E., *et al.* Sexual behavior in aged men and women. *Archives of General Psychiatry* 19(1968): 753–758.

Pierson, E., and W.V. D'Antonio. *Female and male: Dimensions of human sexuality.* Philadelphia: J.B. Lippincott Co., 1974.

Pirages, D., and P. Ehrlich. *Ark II.* San Francisco: W.H. Freeman and Co., 1974.

Ploscowe, M. *Sex and the law.* Englewood Cliffs, N.J.: Prentice-Hall, 1951.

Pohlman, E.G. *Psychology of birth planning.* Cambridge: Shenkman Publishing Co., 1968.

Pomeroy, W.B. *Dr. Kinsey and the Institute for Sex Research.* New York: Harper & Row, 1972.

Pope Paul VI. *On the regulation of birth: Humanae vitae* (Encyclical Letter). Washington, D.C.: United States Catholic Conference, 1968.

Pouillet, T. *L'onanisme chez la femme.* Paris: Vigot Freres, 1897. (Originally published in 1876.)

Pound, E. *Personae.* New York: New Directions, 1926.

Prévost, A.F. *Manon Lescaut.* Paris: Garnier Frères, 1965.

Pribram, K.H. The neurobehavioral analysis of limbic forebrain mechanisms: Revision and progress report. *Advances in the Study of Behavior,* Vol. 2. New York: Academic Press, 1969: 297–332.

Proust, M. *Cities of the plain.* D.K.S. Moncrieff, trs. New York: Random House, 1932.

Rabelais, F. *Works.* T. Urquhart and P. Motteux, trs. London: The Abbey Library, n.d.

Rawson, P., ed. *Erotic art of the East.* New York: G.P. Putnam's Sons, 1969.

Reich, W. *The discovery of the orgone.* Vol. 1: *The function of the orgasm.* New York: Orgone Institute Press, 1969. (Originally published in 1942.)

Reichlin, S. Relationships of the pituitary gland to human sexual behavior. *Medical Aspects of Human Sexuality* 5, no. 2 (February 1971): 146–154.

Reik, T. *Of love and lust.* New York: Farrar, Straus & Giroux, 1970. (Originally published in 1941.)

Reiss, I.L. How and why America's sex standards are changing. *Trans-Action,* 5(1968): 26–32.

——. *Premarital sexual standards in America.* Glencoe, Ill.: The Free Press, 1960.

Repairing the conjugal bed. *Time* 95 (May 25, 1970): 49–52.

Riess, C. *Erotica! Erotica! Das Buch der verbotenen Bücher.* Hamburg: Hoffman & Campe, 1968.

Robbins, S.L. *Textbook of pathology.* 3rd ed. Philadelphia: W.B. Saunders Co., 1967.

Robertiello, R.C. The "clitoral versus vaginal orgasm" controversy and some of its ramifications. *Journal of Sex Research* 6, no. 4 (November 1970): 307–311.

Rose, R.M. Androgen excretion in stress. *The psychology and physiology of stress,* P.G. Bourne, ed. New York: Academic Press, 1969: 117–147.

Rosenbaum, S. Pretended orgasm. *Medical Aspects of Human Sexuality* 4, no. 4 (April 1970): 84–96.

Rosner, F., trs. *Mishneh Torah,* "Hilchoth De'oth," Ch. IV, no. 19. *Annals of Internal Medicine* 62(1965): 372.

Rossi, A.S. Maternalism, sexuality, and the new feminism. *Contemporary Sexual Behavior: Critical Issues in the 1970's,* J. Zubin and J. Money, eds. Baltimore: The Johns Hopkins University Press, 1973, Ch. 8.

Rossman, I. *Sex, fertility and birth control.* New York: Stravon Press, 1967.

Rothballer, A.B. Aggression, defense, and neuro-humors. *Brain Function,* Vol. V: *Aggression and defense,* C.D. Clemente and D.B. Lindsley, eds. Berkeley, Calif.: University of California Press, 1967: 135–170.

Roth, P. *Portnoy's complaint.* New York: Random House, 1967.

Roth-Brandel, U., M. Bygdeman, N. Wiqvist, and S. Bergstrom. Prostaglandins for induction of therapeutic abortion. *Lancet* 1(1970): 190–191.

Rothschild, L., F.R.S. Human spermatozoon. *British Medical Journal* 1 (February 8, 1958): 301.

Rubin, E., ed. *Sexual freedom in marriage.* New York: New American Library, 1969.

Ruch, F.L., and P.G. Zimbardo. *Psychology and life.* Glenview, Ill.: Scott, Foresman and Co., 1971.

Rudel, H.W., F.A. Kincl, and M.R. Henzl. *Birth control: Contraception and abortion.* New York: Macmillan Co., 1973.

Ruitenbeek, H.M., ed. *The problem of homosexuality in modern society.* New York: E.P. Dutton & Co., 1963.

Russell, B. *Marriage and morals.* New York: Bantam Books, 1968. (Originally published in 1929.)

De Sade, D.-A.-F. *Justine. The Marquis de Sade: Three Complete Novels.* New York: Grove Press, 1965.

Salzman, L. Female infidelity. *Medical Aspects of Human Sexuality* 6, no. 2 (February 1972): 118–136.

——. Sexuality in psychoanalytic theory. *Modern psychoanalysis,* J. Marmor, ed. New York: Basic Books, 1968: 123–145.

Sappho of Lesbos. *Lyra Graica.* J.M. Edmonds, trs. London: William Heinemann, 1922.

Schlesinger, A., Jr. An informal history of love U.S.A. *Medical Aspects of Human Sexuality,* 4, no. 6

(June 1970): 64–82. (Originally published in *The Saturday Evening Post,* 1966.)

Schmidt, G., and V. Sigusch. Sex differences in responses to psychosexual stimulation by films and slides. *Journal of Sex Research* 6, no. 4 (November 1970): 268–283.

———. Women's sexual arousal. *Contemporary Sexual Behavior: Critical Issues in the 1970's,* J. Zubin and J. Money, eds. Baltimore: Johns Hopkins University Press, 1973, Ch. 7.

Schneider, R.A. The sense of smell and human sexuality. *Medical Aspects of Human Sexuality,* 5, no. 5 (May 1971).

Schofield, C.B.S. *Sexually transmitted diseases.* Edinburgh: Churchill Livingstone, 1972.

Schroeder, L.O. New Life: Person or Property? *American Journal of Psychiatry* 131 (1974): 541–544.

Schroeter, A.L. Rectal Gonorrhea. *Epidemic Venereal Disease; Proceedings of the Second International Symposium on Venereal Disease.* St. Louis: American Social Health Association and Pfizer Laboratories Division, Pfizer, Inc. (1972): 30–35.

Schwarz, G.S. Devices to prevent masturbation. *Medical Aspects of Human Sexuality,* 7, no. 5 (May 1973): 141–153.

Schwartz, L.B. Morals, offenses and the model penal code. *Columbia Law Review* 63(1963): 669.

Sherfey, M.J. The evolution and nature of female sexuality in relation to psychoanalytic theory. *Journal of the American Psychoanalytic Association* 14, no. 1 (1966): 28–128.

———. *The nature and evolution of female sexuality.* New York: Vintage Books, 1973.

Shiloh, A., ed. *Studies in human sexual behavior: The American scene.* Springfield, Ill.: Charles C Thomas, 1970.

The significance of extramarital sex relations. *Medical Aspects of Human Sexuality* 3, no. 10 (October 1969): 33–47.

Simon, P., J. Gondonneau, L. Mironer, A. Dourlen-Rollier, and C Levy. *Rapport sur le comportement sexuel des français.* Paris: René Julliard/Pierre Charron, 1972.

Singer, I., and J. Singer. Types of female orgasm. *Journal of Sex Research* 8, no. 11 (November 1972): 255–267.

Singer, J. The importance of daydreaming. *Psychology Today,* 1, no. 11 (April 1968): 18–27.

Skinner, B.F. *The behavior of organisms: An experimental analysis.* New York: Appleton-Century-Crofts, 1938.

Slovenko, R. *Sexual behavior and the law.* Springfield, Ill.: Charles C Thomas, 1965.

Smith, D.R. *General urology.* 6th ed. Los Altos, Calif.: Lange Medical Publications, 1969.

Somadeva. *Vetalapañcavimsati.* C.H. Tawney, trs. Bombay: Jaico Publishing House, 1956.

Sorensen, R.C. *Adolescent sexuality in contemporary America (The Sorensen Report),* New York: World Publishing, 1973.

Spiro, M.E. *Kibbutz: Venture in utopia.* Cambridge: Harvard University Press, 1956.

Spock, B. *Baby and child care.* New York: Pocket Books, 1970.

Stearn, J. *The grapevine: A report on the secret world of the lesbian.* Garden City, N.Y.: Doubleday & Co., 1964.

———. *The sixth man.* Garden City, N.Y.: Doubleday & Co., 1961.

Steiner, G. Night words. *The new eroticism,* P. Nobile, ed. New York: Random House, 1970: 120–132.

Stekel, W. *Auto-eroticism.* New York: Liveright Publishing Corp., 1950.

———. *Sexual aberrations.* 2 vols. New York: Liveright Publishing Corp., 1930.

Stephenson, R., and J.R. Debrix. *The cinema as art.* Harmondsworth, Middlesex: Penguin Books, 1965.

Stern, C. *Principles of human genetics.* 2nd ed. San Francisco: H.H. Freeman & Co., 1960.

Stoller, R.J. *Sex and gender: On the development of masculinity and feminity.* New York: Science House, 1968.

Student Committee on Human Sexuality. *Sex and the Yale Student.* New Haven, Conn.: Yale University Press, 1970.

Sullivan, P.R. What is the role of fantasy in sex? *Medical Aspects of Human Sexuality* 3, no. 4 (April 1969): 79–89.

Taylor, G.R. *Sex in history.* New York: Harper & Row, 1970.

Tepperman, J. *Metabolic and endocrine physiology.* Chicago: Year Book Medical Publishers, 1962.

Terman, L.M. *Psychological factors in marital happiness.* New York: McGraw-Hill, 1938.

Thielicke, H. *The ethics of sex.* J.W. Doberstein, ed. New York: Harper & Row, 1964.

Thomas, J.L., S.J. *Catholic viewpoint on marriage and the family.* Garden City, N.Y.: Image Books, 1965.

Thomlinson, R. *Demographic problems: Controversy over population control.* Belmont, Calif.: Dickenson, 1967.

Thompson, G. *Sex rackets.* Cleveland: Century Books, 1967.

Tjio, J.H., and T.T. Puck. The somatic chromosomes of man. *Proceedings of the National Academy of Sciences* 44(1958): 1222–1237.

Tyrmand, L. Permissiveness and rectitude. *The New Yorker* 46 (February 28, 1970): 85–86.

Udry, J.R., and N.M. Morris. Distribution of coitus in the menstrual cycle. *Nature* 220(1968): 593–596.

Van de Velde, T.H. *Ideal marriage.* New York: Random House, 1965.

Van Lawick-Goodall, J. Mother offspring relationship in free-ranging chimpanzees. *Primate ethology,* D. Morris, ed. Chicago: Aldine Publishing Co., 1967: 207–346.

Vatsyayana. *The Kama Sutra.* R.F. Burton and F.F. Arbuthnot, trs. Medallion ed. New York: G.P. Putnam's Sons, 1963.

Vergil (Publius Vergilius Maro). *Works.* H.R. Fairclough, trs. London: William Heinemann, 1965.

Verwoerdt, A., *et al.* Sexual behavior in senescence. *Geriatrics.* (February 1969).

Vidal, G. *Myra Breckinridge.* Boston: Little, Brown & Co., 1968. New York: Bantam Books.

Vierling, J.S., and J. Rock. Variations in olfactory sensitivity to exaltolide during the menstrual cycle. *Journal of Applied Physiology,* 22(1967): 311–315.

Von Krafft-Ebing, R. *Psychopathia sexualis.* C.B. Chaddock, trs. Philadelphia: F.A. Davis Co., 1899. (Reprinted: New York: G.P. Putnam's Sons, 1969.)

Wade, N. Bottle-feeding: Adverse effects of a Western technology. *Science,* 184(1974): 45–48.

Waelder, R. *Basic theory of psychoanalysis.* New York: International Universities Press, 1964.

Wagner, N., and D. Solberg. Pregnancy and sexuality. *Medical Aspects of Human Sexuality.* 8, no. 3 (March 1974): 44–79.

The way of a man with a maid. New York: Grove Press, 1968.

Weinberg, M.S., and C.J. Williams. *Male homosexuals: Their problems and adaptations.* New York: Oxford University Press, 1974.

Weinberg, S.K. *Incest behavior.* New York: Citadel Press, 1963.

Weiss, H.D. Mechanism of erection. *Medical Aspects of Human Sexuality,* 7, no. 2 (February 1973): 28–40.

Weiss, R.S., and H.L. Joseph. *Syphilis.* Camden, N.J.: Thomas Nelson, 1951.

West, D.J. *Homosexuality.* Chicago: Aldine, 1968.

West, N. *Miss Lonelyhearts.* New York: Avon Publishing, 1933.

Westoff, C.F., and L. Bumpass. The revolution in birth control practices of U.S. Roman Catholics. *Science,* 179(1973): 41–44.

Westoff, C.F., and R. Parke, Jr., eds. Sexuality, contraception and pregnancy among young unwed females in the United States. *Demographic and Social Aspects of Population Growth,* Washington, D.C.: U.S. Government Printing Office, 1972.

Westoff, C.R., and R.R. Rindfuss. Sex preselection in the United States: Some implications. *Science,* 184(1974): 633–636.

Westwood, G. *A minority: A report on the life of the male homosexual in Great Britain.* London: Longmans, Green & Co., 1960.

Weyranch, H.M. *Life after fifty: The prostatic age.* Los Angeles: Ward Ritchie Press, 1968.

What are the effects of premarital sex on the marital relationship? *Medical Aspects of Human Sexuality* 7, no. 4 (April 1973): 142–167.

What do you tell parents who are concerned about their children's masturbation? *Medical Aspects of Human Sexuality* 1, no. 3 (November 1967): 12–24.

What is the chief cause of marital infidelity? *Medical Aspects of Human Sexuality* 8, no. 1 (January 1974): 90–110.

The Whippingham papers. London: Privately published, 1888.

Whiteman, R.M. Multiple orgasms. *Medical Aspects*

of Human Sexuality 3, no. 8 (August 1969): 52–56.

Whyte, L.L. *The unconscious before Freud.* New York: Basic Books, 1960.

Wilkins, L., R. Blizzard, and C. Migeon. *The diagnosis and treatment of endocrine disorders in childhood and adolescence.* Springfield, Ill.: Charles C Thomas, 1965.

Willson, J.R., C.T. Beecham, and E.R. Carrington. *Obstetrics and gynecology,* 4th ed. St. Louis: C.V. Mosby Co., 1971.

Winick, C. The desexualized society. *The new eroticism,* P. Nobile, ed. New York: Random House, 1970: 201–207.

The Wolfenden report. New York: Stein & Day, 1963.

Wolpe, J., and A.A. Lazarus. *Behavior therapy techniques.* New York: Pergamon Press, 1966.

Wolpe, J. *The practice of behavior therapy.* New York: Pergamon Press, 1969.

——. *Psychotherapy by reciprocal inhibition.* Stanford: Stanford University Press, 1958.

Wood, H.C., Jr. *Sex without babies: A comprehensive review of voluntary sterilization as a method of birth control.* Philadelphia: Whitmore, 1967.

Woolf, V. *A room of one's own.* New York: Harcourt Brace Jovanovich, 1929.

World Health Organization. *Hormonal steroids in contraception.* World Health Organization Technical Report no. 386. Geneva: WHO, 1968.

——. *Intrauterine devices: Physiological and clinical aspects.* World Health Organization Technical Report no. 397. Geneva: WHO, 1968.

Yalom, I.D., *et al.* Postpartum blues syndrome. *Archives of General Psychiatry* 18(1968): 16–27.

——. Prenatal exposure to female hormones: Effect on psychosexual development in boys. *Archives of General Psychiatry,* 28(1973): 554–561.

Yates, A.J. *Behavior therapy.* New York: John Wiley & Sons, 1970.

Young, W.C., ed. *Sex and internal secretions.* 2 vols. Baltimore: Williams & Wilkins Co., 1961.

Zelnik, M., and J.F. Kantner. Sexuality, contraception and pregnancy among young unwed females in the United States. C.F. Westoff, and R. Parke, Jr., eds. *Commission on Population Growth and the American Future, Research Reports,* Vol. 1. Demographic and Social Aspects of Population Growth. Washington, D.C.: Government Printing Office, 1972.

Zichy, M. *The erotic drawings of Mihaly Zichy.* New York: Grove Press, 1969.

Zola, E. *Nana.* Paris: Fasquelle, 1938.

Zuckerman, S. *The social life of monkeys and apes.* London: Routledge & Kegan Paul, 1932.